The Stephen Cobb
Complete Book
of PC and LAN Security

The Stephen Cobb
Complete Book
of PC and LAN Security

Stephen Cobb

Windcrest®/McGraw-Hill

FIRST EDITION
SECOND PRINTING

Library of Congress Cataloging-in-Publication Data

Cobb, Stephen. 1952 –
    The Stephen Cobb complete book of PC and LAN security / by Stephen
Cobb.
      p.   cm.
   ISBN 0-8306-9280-0   ISBN 0-8306-3280-8 (pbk.)
    1. Local area networks (Computer networks)—Security measures.
  2. Computers—Access control.   I. Ttile.
  TK5105.7.C62   1990
  005.8—dc20   89-70748
                                        CIP

TAB Books offers software for sale. For information and a catalog, please contact
TAB Software Department, Blue Ridge Summit, PA 17294-0850.

Acquisitions Editor: Ron Powers
Technical Editor: Sandra L. Johnson
Production: Katherine G. Brown
Series Design: Jaclyn J. Boone   SCS

Contents

About This Book

Security can be defined as freedom from risk and danger. This book shows you how to make your work with personal computers relatively free from risk and danger. With the aid of this book, you can secure your personal computer equipment, and the data that it holds, from the following:

- Hackers and other interlopers.
- Viruses, worms, and logic bombs.
- Vandals and thieves.
- Competitors and industrial spies.
- Employees, both belligerent and careless.
- Power failures.
- Fires and other catastrophes.

WHAT THIS BOOK OFFERS

While the goal of *complete security* is probably unattainable, this book provides a complete treatment of security issues facing those who work with personal computers, from corporate management, to information technology managers and end users. Because increasing levels of security usually involve increasing costs, this book discusses how to weigh security benefits against security expenses. An increase in security levels can also mean a reduction in accessibility, so this book discusses security measures in light of user comfort levels and administrative feasibility.

Now that more and more offices are connecting their computer systems together, this book looks not only at the security aspects of stand-alone personal computers, but also at the problems facing local area networks, the systems of interconnected personal computers that are of growing importance in the data management strategies of companies, governments, and educational institutions.

If you do not use a personal computer but manage other people who do, you will also benefit from this book. You will gain insight into what your current exposure from personal computers is, and how to reduce it. For those of you who worry about losing data even though you do not understand how a database works, I have taken pains to discuss the problem of protecting data without excessive use of computerese (that strange mumbo-jumbo mumbled by guys with taped-together glasses and one too many pens in their plastic pen protectors). When a special term is used it is explained within the text. An effort has been made to avoid excessive use of acronyms, and those that are introduced are explained.

Of course, if you *do* know where your data is, if the possibility of other people getting at the information you have stored on your personal computer does *not* bother you, if the sudden disappearance of your data in a disk crash would not hurt your business, then you might not need this book. However, if you harbor any doubts about the security of your data, or the equipment that stores it, then this book should help. After all, if you read it from cover to cover and find nothing new, then you will have satisfied yourself that now your data and equipment is about as secure as it can be.

WHAT THIS BOOK IS NOT

This book does not approach security from the mainframe perspective, treating personal computers as annoying interlopers into the previously safe world of terminals and central processing departments. The premise of the book is that personal computers are here to stay and, given a responsible approach by users and information system managers, they can be as secure as any other form of computing equipment.

You might be aware that there are numerous books on the theory and practice of data security as it applies to mainframe and minicomputers. However, most of these do not address in sufficient detail the special issues facing the user and manager of personal computers and personal computer networks. Indeed, some mainframe experts have used the security deficiencies of the personal computer in attempts to reverse the trend away from centralized control of computing resources.

You might also have found that very few books concentrate on the subject of security for personal computers and personal computer networks without veering off into extended discussions of specialized areas like viruses, mainframe connections, data communications, or the morality of hacking. There are several excellent books about viruses and how they work. Indeed, some of them are listed in the resource section of this text. However, such books will not give you the comprehensive approach to data security that you will find here. There are also texts on encryption algorithms, code-cracking, and the art of hacking. Again, these do not cover the broad subject of data protection as it relates to personal computer usage.

While I did seek the advice and input of other computer professionals when putting this book together, this text is not a collection of articles culled from trade journals. A consistent point of view can be found behind the analysis and comments presented here. While you might eventually decide that you do not agree with the perspective, it is presented in sufficient depth to allow you to develop your objections coherently and productively.

This book is not simply a catalog of security-related products. You will find an extensive product listing at the back of the book which should be helpful, but in the fast-moving field of computers, no book can be completely up-to-date. (A few years ago I wrote several computer books that recommended joining The Source, a very reputable on-line database owned and operated by the Reader's Digest group of companies. Today The Source is no more, and the books are outdated.)

For news of the latest security products, including reviews and benchmark tests, you can turn to the extensive array of computer magazines. There are also specialized newsletters on security issues, some of which are listed in the product directory. In general, this text avoids detailed product descriptions, preferring to concentrate on the task of showing you how to determine what type of security products you need. When it is germane, you will find lists of features to look for in certain products and the factors that might affect their pricing. With the aid of this book, you will be able to evaluate which security products you need to purchase, but the emphasis throughout is on creating security through careful planning, simple precautions, and user-training rather than expensive equipment.

This book is not lavishly illustrated for several reasons. Many aspects of security do not lend themselves well to graphic expression. Lists and charts focus attention on specific points of information, but I have included few pictures of security devices. Glossy photos of security equipment tend to emphasize the value of equipment over less expensive strategies like the enforcement of well-designed security policies.

WHY THIS BOOK

This book is based on a commitment to making personal computers work for you, rather than against you. Without underestimating the problem, the general attitude is positive, showing you how to achieve workable solutions to your security problems as quickly and as cheaply as possible.

This book tries to avoid the scare tactics used by some companies that engage in the business of selling products that enhance data security. In some cases, such sales tactics are almost forgivable because they serve to heighten awareness of very real problems that were ignored by many personal computer users, sometimes with regrettable consequences. Yet the tendency to "cash in" on each new wave of concern on this subject has given rise to a plethora of products that are aggressively marketed as solutions rather than tools. These tools are useless unless applied within the type of security strategy that this book advocates.

You might be looking at this book as a text in an institution of higher education; however, the approach taken here is not academic. The canon and maxims put forward are based on "hands on" experience in the real world of personal computing. I have spent a lot of time in the offices of companies, institutions, and individuals who use personal computers, in order to learn what is feasible, what is realistic, when it comes to implementing security measures. When faced with more theoretical matters, like whether hacking is essentially a good activity or an evil one, the text is silent, preferring instead to help you assess your exposure to the adverse effects of hacking.

WHY THIS BOOK WAS WRITTEN

This book was written because many users and managers of personal computer technology are worried about risks and dangers. Obviously, some risks and dangers are very real, but some are imagined, the product of an over-sensational, under-informed media. Effective defense against some risks and dangers is difficult, but many can be thwarted by simple precautions. A very real concern is that the fears and worries of management and end-users will inhibit the spread of personal computing's positive benefits. The mission of this book is to restore some of the sense of security, and spirit of optimism, that has marked previous stages in the growth of personal computing. If your comfort level with the systems you use or manage is increased by what you read here, then that mission is being accomplished.

A NOTE FROM THE AUTHOR

As someone who first encountered microcomputers as an empowering, even liberating tool, I am disturbed by the bouts of fear and dread that seems to grip the worldwide community of personal computer users with increasing frequency. My first efforts with a personal computer in 1980 allowed me to produce better-looking documents quicker. Almost by chance, I found that humble system to be capable of calculations that I had been trying for 12 months to get central data processing to bring on-line. I saw that by using a microcomputer an individual could carry out a wider range of tasks with faster and better results. As this fact sank home in corporations and institutions, the personal computer spread to the point where it is now a universal item of office equipment. These days few people would think about setting up any type of commercial enterprise without a personal computer on-hand. However, because so many tasks have been entrusted to personal computers, the weak points of these machines have become increasingly problematic. To the extent to which personal computers are subject to outside forces, they jeopardize the endeavors of the people who trust them in their work, their recreation, and their self-expression.

Over the past few years, I have written a number of books for personal computer users. All of these books draw on my experience as a trainer of personal computer users, and my work as an information technology consultant to businesses in both the United States and the United Kingdom. Most of these books are what the trade refers to as "software-specific," meaning that their purpose is to explicate one particular piece of commercial software, as in *The Stephen Cobb's User's Handbook to Excel for the IBM PC*. Writing such books allows me to convey what I have learned in the process of teaching the program to others, and pass along what students have revealed to me about the program's capabilities and shortcomings. However, my students have also taught me a lot about aspects of personal computing that are not "software-specific."

One of the recurrent subjects of discussions in the classrooms and offices where I have taught is the politics of personal computing. This might concern the question of who gets the new equipment and who chooses what software should be used, but often the real thrust of the discussion involves access to data. Strictly speaking, *data* is what is given, the given facts. However, a lot of information that we call data we obviously don't want to give away. In this book, I will use the term data to refer to information stored on a computer. Controlling access to that information is one of the central issues in computer security. You can see the issue is a question as simple as "How do I stop other people seeing my stuff?" The broader implications for company politics manifest themselves in questions such as "How do we access the main database on the company mainframe?"

In recent years, I have seen a steady increase in the number of questions that directly relate to matters of security for several reasons. Obviously, the extent to which organizations rely upon personal computers has increased dramatically. The media can now be relied upon to report large-scale security threats. The main reason for my getting more questions is the growing sophistication among users. They can see the broader implications of questions like "How do I stop other people from retrieving my budget worksheet?" and "What if my PC were stolen?" Personal computers have been out there long enough and in sufficient numbers for most users to know of at least one "disaster" in which a lack of security has negative consequences or an organization or individual.

Back when I sold personal computers in one of the more exotic parts of California, I met a client who, according to my manager, was engaged in the world's oldest profession. This explained her particular interest in the password protection systems used by the various database management programs she was considering for the tasks of bookkeeping and maintaining a client list. Subsequent raids by vice squads upon computerized houses of ill-repute have shown our client's concerns to be well-founded. An unprotected database of names and addresses from such an establishment has, on more than one occasion, provided a ready-made arrest list. The moral of the story is that, whatever endeavors we engage in, serious consideration of how to preserve and protect the growing quantity of data that we entrust to personal computers is part of the price we must pay for tremendous benefits of personal computers.

HOW THE BOOK IS ORGANIZED

The book is divided into several parts. In the first part, the overall problem of security is examined, focusing on the issues that are the proper subject of this book. Several inexpensive measures are discussed that allow you to immediately improve the safety of your data. Procedures that you can follow to perform your own security analysis are described.

In the second part, the hardware side of the problem is addressed. Ways of securing hardware from theft, vandalism, and unauthorized access are considered, along with the question of redundancy. The need for reliable power sources is examined, together with alternatives for backup power.

The software side of the problem is considered in the third part where file access, password protection, and encryption are discussed. This section also looks at the question of software piracy and the threat of viruses. Various methods of protection against viruses are examined.

The wider world of personal computing is the subject of the fourth part where the problems of security in local area networks are reviewed. This section also addresses the human factors in security, such as hackers and disgruntled employees.

In the last part, you will find the resource list, a collection of product descriptions and company names that might be of use as you implement a security plan for your system(s). This list is only intended as a starting place because this book needs to go beyond just being a list of security-oriented products that are available at a particular point in time. Through reading this book, you will develop criteria for evaluating security issues, a methodology for assessing the security questions you are faced with and preparing an appropriate response. If this response requires purchasing equipment, then you will already be in a position to evaluate what is currently available and decide if it works for you.

 Scattered throughout the books are tips, anecdotes, and other author's notes which should help enliven and enrich your reading on this rather dry subject. These notes are marked by the icon you see in the margin.

It is 10:00 P.M.
Do you know where your data is?

1
The Need for Security

THIS CHAPTER SEEKS to map out the subject matter of the book. Basic questions of security are reviewed as a preamble to the more specific threat/response suggestions that begin in Chapter 2. While you might already have a high level of security awareness and a strong urge to spring into action, begin with this chapter to help place your actions in a broader context, thus making them more effective in the long term.

GOOD NEWS AND BAD NEWS

On August 2, 1989, a United States federal grand jury indicted 24-year-old Robert Morris, Jr., charging him with one count of violating the Computer Security Act of 1987. The penalty for this crime is up to five years in prison and a fine of up to $250,000. What did young Morris do to get into this predicament? He wrote a software program and then, on November 2, 1988, placed it on a network of computers. The network, called Internet, is very large. The type of program Morris wrote, called a *worm*, is very clever. Within hours almost 6000 computers ground to a halt and were virtually unusable for several days until the worm was identified and destroyed.

Thanks to heavy media attention, this incident quickly became one of the most talked about cases of a computer virus attack (a *worm* is usually considered to be a type of virus). The Internet network is used by many colleges and universities and connects with several other networks, including Arpanet and Milnet, the latter being a Defense Department network. The virus attack and subsequent indictment of Morris hold both good and bad tidings for you, the personal computer user.

First, the good news for personal computers users: This attack did not directly affect personal computer users. The attack was on the operating software of the powerful mainframe and minicomputers that provide computing power and data storage for users scattered over a wide area. These computers work on the Unix operating system. Although some personal computers can run Unix, the worm only attacked software that is used to log on to large systems and communicate between them.

There is more good news: The worm did not damage any important data files. Like many people who write this type of program, Morris seems to have had no desire to damage data, seeking instead to outsmart the operating software that runs the system. His intention might have been, and his effect definitely was, to show up weaknesses in the system. Furthermore, the culprit has been apprehended and prosecuted, a definite deterrent to others who might be contemplating similar attacks.

Finally, the event sparked further activity in the personal computer security market, with new and improved virus detection and prevention programs appearing all the time. Heightened awareness of the need for security makes it that much easier for those of us who endeavor to alert users to the risks, as well as the rewards, of personal computing.

The bad news is that the attack caused a lot of inconvenience to a lot of people and wasted much time and money. However honorable Morris's intentions, the effect of his actions was very negative. That other people might create chaos out of misdirected programming skills and innocent intentions is a strong likelihood. Unix is a mature and sophisticated software system, one that has been developed over a period of more than 15 years. Your personal computer probably runs on a much younger and less complex system, one that is undoubtedly easier to outsmart.

More and more personal computers are being connected on networks, increasing the chances of disruption from forces outside the user's control. While there are steps you can take to protect against viruses, the potential threats are probably increasing in number, rather than decreasing. In the rush to utilize the cheap and convenient power of the personal computer, many organizations have left the door open behind them, providing ample opportunities for interloping, theft, and fraud. Fortunately, it only takes common sense and diligence to close the door. Beyond that you can look at locks, alarms, and the finer points of personal computer security. But first, the subject itself must be defined.

PERSONAL COMPUTER SECURITY DEFINED

Personal computer security can be defined in several ways. In simple terms, personal computer security is about letting personal computers get on with what they do. A more academic definition might be "freedom to enjoy the benefits of personal computers without negative consequences." A more circumspect definition might be "freedom to use personal computers without fear of disruption or outside interference."

As you try to formulate a definition of personal computer security that is appropriate to your situation, you will see that it is a rather difficult subject to pin down. For example, we would all like the freedom from negative consequences suggested in the first definition, but is this realistic? What about something like eyestrain, a negative consequence that many users experience but that is scarcely a question of security?

The last definition is less sweeping but says nothing of the personal computer's use. Concern for security suggests that there is something valuable that needs protecting. Yet how do you access the value of a personal computer? You might argue that the one which computes the fastest route for an ambulance rushing to an accident scene is in a different league from the one which attempts to predict the winner of the next election. This question of value can be addressed after taking a moment to make clear what exactly is meant by "personal computer."

Personal Computers Defined

As computer technology advances, the distinctions between different types of computers continue to get blurred. However, it is possible to roughly delineate three different categories of computer system.

Mainframe Computer. The mainframe computer is a large computer system, consisting of racks of centralized processing equipment supporting multiple users via separate *stations*, or terminals, as illustrated in Fig. 1-1.

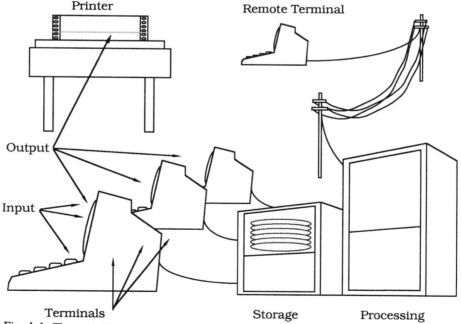

Printer   Remote Terminal

Output

Input

Terminals   Storage   Processing

Fig. 1-1. The mainframe computer system.

This is the original architecture of computing, and it still exercises a powerful appeal. There are administrative benefits to the centralized control inherent in this arrangement, and there is a tendency for other systems, such as personal computer networks, to revert to this type of control. Also, the terminology of personal computing owes a lot to the original architecture. The term *station* is still used to refer to a physical location at which computing tasks are performed, whether they are performed on a mainframe terminal or a personal computer.

To offset the high initial cost of mainframe hardware, it was put to use around the clock. This led to the need to provide access to users at locations other than the central processing unit itself. Access to a mainframe is usually by means of a *terminal*. A terminal is an input/output device with no computational ability or storage capacity.

Because many of the first computers were developed to perform military and financial functions, means to restrict access were inherent in the design. The software used to run mainframe systems has extensive facilities for data protection.

Minicomputer. After the mainframe came the minicomputer, smaller yet still able to support multiple users. The minicomputer offers central storage and processing of information that is entered through inexpensive terminals, as illustrated in Fig. 1-2.

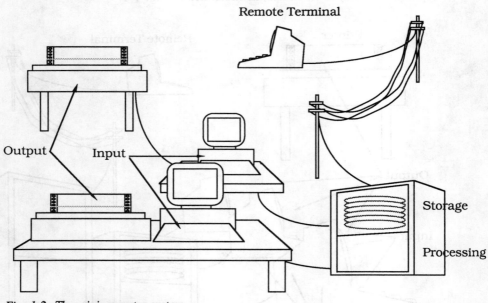

Fig. 1-2. The minicomputer system.

The minicomputer retained many of the security features of mainframe systems, such as sign-in procedures when terminals are used, passwords to control file access, and locks on the terminals themselves.

Microcomputer. Technically defined as a small computer designed around a central processing unit that is contained in a single integrated circuit or microchip, the microcomputer contains all of the basic features of a larger system, but together in a single unit serving a single user, as illustrated in Fig. 1-3.

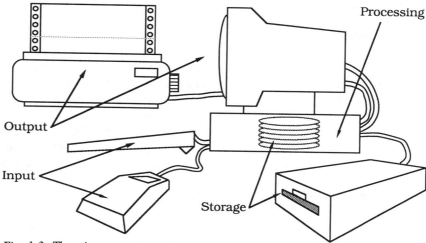

Fig. 1-3. *The microcomputer system.*

The unit might actually be several small boxes cabled together, but the whole thing will fit on or under a desk, providing one person with the ability to enter, process, store and retrieve data, without reference to or assistance from any other facilities.

The term *personal computer* is applied to microcomputers because microcomputers allow an individual to take charge of the entire computing process. None of the components have to be shared with other people for the system to work. Personal patterns and styles of work can flourish without the restrictions of conformity to central control. The situation is not unlike the automobile versus the bus, the personal computer providing freedom for the user to choose the destination, the route, and the schedule. With your own computer, there is no question of waiting for other users to log off, or waiting for the system administrator to install the right software. You are the system administrator.

LANs and Other Permutations

A personal computer does not need other computers or other resources in order to function. However, in some situations, it is advantageous to share or pool resources. This is the case when a personal computer is used as a terminal. Remember that a terminal is an input/output device for a multi-user system. A personal computer might be used to interact with a remote mainframe system and collect information from it, referred to as *downloading*. Alternatively, a personal computer acting as a terminal might transmit data to be stored on a larger system, referred to as *uploading*. The connection from computer to terminal can be made across telephone lines. Devices called *modems* are used so that data can be transmitted instead of voices.

When acting as a terminal, a personal computer does no real processing of data, it merely sends it or receives it, hence the term *dumb terminal*. This role of personal computer as terminal is actually a critical one for matters of security. Most hackers use personal computers with modems as terminals when trying to break in to other computers over telephone lines.

Another way in which resource sharing can be structured in the world of personal computing is a local area network or *LAN*. These have been developed over many years and are now a rapidly growing phenomenon in offices where a lot of personal computers are already in use. As good a place as any to begin the LAN story is with storage facilities. The main form of data storage on personal computers is magnetic media. Data and programs are stored magnetically much like music is stored magnetically on a cassette tape and pictures are recorded on VCR tapes. In fact, the first microcomputers actually used audio cassette tapes to store programs and data. Cheap portable cassette players could be used to write information onto tape and then read it back.

Tapes were followed by floppy disks, so-called because these consisted of a circle of flexible plastic coated with the same stuff that coats cassette tapes. Disks offer the advantage of faster operation. A read/write head can quickly be moved to any part of the disk through a combination of disk rotation and the movement of the head across the radius of the disk. Faster still are hard disks, sealed units containing multiple magnetic coated metal platters. Precision construction allows the data to be packed tighter on the disk, providing greater capacity. It also means higher costs.

When the first hard disk drives for personal computers appeared on the market, they were very expensive, costing almost as much as a complete floppy disk personal computer itself. Justifying the cost of such devices for all users was difficult and so systems of cabling and commands, known as local area networks, were developed to allow several users to share a hard disk. One of the first personal computer LANs, Omninet from Corvus, was designed around hard disk sharing.

The need for personal computer LANs led to the adaptation of software and hardware originally developed for larger computers, and such systems as ARCnet and EtherNet were introduced for personal computers. The hard disk cost justification argument was also applied to letter-quality printers. A single user was unlikely to keep a printer busy all the time but placing such a printer on a LAN of personal computers allowed it to be shared. While plenty of other peripherals are expensive, such as scanners, optical disk drives, and tape backup units, to help justify LANs, the steady decline in hard disk costs relative to the price of network connection has weakened the cost justification argument for networks. However, a much stronger argument has arisen, based on the potential productivity gains made possible by sharing data across a network.

As personal computers spread through offices, people found that several users would be working on the same data. This lead to the *"Sneaker Net"* which involved running between computers carrying floppy disks of vital data from one user to another. Cabling together the computers into a LAN eliminates Sneaker Net and allows much more sophisticated data sharing. You can see an example of a typical LAN in Fig. 1-4.

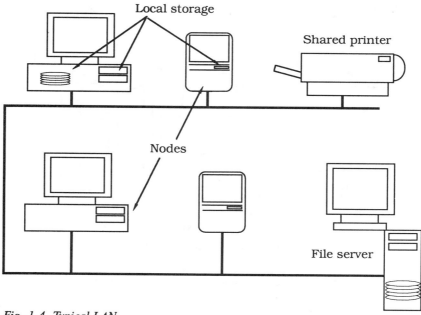

Fig. 1-4. Typical LAN.

Of course, connecting personal computers into a LAN creates its own set of security problems, which are dealt with in detail in Chapter 12.

In some LANs, one particularly powerful computer provides the bulk of the storage capacity on the system and controls the network software called a *file server*. Because of the pivotal role of the file server, extra attention must be paid to its security.

Any personal computer working as part of a LAN can be referred to as a *network node* or a *workstation*. The latter term sometimes causes confusion because it has numerous uses. In its most basic use, *workstation* means a physical location where computing tasks are performed. It was originally applied in the realm of minicomputers to terminals that have their own computing ability. This definition points to a big difference between local area networks and multi-user computers: On a LAN the majority of computing is performed by the stations on the LAN, whereas on a multi-user computer system the central computer does most of the computing. From a security point of view, the workstation can be both a target in its own right or an entrance to the network as a whole. Consequently, workstations require particular attention when securing personal computers.

Of course, there are exceptions to many of the definitions presented here. For example, personal computers can be attached to multi-user minicomputers, not just as dumb terminals, but also as intelligent workstations. In such cases the computing tasks are shared between systems, as diagrammed in Fig. 1-5.

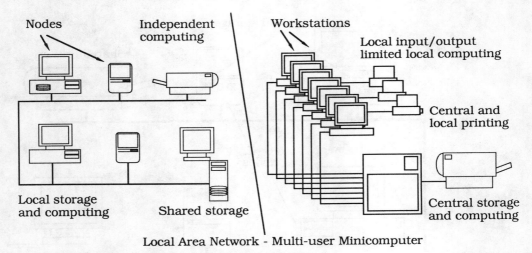

Fig. 1-5. Computing among LANs and multi-user systems.

The newer personal computers can themselves support several users working at terminals, making them micro-minis. Personal computers based on the 80486 chip can be used in a variety of ways, as incredibly powerful stand-alone computers, as file servers for large networks, or even as multi-user computers providing minicomputer level resources to a number of terminals. Indeed, 80486-based PCs have computing powers equivalent to systems that as late as 1985 would have taken up several large filing cabinets.

Types of Personal Computer

This book tries to deal with personal computers in general, rather than just one brand or type. Security is a concern to all personal computer users, whatever model they use. In order to avoid confusion, the term *personal computer* will be used in all situations where a general statement is being made. When comments refer to a specific type or make of personal computer the following terms will be used.

PC. When IBM used the initials PC for its first microcomputer, the stage was set for a certain amount of confusion. Do you use the acronym PC to refer to all personal computers, or just the models that IBM sells? If you stick with a narrow use, the IBM models known as the PS/2 range are not PCs. In this book, the term *PC* refers to any computer that can run PC-DOS or MS-DOS, the operating system developed and marketed by IBM and Microsoft. You will sometimes find such computers referred to as IBM PC compatible systems or IBM clones.

 As you might know, IBM has a thing for initials and order. At IBM the title Marketing Manager is different from Manager, Marketing. When the IBM PC XT came out, the XT standing for *extended technology* followed the letters PC. Similarly when the PC AT came out, it was a PC with *advanced technology*. When IBM developed *reduced instruction set computing* (RISC) and placed it in a compact computer system, it was dubbed the IBM RT PC. This strongly implied that in IBM's mind the RISC factor was more important than the perception of the system as a personal computer.

Within the group of computers known as PCs it is sometimes important to distinguish between *EISA* and *MCA* systems. These acronyms refer to the method used by the respective systems to attach components to the main part of the computer, the *motherboard*. The term *bus* is used for an electrical connection that involves electronic information as well as electricity. The original IBM PC established a *de facto* industry standard for a bus that allows you to integrate additional devices into the system. In IBM's mind, this was superceded by the new bus design it introduced in the PS/2 range of computers, known as the *Micro Channel Architecture* (MCA). However, many companies and users have a vested interest in preserving compatibility with the original architecture. In order to protect investment in existing add-on components and improve the capabilities of their products, a consortium of companies agreed upon bus specifications known as the *Extended Industry Standard Architecture*.

Mac. The Apple Macintosh personal computer, conveniently and affectionately known as "The Mac," is quite different from the IBM PC in many ways. However, at heart, a Mac is a personal computer. Indeed some Macintosh fans describe it as "the only truly personal computer." While such people might object to the term PC being reserved for IBM-compatible machines, they will still find plenty of Mac-related tips and techniques in this book. Whenever appropriate, attention is drawn to the way specific security concerns affect the Mac.

Note that in this text the term *Mac* will always refer to the Macintosh computer, not Message Authentication Coding, a system of security required by the United States Treasury when connecting to its computers.

Unix. These days some personal computers are powerful enough to run versions of the Unix operating system. A multitasking, multi-user operating system originally developed by Bell Laboratories, Unix is not strictly within the purview of this book; however, references are made when appropriate. For example, some companies are looking to Unix as an alternative to the OS/2 operating system, and as a way to avoid the problems of local area networks based on PC/MS-DOS.

Unix has many security features built into it, and it is extensively used in universities and research organizations. You can network widely scattered Unix systems. Ironically, it was a Unix-based network, ARPANET, that suffered the most widely reported virus attack in recent years, the Robert Morris incident.

OS/2. In 1984 IBM introduced the PC AT, which used the 80286 chip. This chip had computing power way beyond the 8088 chip that powered the original PC, for which PC-DOS had been written. While the PC AT and subsequent clones could run PC-DOS, and run it much faster than the basic PC, they could not tap the true power of the 80286 with a new and improved operating system. IBM decided that this operating system would be called OS/2 and went about developing it in conjunction with

Microsoft. With OS/2, you get *multitasking*, the ability to perform more than one task at once. For example, you can be downloading data from the company mainframe while sorting a large database and editing a word processing document. However, OS/2 did not appear on the market until after a new generation of machines, based on the 80386 chip. The 80386 was another leap ahead in computing power, and since OS/2 did not offer a way to tap its full potential we have entered a period of confusion while IBM works on improving OS/2, and users evaluate other alternatives to PC-DOS, including Unix.

Others. Security is also a concern to users of microcomputers such as the Commodore Amiga, the Commodore 64, the Atari ST, and the Tandy 100. While these systems are seldom specifically addressed in this text, it is acknowledged that they are frequently used in important roles. Much of what is said about risk analysis, protection techniques, and security policies does apply as much to these and other systems as it does to Macs and PCs. In some areas, such as viruses, specific concerns for users of these systems are discussed.

Types of User

Clearly, personal computers have a tremendous range of applications, and a correspondingly diverse range of people who can be called personal computer users. While all responsible users will want to protect their systems, there is considerable disparity among users, both in the level of threat and the value of potential damage. The following three categories represent one way of grouping users with respect to their security needs.

Private Users. These people use personal computers for their personal enjoyment or benefit. Work that they perform with the personal computer is for themselves, and not for an organization. These users own the personal computers they use.

Group Users. These people use personal computers as part of their work for an organization. In most cases, these users work on personal computers owned by the organization.

Supporting Users. These people support, assist, or manage group users. They have some level of responsibility for the personal computer resources of an organization.

Obviously these categories are not rigid or exclusive. You might well belong to more than one of them, but in each you will have a different set of concerns when it comes to security. In writing this book, every effort has been made to address the security needs of all three groups, from the private user concerned about viruses on game disks, to the group user anxious not to let down the organization, to the support user coordinating the protection of an organization's resources. However, all the advice given does not apply equally to all groups. The group and support users are most often addressed because they have more problems with which to deal. Some remarks will only apply to the support users because they have a wider responsibility for security than the other two types of user.

Types of Security

Personal computer security has several different aspects, and not all of them are treated equally in this book. On the one hand is the need to protect the computer system itself, together with the valuable data entrusted to it. On the other hand, the personal computer can be a tool for attacks on larger systems, thus being a security threat as well as a risk. The focus of this book is on securing unhindered use of personal computers, rather than on preventing personal computers from being used as tools to defeat larger systems.

WHAT IS AT STAKE

Assessing the value of a personal computer system, the tasks it performs, and the information it handles in order to carry out those tasks is a complex task. Chapter 4 has a more detailed discussion of how to put a price on personal computer systems and the consequences of them failing to perform as usual. For now, it is sufficient to say that there are four main aspects of value in any personal computer system:

- The hardware itself.
- The software used by the hardware to process information.
- The information that is processed.
- The system's ability to continue doing the processing.

The Hardware Itself

Most hardware is easy enough to value. You might well know what you or your company paid for it. You can assign a value to hardware using normal business concepts like purchase cost, replacement value, depreciated value, and so on.

The Software Used by the Hardware

The value of software is a trickier issue. You normally buy the right to use software rather than the raw material of disks and manuals. Someone could steal your copy of the WhizzWriter manual, and even your WhizzWriter system disk, but, under typical licensing agreements, you would still own the right to use WhizzWriter. Of course, you need to be able to prove you really did purchase the program for this right to have any real value.

In the case of software that was custom written, or internally developed, the question of value is murkier still. A program that is very industry- or company-specific might have little value to other users. If you lose all copies of the program and the developer is no longer in business, the program could be said to be priceless.

The Information that is Processed

While the term "information processing" brings to mind piles of accounts receivable, customer orders, mailing lists, and so forth, the reality for some personal computers is quite different. The processed information includes budget projections, letters, memos, proposals, resumes, and so forth. There are several aspects to the value of whatever information is handled by a personal computer:

- The value to you.
- The value to others.
- The negative value.
- The value of immediate access.

The Value to You. Suppose you lose the latest cost estimate worksheet for a major competitive bid. Recreating the worksheet will cost you time and effort. You might also experience a loss in terms of credibility and goodwill within your organization if the missing file means you disrupt the schedule for submitting the bid. This demonstrates the very personal value of the information to you. If the lost file results in a lost bid, then the wider value of the data to you and your organization becomes clear.

The Value to Others. Suppose the file that contains the cost estimates disappears from your personal computer system into the hands of your competitors, who use it to win the bid. This is probably the most obvious demonstration of the value of your information to others. Such data as customer lists and marketing plans fall into the same category. Yet direct competitors are not the only people who might covet the information on your personal computer system. If you are in the business of selling information itself, then there are likely to be those capable of thinking about how to get your information for free.

The Negative Value. Information that is not of direct value to you or your competitors might still have negative value. Many of us have at one time or another used a personal computer to prepare a nice-looking resume. If the resume is intended for a prospective employer, discovery of the resume file on your current employer's personal computer can be embarrassing to say the least.

 Negative value was clearly demonstrated by the infamous Willard Scott/Bryant Gumbel affair. An internal memo in which NBC television presenter Bryant Gumbel expressed personal observations about coworkers was made public, and much was made of Gumbel's negative assessment of coworker Willard Scott. In fact the memo was written by Gumbel at the request of his boss, but this did not lessen NBC's embarrassment. The memo came to light because it was stored on an insecure computer system!

Other examples of information with potential negative value include internal findings about product safety, employee evaluations, environmental test results, and so forth. Indeed, most internal documents that reflect negatively on an organization or individual have potential negative value.

The Value of Immediate Access. Suppose that you come to work in the morning, and your personal computer system does not work the way you expect it to. The file that you need is not where you thought you left it. In a situation like this, you learn the value of immediate access. The file might not be permanently lost, but access to it is delayed, wasting time and effort, causing a dent in productivity.

The System's Ability to Continue Doing the Job

Closely akin to the value of immediate access is the ability of your personal computer system(s) to keep doing the job. As personal computers increase in processing capability, they are assigned increasingly important tasks. Using personal computers for such tasks as order processing, customer reservations, stock management, and data acquisition means that their role is critical. The cost of system disruption, in terms of lost business and goodwill, can be considerable.

Of course, the tasks you perform with your personal computer might not be critical to an organization's profit and loss, but they might still be very important to you. While personal computer security is clearly about letting personal computers get on with what they do, precise statements about the value of personal computer systems are difficult because any respectable list of the different things that personal computers do would be far too long for this book. The approach taken here is to assume that the personal computer system(s) with which you are concerned perform tasks, the importance of which is clear to you.

You could try a theoretical answer to the question, "What do personal computers do?" For example, it is true to say they are used to process information. Yet, as we have seen, the nature of that information is the critical factor. One personal computer might process information about the activities of a simulated airplane as the user attempts to shoot down a simulated enemy. The value of this information to people other than the user is limited. Another personal computer might process information about the activities of a real airplane, information that is of vital importance to the pilot and passengers. What exactly it is that a personal computer does is less important to the discussion than the fact that it plays a valuable role in an ongoing endeavor.

DO YOU REALLY NEED THIS BOOK?

Have you stored valuable information on your personal computer? Are you sure it will be there in the morning? Are you sure it will not appear in the next edition of *The Times* or *The Wall Street Journal*? What will you do if your hard disk crashes right now or the office is gutted by fire overnight? Are you happy letting the clerk from the temporary agency update your payroll files or finish typing that competitive quote? Could your competitors use the information that is on your personal computer to their advantage? Are you sure they are not at this very moment reaping a windfall from the airwaves in your office?

If you are not comfortable with your responses to the above questions, then this book will probably help you. Just buying it and putting it on the office bookshelf might help you feel slightly more comfortable. Reading it and taking its suggestions to heart will definitely help you feel much more comfortable.

The purpose of this book is give you a clear perspective on the problems of security as they relate to personal computers and networks. If you have responsibility for protecting data, either your own, or that of an employer or client, this book will help you meet that responsibility with confidence.

A Simple Test

If you use a personal computer in your work, or at home, try taking this simple test to help you to grasp the security implications of computer usage:

1. Do you use password protection on any of your data files?

2. Do you have a surge protector or some other power line conditioner fitted between your computer and the main power supply?

3. Are your data files free from any references to personal or company bank accounts, credit cards, or phone access codes?

4. Could the contents of all the data files you created in the last six months be leaked to your coworkers without causing you any embarrassment?

5. Is your computer attached to your desk by anything besides cables and gravity?

6. Do you have a written record of your computer's serial number?

7. Do you back up fresh data files every working day?

8. If someone gave you a free copy of a great new game designed to run on your particular brand of personal computer, would you know how to tell if the disk contained a virus?

Now look at the results. If you answered "Yes" to question 3, you might want to check your answer. Are you sure you didn't write any letters or memos that referred to account numbers, perhaps letters of complaint? (I well remember reading a word processing file that contained an internal memo listing company credit card numbers on a floppy disk that was being thrown away!)

If you answered "No" to three or more of the questions, you are probably a typical personal computer user. This means that you have a *low* level of security preparedness. You could do a lot more to protect yourself and your data.

If you answered "Yes" to six or more questions, then you are either very security conscious or you have no faith at all in human nature! In either case, I suggest you persevere with this book. Because you are already one of the converted, you will want to be sure that you have considered all the angles, not just those in the questions above.

Unfortunately, generating a comprehensive security plan is often an exercise in applied suspicion. Only by taking a dim view of people can you be sure that your personal computer and the data entrusted to it are free from risk. Hopefully, you will take such a view temporarily and not become completely jaundiced.

A Tougher Test

The next test is harder. You might try writing down the answers on a piece of paper, but read the questions first. The aim of this test is to put matters into perspective rather than have you provide accurate answers:

1. Without looking at the computer, list of all the programs that are on the computer's hard disk (if you do not have a hard disk, then try the 20 floppy disks that are closest to the computer).

2. Add to the list descriptions of the documents or data files that are on your hard disk or in your collection of floppies (you do not have to list exact file names, but enough of the name and/or contents to identify the file).

3. Write down the date and time of the last complete backup of your hard disk (if you do not have a hard disk, the last time you made backup copies of your six most important data disks).

4. Name three popular programs for your computer that feature password protection.

5. At 3 A.M., how many locked doors are there between your computer and the street?

By now you should see the point of these tests is to increase your awareness of the size of the problem without causing undue alarm. If you think you can answer 1 or 2 successfully, then try. But check your answers against the computer. The fact is that very few people:

- Know exactly what is stored on their computer.
- Perform regular backups.
- Use password protection.
- Use all the locks that exist between their data and the outside world.

ATTACKS, THREATS, AND SCARES

In order to go any further in discussing personal computer security, an agreed vocabulary is needed. In addition to the regular terms and phrases of microcomputer technology, the following terms will be used:

attack—General term for any action or event which threatens to interfere with the proper functioning of a personal computer system, or seeks to achieve unauthorized spread of information entrusted to a personal computer.

attack, active—Action initiated by a person that threatens to interfere with the proper functioning of a personal computer system or causes unauthorized spread of information entrusted to a personal computer. Examples include intentional erasing of files, unauthorized copying of data, or the introduction of a virus designed to disrupt the computer's operation.

attack, passive—An attempt to gain information or resources from a personal computer system without interfering with its operation; such as electronic eavesdropping, Van Eyck phreaking, or placing a tap on a network, all of which can yield important information about the system as well as appropriate the data that is in the system.

breach—A successful thwarting of security measures, such as the theft of a PC or the deletion of valuable data files.

incident—When an attack takes place or a threat materializes you have an incident; some examples are a power failure or an attempt to delete a protected file.

threat—Anything that has the potential to interfere with the proper functioning of a personal computer or cause the loss or unauthorized spread of information entrusted to a personal computer. Examples are power failures, viruses, hackers, or careless users.

A Frightening Possibility

To further assess where you stand in relation to personal computers and security, check how you relate to this scenario.

The Scenario. Next Monday morning you arrive at work to find the office in chaos. There has been a break-in. Your PC has been stolen. What is your first thought?

Like many people you will probably be racking your brains trying to remember what exactly was stored on the computer. While some of us are responsible enough to keep records of our equipment serial numbers, few of us have a clear and up-to-the-minute recollection of what is stored on our computers at any given time. Damage assessment is difficult when you are not sure what exactly is missing in the way of programs and data.

The next thought is probably "When was the last time I made backup copies of my work?" This thought is quickly followed by "Did those get taken as well?" If, like a lot of us, you made your backup onto floppy disks that sit in a disk box next to the computer, the answer might well be "yes."

The next step is to consider how to get on with your job, given that disk files of documents, statistics, ideas, proposals, contracts, estimates, invoices, accounts, and even amorous jottings, are now "out there" rather than safely tucked away on your hard disk.

These days renting a computer is just a phone call away in most cities. When the rental unit arrives, it is time to start to think about backup copies of your favorite programs. If these were not stolen, you might still have to go through lengthy installation procedures to get them up and running. You might have had a lot of small utility programs on your PC, batch files and so forth, that made life easier; do you have copies of them?

Even when you are up and running, you are still not out of the woods. Did they steal the printer? Does the software you are using work with the replacement printer that you rented? If they left the printer, did they leave that custom printer cable that lets an IBM PC print on your Tukidata 180 printer (the one that Fred what's-his-name made up for you, before he left to be a computer consultant in Tasmania)?

After several days of incredible frustration, you might get a call from the local police. They have recovered your PC! Of course, they cannot tell you whether anyone has used it or not, but you're glad to get it back, right? Maybe. You have already cancelled all of the credit cards, account numbers, expiration dates, and current balances of which were stored in that personal money manager program you got for Christmas. Your bank has been warned to watch out for checks on your account, details of which were in that same handy program. You have failed to meet the deadline for bids on that lucrative new contract because the cost estimates were on the computer, not on safely stored floppies. If anyone has read that innocently named word processing document called MYNOTES, your private life could be in for stormy weather. As you drive across town to pick up your recovered PC, you realize that if the culprits have damaged your hard disk, what you are going to collect is a fairly worthless piece of iron.

Lessons Learned

This sort of scenario would sound a lot like scare tactics if it did not sound so typical. Fortunately, it is only a scenario, and several lessons can be learned, all of which will be reviewed in greater detail elsewhere in the book:

- Make the office more burglar resistant.
- Fix your PC to the desk.
- Do the same for printers, cables, and other accessories.
- Make frequent backups of data and programs.
- Keep the backups in a safe place.
- Use the password protection on programs that offer it.
- Use file encryption software on all other sensitive files.

The fact that some of these lessons are fairly obvious does not make them any the less valuable. Security requires common sense more than expensive equipment, commitment more than complexity. For example, your company might have a policy about storing personal data on company computers or locking away backup disks. However, unless such policies are simple to comply with and properly enforced, they are as useless as a slice of floppy disk.

QUESTIONS OF SECURITY

This chapter has asked you to consider how much is at stake when you employ personal computer technology in your endeavors. The fact that you have picked this book up suggests that you are already concerned about issues of data security. You are aware that there are problems and want to know more about them. You probably want to prevent security issues from eating into the benefits you have gained from personal computers.

Many people are alarmed by the sort of questions that have been raised in this chapter. However, these are the questions that you should be thinking about if you are in any way responsible for information handled by personal computers. Fortunately, by the time you finish reading this book, you will not be alarmed by such questions. You might still be concerned. You might realize that you have a lot of work to do to make your data secure, but you should be armed with a realistic understanding of the threat to your data. You will know how to analyze the risks and dangers and how to formulate an appropriate response. You will be able to assess new threats as they arise, because you will have a clear, security-conscious picture of personal computers, and how they handle information.

Questions of security have graduated from the periphery of the personal computer community to the board rooms and management meetings of every company that uses personal computers. They now represent serious anxieties, the sort which, if left unresolved, threaten to discourage prospective users who stand to gain so much from the power of microcomputers. Three basic questions serve to place the subject matter of this book in perspective:

- What do you stand to lose?
- What are the sources of danger?
- How can you protect the former from the latter?

What You Stand to Lose

Several ways of looking at this question were presented in the earlier section, but the question needs further consideration. In 1987, the journal *Government Computer News* asked the National Computer Security Center this question: "What are the greatest security problems facing typical government agency information systems managers?" The reply was unequivocal: "One, lack of awareness among computer users, which leads to problems of neglect . . . ." A major reason for this lack of awareness is the failure to grasp what can be lost through security breaches. The good news is that awareness is a lot cheaper to raise than the cash required to install additional security devices that will be ineffective if users are still complacent. By stressing what can happen to profits and productivity because of lax security, employees can be motivated to attain higher levels of awareness.

Employees are not the only ones going astray. Consider the findings of the British Government's Audit Commission, published in the *Survey of Computer Fraud and Mouse*. Of the more than 1500 companies in the representative sample that responded to the survey's questionnaire, nearly 180 reported being the victims of computer fraud in the preceding five years. The frauds ranged from the elaborate to the simplistic and involved staff from top management down to humble supply clerks.

In a typical case, a supervisor processed bogus purchases from a supplier, sending the check to the supplier who split the proceeds with the supervisor. When other managers questioned the amounts, the supervisor attributed them to computer error and transferred the amount to a different account. In another incident, a clerk discovered that accounts receivable downloaded to a remote terminal could be deleted without the central computer noticing. The clerk deleted records, then collected the debts and pocketed the payments.

This survey was actually carried out in 1990. A more current survey would probably produce an even higher percentage of victims. The survey pointed to the spread of desktop computers and networks as a major factor likely to aggravate the problem. Given that it is inherently difficult to get companies to admit that they were successfully duped, the reported rate of fraud is almost certainly below the actual figure. Compared to the same report in 1987, the number of frauds has risen.

So personal computers that handle accounts stand to lose money. Personal computers that handle valuable data stand to lose data or have it devalued by unauthorized distribution. Personal computers entrusted with sensitive information have the potential to cause tremendous embarrassment if their security is compromised. When it comes to information that is vital to society, we stand to lose a lot from what the NCSC calls the "proliferation of untrusted technology." Whether or not you agree with your government's definition of "national security interests," few people can deny that lax personal computer security in areas such as health and safety puts more than mere data at risk.

The Sources of Danger

This book should answer the many questions that abound among personal computer users concerned about the safety of the data that they have entrusted to a machine that they now realize is fallible and open to attack. For example, does the new telephone connection for your personal computer increase the chance of your files being infected by a computer virus? How likely is it that your personal computer network will be attacked by a hacker? Is it true that data being displayed on your computer screen can be picked up by equipment outside your office? Does the government really try to prevent companies from using any secret codes that it cannot break?

Questions like this received scant attention during the headlong rush to harness the potential benefits of the microcomputers. Those who raised such questions risked being classified as paranoid, reactionary, or possessed of overactive imaginations. Nowadays, thanks to increasingly well-publicized and increasingly ambitious feats of computer tampering, these questions are being asked among rank-and-file PC users.

Limited Reporting. Unfortunately, the questions play better than the answers. Tales of teenage whiz-kids penetrating multinational data networks get more media attention than the simple list of administrative procedures that could have prevented the incident in the first place. When outbreaks of computer virus make national news, people tend to see viruses in every computer malfunction and erroneous result.

In fact, the problems of viruses and attacks by hackers have overshadowed most other aspects of computer security. While researching this book, it was possible to find a lot of headlines like this: "Defense Department Computer Broken Into Again" or "Virus Threat Set to Worsen." It was impossible to find anything along the lines of "Thieves Guess Password, Divert Millions" or "Stolen PC Contained Company Secrets."

Companies do not like to report security breaches that could easily have been prevented, and the fears of computer users are fed by media hype, overshadowing the mundane subject of preventative measures. In some ways, this situation is natural. There is glamour and excitement (of sorts) in talk of computer tinkering, hacking, vandalism, sabotage, fraud, and theft. The other side of the issues is the less than glamorous talk of procedures, rules, audit trails, and paperwork. In fact, as we demonstrate in the next chapter, you can greatly increase the security of the data on your personal computer with a few simple procedures that cost nothing to implement.

Real and Imagined Threats. The potential threats to data security have been exaggerated by the media. Public perception is largely based on news programs that report incidents of computer tampering and fraud in a tone of menace, fueled by a lack of accuracy and detail. Computer magazine articles provide greater detail, but they have a tendency to err on the side of sensation and overstatement. Nevertheless, the need to protect personal computers from outside damage is growing. Only by carrying out the proper kind of risk analysis can you determine the level of danger and thus the "appropriate response."

As we come to rely upon personal computers to carry out an ever-increasing share of the information management tasks within our society, you should realize that the underlying design of these systems has evolved little from the early days. The first personal computers were spawned by a desire to open up computing to the masses, not keep people away from sensitive information. Personal computers are, by their very nature, "open" to all users. With few exceptions, today's typical personal computer can be turned on by anyone, operated by anyone, opened up by anyone, and carried off by anyone. The number of people who know how to operate a computer is growing all the time, as is the number of people who can write programs for them. Clearly the personal computer is made to be used, designed to be accessed freely. Against this must be balanced the growing need to restrict access.

When it comes to determining the possible threats to your system, your best tool is a healthy imagination. Ask yourself what could possibly go wrong and in what ways could you be ripped off. When it comes to determining which of the possible threats are probable, you need a healthy dose of realism. Make an objective assessment of the question: "Is it worth the risk for someone to try this?" To stir your imagination, consider these scenarios:

1. Your organization establishes a "work at home" program in which employees with personal computers at home use modems to dial up the computers at work, receiving and completing assignments over the phone lines. An employee's wallet is stolen, but she is embarrassed to admit that the phone number and password for logging on to the company computer were in the wallet, along with her business cards. An enterprising felon now has a valuable item to peddle, and a computerized felon has access to the company computers. The results can mean damaged data, erased data, or stolen data sold to the highest bidder.

2. In an absent-minded moment, an executive with BIG Corp. leaves his

unlocked briefcase on the commuter bus. An unscrupulous fellow traveller takes the briefcase and the laptop personal computer it contains. Reading the unprotected word processing file describing plans to take over SMALL Corp. the unscrupulous fellow has several options ranging from seeking a "reward" for return of the computer, to blackmail of BIG Corp., to a valuable tip for SMALL Corp.

3. In an absent-minded moment, an executive with BIG Corp. leaves his unlocked briefcase on the commuter bus. An unscrupulous fellow traveller takes the briefcase, and the laptop personal computer it contains. Reading the unprotected checking account spreadsheet, the unscrupulous fellow leaps at the chance to blackmail the executive who has listed several payments to a woman who is not his wife.

4. Personal computers allow you to produce excellent quality documents printed on official company stationery. If you do not control the distribution of stationery, you can be exposed to the negative effects of unofficial mail. While this has always been something of a problem, the speed with which personal computers can churn out documents takes the potential for abuse to a new level.

5. By combining graphics programs, desktop publishing software, and a laser printer, you can fabricate what appear to be official documents, like the one in Fig. 1-6.

2+2+2+2=?

Tired of thinking for yourself? Let someone else do the thinking for you.

The new HAL PC QT does most thinking quicker than you, and much better too.

Why leave business decisions to chance? The technology in the QT (short for Quick Thinking) can do it for you.

Full of so much pre-programmed intelligence we hesitate to call it artificial, the QT is just the latest in a long line of PCs from HAL, makers of personal computers since 1995.

HAL PC QT available next quarter at all licensed HAL dealers. QT is a registered trademark of HAL Corp.

HAL Corp. 2600 Bush Square, Aardvark, NY 10504

Fig. 1-6. Spoof document.

6. By using computer resources, many types of fraud are made more plausible. In one case a sales manager used convincing but phony letters on fabricated letterheads to get bogus suppliers placed on the company master ledger. He then authorized "goods received" notices and payment of the phony invoices, to the drop box addresses he had set up on the letterhead.

7. By combining a high-resolution image scanner with a laser printer, you can fabricate what appear to be exact photocopies of official documents, forms, and statements.

How to Protect What You Stand to Lose from Danger

While the real threats are many and varied, nothing is gained by retreating into paranoia. This book is based on the premise that security is achieved through a balanced reaction to realistically assessed threats accompanied by good disaster-recovery planning.

When security measures go too far, they become burdensome and threaten to choke off the benefits to be gained from using personal computers in the first place. In situations where security measures are nonexistent or too lax, management is bound to face, sooner rather than later, a rude awakening as to the realities of computer crime and computer-inflicted disruption of regular business. While every possible threat to your system(s) cannot be foreseen, you make possible a quick recovery from an attack through advance planning.

This book also stresses the concept of an "appropriate response," finding the right level of precaution to make your data safe, without making your data too difficult to get to. For some users, this will simply mean following a few simple rules. While no PC user can afford to be complacent, in many cases there is little need for expensive equipment to safeguard data.

WHAT IS ASSUMED

This book presents the problems of data security in a realistic, management-oriented style, offering practical solutions based on a balanced approach. When suggestions for action are made, they are presented with a full knowledge of what it will take to implement them in a real office, working with real people.

This book assumes that you do not want to erect so many defenses that your data becomes virtually inaccessible. At the same time, I assume that you have data that needs preserving and protecting. A further assumption is that you now realize there is a problem. You know that these days personal computers handle information that is vital to companies, institutions, and individuals. This can be product specifications, costing and pricing figures, client lists, wage and salary tables, banking transactions, even sensitive correspondence. You realize that controlling access to this information is just as important as getting it organized and computerized.

This book does not assume that you are a computer wizard or a power user who can write assembly language subroutines over lunch, but does assume that you have some idea of the capabilities of personal computers, the roles that they play in enterprises and institutions. In the next chapter, you can read in detail about how personal computers work, which might well improve your ability to protect them.

SUMMARY

The subject of personal computer security is a broad and growing one, increasing with importance as personal computer technology is woven into the fabric of our society. The next chapter examines how a personal computer works, and gives you some straightforward suggestions for quick security fixes.

2
The Basics

THIS CHAPTER LOOKS at how personal computers operate, focusing on their security weaknesses. The chapter also begins to develop the security mindset that you will need if you are to make realistic assessments of the threats posed to your personal computer resources. By describing the basic technicalities of personal computer operations, this chapter and the next will give the nontechnical reader a more confident grasp of where personal computers are vulnerable and what can be done to defend against threats. Suggestions are also advanced for simple but effective security measures that can be instituted at little or no cost.

PEOPLE, PEOPLE, PEOPLE

You might be surprised to see people at the top of the personal computer security agenda. After all, we are talking high-tech problems here. True, but security is a high-tech problem that is also a people problem. Computers are our tools, and if they don't work properly, it is people who get hurt. If they get stolen or are misused, people are the ones who lose out.

 One strain of personal computer virus manifested itself in the United Kingdom on Friday, October 13, 1989. Computer work at a center for the blind and visually impaired was badly disrupted by the virus. The center distributes a program for the IBM PC that displays text in very large characters, opening up the power of the PC to people who would otherwise be excluded.

In America, the National Rifle Association is fond of pointing out that guns do not murder people; people murder people. For the most part, the impediments to successful computing are human in nature, and mechanical. The sad fact is that you will not get far in establishing personal computer security without sometimes taking a dim view of human nature.

It is not the purpose of this text to determine whether man is essentially good or evil. What is taken for granted is that man at times can be pretty devious, grasping, and downright rotten. To establish security from such traits, you must be prepared to think like your adversary and realize that sometimes he is a miserable specimen. (On occasion, the expert in personal computer security is likely to side with Sartre, when he said "Hell is other people.")

People are risks, but they are also resources. It must be said that successful personal computer security depends upon people more than anything else. If you have motivated, diligent, and careful people working with you, then a greater degree of security can be obtained, and with less hassle. Without the cooperation of the people involved, even the most sophisticated security devices will fail. With cooperation, high levels of security can be obtained without recourse to expensive equipment.

What is clear from experience is that both the management and the employees have security responsibilities. Working together, they can be very effective in protecting the company's computer resources. The British Government's Computer Fraud Survey concluded that:

> senior management should ensure that line managers recognize they are involved in the integrity of the firm's computer operations and that all staff are trained to appreciate the need to secure systems . . . In this way the staff will be able to design systems that contain safeguards and the necessary controls.

Support users, those responsible for administering personal computer security within an organization, should consider the following measures:

- *Post security rules.* Write up a basic list of rules that users should follow to preserve security and post prominently. Issue a memo drawing attention to the poster, reiterating the rules in a form that can be kept handy. Consider posting the rules on each personal computer.

- *Circulate regular security warnings.* Use examples of damage and disruption from newspapers, magazines, or this book to illustrate the need for vigilance in maintaining security. Try to make these warnings interesting without providing too much detail, otherwise you might inspire copycat incidents.

- *Formulate security incentives.* Those people who breach security have an incentive to do so. Give people in your organization an incentive to maintain security. Award points for submitting security tips and for compliance with official procedures. Get management to provide substantial rewards for the winners.

- *Institute security checks.* Let people know that security procedures will be checked and tested. Carry out checks on a random basis.

- *Open a security hotline.* Let people know where they can get advice on security issues. Also let people know that they can report security violations or suspicious activity anonymously. On the other hand, offer rewards for lations.

This list is by no means exclusive, but it is a starting place. Chapter 1 human factor in more detail, suggesting further ways to improve security through a variety of personnel management tactics.

BACKUP, BACKUP, BACKUP

Much of what we read in the papers about computer security applies to large mainframe systems and extensive computer networks, particularly the massive electronic fund transfer (EFT) networks that handle payments between banks and large companies. The majority of computer crime that is reported revolves around fraudulent use of these large systems, typically the improper diversion of funds from one account to another. When it comes to personal computer security, the most prevalent problem is not fraudulent use, but damage to or loss of important data.

The good news is that there is a strong antidote to data loss, known as *backup*. In its simplest form a backup is just a copy. By copying programs and data from one disk to another, you double the chances that they will survive an attack. Make a third copy and the odds are further increased in your favor. If you store the backup copies in a safe place, you can get back to work fairly quickly even if the rest of your computer system is stolen. It goes without saying that you should back up your work regularly and store the backup materials safely.

The bad news is that most people find backing up a boring task, and there is a strong tendency to neglect this task. If you are supporting other users, the single most effective security measure you can take is to insist on regular backup. If you are a private or group user the biggest favor you can do yourself is to do your backup diligently. There are ways to make backup easier and faster and these are covered in Chapter 9, along with discussion of how much to back up, how often, and how to restore from backups when your primary data is lost.

UNDER LOCK AND KEY

Besides encouraging the users of personal computers to be more diligent in backing up and more vigilant in general, the most obvious step you can take towards protecting a personal computer system is to lock it up when it is not in use. This helps to prevent unauthorized use and outright theft. At several levels, the lock and key can work for you. In the following sections, some straightforward but often overlooked security measures are reviewed.

Secure Premises

Rooms containing valuable computer equipment and information should be secured outside regular business hours and access to sensitive areas should be controlled even during business hours. Locking the door might seem like a pretty obvious precaution, but the obvious is worth mentioning for several reasons. For a start, the obvious is all too easily overlooked. For example, many companies have a personal computer in their reception area. Between answering phones and greeting visitors, the receptionist can do word processing and data entry. Several risks are involved in this arrangement. The presence of the personal computer alerts all comers to the fact that the office is computerized. There might only be a short distance from the reception area to the parking area, increasing the temptation for a petty thief. Try to keep normal security principles in mind when locating personal computer equipment, as illustrated in Fig. 2-1.

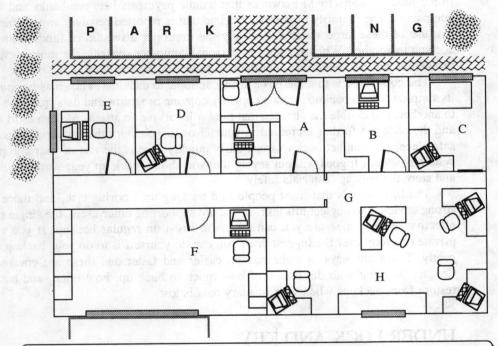

A - Reception area needs to be closely monitored and staffed at all times, controlling access to rest of site, possibly with card i.d. system on inner door.
B - Note poor location of computer in front of window.
C - Better location of computer system away from window, note closed door.
D - Computer location away from window good but watch for open doors.
E - Poor location next to window that is obscured from view by bushes, a prime target for burglary.
F - Warehouse area with loading door needs vigilance. Do not leave unstaffed when doors are open.
G - Open plan work area: hardware should be secured to furniture and system access controls used.
H - Equipment is kept well clear of window for better security.

Fig. 2-1. Diagram of personal computer sites.

 Despite heavy traffic, reception areas might be left unattended at times, leaving unannounced visitors with an unguarded personal computer. I have wandered into several industrial park-type company premises and waited for several minutes before someone came to see what I wanted. Several minutes is all it takes to load a personal computer into a van and drive off.

Another reason for stressing locking the door and other obvious precautions, such as not placing personal computers in front of unguarded street level windows, is that the personal computer has become another piece of office furniture. This is not literally true in any but the saddest cases (dead computer as doorstop). Yet many of today's office workers are so used to seeing personal computers around that they tend to overlook their value.

I have seen office staff carefully lock up transistor radios at the end of the day and yet leave floppy disks on the desk, and give no thought to locking up the computers.

Occasional reminders from management about correct procedures and the need to protect the organization's personal computer investment are a valuable antidote to complacency and the tendency to take personal computers for granted. Note the word "occasional." Bear in mind that reminders made too frequently are themselves likely to be taken for granted. If you are charged with issuing security proclamations, do try to make them interesting, and thus more likely to be noticed. See the example in Fig. 2-2 for some ideas.

Fig. 2-2. Security reminder.

This example was produced with a desktop publishing program on the Mac. Such notices are also a chance to be creative with some of the resources you are trying to protect.

A factor that makes the more obvious security practices more important these days is the rapidly decreasing size of personal computers, illustrated by the Atari Portfolio shown in Fig. 2-3.

Fig. 2-3. The Atari Portfolio, first palm top PC from a major computer company.

This personal computer, introduced in 1989, is arguably more powerful than the IBM PCs sold in 1980. The original PC weighed around 50 pounds (monitor and keyboard included) and took up more than two square feet of disk space. The Atari Portfolio fits in your hand or your coat pocket.

Of course, as some laptop manufacturers have been quick to point out, the ability to slip an entire PC into a lockable desk drawer is a security advantage. The shrinking size of technology can make matters easier for the would-be thief, providing more value per easily lifted pound.

A former computer salesman I know enjoys relating his experience demonstrating one of the first laptop computers, the elegant HP 1100. At a trade fair, his employer's booth was being visited by a high-ranking member of the clergy when the salesman noticed another man pick up one of the highly totable HPs from the display and start walking toward the nearest exit. "C!#%?t, he's got my computer!" yelled the salesman. This was quickly followed by exclamations of "Sorry, Father!" and "Stop that sinner!" A wild but unsuccessful dash in pursuit of the thief ensued and the incident provided a costly lesson in small computer security.

In the days when computers could be measured in cubic yards rather than cubic inches, they were housed in purposely built rooms that had climate as well as access controls. It was natural and fairly straightforward to secure these computer rooms. Today's personal computers can be as powerful as machines many times their size from just a few years ago, but they do not require special rooms. This encourages our tendency to think of personal computers as being akin to telephones or photocopiers. But the consequences of losing a personal computer are potentially far more damaging.

Locked Cubicles

Given the open plan structure of many of today's offices you might be saying, "It's all very well to talk of locking the office door, but I don't have one." In such situations, you might need to resort to different tactics. You can buy all manner of devices for fixing personal computers to desks and otherwise locking them away, and a representative sample is given in Chapter 5.

Typically the responsibility for general security in an open-plan office rests with management. Various strategies are used, the most common of which is restricting access to the office. This can be done through a front desk/back office layout, a card or I.D. badge reader, or a combination lock, to name just a few of the approaches. It is worth noting the generally accepted principle that organizations have a responsibility to provide a secure work environment for employees.

Locked Computers

When IBM introduced the PC AT in 1984 much ado was made about the fact that it came with a lock on the front that disabled the keyboard. Some members of the computer press hailed the "key to the AT" as a new workplace status symbol. Those who got an AT on their desk could lock out less fortunate users. Since then many PCs have been designed and built with keyboard locks on the front, similar to the one shown in Fig. 2-4.

After the initial hype, the reality of day-to-day operations sets in, and the keys were forgotten by many users. Indeed, a good way to test the level of personal computer security consciousness is to check how many who have keyboard locks actually use them.

In fact, these days many people using PCs with power locks would have difficulty finding the keys. (Usually two keys are provided—to score full marks for security awareness you have to know where *both* keys are!) Other people can show you the keys still sitting in the computer. Yet these keys provide one of the most effective low-level deterrents to unauthorized access. If you turn the key to the locked position and remove it, only a determined interloper can use your computer. You can bypass the lock by messing with the system wiring, but this usually involves opening the case of the system unit.

This protection is free to anyone who has this type of lock. You can now see such locks even on cheap Taiwanese XT clones, and they are a feature to look for when

Fig. 2-4. Lock on an IBM-compatible PC.

buying a new system, even if it is for home use. (I have several friends who work at home and use the key to prevent their children using the computer unaccompanied.)

In the well-organized office, a key distribution and control system should be implemented to manage the issue, use, and return of keys. Each user might be issued a key while the supervisor retains the copy. When an employee leaves, the key should be surrendered. For more on physical key management, see Chapter 7.

Locking Up Your Backup

By now, the security role of backup copies of important data and programs should be clear. These copies can be used to recover from security incidents. Even if your computer system is stolen, you can get back to work fairly quickly if you still have backups of your data. However, backups cannot be relied upon to come to the rescue if they are treated carelessly.

The backup media, be it disks or tapes, should be locked away at the end of the day. Most offices have a storage space like a desk drawer or filing cabinet that can be locked. In many cases, locking drawers is sufficient protection. The casual burglar will be interested in hardware rather than data and is not likely to go looking for spare disks. If you fear intruders looking for sensitive information, then you might want to lock backups in a safe. If you are contemplating purchase of a safe for data, consider buying a fireproof model. This will give your data added protection against one of the worst natural disasters an office can experience.

If you feel your office premises are insecure, you might want to store backups at a different location. Consider the construction company that is doing much of its accounting on a personal computer located in a site office. Fearing vandalism, the site manager takes the backup disks home every night. This protects the backups from the perils that might befall the site office. Of course, it is possible that the disks might be damaged or lost while in the care of the site manager, but these are backup disks. For the company to experience data loss, both the original data at the site office and the copies carried by the site manager would need to be damaged.

Removable Disks and Computers

There are definitely tradeoffs between component size and security. A very small computer with large storage capacity offers the chance to lock the whole system away in a desk drawer, but also makes it easier for the whole system to be carried off under someone's arm. Storing a lot of valuable data on small, easily pocketed disks presents the same dilemma. As storage capacities per cubic inch increase, there is less need to split information into small sections. When the IBM PC first came out, a backup copy of a document like the manuscript for this book would have required at least half a dozen floppy disks. Now the backup fits on a disk that will slip into a shirt pocket.

Generally this is very convenient, but consider the implication for company accounts. A high-capacity disk cartridge, such as is used in the Iomega Bernoulli system, and shown in Fig. 2-5, can easily contain the entire accounting system for a medium-sized company.

Fig. 2-5. Disks and cartridges.

The slim cartridge is easier to secure than the pile of floppy disks it replaces, but easier to slip into a pocket and take away.

On balance, the security benefits of easily removable high-capacity disks outweigh the downside. At least, this is what the FBI has concluded since it specifies removable hard disks for critical personal computer applications. Such systems offer advantages in terms of backing up and preventing access that are discussed later.

TURNING ON YOUR COMPUTERS

You cannot lock your computer away all the time. In most offices some personal computers will sometimes be sitting unattended. How do you stop someone using a personal computer once they have got to the point where they are sitting down in front of it? One obvious answer is the lock and key fitted to many IBM compatible PCs. However, not all computers are fitted with such a lock, and on some systems using the lock requires that the machine be turned off.

There are several cheap ways of preventing people from using your computer without fitting a physical lock, and several simple techniques that can keep unauthorized users out. The next few sections review the way in which personal computer systems operate. Armed with this knowledge, you will better understand the security risks, the chinks in the armor as it were, and be better able to thwart attacks.

Putting in the Boot

One of the aspects of personal computing that is both entertaining and frustrating, is the use of strange and obscure terms. A typical example is the *boot disk*. Simply put, this is a disk that contains the essential parts of the computer's operating system. Without this disk you cannot *boot* the computer, meaning you cannot get it started and you cannot use it. Some frustrated users have assumed that this term came from the desire to kick the darn thing to get it working. Images of pioneer computer technicians delivering swift kicks to room-size vacuum tube machines come to mind. In fact, the word is short for bootstrap, as in the phrase "pull yourself up by your own bootstraps."

In a typical personal computer system, the software that controls the hardware, known as the *operating system*, is provided on a disk. Without software to tell it what to do, the hardware is useless. Somehow the operating system software has to get from a disk into the computer's memory, where it remains for the duration of a computing session. In fact, a small amount of software can be stored in the hardware itself so that when the computer is switched on, it knows to read the disk. The first part of the disk that is read is called the *boot sector*, and this contains the information needed for the computer to correctly read the rest of the operating system into memory. By examining what happens when a personal computer is turned on, you can learn a lot about how the system can be protected from unauthorized access.

Powering Up

When you flip on the switch and power starts flowing into your personal computer system, the first actions are carried out by the *BIOS*, short for basic input/output system. In the BIOS of a personal computer, you have the fundamental set of instructions for that particular computer's architecture, including such details as how data is to be presented to the central processing unit, the *CPU* chip.

The BIOS is stored in something called *ROM*, which leads to the eponymous sounding phrase ROM BIOS. An acronym for *read only memory*, ROM is a means of storing computer instructions permanently. The ROM BIOS in your system performs the memory check and other diagnostics that happen before the computer reads from disk. You can prove this with a personal computer that has no hard disk. Turn the computer on with no disk in the drives. Several actions will occur without you typing in any instructions, and without the computer getting any information from disk.

On an IBM PC, one of the first actions performed by the instructions in ROM is a check of the keyboard connection. If no keyboard is attached, a warning beep is sounded. Another action performed by ROM BIOS shortly after power is turned on is a check of the computer's *RAM*. This is *random access memory*, the area of the system where most of the action takes place in a personal computer. Programs and data are placed in RAM while the computer is computing.

Because they both contain information, you measure both RAM and ROM in bytes and kilobytes, the normal measure of data size in a computer. When you turn on an IBM compatible PC, you will normally see a series of numbers in the top left of the screen. These numbers represent the size of the computer's RAM as the actual chips are checked out by the test program stored in ROM. If there are any problems with RAM, the instructions in ROM can provide you with an error code. There are error codes for bad keyboard connections and other problems, such as the absence of a boot disk. When the instructions in ROM have made sure that the computer's memory is in working order, they check the disk drives on the computer for further instructions. You can see the disk lights go on when this happens. If no disks are found, the starting up of the computer comes to a halt. On a Macintosh, you can tell if you have reached this point because a picture of a disk appears with a question mark in it.

In most personal computers, ROM is actually a computer chip or collection of chips into which instructions have been loaded. Unlike the chips that make up your computer's RAM, the ROM chips do not need electrical current to store their instructions. In fact, the instructions in ROM are permanently etched into the chip. When you turn off the power to your computer, the instructions in ROM remain while any information in RAM is wiped out. When power is supplied to the ROM chip, the BIOS instructions are carried out. However, the instructions in ROM are limited. On most personal computers, including Macintoshes and nearly all IBM compatible PCs, they do not include the operating system.

The Operating System

A computer operating system is a program that consists of commands, routines, and conventions that together can be used to run a computer. Essentially an operating system manages the flow of information into and out of the computer, controlling the four main phases of operation: input, processing, and storage, and output. You can see these diagrammed in Fig. 2-6.

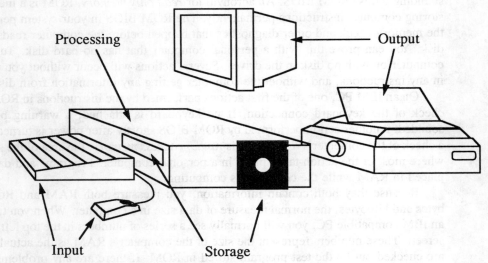

Processing   Output

Input   Storage

Fig. 2-6. Diagram of system components.

While the computer's BIOS sets some of the basic rules for the system, the operating system provides a complete management system with which the user can manipulate data. The operating system controls the opening of files, their arrangement on the disk, the entry of data, the closing of the files, sending files to the printer, and housekeeping tasks like copying and deleting files. Because it does so much, the software that forms the operating system is much larger than the BIOS. This is one reason that most personal computer systems read operating system software into RAM.

Another reason for reading system software into RAM is the high speed with which information can be passed in and out of RAM. When loaded into RAM, the essential operating system software commands can be executed quickly. Also, the practice of reading the operating system from disk allows the operating system to change more easily.

The fundamental programming that has been done in the operating system makes it much easier for programmers to write software. Programs like Lotus 1-2-3 or WordPerfect are called *application software* because they apply the power of the computer to useful tasks. Such applications rely heavily on the operating system to come between them and the raw hardware and BIOS. When you save a file with 1-2-3, it is actually the operating system that carries out the command, deciding where on the disk the file should be placed and keeping track of the location ready for the file retrieve command. You can see this relationship diagrammed in Fig. 2-7.

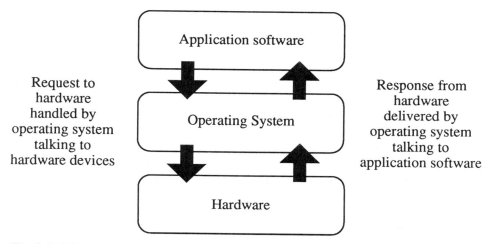

Fig. 2-7. Relationship between hardware, system software, and application software.

The most widely used personal computer operating system is called *DOS*, short for disk operating system. The word "disk" seems a little redundant but might have been used to distinguish the system from more primitive predecessors that were based on tape rather than disk. Also, "disk" implies that the operating system resides on a disk rather than in the system's BIOS. However, some significant exceptions to this are the Toshiba T1000 laptop computer with a version of MS-DOS in ROM and the Tandy Corporation, which has used ROM to store DOS and also a small suite of programs ready to be used without placing any disk in the computer.

You will find that DOS comes in several flavors, the most widely known being PC-DOS and MS-DOS. The term *PC-DOS* is actually IBM's trade name for the version of DOS that they sell. The original creator of DOS is Microsoft, hence the term *MS-DOS*, which is Microsoft's trade name for its own version of DOS. Microsoft licenses DOS to a number of computer makers such as Compaq who get to call their own versions by names like Compaq-DOS. In this book, I refer to PC/MS-DOS simply as DOS.

The IBM PC and its many clones normally use one version or another of DOS, but they do not have to. Other operating systems are run on the same platform (the term *platform* is used to refer to a standard hardware/BIOS combination). Before DOS, a microcomputer operating system called CP/M was very popular with business users. The makers of this system, Digital Research, only narrowly lost to IBM in the battle to provide the operating system for the PC. Digital Research still sells alternatives to DOS, notably Concurrent DOS and DR DOS, the latter being very close to MS-DOS but providing some enhancements like password protection of files at the operating system level.

In some respects, a personal computer built on the IBM PC standard is a generic computer, working on whatever suitably prepared operating system you supply on the boot disk. This flexibility is perhaps one of the reasons that the PC has been so widely used.

In recent years, operating systems more powerful than DOS have been developed in order to use the increased power of newer personal computers. Several versions of Unix will run on PC AT-type systems and PCs based on the 80386 and 80486 chips. IBM has spent large sums of money promoting the OS/2 operating system that was launched with the PS/2 series of personal computers. Both OS/2 and Unix have security features that are dealt with later in the book.

On the other end of the scale, some computer game programmers get around the limitations of using someone else's operating system by writing their own. Games such as Pinball Construction Set and Zaxxon do not need DOS to boot up the system as they have their own graphically-oriented operating system on the program disk. A big advantage of this approach is that there is no question of having to license parts of the operating system from someone else.

The Boot Revisited

Having seen what happens when you first turn on a personal computer, it is time to see how the operating system comes into play. After the diagnostics tests in ROM have been carried out, the BIOS looks for a disk that contains the very first part of the operating system, the *boot sector*.

Using the very basic information in the boot sector, the computer can locate the operating system instructions on the disk and these are read into RAM. The operating system thus takes over control of the system and, in the case of the typical IBM PC, you get to the DOS prompt. On a floppy disk that has been booted from drive A, the DOS prompt might look like this:

```
A>_
```

You can make the prompt more informative than this, but this is what you get when you boot the computer using the standard or default settings. In Fig. 2-8, you can see the screen of a PC that was booted from drive A.

The short flashing line is the cursor. This is where whatever you type will appear. Until you type the name of a command that DOS recognizes and then press the Enter key, the PC does nothing. The letter A represents drive A which, at this point, is the current drive, the one that DOS assumes you are referring to in any commands you issue.

When you boot a PC from the hard disk, the DOS prompt might look like this:

```
Fri Nov 15 1990 C: \ >_
```

The letter C refers to the hard disk and most hard disks are known by the letter C. The date is provided by a customization of the prompt, performed by something called a *batch* file that will be discussed in a moment. In Fig. 2-9, you can see the screen of PC that has just been booted from the hard disk.

```
Current date is Tue  1-15-1991
Enter new date (mm-dd-yy):
Current time is 17:45:23.77
Enter new time:


Microsoft(R) MS-DOS(R)  Version 3.30
            (C)Copyright Microsoft Corp 1981-1987



A>
```

Fig. 2-8. Booting from drive A.

```
HIMEM: DOS XMS Driver, Version 2.60 - 04/05/90
XMS Specification Version 2.0
Copyright 1988-1990 Microsoft Corp.

Installed A20 handler number 1.
64K High Memory Area is available.


V7ANSI.SYS     Version 2.0
Copyright (C) 1987 Video Seven Inc.
Microsoft (R) Mouse Driver Version 7.04
Copyright (C) Microsoft Corp. 1983-1990.  All rights reserved.
Mouse driver installed

Microsoft SMARTDrive Disk Cache version 3.03
    Cache size: 1024K in Extended Memory
    Room for 78 tracks of 26 sectors each
    Minimum cache size will be 256K

Tue  1-15-1991 C:\>
```

Fig. 2-9. A PC booted from the hard disk.

The \ character and colon following the letter C in the hard drive DOS prompt are also added by customization. They refer to the current area of the disk, known as the *current directory*. In this case, the current directory is the main directory, known as the *root*. Directories form part of a hierarchical filing system, branching out like an inverted tree, as can be seen in Fig. 2-10. The directories that are created below another directory are sometimes referred to as *subdirectories*.

In the case of the Macintosh, loading the operating system usually means that the desktop is drawn for you, presenting your files and folders ready for you to begin

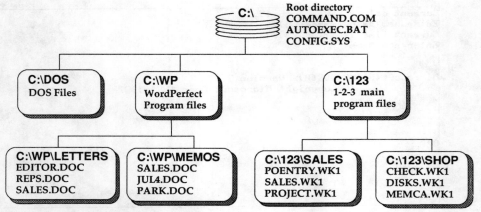

Fig. 2-10. Hard drive directory system.

work. The Macintosh has a filing system equivalent to that on a PC, using folders instead of directories, and folders within folders for subdirectories.

The root directory on a Macintosh is the *desktop*. In Fig. 2-11, you can see the screen of a Macintosh booted from a hard disk. You can also see a series of open file folders forming subdirectories.

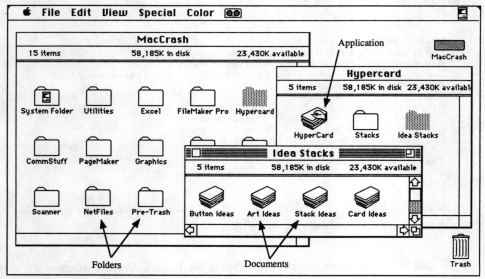

Fig. 2-11. Macintosh file folders.

System Configuration

When the operating system is loaded into a personal computer's RAM, certain assumptions are made about how the operating system is to carry out its work. The assumptions are now as the *default* settings. (In computer terms, *default* refers to what the computer assumes unless you tell it otherwise, and in no way implies that the computer has not been paid for.)

You might want to tell the operating system to use settings other than the defaults. A typical example is the FILES and BUFFERS settings on a DOS system. The FILES and BUFFERS settings determine the total number of files that the system can open at once, and then how many slices of memory should be reserved for juggling programs. The default settings for these two parameters is 2. Many application programs now require around 20 for each setting. Consequently, you need to tell DOS about these variations from the default. You do so with a special file on your boot disk, called CONFIG.SYS. This file is simply a list of statements, each on a separate line, that tell DOS about how you want your system to work.

To tell DOS that you want 20 for the FILES setting and 20 for the BUFFERS setting, you place the following two lines in an ASCII file named CONFIG.SYS:

```
FILES = 20
BUFFERS = 20
```

An *ASCII* file, otherwise known as a *text* file, is one that contains only ASCII characters, and ASCII characters are those that are part of the American Standard for Computer Information Interchange. ASCII is an agreed set of characters to be used by software publishers and hardware makers so that there is some common method of communication between different systems. In all likelihood, your personal computer sends information to your printer in the form of a series of ASCII codes. (Using ASCII codes allows one manufacturer's printers to be used with a variety of makes of personal computer.) For more information on creating ASCII files, see Chapter 5.

Other statements might be required in CONFIG.SYS in order to make a personal computer work the way you want it to. For example, DOS might need to be told how to handle some disk drives and other devices that attach to your PC. This is done through files called *device drivers.* A device driver contains a set of information used by DOS to relate to the device. A typical case would be a special hard disk drive. When the drive is installed a file called something like HARDRIVE.SYS is placed on the boot disk and the statement

```
DEVICE = HARDRIVE.SYS
```

is placed in CONFIG.SYS. This tells DOS how to relate to this particular hard drive. Other examples of special SYS files are RAM disks, print spoolers, and high-resolution monitors.

Operating systems other than DOS use roughly comparable methods to record user preferences and system configuration. For example, on the Macintosh, the user's choice of desktop pattern is recorded in the System file, stored in the System Folder. This preference is actually stored on disk when the Mac is shut down. Unlike most DOS systems, the Macintosh has a formal procedure that needs to be followed when the machine is turned off. Part of this procedure is the updating of the System file to record some of the preferences current at the end of the session. You can verify this by changing the desktop pattern from the Control Panel, then restarting the system. Now select the System file and use the Get Info command from the Macintosh File menu. This will tell you the date and time that the file was last updated, as seen in Fig. 2-12.

This time will be when you restarted the system. Many Macintosh applications also record user preferences in files, some of which are placed in the System folder, like the WordPerfect file called WP 1.0.2 Defaults shown in Fig. 2-12.

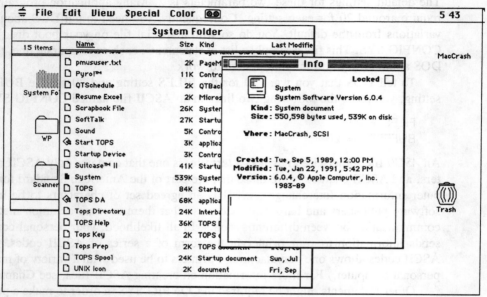

Fig. 2-12. Macintosh System file information.

   Not all Macintosh and PC system preferences are stored in configuration files. The Mac stores such parameters as RAM cache size and volume level in something called *PRAM*, not a perambulator, but a piece of RAM known as *Parameter RAM*. Unlike regular RAM on a Mac, PRAM is maintained by the battery, allowing it to retain information, such as date and time, from one session to the next, regardless of which disk you use to boot the system. On IBM PCs, starting with the AT, a similar arrangement is used to retain information about the type of disk drives installed, as well as the date and time. Unfortunately, these batteries can wear out, which is one reason why AT users sometimes get a message like "Invalid configuration setting, change selection (Y/N)?" when they turn on the computer. Many computer stores sell replacement batteries and long-life battery packs.

The System folder on a Macintosh also contains driver files for special hardware, such as the LaserWriter. These driver files are usually listed as Chooser document when you view the System folder by Name. By including these drivers in the System folder, you ensure that they are available from the Chooser during operation. Mac System folders often contain two other types of file that are important to system startup:

CDEVs and INITs. Both of these are programs, described in the next section, that make useful features available automatically.

The value of configuration files from a security perspective is that they are typically read into memory right after the operating system, and before any programs can be run. By including some sort of key in the configuration file, you can effectively control access. You can also thwart access by keeping the required configuration file separate from the rest of the system. Suggestions on how to do this will be made later.

 Note the file called Tops Key in Fig. 2-12. This is a locked file, one that cannot be deleted (dragged into the trash can). This lock is activated from the File menu with the command called Get Info.

First Programs

When the operating system has been loaded, your personal computer is apt to just sit there, waiting for you to tell it what to do. On some systems, such as the IBM PC, you might be asked to supply the operating system with information about the current time and date, but apart from this, once loaded, the operating system will not initiate any actions. Similarly, the Macintosh will draw the desktop for you, but will do little else. The exception to this is the use of autoexecuting features.

On the IBM PC, autoexecuting is achieved through a specially named file that the operating system always looks for when booting up. Within this file is a series of instructions, telling the operating system to run a program or execute a command. On a DOS system this autoexecuting file is called AUTOEXEC.BAT. A typical AUTOEXEC.BAT might look like this:

PROMPT PG	Customizes the normal DOS prompt.
O'CLOCK /S	Reads the time and data from the system clock.
ECHO OFF	Stops screen repetition of commands.
SK	Loads the utility program SuperKey.
BLANKER	Loads a screen-blanking utility program.
CD \ 123	Changes directory to the area used by 1-2-3.
123	Loads the program Lotus 1-2-3.

For the most part, the instructions in AUTOEXEC.BAT are ones that you would otherwise have to type from the keyboard at the DOS prompt. They are placed one per line with the end of the line acting like the Enter or Return key used to enter the instructions. You can use AUTOEXEC.BAT to read the date and time from the system clock, set a special prompt, set a path, or run a program. For example, many PC users employ small utility programs like Borland's SideKick to carry out tasks that are fairly basic, but not part of the operating system. These programs are loaded into RAM along with DOS, ready to be called upon when needed. Sometimes called RAM-resident utilities, these programs are also known as *TSRs*, for terminate-and-stay-resident programs, reflecting the fact that when they have been used, they remain in memory, unlike major applications such as 1-2-3, which are flushed from RAM when the user exits.

By placing a line in the AUTOEXEC.BAT file, a user can have DOS load the TSR program automatically. The AUTOEXEC.BAT file can also load regular programs automatically. For example, on a PC whose main function is to run costing worksheets, the AUTOEXEC.BAT can load 1-2-3 automatically as soon as the system is turned on. (Some programs, like 1-2-3, have the ability to load data files automatically, permitting a completely automated procedure from power on to data entry.)

Macintosh users who want the system to launch an application when the Mac is turned on can do so with the Special option on the Macintosh menu. First, select the application you want the Mac to launch upon booting (select it, but do not start it). Now choose Set Startup from the Special menu selection and check the Application box. The next time you start up the system, it will open the application. You can disable this feature by checking Finder only or Multifinder only on the Set Startup menu. On some versions of the Mac operating system, you can temporarily disable the auto-launch feature by holding down the Option key while starting or restarting the Mac. Note that most applications will be opened with a blank document, rather than a specific document.

While the Mac operating system does not have the equivalent of an AUTOEXEC .BAT, or of batch files in general, you can use a macro program like AutoMac to execute a sequence of commands. *Macros* are collections of commands and operations that are typically carried out with a single keystroke (*macro* implying many keys under one). With AutoMac, you can create a startup macro that executes when your Mac starts. The subject of macros and batch files for system control will be examined in greater detail in Chapter 5.

Another aspect of auto loading on the Mac are the CDEV and INIT files that, when placed in the system folder, cause software to be loaded automatically when the system starts up. A typical CDEV is the one called Monitor, which is used by the Mac II to allow switching between display modes. Placing the Monitor file in the System folder allows the Monitor icon to appear in the Control Panel. Such files are referred to in the folder directory as a Control panel documents. A typical INIT is Capture, a screen printing utility which I personally like to have available whenever my Mac is running. Such files are referred to in the folder directory as Startup documents. Placing an INIT file in the System folder means that the program is automatically loaded onto memory as the system starts up. This is equivalent to a RAM-resident utility on a DOS machine, otherwise known as a TSR.

If INIT programs and TSRs are loaded when the system starts up, but the system then goes on to something else, how do you access them? The methods vary, but typically a hot key is used. A hot key is a special keystroke combination or sequence which triggers the TSR. For example, you can use Alt−Esc to access the SideKick utility on the PC, or Command−Shift−3 to activate the Capture utility on the Mac. Hot keys are used in some security programs that make use of TSR techniques to keep an eye on operations while a personal computer is running.

The ability to load programs automatically upon booting is a valuable one for programmers seeking to provide security features missing from the popular personal computer operating systems. However, it is important to bear in mind that autoexecuting features can usually be overridden. If you turn on a Macintosh while holding down either the Option key or the Shift key, or both, some INITs will be deactivated, or give you the option to activate them. If you press Ctrl−Break while turning on a PC that has an AUTOEXEC.BAT file you will get this message:

Terminate batch job (Y/N)?

You can type Y and press Enter to circumvent the instructions in AUTOEXEC.BAT.

  You might need to press Ctrl−Break several times during the startup procedure on the PC to get it to work. This is because there are times during the boot process when the system does not accept keyboard input. The correct time to execute Ctrl−Break to interrupt the AUTOEXEC.BAT is just as the system starts reading the boot disk.

SECURE BOOTS

Having seen what happens when a personal computer is turned on, you can begin to see some of the security aspects of the process, and the possibilities for preventing unauthorized access.

The Floppy Boot

Although they are slower and have less storage capacity than hard disk machines, floppy-only personal computers are inherently more secure. This is because any unauthorized use requires a disk, and disks are easy to lock up.

If you are running a personal computer that has no hard disk, you can make it more difficult for someone to use the computer by hiding any floppy disks that contain the system files. Unfortunately, there might be a lot of these disks. It is common for users of floppy-only personal computers to place a copy of the system files on all program disks, so that any program disk can be used to boot the system. However, locking all bootable disks in your desk drawer might well deter casual interlopers.

The more determined attacker is likely to have a boot disk handy. The system files for both IBM and Macintosh operating systems are very easy to get. Nevertheless, if the floppies holding your data files are locked away, there is not much point in an unauthorized user starting up your system, except to put in time on it.

The Unbootable Hard Disk

Normally, one of the first tasks you perform when setting up a hard disk computer is placing the system files on the hard disk. When you are using PC-DOS these files are called IBMBIO.COM, IBMDOS.COM, and COMMAND.COM. If you are using MS-DOS, the first two files are called IO.SYS and MSDOS.SYS respectively. While you are probably familiar with seeing COMMAND.COM in lists of files, you might not have seen the first two files listed. That is because DOS hides them. (There will be more about hiding files later.) All together, the three files enable the computer to be booted by the hard disk, which is the fastest and easiest way to start the system. However, you do not have to place the system files on the hard disk.

If you remove or disable the system files, you can still boot the computer from a floppy disk, and then use the hard disk. This means that a person who does not have the boot disk will have a hard time getting to the hard disk on the computer. This is an effective tactic to use when you are concerned about casual interlopers.

Disk Debooting

The procedure for removing the system files from a hard disk should only be followed after creating a floppy boot disk, and then only by those experienced with DOS. There are two levels of boot-proofing. To get to the first level, you delete or rename COMMAND.COM. If you delete COMMAND.COM from the boot disk, then DOS cannot find it and cannot complete the boot process. Renaming is as effective and can be used in batch files that temporarily deboot a disk (more will be said about batch files in Chapter 5).

The second level of debooting involves deleting the system files. These are called IBMBIO.COM and IBMDOS.COM if you are using PC-DOS; IO.SYS and MSDOS .SYS if you are using MS-DOS. These files are normally hidden so if you simply enter:

    DEL IBMBIO.COM

You will then get the response File not found. You need to unhide the files before you can delete them and this requires DOS utility software, such as Norton Utilities.

In fact, anyone responsible for security on DOS systems would do well to have this software handy. You can use it to recover from accidental file erasing or accidental disk formatting. The Norton Utility program called FA allows you to alter file attributes. Each DOS file has four attributes: read-only, archive, system, and hidden. As you can see from the directory listing in Fig. 2-13, these attributes are not normally apparent when using DOS.

The read-only attribute can be used to prevent important files from being erased or altered. The archive attribute shows whether a file has been backed up or not, and is used by DOS when performing *incremental* archiving, that is, backing up only those files that have been changed since the last backup. The system attribute is assigned to files used by DOS, and the hidden attribute is used to make files invisible to the DIR command. Using FA you can display file attributes and change them. In Fig. 2-14, you can see the FA command applied to the disk shown in Fig. 2-13.

All files on the disk has the Archive status, meaning that they have not yet been backed up, or archived. The first two files on the list carry hidden, system, and read-only status. These two files are the part of DOS that you do not see during normal operations.

As well as showing you the attributes of your files, FA allows you to alter them. For example, you can take the hidden, system, and read-only attributes off the system files, as shown in Fig. 2-15.

```
Tue   1-15-1991 A:\>dir

 Volume in drive A has no label
 Directory of  A:\

COMMAND   COM    25308   2-02-88  12:00a
CONFIG    SYS      215  10-26-90   9:17p
AUTOEXEC  BAT      189   1-13-91   1:33p
COUNTRY   SYS    11254   2-02-88  12:00a
DEBUG     COM    15866   2-09-88  12:00a
EDLIN     COM     7495   2-02-88  12:00a
FORMAT    COM    11671   2-02-88  12:00a
KEYB      COM     9041   2-02-88  12:00a
KEYBOARD  SYS    19735   2-09-88  12:00a
LABEL     COM     2346   2-02-88  12:00a
MODE      COM    15440   2-02-88  12:00a
SYS       COM     4725   2-02-88  12:00a
XCOPY     EXE    11216   2-09-88  12:00a
        13 File(s)    167936 bytes free

Tue   1-15-1991 A:\>
```

Fig. 2-13. Directory of a boot disk.

```
Tue   1-15-1991 A:\>fa
FA-File Attributes, Advanced Edition, (C) Copr 1987, 1988, Peter Norton

 A:\
     io.sys          Archive Read-only Hidden System
     msdos.sys       Archive Read-only Hidden System
     command.com     Archive
     country.sys     Archive
     debug.com       Archive
     edlin.com       Archive
     format.com      Archive
     keyb.com        Archive
     keyboard.sys    Archive
     label.com       Archive
     mode.com        Archive
     sys.com         Archive
     xcopy.exe       Archive

  13 files shown
  no files changed

Tue   1-15-1991 A:\>
```

Fig. 2-14. FA listing.

   This allows you to see the files as part of a regular directory, and also allows you to delete them, as shown in Fig. 2-16.

   Once the system files have been removed from a disk, that disk can no longer be used for booting the system, even if COMMAND.COM is on the disk. Thus, it is not necessary to remove COMMAND.COM to make a disk unbootable, an important point that will be addressed later.

```
Wed   1-16-1991 A:\>fa *.* /r-/hid-/sys-
FA-File Attributes, Advanced Edition, (C) Copr 1987, 1988, Peter Norton

 A:\
      io.sys          Archive
      msdos.sys       Archive
      command.com     Archive
      sec2-14.pix     Archive
      country.sys     Archive
      debug.com       Archive
      edlin.com       Archive
      format.com      Archive
      keyb.com        Archive
      keyboard.sys    Archive
      label.com       Archive
      mode.com        Archive
      sys.com         Archive
      xcopy.exe       Archive

   14 files shown
   2 files changed

Wed   1-16-1991 A:\>
```

Fig. 2-15. Removing system and hidden status.

```
Wed   1-16-1991 A:\>del io.sys

Wed   1-16-1991 A:\>del msdos.sys

Wed   1-16-1991 A:\>dir

 Volume in drive A has no label
 Directory of  A:\

COMMAND  COM    25308    2-02-88   12:00a
SEC2-14  PIX     1819    1-15-91    7:35p
SEC2-15  PIX     1741    1-16-91   12:15p
COUNTRY  SYS    11254    2-02-88   12:00a
DEBUG    COM    15866    2-09-88   12:00a
EDLIN    COM     7495    2-02-88   12:00a
FORMAT   COM    11671    2-02-88   12:00a
KEYB     COM     9041    2-02-88   12:00a
KEYBOARD SYS    19735    2-09-88   12:00a
LABEL    COM     2346    2-02-88   12:00a
MODE     COM    15440    2-02-88   12:00a
SYS      COM     4725    2-02-88   12:00a
XCOPY    EXE    11216    2-09-88   12:00a
        13 File(s)     219136 bytes free

Wed   1-16-1991 A:\>
```

Fig. 2-16. Deleting system files.

A Proper Floppy Boot Disk

To create a floppy disk that will properly boot a hard disk system, you will have to consider what files the system needs in order to operate. In the case of DOS-based machines, the minimum requirement is the system files, but these might not be enough to run the system properly. Most hard disk computers use the two files CONFIG.SYS and AUTOEXEC.BAT in order to give preliminary instructions to the system. If you boot a hard disk computer with just a copy of the system files, then you could be missing important information from the CONFIG.SYS and AUTOEXEC .BAT files. A typical floppy boot disk will have at least the three files COMMAND .COM, CONFIG.SYS, and AUTOEXEC.BAT on it, plus the hidden system files.

Without a correct CONFIG.SYS file on the floppy boot disk, problems in running the system can arise, preventing the interloper with a copy of the DOS disk from getting very far. For example, the correct CONFIG.SYS might contain a FILES= statement without which some of the software on the hard disk will not run. Also, CONFIG.SYS might have a DRIVER= statement that refers to a device driver, without which the system will not operate properly. An example of this might be

DEVICE = HARDRIVE.SYS

which directs DOS to a hard disk device driver file, called HARDRIVE.SYS. Without this file, some hard disks will not even be recognized by DOS, resulting in the response Invalid drive when you enter C:.

In order for your floppy boot disk to work effectively, you need to place on it a copy of the CONFIG.SYS file that would normally be on the hard drive. You should also place on the floppy the SYS files, such as HARDRIVE.SYS, to which CONFIG.SYS refers. Technically, you can refer to drive C for some of these SYS files, but placing them on the floppy disk is safer. To make the system more secure, you can then remove the SYS files from the hard disk (making sure that you have several copies stored away for backup).

For example, if you place HARDRIVE.SYS on the floppy boot disk and remove it from the hard drive, then you have foiled the interloper armed with a DOS system disk. They will not be able to access drive C even though they can get to the A> prompt.

 As with any of the suggestions made in this chapter and the next, you should test them before relying on them. Some device drivers might not be critical to booting the system. I have an 80386 with a Seagate SCSI drive that can be accessed without the file called HARDRIVE.SYS that was created when the drive was formatted with the SpeedStor hard disk management software.

Paths and Programs

The role of AUTOEXEC.BAT is less crucial than CONFIG.SYS when booting a DOS system, but it is still very important. Many AUTOEXEC.BAT files set up the appropriate environment for the applications on the hard disk, including SET and PATH statements. If you boot from a floppy without the correct AUTOEXEC.BAT, then running some applications can be difficult. For example, the PATH statement tells DOS which directories to look in when you ask it to run a program. Take the case of a DOS utility program like CHKDSK, which reviews the use of space on the disk. This is actually a program file called CHKDSK.COM. To use the program you enter CHKDSK at the DOS prompt. Suppose that you do this while the root directory is the current directory. The first thing DOS does is look in the root directory for the file CHKDSK.COM.

Whenever you ask DOS to run a program from disk, it always looks in the current directory first. If the program is not in the current directory, then DOS checks to see if there is a PATH setting. If there is not, you get a message like this:

```
Bad program or file name
```

Suppose that there is a PATH setting, such as

```
PATH = C: \ DOS3
```

This tells DOS to look in the DOS3 subdirectory of drive C, if the program you request is not in the current directory. If the file CHKDSK.COM is in C: \ DOS3, then the program is run. Note that you could run CHKDSK from the root directory without a PATH statement by entering \ DOS3 \ CHKDSK. Alternatively, you could first make DOS3 the current directory by entering CD \ DOS3, then run the program by entering CHKDSK.

To determine the current PATH setting on a PC, you simply enter the command PATH at the DOS prompt. To set a PATH, enter the command followed by a list of directories, separated by semicolons, as in:

```
PATH = C: \ ;C: \ DOS;C: \ 123
```

This tells DOS to look in the root directory of C as well as the DOS and 123 directories. Entering a PATH = statement overrides previous PATH settings.

The AUTOEXEC.BAT on a boot floppy can be the same one used when booting from the hard disk; however, you might want to customize it. Consider this AUTOEX-EC.BAT, taken from system that boots from the hard disk:

PATH = C: \ ;C: \ DOS;C \ CAM	Sets the PATH for DOS to use.
PROMPT PG	Customizes DOS prompt to show path.
O'CLOCK /S	Reads time and date from PC clock.
ECHO OFF	Stops screen repetition of commands.
CLS	Clears screen.
TYPE MENU.MSG	Displays a text menu file.

When transferred to a boot floppy, the file can be altered to this:

PATH = C: \ ;C: \ DOS;C \ CAM	
PROMPT PG	
O'CLOCK /S	
ECHO OFF	
CLS	
C:	Makes C the current drive.
TYPE MENU.MSG	Displays a text menu file.

Macintosh users will note that the Mac operating system does not require any path setting. The system can always find programs. For example, if you double-click on a document called Fred's Memo in the folder called Fred, the Mac attempts to load the application that created Fred's Memo. If the document was created by MacWrite, then MacWrite is loaded if it is present, regardless of which disk or folder contains MacWrite.

Bootless Problems

One drawback to a floppy boot system on DOS systems is that DOS will continue to look for COMMAND.COM on the drive from which you booted. You might wonder why DOS would need to look for COMMAND.COM after reading it from disk in the initial booting procedure. After all, COMMAND.COM is the operating system's command interpreter, loaded into RAM for the duration of the session. Unfortunately, it is not quite as simple as that. Part of COMMAND.COM is always resident in memory, and part is transient. The transient part handles your command requests from the prompt line and is not needed when you are running an application. To give you more memory when running applications, the transient part is unloaded, then reloaded from the COMMAND.COM file when you quit the application. If you boot from a floppy in drive A, load WordPerfect, take out the boot disk (perhaps to insert a data disk), and then exit back to DOS, you might get a message like this: Insert disk with COM-MAND.COM in drive A, and press any key to continue. DOS is simply looking for COMMAND.COM to reread the transient portion into memory, and DOS assumes that COMMAND.COM is on your boot disk.

You can get around this problem in several ways. A popular technique is to copy COMMAND.COM onto a RAM disk then use a SET statement in the AUTOEXEC .BAT file to tell DOS that the RAM drive is the place to look for COMMAND.COM. For example, the following lines in an AUTOEXEC.BAT will do the trick

```
COPY A: \ COMMAND.COM D: \
SET COMSPEC = D: \ COMMAND.COM
```

where D is the RAM drive. The COMSPEC is where DOS looks for COMMAND .COM.

You can set up a RAM drive using one of the many commercial products that come with memory expansion boards, or you can use the file VDISK.SYS that comes with DOS. Enter the following line in your CONFIG.SYS, and you will create a RAM or *virtual disk* that is 128K in size:

```
DEVICE = C: \ DOS \ VDISK.SYS 128
```

This will take 128K away from regular DOS memory. The letter assigned to this drive is the next one after the letter used by the hard disks in your system (if you have two hard disks, C and D, then the RAM disk is E).

If you have an 80286 or 80386 type PC, then you might have extended memory that can be used as a RAM disk without taking up regular DOS memory. You can use the /E option with the CONFIG.SYS entry to place the RAM disk in extended memory, as in:

```
DEVICE = C: \ DOS \ VDISK.SYS 360 /E
```

Because many PC AT type systems have 384K of extended memory, this technique is very useful, giving you a regular floppy disk full of storage space in memory. You can use RAM disks for other tasks besides storing COMMAND.COM.

Another technique to get around the floppy boot "missing" COMMAND.COM problem is to leave COMMAND.COM on the hard disk and then use a SET statement to tell DOS that the hard drive is the place to look for COMMAND.COM, as in:

```
SET COMSPEC = C:\COMMAND.COM
```

You might wonder how you can leave COMMAND.COM on a disk when the disk is not to be used for booting. Bear in mind that DOS requires two other files besides COMMAND.COM in order to boot, as described earlier in the section called "Disk Debooting."

Macintosh users can implement a floppy boot scheme as well, placing the essential programs (System file and Finder) on the boot disk, together with other system files that are needed, such as INITs and CDEVs. The problem with floppy booting a Mac is the large size of recent releases of the operating system. This problem is somewhat alleviated on newer machines that use the high-capacity disks.

Special Cases

A couple of situations deserve special mention when it comes to keeping people out of high-capacity storage devices. Some hard disks are removable, working much like big floppy disks. A prime example is the Bernoulli box system. Using a specially designed floppy disk, this system stores up to 40 megabytes in a cartridge that is little bigger than a CD disk box.

The Bernoulli system offers a good compromise between the high speed and large capacity of a conventional hard drive and the removability of a floppy with all its inherent security advantages. Slip your Bernoulli cartridges out of the drive and into a locked drawer and your data is very safe. You can even do this while your personal computer is still running, so secure lunch breaks are a possibility. Just save your work and slip out the cartridge. Obviously, you cannot take out the cartridge while a program is actively using it. But as long as you are not in the middle of an operation that requires disk access, you can remove the cartridge without having to quit the program. If someone tries to use the program while you are away, they will get an Error reading drive C message.

You can install a Bernoulli system on both Macs and PCs, and newer versions even allow crossreading of disks (the Mac and PC versions can read each other's disk). The cartridge can be set up as the boot device, or you can boot from a different hard disk or a floppy, then access the cartridge. For the operating system to recognize the Bernoulli, a device driver is needed. This means an added measure of security is possible. If you configure the system so that the Bernoulli is not a boot device, you can boot from a floppy on which the device driver has been placed. If you then lock away the floppy, you can prevent people using the system, even if they find a cartridge lying around.

Other removable storage systems include the Tandon DataPak, a fairly conventional hard drive encased in a special box. As hard disks continue to shrink in physical size and expand in storage capacity, removable units become increasingly feasible. Hard drives that attach to your PC via the parallel printer port offer another approach to "removable" storage.

SUMMARY

As you can see, much can be done to achieve a basic level of security by using features and facilities already at your disposal. The next chapter develops the basic theme that a working knowledge of your computer system is the first step to securing it.

3
The First Steps

WHILE CONTINUING TO EXAMINE the basic workings of personal computer systems, this chapter makes some suggestions as to how you might use security resources you already have, or that you can acquire with little cost, to give you a head start in securing your personal computer facilities. Some of the suggestions are not elegant, but they are a good start. The point of this chapter is you can get a lot of security from knowing how personal computers work and applying a good dose of common sense when working with them. Security is as much a question of outlook as it is of outlay. There is no point spending money on security measures if you do not use them, and there is no better place to start than by using the resources that you already have.

BASIC FILE PROTECTION

The terms *read* and *write* are used to signify the complimentary actions of getting information from a disk and placing it onto a disk. Writing to a disk applies to any kind of change to the disk, including erasing files from it. A simple way to prevent data on a disk from being lost or damaged is to use *write-protection*. You can write protect your files either physically or through the operating system. A file that is write-protected is referred to as a read-only file: It can still be read, but it cannot be removed or even replaced by an updated version of the same file. The security benefits of write-protection are that it prevents accidental and casual erasure of files. A reasonably competent user can defeat write-protection, but the innocent user is well-served by it.

Physical Write-Protection

Physical write-protection is a standard feature on floppy disks, but not on hard disks. Write-protection on floppy disks is made possible by a small lever in the drive itself. On traditional 5.25 inch disks, the notch on the right of the disk jacket shown in Fig. 3-1 allows a drive to write to the disk.

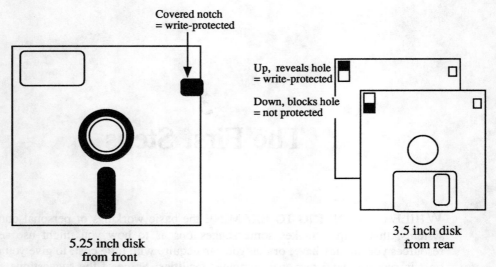

Fig. 3-1. Write-protect features.

A lever in the drive will move into the notch when an unprotected disk is inserted into the drive, allowing the disk to write to the disk. If you close off the notch with a piece of tape or one of the sticky tabs provided in packages of blank disks, then the disk is write-protected. This should be a normal precaution with archive copies.

The newer 3.5 inch disks also feature write-protection, but in a slightly different manner. In the top right of the disk is a square hole, as shown in Fig. 2-12. When you want to allow writing to the disk, this hole must be blocked, which is normally done by turning the disk over and sliding a rectangular piece of plastic across the opening. The drives that read these disks have a lever which allows writing to a disk only if it is kept out of the hole, somewhat the opposite of the system on larger drives. Some 3.5 inch disk drives use an optical system for write-protection. If the light passes through the hole, then writing is disabled.

Of course, write-protection only offers protection against accidental or casual interference, since the system is easily reversed. Furthermore, write-protecting does little help unless you also stick to the rules for disk handling. With careful handling, your disks will retain data for many years. See Fig. 3-2 for the basic rules.

You will also find handling tips on the back of many disk sleeves. Not surprisingly, one of the most basic tips is to always place disks in sleeves when they are not in drives. This wards off fingerprints, coffee spills, and tobacco smoke, all of which

Floppy Disk Care and Handling Information

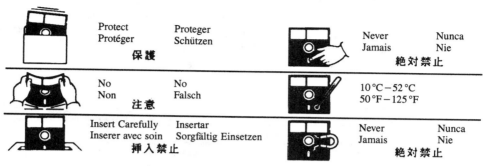

Protect	Proteger		Never	Nunca
Protéger	Schützen		Jamais	Nie
保護			絶対禁止	
No	No		10°C−52°C	
Non	Falsch		50°F−125°F	
注意				
Insert Carefully	Insertar		Never	Nunca
Inserer avec soin	Sorgfältig Einsetzen		Jamais	Nie
挿入禁止			絶対禁止	

Fig. 3-2. Disk protection tips.

pose a threat to the integrity of data on disks. The hard-jacketed 3.5-inch and 2-inch disks are often not supplied with sleeves. Nevertheless, they should be shelved or otherwise removed from the work surface when not in drives because the jackets are by no means water-proof.

Software Write-Protection

When you store information in a file on disk, the operating system might store certain housekeeping information as well. This might include the date and time the file was stored on disk or the name of the program that created the file. Some of this housekeeping information might determine whether or not the user can alter the file. For example, if you select a file on the Macintosh and then select Get Info from the File menu you can check the Locked box, as seen in Fig. 3-3.

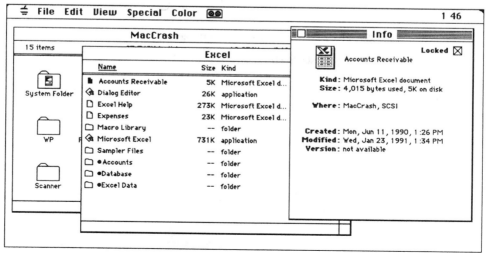

Fig. 3-3. Locking a Macintosh file.

This is the software equivalent of write-protecting the file, preventing from being erased or altered. The file can still be used, but if you read the file into memory and alter it, you cannot store the altered version over the locked original. Locked Macintosh files are shown with the padlock icon in the By Names file listing seen in Fig. 3-4.

If you use the icon method of file listing on the Mac, you can detect protected files by clicking on the name. If the mouse pointer does not change to an edit cursor, then the file is locked.

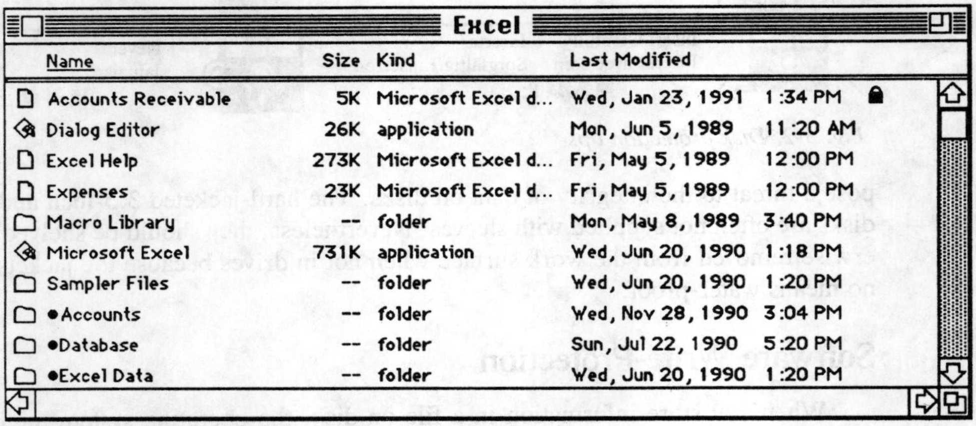

Name	Size	Kind	Last Modified	
Accounts Receivable	5K	Microsoft Excel d...	Wed, Jan 23, 1991	1:34 PM 🔒
Dialog Editor	26K	application	Mon, Jun 5, 1989	11:20 AM
Excel Help	273K	Microsoft Excel d...	Fri, May 5, 1989	12:00 PM
Expenses	23K	Microsoft Excel d...	Fri, May 5, 1989	12:00 PM
Macro Library	--	folder	Mon, May 8, 1989	3:40 PM
Microsoft Excel	731K	application	Wed, Jun 20, 1990	1:18 PM
Sampler Files	--	folder	Wed, Jun 20, 1990	1:20 PM
●Accounts	--	folder	Wed, Nov 28, 1990	3:04 PM
●Database	--	folder	Sun, Jul 22, 1990	5:20 PM
●Excel Data	--	folder	Wed, Jun 20, 1990	1:20 PM

Fig. 3-4. Locked MAC file.

On DOS systems, you can lock a file with the ATTRIB command, which activates the file's read-only attribute. In Fig. 3-5, the user locks a file and then tries to delete it.

```
Wed   1-16-1991 D:\123\DATA>attrib volume1.wk1 +r

Wed   1-16-1991 D:\123\DATA>del volume1.wk1
Access denied

Wed   1-16-1991 D:\123\DATA>
```

Fig. 3-5. The ATTRIB command.

You reverse the ATTRIB command by using − instead of +. Also note that you can alter the attributes of several files at once by using DOS wildcards. For example, give read-only status to all of the program files in a directory that have the EXE extension, you would enter:

```
ATTRIB + R *.EXE
```

This prevents accidental removal of these program files. The read-only status of DOS files is maintained when they are copied from one disk to another.

On a Mac, you can lock several files at once by selecting more than one file, with Shift−click, before selecting Get Info. The locked status of Mac files is preserved when they are copied from one disk to another.

Note that locking files can create its own problems. Some programs write changes to the program file during use. If the file is locked, this is not possible, sometimes leading to unpredictable results. Also, you will need to remove write-protection to perform housekeeping chores such as cleaning up redundant files. Users might find it a chore to unlock files before getting rid of them. On DOS systems, the simple task of moving files from one directory to another is complicated by write-protection since the files have to be copied and then deleted, the latter being impossible until the read-only attribute is turned off. To make extensive changes to the DOS file attributes, you might want to employ a DOS utility program like QuickDOS II which presents a menu-driven file listing with a tag system in order to simplify selective attribute manipulation, as shown in Fig. 3-6.

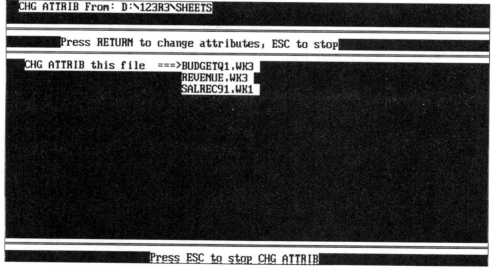

```
CHG ATTRIB From: D:\123R3\SHEETS

      Press RETURN to change attributes, ESC to stop
CHG ATTRIB this file   ===>BUDGETQ1.WK3
                          REVENUE.WK3
                          SALREC91.WK1












                Press ESC to stop CHG ATTRIB
```

Fig. 3-6. Changing attributes with QuickDOS II.

WHILE YOU'RE AWAY FROM ME

So far you have seen some simple techniques for deterring people from stealing or starting up personal computers. However, this does not solve the problem of defending computers that are in the office, turned on, and unattended. In the preceding section, you read how to prevent accidental erasure of files, but typical office practices mean that there will probably be a period of time in every day during which a computer is on but unattended. This might be during bathroom or coffee breaks, over lunch, or while meetings are being attended.

Policy Matters

Most users will object to security policies that would require them to turn off their computers every time they leave their desks. The main objection is that turning the system back on can take several annoying and unproductive minutes, depending upon the amount of RAM, number of utility programs installed, and so on.

A secondary argument can be that it is a pain to have to save to disk all of the current work before leaving the machine unattended, but this argument is less defensible. As a matter of security, all users should always save their work before leaving their desks. This avoids all sorts of problems such as, "Who used my computer without saving what I was working on."

Wear and Tear

In addition to the time saved, a good argument for leaving a personal computer turned on is the claim that doing so saves wear and tear on the components. It seems reasonable to assume that the initial rush of electricity through the circuits, the effort of bringing the hard disk up to speed, the shock of power to the monitor, are all best avoided. On the other hand, leaving systems on for long periods seems to involve few hazards. On most systems, the only moving parts are the fan and the hard disk. While normal hard disks spin continuously, the delicate read/write mechanisms are at rest when the system is not receiving input.

The one question mark concerning extended periods of personal computer use is heat damage. Any properly designed personal computer will maintain the temperature of components within working limits for extended periods. What can cause problems are variations in ambient temperature that exceed those limits. For example, a PC that works fine in the office during the day might have problems at night or on weekends when the normal air cooling systems are turned off to save energy.

A single PC can produce several hundred watts of heat, and a small local area network can act like a two-kilowatt fan heater. Combine that with a hot day and a lack of air conditioning, and you could be looking at heat damage to sensitive circuit boards. Indeed, any time that the temperature in your office gets above 90 °F (32 °C), your personal computer equipment is liable to fail due to heat problems.

See No Evil

One other source of avoidable wear and tear on unattended computer is the monitor. Some monitors are adversely affected by displaying the same image for prolonged periods of time. The image gets "burned in" to the phosphors painted on the inside of the screen. These phosphors normally glow when the electron beam hits them, producing the image that you see. In fact, they can glow very brightly, producing an image that is visible even in broad daylight.

Try this if you are in the office at night: Turn off the lights and turn on a personal computer that was used during the daylight, that is, one with the brightness turned up fairly high. Notice how painfully radiant the image is. Leave it on for about five minutes, then turn it off. The image will appear to linger on the screen. Some monitors that have used 1-2-3 every day for years will retain an image of the spreadsheet outline even when the monitor is left off for long periods. Another trick is to sit at your computer during normal work hours and don a pair of dark glasses. Your view of the rest of the office will be dimmed, but the screen will be perfectly legible.

There are several ways of dealing with the monitor afterglow problem. On some systems, you can very easily turn down the brightness control. Other systems make this adjustment difficult. You could unplug the monitor from the system unit, but this is often awkward and integrated machines like the Macintosh SE do not allow this at all. Turning off the monitor is one alternative but this does impose the on/off wear and tear you want to avoid (on a Macintosh SE you have to turn off the whole system to turn off the monitor). A good solution is to use a *screen blanker*. This is a program which, instead of sending an image to the screen sends no image at all, or a very limited one.

The Blank Screen

Several screen blankers are commercially available. Macintosh users can employ Pyro, available from several sources, including Software Supply who include it with their very useful utility software, Suitcase II. Pyro will blank the screen on command or after a certain amount of time (set by the user) during which there is no mouse movement or keyboard input. A distinctive and useful feature of Pyro is the display of tiny fireworks on the screen while it is otherwise blank. These slowly moving images let you know that the machine is still turned on, without running the risk of screen damage from prolonged display. One problem with screen blanking is the risk that someone might assume a machine to be turned off just because there is no image on the monitor. This can lead to systems being unplugged and moved without proper shutdown procedures being followed.

Users of Microsoft's Windows environment on DOS systems can use a screen blanker that is very similar to Pyro on the Mac. Called Fireworks, this program is distributed as shareware by Synergistic Enterprises. This program will blank the display after a specified period of inactivity or on command. The display is not completely blank, small fireworks erupt from time to time. You can even send a small plane across the screen and launch fireworks yourself.

For those DOS users who work without Windows, a good screen blanking facility is included in the RAM-resident utility called SuperKey from Borland International.

This will do timed blanking, on-demand blanking, and even allows password-protected blanking, discussed in greater detail in Chapter 7.

A super Macintosh program that is not just a screen blanker is Pad-Lock. With Pad-Lock installed, leaving your Mac unattended is not a liability. You simply press a key, then supply a password that will be required of anyone who attempts to access the system. The screen then goes blank except for a bouncing picture of a padlock! When you return, you click the mouse button. You are then prompted for the password. When you enter it correctly, the display is restored. If someone tried to access the system while you were gone, Pad-Lock tells you. You can even customize the warning message that would-be intruders see when they try to enter a password. For more details of Pad-Lock and similar programs see Chapter 7.

To recap: When you leave the computer unattended, you will leave it on, but with nothing on the screen. This saves time, wear and tear, and provides a minimum level of security. To see your work or access files, someone will have to do something besides look.

PASSWORD PROTECTION

Having seen how you can keep data safe from accidental erasure and casual observation, it is time to look at how you keep people from reading your files. Several methods may be readily at your disposal, some of them powerful enough to defeat the most determined snoop.

The Need for Passwords

Suppose you go to lunch, leaving your personal computer on, with the screen turned down. In comes arch-rival Desmond Cry (known to his enemies as Des). He turns up the screen and sees that you are working in 1-2-3. Before you left for lunch, you remembered to save your worksheet, called SALARY91.WK1, which contains sensitive salary data. You also remembered to erase this worksheet from memory so that nobody else would see it, even if they were smart enough to turn up the monitor. However, Des Cry is smart enough to figure that the sensitive salary file is called something like SALARY. Of course, he can use the /File Retrieve command to list all of your worksheet files, and then press the F3 key to show the file names, together with their date and time stamps. He sees that the last file you worked on was SALARY91, and so he retrieves it. In a matter of seconds, your sensitive data is compromised, and all because you did not take a few extra seconds to use the 1-2-3 worksheet password feature.

Like many popular applications, including WordPerfect, Excel, dBASE, Paradox, and Quattro, 1-2-3 offers a simple but effective password option when you store information in a file. To activate this feature in 1-2-3, you simply follow the name of the file with a space and the letter P as you save it with the /File Save command, as shown in Fig. 3-7.

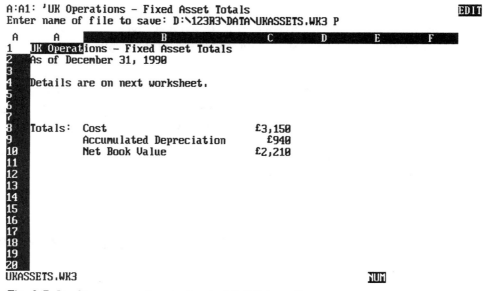

Fig. 3-7. *Invoking password protection in 1-2-3 Release 3.*

When you press Enter, you are prompted for a password. This can be up to 15 characters in length, consisting of numbers, letters, punctuation, and spaces. The password is case sensitive, meaning that Key is different from KEY and key. As you type the password, each character appears as an asterisk on the screen, shielding it from prying eyes, as shown in Fig. 3-8.

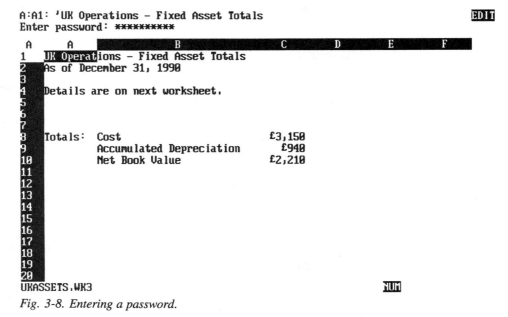

Fig. 3-8. *Entering a password.*

Because what you type is also shielded from your eyes, you have to enter the password a second time to confirm it. If you don't type the password correctly the second time, you have to start again. When the correct password is entered, the file is saved in coded or encrypted form.

Encryption generally means scrambling information based on a key, so that the information is meaningless without the key. In this case the key is the password, and the information is the contents of worksheet file. Once encrypted, the file cannot be retrieved into 1-2-3, nor can the contents be deduced by reading the file with any other program, unless you have the key.

Suppose that you have password protected your SALARY91 file. Sly Des Cry attempts to retrieve it. He gets the message seen in Fig. 3-9.

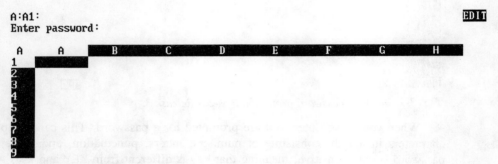

Fig. 3-9. The 1-2-3 password prompt.

Des takes a guess at the password, and types it in. When he presses Enter he gets the response seen in Fig. 3-10, because his guess was incorrect.

Word processing is a personal computer application where the need for security is often overlooked, despite the fact that word processed reports, memos, and correspondence can reveal a great deal about an organization. If you use WordPerfect for word processing, then you can assign password protection with Ctrl−F5, followed by P for password. The password you enter will not appear on the screen and so must be retyped for verification. When you attempt to retrieve a password-protected WordPerfect document, you get the message seen in Fig. 3-11.

Because databases can contain large amounts of valuable information, it is common to apply passwords to them. Indeed, most database management software includes several levels of password protection. For example, in the program called Paradox you store data in special files called tables. If you create a database table with Paradox then you are considered the table owner and can assign a password to it. Only people with the password can change the table. However, the owner of the table can also assign auxiliary passwords controlling the right to view, update, and rearrange the table. In Fig. 3-12, you can see the Paradox auxiliary password form. Several different passwords can be created for a table, each with a different combination of privileges.

Because organizations that develop large collections of data often need to provide many people with access to that data, a lot of database management software is

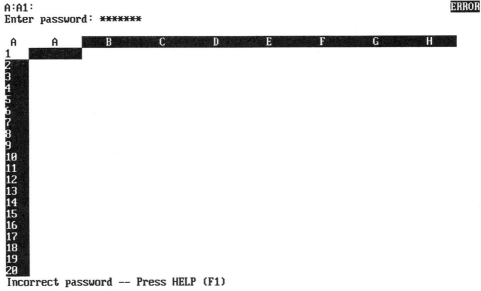

Fig. 3-10. Unsuccessful password guess.

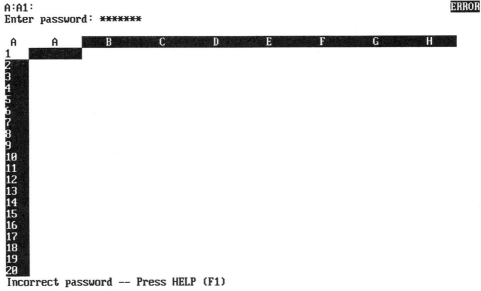

1 Retrieve; 2 Delete; 3 Move/Rename; 4 Print; 5 Short/Long Display;
Enter Password (D:\WP\SECURITY\VIRPROD2):

Fig. 3-11. WordPerfect password protection.

designed to run on a local area network. When the number of users multiplies, so does the task of managing passwords. Paradox contains a special feature called the Protection Generator, which manages passwords for an entire network.

```
Defining auxiliary password 1 of Bookord table                    Password
[F1] for help with setting password options.  [F7] for table view

┌────────────────────────────────────────────────────────────────────────┐
│ Auxiliary password:  @Fred's                               Page 1        │
│ ─────────────────────────────────────────────────────────────────────── │
│ Table Rights  InsDel                   Family Rights  V                  │
│                                                                          │
│ Enter one │ Rights conferred           Enter all that apply, ↵ for none  │
│ ──────────┼──────────────────          ───────────────────────────────  │
│ All       │ all operations             (F)orm       │ change forms       │
│ InsDel    │ change contents            (V)alCheck   │ change validity checks │
│ Entry     │ data entry and updates     (R)eport     │ change reports     │
│ Update    │ update nonkey fields       (S)ettings   │ change image settings │
│ ReadOnly  │ no modifications                                             │
│ ─────────────────────────────────────────────────────────────────────── │
│ Field Rights  Enter ReadOnly or None for each field or leave blank for All. │
│                                                                          │
│ Cust    ReadOnly◄                                                        │
│ Date                                                                     │
│ Item #                                                                   │
│ Vol                                                                      │
│ Quant                                                                    │
│ Emp #                                                                    │
│                                                                          │
└────────────────────────────────────────────────────────────────────────┘
```

Fig. 3-12. Paradox password.

Instead of each user having a different password for each database table, each with a specific assigned level of access, the network administrator can, by means of the Protection Generator, collect each user's privileges under a single password that grants a mixture of access privileges, covering multiple tables. This means that each user only has one password to remember, and changes to passwords can be quick and convenient.

Operating System Passwords

Programmers who write personal computer operating system software have to make compromises between the many different features that some users would like and the amount of space that the resulting program will occupy in memory. Extra memory chips cost extra money. In the IBM compatible world, extra memory chips are difficult to integrate into the overall system design, developed when memory requirements were a lot less than they are today, because software was less sophisticated. In fact, many users do not need all of the features in DOS 4.0, or even 3.3. Small specialized systems, like the Toshiba T1000 laptop, function very well on DOS 2.11.

One feature that many users would like to see in their operating system is password-protect of files. This would relieve some of the burden from application designers who must include such a feature in their software since the operating system itself does not support it. A step in this direction has been taken by Digital Research in its DOS work-alike called DR DOS. This operating system works much the same as

PC-DOS, but DR DOS offers several added features, such as password protection for files and directories from the DOS command line.

DR DOS has several levels of password protection controlled by options used with the PASSWORD command. You can see these options listed in Fig. 3-13.

```
A>password /h
PASSWORD R1.22    Display or change password protection level
Copyright (c) 1987,1988 Digital Research Inc. All rights reserved.

password [/Help] [d:][path][filename.ext] [/R:W:D:P:G[:password]] [/N] [/S]

Valid options are...
  /R[:password] "password" will be required to read, write or delete the FILE
  /W[:password] "password" will be required to write or delete the FILE
  /D[:password] "password" will only be required to delete the FILE
  /P[:password] "password" will be required for all access to the DIRECTORY
  /G[:password] set global default password

  /N            remove password protection from file
  /NP           remove password protection from directory
  /NG           remove global default password

  /S            operate on files or directories in subdirectories

A>
```

Fig. 3-13. The PASSWORD command in DR DOS.

This figure illustrates another nice feature of DR DOS: The ability to get help for any command simply by entering the command followed by /H.

DR DOS allows you to require that a password be entered before a user can even read a file. Alternatively, you can allow files to be read, but not altered. Access to entire directories can be made dependent on a password, effectively shielding a complete application with one password.

A global password can be remembered by DR DOS to allow automatic password entering. If you use the same password for all of your files, DR DOS can supply the password whenever it is needed. This enables a fairly sophisticated protection system to be enabled when you boot up under DR DOS. The AUTOEXEC.BAT can ask you to enter your password, which is then remembered for the duration of session. If you enter the correct password, that is, the one you have used for all of your protected files, then you will have free access to those files. If you enter an incorrect password, file access will be denied. Indeed, you can protect vital system files to make successful booting impossible without the correct password.

In Fig. 3-14, you see a session with DR DOS in which a file is protected and then an attempt is made to access with the wrong password.

```
 /D[:password]  "password" will only be required to delete the FILE
 /P[:password]  "password" will be required for all access to the DIRECTORY
 /G[:password]  set global default password

 /N             remove password protection from file
 /NP            remove password protection from directory
 /NG            remove global default password

 /S             operate on files or directories in subdirectories

A>password d:\123\data\volrev.wk1 /r:@work456
rwd   d:volrev.wk1

A>type d:\123\data\volrev.wk1
Invalid Password
A>copy d:\123\data\volrev.wk1 a:
Invalid Password
      0 File(s) copied

A>copy d:\123\data\volrev.wk1;@work456 a:

      1 File(s) copied
A>
```

Fig. 3-14. Using the PASSWORD command with DR DOS.

Obviously, the correct password is required to remove password protection. Unfortunately, in current versions of DR DOS the PASSWORD command is an external one, meaning that it is not one of the core commands, like DIR, that are permanently retained in memory. This means you cannot perform automatic encryption that can be utilized by application software. Users must add passwords to files outside of the application that creates the file, either after the application has terminated or through a shell command. Future versions of DOS or the Macintosh OS might include password commands that can be called by applications so that whenever files are saved, password protection is an option. Some form of on-the-fly encryption would be a welcome addition to personal computer operating systems.

Third-Party Passwords

If your operating system or the application software that you use for your sensitive data does not have built-in encryption, you can still make use of this security measure by using a third-party program. In the DOS world, one such program is Borland's SuperKey. The main function of SuperKey is to provide PC users with features not found in the operating system or applications. For example, SuperKey provides macro facilities for programs that do not have them, plus, as you read earlier in this chapter, screen blanking.

SuperKey is a memory-resident utility that is loaded after DOS but before applications so that it can be called while you are using DOS or any applications running under DOS. SuperKey provides a encryption feature that works with all types of data files. To encrypt a file, you simply activate SuperKey, usually by pressing Alt — \ ,

```
┌──────────────────────────────────────────────────────────────────────────────┐
│ Macros    Commands  Functions   Options    Defaults  █Encryption█ Layout  Setup │
├──────────────────────────────────────────────────────────────────────────────┤
  ..          <DIR>       10-06-91   11:49a           ┌─────────────────────────┐
  123R3DOS WK3      834    8-20-90    3:13a           │Encrypt file             │
  ACCTNGDB DBF     4255    7-05-90    3:19p           ├═══════ENCRYPTION═══════──┤
  ATOAYEAR WK3   114302    9-09-91    1:07p           │File:         SUMMARY.WK3 │
  CONSOL   WK3     2746    6-19-89                    ├──────────────────────────┤
  CUSTNADB DBF     4214    6-29-90   11:13a           │Keyword:      ****        │
  DATA     WK3     3199    6-19-89                    │Text mode? No             │
  EMPFILE  DBF      666    4-24-89   11:32a           └──────────────────────────┘
  G04AUTO1 WK3     7367    8-22-90    7:32a
  ORDERSDB DBF     4740    6-29-90   11:30a
  SALES    WK3     1890    6-19-89
  SAMPMACS WK3     6862    6-19-89
  SHIPRDB  DBF     4851    6-29-90   11:35a
  SHOES    WK3     2960    6-19-89
  SUM1988S WK3     2293    6-19-89
  SUMMARY  WK3     1568    6-19-89
  TABLES   WK3     4851    6-19-89
  THFSDIR  DBE     5888    7-14-91    5:00p
  UKASSETS WK3     1975   10-20-91    3:29p
        20 File(s)    3461120 bytes free

D:\123R3\DATA>
```

Fig. 3-15. The SuperKey menu.

and select Encryption from the menu bar that is displayed across the top of the screen, as shown in Fig. 3-15.

When you have entered the file name and typed in the keyword, press Enter and retype the keyword to make sure it is correct. Asterisks are displayed in place of the characters you type to prevent the password from being seen. When you enter the keyword a second time, you are asked if you want to use text mode. Typically, you will accept the default answer, which is No. You do this by pressing Enter. At this point the file is encrypted. The contents of the file will be unintelligible unless you unencrypt it.

If you attempt to use an application to read a file encrypted by SuperKey, you will probably get an error message such as Incompatible file format. You can then call up SuperKey, use the Decrypt option, specify the file, and enter the password. Note that SuperKey does not do any of this automatically, which adds a further level of security, but makes the operation somewhat inconvenient. Also, the SuperKey encryption does not prevent the file from being copied, deleted, or renamed.

On the Mac side, you will find third-party encryption is available in a variety of programs. For example, the suite of utility programs called PC Tools Deluxe for the Macintosh (from Central Point Software) contains a piece of software called PC Secure. This program allows you to store files in an encrypted format protected by a password up to 32 characters in length. The program also compresses files, so that they occupy less space on the disk. In Fig. 3-16, you can see the PC Secure menu.

Note the files in the background that have padlock icons. These have already been encrypted by PC Secure. As you can see from the menu, this program has a number of sophisticated features, including the ability to hide files, making them invisible on the desktop. Further applications of PC Secure are discussed in Chapter 8.

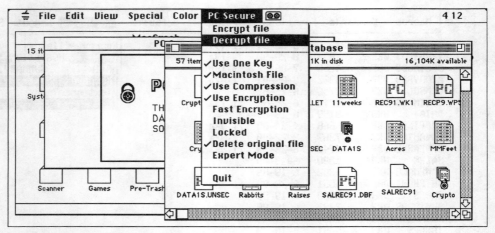

Fig. 3-16. Securing files with PC Secure.

You can use PC Secure as a desk accessory, enabling encryption to be performed from within another application, such as MacWrite. However, files that you encrypt with PC Secure are no longer listed by application File Open menus because their file type has been changed. To compensate for this, PC Secure enables you to launch an application from a secured document, presenting you with the password verification screen shown in Fig. 3-17.

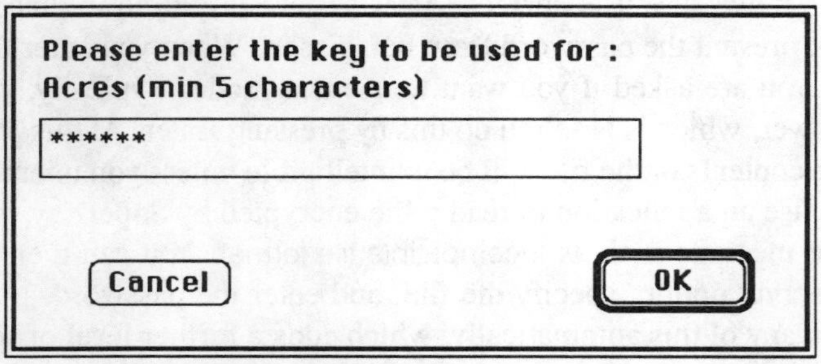

Fig. 3-17. Entering a PC Secure password.

If you enter the correct password, the file is decrypted, the application that created the file is automatically launched, and the document is loaded. You must remember to encrypt the document again. (Note that PC tools for the Mac is now called Mac Tools.)

Password Limits

The protection provided by password schemes is limited. Some simply prevent unauthorized reading of the file. Others prevent unauthorized erasure as well as access. Beyond these limits, the whole concept of password security has limits, which are discussed in greater detail in Chapter 8, where you will find a system for password management. At this point, note that the two main threats to password security are user indifference and hacker initiative. If you forget to use a password or use the same one all the time, such as your first name, then it is unlikely that a persistent interloper will be stopped. Beyond this, it is important to realize that not all encryption schemes are created equal.

Encryption of a file is done with an *algorithm*, a special type of formula. Algorithms vary from simple to highly complex. Not surprisingly, the more complex the encryption algorithm, the longer it takes to encrypt and unencrypt the file. Ironically, the computers themselves set the pace as far as encryption goes. Indeed, the birth of computer technology is closely linked to the efforts to decipher encoded enemy messages, and the same need still motivates much computer research. One measure of the strength of an encryption algorithm is how long it would take for a very powerful computer to "break the code."

If the encryption algorithm used by an application is a simple or common one, then it is likely that someone will develop a means of breaking the code. The encryption method used by 1-2-3 Release 2 can be broken by a personal computer. A much more powerful method of encryption is the U.S. Data Encryption Standard, known as DES, sanctioned and controlled by the U.S. government. Some applications and third-party security products like SuperKey and PC Secure provide DES encryption as an option.

However, because the U.S. government attempts to control the distribution of this cryptographic technology through an export ban on products that provide DES encryption, some software companies have dropped DES in favor of their own algorithms, known as *proprietary* algorithms. For example, copies of PC Secure that are sold outside of the U.S. do not include DES encryption. In typical personal computer work, the proprietary algorithms are sufficient defense against data theft, secure against all but the most expert and ardent attackers. (For more on DES and government intervention in personal computer security, see Chapter 8.)

DISK DISASTER RECOVERY AND PREVENTION

All the locks and keys and encryption in the world is of little use if your operating system scrambles your data for you. Is this possible? Unfortunately, the answer is an emphatic *Yes!* Although most damage to personal computer files is undoubtedly done by negligent or malevolent users, with hardware failures like disk crashes coming a close second, there are times when the operating system itself fails to perform.

Accommodating Data

To understand why a disk can just give up the ghost, you need to know how data is stored on a disk. The disk itself has a magnetic coating that records data in much the same way that VCR tapes record movies. However, while the location of a particular part of a tape is a one-dimensional measurement, that is, the distance from the beginning of the tape, locating data on a disk requires that the information be structured. This structure is called a *format*, a magnetic grid by means of which the disk drive can assign an address to any part of the disk. The basic layout of data on a floppy disk is shown in Fig. 3-18.

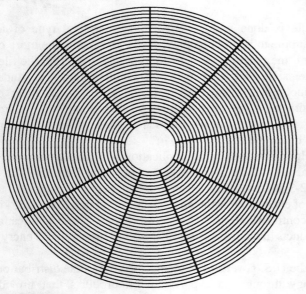

40 circular tracks
9 pie-shaped sectors
9 x 40 = 360 boxes
known as sectors
each storing 512 bytes
= 184320 bytes or
 180 kilobytes per side
180 x 2 = 360K per disk

Fig. 3-18. Disk format.

You can see that the space on one side of a disk is divided into concentric circular tracks which are further divided into sectors. This circular grid, known as a *format*, creates a large number of small sections of disk, sometimes referred to as *blocks*. Different operating systems use slightly different track and sector formats, however, most use both sides of the disk. This is done without you having to turn the disk over, because the disk drive's read/write head scans both sides of the disk at once.

Wipe Out

The format is a set of signals written on the disk by the operating system. Without a format, a disk cannot store files. In the DOS world, you use the command FORMAT to prepare a new disk so that it can store data. In the Mac world, formatting is called *initializing*. For example, when you take a floppy disk fresh from the box and place it in a Macintosh floppy drive, you get the message seen on the left in Fig. 3-19.

If you proceed to initialize the disk, you get the warning seen on the right of Fig. 3-19. If you want to reformat a disk on the Macintosh, you use the Erase Disk command on the Special menu.

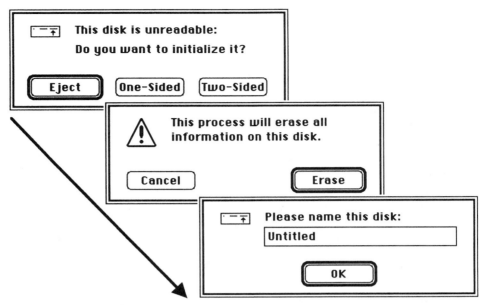

Fig. 3-19. Mac initialize message.

Both hard disks and floppy disks require formatting. In both the Mac and DOS worlds, it is vitally important to bear in mind that the preparation or formatting of disks removes any previously stored data from the disk. Format the floppy disk on which you have stored the accounts receivable database file and you loose that file. While you can write-protect floppy disks to prevent them from being wiped out by the format command, write-protecting hard disks is a different story. You need to be able to write freely to hard disks that are in use.

Many personal computer users know that the format command wipes out the data on a disk. On more than one occasion, the format command has purposely been used to erase critical data files. With a single instruction, a disgruntled employee can trash a hard disk full of data. An ill-informed employee can perform the same operation if not properly trained in the basics of system operation.

One school of thought suggests that you never tell employees about formatting, relieving them of the temptation to abuse this fundamental part of personal computer operation. A more progressive view sees that well-informed operators are less of a threat than those who are stumbling in the dark. But in both views, it makes sense to control the formatting of disks. Several approaches are possible. On DOS systems, the command itself can be removed or renamed. Supplying employees with preformatted disks makes a lot of sense. These tactics are discussed in Chapter 9. At this point it is important to be aware that there is a threat to data from commands that are central to the operating system itself.

The Hotel Register

Most files take up more than one sector. Large files are spread across many sectors. A list is maintained by the operating system showing which sectors are used by what files. If you think of sectors as rooms in a hotel, accommodating a large file is like booking in a rock star with a large entourage. Many rooms are taken up and the entries in the register keep track of who is in which room. The operating system equivalent of the hotel register is called the File Allocation Table, or *FAT*.

When you delete a file, this frees up space on the disk. However, the operating system does not clean out the sectors that were once occupied by a deleted file. This would make deletion a lengthy process. Instead, an alteration is made to the FAT. In the case of DOS, the first letter of the file is removed, effectively removing the file from the directory listing and making it inaccessible to normal applications. However, immediately after a file is deleted, the data is still in the sectors. In fact, the data will remain there until DOS needs the vacated space to add further files to the disk.

Special applications such as Norton Utilities and Mace Utilities, are able to read the FAT and give you a chance to replace the first letter of a file that was "erased." These programs can then use the information in the FAT to find data that belongs to the file, scanning the sectors of the disk until as much as possible of the file has been recovered. If you delete a file accidentally and then use one of these unerase programs right away, you should be able to get all of the data back.

Disks and Data

Normally files are stored in contiguous or connected sectors (adjoining rooms in terms of the hotel analogy). However, as you delete files from a disk, space comes available between files. Eventually this space will be used up by new files. As files are added, enlarged, and erased, the records in the FAT get pretty complex.

Then you delete one or two of the files. Spaces appear in the block of sectors. Now you copy some more files to the disk. Parts of these files are placed into the spaces left open by the removal of previous files. Some files will not be stored in consecutive sectors but split or fragmented across several parts of the disk. The same thing happens if you read a file into memory, add data to it, then resave it onto disk. The file will no longer fit in the original sectors and the added data is stored in a different part of the disk. In Fig. 3-20, you can see a map of a typical DOS hard disk, showing how the space has been used.

This map was produced by a program called Norton Speed Disk, discussed in a moment. Note the large number of unused areas mixed in with the used areas. Also note that the disk area is divided into segments, each of which is 9 clusters in size. A cluster is the smallest area of a disk that DOS will handle. This is usually more than one sector. On a 360K disk, one cluster is 1024 bytes. This means that a file which is 1428 bytes in size will occupy 2 clusters. The 620 bytes of extra space $(2048 - 1428 = 620)$ is unused. On a hard disk, a cluster might be larger. This is why you sometimes run out of space when copying from one disk to another, even though you have

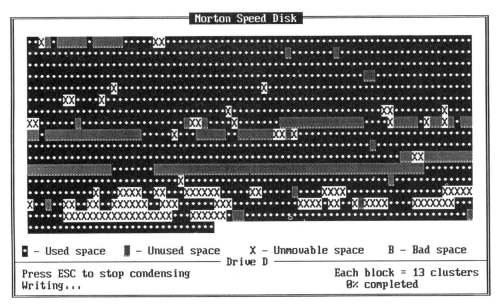

Fig. 3-20. Speed Disk map.

checked that the number of "bytes free" is greater than the total number of bytes in the files being copied.

The fragmentation of files into noncontiguous clusters is generally not a problem for operating systems because they are designed to cope with the phenomenon. Files spread over different parts of the disk can still be read, and the FAT keeps track of where the parts of a file are stored. However, if a disk experiences a lot of adding and removing of files, then the web of connections between files can become quite tangled, and can cause several difficulties.

The more a file is fragmented, the more revolutions of the disk it takes for the entire file to be read into memory. Response time when reading and writing files can slow down dramatically. Both program and data files can be affected. This is particularly noticeable on hard disk systems. Beyond this problem, the fragmenting of files increases the chances that the FAT will not be able to cope. Files can become cross-linked, meaning that the connections between separate part of a file are corrupted.

 I have seen this happen quite often on floppy disks used to move copies of files from one computer to another. If you use the same floppy to take copies of data files home every night to work on them on your home computer the copying on and off of data can wear out the disk's FAT and lead to corruption, even loss of data.

Checking up on DOS

One of the cheapest and easiest preventative measures on DOS systems is to run the CHKDSK utility regularly. This command reports on the use of space on a disk and the amount of memory available in your PC. You can also use CHKDSK to determine how fragmented your disk has become. In Fig. 3-21, you can see CHKDSK used with the DOS wildcard (*.*) that tells CHKDSK to examine each file to see if it is stored in contiguous space.

```
C:\>chkdsk *.*
Volume COMPANY PC  created Aug 25, 1991 10:32a

 32333824 bytes total disk space
   243712 bytes in 25 hidden files
   112640 bytes in 37 directories
 27580416 bytes in 1817 user files
  4397056 bytes available on disk

   655360 bytes total memory
   267376 bytes free

C:\OLDBACK.M_U
    Contains 4 non-contiguous blocks.
C:\BACKUP.M_U
    Contains 4 non-contiguous blocks.
C:\KEYS
    Contains 5 non-contiguous blocks.
C:\LPTX1.LST
    Contains 4 non-contiguous blocks.
C:\HIMEM.SYS
    Contains 2 non-contiguous blocks.

C:\>
```

Fig. 3-21. Using CHKDSK.

You can see that six of the files on the disk are stored in more than one block of clusters. This is not a critical problem, but one that slows down performance. To correct the problem, copy the files to another disk (using COPY or XCOPY, not DISK COPY).

You can also use CHKDSK to analyze the FAT and check for storage problems. Unfortunately, most DOS manuals gloss over the darker implications of the CHKDSK command, using language like this:

> If you specified the /F parameter, you can reply y to tell DOS whether or not to correct the error.
> Depending on the type of error, DOS may or may not be able to recover the data.

Such equivocal statements offer little comfort if you have just tried to load the sales report file that is due to be completed in half an hour and received the message, Error reading drive A, Abort, Retry, Ignore. Nevertheless, CHKDSK can help you determine the problem and even direct you to a solution.

When you run CHKDSK, the program does not actually check the disk space. Rather, it puts together the information in the directory with the information in the FAT to make sure that they match up. In checking the FAT against the directory, DOS will turn up two types of problems: Lost clusters and cross-linked clusters.

A *lost cluster* occurs when a value has been entered for a particular cluster in the file allocation table, but none of the active files in the directory use the cluster. This creates no active danger to existing data files, but it does mean that DOS will not allocate this cluster to any new files.

A *cross-linked cluster* is a more serious matter. In this case, the FAT indicates that a data cluster is being used by two or more different files. This is an anomaly because the data in the cluster should belong to one or the other of the cross-linked files. In the case of cross-linked data, it is highly probable that one or all of the cross-linked files have suffered damage.

The normal cause of such problems is an interruption while DOS is attempting to write information to the disk. This can be the result of a hardware, software, or user error. For example, if a user starts to copy a large data file from the hard disk to the floppy drive but removes the floppy disk before the drive light has gone off, or if there is a power failure at this point, then DOS might be prevented from completing the copying of the file onto the disk.

When you copy a file, DOS first enters the file name into the directory. It then examines the FAT to determine what clusters are free for its use. DOS then writes the data into the clusters. When the writing is done, it returns to the directory and completes the entry for that file by writing the location of the first cluster for that file and its size. This means that if DOS is interrupted while writing a file, you might see the name of the file in the directory with a size of 0 bytes, an indication of an interrupted file-writing process. Some or all of that file was actually written to the disk before the error occurred, but DOS cannot find it.

The DOS program CHKDSK accepts a switch, called /F for *fix*, that causes the program to modify the FAT and directory in order to deal with lost clusters, performing one of two operations on them. For example, CHKDSK A: /F will display a message indicating the number of lost clusters on drive A and asking how you want to deal with the clusters. In Fig. 3-22, you can see the response if lost clusters are encountered.

```
Sun 12-01-1991 A:\>CHKDSK /F

2 lost clusters found in 1 chains.
Convert lost chains to files  (Y/N)? Y

   362496 bytes total disk space
    24576 bytes in 3 hidden files
     4096 bytes in 4 directories
   327680 bytes in 32 user files
     2048 bytes in 1 recovered files
     4096 bytes available on disk

   655360 bytes total memory
   381200 bytes free

Sun 12-01-1991 A:\>
```

Fig. 3-22. CHKDSK dealing with lost clusters.

The program offers you two choices. If you enter Y, you are telling the program that you want to correct the problem by creating a file name in the directory that will correspond to the lost clusters. In that case, the FAT is left pretty much intact and the directory is modified by having a new file name or names added to it.

The term *chain* refers to groups of clusters that are numbered consecutively in the FAT. The assumption is made that all consecutively numbered clusters should be placed into a single file. If DOS finds clusters that are not consecutive, it counts each group as a separate chain and assigns a separate file name for each chain. The file naming convention is to use the name FILEOOOO.CHK for the first chain of clusters, FILEOOO1.CHK for the second chain, and so on.

Note that collecting the lost clusters into files does not free up any disk space. The purpose of the collected files is to allow you to examine the contents of the clusters to determine if you really want to preserve this data. If you do not intend to go through this trouble, it is better to select N. If you enter N to the prompt, the program leaves the directory as it is and alters the FAT by setting all lost clusters back to a value of zero. This also resolves the problem of the lost clusters and, in so doing, releases all the data clusters to be used with other files.

Cross-linked clusters present a more difficult problem. When a disk contains cross-linked clusters, the CHKDSK command will display a list of the cross-links and the files that they relate to, such as:

```
A:\FRED.DBF
    Is cross linked on cluster 123
A:\JOE.DBF
    Is cross linked on cluster 123
```

The list will always contain pairs of entries, one for each file cross-linked to the same cluster. Using CHKDSK, even with the /F parameter, will not affect cross-linked clusters. The reason is that the disk directory or FAT provide no clues as to which file the cluster should belong.

The easiest way to get rid of the cross-links is to delete the files. If the files contain valuable data, another solution is to copy both files to another name on the same disk, or preferably to another disk. Next, you delete the cross-linked files and copy them back to their original disk or file names. This will eliminate the cross-link, but, because DOS copies the cross-linked sector into both files, it does not mean that the files are undamaged. You will have to test the files to see which one, if either, still functions correctly.

Also note that CHKDSK utility does not rearrange files to untangle the fragmentation. For this you need a specialized program called a disk optimizer, discussed next. An advantage of CHKDSK is that you can incorporate it into a batch file, perhaps the AUTOEXEC.BAT, making disk checking a regular preventative measure, rather than waiting to use CHKDSK when you encounter problems reading files.

Optimizing Your Disks

Given the natural tendency of disks to get cluttered by a mass of fragmented files, you would think that the operating system could do something about it. Unfortunately, you need to buy a special type of program called a *disk optimizer* to clean up this problem. Several of these are available for both IBMs and Macs.

The general idea of a disk optimizer is to read files off the disk and then write them back in consecutive sectors. This is a fairly complex operation, and you need to follow carefully the instructions and precautions that come with whatever disk optimizer you use. For example, on DOS systems, you will probably want to make a complete backup of a hard disk before you optimize it for the first time. In the unlikely, but possible, event that the disk optimizer is not compatible with your particular brand of hard disk, you will be protected against the program not working properly.

An optimizing program called Speed Disk comes with more recent versions of the Norton Utilities. Earlier in Fig. 3-21, you saw the display that the program generates when it goes to work on a disk. This shows the way disk space is allocated by representing a small group of clusters with a small rectangle. The number of clusters per rectangle in the map depends on the size of the disk. While the map does not show individual files, it does give you an idea of how efficiently the disk is used. In Fig. 3-23, you can see a map of disk that has been optimized.

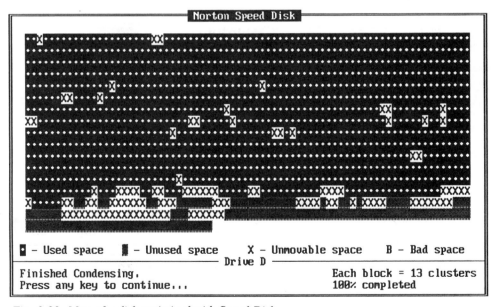

Fig. 3-23. Map of a disk optimized with Speed Disk.

You can see the improvement, with all data stored in contiguous clusters. While optimizing can take a long time, several hours in some cases, the improvements in performance and reliability of files storage are well worth it. Instituting regular optimization sessions, perhaps as part of a backup cycle, is a valuable preventative measure.

 This advice is particularly germane to those using complex software like Windows or Presentation Manager. These "operating environments" make heavy demands on hardware, requiring that your system be kept well-tuned. For example, programs that use hard disk space as virtual memory, rapidly swapping code between RAM and disk, need hard disks that meet the highest tolerances. If the disk fails to locate a critical segment of software, a system crash could occur. If you hear a hard disk rapidly moving the read/write head back and forth for extended periods, (sometimes called *thrashing*), then you know it is time to optimize. If this does not help, then you may need to reconfigure the system, otherwise complete failure of the hard disk can result.

Minding the Mac

Several programs perform hard disk optimization on the Mac. The PC Tools suite of utilities from Central Point Software were mentioned earlier. This set contains the Optimizer program, which performs several important housekeeping tasks, as you can see from the program screen in Fig. 3-24.

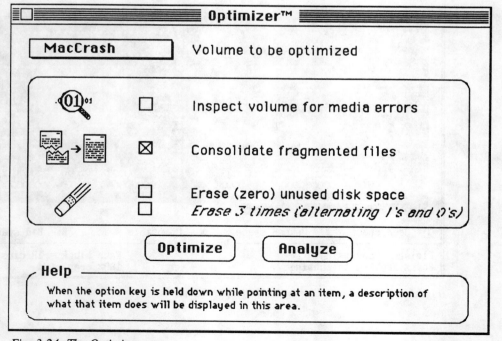

Fig. 3-24. The Optimizer menu.

Until I started daily hard disk optimization on my Mac, I was losing all the data on my hard disk about once a month. Given the difficulty that the Mac operating system sometimes has in keeping its "act together," optimization is a very important preventative measure. In some ways the Mac's occasional crashes are understandable, after all, the graphical nature of the system means that even simple tasks involve complex interaction of software and hardware. When it is working at full tilt, with several applications open at once under MultiFinder, and a dozen desk accessories on hand, the Mac is an impressive machine. But this power has a price, and the delicate harmony can unexpectedly fall apart with unpleasant results. At times it seems like the system software just gives up trying to coordinate things: data files are randomly blended, old files mysteriously reappear, eventually the bomb or sad Mac face tell you contact with the hard disk has been lost.

The first item on the Optimizer menu in Fig. 3-24, indicated by the magnifying glass, inspects the disk for *media* errors or actual physical problems with the storage of data. The program will list bad blocks and note any that contain data. You can then use a utility like MacTools, which comes with PC Tools, to move and recover the files before they are lost.

The second item on the Optimizer menu performs the consolidation of fragmented files. In typical Mac style, the torn page icon is put into motion when the program runs, showing pages being pasted back together. This process can take several minutes for heavily fragmented disks as each file has to be read into memory and then written back to disk.

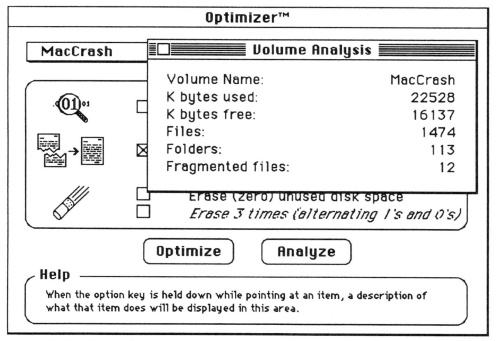

Fig. 3-25. The disk analysis report.

In order to perform the optimization, you must first select Analyze. This operates much like CHKDSK on DOS systems, giving you a report like the one seen in Fig. 3-25.

Like DOS, the Macintosh OS does not actually erase files when it deletes them, it simply alters the directory so that deleted files are not listed and the space they occupy can be used for new files. This feature of file handling in the operating system makes possible the recovery of deleted files, described in Chapter 9. However, it opens up a security window, through which the clever interloper can gain access to data that you thought had been removed. For example, programs like MacTools on the Mac and Norton Utilities on the PC make the reading of deleted data files quite simple. To prevent anyone from reading remaining file fragments on the Mac, you use the option on Optimizer menu represented by the pencil tip eraser. A slower but even more secure option is the last on the menu, which performs the erasure three times. Similar utilities exist for the PC, some of which are described in Chapter 9, where the problem of secure deletion is discussed in further detail.

The only defense that is more than pretense
Is to act on the fact that there is no defense
Piet Hein

4
Analysis and Planning

THE FOCUS OF THIS CHAPTER is how you go about analyzing personal computer security risks and planning appropriate defensive measures. How do you value personal computer assets? How do you quantify the risks of attack? How do you weigh the potential losses from an attack against the cost of security measures? How do you go about developing personal computer security policies for yourself and/or your organization? How should you respond to a major breach of security?

This chapter will help you answer these questions. In doing so, three important documents will be discussed: the Risk Evaluation, the Security Policy, and the Contingency Plan. Any organization that has computer assets should have all three. By the very act of preparing these documents, an organization can improve its ability to defend personal computer resources and cope with security problems. Also, personal computers can be applied to some of the tasks of security analysis. Reports and questionnaires can be created with word processing and desktop publishing packages. Database software can organize details of hardware and software resources. A spreadsheet can be used to analyze risk factors.

THE TERMINOLOGY OF RISK

Concern about security is a fairly recent phenomenon in the microcomputer world. The more established environment of mainframe computing has been involved with security issues from its very inception, largely because much of the early development of computer systems was carried out by intelligence agencies. Specialized terminology has been developed with which to discuss the analysis of mainframe security, and it is natural that some of the terms should be carried over into the realm of personal computer security. However, it is all too easy for specialized terminology to obscure what is at the heart of personal computer security: common sense. While this chapter uses numerous specialized terms, the intent is to provide a suitable vocabulary for the subject matter, not to suggest that fancy phrases are a substitute for following the straightforward procedures that form the basis of security planning.

Mainframe vs. Micro

Quite a few texts deal with risk analysis for large computer systems. In some cases, the methodologies developed are very sophisticated. However, significant differences between the world of the mainframe and the world of the micro can make it difficult to adapt mainframe risk analysis techniques to personal computers.

Consider the concern among managers of mainframe systems about the unauthorized use of computer time. Mainframes support many users, whose work places demands on the processing capacity of the system. The system then has to allot resources to the various tasks competing for its attention. With a personal computer that supports one user at a time, you can usually see if the computer is being used. If someone else is using the personal computer you normally use, then either they have to "get off" or your work has to wait. On a mainframe system, the distribution of resources is not such a discrete variable. For example, a typical airline reservation system can accept thousands of users at once, and the number of active users varies greatly according to the time of day. If activity is heavy, say on a Friday afternoon, response time for each user slows down, but the system keeps working (hopefully!). Seldom is the functioning of the system dependent upon one user kicking off another in order to be accommodated by the system.

As a consequence of the multiple-use that is characteristic of a mainframe system, and in order to cover the high cost of creating such a system, mainframe processing time is assigned a value. This can be expressed as so many dollars per minute. Someone who takes up time without proper authorization, and without paying for it, is thus considered to be stealing a valuable resource. In some ways, this is analogous to stealing into a movie theatre through an unlocked exit. The theater was showing the movie anyway; the interloper has not physically taken or damaged anything. Nevertheless theater management can easily determine what the nonpaying customer has "cost" the box office (the price of a ticket).

Consider a biology student who gains unauthorized access to company mainframe. The student uses the mainframe to perform a statistical analysis of some tests he has been running. No company programs or data are altered or damaged. Nevertheless the student has stolen computer time, and the consequences could be more serious than crashing a movie. The student's program, competing for the processing resources of the mainframe, is likely to slow down other programs. Suppose the company uses the mainframe to perform account posting overnight. Company operations might rely on having accurate balances available at 8:00 A.M. There could be a loss of business, goodwill, and productivity if normal overnight processing is not completed on time, fairly heavy consequences from such seemingly harmless unauthorized use.

A manager of personal computer systems is probably less concerned by this type of unauthorized use since personal computers are seldom used around the clock. Indeed, some companies allow employees to use systems for their own projects in the evening or on weekends, figuring that this creates goodwill, more competent users, and the occasional productivity bonus. Management does need to be concerned about unauthorized use if there is the possibility of data loss, data damage, or other ill-effects from unsupervised use. As far as the actual cost of time used, unauthorized use is a minimal cost if it does not interfere with normal operations.

You can see that the mainframe poses quite different risks from the personal computer. If you are considering applying mainframe-oriented risk analysis techniques to personal computers, you should realize that in many ways, personal computers are inherently less secure than larger systems, and thus pose a greater challenge when it comes to risk evaluation.

End Users vs. Administrators

The chapters that come after this provide details of different devices and techniques that can be used to increase security. Some of these devices and techniques can be put in place by individual users, while others must be or are best implemented at a group level by someone in an administrative capacity. This is not an endorsement of centralized computer bureaucracy. The fact is that many security measures are only effective if they do form part of a comprehensive approach to the matter. Only after careful analysis of the need for security, the current level of security, and the current capacity to cope with a breach of security can a group of users make effective decisions about how to improve matters.

You will recall that in Chapter 1 three types of personal computer users were identified: Private user, group user, and supporting user. Of these three types, the supporting user is most often addressed in this chapter. This is because the activity of risk assessment and security planning needs to be done on an organization-wide basis. The private user should carry out these activities, albeit on a much smaller scale than the supporting user. Group users need to think about the value of the personal computer resources they use. Their input on matters of security should be sought by supporting users. But group users cannot be held responsible for overall security strategy. Their role is to implement the strategy developed by supporting users.

Methodology

Personal computer systems are used to perform such a diverse array of tasks, in such a vast variety of organizations, that it is very difficult to lay down any hard-and-fast rules as to the best way to ensure the security of those systems. Much of the important information in this chapter appears in the form of lists from which you can select the parts you need for your specific situation. Indeed, the assessment of risks and formulation of responses must be tailored to each organization, which is why this chapter precedes detailed discussion of the many security devices and techniques that are available.

Coming to Terms

To talk about security risks just in terms of "the company" is a real temptation. But terms like *corporate exposure* tend to give the false impression that only commercial entities use personal computers. Local and national government departments as well as nonprofit agencies form a very significant group of computer users with very real security concerns. For this reason, it is helpful to talk in terms of the *organization*, rather than the company. One term that helps to focus on the universal nature of security measures is *mission*. Thus the effect of losing data can be assessed as a *mission threat*, meaning the extent to which this computer problem prevents the organization from functioning normally, or the extent to which the purpose of the organization is thwarted.

You might come across the term *mission-based risk analysis*. This is used to describe a particular approach to security analysis, sometimes distinguished from *threat-oriented risk analysis*. According to David Snow, writing in *Government Computer News*, threat-oriented methods "apply a predefined set of adversary capabilities to determine whether possible system security failures can be exploited."

According to Snow, threat-oriented methods have several drawbacks. First of all, "Analysis can only be done when the system is well-defined." If you are trying to decide what risks are posed by your current personal computer systems, it might be adequate to check off a list of possible threats, like the ones given in this chapter. However, if you are introducing personal computers into an organization, or supervising the growth of a personal computer installation, then you will want to adopt a mission-based approach.

The second drawback of threat-oriented thinking is that "Only the insecurity of the system is demonstrable—not its security—and there is always uncertainty about additional unidentified impacts on the mission." By contrast, mission-oriented methods "attempt to identify all mission hazards early on. The hazards are then used to define the systems' basic security requirements." There are four elements to mission-oriented risk analysis.

Security Fault Analysis. This means looking at the computers, their software, their location, and their purpose, in order to identify security loopholes that could lead to a *mission hazard*. For example, a new personal computer is being installed that will receive inventory reports via modem from other PCs at remote locations. Because the modem will have to be set up to receive data, a path into the computer system is opened up. This will need to be guarded by security measures such as password authentication because unauthorized access to this path could allow someone to steal/damage/compromise data. A weakness in the safeguards placed on the modem connection poses a mission hazard.

Threat Analysis. This means looking at the capabilities of potential adversaries to determine whether or not they could cause or exploit a security failure. Suppose that a modem-equipped personal computer is used to store central inventory records for several branches of a jewelry store. A password is required before an incoming phone connection can be established with the inventory computer. Threat analysis looks at how likely someone is to try and make an unauthorized connection to the computer, what are the chances they will persist in trying to guess the password, how strong the password is, and what sense or use could be made of the inventory information if the password was broken. A further factor would be what damage to business could be caused by the corruption or loss of the data rather than its exploitation. The chart in Fig. 4-1 shows the basic assumption that the greater the capabilities of potential adversaries, the greater the justification for strengthening the system.

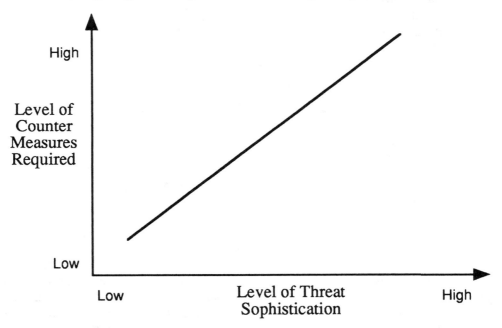

Fig. 4-1. Threat analysis assumptions.

Risk Reduction. If analysis of the weaknesses in the system and the strengths of adversaries reveals risks that are deemed unacceptable, then further risk reduction is necessary. Further *countermeasures* can be considered, and an assessment made of the relative *cost-effectiveness*. The chart in Fig. 4-2 shows the basic assumption that the greater the possible loss from a security failure, the greater the justification for further risk reduction.

Security Evaluation. Because absolute security is an unobtainable goal, a given set of security measures can be tested until the weak points are revealed. Evaluation of the security of the system with safeguards in place is an important part of the risk analysis process.

Suggested Procedures

The first stage in a review of personal computer security can be accomplished by preparing a document called the *Risk Evaluation*. This is an exploration of the poten-

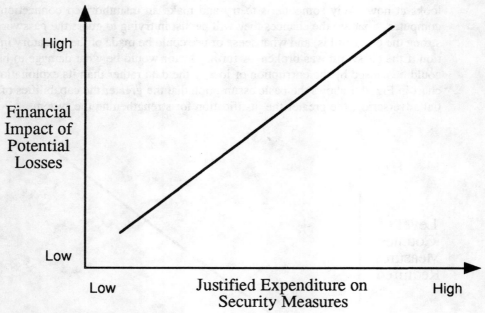

High

Financial
Impact of
Potential
Losses

Low

Low   Justified Expenditure on   High
                          Security Measures

Fig. 4-2. Risk reduction assumptions.

tial for loss, the consequences of a loss, and the likelihood that a loss will occur. The task of risk assessment can be anything from a sole proprietor making notes about what could go wrong and what the cost would be, to a major survey performed by a team of consultants. The end result in either case should enable management to prepare the *security policy*. In a security policy, you lay out rules and regulations for users, including those techniques, devices, and practices that will be implemented to maintain the desired level of security. When the security policy is in place, you can develop the *contingency plan*. In the contingency plan, you describe proper responses to security incidents, giving procedures for users to follow in the event of a breach of security. This approach to security can thus be summarized:

- Risk evaluation—what are the risks, what is the value of what is at risk.
- Security policy—what practices should be followed, what devices used, and what is the allocation of responsibility.
- Contingency plan—what should be done to recover from a major security incident.

More about Risk Analysis

The analysis of risk is an inexact science, dealing as it does with estimated values, chances, and probabilities. A fair amount of literature is on the theoretical side of this issue. Tables of probabilities have been developed showing the likelihood of a certain type of disaster occurring in a particular location. There are even computerized risk analysis systems, such as the BDSS program (short for Bayesian Decision Support System), which are discussed later in this chapter. However, these programs are focused on larger computer systems and tend to be inappropriate or overkill for personal computer users. What you must do is make an objective assessment of the likelihood of negative events in your location. One simple method for doing this is outlined in the section called "Performing Your Own Risk Evaluation."

Risk analysis is more than figuring the chances of bad things happening. You will need to put a dollar amount on the possible impact of bad things. This can then be used to weigh the cost of defense against the value of what is being defended. Essentially the risk evaluation you need to perform for personal computer systems should attempt to answer, as reliably as possible, the following questions:

What are you trying to protect?
What is its value to you or your organization?
What are you trying to protect against?
What is the likelihood of an attack?

About Your Security Policy

Like a personnel or employment policy, a security policy is an essential document for a company that relies on personal computers. In this document, you lay out the responsibilities of each staff position with respect to security measures. Rules are set down for ongoing security practices and for additional actions to be taken by key personnel. For example:

Everyone who uses a personal computer must save work and turn down the screen whenever they leave the computer unattended.

The manager of information services will perform spot checks to ensure that backups are performed according to agreed schedules.

The security policy should also describe how security devices work and how they are administered. For an example, consider the simple device, keyboard locks. The security policy might state:

All users will lock their keyboards whenever leaving their system unattended.

But this is not enough. You must have rules about who keeps the main key and who keeps the copy. When an employee leaves the premises at night, should the key be left at work, locked in the employee's desk, or can employees take keys home? Who is responsible for retrieving the key when an employee is terminated? Who assigns the key to new employees? In-depth treatment of complex systems, like smart cards or sign-on passwords, can be very time-consuming, but once procedures are clearly established, they are easier to maintain effectively.

About the Contingency Plan

Even if everyone adheres to well-defined security procedures, problems can arise. In addition to determined data thieves, natural disasters are difficult to prevent. In the contingency plan, you lay down procedures to be followed in the event of a problem. You might begin with a list of all possible problems, taken from your risk analysis, and then decide who should do what when the problem happens. For example, each user should know to whom he or she should report missing data files. While this might be a natural extension of the normal chain of command or the usual lines of communication, the administration of security matters cannot be taken for granted. Suppose that the immediate supervisor thinks that a loss of data files would be a negative reflection on his or her performance. This perception might act as an impediment to prompt reporting of a loss to more senior management. Similarly, a corruption of data files might be dismissed as a minor computer malfunction by a supervisor who is not technically competent. You should consider setting up special channels for reporting matters of security, perhaps through a central security coordinator. A contingency plan will address these issues, as well as such questions as where to hire replacement equipment, how to recreate accounts in the event of a complete loss of files and backups.

PERFORMING RISK EVALUATION

Risk evaluation involves imagining what could go wrong and then estimating what the cost could amount to. For each of the possible problems the question of probability needs to be considered. In this way, the problems and their potential costs can be prioritized and an appropriate plan of action developed.

A Basic Example

When it comes to specifics, there are several ways of going about the task of risk evaluation. Consider a small consulting company of six people that uses personal computers for its billing and accounting, as well as for the preparation of proposals, contracts, and reports. The company has few rivals in the area. The company is located on the ground floor of an office building on the fringe of the central business district of a large metropolitan area. The office is not visited by the general public. The company has three PCs, a laser printer, and a modem to call up a specialized on-line database. The company recognizes that the information that is its lifeblood flows through its personal computer equipment. The office manager sits down with the other employees and makes the following set of notes, which have been annotated for your edification.

What personal computer security risks does the company face?

- Fire, destroying equipment and files.
- Common theft, taking equipment and files.
- Vandalism, damaging equipment and files.
- Equipment failure, damaging files.
- Screw-ups, damaging files.
- Virus damage, damaging files.
- Earthquake, destroying equipment and files.
- Unauthorized access, leaking sensitive data.

- Data theft, spreading data without fee.
- Fraud, diverting funds by computer.

This is a rather short list, but the company is fairly small and fortunate in that it is not open to the public and does not have extensive connections to outside computers.

How likely is it that any of these mentioned risks will happen?

- Fire, destroying equipment and files: building recently refurbished to code with sprinkler system, plenty of extinguishers and smoke detectors. Risk factor—very low.

- Common theft, taking equipment and files: neighborhood is not the best, some drug dealing, computers visible from street during daylight hours. Risk factor—high.

- Vandalism, damaging equipment and files: possibility of damage from disappointed or thwarted burglar, otherwide malicious damage unlikely. Risk factor—medium.

- Equipment failure, damaging files: even the "best" equipment seems to wear out/break down from time to time. Most hardware was purchased with "loaner" provision in case of failure, but fall-out from critical failure hard to predict. Risk factor—medium.

- Screw-ups, damaging files: most current employees well-versed in computers, those who are not know to ask for assistance. This factor would be very low except for need to bring in temp help during vacations. Risk factor—low.

- Virus damage, damaging files: a lot of software used to be tried out in the office before "vetting" was introduced. Even with precautions, infection still possible through commercial software, client data disks. Risk factor—medium.

- Earthquake, destroying equipment and files: location is earthquake prone, building is supposedly earthquake proof. Major quakes produce many unforeseen problems; it could affect us, but chances of a quake are small. Risk factor—low.

- Unauthorized access, leaking sensitive data: few rivals, unlikely that a competitor would try to get at our files. The modem is used to call out, cannot be used to call in. Risk factor—low.

- Data theft, spreading data without fee: some of our databases are now quite valuable, could lose revenue if they were made public, but list of suspects is short. Risk factor—low.

- Fraud, diverting funds by computer: unlikely given small size of company and the fact that one person does all of the accounting. Funds paid out are to suppliers and there are only a few of these. Risk factor—very low.

The company is fortunate in having good fire protection in the building and well-trained employees. However, the building location poses problems. The concern over hardware is typical reflecting what many users see as a relatively low level of hardware reliability in personal computer systems. The lack of concern about user-errors smacks of over-confidence.

Summary of risks, ranked by risk factor:

- Common theft: high.
- Vandalism: medium.
- Equipment failure: medium.
- Virus damage: medium.
- Screw-ups: low.
- Earthquake: low.
- Unauthorized access: low.
- Data theft: low.
- Fire: very low.
- Fraud: very low.

This ranking will be important when they enter the cost/benefit phase of the evaluation. Note the terms low, medium, and high. While these might seem subjective and unscientific, the alternatives are scarcely any better. If you assign a scale of 1 to 10, does 8 mean 4 times more likely than 2? Does 1 mean it will happen once in the next ten years? If you use percentages, what are they measuring? The field of probabilities is a vague one at the best of times. Later in this chapter is a discussion of a formal measurement called *annualized rate of occurrence*, but this is of limited practical value.

What do we stand to lose?

- Common theft: Equipment is insured, but data is not. Reconstructing data and getting "back to normal" could take up to ten person-days. Some business might go unbilled and some work might be lost. Potential per incident loss: $5000.

- Vandalism. Same as above. Potential per incident loss: $5000.

- Equipment failure. No single piece of equipment would cost over $3000 to replace. Potential per incident loss: $3000.

- Virus damage. Given current means of early detection, could cause one day disruption for four people. Potential per incident loss: $1000.

- Screw-ups. Given current levels of expertise, could cause half day disruption for one person. Potential per incident loss: $500.

- Earthquake. Loss of equipment and interruption of business covered by insurance. Potential per incident loss would be limited by deductible: $5000.

- Unauthorized access. Revealing some of our internal comments could cause loss of goodwill. Losing a major client could have a serious impact. Potential per incident loss equal to annual revenue from largest single client: $50,000.

- Data theft. Loss of revenue in one year could probably amount to one quarter of total revenue (currently $280,000 per annum). Potential per incident loss: $70,000.

- Fire. Loss of equipment and interruption of business covered by insurance. Potential per incident loss would be limited to deductible: $5000.
- Fraud: Total cash turnover per month is $40,000 but this is closely watched. Potential per incident loss: $10,000.

This casts an interesting light on the relative importance of each threat. Consider the spreadsheet in Fig. 4-3 that lists Threats, Risk Factors, Loss Potentials, and Loss Exposures.

Risk Analysis - Loss Factors

Threat	Risk Factor	PPIL (K)	Loss Exposure
Fire	1	$5.0	$5.0
Equipment Theft	4	$5.0	$20.0
Vandalism	3	$5.0	$15.0
Failure	3	$3.0	$9.0
Screw-ups	2	$5.0	$10.0
Virus	3	$1.0	$3.0
Earthquake	2	$5.0	$10.0
Leaks	2	$50.0	$100.0
Data theft	2	$70.0	$140.0
Fraud	1	$10.0	$10.0

Fig. 4-3. Spreadsheet of loss factors.

You can see that Risk Factor column assigns a value to the terms very low, low, medium, and high. The column headed PPIL lists the values identified in the above list as potential per incident losses, given in units of $1000. The Loss Exposure column multiplies the Risk Factors by the Loss Potentials. When you sort this table according to the Loss Exposure column, you get the very interesting results seen in Fig. 4-4.

This tells the company that the highest risk factors do not necessarily create the largest exposures. Another approach would be to replace the high-low risk factors with estimated rates of occurrence. The table you see in Fig. 4-5 shows the estimated incidence of each threat for each year, based on management's best guess.

The results can be termed the *annualized loss exposure* (ALE) and, as you can see, they differ significantly from the estimates based on risk factor. This table will help the company decide which threats should get the most attention.

Risk Analysis - Loss Factors

Threat	Risk Factor	PPIL (K)	Loss Exposure
Data theft	2	$70.0	$140.0
Leaks	2	$50.0	$100.0
Equipment Theft	4	$5.0	$20.0
Vandalism	3	$5.0	$15.0
Screw-ups	2	$5.0	$10.0
Earthquake	2	$5.0	$10.0
Fraud	1	$10.0	$10.0
Failure	3	$3.0	$9.0
Fire	1	$5.0	$5.0
Virus	3	$1.0	$3.0

Fig. 4-4. Results sorted by exposure.

Risk Analysis - Loss Factors

Threat	ARO	PPIL (K)	Loss Exposure
Leaks	0.0140	$50.0	$0.700
Data theft	0.0070	$70.0	$0.490
Screw-ups	0.0340	$5.0	$0.170
Fraud	0.0090	$10.0	$0.090
Failure	0.0270	$3.0	$0.081
Equipment Theft	0.0080	$5.0	$0.040
Fire	0.0075	$5.0	$0.038
Vandalism	0.0060	$5.0	$0.030
Earthquake	0.0010	$5.0	$0.005
Virus	0.0015	$1.0	$0.002

Fig. 4-5. Exposure sorted by rate of occurrence.

Defenses currently in place:

- General: backup to floppy disks is performed on most machines on an "almost daily" basis with backups stored in locked drawers.
- Common theft: front door lock, blinds closed at night.
- Vandalism: front door lock.
- Equipment failure: tender loving care, regular maintenance, no-smoking rule, "loaner" provisions.
- Virus damage: all incoming software vetted on one system, using vaccine software. Public domain and shareware programs only used if from reliable sources.
- Screw-ups: well trained employees, try to get good temp help when needed.
- Earthquake: none apart from fire protection, which is good.
- Unauthorized access: lock on front door. Some of the personal computers have keyboard locks.
- Data theft: lock on front door. Some of the personal computers have keyboard locks.
- Fire: fairly good systems installed at present, no-smoking office.
- Fraud: password protection on accounting system. All reports closely held by accountant.

Defenses that could be added:

- General: fast tape backup system for the PC that runs accounting program, making daily backup less of a chore; get "fast backup" software for other systems and insist on daily backup for all users; get a fireproof filing cabinet for storage of backup media and printed accounting reports, billing slips, and invoices.
- Common theft: install alarm system; arrange office so that computers not visible from street; attach computers to desks with cable system.
- Vandalism: as above.
- Equipment failure: possibly replace equipment that is getting old.
- Virus damage: keep antivirus software up-to-date; watch computer press for virus news.
- Screw-ups: make sure that undo facilities are active in programs used. Install system level rebuild facilities; install unerase programs; install unformat programs; hire temp help from bonded agency specializing in personal computer workers.
- Earthquake: fireproof filing cabinet, as above.

- Unauthorized access: office alarm system; install system access control software; use passwords on important files; improve handling of keyboard lock keys.
- Data theft: as above.
- Fire: the fireproof filing cabinet.
- Fraud: review accounting procedures.

The next step would be to place a price tag on each defensive measure and total up the cost. You can see that some of the suggested measures will be effective on several fronts. The company would need to weigh the security benefits of each item against the cost, relative to other demands on the budget. In Fig. 4-6, you can see a worksheet of costs relative to potential loss/savings.

Planning For Risk Reduction

Additional Defenses	Cost	Description	Cost Shared	ALE	Cost/Benefit
Common theft	$500	Alarm system	$250	$0.040	0.0160
Vandalism	$0	As above	$250	$0.030	0.0120
Euipment failure	$1,000	Upgrades	$1,000	$0.081	0.0081
Virus damage	$100	Software/magazine	$100	$0.002	0.0020
Screw-ups	$1,500	Tape backup	$1,500	$0.080	0.0053
Earthquake	$250	Fire-proof safe	$125	$0.005	0.0040
Fire	$0	As above	$125	$0.038	0.0304
Fraud	$850	Accounting review	$850	$0.090	0.0106
Leaks (unauthorized access)	$100	Software	$50	$0.700	1.4000
Data theft	$0	As above	$50	$0.490	0.9800

Notes: Cost Shared column spreads costs of items that have an effect on several areas. The Cost/Benefit column is fairly crude since some items, notably the tape backup unit, offer defense against a wide range of threats.

Fig. 4-6. Costs and benefits.

From this example you get an idea of what is involved in a risk evaluation, even if your organization is much larger. The final decision on which measures to adopt will depend on a variety of factors beside cost. Consider the following variables.

Productivity. Personal computers were introduced to increase productivity. Some security measures are so inconvenient that they can impair productivity. Any loss in productivity from a specific measure will need to be weighed against the perceived benefits of the measure.

Feasibility. Some security recommendations that sound good in theory might just not be feasible, given the practical implications. For example, "keep personal computers away from members of the public" is a good idea, but clearly not feasible if the personal computers are being used in a front-line operation like point of sale. Alternatives and compromises will have to be considered. (For example, the security of a personal computer that is exposed to the public might be improved by bolting it down and fitting the keyboard with a protective cover to prevent damage from spills and dirt.)

Aesthetics. All houses would be more secure if they had iron bars across all the windows, but most houses do not. This is because there is a quality-of-life factor to consider in any security decision. There is little point in adopting security measures so ugly that they have a negative impact on morale. Placing trust in employees usually bears more pleasant and profitable fruits than starting out with an adversarial attitude.

Methods in General

For a larger company, the tasks of assessing security is more complex, but can usually be accomplished with an expanded version of the approach outlined in the example above. Probably the best place to start in a large organization is with a station-by-station review of the current deployment of personal computers. Until you have a clear picture of what each personal computer does, you cannot formulate effective strategies. You can use a personal computer to assist you in this survey. In Fig. 4-7, you can see a sample questionnaire printed with a desktop publishing program. This includes many of the questions that should be asked, but you might need to add other organization-specific questions.

Once the questionnaires are completed, the responses can be compiled and analyzed with software. Most database or spreadsheet programs can be adapted to the task of collecting answers. Some basic statistics can then be developed, such as the total number of stations, the percentage that have modems, and so on. Reports that list comments can be printed out for review. As a whole, the data collected will give you a detailed picture of the current situation. You can then draw up a list of potential threats and begin to assess the degree of risk posed by each one. With survey responses about the type of data processed and basic figures on the organization's revenues and expenditures you can begin to assign values to data, equipment, and potential losses.

In Fig. 4-8, you can see a Quattro Pro spreadsheet from an IBM PC, designed to accept survey responses keyed in by a data entry operator.

What type of software you use to collate your information will depend upon what you are used to and what reporting capabilities it has. For example, on the Macintosh, the FileMaker database manager allows you to set up very friendly data entry forms like the one shown in Fig. 4-9.

Indeed, you might want to set up a live questionnaire on computer. A disk with the questionnaire program could be distributed to employees, allowing them to enter their responses "on-line." If your organization's personal computers are networked, the survey could be carried out over the network. Alternatively, you could make the rounds interviewing employees face-to-face, but entering their responses directly into a database on a portable computer.

THE QUESTIONS TO ASK

Some idea of the questions that need to be answered to get a clear picture of an organization's personal computer security exposure can be gained from Fig. 4-7. One

Workstation Review

CQR DATA COMPANY ™

Client Name: _____

Review Date: _____ Location: _____

A. Equipment Details

Workstation Name or Number: _____

This workstation consists of the following equipment:

Personal computer ☐	3.5 inch floppy disk drive(s) ☐	Mouse ☐
Separate monitor ☐	5.25 inch floppy disk drives ☐	Other input device ____
Printer ☐	Internal hard disk drive(s) ☐	
Modem ☐	External disk drive(s) ☐	Other output device ____

B. Equipment Identification

	Make	Model	Serial Number	Company I.D. Number
System unit				
Monitor				
Printer				
Modem				
Other				
Other				
Other				

C. User Details

Name of principal user: _____

Uses system for: _____

Other users: _____

Uses system for: _____

Uses system for: _____

Normal user hours: _____

D. User Classification

	1	2	3	4	5		Yes	No
Skill level of nornal user	☐	☐	☐	☐	☐	Is there a keyboard lock?	☐	☐
Skill level of casual users	☐	☐	☐	☐	☐	Is the lock used regularly?	☐	☐
Security awareness of users	☐	☐	☐	☐	☐	Is boot security installed?	☐	☐
Regularity of backup	☐	☐	☐	☐	☐	Is any encryption used?	☐	☐
Sensitivity of data handled	☐	☐	☐	☐	☐	Is a modem used?	☐	☐
System exposure to public	☐	☐	☐	☐	☐	Locked drawer for backups?	☐	☐
Level of user consistency	☐	☐	☐	☐	☐	Is personal software in use?	☐	☐

E. Other Comments _____

_____

_____

CQR Data Company, Form: SR0001 Revised 1/1/90 Copyright, 1990

Fig. 4-7. Security questionnaire.

place to start is with an inventory of personal computer resources. Most larger organizations have, or should have, centralized records of all personal computer equipment with serial numbers and current assignments.

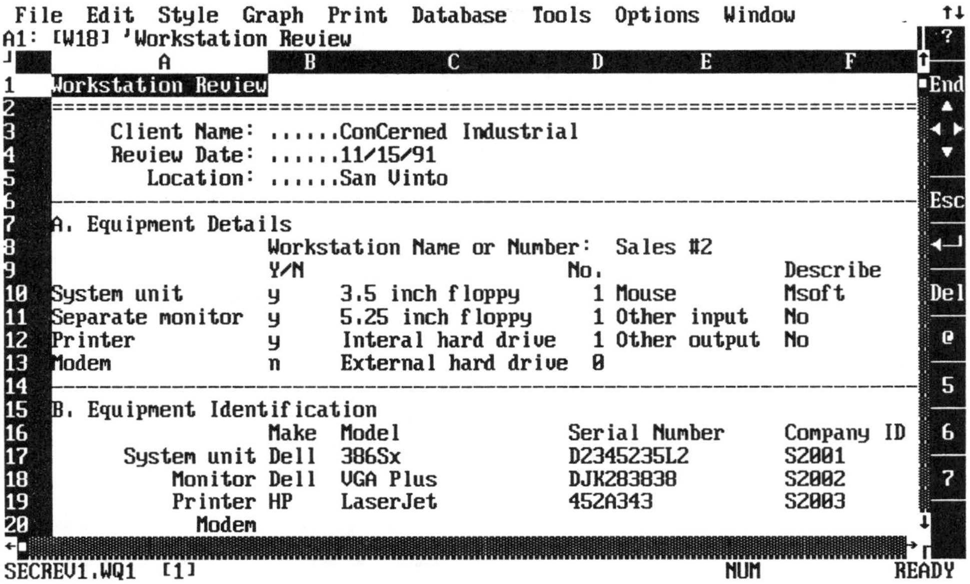

```
 File  Edit  Style  Graph  Print  Database  Tools  Options  Window       ↑↓
A1: [W18] 'Workstation Review                                              ?
 ⌐          A              B          C          D         E        F      ▮
 1  Workstation Review                                                    ■End
 2  =================================================================      ▲
 3       Client Name:  ......ConCerned Industrial                       ◄ ►
 4       Review Date:  ......11/15/91                                      ▼
 5          Location:  ......San Vinto
 6  ----------------------------------------------------------------      Esc
 7  A. Equipment Details
 8                      Workstation Name or Number:  Sales #2              ↵
 9                      Y/N                     No.          Describe
10  System unit         y     3.5 inch floppy   1 Mouse      Msoft        Del
11  Separate monitor    y     5.25 inch floppy  1 Other input No
12  Printer             y     Interal hard drive 1 Other output No         @
13  Modem               n     External hard drive 0
14  ----------------------------------------------------------------      5
15  B. Equipment Identification
16                      Make  Model             Serial Number  Company ID  6
17       System unit Dell  386Sx             D2345235L2     S2001
18          Monitor Dell  VGA Plus          DJK283838      S2002          7
19          Printer HP    LaserJet          452A343        S2003
20          Modem                                                          ↓
 ←▪                                                                  →▪
SECREV1.WQ1  [1]                                     NUM        READY
```

Fig. 4-8. Spreadsheet for survey responses.

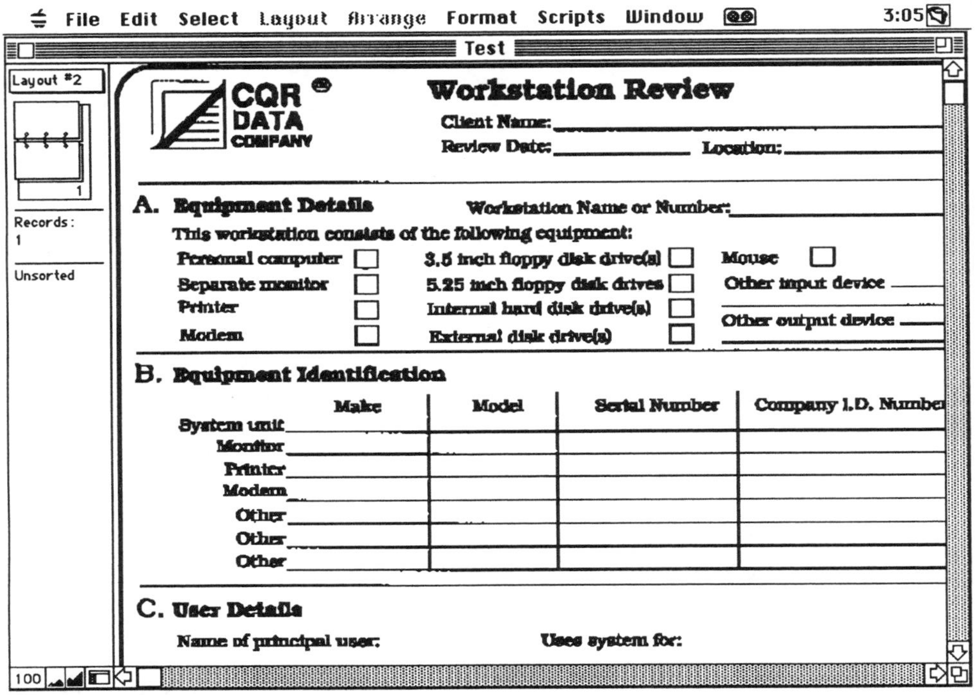

Fig. 4-9. FileMaker data entry form.

The Joys of Being Organized

In some cases personal computers have been incorporated into the fabric of an organization so quickly that proper controls have been overlooked. Indeed, it is possible to find companies where staplers are more carefully accounted for than computers, software, and peripherals, all of which cost far more and open far greater avenues of potential loss. Considering the ease with which a simple database management program or electronic spreadsheet can handle the tracking of such details, there is really no excuse for not having a thorough record of all personal computer equipment. In Fig. 4-10, you can see a typical Mac-based database manager, FileMaker from Claris, set up to record equipment details.

Fig. 4-10. Personal computer equipment database.

Among the hardware details to track for security, as well as general management purposes are:

serial number
date of purchase
vendor
warranty period
maintenance contract
current location of equipment
current location of manual

Keeping track of software is definitely a more challenging task, given the ease with which it can be installed/discarded by different users, the frequency with which upgrades appear, and the lack of consistency between vendors when it comes to upgrade methods. Nevertheless, a well-maintained database that reflects current software status will help immensely should there be a theft or security problems arising from software deficiencies. Among the software details to track for security, as well as general management purposes are:

serial number
original version number
date of purchase
vendor
is the software registered
current location of manual
current version number
date of last update

Typical Questions

When preparing a security survey, you should consider the following questions on a station-by-station basis:

- Is there a keyboard lock?—this should be used.
- Who has the keys?—these should be controlled.
- How skilled is the user?—low level of skill means a potential source of data loss, high skill level could weaken effectiveness of simple defense.
- Does the software being used have undo capability?—this should be turned on.
- Does the system have format capability?—remove if practical or install protection.
- Does the system have unformat capability?—if not, install.
- Is a disk optimizing program installed/used?—if not, install.
- Is personal software used?—if so, is it guaranteed/approved?
- How complex is the operating environment?—the more complex, the greater the potential problems.
- What type of backup device is installed?—the first line of defense (only diskless personal computers lack a backup device).
- Is there an automated backup procedure?—if not, install one.
- Is the backup media stored securely?—if not, why do backup?
- Is the backup performed regularly?—use backup file dates to check this.

One specialized but very serious window of vulnerability is any connection between a personal computer and other computers. This could be a local area network, a micro-mainframe link, or a modem for uploading and/or downloading data. The security exposure presented by such connections will be addressed in detail in Chapter 12, but the important questions to ask are listed here.

- Is a modem attached?—a potential window into the system.
- Does the modem accept incoming calls?—an actual window into the system.

- Is the modem used for downloading data?—it could be intercepted.
- Is downloaded data packed?—compressed data is harder to read.
- Is the data encrypted?—this can ensure that intercepted data is not revealed.
- Is the modem used for downloading software?—a possible carrier for viruses and trojan horses.
- How reliable is the software source?—only use proven sources.

How Personal Computers Are Used

The most basic question to ask is, "What are the personal computers used for?" The answer to this allows you to determine what data is involved, what tasks will be interrupted by a security incident, what aspects of the organization will be affected by data loss, misappropriation, or corruption. In some organizations, each personal computer has a different mission and so a system-by-system survey is necessary to answer this question. You might want to group systems by category of activity.

Receive Information. Personal computers used for data entry, transaction recording, data acquisition, and even word processing, are all fulfilling the role of receiving information. The security problems associated with such systems concern corruption or intercepton of incoming data, and the disruption of processing capability.

Store Information. The same computers might be the store place for information, or they might hand it on to other systems. For example, a personal computer used for point of sale transactions might be the front-end of a store accounting system and not retain much information for long. A word processor might receive a lot of information but store little of it beyond approval of the final document. However, it is important to bear in mind that many systems store quite a lot of data temporarily, even if they are not the data's final resting place. The security implications for systems that are used for storage center on the possible loss/theft/corruption of data.

Produce Information. The primary task of some computers is to take produce new information out of stored data. Such information might be new contracts assembled from boiler-plate text or revenue projections based on past performance and assumptions about the future. The security concerns for such systems are corruption of data due to errors and service interruptions, plus possible misappropriation of data for gain.

The Impact of an Interruption in Use

Whatever role a personal computer fulfills, continued fulfillment of that role is presumably of some value to the organization. You might have an old floppy disk PC that is used for occasional word processing, the loss of which might not seriously affect business as usual, but the smooth and continuing operation of most personal computers is considered essential to mission fulfillment in most enterprises.

To examine the impact of an interruption in use due to virus infection, hardware loss or damage, or some other breach of security is to engage in "what-if." You have to use your imagination to list what ramifications an interruption might have. You can proceed on a station-by-station basis, assuming that each system in turn is rendered unavailable for one day.

A Cost of Loss Example

As an example of costing an incident, consider a supermarket chain that operates its own fleet of trucks and uses personal computers to manage the trucking operation. All maintenance information for the trucks is stored on a personal computer, including miles and hours logged, service performed, and so on. Vehicle maintenance schedules are produced and reports to management are generated detailing age and history of vehicles. Early one morning, the personal computer and printer are stolen. The backup disks from the day before are safe. Determine the cost of this incident:

- Three people spend four hours each determining what has been stolen, arranging delivery of a rental unit, reporting the crime to the police, and briefing management on the problem: 12 hours.

- Maintenance staff do not get their computer-generated work orders and have to figure out a schedule by hand, taking four people three hours: 12 hours.

- One person spends three hours setting up the rental unit with software, backup data, and printer interface (rented printer not the same model as the one stolen): 3 hours.

- Normal day is now over, but schedules need updating, daily entries made. Takes two people three hours at time and a half: 9 hours.

- Insurance claim for loss of computer is prepared and pursued until paid: 8 hours.

- Replacement computer is installed: 3 hours.

- Cost of replacement computer and printer is $6500 of which the insurance covers $5000, leaving the company to cover a balance of $1500.

- Rental computer and printer returned: one week at $200 per week.

Total cost of theft is thus $2170 (47 hours at $10 per hour, plus $200 for rental and $1500 insurance shortfall). This is a fairly simple example, but it gives you an idea of how to proceed when evaluating the impact of a loss.

To make this example more interesting, you could add in the Fred Factor. Fred is a route driver delivering the supermarket's baked goods, which are sold to restaurants, as well as the bakery departments of the chain's own supermarkets. Fred earns a bonus for attracting new customers. He has spent weeks wooing a new restaurant that is near the end of his route. The restaurant owner's main concern is getting goods early enough in the day to meet the lunchtime rush. Fred has promised a first delivery the day of the computer theft. Because of the disruption to the maintenance schedule caused by the theft, Fred's delivery van is not ready on time. Fred is late getting to the restaurant; the deal is off. Fred loses his bonus, the supermarket chain loses a sale that day, as well as a new chunk of business. While losses like this are hard to predict and to cost, they are very real. You can clearly see the importance of determining how critical each personal computer is to the organization's mission.

How Important the Information Is to the Organization

There are several ways to look at the importance of information to an organization. If you consider the impact of different forms of attack, this will help you realize the relative value of different types of information.

Damaged or Destroyed. When data is lost and backup copies are not available, you can either recreate the data or live without it. In practice, you will find that a lot of disk space is taken up by files that are useful to have around, but not important to ongoing operations. A typical example is copies of correspondence in word processing files. Such files are often kept for reference purposes, or in case similar letters need to be sent in the future. However, these letters probably exist in hard copy as well. If the files were deleted, it might be inconvenient, but the impact on the organization might well be minimal.

Accounting files present quite a different picture because recreating them can be very time-consuming. Furthermore, many organizations rely on such files in day-to-day decision-making. Without current data, operations could be severely impacted.

Altered or Amended. The importance of data that is modified illicitly depends upon the extent to which the organization relies upon the data for operations and decision-making. If there is any possibility that it could be tampered with, data from personal computers that forms the basis of decision making must be verified before decisions are made. There must be safeguards against the tendency to assume that "It came off the computer, so it must be right."

Compromised or Communicated. The importance of data that is disclosed against the wishes of an individual or organization depends upon how much damage the disclosure could cause. While losing your accounting files completely could bring your operations to an abrupt halt, having someone else reading them might have less immediate consequences. On the other hand, the word processing files that are relatively low in importance when destroyed, might be high in importance when disclosed. Indeed, this difference in emphasis can lead to damaging misjudgment. If a file that is of little importance to current operations is given minimal protection, this can lead to its disclosure, possibly with negative results. Like distilled liquors, files retained merely "for the record," can actually gain potency over time. Circumstances and opinions change, and material that was innocent enough when it was archived might prove to be incriminating a few years later.

In order to decide how much security to accord the data that your personal computer(s) handle files, you can categorize or grade it. This will help set priorities if you cannot afford total protection for everything, or if you find that according all data maximum protection would have a negative impact on productivity. You might want to use the following categories, bearing in mind that some data will fall into more than one category:

- Decision-critical: data that is used as the basis of decision-making, for example, budget projections, or current inventory.

- Operational: data that is an integral part of operations; for example, daily transaction accounts, timesheets.
- Archival: data that is retained for record-keeping purposes, such as purchase orders, invoices, and correspondence.
- Convenience: data that is retained because it might be useful at some point in the future, such as keeping expired contracts because the language might be used in new contracts.

Application Software Used

Several questions of security can affect your choice of software. How reliable is the source of software? Is the software guaranteed to be virus-free? How strong are the security features built into the software? Does the software work with third-party security systems?

These questions are the first line of inquiry about the software upon which the organization is relying. A second round of questions should be considered. To what extent is the software customized? If so, who did the customizing? Are the persons reliable? Are they still around? Are they/their works bonded/insured?

Questions about customized software are particularly poignant given the prevalence of the "errant knight" syndrome in personal computer consulting. You will recognize this syndrome if you have ever encountered a personal computer that is supposed to perform a certain task and was "set up by this guy (the errant knight) who was a real whiz at these things." The personal computer is no longer performing the task correctly and this "whiz-kid" has long since whizzed off. These knights are errant in that they seem bound to wander and bound to leave a trail of used and confused users in their wake.

In fact, unscrupulous or merely unreliable consultants pose a very real security threat. Unless someone reliable within an organization has a handle on what is being done to and with the organization's personal computer resources, the organization can hardly rely on those systems performing correctly. For more on security exposure from software see Chapter 10.

The Skill Level of the Users

This question requires more tact than most and is quite likely to bring a security survey into contact with personnel policies and organizational politics. Many users feel that they do not get enough training, while some managers feel that users "know too much already." There is something of a dilemma between a low skill level, at which accidents are more likely to happen, and high skill level at which the ability to break simple security barriers is obtained. What you and your organization make of this dilemma will have a significant impact on security policy. Fortunately, some of the most straightforward security measures, such as file encryption and hardware locks, take exceptional skill to defeat.

 Opinions vary greatly on the question of how much knowledge is a good thing. I happen to think that there is little to be gained by keeping people in the dark. For a start, the fewer secrets an organization has, the less it need worry about security at all. Secondly, time and the lessons of history oppose those who base their security on the ignorance of others. The benefits of personal computers are best realized by those who best understand them, and the more such persons you have in your organization the more likely the organization is to succeed in its mission.

The organization that employs its own programmers might have a particularly tough time with the question of skill level and the following questions concerning ethics. For more on the personnel aspect of security, see Chapter 13.

The Ethical Level of the Users

Not many people will want to make the call on this subject, but it must be considered. Casting a suspicious eye over colleagues you normally trust is no fun, but neither is losing data. There are really two levels of concern: The organization's defense against an attack by an unethical employee and the individual user's defense against an attack from within the organization. To what extent you trust those working alongside you will determine how keen you are to implement some of the hardware and file access control methods discussed in this book. To what extent the organization inspires and rewards loyalty will determine how far it has to go to protect itself from internal threats.

The Hardware

A line once popular among personal computer salespersons went something like this:

Technically speaking, personal computer hardware never becomes obsolete. Sure, things break and people don't bother to fix them, but if you buy this personal computer to perform task A, then as long as it performs task A, it is not obsolete. New hardware may perform the task faster, or run software that performs task B, which is all of A plus a whole lot more, but there may still be a need for task A and the old hardware can be kept in service long after its level of performance has been surpassed.

There is a lot of truth to this. The problem with using older hardware is not that it doesn't do the job, it is the difficulty you will have replacing it if it goes missing. If your operations depend upon older hardware, or purpose-built hardware, then you need to make sure that service, repair, and replacement remain available. Otherwise, you might lose the use of hardware in which valuable data is stored, effectively creating a technological tomb for your data.

Insurance

The insuring of personal computer resources is a fairly recent phenomenon. Insurance can be obtained at several levels and not all policies cover all of the losses that can accrue from a breach of security. Some other forms of insurance, like household contents, might actually exclude personal computers. Certainly a review of personal computer security should include a clear picture of what losses are insured, together with the records needed should it be necessary to file a claim. See Chapter 6 for more on insurance and personal computer resources.

Current Practices

Having evaluated an organization's personal computer security risks, assigning values to what might be lost, the process moves on to reviewing current practices. The goal is to get a clear picture of how existing security systems are used. While a survey will give you responses to questions, only by observing what actually happens in day-to-day operations will you get an honest picture of current exposure.

For example, if it appears from observation or spot checks that employees conscientiously make daily backups which they store in a fireproof safe at the end of the day, then you have less to worry about than if you find backup media lying around on desks after hours. Indeed, a walk around the office when everyone else has gone home can be very revealing. If you see a lot of floppy disks left on desks, keys left in locks, systems left turned on and unprotected, then you know that current practices leave a lot to be desired.

 The story is told of a consultant who was having great difficulty interesting a potentially lucrative client in his security services. After being rebuffed several times, he scheduled a last-ditch presentation late one afternoon. On the pretext of visiting the bathroom, he managed to make a quick unaccompanied tour of the premises. When he returned to the conference room, he began his presentation by showing a handful of keys. His audience was finally convinced that there was a security problem when the consultant revealed that these were the keys to the company's personal computers, left in the locks by employees who had left for the weekend.

ASSESSING PROBABILITY

Assessing probability is one of the most subjective areas of the entire risk analysis. Few people claim that they can reliably predict fire, flood, hurricane, earthquake, burglary, arson, or random acts of violence. The random factor in existence makes uncertainty the only certainty. This is your saving grace if you are attempting to be a responsible steward of valuable resources: you cannot fairly be blamed for not anticipating what could not be foreseen. However, you do have a responsibility to know what is likely and what is not, and you can establish a statistical basis for this knowledge.

Somewhere to Start

You begin by making up a list of all imaginable threats. You then find out how many times each threat has materialized in your area in the last ten years. This will allow you to create a weighted list of probabilities. While this information is not easy to gather, commercial sources are available, some of which are mentioned later in this chapter.

Unfortunately, fate is not kind to those who rely on statistics. Some statistics only lead to further questions. For example, the fact that a particular threat materialized only once in the last ten years might be taken to mean that it is likely to happen again only once in the next ten years. However, some people might say that once in ten years was below average, implying that a fresh occurrence is more likely now, since "We've only had one in the last ten years."

To avoid getting too deeply mired in statistical conundrums, it is wise to apply a good dose of common sense. You need to distinguish the likely from the unlikely, and to realize that you cannot anticipate all instances of the latter. A lesson may be taken from events in Silicon Valley during the period 1985-90. During this time many hi-tech companies, using thousands of personal computers, moved into large industrial parks, occupying sprawling office complexes. These offices complied with the latest building regulations. Traffic through these parks consisted mainly of employees, deliveries, and shipments. Most office buildings had front desks where visitors registered. Some companies used ID card systems to control access to their premises.

Most companies had clearly covered most aspects of security. However, in 1987 and 1988, there was a rash of mass murders in this area. In each case, heavily armed individuals entered offices and fired on employees and equipment. No one could have planned for this tragic eventuality. Nobody could blame the companies involved for lax security. A normal business operation simply cannot anticipate having to deal with deeply disturbed and heavily armed intruders.

The Earthquake Example

As an example of the problem of risk assessment, consider one particular threat, the earthquake. Depending upon where in the world your personal computers are located, the threat from earthquakes can be anything from minimal to considerable. Yet, even in high-risk areas like California, no respectable scientists are prepared to give specific predictions on earthquake occurrence. About all you can get by way of prediction is a statement along these lines: "There is an X % chance of quake of Y magnitude occurring in the next Z years." So placing any kind of figure on how likely it is that your personal computers will have to withstand an earthquake is going to be difficult.

Suppose that you have decided that a moderate quake could strike. The next question is, "What kind of threat does this pose?" There are several levels to the answer.

Initial Shock. The direct effect on the computer can be hard drive damage and data loss. All users need to know that jolts to a hard disk that is in operation, whether from earthquake tremors, swift kicks, or sudden descent (as in dropping) can cause the read/write head to come into contact with the disk platter. This in turn can cause physical damage to the special magnetic coating on the platter that actually stores data. In this manner, data literally can be wiped out, rather like a paint scraper removing lettering from a painted sign. Whatever the source of the blow, if it is hard enough and comes at just the wrong time, the effects can be serious. Data can be damaged or, in a worst-case scenario, the entire disk can be rendered useless.

After-effects. The shaking caused by an earthquake is only the beginning of the problem for personal computers. Falling masonry might damage systems. Electrical power supplies are often interrupted. Sprinkler systems might be activated. Fires can break out. Looting may take place. Buildings that have become structurally unsafe might later need to be destroyed. Each of these effects can threaten the security of personal computers. The problems of data loss through loss of power are dealt with in Chapter 6. Fire damage to personal computers is often disastrous, heat and smoke can ruin hardware and backup storage media, such as tapes or floppies. Because a serious quake can render normal security systems useless, theft is also a possibility.

Unforeseen Effects. Beyond specific factors, the general disruption that follows a quake is itself a danger. After the October 1989 quake in northern California, a publishing company's personal computers were damaged by a series of events that would have been hard to predict. As soon as the quake struck, the electricity was cut off. The building was rapidly evacuated and, quite understandably, people did not stop to make sure that the computer equipment was turned off. Several hours later, power was restored, but by that time the office was empty. The building's air-conditioning system had been damaged and did not start up, but the personal computers did. The result was overheating in some offices, and several computers suffered heat damage, requiring circuit boards to be replaced.

If a quake is a possibility, then what is a reasonable level of response? The first line of defense for data is, as always, regular and secure backup. For hardware the best defense is probably insurance, followed by common sense. The latter will tell you that computers can be damaged by falling objects, toppled bookshelves, and so on. This means you can take some elementary precautions against shock damage, but, since there is no way to predict the exact nature of problems arising from an earthquake, insuring your equipment against damage caused by an earthquake is probably the only real defense you have.

ASSESSING VALUE

In the case of the earthquake example, the publishing company was faced with an expense of several thousand dollars to replace heat-damaged circuit boards. However, the company counted itself lucky that nobody was injured. Relative to the size of the threat, the damage was light. In the earlier example of a trucking company computer being stolen, you saw how the cost can be assessed by adding the value of the lost time to the replacement cost of the hardware less the amount recovered from insurance.

The Time Factor

Because we all know that time is money, and most of us know that computer problems are invariably time-consuming, it should come as no surprise that time is one of the most expensive elements when there is a breach of personal computer security. When you attempt to place a dollar amount on what a security problem might cost, it is important to bear the time factor in mind.

Administrative. Even if you are insured against most negative aspects of a security breach, time is always involved in filing claims and organizing a return to normal operations. Uninsured losses, such as accidental data loss, can involve extensive recovery time.

Recreating Data. You might find that some data which is lost is not worth recreating; however, when data has to be recovered, you must put a total cost on the time involved.

You calculate the cost of time lost by multiplying person-hours by dollars-per-hour. Remember that the dollar-per-hour figure is not just an hourly wage, but should include employee overhead as well.

The Opportunity Cost

The term *opportunity cost* has a special meaning in economics, but in the case of a security problem, it can simply mean what the organization loses out because of the problem. This could be a bid deadline or delivery data that is missed, resulting in loss of business. If employees are kept busy repairing a security breach, they will not be able to continue with normal operations, and this can have a snowball effect. One potential benefit of a contingency plan, discussed later in this chapter, is an orderly and speedy return to normal operations after a problem.

The Confidence and Goodwill Cost

Most organizations need both internal and external confidence in order to flourish. The confidence and goodwill of clients and suppliers is essential for continued operation. Employees within an organization need to have confidence that the organization will continue to fulfill its obligations to them. An organization's backers, such as investors and bankers, need to have confidence in its integrity and continued prosperity. Confidence at all these layers can be badly shaken by a serious security breach. The breach does not have to involve massive data loss or serious system damage. The very fact that a breach occurred can be sufficient to threaten the confidence upon which the organization depends.

The Cash Cost

When you place a dollar amount on the material cost of security breaches, also consider some important accounting principles. Suppose that the IBM PC XT that you bought for $3500 in 1985 is stolen in 1990. Have you lost $3500 worth of equipment? In most cases the answer is no. The *replacement* cost of machine with the capabilities of a 1985 IBM PC XT is around $1000. Over the years since you bought the old XT, you have probably gained tax benefits from depreciating the *original* or *purchase* cost of $3500. Using *straight-line depreciation* over 5 years the *salvage* cost of the XT in 1990 is $0 because you will have depreciated the entire cost (5 years × $700 per year). This probably means you could not use the loss of the XT as means of reducing your taxes. (In fact, some personal computer equipment can be expensed rather than depreciated, further complicating the tax implications of a loss.)

If you file an insurance claim to replace the XT, you will find out its *insured* value. This might be based on replacement cost, a depreciated amount, or *market* value. The last of these is what you could get for the XT on the open market, which is probably only a few hundred dollars. The wide disparity between the different methods of valuation makes it very important to be clear which values you are referring to when you estimate loss exposure, take out insurance, or count your assets. If in doubt, you might want to consult your accountant, particularly if questions of tax are involved.

SECURITY POLICY

A cornerstone of effective personal computer security in an organization is a security policy. This can be defined as a set of rules, principles and procedures that regulate how an organization manages, protects, and controls personal computer resources and the information they contain.

By assembling such a policy document, an organization is forced to face up to questions of security. Obviously, a security policy does not provide security in itself. But it is a very effective tool, a measure of current levels of security, a standard that can measure compliance, and basis for further improvements.

Implementing Security Policy

Once a security policy has been drawn up, management can issue regulations to the troops and set about installing any additional devices that are required. Only by implementing a policy will its practical value be realized. It might be that through policy implementation, new measures and methods will be worked out.

A CONTINGENCY PLAN

A close corollary of planning for security is planning for security failures. While it is not much fun to think about what will happen when security is breached, failure to do so will only make matters worse if a "worst-case scenario" materializes. In the contingency plan, you lay down procedures to be followed in the event of a problem. A list of all known threats, possibly taken from your risk analysis, can be used to ensure that all eventualities are considered.

In larger organizations, a contingency plan should have two aspects: operational and administrative. At the operational level, each user should know what to do when a problem arises. At a minimum, this knowledge will include an answer to the classic question, "Who you gonna call?" At the administrative level, the plan will cover such questions as where to hire replacement equipment, how to restore data from backups, what documentation is needed for an insurance claim, and how to recreate data in the event both files and backups are destroyed.

As mentioned earlier, organizations are well advised to set up special channels for reporting matters of security, perhaps through a central security coordinator, rather than use existing lines of communication. This can lead to quicker and more appropriate response. For example, in the case of a new virus appearing within an organization, reporting to a single individual with security responsibilities can save a great deal of duplicated effort and can head off widespread infection.

BEGIN AGAIN

The task of maintaining personal computer security is a cyclical one. The cycle of analysis and planning outlined above is really only the beginning. Once equipment is placed, administration must see that it is used. Once rules are laid down, administration must see that they are adhered to. In larger organizations, it is wise to assign specific responsibility for these enforcement tasks, otherwise compliance will slide, a breach of security will occur, and there will be a lot of finger pointing without any useful decision as to who was to blame for the lax state of affairs. By giving final responsibility to one person, you will probably assure more diligent enforcement of security measures than if a group or committee is held accountable.

Once the ongoing enforcement of security policies is well in hand, it is time to consider beginning the cycle of planning and risk evaluation all over again. Certainly this is the case in large organizations. Circumstances change and so does equipment. The range of threats might increase. You have to assume that the sophistication of would-be intruders is steadily increasing. Revised assessment of risks, a review of current practices, redefining of policy—all these are part of the ongoing task of ensuring personal computer security.

The Cyborg scheme, launched at the end of 1989, is a good example of how the range of threats can suddenly increase overnight. In this case, described in detail in Chapter 9, a Panamanian company called PC Cyborg Corporation, mailed thousands of copies of "free" software to personal computer users all around the world. People who loaded this software onto their PCs found data was disappearing. The "free" software then presented demands for payment which amounted to blackmail ("If you want your data back, send the money to . . ."). The scale of this scheme and the trouble to which its perpetrators had gone to gain access to innocent PCs marked a new level of threat. From now on, virtually any unsolicited software must be suspect. Before the Cyborg incident, this simply was not the case.

One of the dangers of expensive and elaborate security systems is that, once installed, they give a false sense of security. In some respects, you cannot allow yourself to get too comfortable with the status quo. Remember that complacency is the curse of comfort. On the other hand, those responsible for security within an organization must avoid creating a constant state of paranoia, since this is as self-defeating as complacency. As Marshall McLuhan said "The price of eternal vigilance is indifference." Issuing occasional security reminders to users and running the odd security awareness program should serve to keep attention to this problem at the right level.

COMMERCIAL ANALYSIS AND PLANNING SYSTEMS

You will probably not be surprised to learn that there are numerous companies who will, for a fee, assist you with the tasks of security analysis planning. Some of these companies provide straightforward consulting services, while others sell software and other materials that help you to undertake the work yourself. The usual rules of "buyer beware" and "look before you leap" apply as much in this area as well as any other. A sample of available services and products are described in this section, but no claim is made as to their suitability to the needs of your organization.

The best approach to finding the right product or service is probably to begin with a source of information that you have already found to be reliable. For example, your organization might use the services of an accounting firm that it trusts. This firm might be a good source of assistance when it comes to retaining the services of a reliable security consultant. Indeed, many large accounting firms have their own security departments. For example, the British firm of Coopers and Lybrand operate a full range of services covering access control, acceptance testing, audit software, contingency planning, encryption, and corporate security. Similar services are provided by Touche Ross, Price Waterhouse, Peat Marwick McLintock, and Ernst & Whinney (Ernst & Young in the U.K.).

Another familiar source of security assistance could be your telephone/communications provider. Such companies as AT&T have extensive experience not only in secure communications but also in computer system security. In the United Kingdom, British Telecom operates a complete security and contingency planning service.

Computerized Risk Analysis

The Bayesian Decision Support System (BDSS) is a full-support automated package for quantitative risk assessment in the information processing environment. It runs on an IBM PC XT, AT, or compatible and supports all tasks of a complete, detailed quantitative risk assessment, a summary-level risk assessment, or any level in between.

According to the literature about BDSS, the question is not whether one should be concerned about information security. Threats are real, vulnerabilities exist, and potentially adverse consequences are too great to be ignored. The real questions are:

> What can go wrong?
> How often can it happen?
> What will be the consequences?
> How certain are the answers to the first three questions?

Risk analysis means answering these questions, nothing more or less.

To answer the first question, BDSS develops a logical risk model of your information processing environment, based on your responses to the questions it asks. Powerful internal logic controls the questioning process, so that questions posed by the system are largely determined by answers to previous questions. In this way, BDSS develops a risk model tailored to the specific information processing environment of the client organization.

Using this risk model, BDSS identifies vulnerabilities and maps them to applicable threats.

Answering the second question, BDSS develops rate of occurrence distributions for various risk scenarios. This is done by integrating, three types of information, using complex mathematical and logical algorithms:

- The logical risk model.
- A large internal database of threat frequencies and safeguard effectiveness.
- Historical data on the occurrence of various threats at your site.

To answer the third question, "What will be the consequences?" BDSS addresses both tangible and intangible resources, everything from computers to mission/business impact. The user is guided through a process that identifies and assesses the value of resources, as well as the immediate and consequential impact of their loss.

The answer to the fourth question, "How certain are the answers to the first three questions?" is achieved by the Bayesian integration of uncertainty within the BDSS analysis of your logical risk model. This realistic portrayal of the uncertainties in calculated values is a central attribute of the BDSS risk analysis.

The BDSS system then goes on to propose safeguards based on its analysis of your risk model. You are free to select the safeguards you want, and the program will then evaluate the reduction in risk attributable to that selection. The results are graphed, showing the risk levels both before and after the safeguards are applied. This is done with "risk curves" that present the true range of loss exposure and the associated range of probabilities. After reviewing these "before and after" graphs (without regard to cost at this point), you select the most effective combination of safeguards. Finally, BDSS performs, based on cost parameters you provide, cost-benefit analyses for the safeguards you have identified as being most effective.

With BDSS, risk quantification results are no longer presented as the misleading product of threat frequency times exposure factor times asset value. The risk curves, ranked threats lists, and other summary data help clarify decision issues. The information is presented in a three-part, management-oriented report, with the first part giving an executive summary, the second presenting decision support information, and the third giving technical detail.

How reliable is this system? Well, its creators claim it took 3 years and a team of 12 experts with over 125 years of collective experience in information security, risk analysis, and software development. The result is described as "a risk management tool that is remarkably simple to use while exercising (internally) the most advanced risk assessment technology."

To show you how this particular system approaches risk analysis, the following paragraphs describe the various program modules and their roles.

Project Sizing. This module provides text editing support enabling the user to draft language for the following areas of the project report:

Problem statement/background.
Objectives.
Purpose.
Scope and constraints.
Responsibilities.
Risk acceptance criteria.

Sample statements are provided in the documentation to be used as models and for reference.

Loss Valuation. This module provides input screens on which the user identifies in detail all assets within the scope of the assessment. Manufacturer, vendor, model number, quantity, low and high estimates of value as applicable for each tangible item, from modems to mainframes, and intangibles such as data, business loss, and so on, are input to the asset files. Alternatively, you can enter summary-level low and high estimates of loss value for each of the categories of assets.

It is interesting to note that BDSS sees application and system data and software as having two values. First is the replacement cost. Second is the impact on an organization's line of business, mission, or business/mission function. This must be assessed over time if data cannot be processed. The BDSS package helps develop defensible estimates of application and system data and software value ranges by means of proven techniques and rules of thumb. For each category of asset and each threat occurrence frequency distribution, BDSS recognizes associated confidence levels. These levels of confidence assist in representing the uncertainties associated with asset loss values.

Threat Vulnerability Mapping. This module scrolls a series of qualitative and quantitative questions. The answers to these questions provide BDSS with a map of the vulnerabilities and related threat exposures existing within the scope of the analysis. Each question sequence begins with relatively general questions and proceeds with increasingly detailed questions. The user's answers determine subsequent questions posed by BDSS.

For each threat, BDSS provides the option of entering site-specific threat occurrence frequency data. This data is used to develop Bayesian posterior distributions of threat frequency. In this module, users can review on-screen or print all of the vulnerabilities organized within their associated threats.

Impact Analyzer. This module maps question responses with the question/threat database to develop a risk model of the subject environment, including loss value distributions, threat frequency distributions, and exposure factor distributions, as well as other information pertinent to risk quantification.

This module has no user interface. It is internally executed as necessary. Output, which is provided to the evaluate and revise module and the risk analyzer, includes six items for each of the affected asset categories of each threat: derived annualized rate of occurrence (ARO), national ARO frequency distributions, summary single loss exposure

(SLE) distributions, summary exposure factor distributions, derived SLE distributions, and exposure factor distributions.

Risk Analyzer. This module accepts the risk model produced by the impact analyzer and submits the data to a series of sophisticated statistical algorithms, including Bayesian algorithms addressing uncertainty. This module has no user interface and is internally executed as necessary. Output from this module is a file of data representing the risk curve and the average annualized loss exposure (ALE) for each threat.

Safeguard Analyzer. This module affects the selection and application of safeguards to vulnerabilities derived in the threat vulnerability mapping module. When you enter this module, it analyzes your responses to questions in the threat vulnerability mapping module, presents indicated vulnerabilities, and suggests appropriate safeguards. Users can select the safeguards they wish to consider implementing. Loss exposures associated with the affected threats are reduced accordingly. Results of safeguard analysis can be previewed in the Evaluate and Revise module by looking at a single threat with all suggested safeguards applied or, conversely, at a single safeguard with all affected threats represented.

Safeguard Cost/Benefit. In this module, costs of selected safeguards are developed. The cost/benefit analysis is completed by BDSS through present value techniques applied to the projected implementation and maintenance costs of subject safeguards versus expected savings (loss reduction) over the life of the safeguards. Then, based on expected loss reduction, users select those safeguards that best address the vulnerabilities and associated loss exposures. Alternatively, users can allow BDSS to present all analyzed safeguards for management to review and select for implementation.

Evaluate and Revise. This module allows evaluation of the tabular frequency distribution and exposure factor data from the impact analyzer. It also permits review of the risk curves for any given threat, combination of threats, or safeguards. The non-reduced risk curve for any given threat or combination of threats can be viewed. If the safeguard analyzer has been executed, users can review the loss reduction achieved by applying safeguards via the superimposed reduced risk curve. This module can also provide a list of the threats ranked according to their loss potential (contribution to overall risk as denoted by the average ALE for each threat) before and after the application of safeguards.

Report Generator. This module assembles all of the information provided by the users, as well as calculated information, and generates a set of reports. The reports are described here because they give you a good idea of what type of information needs to be assembled to make fully informed security planning decisions.

The executive summary reports present:

- Project problem statement and objective(s).
- Scope and constraints.
- Overview of the Bayesian Decision Support System methodology.
- Discussion of key vulnerabilities and their significance.

- Graphic display depicting the unacceptable risk region, a summary nonreduced risk curve for all threats with a superimposed summary reduced risk curve representing all threats with risk reduction measures applied, plus an incremental curve representing summarized safeguard costs.
- General recommendations.

The executive decision support report provides the decision-making executive (and other interested parties) with all the information needed to make well-informed and defensible decisions regarding the purchase and/or development and implementation of safeguard measures. The parts of this report are:

- Introduction, with problem statement, objectives, scope and constraints, and recommendations rationale as entered originally in the project sizing module.
- Approach, describes the BDSS methodology, and its application.
- Graphic threats summary, summarizing safeguards are applied to summarized threats, and the resulting reduced risk curve and safeguard costs curve are depicted superimposed on the summarized threats' nonreduced risk curve.
- Threat graphics, graphs of the nonreduced risk curve for each single threat with superimposed reduced risk curve and associated costs curve representing applicable recommended safeguards, with supporting tabular values for the subject threat and mitigating safeguard.
- Safeguard graphics, graphs each recommended safeguard via a reduced summary risk curve for all affected threats superimposed on the nonreduced summary risk curve for the same threats, with supporting tabular values and costs for the subject safeguard and affected threats.
- Asset inventory summary, a list of assets summarized by category.
- Ranked threats summaries, a list of all threats identified in the assessment and their associated loss exposures before safeguards are applied, and the same threat list resequenced as appropriate after safeguards are applied to reflect their reduced loss exposure.
- Detailed recommendations, user-generated narrative detailing the safeguard recommendations as desired.

The technical analysis reports provide all the information, fully detailed, that was generated by and supported the Bayesian Decision Support System.

- Detailed asset inventory, organized by category.
- Threat/vulnerabilities summary, a brief discussion of each vulnerability and associated threats identified in the assessment before and after safeguards are applied.
- Threats and loss analysis, a list of all threats and identification of those threats having the potential for impacting the subject information systems environment, based on responses during the threat vulnerability mapping. Both

national and localized ARO distributions are presented for each threat. The assets potentially impacted by each threat are also identified here along with the associated loss values and exposure factor distributions.

- Safeguards selection and cost/benefit analysis, correlates vulnerabilities with applicable threats and presents an analysis of that information with the selected combination of safeguards that will minimize the loss potential for the subject information systems environment.

Securing Your Analysis

The information assembled in a typical risk assessment effectively presents a map of vulnerabilities that a malcontent or other individual with destructive intentions could use to damage or destroy the organization. A programmed analysis such as BDSS must allow the owner or project manager to control access to the various projects and "what if's" within a project. With its system functions module, BDSS provides this function, allowing the owner to prevent access to specific information by all except those with a need to know.

Further Risk Analysis by Personal Computer

The U.S. company Computer Security Consultants, Inc. (CSCI), has developed a product called RISKPAC, which is an interactive, automated risk assessment program that runs on PCs. RISKPAC is an expert system incorporating the experience of CSCI into a questionnaire that forms the basis of the user interface. As you answer the questions, rules developed by CSCI score the answers and provide a set of descriptive conclusions and recommendations for action. The company's expertise in information security, computer technology and auditing are captured in a series of specific questionnaires. You can use these as is or tailor them to suit your environment.

If you have your own inhouse experts, you can use RISKPAC System Manager to create your own custom questionnaires that focus on your corporate philosophy, organizational standards, or semantics.

Recovery Pac allows disaster recovery plan developers to produce effective, tailored, testable plans. It integrates the power of a relational database with graphics-oriented project planning programs to provide a solid set of tools for collecting and updating data, defining and sequencing tasks, and tracking and evaluating tests in real time. Over 100 report formats, available at the press of a key, ensure that recovery plans are easily interpreted and distributed throughout the organization. Reports can be produced on screen, on paper, or in the ASCII file format accessible through most word processors. The product is targeted toward medium to large data centers or total organizations.

Recovery Pac II is a downsized version of Recovery Pac with over 40 report formats available and all other Recovery Pac capabilities, with the exception of tracking and evaluating tests in real time. The product is targeted toward small data centers or single organizational departments.

Comprehensive Computer Security Software

The Dutch company called Computer Security Consultants International (Coseco) has developed a product called the *Security Computer*. This is a system of computerized tools for security staff in an organization, consisting of a number of modules. Currently available modules include contingency plan, directives and procedures, audit and review diary. The Security Computer is available for the IBM PC/ XT/AT, PS/2, and compatible computers. The system requires a hard disk and Word Perfect 5.0.

A contingency plan is created by the contingency plan module of the Security Computer that describes the specific activities to be carried out in an organization after a disaster has caused serious disruption to the operations of data processing. When it is necessary to adjust the plan to accommodate changes, they can be easily maintained through the system. The contingency plan is carried out by 3 to 13 teams, depending on the size of the organization. The description of the tasks of the teams forms the core of the plan. Besides this, the plan contains information on aim and structure of the plan, assumptions made, description of the team organization, timetables, methods for activating the plan, and so on.

The directives and procedures module of the Security Computer enables the user to compile a consistent set of procedural security measures, tailor-made to the organization. The final text can be adjusted to organizational changes through the system. The text as compiled by the module consists of a maximum of 543 procedures, divided into 14 sections: general, access control, personnel, equipment, maintenance, system programming, system development, application programs, data security, data processing, contingency planning, offsite storage, backup and insurance.

The audit module of the Security Computer is used to gain insight in the quality of security measures taken. To that aim, the audit module consists of over 1700 multiple choice questions divided into clusters and main clusters. Each cluster represents a subject of security. This division makes it possible to draw up an inventory of the level of security for one or more subjects. The results are measured on a scale from 0 to 10, and can be displayed in text or graphically on screen or printer. Comparison of results and testing of "what-if" situations are made possible by this system.

The aim of the review diary module is to examine security measures in a structured way. This is to be considered an essential part of security management. Within the framework of the Security Computer, the review diary offers the possibility to register by cluster what reviews should be executed and at what time. A cluster represents a subject of security. You can record which department or functionary will execute the review and which review approach will be used.

The risk analysis program *RISAN* provides a model to analyze risks in the organization in an automated way. RISAN is used for inventorying and quantifying the risk situation of an organization and establishing priorities when implementing security measures. By using the program, threats, risk areas and processes are defined, and single and annual expectations of loss are calculated. This program requires a hard disk and is available for IBM PC/XT/AT, PS/2, and compatible computers.

Another product is called *RISKETTES*. This is used to gain insight into vulnerabilities and security measures. The system consists of a total of 14 floppy disks, each of which treats a specific subject of security such as access control or fire protection. Each disk contains a full system and can be used independently. The core of the system is formed by a number of multiple choice questions. The results are measured on a scale from 0 to 10 and can be displayed in text or graphically on screen or printer. Comparison of results and testing of "what-if" situations are only two of the advantages of the system followed. This program does not require a hard disk and is available for IBM PC/XT/AT, PS/2, and compatible computers.

The *System for Security Audit* (SSA) is intended for gathering and analyzing information from a large number of departments or subsidiary companies (up to 10,000). SSA consists of a central system where floppy disks are sent to and received from remote systems. These floppy disks contain a centrally generated list of queries and the programs necessary to answer them. After having received the floppy disks, the results are entered in the central system, whereafter the data can be analyzed, stored and/or printed in a number of ways. This program does not require a hard disk and is available for IBM PC/XT/AT, PS/2, and compatible computers.

The *Structured Approach for Security Management* is an overall method to achieve and maintain an optimal security situation, carried out for clients by CSCI. The Approach consists of 6 steps:

1. An inventory of the actual security measures is drawn up; this inventory shows the weaknesses in security.
2. With a risk analysis, the consequences of threats on the organization can be quantified.
3. The goals and points of view of management on security are laid down in a security policy.
4. The security measures to be implemented are described in a security plan. Priorities in implementing security measures can thereby be established on basis of the risk analysis.
5. The security measures additionally required are implemented.
6. The security measures are then reviewed and checked on a regular basis.

Large-Scale Disaster Planning

For larger data processing systems the American company EDP Security offers *DISASTER PLAN/90*, an automated methodology for disaster plan development. By combining an expert system and a basic customizable contingency plan document, an organization- and site-specific plan can be created that provides a basis for business resumption planning in the event of a large-scale disruption in computer service. Clients can test the plans they develop with the system by using DISASTER PLAN/90 to run simulations of disasters. Using typical scenarios developed from EDP's experience in this field, the performance of the contingency plan can be assessed.

SUMMARY

As you can see, the commercially available security analysis and planning tools follow a pattern that is similar to the one outlined in this chapter. Clearly these commercial programs will enable larger organizations to perform review and analysis tasks much quicker than if in-house personnel start from scratch. Even smaller organizations can benefit from outside assistance, either a computer program or a consultant, if they do not have the human resources or expertise needed to undertake a review of security themselves. However, just about any organization can find within itself enough of the vital ingredients of security planning: imagination, clear thinking, and common sense. Apply these to the following questions, and your organization will be better equipped to gain, rather than lose, from its investment in personal computers:

A. What could go wrong?
B. What would the impact be?
C. What should be done to minimize B and prevent A?
D. How should we react if A happens anyway?

Don't it always seem to go,
That you don't know what you've got till its gone.
Joni Mitchell

5
Securing Hardware

THIS CHAPTER, THE FIRST OF THREE that deal with hardware aspects of personal computer security, concentrates on preventing hardware from being stolen, vandalized, or otherwise damaged. This does not cover the question of maintaining a proper supply of power, which is covered in Chapter 6, or how to stop people from using your hardware, which is covered in Chapter 7. In Chapter 8, you will also read how to stop people from using electronic eavesdropping techniques from getting information out of your hardware. Since this chapter provides an example of theft deterrence that uses a batch file running under DOS, a short review of how to write batch files is included.

A SECURE EXAMPLE

For several years, beginning in 1986, I taught seminars at the IBM offices in a large high-rise building in downtown San Francisco. The security arrangements already in use by IBM at that time are some indication of how seriously the world's largest computer maker takes the subject of hardware security. The classroom was on the third floor and all elevators that accessed that floor were monitored by security personnel.

Only badge holders were allowed onto the elevators. This meant that all seminar attendees had to sign in with a security officer and get a badge before going up to the classroom. You had to be pre-registered for the class and the security officer had a list of pre-registered attendees. When you reached the third floor there were two doors. One led to the area containing the classroom and the other led to IBM's internal computer facilities. This second door was controlled by a magnetic card reader and operated by employees with the correct ID cards.

In the classroom itself, the PCs were set out on proper workstation desks. All of the monitors and system units were attached to the desks by cables anchored on the underside of the work surface. The cables were connected to the monitors and system units with adhesive pads. The monitors could be moved for better viewing and the system units could be opened for quick repairs, but neither could be removed from the room without the use of a screwdriver.

When students took a break they were issued with special cards that enabled them to unlock the door that led to the section of the floor that contained the bathrooms. These cards did not unlock any other doors. All cards were collected at the end of the class.

This arrangement was not entirely convenient, but it was secure. Only a determined intruder would persist in face of the security barriers IBM had erected. Whether you need to go to such lengths or not, the best frame of mind in which to read this chapter is a suspicious one, reflecting on the ways in which your personal computer hardware could be ripped off, and the best defense against that eventuality.

Protecting your hardware from disappearing is known as physical security, and, as you saw in Chapter 2, it is largely a matter of common sense. Making sure that your personal computer hardware stays where it should, can be as simple as securing the hardware to the desk. Yet even simple solutions need to be thought out and can only be effectively implemented after careful analysis of the potential threat. Going to the trouble of attaching an expensive personal computer and printer to a chic computer work desk might be of limited value if the work desk has wheels and is located near the elevator. Writing in the 1989/90 Information Security Guide, security consultant Gerry Faulks describes the four-fold role of physical security: to *deter*, to *delay*, to *detect*, and to *defend* (respond). As different strategies are reviewed, their performance in these four areas will be assessed.

HARDWARE RESTRAINT

One of the most straightforward approaches to preventing personal computer equipment from disappearing is to attach it to the desk upon which it is used, provided that the desk is large, heavy, awkward, or otherwise difficult to move. The idea is that the equipment is that much harder to steal if it requires that the furniture goes with it, or if it first has to be detached from the furniture.

Some Possibilities

A variety of commercially available devices perform this function, using a variety of methods. For example, the PadoLock system from Doss Industries of San Francisco consists of interlocking steel plates. One plate, containing a lock, is attached to the desk. Another plate is secured to the bottom of the computer system unit. The system unit is then "docked" onto the desk plate and the key turned, locking the two plates together. Removal of the computer for servicing is still fairly simple—turn the key and lift it off. The only administration involved in the system is looking after the keys.

You can already see where some of the tradeoffs occur with hardware restraint systems. While the PadoLock does not mar the aesthetics of your equipment, it does make rearranging it rather difficult. The base unit will have to be relocated in order for you to move your system unit. Because most keyboards are detachable you still have flexibility in adjusting your typing position. However, using this product with a personal computer like the Mac SE, in which the monitor is integrated into the system unit, limits your ability to adjust the position of the monitor, say to avoid the glare of late afternoon sunlight.

Many companies sell an alternative system of restraint based on cables and padlocks, rather reminiscent of bicycle locks. Some products use the Mac security retention socket in the component case to retain a tab through which cables can be passed. You can see how this works on a Mac II in Fig. 5-1. Other manufacturers should follow Apple's lead and include this feature on their products.

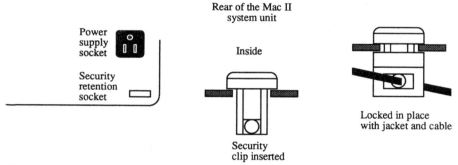

Fig. 5-1. MAC Lock SE.

With a little ingenuity, it is possible to secure all the Macs peripherals with one lock, including the mouse, external drive, and keyboard. The flexibility of the cable system allows minor adjustments to the system configuration without a lot of fuss. The padlock means that the hardware can be released fairly easily, thus retaining the benefits of the original Mac's semiportable design. Clearly there is an aesthetic penalty involved in this system, which adds to the already annoying clutter of cords and cables that most personal computer systems create. One advantage is that nothing is permanently glued to the computer equipment.

For more general applications Secure-It, Inc., supplies a kit consisting of cables, locks, and fasteners through which to loop the cable. Each kit will secure up to six items. The fasteners are designed to use screws that already exist in the hardware, rather than adhesive pads. You can order several of these kits with identical keys to make life easier for the administrator.

The Grabber from PC Security Limited is a conventional cable restraint system consisting of steel plates that attach to the various components, plus a steel cable and padlock. The British company Satellite Electronic Services markets a similar system of steel plates and vinyl-coated steel cable for hardware restraint. The steel plates affix to components with 3M industrial adhesive.

Elements of Restraint

Most attach-to-desk systems are made up of one or more of the following components.

Cable. A steel cable is passed through an existing opening in the hardware or through an eyelet attached to the hardware with a sticky plate or bolts. The cable is attached to the desk with screws, bolts, or a sticky plate, as shown in Fig. 5-2.

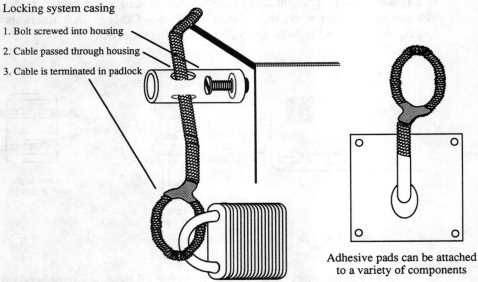

Locking system casing

1. Bolt screwed into housing

2. Cable passed through housing

3. Cable is terminated in padlock

Adhesive pads can be attached to a variety of components

Fig. 5-2. Cable system.

To prevent scratching from bare metal, some companies supply plastic coated cable. This also reduces the possibility of electrical problems such as short circuiting.

Sticky plate. When hardware has no obvious place to which a lock can be attached or through which a cable can be passed, you can create one by using a large area of adhesive, as shown in Fig. 5-2. The industrial adhesive used on these plates is pretty effective, withstanding thousands of pounds of force. However, you might not want your equipment permanently marred by such additions.

Screws. To attach cables or loops to a piece of hardware, you can use screws that are already holding things together. This has the advantage and disadvantage of making the attachment readily reversible. Also, you might consider the role of the screws you press into service for restraining devices. They might not hold things together as well after you give them the added task of holding a loop or fastener. Screwing a cable system terminating plate to a desk can be fairly effective (more effective the more screws you use) and using the underside of the desk can keep things fairly tidy.

Bars. Some restraint systems use a locking bar that goes over or around the system unit. For example, The Muzzle from Ergotron fixes your Mac Plus or SE to a swivel base using a bar which obscures the floppy drive opening. Not only is a key required to remove the computer, but also to access the internal floppy drive.

Keys. Any device that uses a removable key requires a system of key management to ensure that keys are not lost, improperly distributed or copied, or retained by departing personnel. Combination locks are sometimes preferable, if you can operate them quickly and can administer the codes effectively. Combination locks with user-defined codes are preferable to fixed code devices.

The Value of Restraint

When evaluating an attached-to-desk system, you need to see how it performs in the four categories:

- *Deters:* Probably. A good deterrent to the casual thief who is not familiar with the restraining device. Less of a deterrent to the employee or other person with the time and means to unscrew/unstick/unlock.

- *Delays:* Definitely. Makes running off with a PC a lengthier procedure, however adept the thief.

- *Detect:* No, While the restraining device may show signs of tampering it has no inherent ability to tell you who did the tampering and so cannot contribute much to the detection of thieves, whether would-be or successful.

- *Respond:* Possibly. Some restraining devices can be connected to alarms, setting them off if tampered with. The response to the alarm depends upon the sophistication of the device and the priority assigned to the alarm.

You might want to bear in mind several nonsecurity factors. Most cable/connect systems are lacking in aesthetic appeal. They look cumbersome and give off an air of paranoia. To some users, they are about as appealing as finding the chairs in a motel room bolted to the floor. These systems do not prevent damage such as vandalism. The convenience factor should also be considered. Servicing and moving components is made more complicated. If padlocks are used, then keys or combinations will need to be managed.

POWER AND INTERNAL CONTROL

Another form of theft deterrence is provided by the Unilock from Europa Systems. This is a locking device that prevents the unauthorized powering up of the computer. Once fitted, which only takes a screwdriver, the device is captive to the input power socket and can only be removed by an authorized key holder. The system will fit a wide range of makes and models including IBM PS/2, Apple Macintosh, Compaq, and so on.

The Stopper from PC Security Limited is a device that gives two types of security: it prevents unauthorized power-up and unauthorized opening of the system unit. The Stopper fits over the power switch on a conventional PC and around the back of the system unit casing. A keyed lock gives you control of the supply of power to the PC and of access to internal components. The Stopper also controls the power output from the PC power supply to the CRT.

There are few statistics available on the incidence of theft of internal components from a personal computer. During the last shortage of RAM chips, several large-scale thefts of chips from manufacturing and warehouse facilities, were reported, but few reported people stealing the chips from inside a machine.

Nevertheless, some components could be targeted by enterprising individuals and a locked case also discourages would-be technical experts from interfering where they shouldn't. As you might know, most personal computers are made up of a small number of basic components, as shown in Fig. 5-3.

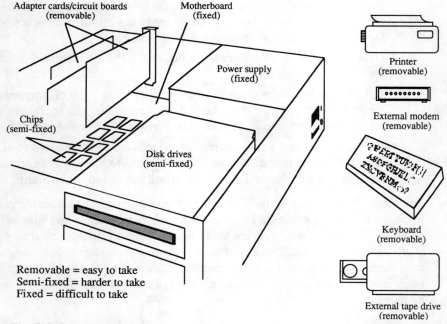

Fig. 5-3. Basic system components.

These are slotted together and held in place by screws or bolts. Some components are relatively easy to take out and could be stolen with little or no discernible change in the outward appearance of the unit. Worries about open cases used to be the confined to users of IBM clones, but now several models in the Apple Macintosh range are "open" in design.

One way to discourage users from opening the computer casing is a seal. While less drastic than a lock, and probably not a deterrent to a determined thief, a seal will make most employees think twice about opening or breaking it. The personal computer administrator could simply place a printed adhesive label across two parts of the case that come apart. You can print such labels on the PC itself, using a design like the one in Fig. 5-4.

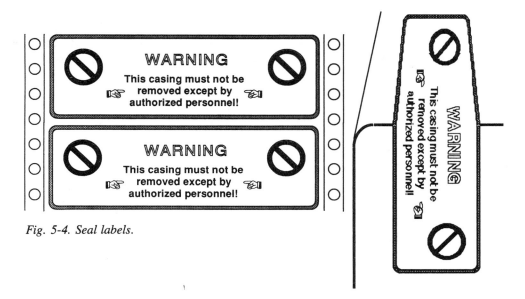

Fig. 5-4. Seal labels.

If the system is properly administered, a torn seal will mean there has been an unauthorized entry into the system unit. Persons requesting legitimate access to the innards could be issued with a fresh seal from the administrator. Of course the seals should be serialized or difficult to copy.

Consider the way this idea meets the four protection criteria.

- Deters: Probably. A good deterrent to the casual thief or meddler.
- Delays: No. Unless you use one of the more sophisticated commercial systems a seal does not slow down entry into the system unit.
- Detect: Yes. Will show that security has been breached.
- Respond: No. Hard to tell who broke the seal and when without heavy surveillance.

DAMAGE PROTECTION

Some personal computers have to serve in less than hospitable environments and simply securing them to the furniture might not be enough. You may feel safer locking the entire unit away when it is not in use.

The Mynda Marketing Company makes and sells a product called the MYNDA PC, designed for the safe storage of computers, word processors, and similar valuable equipment. Features include steel plate construction, completely enclosed locking mechanism, heavy-duty high-security lock, antileverage channels, secure steel roller shutter, cable tidy and electrical distribution board, heavy duty castors, and adjustable shelves.

For the storage of disks and other backup media, paper records, and so forth, Mynda makes the SYSTEM 5000 high-level security cabinets. Specially designed to provide the safe storage of valuable portable equipment and documents, they are suitable for almost any application, in schools, hospitals, shops, factories and building sites. Features include continuously welded, fully rebated steel plate construction. Units can be made to order.

How does the practice of locking up a personal computer system in a steel case perform against the physical security criteria?

- Deters: Yes. A very good deterrent to all but the most determined thief.
- Delays: Definitely.
- Detect: Yes. Any attempts to force the unit open will probably leave visible evidence.
- Respond: Possibly. It would not be difficult to fit an alarm to the case that would let you know if it was being attacked.

MAKING YOUR MARK

One of the quickest and cheapest ways to defend your personal computer hardware is to mark it. By placing a hard-to-remove serial number, identification number, or statement of ownership on your hardware, you decrease its value to the thief. Several systems are available. You can scratch or etch an identifying mark or use a special ink that is visible only in certain light.

You need to strike a compromise between conspicuous marking, aesthetics, and resale value, which can be affected by badly done marking.

The effectiveness of a marking system is greatly enhanced by prominent notices in the office, such as the one shown in Fig. 5-5.

This warns would-be thieves of an added obstacle to fencing the goods and an added means of detection should the goods be intercepted. The notice should indicate that a marking system is in use, but not be specific about the system used.

Of course, some of your hardware, like monitors, printers, and system units, has fairly good identification already in the form of a manufacturer's serial number. However, while you should diligently keep track of all serial numbers, you should not rely on this for your marking because some of the numbers can be removed. Furthermore, some systems, notably hand-built PC clones, might lack any form of serial number.

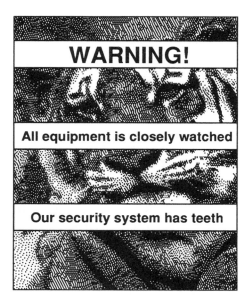

Fig. 5-5. Notice of equipment identification.

Consider the way that equipment identification stacks up in the four categories:

- Deters: Definitely. Makes the hardware harder to unload. A sign pointing out the use of a marking system can be preemptive.
- Delays: Definitely. A thief might think twice about running off with your marked hardware as opposed to someone else's unmarked equipment.
- Detect: Possibly. The authorities can better trace and identify your property if it is marked, and this might help them build a case against a perpetrator.
- Respond: Yes. Enables potential buyers and the authorities to spot stolen goods and return to rightful owner.

SECURING THE PERIMETER

The need to lock your computer to the desk and mark it with your company name is somewhat reduced if you have a secure facility, or one that denies access to all but authorized personnel.

Securing the premises is not simply a matter of personal computer security, and your organization may already have site security systems installed for other reasons than the proliferation of PCs.

The growing concern about personal computer security has given rise to a rapidly expanding range of commercial products offering to solve one or more of the problems raised in this chapter. Of course, the pace of change and innovation in the personal computer industry in general is so fast that no printed publication can provide a complete listing of the products available in any particular category. This is especially true in the case of physical security products. Some products are transferred from other markets, supplied by established companies who see a new market for existing merchandise. Other products are rushed out by astute entrepreneurs who have glimpsed the potential of this market. The products mentioned in the next few paragraphs are merely a representative sample of what is available.

Typical Commercial Products

When considering personal computer security in large organizations, one of the first lines of defense is site control; that is, control of access to company premises and screening out unauthorized persons. Systems to provide this type of security are becoming increasingly refined, and many use personal computers to provide the administrative processing required. Indeed, this is a classic case in which the cheap processing power of the microcomputer makes it an ideal tool, allowing installation of a sophisticated access control system, without imposing any strain on an organization's mainframe or minicomputer resources. Of course, a PC used to run a security system will itself have to be properly secured!

Examples of this type of equipment are the photo image management systems made by the Kodak subsidiary EDICON. These systems integrate color or black-and-white photographic images with text and graphics in a computerized database. Records can then be stored, sorted, retrieved and displayed, which is especially effective for corporate security, personnel badging, and access control. For example, this system is used by Los Angeles International Airport to control personnel access to secure areas.

The EDICON Electronic Badging System and Personnel Photo Database System provide improved facility security through the use of a personnel database consisting of photographic images combined with textual information. When used with the badging application, a visual image of the employee is printed on a laminated badge to be worn by the employee. At the same time, the visual image and employee record is stored in the personnel database for use by security personnel monitoring access to buildings and facilities. The badge information can then be compared with the computer record and image for confirmation of access and appropriate security clearance. Thousands of images can be stored on a personal computer.

The EDICON Access Control System integrates badging and access control through the use of employee badges and badge readers linked to the personnel database. Employee badges with photographic images and textual information can be used as a security pass when worn, as well as a key to facilities through bar coding and magnetic strips. Specific access limitations such as physical boundaries, time and date restrictions, security clearance requirements can be defined on the badge. The system can also be tied into existing surveillance mechanisms or customized for each client, with unlimited expansion capabilities.

The Cotag 2030 Plus System from Cotag International provides a convenient system of access control using what is referred to as proximity technology on tags worn by employees. The employee merely has to wear or carry a tag for quick and easy access control by means of an electronic reader. Because it reads information from the card at the distance, the 2030 Plus System uses no slots or keys and allows simple hands-free operation with no need to remember security numbers or PINs. The system is expandable up to 16 reading heads and 3000 users.

Each user is issued with a Cotag Card, which can have optional photo ID. Cards can be clipped to clothing or carried in pockets or handbags. Discretely designed reading heads are installed at each door where access is to be controlled. Users are individually identified as they approach the door. If they are authorized, the LED indicators turn from red to green and access is granted. Administrative software runs on IBM PCs and provides control of time zones and management reporting. New staff can be added to the system and lost cards can quickly be invalidated using the menu-driven program.

Of the many different site access control systems, some use passwords, keys, magnetic cards, infrared cards, and so on. All of these systems require extensive administration to control the keys/cards/passwords. One such system, the CASS 1600 controlled access system from the white group, uses a PC AT to streamline the administrative procedures and can control up to 64 doors and 16,000 badges at up to 8 different sites using a menu-system accompanied by graphic displays. The system works with a wide range of badges, including the Cotag system described.

Understanding Access Controls

Some authorities credit the Chinese with the first comprehensive access control system. Apparently, around 1000 B.C., the Emperor began to require servants at the Imperial Palace to wear rings engraved with intricate designs that identified areas of the palace where they were permitted to enter. The premise of site access control remains the same today. Organizations of all sizes are erecting access control systems to control people flow and access to sensitive areas. As far as computer security is concerned, it is obviously easier to implement security if an organization can control who gets near enough to computer equipment to steal/abuse it.

Several aspects to access control are allowing access to those who are authorized, denying access to the unauthorized, and knowing who has used access privileges and when. All access control systems must be able to assign access privileges to individuals and also revoke those privileges. More sophisticated systems can vary the extent of privileges (you may enter this room, but not after 6:00 P.M.). They can also track use of privileges (card number 21 entered room A at 6:49 A.M.). Some can even report attempted abuse (card number 21 attempted to enter room B after hours on three occasions this week). However, it is important to bear in mind that, apart from those using biometrics, a concept described in detail in Chapter 7, few access control systems can guarantee the identity of a person using an access privilege. Badges can be borrowed, numbers shared.

From the most basic access control hardware still around today, lock and key, access control technology has grown to include keyless systems. For example, many fast food restaurants guard restricted areas from the public with door locks activated by a keypad. On the keypad is entered a five- or six-digit number. Access is allowed to everyone who enters the correct number. The correct number can be changed by the manager at a moment's notice.

Many of us experience access control when we get money from an automatic teller machine. This system uses a two-key approach. The first key is a public key, a unique card number. The second key is a personal identification number (PIN). The bank's computer knows which PIN goes with which card number and only allows access to the account to persons who have both the card and the PIN number. Again, the PIN number can be changed if it is revealed or compromised.

Card Control Systems

Introduced in the early 1960s, card access control systems now have capabilities never dreamed of 25 years ago. They are capable of database management and even biometeric functions such as voice, fingerprint, retina, and signature identification. Time and attendance figures can be included in the information provided to system managers. Employees who use a card access control system are issued with cards to enter an area instead of a key. Management installs card readers on each door where access will be limited, and it can decide which employee goes where and at what time in the facility, regardless of whether it is a sensitive communications area or a warehouse. Manufacturers are producing systems that can control from eight card readers and 1000 cards, up to extremely large systems that monitor several thousand readers and more than 60,000 cards.

While a typical card system will have a computer as its brains, other components of an access control system can include card readers, PIN pads, door contacts, a CRT display with a keyboard, a printer, and the cards themselves. Using the keyboard and a menu-driven program, a security manager can define which cards are allowed to enter a particular entrance on particular days of the week at a particular time. Readers can be installed inside or outside, on glass doors, turnstiles, parking gates, wherever convenient and necessary. The basic entry procedure when such a system is installed would go like this:

1. An employee seeking admission runs a card through the card reader at the entrance, either pushing it through the reader or inserting it. (On a proximity system, the card only needs to be held close to the reader, which then scans the electronics on the card.)

2. Once the reader has obtained the identification information from the card, it checks with the computer to see if this particular card is authorized for this facility.

3. If the answer is yes, there may still be questions for the computer. For example, is an employee holding card #21 allowed to enter Door A at this particular

time? The computer searches its database and sends the answer to the card reader.

4. If the answer is yes, the reader electronics alerts the door release. At the same time the computer records that card #21 was inserted in Door A and date/time stamps the record, for example, at 6:45 A.M. on January 13, 1991. On more sophisticated systems, the computer might also register the employee name and door location.

5. If the system refuses entrance, it prevents the door from opening and the computer notes that card #21 was refused access at Door A and the reasons for denial, such as the wrong time or the wrong door.

Some access control systems just print out activity reports while others use disk storage to keep extended records. The capability to store each event on the system from the first day of operation helps when you need to develop a complete picture of personnel movements. Using the software to search for specified parameters, management can recreate the use of the system to review security procedures. Furthermore, an organization may want to track the use of a particular card over a period of time, if the user is suspect. Such audit abilities allow you to know who entered or attempted to enter at a particular location. Conversely, the computer audit trail can alert management about all employees who tried to enter a location but could not enter because it was the wrong time. This may indicate a need to review entry times.

A PIN entry pad adds another level of security when used in conjunction with a card reader. This produces access security similar to that of ATMs. With a PIN pad alone, the employee must be permitted to go through an entrance at a certain specified time. If, in addition to an identifying card, a correct personal identification number must be punched in, tighter control is possible. An intruder who happened to pick up the right card for the right door could not get inside because he would not know the correct PIN.

The most secure access control systems combine card systems and PIN pad. When a large number of people are adverse to ID cards and prefer to punch a number, management might have to opt for just a PIN system. Sometimes employees can be in favor of ID cards because they can double as photo identity for check cashing and other purposes.

System Control

The normal situation when a electronic locking mechanism is installed on a door, connected to the electronics of a card reader package, is that the door will only open when the computer tells it to. This has some disadvantages when unusual events occur. There are two types of electronic door: fail-lock and fail-safe. A *fail-lock* door prevents people from entering or leaving the building when the power is turned off. A *fail-safe* door does the opposite: when power is cut, the doors are unlocked, a highly desirable choice in a fire/emergency situation. Many local building codes now require fail-safe doors.

The normal situation, in which only valid cards can open doors, and only valid personnel pass through, breaks down if the door is not closed after that person has entered. A door could be propped open to permit theft of equipment. Electronic strike plates on doors, often located at the top of the door, can notify the computer if the door stays open too long. This event can thus be the basis for an alarm and/or alerting a guard. However, in special situations, it is desirable to be able to program the control software to disarm the door contact, for example, when new office furniture is being delivered.

Software can also be programmed to drop the required identification procedure on certain doors at different times of the day. You might not want visitors and employees to have to use the access control system at the door leading to the receptionist during normal business hours. So you tell the system to lock the door after 5:30 P.M., and only unlock to specific cards.

One big benefit of card access systems is that they can instantly and permanently eradicate a card from the system. If, for example, an employee has lost a card or ceases to be employed at the company and fails to return the card, management can immediately void that card. If someone tried to use that card to enter, not only would that person be denied access, but management would receive a report showing that someone tried to enter with a voided card. It is helpful if the level of access privileged can be changed easily so that management can program the computer to allow employees to enter different areas and at different times, useful in cases of promotion or a change to shift hours.

Choosing a System

If you are considering a card access system, you face a variety of actual card technologies including magnetic stripe, Watermark, barium ferrite, Wiegand, infrared, and proximity. Whatever the technology, the information on the card should include a client or site code, a card number, and several bits of parity. The site codes ensure that the information is unique to the client or installation, making certain that cards issued by one company cannot be used elsewhere.

To allow different access authorizations to be applied to each card and permit accurate tracking of card use, the individual encoded card number must be unique. The provision for parity information is to allow the card reader to verify that the number just read is in fact the number encoded on the card so that no card numbers are misread.

Magnetic stripe and Watermark cards employ a magnetic stripe similar to those found on credit cards. One advantage of these cards is that they can be encoded on site. Of the card technologies available today, only the magnetic strip and Watermark card can do this. The negative side to encoding your own cards is that persons trained to use this part of the system can then abuse it, copying or modifying cards without authorization. To combat this, each Watermark card comes with a permanently encoded number that cannot be changed or copied. This means that each piece of plastic can be traced, making it extremely difficult to create undetected unauthorized copies.

Typical information placed onto a barium ferrite card includes site codes, card numbers, and parity bits encoded in a soft pliable magnetic material sandwiched between layers of plastic. The Wiegand card uses metallic rods or wires embedded invisibly inside the card. Using a pattern of shadows inside the infrared card, a low-level infrared light in the reader detects the pattern and determines whether to grant entry.

A more recent development is the proximity card, which uses radio frequency signals to check the card without it having to touch the reader. The card can be read even if it is in a purse or pocket. This saves the user from having to do anything with the card and means that readers can be hidden from view. This lowers the security profile considerably and counteracts the problem inherent in the observation, "looks like they have card controlled electronic locks on those doors, so there must be something worth stealing inside."

When considering a card control system the following points should be kept in mind:

- System capacity: How many entrances and exits must be controlled today, and how many five years from now? How many employees will receive cards today and five years from now?
- System strength: How stringent must security be at the various entrance or exit locations where access control will be installed?
- System flexibility: Do you need to be able to program different authorization levels for various groups of employees?
- Audit capacity: What information on activity needs to be retained and for how long? Is disk storage of system transactions needed?
- User interface: Will the system be comfortable for users? How intimidating will it be?
- Power problems: Does the system have to stay fully functional during power failures?
- Can additional functions within the building or complex be integrated into the system?
- Expandability: Do you want to be able to add to the system as your organization grows?
- Current resources: Are special pieces of hardware required, such as turnstiles or parking gates? Can existing doors be used? Can existing personnel operations be taken up by the system, such as photo ID cards combined with access cards?

When choosing between prospective suppliers you need to focus on two areas: support and training. You need help to plan, install, and implement the system. Administrators of the system will need to be trained. You want to buy from a security company that is going to be around for a while, so that they can maintain the system over the years, and help you expand on it if need be.

Preparation. In addition to planning where the access control points should be and where to locate the central control unit, you need to do preliminary work with employees to present the system in the best light. Seek to get employee consensus behind the need for the system, then get input on the most convenient way to implement it.

Installation. This is no small task. Cable from the reader to the central control unit signal must be installed in a conduit separate from the wiring that controls the electrical door strikes. The central control unit must be cabled to the readers and PIN pads according to manufacturer's specifications. There might be limitations on cable distances between the main components. Poor installation can result in marginal operation leading an otherwise good quality access control system to be discarded as unsatisfactory.

Training. Providing the right level of training for users of the system is important, helping to break down resistance to the system and show how little it actually interferes with normal business. The natural antipathy to restrictions needs to be countered by stressing the positive aspects (increased profits from reduced losses, reduced risk to jobs from loss of valuable data). Incentives and rewards for making the system work tend to work better than threats of punishment if it doesn't. Care needs to be given to the training of system administrators. Ongoing securing of the system will depend on controlling detailed knowledge of how it works. For example, avoid training high turnover clerical staff in how to make access cards.

Maintenance. The cost of setting up an ongoing maintenance scheme should not be skimped because the system will not be secure if even one defective component goes unrepaired.

PROTECTING THE WHOLE COMPUTER SYSTEM

One of the first computer-related crimes I encountered was a night-time break-in at the office of a planning consultant. This particular case illustrates the need to consider the security of the personal computer system as a whole, and the need to think carefully about what needs protecting.

The consulting business used two IBM PC-XTs. One of these was on the desk of the receptionist/administrative assistant who did most of the typing of the lengthy planning documents that the consultant prepared for his clients. This desk was visible from the path that led to the car park that served the building in which the office was located. This was probably where the thief got the idea for the break-in. An alarm on the premises did go off when the burglars entered. This probably accounted for the fact that only one PC was taken, and that it was very hastily ripped off the desk, with some cables still attached. However, the police response was not quick enough to be of much use in apprehension of the criminals.

When the consultant arrived at the office to survey the damage he was relieved to find the set of backup data disks in his desk had not been taken. He arranged for a rented PC XT to be delivered to replace the stolen one. The large letter quality printer, an IBM 5218, was still in place. When his assistant arrived, they thought they would be back in business very quickly. However, when they installed the renter computer, they realized that the printer cable was missing. It only took a few phone calls to discover that this was no off-the-shelf cable. As the consultant tried to contact IBM for a cable from an IBM PC XT to an IBM Model 5218 printer, his assistant installed their word processing software, DisplayWrite 3, on the rented XT. A bid submission deadline was fast approaching, and the office had no printing capability.

The consultant called around to rent a printer and found himself sinking into a nightmare. Very few printers were compatible with DisplayWrite 3, none of the units on offer from rental companies. At that time DisplayWrite 4 had just been released, and it supported more printers. DisplayWrite 4 reads DisplayWrite 3 files. They could upgrade to DisplayWrite 4 and use it with a rented printer, but upgrades took weeks to process. They could go out and buy DisplayWrite 4, but there would be a learning curve to get used to the program changes. Besides, DisplayWrite 4 did not support the IBM 5218 printer that they wanted to use as soon as a cable was found.

Finally a man from IBM arrived. He installed and tested a cable. It did not work. A new serial card was installed. A second cable was tried. It did better. A configuration file used to redirect print output to the serial port had to be fine-tuned. Finally, the printer communicated with the PC. However, DisplayWrite 3 would still not print pages properly. Another cable was tested. Finally, it was determined that IBM had issued a special memory-resident driver program for the 5218 printer. This was needed because the 5218 printer had been created for the original DisplayWriter dedicated word processor, which did not use DOS. A copy of that driver program had been installed on the stolen PC. After a frantic search, the consultant found the master copy of the driver. But simply installing it did not solve the problem. To run correctly, the driver program needed certain settings, and the documentation was nowhere to be found.

Eventually, several calls to IBM later, the correct settings were determined and the problem was resolved. Yet this was two agonizing, frustrating, and expensive days for the consulting company. What lessons were learned?

Backup data files are good. But backups which include program files are also important. The vital driver software and configuration file that let the printer and computer understand each other took hours to fine-tune by trial and error, while obviously already installed correctly on the missing computer.

The stolen cable was a custom job, very hard to replace, valuable far beyond its dollar cost. Without it, the office lost its printing capacity. The harder something is to replace, the more closely it should be protected. The other side to this is to avoid specialized hardware. Clearly this goal cannot always be achieved, but there are definite advantages to using readily replaceable components.

Do not overlook basic security. For example, placing personal computers near the front door makes them that much more tempting. In this case, the alarm system did help. Only one computer was taken. Even that might have been left behind if it had been further from the front door or attached to the desk.

FAKING IT

You can probably attain the greatest amount of deterrence for the least amount of money by installing conspicuous warning signs and messages of foreboding. A sign like the one in Fig. 5-6, or the one seen earlier in Fig. 5-5, posted on the outside of an office door, will cause most intruders to think twice.

Fig. 5-6. Warning sign.

If just a few people know that the message is not entirely true, then you can deter would-be wrongdoers without spending a lot of money. Only those on the inside need know that the company cannot afford the real thing.

Sign Making

The signs themselves are easily obtained by most personal computer users, using the computer itself. Now that many personal computer printers can create practically typeset quality output, signs like those in Fig. 5-5 and 5-6 can be fabricated very quickly. You can use clear plastic adhesive tape to fix the signs onto equipment, furniture, walls, or doors. If you use wide sheets of plastic that cover the sign without joints then the sign appears to be laminated, and a very convincing result can be obtained. If your office actually has a laminating device, then enclosing signs in stiff plastic will add to the realism.

A Moving Sign

A colleague who works out of an office in his home finally got a chance to take a vacation and, worried about the possibility of a burglary, he planned to lock his personal computer system in a closet before he left. However, he realized that, because his personal computer operated his phone answering machine, he would have to leave it turned on while he was away. Faced with this dilemma, he devised an ingenious means of discouraging burglars. He wrote a small batch file program that displayed the screen seen in Fig. 5-7.

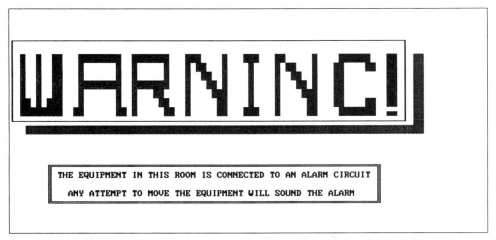

Fig. 5-7. Warning screen.

The only way that you can test whether this message is true is to risk setting off the alarm. Realizing that there could be power failures while he was away, the wily user altered the computer's AUTOEXEC.BAT so that the message was displayed whenever the PC was turned on. However, he realized that simply displaying the message would not be a good idea because prolonged display of any single image can damage the monitor.

To get around this problem, several different messages were created and displayed in turn, with a short gap between them. In fact, the effect of screen movement added to the realism of the warning. This was further augmented by using beeps from the computer's speaker. The final result was an impressive message that would probably discourage all but the most sophisticated burglar. Not only was the result imposing, but any PC user can create a similar system.

AN INTRODUCTION TO BATCH FILES

Because a large percentage of the readers of this book will be users of MS-DOS based systems, it is worth taking a moment to review the use of batch files. You can implement several effective security measures with batch files, including the warning system described in the previous section. Because batch files are not central to this book, the following notes cannot be exhaustive. For an excellent treatment of the subject in detail, look no further than *MS-DOS Batch File Programming*, by Ronny Richardson, Windcrest Books. More experienced users will also enjoy Dan Gookin's *Advanced MS-DOS Batch File Programming*, also from Windcrest.

About Batch Files

A batch file contains a series of commands that will be executed as a group or batch (in parts of England small round bread rolls are called *batches* because they are baked in a batch). In DOS, these files have the extension .BAT as in Q.BAT.

In Chapter 2, mention was made of the file called AUTOEXEC.BAT. This is a batch file that DOS looks for whenever a PC is booted. If DOS finds a file called AUTOEXEC.BAT on the boot disk, it carries out the instructions in the file. A typical AUTOEXEC.BAT file might contain the following:

```
O'CLOCK /S (sets time and date to internal clock)
PATH = C:\DOS;C:\123 (sets PATH for DOS to use)
PROMPT $P $G (sets DOS prompt to show current directory)
DIR *. (lists all subdirectories of the root directory)
```

As you can see, this series of commands could be carried out from the DOS prompt by the user typing each line and then pressing Enter. However, the batch file feeds the commands to DOS much faster than typing and introduces a level of convenience. Because batch files will also accept special commands that perform tests based on user input or user-specified conditions, they offer a basic level of programming, or programmed control of the PC.

Making Batch Files

Batch files would not be so popular if it were not so easy to create. A batch file is simply a text file, one that contains nothing but simple text characters. There are several ways to create BAT files:

- The COPY CON command.
- The line editor that comes with DOS, EDLIN.
- A text editor included in a utility or shell program, such as: the SideKick Notepad, the QuickDOS II editor, or the Windows NOTEPAD.

- A word processing program that can store files in ASCII:
    WordStar, using nondocument mode.
    WordPerfect, using the Text In/Out, DOS Text command.
    DisplayWrite 4, using the Get File command.
    Microsoft Word, using Transfer Load.

The simplest method to use is the COPY command. For example, to create a batch file called TEST.BAT type the following at the DOS prompt:

```
COPY CON TEST.BAT
```

Now press Enter. This will move the cursor down one line on the screen. This is the first line of the file. Type the first command that the batch file is to execute, in this case, CLS, the DOS command for clearing the screen. After typing CLS, press Enter. You are now on a new line, the second line of the file. Type as the second command

```
ECHO Here is a list of files. . .
```

and press Enter. Now type the third command of the file

```
DIR /W
```

but do *not* press Enter. You need to tell DOS that the file is complete. You do this by striking Ctrl−Z or pressing F6. This is called the End-Of-File command, or *EOF*, and it will look like this:

```
DIR /W^Z
```

Now press Enter and the DOS prompt will reappear. Type

```
DIR *.BAT
```

and press Enter, and you should see the new file listed on the screen. To run a batch file, you simply type the name at the DOS prompt and press Enter. In this case, type TEST and press Enter and the results will look something like Fig. 5-8.

Note that the message you entered is repeated on the screen as are all of the commands. To eliminate this problem, you use the command ECHO OFF at the beginning of your batch file.

Altering Batch Files

To add a line to or otherwise alter an existing batch file is to edit it. You cannot do this with the COPY CON method. Using COPY CON, you simply create the file again, this time incorporating the changes. The file should now contain the following:

```
ECHO OFF
CLS
ECHO Here is a list of files . . .
DIR /W
```

If you are using EDLIN or another editing tool, you can simply insert a new line in the

```
C:\>ECHO Here is a list of files...
Here is a list of files...

C:\>DIR/W

 Volume in drive C is COMPANY PC
 Directory of  C:\

123R23           BAT             COL             DOS             INSET
KEY              NU              PHONE           QDOS            QT
QUATTRO          SK              SYTOS           TOPS            TP
VACCINE          23      BAT     ANSI    SYS     ART     BAT     AUTOEXEC B00
AUTOEXEC BAT     AUTOEXEC OLD    BACKUP  LOG     OLDBACK M_U     BAK     BAT
BETA     MEN     COMMAND  COM    CONFIG  OLD     CONFIG  SYS     CR
CR       DAT     DMOUSE   COM    DT      EXE     ENHKEYBD COM    ENHKEYBD DBG
HARDRIVE SYS     HIMEM    SYS    KEYS            LPTX1   LST     MAIN    MEN
MAIN1    MEN     MENU     DAT    MOUSE   SYS     NEW     DAT     NOW
NU       EXE     BACKUP   M_U    PMAP    EXE     PMINFO  DAT     QD2     EXE
QD2      LOG     QDCOLOR  COM    QDSTART EXE     RUFF    WQ1     SIMP    MEN
START            STOP            SYM     BAT     TEST    BAT     TOPSTART BAT
TREMEMBR BAT
        61 File(s)   2631680 bytes free

C:\>
C:\>
```

Fig. 5-8. Running TEST.BAT.

existing file; there is no need to create the file over again. Now run the amended TEST.BAT, and you will see the difference. The commands are not echoed on the screen.

You can control the executing of commands in a batch file in many ways. For example, if you edit the TEST.BAT to include the following changes, you will allow the user to control whether or not the commands after PAUSE are executed:

```
ECHO OFF
CLS
ECHO Do you want to see a list of files?
ECHO If No, then type Ctrl – C, otherwise . . .
PAUSE
DIR /W
```

When you run this file, a question is posed before the DIR command is executed. Pressing Ctrl – C interrupts the batch file (as does the equivalent key Ctrl – Break). If you press Ctrl – C, you get the further message:

```
Terminate batch job (Y/N)?
```

You enter Y to stop the commands in the rest of the file from being executed. If you enter N, the execution of the file resumes.

Typing Messages

Your personal computer might already have some batch files. Several software packages create batch files when they are installed. To find out what a batch file does without running it, you use the TYPE command, as in:

```
TYPE AUTOEXEC.BAT
```

The TYPE command displays the file contents on the screen.

This command is also useful for displaying messages. If you create a message file that is pure ASCII code just like a batch file, then the contents can be typed on the screen with TYPE. As an example, create the following two-line file, MESSAGE .TXT, in the same way you created TEST.BAT:

```
You are not an authorized user!
Further input will sound the alarm!
```

Now create a batch file called WARNING.BAT that contains the following instructions:

```
@ECHO OFF
CLS
TYPE MESSAGE.TXT
PAUSE
```

When you run this file the screen will go blank except for the following lines:

```
You are not an authorized user!
Further input will sound the alarm!
Strike a key when ready . . .
```

In this example you could have used two ECHO commands to display the message lines, but the TYPE method offers several advantages. You can alter the message file without having to alter the batch file. If you want, you can make a very elaborate message file, using the techniques described in a moment.

 Note the @ECHO OFF command. The @ sign in front of a batch file command tells DOS not to display the command. Thus, @ECHO OFF does not even show the "echo off" message. This results in a smoother appearance when the batch file runs. Using the @ sign is valid in DOS 3.3 or greater. Just leave it out if you are using an earlier version of DOS.

What actually happens after you run the WARNING.BAT and the message appears? If you press any key, the DOS prompt returns. Of course, you know that, but many other users would not. You have just created your first security batch file. If you run WARNING from the DOS prompt before you leave your computer unattended, you will have some level of protection against casual snoops.

If someone does press a key you will know it, because the message will disappear. The only way to restore the message is to run WARNING.BAT again. The clever intruder who knows an alarm will not sound, might press a key, then press F3 to check the last command you gave to DOS. This will reveal the name of the batch file, which can then be run by the intruder after he or she has finished snooping.

Creating Loops

One weakness of this batch file is that even an accidental tap of the keyboard removes the message. To overcome this, you can place a loop in the batch file, meaning that the program will go back to an earlier section and repeat it. You do this by using a GOTO statement together with a named line in the file. The named line consists of a word preceded by a colon. Edit the WARNING.BAT file so that it reads thus:

```
ECHO OFF
:START
CLS
TYPE MESSAGE.TXT
PAUSE
GOTO START
```

Now when you run the file the message will not go away. You can only get back to the DOS prompt by pressing Ctrl−C and terminating the batch file. You can see that the level of knowledge required to defeat the batch file has increased considerably.

Fancy Messages

To display a more impressive message, you can use a word processing program, such as WordPerfect or DisplayWrite 4 that has a "cursor draw" feature. This is simply a method of creating shapes by arranging those ASCII characters which represent lines, blocks, and shading. In Fig. 5-9, you can see cursor drawing at work in Word-Perfect.

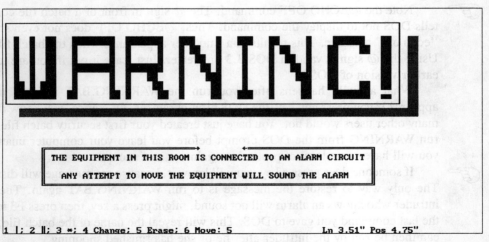

Fig. 5-9. Cursor draw.

When this file is completed and saved in DOS text (ASCII) format, it can be displayed with the TYPE command. This is how the message in Fig. 5-7 was created.

A Short Wait

Several messages can be displayed one after another using a series of TYPE commands. However, you might want DOS to pause between messages. This is not a pause for user input, but a waiting period. You can create waiting periods in batch files by using a small DOS utility like WAIT.COM that comes with the Norton Utilities. This program is executed from DOS followed by a number which is the number of seconds that DOS must wait until carry out the next line of batch file. The number is called an argument, and many DOS programs use them. The following batch file using WAIT will display three messages (in files called M1.TXT, M2.TXT, and M3.TXT):

```
ECHO OFF
CLS
:START
TYPE M1.TXT
WAIT 10
CLS
WAIT 5
TYPE M2.TXT
WAIT 10
CLS
WAIT 5
TYPE M3.TXT
WAIT 10
CLS
WAIT 5
GOTO START
```

Each message appears for 10 seconds, followed by 5 seconds of blank screen. The batch file is looped so that it keeps repeating. The effect is quite professional and suitably worded messages should discourage casual interlopers.

Sounding Off

To add to the impression made by the above batch file, you might want to add some sound. You can do this with the BEEP.COM program that comes with Norton Utilities. This program makes a sound through the PC's speaker. For example, you could add it to the above batch file like this:

```
TYPE M3.TXT
WAIT 10
BEEP
CLS
WAIT 5
```

This would mean that a sound was made just before the screen went blank. The sound that BEEP normally makes is fairly short and high pitched. By adding *F*requency and *D*uration arguments to the BEEP command you can alter the sound, as in

```
BEEP /F45 /D10
```

which is a longer and deeper sound. The Norton Utilities manual explains the arguments (and even shows you how a tune can be composed and stored in a text file to be played by BEEP).

By using the power of batch files inherent in DOS plus some small utility programs, you can develop some useful routines. These can be used to discourage theft, and, as you will see in Chapter 7, access to the system.

A RANGE OF PRODUCTS

An indication that security concerns have reached the mainstream of the personal computer community can be seen in the catalogs of major office supply companies. For example, through their catalog of computer supplies and data communications equipment, Inmac provides a range of furniture and security equipment for PCs and media. Such equipment includes security installations, safes, PC locks, and compatible power supplies.

Inmac's PC LOCK KIT is a hardware restraining kit designed to attach objects such as monitor, CPU, printer, keyboard, modem, fax machine to your desk, terminated with a resetable combination lock. A companion product is LAPTOP LOCK designed to attach your laptop to your desk using a combination lock. Inmac also sells a digital push button door lock designed for use on office doors. Featuring 13 buttons with 5500 combinations in codes of between 5 and 7 digits, the unit comes in manual or automatic versions with a deadbolt lock.

Inmac can sell you two sizes of fireproof data safes, a lockable storage cabinet with multi-locking roll-up doors, a mobile security workstation to house your PC, printer and accessories, also lockable with a roll-up door. The same catalog also features a wide range of standby power supplies, power breaker rugs, surge breakers, power filter plugs, and transient isolators, discussed in the next chapter. Another large supplier of computer related products, Misco, has a similar range of security devices in its catalog.

SUMMARY

Physical security is the most basic level of security. This is important to bear in mind as you get further into data and program security. The most sophisticated password file protection is of little protection against vandals breaking into your office and trashing your machines. Overall office security is the first line of defense. The safety of an organization's personal computer equipment and the data stored on depends upon the organization taking appropriate steps to secure the premises. Beyond this lies protection from the enemy within, and methods to minimize the impact of a failure to secure the premises.

Uncertainty and expectation are the joys of life.
Security is an insipid thing.

William Congreve

6
Keeping the Computers Running

FEW PERSONAL COMPUTER USERS would agree with the above quotation, at least not while using their personal computers. This chapter could be subtitled "secondary power supplies and other forms of insurance against uncertainty and the unexpected." It deals not only with keeping the supply of power to your computer smooth and constant, but also with the possibility of insuring against the harmful effects of relying upon computers.

You might wonder about the inclusion of computer insurance in a chapter about hardware, but the subject needs to be addressed somewhere if the content of the book is to match its title, and, as it happens, hardware is the easiest part of a computer system to insure. Indeed, some insurance policies only cover hardware. Before discussing what to look for in a personal computer insurance policy, the chapter explores surges, spikes, and overloads. These terms refer not to your emotional state when you learn "That's not covered," but the state of the electrical current that keeps your personal computer running.

POWER TO THE COMPUTER

To work properly, personal computers need a reliable source of electricity, one that is maintained within specific parameters. If the supply of power is interrupted unexpectedly or varies significantly from the normal parameters, the consequences can be serious. Data in memory can be lost or corrupted, hardware can be damaged, operations interrupted, and information rendered temporarily or permanently irretrievable. Devices can help protect against these dire consequences. They go by names like *surge suppressor*, *line conditioner*, and *uninterruptible power system*. Before examining how these devices can help, it is important to be clear on some of the basics of electricity.

Electricity 101

Personal computers consist of a large number of electrical circuits. Some circuits, such as those that hold information in memory, use only a small amount of power. Other circuits, such as those that power the disk drives, require more electricity. The electricity used by the internal components of the personal computer is known as *direct current* (or dc) because it is always travelling in the same direction (the wire supplying the electricity is positive, the return wire is negative).

As a rule, personal computers get their electricity from normal domestic electrical circuits, sometimes referred to as *mains current*. This mains current is fairly strong and is known as *alternating current* (or ac) because it alternates between positive and negative. Within most personal computers is a piece of equipment called a *power supply*. This takes in the ac current from the mains and converts or transforms it to low-powered dc current used by the computer components. You can see this diagrammed in Fig. 6-1.

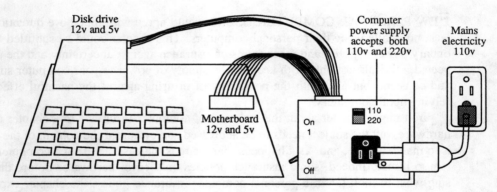

Fig. 6-1. Supply of power to a personal computer.

The power supply is a vital component in any personal computer system, and the one that bears the brunt of abnormalities in the mains supply. (The term *power supply* will be reserved for this component and will not be used for other devices, discussed later, which can also be said to supply power.)

A notable and growing exception to these observations are laptop computers which run on batteries. Laptops are discussed later in this chapter.

By and large, electricity is useful only when it is allowed to flow through a device or appliance. For example, if it flows through a lamp, it produces light. If it flows through a disk drive motor, it produces rotation. Whatever it flows through, electricity produces heat, in quantities that vary according to the appliance. For example, when electricity flows through a normal household bulb, the bulb gives out light *and* gets hot. An electric blanket is an appliance in which electricity does nothing else besides produce heat. The electrical circuits inside a personal computer generate heat, which is why many systems are fitted with fans that provide air flow for cooling.

Measuring the Power

What causes electricity to flow through an appliance is the existence of a difference in electrical *pressure* between the wire supplying the electricity, the *live* wire, and the wire taking it away, the *neutral* wire. The greater the difference in pressure, the greater the flow. But the flow is also determined by the electrical *impedance* of whatever lies between the live and neutral wires. If this impedance is low, a given pressure difference will result in a much higher flow than if the impedance is high. The term *resistance* is sometimes used instead of *impedance*, although there is a technical difference between the two. If the live wire is carrying a lot of electricity to an appliance, and the appliance uses that electricity, it creates a resistance.

The flow of electricity is usually called *current* and can be measured in *amperes*. The abbreviation *amps* is usually used, designated simply as A. The more amps an appliance uses, the more electricity it consumes. You will find the amperage of many appliances listed close to where the power cord enters the casing. For example, the Apple LaserWriter IINT says 7.5 amps. The pressure difference in a circuit is called *voltage* because it is measured in *volts*. The higher the volts, the more pressure there is to make the electricity flow. Volts are often designated as V and large quantities are measured in kilovolts (kV) so that 2000 V = 2 kV. Impedance, or resistance to flow, is measured in *ohms*, represented by the symbol Ω. The relationship between the three quantities can be expressed mathematically: resistance is equal to the pressure difference divided by the rate of current, or

ohms = volts / amps

This means that if you know two of the amounts involved, you can work out the third.

In measuring electrical devices such as computers, a fourth quantity often enters into things: power. This can be measured in *watts* (designated W). For example, the bulb in a desk lamp might be 60 watts or 60 W. For larger appliances the watts are measured in thousands, or kilowatts, designated kW. You can see this and other terms diagrammed in Fig. 6-2.

The power or wattage of an electrical appliance is a measure of how much electrical energy it consumes in a given period of time. For example, the original floppy disk IBM PC systems had power supplies rated at about 50 W, less than many light bulbs. This was not sufficient to run the early hard disks, which used a lot of power. A typical AT-style IBM compatible of the late 1980s might have a 220 W power supply. For most practical purposes, wattage is equal to the voltage (volts) of the supply multiplied by the current that the appliance draws from that supply (amps). The equation looks like this:

watts = volts * amps

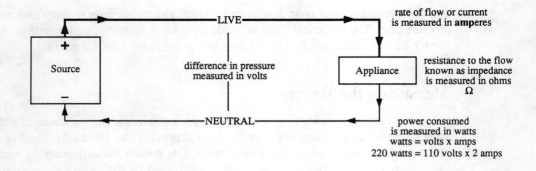

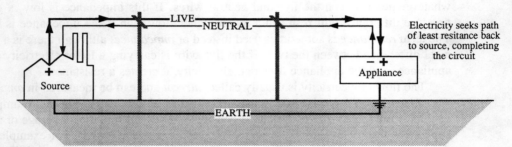

Fig. 6-2. Diagram of terms.

Suppose you have a laser printer rated at 7.5 amps. Operating at 120 volts this appliance will draw 900 watts.

To turn the equation around, amps are what you get by dividing volts into watts, thus

amps = watts / volts

If your personal computer has a 120 watt power supply and you are running on 120 volts, then you might put the amperage at 1. However, this is not always an accurate equation, because the appliance might not consume the entire current that is fed to it.

For this reason, a further measure is used in discussions of computer power supplies: volt amps or va. Like watts, this measurement can also be defined as volts times amps, but takes into account something called the *power factor*. An appliance like an electric heater represents what is termed a *purely resistive load*, one that consumes all of the power supplied to the appliance. But a power supply is computer system appliance is *partly capacitive* and *partly inductive*. Simplistically put, this means that the computer system appliance doesn't use all of the power it gets; it sidelines some of it and stores some of it. This gives rise to a power factor for appliances that are not completely resistive, based on their relationship to a power requirement of 1, which represents a purely resistive appliance. Typical personal computer power supplies have a power factor of around 0.65. The equation for volt amps is thus:

volt amps = volts ∗ amps ∗ power factor

When amps are not known, then you can use this equation:

volt amps = watts ∗ power factor

Suppose your personal computer's power supply is rated at 200 watts, operating on 120 volts. With a power factor of 0.65 the volt amps would be 130.

A unit of measurement you might see mentioned in product literature for power conditioning products is *joules*. A joule is a fairly complex measure of energy. In electrical circuits you can assess the energy in a flow of current for a period of time. This is sometimes useful when comparing sudden rushes of power across a circuit.

A Matter of Time

The time during which an electrical current flows can be of considerable significance. Your electricity bill probably shows the amount of electricity you have consumed since the last bill, measured in thousands of watts per hour or kilowatt hours (kWh). If you leave 10 lamps on, each burning a 100 W bulb, for 10 hours, you will have consumed 10 kWh.

Electrical activity within a computer takes place at very high speed and so it is often measured in parts of a second. For example, one thousandth of a second is one millisecond (ms). The time it takes for a hard disk drive to read a piece of information from disk into memory is often measured in milliseconds, as in "40 ms access time." A millionth of a second is called a microsecond and a thousandth of a millionth of a second is called a nanosecond. These terms are sometimes used in describing the performance of such devices as surge suppressors and standby power supplies.

A particularly important area of time measurement in computers involves the time taken to complete a cycle of events. Periodic time, or frequency, can be measured in cycles per second, or *hertz* (Hz). If you measure in millions of times per second, you use *megahertz* (MHz). The relative speed of the central processing chip of your personal computer is measured in megahertz. This is actually the number of "ticks" generated in one second by the clock crystal controlling the chip. The chip processes a single instruction each time the clock ticks. For example, the original IBM PC had a clock speed of 4.77 MHz. A typical 80386 system of the late 1980s has a clock speed of 20 MHz.

As far as the ability to process information is concerned, clock speed is not everything. The amount of data that is processed during one tick is also very important. The original IBM PC had the capacity to process data 16 bits at a time while earlier systems could only manage 8 bits. The 80286 chip in the IBM AT processed 16 bits at a time, while the 80386 chip can handle 32. Theoretically, an 80286 chip operating at 12 MHz can process data at the same rate as an 80386 operating at 6 MHz.

An interesting phenomenon occurs as clock speeds for computer chips are increased. When the clock ticks, the power level in the clock goes from zero to five volts. Theoretically this happens instantly, but in fact the voltage takes time to build up. The more ticks per second, the less time there is for the power to build up. To overcome this problem, the circuit is designed to apply greater pressure to the circuit to get the clock voltage to rise faster. Unfortunately, this often results in the voltage overshooting the level actually needed, placing a strain on the chips in the system. This stress, together with other design problems associated with high-speed processors, such as the creation of harmonics, has a practical reliability/security implication. If you are attempting to choose between competing personal computer systems, the goal of long-term reliability is more likely to be assured by a large capacity chip operating at modest speed, rather than a moderate capacity chip working very, very fast.

 This problem has been acknowledged for many years in mainframe design, and it accounts for IBM's controversial decision to set the clock speed of the 80286 chip in the original AT at 6 MHz, despite the fact that the same chip was capable of operating at higher speeds. IBM doubted the reliability of the supporting chips under the stresses imposed by higher speeds. When 33 MHz systems based on the 80386 were announced, many companies had problems getting them to work reliably. An associated problem with higher frequency chips is that, at higher speeds, the wires in the system start to hum and resonate, affecting integrity of the circuits, resulting in all sorts of unpredictable behavior.

The Wave

Another important area in which hertz are used is in the measurement of the alternating current that flows through the mains. This current goes from positive to negative and back to positive many times a second. In U.S. current, the complete cycle is carried out 60 times a second (60 Hz). In Britain the mains current is 50 Hz.

You might wonder why there is a difference in frequencies between the two countries. The answer has to do with what happens when electrical current is raised or lowered. The stronger current that is being alternated, the harder it is to control the change. You might think of kinking a garden hose to turn on and off the flow of water. The more pressure in the hose, the harder it is to cut off the flow quickly and cleanly. Alternating 240 volts of current 60 times a second would make the cycles more abrupt than they are at 50 cycles.

Measurement of a smoothly alternating current should produce a smooth graph, like the first one seen in Fig. 6-3. This is called a *sine wave* since the cycle follows the mathematical curve generated by plotting the sine function.

Abrupt cycles appear more like square waves and electricity following this pattern is more likely to create disturbances in electrical equipment. A phenomenon known as harmonics can occur at the "shoulders" of a square wave, frequencies related to but higher or lower than the normal frequency. Harmonics are a primary source of *elec-*

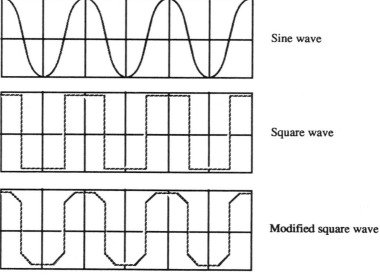

Sine wave

Square wave

Modified square wave

Fig. 6-3. A sine wave.

tro-magnetic interference or (EMI), which can seriously disrupt electronic components. An engineer using an oscilloscope can check the wave form of your current.

FUSES, GROUNDS, AND BREAKERS

To understand some of the things that can go wrong with electrical circuits, it might help you to think of electricity coming from the power station to the outlets in your office, borne on the live wire, then returning to the power station on the neutral wire after it has performed its work. Materials along which electricity flows freely, such as the copper in your office wiring, are called *conductors*. Electricity is essentially lazy, attempting to get back to the power station as quickly as possible through any available conductor.

What keeps electricity from getting back too soon is insulation, which restricts the flow of electricity. Rubber, plastic, and a large variety of nonmetal materials make good insulators. Insulators make it possible to contain the flow of electricity, enabling us to make electrical appliances out of materials are good conductors. For example, the casing of many personal computers is made of conductive metal, but touching the case should not give you a shock since insulators keep the current within the internal components of the system.

However, under extreme conditions, such as high voltage, even good insulators will break down, allowing electricity to flow where it should not. Faults in electrical circuits are usually caused by either an insulator or a conductor not working properly.

Faults usually result in high temperatures, and the results can be disastrous for sensitive equipment. There are ways to prevent faults and technologies which minimize the impact of faults.

Grounding

Two alternative paths for the completion of an electrical circuit are down the neutral conductor of the supply cable or via the earth. In simple terms, the latter path exists because the neutral side of the electrical supply from the power station is connected to earth. This is why, if you touch a live conductor and are attached to the earth with no insulation, you will get a severe shock. The current passes through you to the earth.

The tendency of electrical current to return to earth has positive uses, called *grounding*. To ground an electrical device, you should make sure that any conductive materials in it that should not become live, such as the metal case of a personal computer, can be easily connected to the ground. This way, if insulation breaks down, the live current will be quickly directed away harmlessly to the ground as the electricity seeks the fastest way home. In the process, the leak of electricity to ground should be detected, and the equipment turned off to prevent further damage. This task is usually accomplished by a fuse or circuit breaker, as diagrammed in Fig. 6-4.

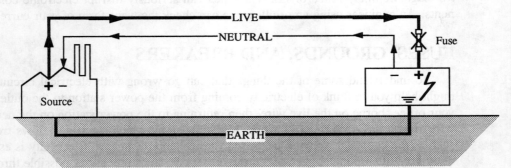

When electricity leaks to ground it causes a sudden increase in flow which blows the fuse

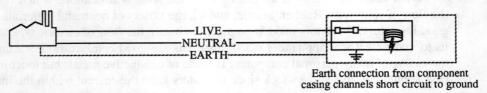

Earth connection from component
casing channels short circuit to ground

Fig. 6-4. Grounding electrical current.

Electricity leaking from your computer onto the casing could be conducted to the ground in several ways. In some countries, such as Britain, where voltage is quite high, all appliances must be fitted with a three-pronged plug. There is one prong each for the live and neutral wires, and a third for the earth or ground. In the wiring of sockets, the wire from the ground prong is connected to a special cable called an *earth continuity conductor*. Several such conductors might be in a house or office. The metal casing of light sockets and any metal plumbing pipes will also have earth conductors attached to them. All such conductors will lead to a central point. Here the earth cable might literally go into the ground. Newer American buildings are supposed to be wired in the same way, with the third prong leading to earth.

An alternative to running the cable into the ground, called *protective multiple earthing*, is to connect the central earth of the building to the neutral wire of the electricity company's service cable. This method is the basis for grounding when you only have two prongs on your plug. The neutral side can be used as the ground. However, this only works if the plug is put in the right way around, as diagrammed in Fig. 6-5, and the sockets are wired consistently.

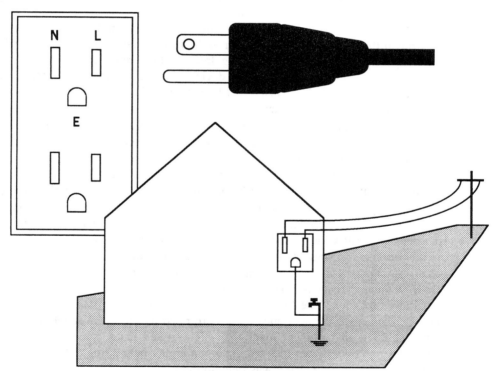

Fig. 6-5. American plugs and sockets.

This is why many American two-pronged plugs have one prong larger than the other, and receptacles will only accept the plug when it is correctly aligned (just so that we are clear on this, the small prong is the live side). Failure to follow the correct orientation can be dangerous.

Suppose you are in an older building and do not have a three-prong outlet handy for your computer. You might be tempted to place a "cheater" or adapter that allows you to use a two prong outlet for a three-prong plug. This alone is bad enough as you are giving up the grounding of the computer. (Some adapters feature a wire that can be attached to a screw on the socket, which might establish a ground.) However, if you accidentally get the plug reversed, the results could be serious. If the computer has been designed to use the neutral wire for grounding, and the neutral wire is now the live wire, a leak of electricity within the computer could be disastrous.

Grounding within personal computer equipment is part of the designer's job. However, as you can see, the user can thwart the design in some ways, and you can take steps to help it work effectively.

Fusing

In the wiring of the computer, the casing is normally connected to the third prong of the supply cable. In some cases, the ground might also be connected to the neutral wire. If electricity should leak through insulation to the computer casing, then it will run straight through the earth conductor to the ground. At the same time, this leak of electricity will increase the current being drawn by the circuit. This increase should be sensed by a fuse or circuit breaker, two devices that are designed to interrupt a circuit if it becomes overloaded. (A *fuse* must be replaced after it has be *blown*, whereas a *circuit breaker* can be reset after it has *tripped*.)

When the live and neutral wires of a circuit are connected before the current has completed the work that the circuit was designed for, then you have a *short circuit*, an unexpectedly heavy flow of current that, like a flow of current to earth, generates heat. Because a short circuit or leak to ground indicates some form of component failure, you want the system turned off before any further damage is done. A fuse or circuit breaker, either the computer or in the supply wiring, should accomplish this. Some computer peripherals, such as printers, have their own fuses. The multiple outlet extension cords widely used for personal computer systems often contain fuses or circuit breakers. In some countries, such as Britain, the appliance power cord plug has a fuse, as do most sockets, as diagrammed in Fig. 6-6.

How much damage is done before the fuse blows will depend upon the size of the fuse and its location. The further away the fuse from the appliance, the greater the potential damage to the appliance. Fuses are rated in amps, lower ratings, such as 1 amp, will blow under lower loads than higher-rated fuses, such as 13 amps. You should not replace a blown fuse with one of a higher amp rating unless you are absolutely sure that the blown fuse was rated too low.

If a piece of computer equipment blows a fuse or trips a circuit breaker, you should first turn off the equipment. Then unplug the power supply cord leading to the equipment, and find the fault that caused the fuse to blow. Remedy the fault, and plug the equipment back in. Turn on the equipment, but be prepared to turn it back off again quickly if the fault was not properly remedied.

Among the more benign causes of blown fuses and tripped circuit breakers is

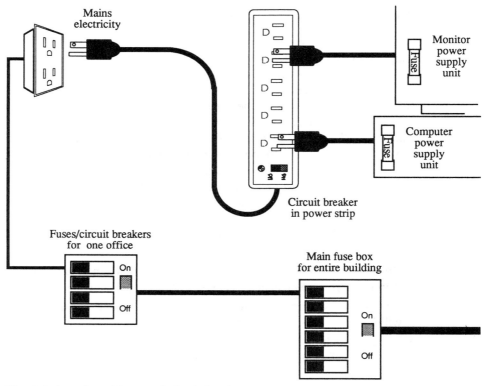

Fig. 6-6. Location of fuses and circuit breakers.

overloading of a wiring circuit. For example, if you have an extension strip proving multiple sockets from a single wall socket, you could plug in equipment that draws more current than the single wall socket was designed to carry. To correct this condition, you will need to rethink your plugs/socket arrangement, spreading the load more evenly.

More serious faults include damaged cables in which the insulation between conductors has broken down. Within appliances, insulation can wear down or melt down, leading to short circuits. Exercise great care when replacing fuses within computer equipment. All equipment should be turned off and disconnected before the fuse is removed. Bear in mind that some pieces of equipment, such as monitors, can hold a high voltage charge even after they have been turned off.

You must make sure that the replacement fuse is the same capacity as the blown fuse. For example, if the blown fuse is marked 2 amp, you should not replace it with a 3 amp fuse. A 2 amp fuse means that the equipment will not be subjected to current above 2 amps. A 3 amp fuse will pass through 1 amp more current than the designer of the equipment intended. If a device keeps blowing a fuse, then something is wrong with the equipment.

Extension Cords and Capacities

Personal computer systems sometimes gobble up electrical outlets. Consider the following configuration which is by no means untypical, and which takes up six outlets: personal computer system unit, monitor, printer, scanner, transformer for mouse, and transformer for external modem. Few offices are equipped with enough wall sockets to handle this. Given the need to plug in a desk lamp or other noncomputer appliance at the same location as the computer, and it is easy to see a big need for extension cords. The use of such cords needs to be carefully monitored by office managers. Not only do they tend to look unsightly, but also they can present considerable danger to those who are apt to trip over them. Apart from the physical damage that can result from a sudden tug on the cord, it is a quick and nasty way to power down an entire system. For safety and security consider implementing the following rules:

- Extension cords should be kept out of pedestrian areas whenever possible.
- Use proper rubber mats to cover cords if they must cross pathways.
- Do not daisy chain extension sockets because this can result in more current than the cords are designed to carry. Use wall sockets whenever possible.
- If possible, use extension units that have fuses or circuit breakers in them. This will help limit any damage from electrical faults.
- Always match extension units to the load. Most have an amp rating on them, and the total amperage of appliances supplied by the cord should not exceed this figure.

REGULATING THE POWER SUPPLY

Once you have taken the basic security measures of correctly plugging in your computer equipment and making sure that it is grounded properly, you just need to make sure that the electricity flowing through the wires is free from interference, fluctuations, or complete disappearance known as *outage*. This is easier said than done. You can buy devices that will help, but you need to know something about how they work and what they do before you can decide which you need.

Sags and Surges

In the United States, and Canada, mains current is nominally 120 volts. In the United Kingdom, it is nominally 240 volts. Most other countries use are on one of these standards. The term *nominal* is significant because the actual voltage can vary. While U.S. voltage is sometimes quoted as being 110 V, or 115 V, the voltage actually delivered to your office can easily be from 105 V to 125 V. The voltage in Britain is usually listed as 240 V but actual measurements are often from 230 V to 250 V. Parts of Ireland use 220 V. Equipment rated at 220 V will usually work fine at 240 V. Fortunately, a lot of personal computer equipment can tolerate a range of voltages. A typical personal computer designed to run on 110 V – 120 V will probably work acceptably on anything from 85 V to 135 V.

What causes problems for personal computer equipment are large swings in voltage, for example, a *sag* below 80 V and a *surge* above 140 V. If a sag lasts for more than a fraction of a second, it can cause enough of a drop in power supplied to the random access memory for the data there to be lost or at least scrambled. Furthermore, the effect of current returning to full strength can also have a disruptive effect.

The effects of a surge are harder to predict, and they depend to a certain extent on the power supply unit within the computer. This has a moderating effect on the rise in current but it might not be enough to prevent temporary shorting of components leading to scrambled data or even damage to chips. Erratic performance is the primary symptom of a surge.

As long as you are careful, it is fairly safe to measure your voltage. A typical digital multimeter, available from any electronic store, will give you a readout of voltage when you insert the test probes into a socket. In Fig. 6-7, you can see a multimeter being used to check the current supplied to a PC.

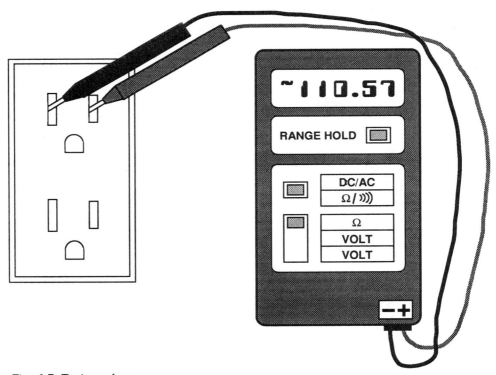

Fig. 6-7. Testing voltage.

The power supply cord can be disconnected from the back of the PC, and the test probes inserted in the openings of the power cord. This is usually more convenient than testing the actual wall socket, and most personal computer equipment has similar detachable power cords. Some meters take a moment to stabilize but the readout should register a steady number after a few seconds. (Also note that many digital multimeters will tell you which wire is live and which is neutral, allowing you to check the integrity of the mains circuits you are using.)

If the voltage readout continues to fluctuate, note the high and low measurements. If these are within six percent of the expected voltage, they are probably not going to cause a problem. If the swings are outside this range, it would be worth getting an electrician to check your wiring, and investing in some power conditioning equipment.

Surge Suppressors

A relatively inexpensive cure for surges is a *surge suppressor*. This is an electrical device placed between your personal computer equipment and the mains supply. Containing special circuitry that clamps down voltage when it starts to rise beyond an acceptable level, a surge suppressor prevents dangerously high mains voltage from reaching equipment.

The circuitry in a surge suppressor is fairly compact and so these units can come in many shapes and sizes, a sample of which are shown in Fig. 6-8.

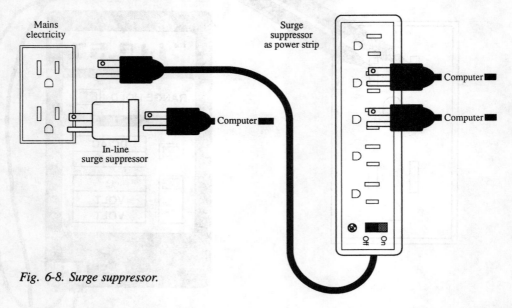

Fig. 6-8. Surge suppressor.

Unfortunately, performance as well as outer design varies a great deal between makes and models, and it is difficult for the nontechnical buyer to assess the design and its capabilities.

What do you look for when buying a surge suppressor? The first consideration has to be the reliability of your source. Do you trust the dealer you are buying from? If the manufacturer is selling direct, can you get references from other users? Check the personal computer press for product reviews that include realistic bench tests. Beyond this, you need to look for suitable features and configuration. Do you want a unit that acts as an extension cord or do you want to insert the unit at the wall socket? You should also consider the following features.

Circuit Breaker. All surge suppressors should have a circuit breaker, a resettable switch that turns the supply off if the circuits become overloaded. This is the minimum level of protection in any device and even a simple multiple outlet extension box should have a circuit breaker. Note that fitting a circuit breaker to an extension box does *not* make it a surge suppressor. You need additional circuitry to effectively protect against surges. Also note that you should not reset a circuit breaker that has been tripped until you have determined what caused it to trip in the first place.

Separate Protection. Many surge suppressors provide multiple sockets for plugging in your equipment. The design of the unit should be such that each socket is protected separately. This design is more likely to successfully clamp heavier surges than a design simply protects the single line running to multiple sockets. Separate protection can also contribute to the reduction of noise interference between pieces of equipment plugged into the same supply circuit (see the following section for more on the noise problem).

Measurements. You might see several measurements in product literature describing surge suppressors. A basic measurement is *capacity*, in terms of the total current the device is designed to protect. This measurement works the same as for a simple extension socket. If the socket or suppressor is rated at 10 amps, then the total draw from all the equipment that you plug into it should not be more than that. *Initial clamping voltage* is the level of current at which the clamping effect of the suppressor's circuitry is applied. For example, in the U.S., this might be 140 V. *Clamping response time* is the length of time it takes for the suppressor's clamping circuitry to take effect. This could be stated as nanoseconds, and a 5 nanoseconds response time is good. The response time might also be stated in terms of cycles. Bear in mind that the ac mains in the U.S. alternates at 60 Hz or 60 times a second. This means that 1 cycle lasts one sixtieth of a second, or 16.66 milliseconds. A response time of $1/10$ of a cycle would thus be 1.66 milliseconds, far longer than 5 nanoseconds.

Response time can sometimes be distinguished from *detection time*, how quickly the suppressor detects that there is an over-voltage. Some makers argue that a short response time is of no use if detection time is too long. Obviously, makers will play up those measurements that reflect most favorably on their designs.

If you are going to spend money to protect against surges, you will probably want to get a unit that also has spike and noise protection. Protection against sags is typically provided by supplementing the mains voltage with battery power. This task is performed by an uninterruptible power system, or UPS, discussed in a moment.

Spikes

A more dangerous and difficult to measure variation in current is the spike. This is a very sudden rush of current to very high levels. Mains circuits can carry damaging impulses as much as 2 kV (2000 V) that are very brief, a few microseconds in duration. Several different events can give rise to spikes. Many are caused by the switching on and off of large electrical appliances. Spikes come in two different varieties: normal mode and common mode. *Normal mode* events can be measured between the hot wire in a building's electrical circuits, and the neutral wire. *Common mode* events are measured from the neutral wire to ground.

A normal mode spike of high magnitude can affect the power supply of the microcomputer. However, a common mode spike of only a few dozen volts can also blow out logic circuits or cause errors between microcomputers. Surge suppression circuits offer good protection against normal mode spikes, but some experts say that their clipping action can actually cause common mode spikes. For this reason, many surge suppressors also contain separate spike blocking circuitry and are marketed as surge/spike protectors.

The criteria for purchasing a spike protector are much the same as for a surge protector, and usually a single unit will provide protection against both, although you must check the labelling carefully to make sure. The ability to block spikes from reaching your equipment is sometimes measured in joules. A joule is a measure of energy, power expended over a period of time. For example, a product might be advertised as suppressing up to 140 joule spikes. You will also see measurements in amps, such as "140 joule spikes at 6500 amps." In general, the higher the voltage/joules/amps that the spike protector can block, the better.

Switching Problems

Earlier you saw that switching electricity on and off presents difficulty for chip designers as it is difficult to raise voltage from zero to a set level, then reduce it back to zero in a very short period of time. Switching current is not only a problem for computer designers. In fact, anytime an electrical circuit is completed or broken, it can have negative side effects.

To understand this, think of electrical flow as a water supply that flows through a pipe until it meets a tap. The effect of a tap is like that of a switch in that it turns supply on and off, but a tap acts differently from a switch in that it operates gradually. Turning on the tap gradually opens a valve which slowly increases the flow of water. Electricity also flows under pressure, but most electrical switches do not act like valves. Switches act more like jamming the flow of tap water with your thumb to turn it off, which usually results in water escaping around it, spraying out under pressure as you try to seal off the flow.

When switches are turned on or off, some of the electricity might still "spurt out" in a spark, short, surge, or spike. Turn a hair dryer on and off in a dark room, and you will probably see this phenomenon. Unplug the hair dryer when it is still turned on, and you will probably see a spark at the socket.

These flashes of current can have two negative impacts for sensitive personal computer equipment. First is the spike, the sudden rush of voltage that spike protectors defend against. You can help cut down on this problem by following a few rules.

Do not plug or unplug appliances that are turned on, particularly computers, printers, and monitors. Often these appliances will have some form of protection on their switch circuits that you bypass if you leave the switch on and then plug it in or unplug it. Because separately switching on each piece of equipment is a chore, you might want to use a power center, a surge/spike protection unit in a console design that pulls together the supply for each part of the system and can handle the current flows needed at system start up. You can see an example in Fig. 6-9.

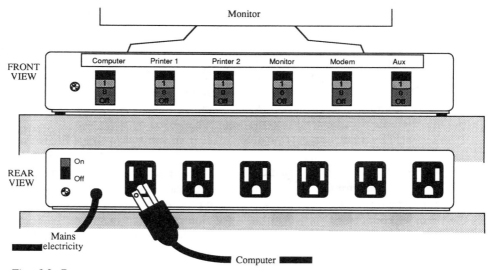

Fig. 6-9. Power center.

The second negative effect of switching is the more complex matter of harmonics, electrical frequencies substantially higher than the current that produced them. The sudden action of switch is like the sharp flick of the finger that produces harmonics from a guitar string. Emanation of these unintended frequencies from one piece of equipment can interfere with the operation of neighboring equipment. Good surge/spike protectors that supply electricity to more than one piece of equipment will offer some form of isolation for each piece in order to cut down on this problem, sometimes described as "noise" and discussed in more detail in the next section.

THE NOISE PROBLEM

Surges, sags, and spikes are not the only electrical supply problems facing personal computer users. There is also the matter of *noise*, not the sort of noise you can hear, but the electronic noise that interferes with the performance of electronic components. To understand this problem and place it in perspective will take a few paragraphs, but understanding noise will help you to stop it from interfering with your data, and also prepare you to combat electronic eavesdropping on the noise that your personal computer emits (a problem described in greater depth in Chapter 7).

Terms and Concepts

Two terms are used to describe this noise: *radio frequency interference* (RFI) and *electromagnetic interference* (EMI). You can literally see this noise if you use an electric drill close to your television set. The electric motor in the drill causes lines, snow, or other patterns to appear on the screen. Similar EMI can be caused by spark plugs in a car outside. Radio interference can result from cordless telephones that use radio waves to communicate between the hand unit and the base. Not only TV reception, but also the integrity of data within personal computers, is at risk from these and other sources of interference. The mains supplying electrical current to your personal computer can act as a transmitter, carrying EMI and RFI into the computer system.

Whenever an electric current flows through a conductor, it generates a force field, waves of energy that create an electromagnetic field. The frequency of the waves in this force field can extend into the frequencies used by radio waves used to transmit radio and TV signal waves. You do not need high voltages to create EMI. The strength of an electromagnetic field is more directly related to the acceleration of the electric charges, the rate of change in the current, rather than the strength of the current itself.

Any conductor that carries an electric current acts as a broadcasting antenna radiating a field produced by that current. A typical electrical appliance can contain hundreds of conductors, varying from a fraction of an inch to several inches in length. Probably, at least one of these conductors will resonate with one of the frequencies generated by the electronic components within the appliance, turning the conductor into an antenna emitting signals that interfere with other appliances. Good design can cut down on these electronic emissions or radiation. Metallic casings can be used as a shield to stop emissions from escaping. However, achieving complete protection is impractical and design flaws and faulty components can result in extensive emissions.

Their Own Worst Enemy

Personal computers are at risk both from outside interference, as well as from the disruptive radio and electromagnetic emissions created by personal computers themselves. Many of the circuits in computer equipment generate EMI and RFI. You might have seen a notice like the one in Fig. 6-10 in the manual accompanying such components as monitors and system units.

This notice is required by the Federal Communications Commission whenever a product is sold that can interfere with a radio and television reception.

Personal computers make extensive use of digital switching, the turning on and off of electrical current. As described earlier in the chapter, the central processing chip in a typical PC might turn on and off 12,000 times a second, and that is one chip. The processing of information in a personal computer creates what is described as a digital pulse train, a string of current changes. Thus personal computers have the potential to create extensive EMI.

RADIO FREQUENCY INTERFERENCE STATEMENT

This equipment generates and uses radio frequency energy and if not installed and used properly, that is, in strict accordance with the manufacturer's instructions, may cause interference to radio and television reception. If this equipment does cause interference to radio or television reception, which can be determined by turning the equipment off and on, the user is encouraged to try to correct the interference by one or more of the following measures:

- Reorient the receiving antenna.
- Relocate the computer with respect to the receiver.
- Move the computer away from the receiver.
- Plug the computer into a different outlet so that computer and receiver are on different branch circuits.

If necessary, the user should consult the system owner's manual, the dealer, or an experienced radio/television technician for additional suggestions.

The user may find the following booklet prepared by the Federal Communications Commission helpful: "How to Identify and Resolve Radio-TV Interference Problems." This booklet is available from the following sources for $5.00 postage-paid, price and availability subject to change:

U.S. Government Bookstore
World Savings Building
720 North Main Street
Pueblo, Colorado 81003
(303) 544-3142

Consumer Information Center-V
P.O. Box 100
Pueblo, Colorado 81002
(303) 948-3334

Fig. 6-10. FCC notice.

As you saw earlier in the chapter, changes in electrical current are measured as a wave. The waveform of a digital switching circuit rapidly turned on and off is a very square one, which tends to radiate *harmonics*, variations of the basic frequency at which the energy is pulsing in the current. Currents with pulse frequencies in the 1 to 25 MHz range common to personal computers and mainframe terminals, radiate a significant amount of harmonics that extend into the UHF range. Square waveforms and the digital pulse trains of personal computers are said to be rich in frequency content. This radiates from the circuits in the personal computer's motherboard, keyboard, expansion cards, and monitor. The cathode ray tube (CRT) in the last of these puts out a particularly large amount of EMI.

Conductors carrying electric current act as broadcasting antennas and radiate a field produced by the current. Because a typical personal computer contains thousands of conductors of varying lengths, the probability is high that at least one of these conductors will match one of the frequencies generated by the personal computer's components, turning the conductor into an antenna with a signal-to-antenna coupling efficient enough to send out a signal that can be picked up by a simple radio receiver.

 I found that my pocket radio was able to detect keystrokes from a "Made in Taiwan" extended PC keyboard at 93.2 MHz on the FM dial! However, I should not fault the keyboard manufacturer because I have heard reports of the original IBM PC keyboard being picked up on 95.4 MHz, with sufficient clarity to distinguish different keystrokes.

Noise Protection

To protect your personal computers from EMI and RFI, you need to consider three aspects: the power line input, placement of noncomputer appliances, and shielding of computer equipment.

Power Line Noise. Some surge and spike suppressors are designed with circuitry that filters out noise from the power supply. Noise suppression is measured in decibels, as in "offers high frequency noise suppression of 20 dB @ 50 kHz." While it is difficult to put the meaning of such measurement in practical terms, it is useful as a relative measure of effectiveness, a higher dB rating being better.

Placement of Appliances. As a general rule, personal computers and heavy electrical equipment do not mix well. When setting up personal computer workstations, you should try to keep them away from such equipment. It is difficult to suppress interference from the powerful currents running through such machinery as overhead cranes, printing presses, and electric welding tools. For most offices, this is not a problem. Other office equipment, such as photocopiers, are usually well shielded. However, elevators can be a problem in office buildings, and the industrial use of personal computers is growing rapidly. Therefore, in some situations, it might be necessary to place a metal enclosure around a personal computer to protect it from electrical noise interference. See the section on electronic eavesdropping in the next chapter for more on shielding.

Other Computer Equipment. A good surge/noise suppressor will filter out the noise interference between the various components plugged into it. However, the outer casing on some components might not be properly shielded, resulting in interference between devices. It is useful to bear in mind that noise incompatibility problems do arise from time to time, even among components from the same manufacturer. You might be familiar with the rule of external disk drive placement with older Macintoshes: always below the Mac or on the right of it. Because interference from the Mac's power supply, which was on left of the original Mac body, was so strong, it disrupted the read/write activity of the drive heads. If you have erratically performing equipment, you might consider rearranging it with respect to other parts of the system. This might just solve the problem.

Phones and Faxes

Electrical noise also affects telephone transmissions. You can get filters for phone lines that carry data and fax transmissions. In some cases, these are combined with regular surge/spike suppression. You plug the phone line from the wall into the suppressor unit, then connect the phone/modem/fax to the unit. The phone line is then filtered and protected.

The other side of the phone noise problem is interference from phones affecting personal computers. This often happened with the early cordless phones, and you might still need to keep a cordless base station away from the computer. Do not be surprised if speaking into a cordless phone while looking closely at your personal computer monitor causes some disruption to either the phone or the computer.

Coping with Static

In some parts of the world, at some times of the year, static electricity is a major problem for personal computer equipment and data. This is not the place to go into the physics of static electricity. Most people are aware that an electrical charge can build up in the human body, which acts rather like a capacitor. When the skin, a conductor, contacts another good conductor like a metal desk, the static charge can be released, sometimes at quite high voltages. If a strong static charge is grounded through your computer equipment or a floppy disk, then severe disruption of processes and data can result.

The antidotes to static are numerous. Dry air aids static buildup so maintaining proper humidity in an office will cut down on static (as well as improve sinuses). Badly affected offices can be fitted with special carpeting, rugs, and mats, which cut down static buildup. An antistatic mat can be placed under your chair to help prevent a charge building up. Static grounding has now been designed into a variety of accessories. Small antistatic mats can fit under the personal computer keyboard. Touching the mat before typing or handling disks will ground the static in your body, leaving you safe. Monitor screens and mouse pads with similar protection are also available from many office supply houses.

Before investing a lot of money in antistatic products, bear in mind that static is not a problem everywhere. Unless you have seen or felt sparks around the office, you probably have nothing to fear. A rough test can be done by taking off a sweater in the office at night with the lights out. Walk around the office for a few minutes in stocking feet, then take off the sweater while keeping your eyes open. If you see sparks, then you know that there is static around, and some basic precautions are probably in order.

LINE CONDITIONERS

An all-around device that offers to clean up surges, spikes, and noise, is a *line conditioner*. There is no clear distinction between a powerful surge/spike/noise suppressor and a line conditioner, although some line conditioners can actually protect against sags. In some circumstances, it might be economical to install a line conditioner directly into the mains circuit supplying an office ahead of the outlets used by personal computers. This will avoid the need for a lot of individual protectors and can be feasible when building or remodeling an office.

One technology used to accomplish line conditioning is a ferroresonant transformer, described in more detail later, in the section on "A Special Transformer." By placing a ferroresonant transformer between the mains and your personal computer, quite severe drops on voltage can occur without affecting the computer.

If you are worried about complete power outages, you might be thinking of getting some form of backup power device. These are described in a moment, and some of them offer surge and spike protection so you can solve several problems with one purchase. However, all such claims should be checked out, as the following section suggests.

BUYER BEWARE

When the market for personal computers really started to boom, some unscrupulous souls saw a great opportunity in surge and spike suppressors, which were sold like the cans of special polish that some shoe stores thrust at you every time you buy a pair of shoes. Faced with the salesperson's line, "How about a surge suppressor, only $100, and it could save your $5000 system from getting fried," the average personal computer buyer, often succumbed. However, most buyers lacked the expertise in electronics to judge the contents of these "little black boxes." Besides, many of them were sealed units. Chances are the user would never know whether or not the product worked properly.

If the surge suppressor did fail to protect the equipment and the user could remember where the suppressor had been purchased, the seller could place the blame on the mains supply and sell the user a bigger and better suppressor. The appeal to dubious ethics was powerful. Unlike other components of a personal computer system, here was a product that required no training or support, that could be sold at a terrific markup if cheap or useless components were used, and that generated very little blowback.

These days most peddlers of worthless protection have been weeded out, and a number of brand names have established themselves as reliable and worthwhile. Nevertheless, it is important to buy your surge suppressor from a reliable source, examine carefully the claims that are made for the product, and read any comparative tests you can find in the trade literature. If you are going to make a large-scale purchase for a department or organization, consultation with an electrical engineer will probably pay dividends.

GUARANTEEING THE POWER SUPPLY

There are ways of making sure that your computer does not lose power when there is a blackout. These vary considerably in price and capability. You will need to weigh these factors against the potential loss of data and damage, as well as inconvenience that a power outage can cause.

A Measure of Protection

The sags, surges, and spikes discussed earlier can have a negative impact on all types of electronic equipment. This includes personal computer system units, monitors, printers, and other peripherals. However, the negative effects of a complete loss of power primarily concern the system unit. Unexpected powering down of the system unit can:

- Wipe out information in RAM. Newly entered data or recently edited data that has not been saved to disk is lost.
- Interrupt writing of data to disk. Important information required by the operat-

ing system, such as file location, can be lost, resulting in files being lost or scrambled.

- Causes a hard disk "crash." The read/write heads of most hard disk drives automatically retract from the disk when the unit is turned off, but possibly in some systems the heads will "crash" onto the disk surface and damage it, causing a loss of data and even physical damage to the disk.
- Interrupt printing. When power is returned, uncompleted print jobs must be resumed. This can be a very tiresome chore unless you have good print management software. In some cases, the entire print job must be redone.
- Interrupt communications. When power is returned, data that was being transferred between computers must be checked for accuracy and files that were in the process of being transferred might need to be transmitted again.
- Bring operations to a halt. In organizations that depend heavily upon computers, a power outage and the temporary lack of computer facilities could adversely affect productivity and profitability.
- Expose the system to spikes and surges when power is returned. Normally you will want to switch off computer equipment when the power goes out, but this is not always possible. When the utility company restores power, it often returns in surges, which could damage appliances that were not switched off.

Clearly such events are to be avoided if possible. While power from the mains is susceptible to all manner of fluctuations, down to complete absence of current, batteries provide much smoother power, independent of the mains supply. However, batteries do not last forever and will eventually run down, at which point they are disposed of or recharged, depending upon their design. Given these factors, it would seem logical to power a personal computer from batteries that are recharged from the mains. This is a good idea in principle. You can buy equipment, known as an Uninterruptible Power System (or UPS), that will provide power in this way, offering protection from power outages.

When the mains power disappears, the battery in a UPS continues to supply power. This power is limited by the battery capacity in both duration and strength. Powering all of your computer equipment from a UPS during an extended power outage is probably not feasible unless you are going to invest in some very expensive equipment. Typically the role of the UPS is to provide enough power to see you through brief outages of a few minutes duration, and to enable you to carry out an orderly shut down of your system during prolonged outages. A good UPS system will be able to warn you when the battery is getting low so that you can save files and power down.

The Need for a UPS

Numerous factors will determine whether you think a UPS will improve the security of your data. You will probably be influenced by the number of times you have experienced a power failure while computing. Obviously some places get more unscheduled outages than others, with remote and rural locations generally faring worse, although urban areas with heavy construction activity can experience more than their fair share of interruptions. However, it only takes one outage in the middle of a crucial project to convince you of the desirability of a backup power system.

The main question will probably be, "Is the protection worth the price?" Details of pricing will be discussed later, after a review of the features available in UPS equipment, but about $1000 should buy a reliable UPS large enough to keep a pair of hard-disk color PC-AT-type systems running for ten minutes without mains power.

Thinking about a typical power outage scenario in an office without a UPS might help you decide whether or not you need one.

Some power failures are announced so that precautions can be taken. Others strike without warning. Typically, the loss of power in an office without standby systems is accompanied by a general groan and the odd expletive. Users who have not recently stored their data on disk have just seen their work disappear from RAM as well as from the screen, wasting valuable time that could run into hours. As the office manager frantically reminds users to turn off their systems to prevent damage from the surge of returning power, people begin to consider what they have lost.

Communications sessions, such as downloading data from other computers, have been broken. Print tasks have been aborted in mid-line. File transfers across networks have been disrupted. File save operations have been interrupted. There is the possibility of damage to hard disks. When power is returned, users will need to restart their systems and make sure they were not damaged. They will need to check for data that might have been scrambled. Print jobs will need to be sorted out, completed or resubmitted. Work that was lost will need to be repeated. The major impact of productivity thus becomes the recovery from the effects of the outage, rather than merely the computing time lost due to lack of power.

A Power Outage Scenario

What is computing like when you have a UPS? A typical UPS will sit quietly in your office largely unnoticed while the mains power is on. A power cord leads from the mains to the UPS and a variety of PC system units and monitors are plugged into the back of the UPS. Most UPS systems have one or more warning lights to let you know that the mains are okay and that the battery is charged or charging. Suppose your mains power is cut off. An alarm in the UPS is sounded. A warning light shows that you are running on the battery, that continues to power the equipment connected to the UPS.

Following procedures laid down in the organization's contingency plan (described in Chapter 4) the employees using the PCs react to the alarm by starting to save their work. This is not always a case of picking Save from a program menu. The computer might be in the middle of a lengthy operation, such as database sorting, and the user will have to decide whether the process can be completed within the time remaining before the batteries are depleted. As work is being saved, the UPS reports on battery status, sounding a new alarm when only a few minutes of power remain.

Suppose that the mains power is restored at this point. Work can carry on with virtually no interruption or loss of productivity. Any computers that have already been turned off can simply be restarted. It is not difficult to see that an UPS makes life a lot easier.

A Word of Caution

As you can see from the drawing in Fig. 6-11, a UPS looks like a box with wires and lights. Indeed, while there are several different types of UPS, and hundreds of different products that are advertised as UPSes, they all tend to look like boxes with wires and lights.

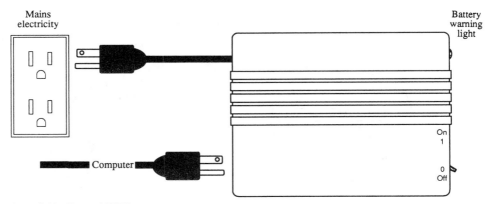

Fig. 6-11. Typical UPS.

The simple appearance of a UPS, combined with the fact that its performance is difficult to test without special equipment, means there is considerable potential for ripoff. Many other computer products require support and training, leading to sales through reputable dealers who will be around to provide these added value services. However, some salespersons look at a UPS sale as having few strings attached. Many sales are made through the mail. It is quite possible that the customer will plug it in and never have occasion to find out how well it performs. To protect against unscrupulous vendors follow these two guidelines:

- Do not buy a product unless you have read a technical review of its abilities, such as you will find in *PC Magazine* or *BYTE Magazine*.

- As soon as you have bought and installed a UPS, test it by turning off the mains yourself. You can do this after hours or on the weekend to avoid disturbing normal working conditions. Be sure to test the full load that will be placed on the UPS.

How a UPS Works

Providing electricity to your personal computer at full mains strength is a difficult task for a battery to perform. Batteries produce direct current while mains-powered PCs consume alternating current. Furthermore, batteries work more efficiently at lower voltages, such as the 12-volt systems in cars. Alternative power supply systems, such as wind-powered electrical generators, typically produce 12-volt direct current that is stored in batteries and then converted to alternating current when required by normal household appliances. The conversion from dc to ac is carried out by an *inverter*. One approach to providing uninterrupted mains level power to a computer involves converting mains power down to 12 volts dc and using this current to charge a battery. The battery output is then inverted back to mains level when the computer draws from the battery. The entire chain of activity can be seen in Fig. 6-12.

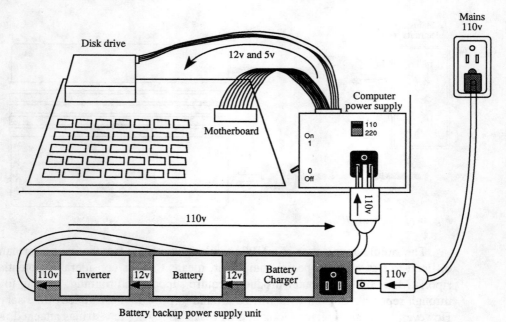

Fig. 6-12. A battery backup system.

As you can see, most components of a personal computer system run on just a few volts of dc power (usually from 3 V to 12 V). There is considerable irony in this. Makers of personal computers who are looking to distinguish their designs from the crowd might find that it pays to build battery backup into their personal computer systems, offering their customers added value. In effect, this is what is happening with battery-powered laptop computer that is left on constant recharge from the mains, as diagrammed in Fig. 6-13.

The total cost of components in this arrangement is considerably less than when an independent UPS is used to provide ac power to a conventional personal computer.

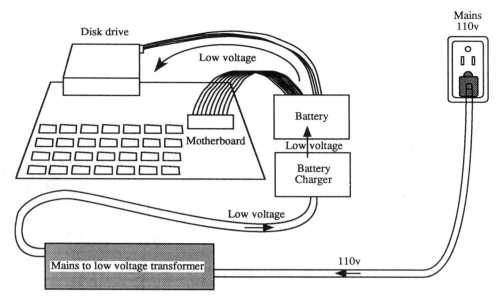

Fig. 6-13. A computer powered by rechargeable batteries.

UPS Terminology

Note that the acronym UPS stands for uninterruptible "power system" and not "power supply." A UPS is an external system for providing continuous power when the mains supply fails. A power supply is a component inside the personal computer that converts the utility's ac power to dc, which is what the logic circuits of the microcomputer need for working energy.

The correct terminology is even more complicated because not all UPSes are truly uninterruptible. Some experts divide UPSes into *on-line* or *off-line*. While an on-line UPS is always drawing power from a battery, meaning that the backup supply is always "on-line," the off-line system kicks in backup power only when the mains current fails. Some people would argue that an off-line unit is more correctly called a standby power system (SPS). However, some SPS designs are virtually uninterruptible, further blurring the distinction.

One reason for this blurring of terms relates to the personal computers itself. A personal computer power supply has what is called *ride-through*: The amount of time that the power supply can deliver stored energy to the logic circuits with no electricity being fed to the supply. This energy storage is directly related to the size and quality of the power supply components, particularly the filter capacitors. The ride-through of typical personal computer is from 20 to 40 milliseconds. This is a long time in the terms of electronics since a single cycle of ac current at 60 hertz takes only 16.66 milliseconds (1000 / 60). To put it in nontechnical terms, the electricity reaching the computer power supply could probably skip a beat without affecting the flow of power to the computer's logic circuits.

The SPS Solution

This long ride-through has enabled the SPS to become the most popular of the power loss protection devices for the personal computer market. In Fig. 6-14, you can see a block diagram of an SPS.

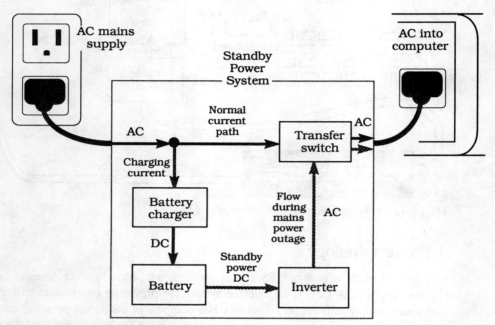

Fig. 6-14. How an SPS works.

The incoming mains power (ac) is fed directly into the microcomputer under normal conditions. When mains power fails, the transfer switch senses this happening and turns on the inverter, which converts battery power (dc) into an ac source that keeps the microcomputer running. When mains power returns, the transfer switch returns the microcomputer to mains power. This is called standby technology because the inverter is literally "standing by," waiting to be turned on.

The UPS Solution

In Fig. 6-15 you can see a block diagram of a true on-line UPS in which the incoming utility power is converted from ac to dc by a rectifier/charger.

As the name implies, this component performs two functions. The functions are changing the power to dc (the rectifier) and charging the battery. The battery is said to float on a dc bus, meaning that a single conductor connects the rectifier/charger and the inverter. If the battery needs charging, it draws power from the bus. If, on the other hand, the bus voltage level falls below the battery float voltage, the battery delivers energy to the bus. The energy conducted through the dc bus provides power to the inverter which then provides power to the microcomputer. In other words, the system is on-line all the time, and a full-time ac-to-dc-to-ac conversion takes place.

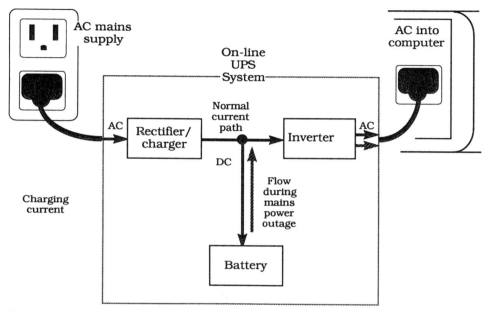

Fig. 6-15. A true on-line UPS.

The advantage of this design over a standby system is that no switching takes place if utility power fails. Because the inverter is always providing power to the personal computer, it never sees an interruption of power. This feature is not without its drawbacks. The duty cycle of the components, the percentage of time that they have to work, is 100 percent. This means that they must be bigger and with higher reliability ratings than the equivalent components in an SPS of similar output. Particularly affected is the battery, which is working all the time in a UPS. The battery in a UPS is likely to wear out sooner than that in an SPS. An on-line design can cost twice as much or more than a standby unit of the same rating.

A Special Transformer

One technology, the ferroresonant transformer, offers a middle ground between the expensive but ever-present power of the UPS and the cheaper standby systems. Interestingly enough, ferroresonant transformers have been around for a long time. They have the unique ability to store energy for a few tens of milliseconds. In Fig. 6-16, you can see how this device can enhance the performance of the simple SPS.

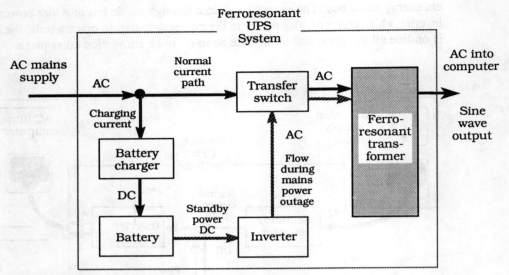

Fig. 6-16. An SPS with ferroresonant transformer.

Notice that all the blocks are the same, but that the transformer has been added at the output. With this design, the time that it takes to switch on the inverter is covered with the ride-through capability of the transformer. Because the personal computer's own power supply unit also has a ride-through factor, the computer is unaware that any switching has taken place. Companies such as BEST technology are pushing this type of system as a good price/performance compromise between a true UPS and a regular SPS.

As you might expect, a ferroresonant transformer does tend to add cost to the basic SPS, but this is partly offset by the fact that it adds some real power conditioning to the current it supplies. You can expect to see an increasing number of SPS units with ferroresonant technology, priced between the UPS and the regular SPS units.

In fact, many manufacturers claim surge and spike protection benefits for their SPS and UPS models. This is natural, because many buyers are looking to avoid spikes and surges as well as complete power loss. However, such claims need careful examination. See the section called "Power Conditioning" for more on UPS units and power quality.

Choosing a Design

The variations of the uninterruptible designs on the market are virtually limitless. Expect to see hybrids of the technology discussed above, plus innovations and exceptions. However, a working knowledge of the basic designs shown here will prepare you for choosing a design for your own purposes.

There is considerable argument between proponents of the various UPS technologies. Supporters and manufacturers of on-line models claim they are better because the inverter is on-line all the time. They point to thermal stress that can affect inverters when they are started from cold. This is not a worry for an on-line system because the inverter is always on. Fans of standby designs say that they are more reliable because the inverter is only on when power is out and thus subject to less wear.

To the consumer seeking reliable protection for data, the main concern is not whether to side with one point of view or another. The question is how well the system is designed and constructed. If an SPS is not designed to pick up the load gracefully, even the most reliable components will not cope. If an on-line unit is not carefully engineered, then thermal stress will cause premature failure while the unit is running. The inverter is not necessarily the weak link in a UPS. More important factors are quality control and batteries. Systems can reach the shelves unopened and untested. Any unit you buy should have a test certificate and a long warranty, including free replacement if the system fails within the first year of service. Batteries are the single most frequent point of failure for any UPS, so you should check the battery source and specifications thoroughly.

What Type of System to Buy

With some idea of how they work and what level of protection they provide, it is time to assess whether you need a UPS or an SPS, and if so, how you select one that is suitable for your needs. You should look for several important features when purchasing a UPS.

Warning Lights and PC Interface. You need some way of knowing what your UPS is doing. Many designs feature indicator lights that let you know when the battery is being used and what kind of charge the battery is holding. Look for indicators that are functional rather than just decorative. You will probably want audible as well as visible warnings when the system switches to batteries and when batteries are low.

Many systems now offer a personal computer interface, a means of sending signals to a personal computer to warn of impending shutdown. This is particularly useful if you are using a UPS to protect a network file server. For the feature to be of any use, the personal computer must be running software that can interpret the signals sent from the UPS. Various programs can do this, and they are described in the context of network security in Chapter 12.

A Switch in Time. A major factor in the performance of any SPS is switching time. The unit must be able to switch its inverter on and smoothly, some would say gracefully, take up the electrical load before the personal computer's internal ride-through expires. Typical switching times are from 4 to 10 milliseconds. Times within this range mean that the computer's power supply will not notice any change in current. However, when checking product specifications, you should make sure that quoted switching time includes the time it takes for the SPS to sense an outage and complete the switching process.

Adjustable Transfer Point. An SPS will switch to battery power according to a predetermined transfer point or voltage level. When the mains voltage (say 120 V) falls below the transfer point (say 100 V), the SPS begins the switching process. This ensures that by the time voltage reaches a dangerously low level (say 80 V), the micro-computer will already be on battery. A selectable transfer point is an important feature. The power supply inside most microcomputers has a working voltage window that is enormous, from about 80 V to nearly 140 V. If your site experiences chronic brownouts or low-voltage conditions, you might want to buy a unit that lets you select a low transfer point (possibly as low as 90 V) so that the SPS does not transfer to battery power unnecessarily.

Hysteresis. The voltage at which the SPS switches back from battery power to mains when the latter returns is called the retransfer point. You should be able to set this above the transfer voltage so that, if the utility voltage hovers near the transfer point, repeated switching on and off of the battery does not occur. This feature is referred to as *hysteresis* (literally meaning that the effect lags behind the action that causes the effect). A typical hysteresis window might have a low of 102 V and a high of 107 V.

Waves. The ac current from the mains has a smooth sine waveform. Many SPSes do not put out a sine wave because it is considerably cheaper to put out a square wave, a rectangular wave, or some quadrilateral in between. The inverter which creates ac from dc is basically a very fast switch. The switching process of the inverter creates a lot of high-frequency electrical noise. To produce a sine wave, most of this noise is eliminated by a filtering process. (To produce a sine wave, a special switching scheme is needed to build some kind of approximation to a sinusoid using a series of pulses that can then be filtered to produce a smooth product that looks like normal mains power.)

With a square wave, no such filtering is necessary to produce a power output that the microcomputer will run on. However, the chance that inverter noise will be present in the SPS's output is far greater with a square waveform. Also, a square wave is not a fundamental of 60 Hz as is a sine wave. The "shoulders" of the square wave-form contain odd harmonics of the fundamental 60 Hz signal. This means that the manufacturer must take care to eliminate noise from the non-sine wave of an inverter. If this is done, there is no real reason to shy away from non-sine wave products, but true sine wave units typically put out less interference and cost more money.

Synchronizing. When an SPS retransfers to mains power, the waveform output of the inverter needs to be adjusted to match the phase of the incoming utility power. This is called *synchronizing* or *phase matching*. When the two waveforms are in phase, no gap will occur when retransfer takes place. A small gap will probably not affect the computer's power supply, but phase matching is a feature that is indicative of good design and possibly makes for more reliable performance.

Low Battery Warning/Shutoff. When batteries power a load during a power outage, their stored energy is slowly depleted. At some point, the depletion is so dramatic that the voltage level of each cell in the battery begins to drop. At a level called *end voltage*, further discharge will permanently damage the cell. To preserve the life of the battery, most quality SPSes shut off the inverter before this happens. Without this feature, called low battery shutoff, the SPS may survive only a few long-term outages. Ideally, of course, you will shut down the microcomputer and the SPS before this happens. An audible/visible low-battery warning signal is essential to enable the shutdown to be performed in time.

Power Conditioning. A big sales pitch for UPS makers is that their units are also power conditioners, removing spikes, surges, and noise interference. However, bear in mind that while some systems might do this, there is little inherent protection in most SPS and UPS technology. Indeed, an off-line or SPS unit will pass all spikes and surges straight through to your computer unless the design incorporates proper filtering circuits. The switching activity of the inverter in an on-line system can generate interference over and above that present in the mains supply.

You will recall that the two types of spikes are normal (line/neutral) and common (neutral/ground). The double conversion process of an on-line UPS will suppress high-energy impulses appearing between line and neutral, but on-line technology does nothing to prevent common mode impulses from getting to sensitive equipment. As a matter of fact, all UPS and SPS units generate significant common mode noise. A transformer can solve this problem because a transformer has its neutral and ground bonded together, thereby shorting out common mode noise. The transformer itself can be part of an excellent design to thwart common mode events. The ferroresonant design mentioned earlier is a good power line conditioner for both normal-mode and common-mode events, making the ferroresonant SPS design an increasingly popular choice. However, you can buy separate line conditioners that plug in downstream from an SPS to provide similar benefits.

SOFTWARE ASSISTANCE

The unexpected loss of power is a hardware problem, but there are some solutions. The main impact of a power outage is the loss of unsaved work. Many popular personal computer programs do most of their work in RAM, the memory area that receives your input from the keyboard. Your software must arrange for the computer to store your input onto disk, otherwise the input is simply not recorded.

Whatever information is in RAM when the power goes out is wiped out. This includes the operating system and the software application you were using at the time. Of course, you have copies of the application and the operating system on disk. The unsaved input in RAM is what is at risk. You know you are supposed to save your work on a regular basis, but human nature means that this rule will never be adhered to with the diligence required to prevent at least one disaster per user per lifetime.

While you can buy battery-backed RAM, it is more expensive than regular RAM and still quite rare. Most personal computers are simply built with the major weakness of regular RAM as part of the design. To cope with this design weakness, plus human weakness, as well as the fact that UPSes are not universal or cheap, some software provides the user with help in issuing save-my-work commands on a regular basis.

A typical example of a popular application with automatic saving is WordPerfect, which saves the document you are editing every so many minutes. The time period is up to you. The actual saving only takes a fraction of a second when you are editing a two- or three-page document. On longer documents or older computers, you might find that you cannot keep typing at high speed throughout the saving process, but it is likely that the automatic save will sometimes occur while you are not actually typing. The minor inconvenience is vastly outweighed by the added piece of mind that comes from knowing that you will not lose a lot of effort when the power goes out. Several third-party products that provide software backup for those times when things go wrong or the power goes out.

BATTERIES INCLUDED

As owners of many laptop computers know, you can run a computer on batteries. Unfortunately, only specially designed personal computers, like laptop models, are able to run for extended periods on batteries that are small enough to carry around. Indeed, some laptop computers with a hard disk and bright screens can only last a few hours on batteries alone. Most laptops use rechargeable batteries that are kept topped up by plugging the system into the mains most of the time.

In fact, as laptop computers continue to improve, matching the performance levels of desktop machines, it is likely that their built-in ability to survive power supply problems will become an increasingly important factor when users choose between a laptop or a desktop model. After all, a laptop offers the benefits of portability, the security of being easily locked up, as well as the capacity to keep going when the power is out.

While the screens on laptop systems have tended to be inferior to larger monitors, most laptop systems can be attached to desktop monitor, giving the benefits of a full-size screen. Besides, as you will see in the next chapter, security weaknesses in regular CRTs are leading some users to replace CRTs with laptop-style displays on desktop personal computers. As flat screen technology improves, this trend will probably continue.

Battery technology is limited by size and weight relative to storage capacity. The larger the capacity, the larger and heavier, the battery. Because the main idea behind a laptop is portability, much research has been done to cut down the amount of power needed to run the computer, so that the batteries required are not too heavy.

Some designs do away with batteries in order to make a powerful computer that is still very portable. Toshiba did this with the T3200SX. The lack of batteries is partly compensated for by a universal power supply that can be plugged in to any mains, from 100 to 250 volts. This makes the machine capable of travelling just about anywhere. Other designs simply accept that the computer will only run on the battery for a short time. Most of the time, these systems are like a regular personal computer hooked up to an on-line UPS. They draw mains power through a battery until such time as the mains is turned off or they are disconnected. This provides a high level of power conditioning, protection against surges, sags, and outages.

The power supply facilities of a laptop can be enhanced with add-on products such as extra battery packs. Automobile adapters are available to allow the laptop to be run and its batteries to be recharged from a cigarette lighter socket. Travelling Software of Bothell, Washington, even offers a solar charger for laptop batteries. ADA Computer Systems in the United Kingdom offers a line of laptop power supply products, as well as other enhancements for portable computers.

GLOBAL VILLAGE?

As economic enterprise, and other forms of human activity that improve personal computers, becomes increasingly international, so must computing. For years now computer magazines, and the advertisements with which they are crammed, have trumpeted the international aspects of computing, the global electronic village in which we are connected by computers, sharing information around the world. As with most other subjects that are treated to heavy doses of Madison Avenue hype, the reality lags behind the concept.

The Power Problems

Anyone who wants to move around the world with their computer in tow, faces numerous difficulties. Beyond the problems of packaging sensitive equipment for a move and checking hardware through airports, there is the problem of plugging in to a foreign power supply when you get there. There is a physical aspect to this and an electrical one. Physically, the sockets might not accept the plug on your power cord. Electrically, the current might not be what your personal computer is used to.

The problem of plugs and sockets is fairly easily solved by purchasing plug adapters which mate your plug to the foreign socket. Do *not* confuse plug adapters with power transformers! For example, an adapter that allows you to insert a U.S. plug into a U.K. socket is a dangerous thing. The voltage in the U.K. is twice that in the U.S. and will probably fry any appliance that is not prepared for it.

An alternative to plug adapters is actually changing the plugs to match the local standard. Alternatively, if you have detachable power cords, you can buy spare cords with local plugs on. These are usually available from electrical and computer stores at low cost. However, before you go to the trouble and expense of adding foreign plugs or buying adapters, consider the extension box you probably already have for your domestic supply. You only need to change/adapt one plug in order to gain multiple outlets in the correct style.

A welcome trend in personal computer design is to use autosensing power supplies. For example, a Macintosh II or a Toshiba T3200SX can be plugged into any domestic mains from 100 to 250 volts. For those with computers that do not have this feature (and you should be *sure* you have it before you test it), many newer personal computer's have a switch on the power supply unit that slides between 110 and 220. Check for this switch near where the power cord enters the casing. You might need to open the system unit case to reach the switch, which you will probably find on the shiny metal box that is connected to the power cord.

Fixed Voltage

Unfortunately, the trend to autosensing and manually adjustable power supplies has been slow to reach beyond actual system units. To display your work or print it out you need a monitor and printer, chances are that one or both of these will operate at fixed voltage. For example, the Apple LaserWriter IINT, which is often sold along with a Macintosh, has a fixed voltage, even though many Macs are now autosensing.

The problem for fixed voltage equipment that ends up in places that don't have that voltage is to find the right kind of transformer to convert the foreign current to the level required. Several factors need to be considered. You need the right voltage in and out, as well as sufficient capacity, in either watt or amps, to properly power the equipment. *Beware* of the small voltage adapters sold in travel agencies. These seldom work with appliances larger than electric shavers, but they are useful for converting the small low-voltage transformers used by some personal computer components, such as modems and mice. (Do not be taken in by warranties and guarantees for a voltage adapter unless they cover the full cost of the appliances that you want to connect to it.)

Transformers capable of running computer equipment are unlikely to be light in weight, low in price, or available in general stores. You will probably need to consult an electrical contractor or specialist to get what you need. To run a laser printer, you will need about a 1000 watts, or 8 amps, of power. A high-resolution color monitor will need 100 watts or 2 amps. Add up the watts or amps of equipment that you will be running off the transformer and give that figure to the supplier.

If you are taking 110 voltage equipment to countries running on 220 or 240, you will be happy to know that many building sites in those countries use 110 volt equipment for safety reasons. Therefore, a good tool supply company should be able to sell you a fairly powerful transformer at a reasonable price. Using an industrial strength transformer to run computer equipment at 110 V rather than 240 V has the side effect of inserting a level of surge/sag protection between the computer and the mains power supply. Since a transformer has its neutral and ground bonded together, common mode spikes are also eliminated.

Monitor Problems

Monitors based on CRT technology create images by scanning display area with a beam of electricity that charges the chemicals coating the inside of the screen. The frequency with which this scanning occurs determines how detailed an image may be displayed, referred to as *image resolution*. Some older monitor designs of low resolution use the ac frequency of the power supply, for example 60 Hz in the United States, to provide the scanning frequency of the display circuitry. This design shortcut meant that monitors could be built at low cost, but it also meant that those monitors will not work properly on power of another frequency, even if it is the correct voltage. Damage from running on the wrong frequency is unlikely, but you should check the monitor manual first. Models that can run on a range of frequencies should be marked that way somewhere on the casing. You will find that many of the more recent, high-resolution color CRT displays, such as the Priceton Ultra-Sync, are now available in dual voltage (110/220). This is possible because a full power transformer in the monitor does not directly employ the ac frequency to create the image.

Communication Problems

Apart from the language barrier when travelling, you will find some significant differences in phone systems that can make the use of a modem difficult. These problems are really beyond the scope of this book, but modem users in the United States should be aware that most of the rest of the world is on a different standard for phone signals. While United States modems use a standard known as Bell 103 (also 202 and 212A), many other countries conform with the CCITT standard (Committee de Communications International Telecommunication Transmission). Needless to say, this makes it difficult to use U.S. modems and communications software in Europe.

COMPUTER INSURANCE

A nontechnical defense against some of the negative aspects of relying on personal computer technology is to take out an insurance policy. At no time should this be your first line of defense. Claiming on an insurance policy company is a chore even when dealing with the best of insurers. Furthermore, many insurers will want to know that you have taken risk management seriously before they will offer full coverage. Insurance is a complex subject, and this book can only give pointers on what to look for when looking to insure the personal computing aspect of your activities. If you have an insurance broker that you trust, he or she is the best person to advise you on right policy for your particular circumstances.

The Value of Computers

Computers are quite different from cars, photocopiers, or other major appliances. They represent not only the value of hardware that can be resold, but the product of putting that hardware to work. Steal a hard disk computer, and you have taken the equivalent of the sculptor's chisel, block of marble, and finished statue, all rolled into one. Of course, unlike hardware, software and data can be copied inexpensively. In all discussions of computer insurance, you need to make sure that the distinction between hardware and software/data is understood. Ask directly whether or not your data and software are insured as well as the hardware. Do not get stuck paying for a policy that does not cover everything you think it should.

Like a piece of sculpture, and unlike a piece of hardware, the data that is stored on a computer might not have a street value and so placing an insurable value on it is going to be difficult. You might be able to calculate the data entry hours to rebuild a database, but the hours that it takes to create specialized software might be much harder to figure. Nevertheless, you need to make sure that whatever software you have that is hard to replace is fully insured. Of course, unlike many forms of sculpture, software and data can be copied many times over. Stored judiciously, archive copies can overcome all but the most global of catastrophes.

The Basics of Computer Insurance

The subtle differences between a computer and other appliances accounts for the fact that many policies used to insure office contents and household contents do not cover computers.

Household policies often exclude any equipment used for business purposes. Even in office policies that cover such items as photocopiers, personal computers are often specifically excluded. The easiest way to find out if a policy covers personal computers is to call the broker who sold the policy and ask.

Many household or apartment contents policies require that you list individual items, such as jewelry, that are over a certain value. Insurers may require *riders* for particularly risky items, resulting in an increased premium. This might also apply to personal computers. Reimbursement on these items might be limited in some way. Even if you see no specific exclusion for personal computers in your policy, you should let your insurer know that you have personal computers in your home or office and get a written determination as to whether or not they are insured.

On the other hand, do not overlook some of the coverage your personal computers might already get under special circumstances. For example, if you have an automobile policy that covers "theft of items from inside a locked vehicle," it might cover loss of computers that are in transit. Laptops present a particularly interesting case as they are more prone to travel and to get dropped. Special policies can be obtained for laptops.

Most insurance policies are likely to have a deductible, an amount you have to pay towards a loss before the insurer will pick up the balance. If you are prepared to accept a higher deductible, you can probably get a lower premium.

Sources of Insurance

If you find that your current insurance does not adequately cover your personal computer resources, you can purchase special computer-related policies. Apart from calling the broker you use for your other insurance needs, you can get computer insurance policies by mail order. These policies should be approached with caution. They might only insure hardware, and the premium might be quite high. The more established mail order companies, would appear to have been around long enough to be trusted, particularly as a source for work-at-home situations where household policies do not provide adequate coverage. Carefully check the resources of any mail order insurance company if you are insuring a large number of personal computers.

You might be able to get a better rate on insuring a large installation if you have your insurance broker shop around. Larger organizations, such as publicly-held companies, can sometimes create self-insurance schemes, setting up their own "captive" insurance company subsidiaries.

The rapid increase in businesses run from the home has given rise to several associations of home-based entrepreneurs. Check these groups, or other trade organizations of which you are a member, for possible access to computer coverage at group rates.

What to Buy

Whatever the source of your computer insurance, you are going to be looking for a number of different types of coverage. You might want insurance to cover three areas, discussed next.

Loss of/Damage to Computer Hardware. This should include ancillary equipment, like modems, scanners, surge protectors, and cabling. Make sure that everything that needs to be covered is included in the policy, and obviously keep the insurance company informed of any changes. When disaster does happen, users often find they have forgotten to mention new acquisitions and are thus underinsured. Also check that the policy does not exclude threats that might be common in your area, such as damage from power outages.

Loss of/Damage to Data-Carrying Media. This should include the cost of restoring data and replacing files, software and other programs. Quantifying the amount of cover to take out can be problematic. There is the physical aspect of paying people to rekey data, but there is also the task of actually recreating that data afresh. Take advice on this point from an insurance broker or accountant, and then estimate a ballpark figure. Steer away from outrageously high figures as it just means exorbitant premium charges.

Business Interruption. This is usually regarded as having two distinct elements. First is the "increased cost of working," which means the cost of getting through the usual workload without the computer, which would include the cost of renting new equipment and hiring temporary staff. Second is the "consequential loss," for example, loss of revenue because files cannot be accessed and so invoices cannot be sent to customers. Business interruption is another area where quantification is difficult, and professional advice is probably essential for all but the smallest of businesses.

What to Pay

Determining the likely cost of insurance is rather like asking how long is a piece of string. A lot will depend on the value of the hardware insured, along with the other risks insured on the policy, particularly business interruption. A further factor will be the individual circumstances of the policyholder, users with bad claims records or businesses located in high-risk areas will pay more.

As a guideline, a generic mail order policy that offers replacement cost coverage of hardware and off-the-shelf software against fire, theft, power surge, lightning, flood, and earthquake damage, will cost around $100 for $10,000 insured value. For larger coverage, it is probably easier to get an independent insurance broker or intermediary to find the best quotes for you. An agent should be prepared to "rebroke" for better quotes when the policy comes up for renewal. Make agents earn their commission by handling any claims you subsequently have to make. They know the shortcuts through the insurance industry red tape and can speed things up considerably.

The Finer Points

You should check what the policy says about taking reasonable precautions to prevent or minimize loss. These should be genuinely reasonable. They can include due care in selection and training of staff, compliance with hardware maintenance agreements, and normal antitheft precautions. Make sure the provisions are not so extensive as to provide obvious loopholes for an insurer looking to avoid paying a claim.

For example, an insurer might refuse to pay the full cost of recreating data if a hard disk computer is damaged by a power surge and a proper backup regimen was not followed. If the entire office is destroyed by fire, including the backups, you might think that the full replacement cost of the data is a reasonable claim. However, the policy might specify that backups be stored in a fireproof safe. In general, following a good risk management plan and sound security policies is both a prerequisite to reasonable claims settlement, as well as the best way of avoiding the need to claim.

Check what the policy says about reinstatement of damaged equipment. Typically, goods are replaced on the basis of "similar equipment in a condition equal to but not better or more extensive than its condition when new." With the rapid rate of change in computer technology, you might be claiming for equipment that is somewhat obsolete or even out of production. This means that the replacement model is likely to be better, and the policy may require you to pay all or part of this difference. For larger policies, this point might be negotiable.

SUMMARY

One of the main reasons that the use of personal computers has spread so far so fast is the low cost of hardware and software relative to mainframe and minicomputers. In part, this low cost has been achieved by simply ignoring some aspects of design that are considered essential in larger systems. Power conditioning and backup are either built into mainframe computers or installed as a matter of course when the system is first set up. Many mainframes have disaster recovery routines built into their operating system software or provided for in their application programs.

As personal computers take on more and more of the tasks previously performed by larger systems, the true cost of personal computer systems becomes increasingly apparent. Serious applications require disaster recovery features. Most installations need some form of power conditioning. All vital systems should have power backup so that they can keep computing during brief power failures and accomplish an orderly shutdown during prolonged outages. While provision of these features increases the price tag for personal computer technology, most users will consider the money well spent, providing a valuable security against data loss, hardware damage, and costly interruptions in normal operations.

The effectiveness of most security systems
is somewhat akin to that of contraceptives:
The more you challenge them to do their job,
the more likely it is that they will fail.

Stephen Cobb

7
Controlling Computer Access

HARDWARE SECURITY is not only a matter of preventing equipment from disappearing. You need to be able to regulate who uses the hardware, locking out unauthorized users. This chapter deals with access control, examining such subjects as biometric user authentication and batch files that require passwords from would-be users. These security measures vary from the inexpensive to the exotic. Which of them will be appropriate to your needs will depend upon the level of threat and the value of the resources you are defending. This chapter also examines some comprehensive approaches to personal computer security that address the problem from a hardware perspective, such as the Opus Datasafe, an IBM-compatible designed with security in mind.

SITE ACCESS CONTROL

The first line of defense against unauthorized personal computer users is the same as that raised against theft of personal computer equpment, namely, site access control. If you can be reasonably sure of who can even get close enough to your personal computers to use them, then you have gone a long way to controlling computer access.

Site security was considered in some detail in Chapter 5 and there is no need to go over the same ground here, except to note the trend in personal computer security to apply techniques developed for site access control to computer access control. The technologies used for controlling perimeter security are getting more sophisticated and more compact, allowing them to be applied directly to personal computers. In Fig. 7-1, you can see an example of a personal computer access control system that uses a magnetic card reader.

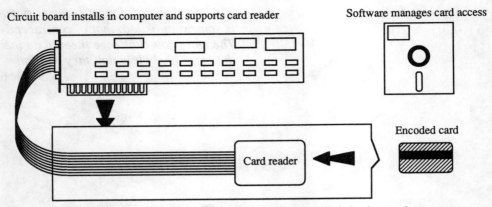

Circuit board installs in computer and supports card reader   Software manages card access

Encoded card

Card reader

Card reader attaches to adapter card - access to computer denied unless card present

Fig. 7-1. Personal computer access card system.

The card must be inserted into the reader and the correct PIN (personal identification number) entered in order for access to be granted. Devices of this type that can be fitted to personal computers will be discussed in greater depth later in this chapter.

The goals of site access control are to restrict access to authorized persons, to ensure that you know who is inside the premises, and to alert you to an unauthorized presence. The goals of computer access control are to restrict access to authorized persons, to ensure that you know who is using the computers, and to alert you to an unauthorized user. In a sense, site access control acts as the first level of computer access control. Indeed, in some small offices, site control might be the only form of computer access control. On the other hand, companies using highly expensive identification systems might find it cost-effective to use them to control a group of computers in a special room rather than fit a device to every computer. A variation on this is for an expensive identification system to provide limited duration passwords rather than direct room or computer access. The password must be used right away and will be invalid after the user has logged on.

PHYSICAL KEYS

Chapter 2 pointed out that a sizable percentage of personal computers sold today have a very nice access control feature built into them: the keyboard lock. Usually located on the front of the system unit, this lock controls the connection between the keyboard and the motherboard, the latter being the main circuits of the computer. Many front panels on personal computer system units contain a small icon indicating the two positions of the lock, as shown in Fig. 7-2.

When the lock is in the open or unlocked position, the circuit between the keyboard and the motherboard is complete and keystrokes are accepted by the computer. In the closed or locked position, this circuit is broken, meaning that you can press keys but nothing will happen.

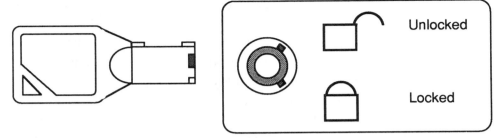

Fig. 7-2. Keyboard lock.

For the keyboard lock to be an effective security measure you must:

- Lock the keyboard whenever the computer is unattended, particularly during nonworking hours.
- Only place the key in the lock when you must. Do not leave the key in the lock.
- Store all copies of the key in a safe place (usually two keys come with each computer).
- Test the lock whenever you use it. Turn the keyboard off before powering down your system, so that you can try typing to make sure that the system is locked.

On some designs, it is possible to disconnect the wires leading to the lock or short circuit them so that it is ineffective. This is difficult, usually requiring that the system unit case be opened, but someone could possibly sabotage the lock. The best defense against this is a secure system unit and regular testing of the lock.

For systems that do not have a built-in keyboard lock, add-on locking devices are available. Some of these just control the power switch and so offer no defense for systems that are on but unattended. For tips on defending the unattended working unit, see the next chapter.

PHYSICAL KEY MANAGEMENT

Possession of a key does not guarantee the identity of the key holder. Keys get lost. They can be stolen. Some can be duplicated. A serious security program that relies upon physical keys will include some form of key management system. There is nothing exotic about such a system, it is simply one of those tedious record-keeping systems that only works *if* you work at it. You might find that a personal computer database can help keep track of key assignments. In Fig. 7-3, you can see an example of such a database, created with FileMaker on the Macintosh.

The main elements of a key management system are as follows, with some applying specifically to keyed equipment, while others apply to keys in general:

- Separate keys from equipment as soon as it arrives. Make sure that all the keys that come with a piece of equipment are controlled.

- Cross reference keys to machines using a protected code. Do *not* label keys so that they can be matched with machines without the code.

- Only issue keys as they are needed. Do not leave keys with the equipment.

- Collect *all* keys from employees who are leaving, as they are leaving.

- Be prepared to change locks if keys are missing.

- Be alert to the fact that keys can be duplicated. Mark keys with "do not duplicate without permission" and get to know the locksmith nearest the site.

- Mark internal keys, such as those for keyboards, with the name of your organization. This will help tracking and retrieval, and alert locksmiths. Do not mark the front door keys in this manner.

- Reward employees for looking after keys. Penalize them for negligence. Let employees know that they will be held responsible for fraud/abuse carried out on a system for which they have a key.

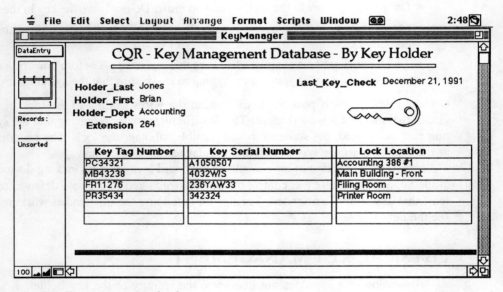

Fig. 7-3. Key management database.

AUTHENTICATION HARDWARE

One of the most neglected areas of personal computer security is policy towards, and knowledge of, who is actually involved with the handling of the data. We have already seem that possession of a key does not guarantee the identity of the key holder because physical keys get lost, stolen, shared, and duplicated.

The limitations of physical keys have given rise to a specialized type of equipment sometimes referred to as authentication hardware. Much of this hardware has been borrowed from the general field of site security, downsized, and applied directly to computer access.

While some access controls rely on passwords and PINs, these techniques, referred to as "memory-based," do not guarantee the identity of persons using them. Use of a PIN only proves that someone has knowledge of the PIN, the supposedly "secret" identifier. Such techniques of identification rely on absolute secrecy as well as above-average file management. To overcome these limitations, security professionals have sought identifiers that, unlike secret memory tricks, cannot be transferred or taken.

Biometric Devices

One type of authentication system that has been revolutionized by microprocessor technology itself is biometrics. As defined by the International Biometric Association, a biometric is ". . . a measurable physical characteristic or personal trait used to recognize the identity, or verify the claimed identity, of a person through automated means." Biometric identifiers, unlike memory-based secrets, cannot be transferred either by theft or gift. They cannot be altered or lost. A properly implemented biometric ID method is positive identification of an individual person. In the event of a security breach, the audit trail can be completed, and the breach traced to an individual.

By definition, biometric excludes PINs and passwords. Also excluded are cards, tokens or keys, and imprecise recognition features, such as when security personnel make a judgment, for example concerning facial features or signature similarities. Biometric does include behavioral traits such as handwriting and speech characteristics that can be recognized "by automated means." An almost perfect example of a biometric identifier is DNA. The procedures for DNA typing involve a lot of effort but matching involves no human judgment. (While DNA is an excellent biometric identifier that is becoming a valuable tool in law enforcement, it is unlikely as an identifier in access control due to the complexity of the process.)

For centuries, those involved in enforcing the law have tried to find the truly unique physical characteristics of human beings in order to identify them quickly and beyond all reasonable doubt. The most widely used characteristic is still fingerprints, which were known as a form of identification in ancient China. Today the FBI compares fingerprints by using minutiae, points where fingerprint ridges fork or end. Each person has unique number and spacing of minutiae.

Many other forms of identification are used today, such as voice prints, handprints, teeth prints, retinal scans, other measurements such as height and weight. These features can be recorded, analyzed, and compared. For some time, those interested in verifying identity for purposes of controlling access to buildings have looked at one or more of these factors. Some highly secure government installations, such as parts of the Lawrence Livermore National Laboratories in California, use a combination of factors. For example, an individual wishing to enter a secure area might have to speak in order for a voice print to be matched, while at the same time being weighed. With biometrics, the key to the access control lock, either on a personal computer system or the room in which it is located, is literally at the user's fingertips. While they might strike many of us as very futuristic, turnkey biometric systems that are available today offer a very high level of security that is worth considering if security is a priority for your organization.

Biometric Implementation

What are the components of a biometric security system? First there is the *reader*, a physical device that reads or scans the feature being measured or "printed." You can see a typical example in Fig. 7-4.

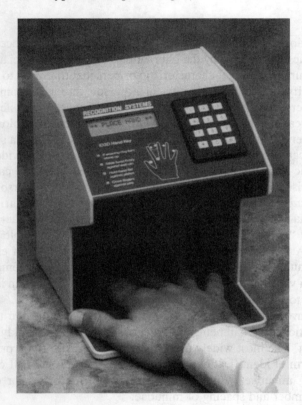

Fig. 7-4. Biometric reader.

When a system is being installed the reader scans the prints of authorized personnel. These are recorded and cataloged by a computer. This phase of operations is called *enrollment*. The reader is then used as a log-on device or lock. The would-be user presents hand/voice/eye for scanning by the reader. The print is matched against those cataloged in the computer. A match opens the lock. If a match is not made, the user is rejected. The biometric system can be used to secure a single personal computer, terminal, or LAN workstation, or a room in which secure computing is carried out.

The cost of biometric systems is currently very high, typically upwards of $1000 per installation, but in some applications, the need for security is so great that the cost is justified. This is because biometric devices offer unparalleled security. They have none of the weaknesses of password and traditional key systems. Even for the most determined hacker, there is no obvious way past biometrics. Everyone has a unique fingerprint, voiceprint, retinal pattern and so on. Changing your biometric, the feature that is being scanned, is more expensive, dangerous, and difficult than simply copying a key or breaking a password. Biometrics might not be the answer for every situation, and they might be overkill for low-risk applications, but they are becoming the approach of choice for high-level security in government installations, laboratories, banks, and so on.

Besides being expensive, biometric systems have some other weak points. If you install a biometric system, you run the risk of intimidating users. The reader devices themselves are somewhat frightening. Putting your face up to a retinal unit before starting work in the morning can be rather daunting, as can talking to a box that wants to check your voice. Of the biometric systems available today, signature recognition is probably the least disconcerting.

There are also questions of reliability and practicality. A user with a plaster bandage on his/her thumb cannot give a thumb scan. A user with a case of laryngitis might not produce a voiceprint that is acceptable. Ways around such problems exist, but the problems need to be acknowledged and dealt with when you are considering a biometric system. Override capability should be built into the system for use by the system controller when anomalies occur.

In the past, biometrics gained a reputation for ineffectiveness. People who should have been accepted were rejected, while those who should have been rejected were accepted. However, biometric technology today has improved accuracy levels. Typically, a biometric device will reject the right person a little more than one percent of the time, and admit the wrong person less than one percent of the time. If the biometric is combined with a password and identification number system, then the system almost guarantees the exclusion of unauthorized users.

Biometrics in Operation

Until biometric readers come down in price, securing each personal computer with a reader is expensive. An alternative use of the biometric technology is to secure a group of users with one machine. Recognition Systems of San Jose, California, enables users to have one hand geometry reader per room or department. After a user's hand is scanned, he or she is assigned a password. The password is only effective for a few minutes at a particular workstation. Every password is randomly generated. This way you get the security of biometrics for a fraction of the cost. Some biometric devices include an identification pad. Before or after matching his biometric, the user enters his secret identification number. If both the number and the biometric are verified, the person is admitted. Otherwise, the person is rejected.

A rapidly expanding range of biometric readers are coming onto the market. It is perhaps not surprising that these devices use microprocessor technology to speed the measuring and matching process. As this technology gets faster, smaller, and less expensive, biometric readers will come down in price, and new systems will be developed.

Fingerprints. Readers for fingerprints benefit from the long familiarity with the science of fingerprinting and are now remarkably small, and accurate. They identify a user by the shape and number of *minutia* points on a finger. The minutia points are the points where ridges fork or end, as shown in Fig. 7-5.

Fig. 7-5. A fingerprint.

This is the same process used by the FBI and Scotland Yard, but law enforcement systems are designed to search for fingerprints, while biometric readers are designed to identify fingerprints.

The fingerprint method is known to be uniquely related to only one individual, and thus is a strong deterrent to computer system fraud. However, a certain stigma is associated with fingerprints because they have been the staple of criminal identification for most of this century. Some people feel it an insult to be fingerprinted, even for their own safety. This attitude is fading as more governments are putting fingerprints in driver license files, and employers, such as banks and nursery schools, are requiring fingerprints with job applications. Use of fingerprinting in an employee situation does not present the stigma that it might in public use. Some systems use just the thumbprint, and there is no need to go through messy ink printing to register the print in the system.

Several companies now manufacture fingerprint readers that can be used with PCs. Identix of Sunnyvale, California, offers a Touch Net system for keyboard operator ID. The Ridge Reader Mint for PCs from Fingermatrix ranges in cost from $1300 to $3300 per entry point dependent upon configuration. The ThumbScan system is described by its maker as "a compact, cost-efficient biometric authentication system which acquires and analyses unique fingerprint data to ensure that only authorized computer users gain access to valuable information or a system." The ThumbScan system includes a fingerprint scanning device connected to the user workstation (PC or CRT terminal) and software installed on the host computer. To gain workstation access, the user's fingerprint is analyzed and compared with stored data from authorized personnel fingerprints.

One variation of this sytem that adds features to the basic protection of fingerprint matching is Lanboot. This product is designed to prevent unauthorized access to individual PCs or local area networks by allowing owners to boot up, then lock the software and scramble the data. Lanboot includes the ThumbScan Access Key coupled with a half-slot board that plugs into a LAN file server. A menu screen prompts the user through the option selection process, which establishes rules for access and usage. The user places the Access Key against the display terminal screen where the Key optically reads.

The same company also makes Dealerboot, which helps retailers use access control to stimulate the PC purchase decision. Dealerboot includes the ThumbScan Access Key coupled with a half-slot board which plugs into a PC filer server. The Dealerboot can program the Access Key to function for a specific number of days, enabling a dealer to lend hardware and software to a prospect for trial and evaluation for a specific time period.

PC Boot prevents unauthorized access to individual personal computers by allowing owners to control bootup, lock the software and scramble the data. The PC Boot system includes the ThumbScan Access Key coupled with a half-slot board that plugs into the PC. A menu screen prompts the user through the option selection process that establishes the rules for access and usage. An authorized access code (password) from the Access Key is required to access the PC. The user places the Access Key against the display terminal screen where the Key optically reads an encoded pattern from the host and generates an alphanumeric password. The ThumbScan AMS-PC (Access Management System PC) with Fingerprint Reader costs around $1500 per PC.

Hand Geometry. The shapes and sizes of fingers vary considerably from person to person. Finger lengths vary, as does the profile of the knuckles, in ways that are difficult to fabricate or copy. Measurement of the hand is referred to as hand geometry. Using ordinary light, the reader constructs a three-dimensional image of person's hand. This was the basis of one of the first automated biometric devices. The Identamat was introduced in 1973, and it measured finger length. Somewhat larger and unwieldy, the system is no longer available, but is still in use. A more recent device is the ID-3D hand geometry system from Recognition Systems of San Jose, California. The unit is about the size of a lunch pail and uses both finger dimensions and a knuckle profile. The RSI unit is available for $4000 to $5000 per station.

 As with fingerprint readers, the hand measuring device is actually separate from the keyboard. This does open up the possibility of *operator substitution fraud* in which an authorized user logs on for an unauthorized user. The deterrent to this is that the activity of the unauthorized user will be attributed to the person who permitted the substitution.

The Mark V Personal Identity Verifier, from PIDEAC, also uses hand measurement as part of systems designed to control access to rooms or workstations. To set up access, an authorized person first inserts a memory card into reader/writer slot. Then each hand in turn is placed under scanning camera which records a digitized silhouette of four fingers on a card. A security officer adds name, permitted locations, hours, days and so on, when the card can be used. To gain entry, an authorized person inserts the card and places either hand under a camera. The live silhouette, matched to the appropriate template, yields a match score. If the match score exceeds a preset threshold, the person is accepted as the true card owner. According to the manufacturer, no PIN is needed for this system.

Keystroke Dynamics. The principle of keystroke dynamics is that there is a consistency of timing in striking letter groups when a person uses a keyboard. The method is most effective on professional typists, but can also work on those of us who operate personal computers with only two fingers. The use of keystroke rhythm to identify a person seems a natural method for identifying keyboard operators. The reader is the keyboard itself, making the system transparent to the operator. Indeed, the method can check constantly on the operator, thus preventing operator substitution fraud.

To implement the system, you type several short sentences several times over. The system senses and records the precise relative timing of your keystrokes. This recording creates a template that is placed in the system by the administrator. Tedious as this enrollment is, taking as much as a quarter of an hour, it uses no "scary" high-tech apparatus like some other systems. When the operator wishes to work with the system, he or she enters a PIN or employee name that declares a claimed identity. One of the enrollment sentences then comes on screen, and the operator enters that sentence by keying the letters into the keyboard in the usual way. A software program compares the speed and timing of the entered sentence with the template that was put on file at the time of enrollment. If the patterns match, the operator is presumed to be as declared, and he or she is allowed access to the network or system. If the match is close, but not over the threshold, the operator might be prompted to try a second or third time.

Some systems then continue to monitor the keystrokes during the session to prevent operator substitution. Ongoing monitoring is not as detailed as the original sign-on matching and is based on frequently used three and four letter groups, such as *tion* or *ing*. If mismatches are found, the system stops the session and requests another log-on test.

The nuts and bolts of keystroke dynamic systems are available from the Electronic Signature Lock Company in San Francisco, while International Bioaccess Corporation in New York sells complete keystroke dynamic systems built on PC expansion cards. These are priced under $500.

 In common with other behavioral biometrics, a physical injury or extreme emotions might cause an operator to be rejected in error, but acceptance of impostors is claimed to be under one per cent. It should also be noted that operators can misrepresent themselves to the system by typing in an unusual manner, thus forcing the system to reject them.

Retinal Scanners. Every person, even identical twins, has a unique blood vessel pattern in the retina. Retinal scanners, like the EyeDentification System from Eye-Dentify of Oregon, scan the pattern of the user's retina. The principle of the eye scan is to record a template pattern of the blood vessels which appear on the rear wall of the eyeball. These patterns are as unique as fingerprints and not nearly as complex. The pattern never changes unless there is major brain damage.

To read the pattern, a pencil beam of low-intensity red light is made to track around the edge of the eyeball, measuring reflected light as it crosses a blood vessel. These vessels are irregular shaped spokes radiating from a central core and thus easily measured as to radial location and size. During the scan, a low-intensity infrared light is bounced off 320 data points within a 450-degree scan. The circuit takes about half a second.

This might sound somewhat frightening, and at first using the system can be intimidating. However, it is quite safe. The light used has an intensity about equal to one Christmas tree bulb. A number of organizations have used readers without a problem. For example, EyeDentify has been approved by Underwriters Laboratory, The Health and Safety Section of the Australian Radiation Laboratory, Oregon Health and Sciences University, Workers Compensation of the State of Oregon, Sweden's National Institute of Radiation Protection, the organization that has spearheaded higher standards for VDUs.

To use the system, you look into a dark barrel and focus on a target at the end of the darkness. When the target appears clear, you press a button and the circular peripheral scan commences. If the pattern matches the template that was created for you when you enrolled, the identification is successfully completed. The maker claims that the quantity of light is not affected by contact lenses, even tinted ones. However, eyeglasses must be taken off during enrollment and log-on.

As with fingerprint systems, enrollment in retinal scan systems is a fairly quick procedure. Unfortunately, the cost is still fairly high for use with personal computer access systems.

EyeDentify manufactures two retina readers. One stand-alone unit retails for about $6000, generally used in securing room access. The other reader, EyeNet can be used with personal computers, with the cost dependent on the particular installation.

Voice. Another area where biometrics have become popular is voice. A voice verifier works by analyzing the unique characteristic of a person's voice. A mathematical model of a speaker's vocal tract is constructed. If the vocal tract matches the one on file, then access is granted. The identification can be handled centrally by a phone system or at each station by a small device attached to the terminal. While early voice analysis systems had problems with interference on telephone lines and with background noise, the problems have been largely solved. By placing the receiver in a quiet location, the problem can be avoided even in cases where there is a background of voices. It is claimed that neither a recording nor a cold affects the system. This is because the voice recognition itself is not the key, but simply the vocal tract.

Voice ID systems that use a telephone work well with network and remote terminal situations where the voice can be transmitted over the same cable system as the data. Because no training is required to use the system, voice ID is quite popular with both users and administrators. A typical system can be installed for under $1000 per unit.

Since voice ID uses a reader that is not part of the data system, there is the risk that the voice used for ID is not that of the operator.

To enroll into a voice system, you repeat a set of words into a receiver, as prompted by the system. Words are spoken several times to establish a template. Before you can log on, you identify yourself to the system, sometimes by entering a PIN, then the voice ID system asks you to speak selected words, choosing the words at random from those previously recorded. Immediate response is required, thus defeating attempts to use recordings. Several systems are available. Ecco Industries, of Newton, Massachusetts, manufactures VoiceKey for securing rooms and installations, at a cost of approximately $1000 to $1500 per reader. Voice Prints of Santa Ana, California makes a similarly priced unit.

Signature. One popular way of identifying someone is through his or her signature. This is usually unique in appearance. Nevertheless, in the past, a signature was often accompanied by visual identification. You knew the signer and watched him or her sign. After all, signatures can be forged. Important signatures still require witnesses today, but more typically, the signature is used as ID by comparing a recent signature with one that was previously filed or enrolled. While most of these matches are done by a specialist making a visual comparison, image processing machines for check accounting can electronically match signatures. Such machines are very costly and are designed for a throughput of many signatures per second. The recognition of completed signatures is not really suited to access control devices.

A more suitable method of using signatures for instant ID is signature dynamics, which identifies a user by a variety of writing characteristics, including pen pressure, character shape and pen acceleration. Instead of looking at the finished product, this form of ID uses the uniqueness of the writing action that creates the signature. A would-be forger is unlikely to know the time a person takes to sign, at what point the *i* was dotted or the *t* was crossed, or how long the signer paused between first and second names. A sensitized tablet or pen tip can record these time intervals and thus distinguish true signer from impostor while the signature is in progress. As the pen moves, it is measured, and the decision to accept or reject is made immediately upon completion of the signature.

Unfortunately, as in keystroke dynamics, signature dynamics involves a relatively lengthy enrollment procedure. As many as ten performances of the signature must be measured. The time or speed value of the pen strokes is taken as a template from these. AutoSig's Sign/On compares the generated X-Y coordinates to a template held on disk. AutoSig offers several different models of their product. Its versions for securing a personal computer or a room range from $700 to $1260 depending on volume. The weakness of signature ID for access control is that a separate sensor such as pad, tablet, or wired pen, is used and so control over operator substitution is difficult.

The Biometric Bottom Line

While biometric devices offer highly accurate authentication of identity, some systems fail to overcome the possibility of operator substitution. Because biometric systems tend to be expensive, you will need to weigh the possibility of substitution against the weakness of physical key, electronic card, and password systems (that is, the likelihood that they will be shared or revealed to others). Assessments of this type will depend upon the type of operation you are protecting, the potential benefits from fraud, and your estimation of users and their ability to resist the temptations.

Some biometric systems are likely to be resisted as intimidating or intrusive and, while some devices substantially improve a system's security, not even their makers would claim they are a solution in themselves. Security problems go beyond proper user identification. Corrupted authorized users accessing secret data is a prime example. User integrity cannot be programmed or scanned. If authorized people log on and then share their account with others, the best biometrics are defeated. Proper data security, user education, and transaction tracking are equally important.

THE UNATTENDED SYSTEM

Not all problems of access control are solved by installing a means of verifying the identity of persons starting up the computer. Some systems are primarily geared to controlling initial access, which still leaves the question of interim access control. Once a system is up and running and a user is logged on, you need to be able to prevent unauthorized users from eavesdropping, looking over your shoulder, or simply waiting until you are out to lunch.

Eavesdropping is considered in the next section of this chapter. The question of peeking is considered in the next chapter where techniques for blanking the screen are discussed. The question of unauthorized program and file access is also considered in the next chapter. Many of the systems used to secure against this depend on passwords, just like some site and system access controls. For this reason, the next chapter has a discussion about effective password selection.

As with many other aspects of security, the problem of people using unattended systems when they should not is mainly a people problem. We people being what we are, the problem is minimized when the temptation is minimized. This means that such diverse factors as office design and personnel policy can greatly affect security. The old saw "out of sight out of mind" is well applied to the location of personal computers that carry sensitive information. Unfortunately, open-plan offices were developed when people did paperwork that was flat on the desk and easily slipped inside it. Nowadays, many people do their work on screens that glow in the dark and are visible from quite a distance. A bright color display is much more of a magnet to human curiosity than a pile of papers.

As for personnel policy, it may well be said, "The more content the workers are the less they work at defeating security systems." A lot of prying, with its attendant risk of inadvertent damage, is done by those who feel the organization is hiding something from them. The classic case is salary and wages, which generate attempts to uncover them in direct proportion to the secrecy with which they are guarded and the perceived inequalities between them. Resolving this problem is not a matter of personal computer security, but having the good sense to keep personal computers that store this type of information out of the way of most employees certainly is. The observation made the beginning of the chapter should be kept in mind. The cost-effectiveness of expensive security measures is needlessly diminished if simple precautions against temptation are ignored.

ELECTRONIC EAVESDROPPING

All of the access control and user verification techniques described here are no defense against the determined interloper who can afford sophisticated electronic eavesdropping equipment. We are not talking about bugging devices that listen in to conversations. In this instance, electronic eavesdropping refers to remote interception of computer data, a feat made possible by the fact that a lot of computer equipment gives off faint signals which, if correctly interpreted, reveal the information being processed by the computer. Indeed, unless you have taken measures to prevent this eventuality, someone could be sitting in a van outside your office right now reading everything that comes onto your screen or is sent to your printer.

The U.S. government is so concerned about the security risks posed by such eavesdropping that a set of tests have been developed to certify that electronic equipment is secure against such attacks. The tests and how they are carried out are classified. So sensitive is this subject that the name by which it is know, *Tempest*, was itself classified until quite recently. (Try calling up the government and asking, "What exactly is Tempest?" You will probably get a very tight-lipped response, although the magazine *Government Computer News* regularly carries advertisements for "Tempest-certified" versions of many popular printers and personal computers.) The term *Tempest* will be used here to refer to this particular aspect of personal computer security.

The Appropriate Response

Before describing *how* it is possible to "tune into" someone else's computer and surreptitiously read their data from afar, it is important to discuss *why* someone would go to this trouble. Realistically, you are only at risk from Tempest-type electronic eavesdropping if you are working with *very* valuable data. A combination of equipment and expertise is required to successfully perform Tempest-type spying. The correct combination is currently quite rare, although it would only take one enterprising individual to market a suitable device complete with instructions for this situation to change.

As things stand today, you have to be processing data that is of considerable value before it becomes worthwhile for someone to tune in to your personal computers. However, if your personal computer carries any of the following information, then you need to be concerned about Tempest-type intrusion:

- Government secrets.
- Trade secrets.
- Banking and financial data.

- Account numbers.
- Personal Identification Numbers, access codes or passwords.
- Incriminating or potentially embarrassing data.

Whether you need to explore some of the defensive measures described later in this section will depend upon your assessment of the determination and resources of potential attackers, bearing in mind that they could range from teenage students of electronics, to well-financed agents of foreign governments.

The EMI Problem

In the last chapter, the problems of radio frequency interference (RFI) and electromagnetic interference (EMI) were described from the point of view of interference with the electrical activity within a personal computer. It was also pointed out that personal computers themselves produce RFI and EMI. The normal high speed pulsing of electrical current through the circuits of a personal computer gives rise to harmonics, electrical frequencies strong and high enough to be tuned in by radio receivers. As a consequence of this phenomenon, activity on a personal computer or terminal can be detected from some distance if you have the right equipment.

If you have some difficulty believing this, you can perform a test that demonstrates the principles at work. Using a typical FM pocket radio, preferably one with headphones, you can probably detect EMI when your personal computer accesses the disk drive. First, set up a macro or batch file on your personal computer that carries out a continuous loop of disk access activity. On a PC, you might write a batch file like EMI.BAT listed here:

```
:START
ECHO Testing EMI
DIR/W > EMI. DAT
DEL EMI.DAT
GOTO START
```

When you run this batch file, it will continue reading the directory into a file called EMI.DAT and then erasing the file. The loop will continue until you press Ctrl−Break.

Now tune the radio so that it is between stations, at around 93 MHz on the FM dial. You should get a fuzzy static sound (this is why you want the headphones—the noise can be quite annoying to others). Next you run the batch file while sitting at your computer. While the batch file executes slowly adjust the tuning on the radio until you hear a rhythmic buzz or crackle that matches the rhythm of the batch file. (Try tuning up from 92 MHz to around 96 MHz; the test works best in areas with relatively few radio stations, but you should detect a signal of some sort, even if it is interference with an actual station.) Try placing the radio close to the personal computer if the signal is faint.

When you do pick up the noise of the disk access, try moving the radio away from the computer to see how far away you can detect the signal (you might need to twist the radio through different angles to keep the signal). You will probably find that you can still get the signal several yards away.

What you are hearing is EMI, radiated harmonics of the circuits accessing the disk. You can do a similar test for emissions from your keyboard. Try typing while tuning your radio and you will probably be able to pick up keystrokes as blips or abrupt changes in the background static. With specialized equipment, it is possible to record such signals, analyze them, and determine what is being typed.

The Weak Link

While various parts of the typical computer system such as the drives, keyboard, and printer connection emit detectable signals, it is difficult, although not impossible, to make sense of these signals. The easiest way to tell what a personal computer is doing is to look at the screen. One of the strongest sources of EMI in your personal computer system is the cathode ray tube (CRT) in a typical monitor. This is because the video signal from the personal computer is boosted to several hundred volts to drive the electron beam of the CRT.

As it happens, the radiated harmonics of the personal computer's video signal are fairly close to that of a typical broadcast TV signal. All that is required to pick up and read this signal from some distance is a directional antenna and a television. The signal will appear as a scrambled TV station because the signals that provide horizontal and vertical synchronization do not transmit very well. However, if you add special circuitry to supply the missing synhchronization signals, then it is possible to read on a remote screen what is displayed on a personal computer monitor.

In 1985, in a now legendary piece of hacking, Wim Van Eck, a Dutch electronics researcher, proved to a number of banks that is was possible to read information from their CRTs at distances of almost a mile away, using an ordinary TV, with two simple electronic extras—a directional antenna and an external sync generator. This incident gave rise to the term *Van Eck phreaking*, which is an alternative to "Tempest-type electronic eavesdropping." The incident also contributed to a growing awareness on the part of many organizations that they must take defensive measures. Defenses are necessary both to avoid direct losses and also to head off accusations of negligence, should the weakness become widely known. The rapid spread of personal computers has greatly exacerbated the problem becuase it has significantly increased the number of displays on which sensitive information appears. Furthermore, as in other areas of security, most personal computer designs are woefully lacking in protection features.

Defensive Action

You can use several techniques to defend against EMI eavesdropping. These range from simple and inexpensive to very costly and sophisticated, depending on how much security from this type of intrusion you think you need.

NON-CRT Displays. The cathode ray tube has been such a prevalent part of computer technology over the last 30 years that terminals and monitors are regularly called

CRTs. This might change in the coming decades as new technologies emerge that can present images without a CRT. Because the CRT is the weak link when it comes to EMI eavesdropping, you can improve security by using a different type of display, such as the LCD and gas plasma screens found on laptop computers. These are driven by much lower voltages that emit far less powerful signals than the standard CRT. Indeed, some companies, such as Emerald Systems, are selling network terminals with non-CRT displays, like the one pictured in Fig. 7-6.

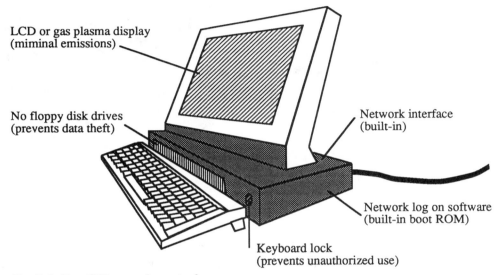

LCD or gas plasma display
(miminal emissions)

No floppy disk drives
(prevents data theft)

Network interface
(built-in)

Network log on software
(built-in boot ROM)

Keyboard lock
(prevents unauthorized use)

Fig. 7-6. Non-CRT network terminal.

Some companies now sell flat panel displays with non-CRT technology as replacements for regular monitors. These appeal partly for security reasons, and also for reasons of design and space because they take up far less room than a conventional display. For example, Sygnos Technologies of London, offers a VGA compatible flat screen display shown in Fig. 7-7 that plugs directly into the video port of your PC or Macintosh.

The light weight and small size make for savings on desk space. Hanging such a display on a wall or vertical arm for a zero footprint would be very easy. Users of laptop personal computer systems are already familiar with non-CRT technology and are probably aware that it is rapidly improving, with VGA and color systems coming onto the market at steadily decreasing prices.

Manage the Monitor. If you are stuck with a CRT display, you can take steps to minimize EMI security risks. Obviously, you should keep to a minimum the amount of sensitive data that is displayed on the CRT. Such information as account numbers, access codes, and passwords, should not be displayed at all if it can be avoided. If you adjust the CRT's brightness and contrast controls to give low contrast combined with

Fig. 7-7. Flat screen monitor.

high brightness, this makes it harder for a would-be eavesdropper to tune in, although you need to consider the question of comfort and potential eyestrain. Also bear in mind that the higher the resolution of the screen display, the harder it is to decipher the image when receiving it remotely. Using the 50-line mode available with a VGA monitor instead of the traditional 25-line mode should help to thwart eavesdropping.

Cable Connections. Another weak link is the cabling used between personal computers components and between multiple personal computers on a network. A determined eavesdropper could tune in emissions from such cabling and make sense of the data it carried. If the cable is heavy-duty *coaxial* cable (like the cable used between a TV and a VCR or antenna), then it is probably fairly well insulated. However, the expense of coaxial cable for networks has led to many companies using lightweight cable, called *twisted pair* that is similar to that in telephone wiring. This is not as well shielded, and so emissions would be easier to tune in.

The cables used to connect personal computers, printers, keyboards, and monitors should be the round type, rather than the flat ribbon cables. You should only buy cables marked "shielded" on the package, meaning that they have a layer of foil wrapped around the wires beneath the plastic outer skin. While this is hard to check for without cutting into the cable, buying cables marked "shielded" from a reputable supplier should be sufficient safeguard. The older ribbon cables are not shielded and can give off considerable emissions.

A technology that transmits data without EMI is fiberoptic, which uses pulses of light rather than electricity. Fiberoptic cable is currently replacing traditional copper phone wiring in many parts of the world. You can network computers with fiberoptic cabling and thus eliminate the chance that data will be overheard as it travels between computers.

Shielding the Box. Most personal computer equipment has some form of shielding designed to keep emissions from escaping. The use of a metal casing for the system unit, as in the original IBM PC, is one level of shielding. Plastic-cased components will often have a metal inner shell, like the Apple Macintosh II. Both plastic and metal cases can have a black metallic coating on the inside for further protection. Openings in the casing should be kept to a minimum, which is why blank plates are placed over unoccupied expansion slots (and should be replaced when expansion cards are removed). Openings for ventilation should have metal baffles.

Equipment varies greatly when it comes to the level of shielding because this is an area where manufacturers can cut costs without reducing apparent performance. In the United States, the Federal Communications Commission is charged with regulating emissions from computer equipment and making sure that corners are not cut. The FCC classifies equipment based on how well it performs in this area and has the power to prevent the sale of equipment that gives off too much interference. Many products are sold with a Class B rating, which means they are known to emit interference but at levels that are "reasonable."

The flood of cheap personal computers from the Far East has outpaced the FCC's ability to regulate these products, so enforcement tends to be uneven. Often the larger companies have to make the most concerted efforts at compliance with FCC standards because their products have a higher profile. As a rule of thumb, a private label PC compatible made from generic components imported from the Far East will emit far more than an IBM or Compaq. However, this is no guarantee that the IBM or Compaq is in any way immune to eavesdropping.

A Safe Position. Radiated signals from electronic components can be reflected from flat metal surfaces, actually increasing the power of the signals. When locating your personal computer equipment, avoid placing it on metal desks or work surfaces, and avoid proximity to metal doors, filing cabinets, and dividing screens. On the other hand, a metal box placed around the equipment can prevent signals escaping; the thicker the metal, the greater the protection. Air vents and openings for wires entering the box would need to be baffled. If you are considering going this far, then you might consider the Tempest standard, described next.

The Tempest "Standard"

The United States government has developed a method of testing computer equipment to measure any emissions that can be used to obtain useful information. Equipment that passes these tests is considered to be secure enough for use in sensitive government applications where the computer data being handled is classified. The tests, or rather the problem they address, are referred to as *Tempest*. The tests themselves are classified, and so cannot be described. The Tempest tests exist in two very similar forms, one for the United States government (referred to as NACSIM5100A) and another for N.A.T.O. (referred to as AMSG720B).

To get Tempest certification for a product, a manufacturer submits it to the government. The government then places it on the Tempest Preferred Product List. Contracts to supply the government with computer equipment or to carry out data processing tasks for government agencies can specify Tempest-certified equipment. Nongovernment organizations can purchase equipment that is modified to protect against Tempest-type attacks although they are apparently denied details of government Tempest specifications. Not surprisingly, modifying a piece of personal computer equipment so that it passes Tempest testing adds considerable cost to the equipment. However, it is possible for anyone to secure their computer activities from electronic prying. Some banks are known to use Tempest-level protection on personal computers involved in sensitive applications. Outside of the United States, it is possible to buy equipment with "Tempest-type" protection.

Finally, it is worth noting that some countries have laws which set minimum levels of security for organizations storing data about individuals on personal computers. For example, the United Kingdom Data Protection Act extends this protection to basic name and address information. Future legislation along these lines might well set minimum levels for security from eavesdropping, placing the burden of protection on those who use personal computers for database management.

BATCH FILES FOR BOOT CONTROL

In Chapter 5, you saw how you could program DOS-based personal computers to present a warning to would-be thieves and intruders. Expanding on those examples, you can create a password or passkey system to prevent unauthorized access to your hardware. The techniques described in the following sections will also be useful when creating protection against snooping, as described in the next chapter.

A Basic Example

The examples in Chapter 5 showed you how to write and run a batch file that left a message on the screen that could only be cleared by pressing the Break key (this is the combination of Ctrl and the key called Break, also activated by Ctrl and the letter C). By looping the batch file with a GOTO statement, any key besides Break simply caused the main instructions in the file to repeat. You could incorporate a similar system in the AUTOEXEC.BAT to stop someone from turning on a system and then using it. Consider the following AUTOEXEC.BAT file:

```
@ECHO OFF
PATH = C: \ ;C: \ DOS
PROMPT $D $P$G
:START
CLS
```

```
ECHO Enter password, then
PAUSE
GOTO START
```

The first line (@ECHO OFF) turns off the screen repetition of commands. The second line uses the PATH command to set the DOS PATH that the user requires. The PROMPT command is then used to set the preferred prompt: date ($D) followed by path ($P) and the greater than sign ($G). Next a line called START is named for use by the later GOTO statement (:START). The screen is then cleared and the cursor placed on the top line (CLS) before a message is displayed (ECHO Enter...). When the batch file is run the screen will show the following:

```
Enter password, then
Strike a key when ready . . .
```

The PAUSE command is used to display the second line of this message, telling the user to press a key. Right after this is the GOTO statement that sends DOS back to the second line. Only if the Ctrl−Break key is used to interrupt the batch file can the user get to the DOS prompt and access to files. Resetting the system will only get the user back to the batch file message because it is in the AUTOEXEC.BAT, which is run whenever the system boots.

There are several weak points in this protection system. First is the weakness common to most batch files: they can be terminated by Ctrl−Break. This fact will be dealt with later in some detail, but suffice it to say that by employing Ctrl−Break as the key to access this batch file only serves to expose the weakness of the system. Furthermore, the key to the system cannot be varied. Only Ctrl−Break works. Finally, the design of the file means that the real work of the batch file is completed before the security routine is invoked. You will probably want to make the security check the first thing that an AUTOEXEC.BAT does.

User Input

An essential feature of a good access prevention batch file is the ability to work with a variable key. The user or administrator should be able to specify the key that permits access. So far you have seen that batch files can accept "a key when ready" or Ctrl−Break. Unfortunately, within the batch file language, this is the limit as far as user input is concerned. In order to make them respond to a wider range of specific keys, batch files need some assistance from other programs, known as DOS utilities. Several of these are available:

REPLY.COM—Created from instructions later in this chapter, reads all keys, activated by a single key, although up to three may be used for a password.

GETKEY.COM—Public domain utility available from many bulletin boards, reads typewriter keys only, otherwise works like REPLY.COM.

GETFUN.COM—Public domain utility available from many bulletin boards, reads only function keys.

ANSWER.COM—Public domain utility available from many bulletin boards, can handle lengthy passwords.

ASK.EXE—Comes with Norton Utilities, handles 10 different keys, defined by the user, but only a single key password.

Which of these you want to use will depend on the level of security each one offers, as well as their availability.

USING THE ASK COMMAND

A small utility program called ASK.EXE comes with the Norton Utilities. This program can be run by a batch file, allowing the file to evaluate single key user input from up to nine possible choices at once. The user defines which keys can be accepted as a response, and what the batch file does with the response.

How ASK Works

The ASK command is entered in a batch file followed by a piece of message text and a list of acceptable keys chosen by the user. For example, the following line in a batch file would give the user an opportunity to enter L, D, or Q and thus activate one of two programs or the quit option:

ASK "Run (L)otus 123, (D)base, or (Q)uit: ", LDQ

Typing L or D in response to this statement could direct the batch file to a subroutine that loads the appropriate program. A *subroutine* is a section of instructions or code within a program that is called on by the program under certain circumstances.

Note that the message is enclosed in quotes due to the comma in the message. If there are no commas in the message, the quotes are not needed. Also note the space after the colon. This causes the cursor to flash one space past the colon, which is generally more legible. The possible responses are simply typed at the end of the line. When the above line appears in a batch file the screen displays the following:

Run (L)otus 123, (D)base, or (Q)uit: _

As soon as the user enters one of the keys listed in the ASK command (the letter L, D, or Q), the batch file continues to the next line.

Using ERRORLEVELS

The next line of the batch file must evaluate the user input. This is done by using the ERRORLEVEL feature of DOS. The ERRORLEVEL is a single digit code from 0 to 9 that can be left in memory by a DOS program or command when it is completed. The ASK program assigns ERRORLEVEL 1 to the first key defined by the ASK statement. The second and third keys are assigned to ERRORLEVELS 2 and 3. If you type L in response to the above ASK statement, the ERRORLEVEL is set to 1. If you type

D, then the ERRORLEVEL is 2, and so on. If you type any other character besides the ones listed, then the ERRORLEVEL is 0, which causes a beep and prevents the batch file from continuing. That is why the ASK statement needs a Quit option. You can use the batch command IF to check the ERRORLEVEL and then branch to a subroutine. The following lines could be used after the ASK statement to create a menu batch file with three subroutines:

```
IF ERRORLEVEL 3 GOTO QUIT
IF ERRORLEVEL 2 GOTO DBASE
IF ERRORLEVEL 1 GOTO LOTUS
:LOTUS
CD \ 123
123
GOTO :QUIT
:DBASE
CD \ DBASE
DBASE
:QUIT
END
```

Note that the ERRORLEVEL is evaluated in declining values. In fact, the statement IF ERRORLEVEL 1 GOTO LOTUS means IF the ERRORLEVEL is 1 or above, then GOTO LOTUS. By dealing with the highest ERRORLEVEL first, ambiguity is eliminated. Also note the use of the END command. This terminates a batch file. It is not strictly necessary in this case because going to the line called QUIT has the same effect, but the END statement is good programming form and makes the purpose of the batch file clearer. The END statement is useful when you want to call a subroutine that terminates the batch file but is not located at the end of the file.

Pass Keys with ASK

If the user responds to the above ASK statement with a key other than the three in the list, a beep will sound and the message will remain. This allows you to set a pass key, using just one possible key in the ASK statement's key list. For example, the following AUTOEXEC.BAT presents a message that will not go away until the letter K is typed:

```
@ECHO OFF
:DENIED
ECHO Correct password required!
ASK "Enter password: ", K
IF ERRORLEVEL 1 GOTO OKAY
GOTO DENIED
:OKAY
CLS
PROMPT $D $P$G
```

Note that the letter K can be typed upper- or lowercase. One nice feature of this sytem is that all keys besides the correct one cause a beep. Someone trying to type in a password will get a succession of beeps. Also, the fact that the key letter is at the end of the batch file command line makes editing in a new letter very easy. You might think that a single key is pretty easy to guess, particularly if it is not case sensitive, all you have to do is type all the keys. However, you will cause a warning beep if you do this, and you can use characters besides the regular letter and number keys. For example, you can use Ctrl plus a letter or number, such as Ctrl−Q. This will appear as ^Q when you enter it in the batch file in an ASCII editor such as EDLIN. (Note that you cannot enter Ctrl−C or Ctrl−Break in this way.)

An even more challenging key is a special character entered as an ASCII code number. All characters you can type from the keyboard, plus others that are used for shapes and foreign characters, have an ASCII code number. For example, the ASCII code for *q* is 113. You can create characters from their ASCII code numbers by holding down Alt, typing the code on the numeric keypad, then releasing Alt. If you do this at the DOS prompt, hold down Alt, type 113, release Alt, then the letter *q* will appear. The ASCII code for the pounds sterling sign (£) is 156. This character does not appear on a United States keyboard, so if you use it for the ASK key, the user will have to enter it as just described, Alt−156; otherwise, access will be denied. This makes it tough to guess a three-digit pass key.

THE ANSWER COMMAND

An alternative to ASK.EXE is provided by Frank Schweiger, a programmer and PC user who realized there was no way within strictly DOS batch files to ask a user to input a directory and program file name. Mr. Schweiger wrote, and released to the public domain, ANSWER.COM which takes care of this DOS deficiency. You can find ANSWER.COM on many bulleting boards.

The Workings of ANSWER

The ANSWER.COM program makes use of a small area of memory set aside by DOS for user input and other information and referred to as the *environment*. The syntax for using ANSWER is as follows:

ANSWER [optional prompt]

When you include this command in a batch file, ANSWER will display the optional prompt, and then accept input from the keyboard. The input is placed in the environment area and named as ANSWER. (Advanced users might note that if ANSI.SYS has been loaded, the optional prompt can contain any valid ANSI sequences to position the cursor, change color, and so on.)

Parameters in the environment area can be accessed similarly to command line parameters. A *command line parameter* is a piece of information, a variable or argument, that you provide to a program. For example, when you enter DIR A:, the A: is a parameter, telling DOS which drive to read. You can use numbered parameters in a batch file by enclosing them with percentage signs. Consider this batch file, called DW.BAT, which uses a parameter %1% for the letter of a drive:

```
@ECHO OFF
CLS
DIR/W %1%:
```

To run this batch file, you enter the file name followed by a space and then the parameter. Thus you could enter DW A to tell the program to produce a wide directory listing for drive A, or DW C to create a wide listing for drive C.

When you use ANSWER, the parameter or variable is named as %ANSWER%. For example, suppose you want the batch file to ask for the name of a file on drive A that is to be copied to drive C. You would use this sequence of commands:

```
ANSWER Enter name of the file on drive A:
COPY A:%ANSWER% C: \ DATA
```

Suppose you wanted the batch file to ask for a drive letter, directory, and file name, in turn. You could use this sequence of commands, which employs the SET command to copy the information in the variable called ANSWER into a variable of another name, also stored in the environment area:

```
ANSWER Enter the drive ("d:") that the file is on:
SET DRIVE = %ANSWER%
ANSWER Enter the path ("path \ ") for the file:
SET COPYPATH = %ANSWER%
ANSWER Enter the filename:
COPY %DRIVE%%COPYPATH%%ANSWER% C: \ DATA
```

Note that this example uses three named parameters in the environment area. The SET DRIVE = %ANSWER% tells DOS that the variable called DRIVE should equal the variable called ANSWER. If you have not expanded your environment area from the default of 127 bytes, you might run out of environment space. You use the SHELL command to expand environment space. Enter this command in your AUTOEXEC.BAT to expand the environment to 1024 bytes:

```
SHELL = C: \ COMMAND.COM /P/E:1024
```

Note that ANSWER sets a return code that can be examined by the ERRORLEVEL option of the IF statement. The ERRORLEVEL will be 0 if ANSWER was successful, or 1 if there was insufficient room or the environment area was corrupted. Also note that before the ANSWER command is issued, you must display some indication that keyboard input is expected or include the optional prompt to do so. If the optional prompt is not present, ANSWER will not display anything that tells the operator that input is expected.

Security with ANSWER

You can use ANSWER to create a batch file that locks out any user who does not know the correct password. The following code shows how you would set this up if the password was 999 (see line 5):

1. @ECHO OFF
2. :DENIED
3. CLS
4. ANSWER Enter password, then press ENTER:
5. IF %ANSWER%= =999 GOTO OKAY
6. GOTO DENIED
7. :OKAY
8. CLS

Note the use of double equal signs in the IF statement that compares the %ANSWER% variable to the password. This is required because the variable is being compared to a string of characters that are not stored in the environment. This method of password protection gives you the use of a lengthy password instead of a single key. The password could be as long as 100 characters, but this would be overkill. Spaces in passwords are not allowed, but because the password detection is case sensitive and you can use any of the keyboard characters and numbers, even an eight-character password would be very difficult to guess.

USING REPLY.COM

Another short program that identifies the key most recently pressed is REPLY .COM. This allows batch files to carry out different commands depending on what key is pressed. You have already seen that DOS stores a number, called *errorlevel*, in memory, and that you can test the value of errorlevel with the IF command. All that REPLY.COM does is wait for you to press a key, then it sets the value of errorlevel to the key code of the key that you pressed. Because the IF command checks for an errorlevel equal to or greater than the number you specify, you must check for key codes in descending order, starting with the highest and proceeding to the lowest.

The key code of the standard typewriter portion of the keyboard is the ASCII code of the character. The extended key code of the special keys, function keys, keypad keys, and combinations with the Alt and Ctrl keys, is two numbers. Because the first number of an extended key code is always 0, REPLY.COM sets the errorlevel to the second number. Some ASCII codes are the same as the second number of the extended key code of other keys. This creates some duplications: the semicolon and function key F1, for example, both set errorlevel to 59; Alt−B and 0 both set errorlevel to 48. This should not be a problem in most cases because the duplicated keys are generally unrelated.

Creating REPLY.COM with Debug

You can use the DOS program called DEBUG.COM to create REPLY.COM. In fact, DEBUG.COM is a program editor, used by programmers to find bugs in programs. However, you can use it to write short assembly language programs like REPLY.COM. Simply follow the instructions given here. You will probably find DEBUG in the DOS directory of your hard disk or on the original DOS disk that came with your PC.

To start DEBUG, you simply enter DEBUG at the DOS prompt. The program will reply by placing a hyphen on the next of the screen. This is the DEBUG prompt. Now type the following lines to create REPLY.COM:

```
a 100
mov ah,8
int 21
cmp al,0
jnz 10a
int 21
mov ah,4c
int 21
```

Now press Enter. Check that your work so far matches the first part of Fig. 7-8.

```
C:\>debug
-a 100
5314:0100 mov ah,8
5314:0102 int 21
5314:0104 cmp al,0
5314:0106 jnz 10a
5314:0108 int 21
5314:010A mov ah,4c
5314:010C int 21
5314:010E
-r cx
CX 0000
:e
-n reply.com
-w
Writing 000E bytes
-q

C:\>
```

Fig. 7-8. Using DEBUG to make REPLY.COM.

If it does not, you simply enter the commands in again. To complete the program and write it to disk you enter the following:

r cx

DEBUG responds with

CX 0000
:

and you enter e followed by

n reply.com

followed by

w

DEBUG responds by saying Writing 000E bytes, and you simply type q and press Enter to quit DEBUG.

Accepting any Key

All that REPLY.COM does is set the errorlevel equal to the key code of the next key pressed. You have to include instructions to check the errorlevel in your batch file. Otherwise, REPLY.COM behaves just like the PAUSE command. That is, it stops processing until a key is pressed, but without the Strike a key when ready message.

In fact, to test REPLY.COM, just enter REPLY at the DOS prompt. Nothing should happen, there should be no system prompt. If you have a system prompt, something has gone wrong and you should go back and try creating the program again. There should be no system prompt because REPLY.COM is waiting for you to press a key. When you press any key, DOS should display the system prompt.

The first demonstration of REPLY.COM is a batch file called TESTME.BAT that displays a two-item menu and waits for you to reply. If you press F1, it clears the screen. If you press F2, it displays the directory. If you press any other key, it returns to DOS. Here is the code for TESTME.BAT (do not enter the line numbers):

1. @ECHO OFF
2. CLS
3. ECHO F1 - wide directory
4. ECHO F2 - paused directory
5. ECHO Press any other key to quit
6. REPLY
7. IF ERRORLEVEL 61 GOTO END
8. IF ERRORLEVEL 60 GOTO F2
9. IF ERRORLEVEL 59 GOTO TO F1
10. :F1
11. DIR/W
12. GOTO END

```
13.  :F2
14.  DIR/P
15.  :END
```

The first six lines clear the screen, display the menu, and run REPLY.COM. The seventh line checks whether the key code is equal to or greater than 61 (to see if a function key other than F1 or F2 was pressed). In this way, the batch file does something only if F1 or F2 is pressed, so the first IF command tells DOS to go to the END if the key pressed was F3 or greater.

The eighth line tells DOS that if the key code is 60, corresponding to F2 being pressed, go to the line labelled F2. Because the seventh line eliminated the possibility that any key whose code is higher than 60 was pressed. This IF statement isolates the F2 key. The following line says that if the key code is 59, function key F1, DOS should go to the line labelled F1. This IF command isolates the F1 key. The tenth line (GOTO END) tells DOS to exit the batch file without doing anything. Just as the IF command in line 7 ignores all keys higher than F2, this command tells DOS to ignore all keys lower than F1.

The rest of the field defines what happens if F1 or F2 is pressed. Pressing F1 should produce a wide directory while pressing F2 should produce a paused directory.

Accepting Only Certain Keys

The above batch file accepts any key, but acts on only F1 and F2, returning to DOS if any other key is pressed. For security batch files this is not the best way to handle replies. The following version of TESTME.BAT will do nothing unless either F1 or F2 is pressed.

```
 1.  @ECHO OFF
 2.  CLS
 3.  ECHO F1 - Wide directory
 4.  ECHO F2 - Paused directory
 5.  ECHO Press F1 or F2
 6.  :REPLY
 7.  REPLY
 8.  IF ERRORLEVEL 61 GOTO REPLY
 9.  IF ERRORLEVEL 60 GOTO F2
10.  IF ERRORLEVEL 59 GOTO F1
11.  GOTO REPLY
12.  :F1
13.  DIR/W
14.  GOTO END
15.  :F2
16.  DIR/P
17.  :END
```

The only way to end this batch file is to press F1 or F2 or Ctrl−Break to cancel it.

Isolating a Pass Key

You can isolate a single key entered in response to REPLY.COM so that unless the correct key is pressed, the batch file will stay in a loop. If you were to choose F1 as the pass key, then you could use this batch file code in your AUTOEXEC.BAT to lock out any other key besides F1:

1. @ECHO OFF
2. CLS
3. ECHO Enter pass key
4. :REPLY
5. REPLY
6. IF ERRORLEVEL 60 GOTO REPLY
7. IF ERRORLEVEL 59 GOTO END
8. GOTO REPLY
9. :END

When this code is executed by DOS, the screen will be blank except for the prompt Enter pass key at the top of the screen. Only pressing F1 or Ctrl−Break will get you back to the DOS prompt.

A slightly smoother way to accomplish this is to use an IF statement that includes a second IF command. The first IF command selects all keys whose code is equal to or greater than 59, and the second IF command selects all keys whose code is less than 60. You can see this modification here:

1. @ECHO OFF
2. CLS
3. ECHO Enter pass key
4. :REPLY
5. REPLY
6. IF ERRORLEVEL 59 IF NOT ERRORLEVEL 60 GOTO END
7. GOTO REPLY
8. :END

Only key code 59 actually passes both tests on line 6. If you change line 6 to the following, the pass key becomes 156, typed from the numeric keypad while holding down Alt:

6. IF ERRORLEVEL 156 IF NOT ERRORLEVEL 157 GOTO END

Note that nothing appears on the screen when you enter the code in response to the batch file prompt. Using this technique there are hundreds of codes to choose from, making it very hard to guess the right pass key.

SAFETY VIA CONFIG.SYS

So far you have seen how DOS can be used to give you a measure of access control through batch files. Unfortunately, batch files can be broken with Ctrl−Break.

An interloper who knows this will defeat the protection the batch file provides. Fortunately, you cannot break into the very first user file that DOS reads, CONFIG.SYS. Several programs use this fact to establish password protection above the AUTOEXEC.BAT level.

One such program that is in the public domain and available on many bulletin boards is called PW.SYS. This works with a companion program called CP.COM. To use this system you enter the following line in your CONFIG.SYS:

```
DEVICE = PW.SYS
```

The file called PW.SYS should be in your boot/root directory. Using the program called CP.COM, you enter your password. This is not shown on the screen as you type, and you must enter it twice to make sure you type it correctly. The CP.COM program them rewrites PW.SYS so that it contains your password. From now on, whenever you boot the computer, you are required to enter the password. Pressing Ctrl−Break has no effect except to produce a telltale beep. Quite simply, DOS cannot proceed past the CONFIG.SYS file, and all attempts to use an incorrect password produce a warning beep.

Cost conscious PC users owe a debt of gratitude to KJ Consulting who wrote this program back in 1985. The program has a lot to recommend it. You can change the password at any time, and must know the current password before you can enter a new one. Nobody can see what you type for a password when you do change it. If there is a weakness to the program, it is that you can use some utility and editing programs to view the password in the PW.SYS file. However, an unauthorized user would need to get access to the system before PW.SYS could be discovered in this way, and the password cannot be seen with the simple TYPE command. These days there are several similar programs available on bulletin boards such as CompuServe.

BOOT DISK PROBLEMS

Taken on their own, the above methods of access control for hard disk DOS machines provide moderate levels of protection. Casual interlopers and the office snoop are likely to be discouraged. The determined and knowledgeable attacker armed with his/her own DOS boot disk will simply boot from the floppy drive and bypass both CONFIG.SYS and AUTOEXEC.BAT protection.

Chapter 2 mentioned making your personal computer unbootable. Basically, this can be at two levels.

1. Make it impossible to boot from the hard disk, requiring any would-be user to have their own floppy boot disk.

2. Make it impossible to boot from the hard disk, even if you have an ordinary boot disk handy.

The first level is easy enough to achieve, as described in Chapter 2. You could place one of the above access control programs on any floppy boot disks you use and further strengthen access control. However, level 2 boot protection is more difficult to attain.

Some specialized hard disk format programs require the presence of a driver file before they can be recognized by DOS. Removal of this driver to a floppy boot disk can create level 2 protection, but most hard disks are accessible to plain DOS, leaving them prey to interlopers armed with DOS disks. In the next few sections, techniques for closing this loophole are discussed.

A SECURE DESIGN

From the point of view of basic design, "personal computer security" is really an oxymoron. Relative to the levels of security built into mainframe systems, today's typical personal computer design is, as Shakespeare very chauvinistically put it, "as leaky as an unstaunched wench." The problem is that personal computers are taking over the work traditionally done by mainframes. Computer makers are beginning to realize that there is considerable profit potential in this problem.

In the late 1980s, the technology of IBM AT clones was becoming very commonplace, and it was getting harder for clone makers to distinguish their designs from the crowd. One manufacturer who has sought to correct the security weakness of standard designs is Opus Technology. In late 1989, they introduced the Opus DataSafe, an AT compatible that was built for secure operation. In fact, some of the security features resulted in an unexpected performance bonus, giving this 80286-based machine performance levels equal to an 80386 in several respects.

The Opus Datasafe

As you can see From Fig. 7-9, the Opus Datasafe is not an unusual looking computer, and its basic specifications are fairly standard: an 80286 processor running at 12 MHz, just twice the speed of IBM's original AT; 1 megabyte of RAM; and VGA graphics.

However, when you turn on the Datasafe and try to use it, you immediately notice a difference. Instead of a DOS prompt, you get a menu asking for a user name and a password. If you do not provide an authorized name *as well as* the correct password for that name, you can get no further. After three unsuccessful attempts at logging-in, the system shuts down until it is powered down or reset. A determined interloper might try restarting the machine with a floppy boot disk but this does not work. The Datasafe does not check the floppy drive before carrying out the login sequence.

Security Measures

The Datasafe has both hardware and software security features. Like most post-AT designs, the Datasafe has keyboard lock on the front panel. However, a second lock is at the back of the case, referred to as the security key. This key controls access to the computer's case. Lock it, and the cover cannot be removed: a sturdy metal tongue latches into the case top to prevent tampering. The security key also activates what is referred to as Secure-mode, turning on BIOS-level security features.

Fig. 7-9. Opus Datasafe. Opus Technology, Ltd.

As described in Chapter 2, BIOS is the most basic piece of software. Permanently written into a chip within the computer, BIOS provides the connection between the operating system software and the hardware. In secure mode, the Datasafe ignores the floppy disk drive during the installation sequence. Furthermore, the Ctrl−Break key, dreaded foe of AUTOEXEC.BAT security systems, is deactivated, along with Ctrl−C.

The ingenious hacker might be aware that the BIOS on AT-style systems can be accessed via the SETUP program. These days many systems, including the Opus, let you access SETUP during startup by pressing a special key, often Del. However, when you do this on the Datasafe, you find that the specially written BIOS is password-protected, requiring a preassigned number between 0 and 65535 to be typed in before access is granted.

The BIOS used by OPUS is a special version of the AMI BIOS (American Megatrends International) with extensions written for Opus by a company called GSI, who also designed the motherboard.

Me and My Shadow

One particularly interesting design feature of the Opus system is the fact that the hard disk controller is built into the motherboard. This can control up to two hard disks, in either normal or shadowed modes. For disk drives, *shadow* mode means that instead of one disk, you have two, with the second one duplicating every operation of the other. When you save a file, it is automatically written to both disks. The Datasafe uses two identical disk drives, located one above the other, as seen in Fig. 7-10.

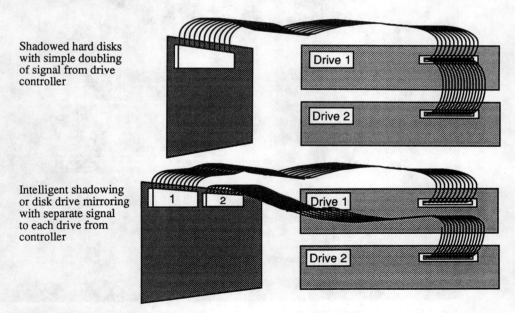

Shadowed hard disks with simple doubling of signal from drive controller

Drive 1

Drive 2

Intelligent shadowing or disk drive mirroring with separate signal to each drive from controller

1   2

Drive 1

Drive 2

Fig. 7-10. Twin drives for disk shadowing.

Disk shadowing was first used on large mainframe systems that simply could not afford to "go down." Shadowing is part of an approach to computer design and operations known as *fault tolerance*, meaning that the system as a whole can keep working despite a fault or error in a part of the system. The system literally tolerates faults. To achieve fault tolerance, and improve the speed and reliability of disaster recover designers introduced the concept of *redundancy*, equipping the computer with two of each of the vital parts, much the same way that some cars have dual braking circuits.

The primary security advantage of disk shadowing is that if one hard disk breaks down, you have a current backup immediately available. The system can be designed so that a disk crash will result in little more than an error message, with disk read/write activity unaffected. Of course, disk shadowing does not protect against user error: Mistakes such as accidental file erasing are faithfully duplicated. Nor is shadowing a replacement for normal backup procedures. Indeed, one could wish for a secure tape backup unit to be included in the Opus design. However, by itself, shadowing is very convenient and fault-tolerant.

While many security measures tend to slow down operations, performance gains can be had from disk mirroring. All writing to the disks occurs in parallel for data integrity reasons, but there is no reason why reading should be mirrored. With an intelligent disk controller, one disk can read data from one area and the other read from somewhere else. This means that each read/write head does not have to move as far to reach the information you request, resulting in improved read times.

As you saw in Chapter 4, formatted MS-DOS disks are divided into concentric tracks, which are themselves divided into sectors. These combine to form a grid by which the disk controller and software can locate any area on the disk. To keep track of where in this grid the files stored on the disk are placed, MS-DOS writes the *File Allocation Table* (FAT) onto the disk. The FAT is placed in a consistent and contiguous location on the disk. Files are written onto the disk wherever there is space, meaning that some files will occupy sectors scattered around the disk. To read a file, the disk head has to move to the FAT, find where the first part of the file is, move to that part of the disk, read the file, and then repeat the process until the entire file is in memory. Reading a large file, or a group of small files can take a disproportionate amount of disk head movement.

A pair of mirrored disks can be arranged so that one head does the reading of location information from the directory or FAT, while the other is off reading the file itself. Because moving the heads is the slow part of disk operations, the speed advantages to splitting the task this way are considerable. Combined with other design features, this unique approach to hard disk access allows it to perform many routine tasks faster than an 80386 system running at twice the clock speed.

Another interesting feature of the Opus disk system is called *skewing*, meaning that instead of being truly radial in arrangement, the sectors divide each track slightly after the one before it, as shown in Fig. 7-11. This means that the head has time to move from the end of the outer track to the beginning of the inner one while the disk is spinning.

When the tracks are lined up exactly, a head moving from a sector on the outer

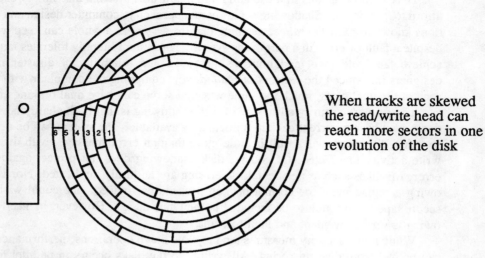

When tracks are skewed the read/write head can reach more sectors in one revolution of the disk

Fig. 7-11. Skewed disk tracks.

track to one on an inner track would have missed the start of the second sector on the first try and have to wait for a complete revolution of the disk before starting to read data. The Opus uses other tricks to speed disk access, including *caching*, which keeps recently read data in memory for as long as possible to avoid unnecessarily rereading from disk, and *zero latency*, which is a form of anticipatory reading of data from sectors as they pass the read/write head.

Security System Software

The Datasafe uses special system software to provide security features not normally standard on DOS machines. Its purpose is to restrict access to the computer to reigstered users only, and then to limit the areas and files such users can access. The software depends on the Datasafe being installed and set up by the person responsible for its security. Opus envisages the hardware and software being delivered separately, the software being sent directly to the system supervisor. Once the system is set up by the administrator, nobody can change the way the computer works without authorization.

The software is in two parts: resident and nonresident. The resident routines are loaded by CONFIG.SYS and AUTOEXEC.BAT when the computer is booted. In secure mode, there is no way of preventing this software from loading. The three main parts of the resident software are a small keyboard driver and two programs, RESIDENT and DIRLOCK. These stay in memory at all times, and perform the tasks of monitoring the user's requests to access files, checking them against the list of activities permitted to that user.

The nonresident software, ACJRMGR, is run by the administrator as part of the system security management. The program adds, removes, and modifies the details of users in the system's security files. The program LOGIN gives a user access to the system in the first place, while PCHANGE is used to alter a user's password. A further program, GBREAK.COM, reenables the keyboard break keys.

When the supervisor runs ACJRMGR, it asks for a user name. This is a named set of privileges. If the name supplied is a new one, a new set is created. An existing name can be modified. Once a name has been supplied, a QuickDOS II style disk map is displayed. Directories, and files ending in .EXE, .COM, and .BAT within the directories, can be either tagged to give the user access rights or untagged to deny access. After selections have been made, the Create User option writes files to disk that contain the details of the authorized files and directories, including file size, date, and time of creation as well as the file name. The ACJRMGR then asks for a password for this user. In the usual fashion, this must be typed in twice without appearing on screen.

A user created in this way can now get into the computer by typing the name and password on startup. To the user, the computer and any application programs look normal. However, any attempt to change directory to an unauthorized area results in a Directory Inaccessible message. Similarly, attempts to load prohibited programs return Access Denied.

These messages are the work of the two resident programs mentioned RESIDENT and DIRLOCK. RESIDENT monitors requests for access to program files and compares the name of the user making the request with the list generated by ACJRMGR when the account was set up or modified. If the requested program file does not exactly match those details, then the request is refused. Remember that the original length, time, and date of authorized files have all been recorded. This prevents you from circumventing the system by renaming a file to something innocuous. Also caught are files that might have increased in length. Becuase this is a telltale sign of virus infection, viruses can be quickly caught. The DIRLOCK program works the same limits on directories that a user attempts to get to. Even if the user creates a new directory, access will be denied because it is not in the list created by the security controller.

The Datasafe in Action

As you can see from this description, there are some tradeoffs in achieving security. The Opus system must be administered and even a simple task like creating a new directory will require intervention. Of course, in applications where the personal computer is set up once and rarely modified, which is the case in a wide range of office tasks, this might not be much of a problem and will actually be welcomed by some office managers trying to control an unruly herd of users.

There are also weaknesses. The memory-resident programs used by the Datasafe work by intercepting the program calls that are made to DOS by applications. This works much the same way as some network software such as TOPS. The application thinks it is making a perfectly normal filing system request, and MS-DOS thinks the request is coming directly from the application. However, RESIDENT and DIRLOCK are busy screening the flow of calls and checking everything against the lists. This results in a high degree of compatibility for software that sticks to standard DOS calls.

Unfortunately, some software, like the Norton Utilities, make calls directly to the disk and screen BIOS, and this bypasses the software. A hacker could use this to access the memory-resident files this way and alter them. Of course, if the security program files are themselves encrypted, this would be very difficult. System disruption rather than useful cracking would be the likely result.

The Datasafe is not safe unless it is administered, preferably as part of a planned security system. For an individual user who is his or her own supervisor, it is approaching overkill. But properly used, it offers large organizations levels of control that just do not exist on regular personal computers without the addition of expensive third-party hardware and software. The integrated approach of the Datasafe, combined with competitive price and performance, suggest it will successfully establish a new genre.

OTHER HARDWARE APPROACHES

At this point in time, few personal computers come with anything like the level of security built into the Opus Datasafe. Practically speaking, not all personal computers need that level of protection. One of the reasons that personal computers have flourished is that they are so flexible, with an almost infinite ability to accept extra devices and refinements. A healthy market exists in security hardware that can be added to personal computers to create an appropriate level of protection. These products range from the simple to the sophisticated, each covering a slightly different niche in the market.

The IBM PS/2 Floppy Disk Drive Lock, from Europa Systems, is an example of a very physical device. It prevents either the unauthorized insertion or removal of a floppy disk. The device consists of a metal casting that replaces the plastic panel covering the disk drive. According to the maker, "Effective protection is provided against removal of data from hard disk, use of unauthorized software, and the introduction of viruses into the system."

Damage to hard disk files can be prevented by hardware devices such as the Disk Defender, from Director Technologies, of Evanston, Illinois. Unlike floppy disks, hard disks in PCs have no device that stops write signals from reaching disk and corrupting or erasing its stored programs. The Disk Defender uses an expansion card and an external control box to overcome this design deficiency.

Disk Defender operates independently of any software and cannot be circumvented by any software. It lets you select part or all of the hard disk as a protected zone. The programs and data files to be secured are then placed in this protected zone of the hard disk. Disk Defender works with disks that have the ST-506/412 interface, which includes most PC compatible hard drives.

All or part of the disk can be write protected. While software defenses can detect intruders and viruses and minimize their effects, only hardware solutions give you complete protection against all efforts to erase or corrupt data. Once installed, the Disk Defender system is activated through the external control box, which can be placed up to five feet from the computer system. The operator turns on protection by placing the switch on the face of the control box in the desired protection mode. Status lights keep the operator advised on disk access, reading, and writing functions. The external control box can easily be removed if you do not want the operator to have access to the protected portion of the disk. Without the control box in place, the unit is in the protect mode at all times, and no one can get access to the protected portion of the disk.

A similar approach is taken by Guard Card, from NorthBank Corporation of Richmond, Virginia. Guard Card is an expansion board that provides hardware-based write protection for hard disks. The Guard Card prevents accidental erasures and formats when persons share a PC, such as in a networked system. The card supports one or two drives. Protection for one of the drives can be selective areas, if the disk is partitioned. Guard Card works with any ST-506 controller.

Stoplock 1 from PC Security is a printed circuit board that prevents access to your PC by unauthorized users. It will support up to six user IDs plus that of the system security administrator (SSA). The SSA is responsible for authorizing and distributing user-IDs. Once installed, Stoplock 1 takes control of your PC on power-up and will not allow the PC to be accessed until a valid user ID is entered, at which time the PC operates normally.

The Guardian Angel system from Protection Systems combines access control and encryption techniques to give you what the manufacturer refers to as "all-round protection from the assaults of the enemy!" Having restricted the use of the PC to specific people, Guardian Angel then gives access to particular files only according to each user's security profile. This is done by password systems or by subdirectory management. The full range of encryption facilities are available such as automatic or manual encryption, audit trails, and so on. Guardian Angel can be tailored for specific protection needs.

The DataSentry security system from Rainbow Technologies is an integrated hardware/software solution for protecting sensitive data from unauthorized access. The system is based upon a cryptographic algorithm and uses proprietary technology. Each user is assigned an individual DataSentry hardware key that quickly plugs into the personal computer's parallel printer port. The device is transparent to the printer and so does not prevent normal print activity. This type of hardware system is referred to as a *dongle*. The DataSentry software checks for the presence of the dongle and will not allow access unless it is present. In addition to providing system access control, the software can encrypt and decrypt sensitive files. Primarily used by software developers to prevent unauthorized use of proprietary software, dongles are discussed further in Chapter 11.

Another dongle system comes from Vault Corporation whose Romlok-P is a physical solution to the problem of software protection that can be applied to maintaining security of data. Attached to the parallel printer port, Romlok-P is known as a pass-through device, in that it does not interfere with any peripheral that might be currently using the port. Romlok-P requires few programming skills. Unless the user wants to, it is not necessary to make any modifications to the original source code that controls the system. Vault supplies a utility program with your initial Romlok order. This program will automate the necessary access control routines to check for the Romlok device.

PC-Guard Plus from Savtec Computer Technology is a hard disk security system designed to bring total control over access to IBM compatibles within a working environment by means of password protection. PC-Guard Plus will deny unauthorized users access to the PC or, if required, will offer only restricted access. As with many such systems, this has the added benefits of preventing unauthorized duplication of application software programs and aiding protection against viruses. Incorporated into PC-Guard Plus is a hard disk menu management system that complements PC-Guard Plus and ensures the same user interface throughout.

A series of products from Security Microsystems of Staten Island offer various levels of access control. The Lockit 1 system protects a computer from unauthorized use by requiring a user to enter a password before the computer will complete bootup. Once the correct password is entered, the computer can work normally. The program is available as a software-only system or as a combination hardware/software system. Both versions of Lockit 1 function similarly, the difference being the way each product handles floppy disk booting. Without a customized BIOS, there is no way to prevent a computer from booting from the A drive by means of a software-only product. This is a consequence of the way the BIOS ROM code was designed.

The Lockit 1 software does prevent access to the hard drive if bootup was achieved via a diskette in drive A. Thus, even if someone tries to get around Lockit 1 by booting from their own diskette, they will not be able to get at your data on the hard disk. However, with Lockit 1 hardware (an expansion card installed in the system), there is no way to get around the password protection because booting from the A drive is completely controlled.

Another feature of Lockit 1 is what the maker calls a "Lunch Break" screen and keyboard lock which allows a user to leave the computer on and running, but prevents anyone else from using or disrupting it. Reentering the user's password unlocks the Lunch Break feature. Lockit 1 hardware also prevents the breakout of the AUTOEX-EC.BAT file and can provide branching within a batch file based on which password has been entered.

Lockit 1 software is available with a single password for use on a computer that is only used by one user, or it can be obtained with an administrator option, which allows four user passwords and one system administrator or master password. Lockit 1 hardware comes standard with four user and one master passwords, but can be expanded up to 200 passwords with optional 50 password modules. An optional software encryption program is also available with Lockit 1, and a DES encryption chip is available for Lockit 1 hardware. Lockit 1 hardware or software does not require reformatting or encrypting of the hard disk.

Finally, a comprehensive hardware-based package that uses an encoded card to control bootup, is the Lektor 3600 (Fig. 7-12) from British Telecom. Before system startup can be completed, a unique encoded card must be placed into the card reader attached to the PC and the user's PIN number entered from the computer keyboard.

Fig. 7-12. Lektor hardware control unit.

The card reader is connected to an expansion card inside the personal computer. This card prevents booting from the floppy drive and also provides for proprietary file encryption. Once a user has logged on, special software controls the automatic encryption of files on both hard and floppy disks. The encryption can be extended to network and communications links. The Lektor system also provides true file erasure to prevent intruders from recovering data that the user thought was deleted.

SUMMARY

As you can see from this chapter, the inherent security weaknesses of personal computer design are being counteracted on a variety of fronts, from personal computers

puters designed around security features to a variety of add-on products. For those needing high levels of security, advances in technology are bringing biometric authentication systems into the realm of personal computers., Access control systems at the site and workstation level are becoming much more manageable, thanks to the database management capabilities of the personal computer itself. For those who need less than ultimate security, a variety of options are available to stop unauthorized persons from using your computer, right down to batch files that you can write yourself.

Come on Jack, just give me the password, then we can bring all of the boys back safe and sound.

Dr. Strangelove,
The Movie

8
Controlling File Access

WHEREAS THE PRECEDING CHAPTER discussed measures to keep people from using personal computers, this chapter examines control of access to files once someone, authorized user or successful imposter, has gained access to a system, or has intercepted a file being sent from one system to another. In discussing file access control, this chapter looks at available methods of file encryption, and the finer points of password selection and management. Many of the comments about password protection apply to both files being communicated over phone lines as well as to files stored on disk.

THE ROLE OF FILE ACCESS CONTROL

Some of the hardware and software techniques designed to prevent unauthorized users from booting up or logging on to a personal computer system do not perform ongoing user verification. This means that once the initial system access control requirements have been met, by either an authorized user or a successful imposter, the system is wide open to attack. The potential then exists for files to be deleted, copied, or examined. How serious this fact is in any given situation will depend upon an assessment of the need for security. When the need for security is low, basic system access control alone might be sufficient protection. However, in many situations system access control needs to be backed up by some form of file access control.

Introducing Cryptography

A good file access control system should have the power to render files useless to those without authorized access. Typically this means that the data in the file is scrambled or *encrypted*, using some form of password as a key (encrypt comes from the Greek *kryptos*, meaning key). Without the key the scrambled data cannot be unscrambled or *decrypted*. The science of designing systems for encrypting and decrypting information in order to make it secure is known as *cryptography*. In cryptographic terms, the contents of a file before encryption are *plaintext* while the scrambled or encoded file is known as *ciphertext*. This is a field of study that goes back many centuries, with the first European treatise on the subject appearing in the fourteenth century. The subject assumed immense historic importance during the World War II. The concentrated (and eventually successful) efforts of the British to break the codes used by the Germans to protect their military communications was a major factor in both the outcome of the war and the development of the first electronic computer systems.

Ever since WWII, cryptography and computer science have developed hand-in-hand. Beginning in 1956 in the United States, the National Security Agency (NSA), the government department in charge of monitoring the worldwide flow of information "in the interests of national security," provided tremendous impetus to improvements in computer hardware, pumping some $25 million into Project Lightning. This five-year development effort, intended to produce a thousand-fold increase in computing power, resulted in over 150 technical articles and more than 300 patent applications, and succeeded in advancing the frontiers of hardware design. Today, the NSA is widely believed to have the largest collection of super-computers in the world.

Much of the language and literature of cryptography is still oriented to protecting messages and communications. This fits the traditional data processing perspective where the weak link is communication between secure terminals and closeted mainframes rather than stolen copies of PC data files. This orientation can be seen in the definition of encryption, given by Seberry and Pieprzyk in *Cryptography: An Introduction to Computer Security* as, "a special computation that operates on messages, converting them into representation that is meaningless for all parties other than the intended receiver."

When applying cryptography to the world of personal computers, it might be appropriate to substitute the term "files" for "messages." Data does take the form of messages on personal computers when it is transferred from one computer to another across a network, or via phone lines. Practically speaking, data being transferred in this manner is exposed to a somewhat different set of dangers from those which threaten data residing on personal computer in an office. (The dangers inherent in communicating data between computers are specifically addressed in Chapter 12.) However, the role of encryption, to render files useless to anyone other than an authorized user, applies to both transmitted files and those sitting on a stand-alone personal computer. What is important to note at this point is that cryptography does not present itself as the primary defense against data theft or tampering. Encryption merely represents a third line of defense for computer information, after secure sites and secure terminals.

Nevertheless, classical cryptography is of considerable relevance to personal computer security. It provides a useful set of terms with which file access control operations can be discussed. Information that has been deciphered is said to be *com-*

promised. Deciphering coded messages is work of *cryptanalysis*, which is, according to Seberry and Pieprzyk, "a highly specialized facet of applied mathematics, drawing from such disciplines as probability theory, number theory, statistics and algebra." The history and study of codes and ciphers is known as *cryptology*, and many computer users will find it a fascinating subject, involving equal doses of mathematics, intrigue, and intellectual skill. Unfortunately only the surface of the subject can be touched upon here (Appendix C lists some excellent texts on the subject for those seeking more detailed coverage.)

The Role of File Access Control

Even though applied cryptography can provide personal computer users with levels of security that cannot be overcome without specialized knowledge and powerful computers, file access control should not be thought of as an alternative to, or substitute for, system access control. According to Seberry and Pieprzyk, the role of cryptography is to protect "information to which illegal access is possible and where other protective measures are inefficient." File access control should be a third barrier after site and system access controls, if for no other reason than that most file access control systems cannot prevent files from being stolen or deleted. In many cases, losing files can be as bad as having their contents compromised.

For personal computer users file access control is necessary not only as a defense against intruders who have defeated the site and system access controls, but also in situations where strict control over system access is difficult to enforce. For example, several users might share one personal computer system, or a system might have to be left running in a location where physical access is not controlled. Access control can be in place to prevent unauthorized users from starting up the computer, but once the system is up and running there might be times when the authorized user is not around, and an unauthorized user can spend time on the system. Additionally, as discussed in Chapter 12, files are at risk when they are communicated, over the telephone, via a network, or on disk sent through the mail. In such cases, file access control provides a valuable defense.

You might have observed that some of the system access control schemes mentioned in the last chapter also included file access control. In some cases, an integrated security system that provides both types of protection is appropriate. In other circumstances, separate file access control might be suitable. Some commercial access control systems will be reviewed later in this chapter.

A FILE ACCESS SCENARIO

To better understand the role of file access control, consider a typical scenario. Suppose it is widely known that you, the department manager, are preparing proposals for salary increases covering the staff in your department. You are using a spreadsheet program to do this. Staff members are naturally curious about your proposed figures, but you do not want to reveal them.

The Barriers to Access

As an initial precaution, you turn off your computer when you go to lunch. You also lock the keyboard, slipping the key in a drawer of your desk. While you are out, a particularly curious employee cannot resist temptation and enters your office, hoping to find the salary recommendations. Because you have left no tell-tale paperwork on your desk, the employee decides to look for the information on your personal computer. The machine is turned on. Finding the keyboard locked, the interloper, no respecter of privacy, checks your desk drawers, sees the key, and uses it to unlock the keyboard. Your computer has no other access control system and so the employee, having turned on your machine and unlocked the keyboard, is free to browse the files and directories on the system to find the information that is the target of his or her curiosity.

This is the point at which to ask: What barriers remain between the interloper and the desired data?

- File type. If the interloper does not know which application you used to create the file, this will slow down the search.

- File name. If the interloper does not know the name of the target file, the name will have to be guessed or deduced.

- File access control. If you have used some form of file access control, the interloper will have to defeat it.

Relative Effectiveness

The next question to ask is: How effective are these barriers, in terms of normal office practice? As far as file type is concerned, the interloper is likely to know this already, or be able to figure it out fairly easily. The names of the programs that you use on your PC are not likely to be a secret. Indeed, the department or entire organization might have a computing standard that dictates which programs you use. Apart from this, many personal computers have a menu system that facilitates access to the main programs when the system starts up, further simplifying the task of getting to where the target file is likely to be. Given a known collection of programs, determining the one you have used to come up with salary recommendations is likely to be an easy task. The most likely candidate is a spreadsheet. In other words, the first barrier is not very effective.

The second barrier, file name, pits convenience against caution. In general, your work as a computer user is much easier if you are free to name your files in a logical manner, using names that reflect the contents. Thus a worksheet containing salary recommendations for 1991 might be called SALREC91.WK1. Of course, this makes it fairly easy for an interloper to find the file, but what is the alternative? If you start adopting file names that are deceptive, or uninformative, then you will have to develop a cross-reference system for your own use. This is inconvenient to say the least.

The third barrier, file access control, is the one that really works. There is a measure of inconvenience with all file access control systems, but this is justified by the effectiveness of the barrier. Suppose that, in the above scenario, the interloper has loaded your spreadsheet program and has used the program's File Open command to look at a list of your files, as shown in Fig. 8-1.

Fig. 8-1. Opening a file in 1-2-3 Release 3.

In this case, the spreadsheet program is 1-2-3 Release 3. The salary file is clearly visible in the list, and the interloper is dangerously close to succeeding. However, you have used the program's password protection system. This means that the file was saved using a variation of the normal File Save command in which a password was entered. The data in the file was scrambled or encrypted using the password as a key. Without the key the scrambled data cannot be decrypted. The interloper attempts to complete the File Open command, typing in a five letter password, only to get the ERROR message shown in Fig. 8-2.

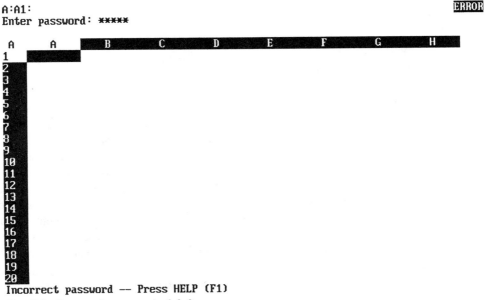

Fig. 8-2. Protected message in 1-2-3.

At this point, the interloper really has only one option: guess the password. As you can see, the password itself is not shown on the screen as the user types it. This prevents the password from being revealed, and makes it difficult to type if you do not know the correct word. The potential strength of this barrier is considerable. Even if your password only used four letters out of a possible 26, the number of possible passwords is 4^{26} otherwise known as 4,503,599,627,370,500. If the password system is case-sensitive, then the number of possible words soars to 4^{52}. However, it must be emphasized that this is *potential* strength. If you use a "soft" password, such as your last name or your initials, then the password will not be much of a barrier to an interloper with initiative.

Later in this chapter you find tips on how to avoid "soft" passwords and more about how encryption systems work. Note that there is another option besides guessing the password and that is cryptanalysis, although in terms of casual office snooping this is not a "real" option. *Cryptanalysis* uses a variety of measures to analyze the encrypted data and attempt to decipher it without guessing the password. Only a professional interloper is likely to have the knowledge and skill needed to apply this approach to even the most basic password protection system. Cryptanalysis takes time and requires advanced programming techniques and powerful computer systems.

In the case of 1-2-3 Release 3, entering an incorrect password causes the file opening process to be cancelled. The only recourse is to try again. While it is not difficult to imagine a simple program written to automate the "guessing" of passwords, such a program would need time to run, given the large number of possible passwords. Some password schemes beep when given an incorrect password, further complicating matters for the interloper.

Lessons Learned

Before examining password protection systems in greater detail, it is important to see what conclusions can be drawn from this scenario. The first question that you might ask is, why turn off the computer before going to lunch? Most keyboard locks work without having to turn the system off. In this case it sounds as though the keyboard was locked as an afterthought, an impression reinforced by the casual handling of the key. If the key had been better guarded, for example, taken to lunch by the user instead of left in the office, then the interloper would have been quickly defeated. Given that the interloper can successfully boot up and use the computer the next factor to consider is the level of computer literacy the interloper possesses. Even to get as far as finding the file that contains the target data, the interloper must possess a basic working knowledge of the system. At this point, two different managerial attitudes can be detected. On the one hand there is the "the less they know, the better" school of thought, otherwise known as the "mushroom" method of management (keep them in the dark and only open the door once in a while to "dump a fresh layer of fertilizer" on them). On the other hand there is the "a little knowledge is a dangerous thing" or "a smarter employee is a better employee" lobby. This text finds itself in the latter camp, for the following reasons:

- You cannot master information technology with ignorance. While previous upheavals in commerce might appear to have thrived on the exploitation of ignorance (see information about the Industrial Revolution), the spread of knowledge is what drives the information age that is now upon us. Superior technical skills and knowledge are increasingly important keys to commercial and organizational success.

- Better skilled workers make a difference. While the direct productivity benefits of increased computer literacy in an organization are notoriously difficult to measure, there are numerous examples of the overall effect that widespread computer savvy can have. Government-fostered computer literacy programs in Singapore, Ireland, and India have started to pay handsome commercial dividends, snatching major software and hardware contracts from more established contenders.

- People will find out anyway. Attempts to keep employees from gaining technical skills and knowledge are bound to be futile. The individual who, driven by the prospect of higher earnings, seeks to learn about computers but is denied access at work, can learn at home or at any number of public training facilities.

Given that you have opted to foster computer literacy among staff, this does raise the specter of the interloper who knows his or her way around a computer system. However, the use of any of the password systems built into popular personal computer software is going to defeat an interloper who is not skilled in cryptanalysis and programming.

In situations where an interloper with cryptanalytical skills is a possibility, further measures must be taken. This means proper site and system access control. Because all cryptanalytical techniques involve a time factor, limiting the time during which such an attack can be mounted is critical. Furthermore, because the interloper would prefer to take a copy of the file that can be inspected elsewhere at leisure, techniques to prevent file copying are also an effective barrier.

A further lesson to be learned from the scenario described is the importance of password selection and management. This will be discussed at length later in the chapter.

FREE PASSWORD PROTECTION

The title of this section was chosen to emphasize that password protection is a level of security that is already in place on many personal computers. This is because many of the best-selling software programs offer password protection on their files. The list includes all major spreadsheet and database management applications, as well as leading word processing programs, such as WordPerfect.

Passwords in Action

In Fig. 8-2, you saw what happens when you try to retrieve a 1-2-3 worksheet that is password protected. In Fig. 8-3, you can see the way that WordPerfect reacts to a file retrieve request when the file has been assigned a password.

```
Dear Frank:

Here are the Salary Recommendations for 1991, based on the agreed ranking
system:

First     Last     Hired     Salary   Rating   Raise
Alan      Chan     08/14/87  3,301        1      297
Bill      Front    08/05/87  1,905        4      114
Emma      Wong     05/08/90  2,844        2      228
Jane      Dobbs    06/06/88  2,302        7       69
Jane      Folsom   08/11/87  3,091        2      247
Joe       Smith    07/25/87  2,750        3      193
Erin      Marissa  08/23/87  2,171        2      174
Nancy     Blass    10/20/89  2,052        3      144
Nina      Smith    08/21/87  1,850        7       56
Peter     Green    08/11/87  3,388        6      136
Sue       Wong     07/27/87  3,390        1      305
Will      Right    11/09/88  1,568        2      125

Please let me know if you have any changes to make.

Fred

Enter Password:
```

Fig. 8-3. Password request in WordPerfect.

This type of protection is available in both Macintosh and PC applications. A typical Macintosh example is provided by the popular database management program, FileMaker. In Fig. 8-4, you can see that FileMaker provides several levels of access controlled by passwords, from being able to browse records without altering them, to access to the entire file.

Note that in this case the user has typed the password, and the characters are not visible on the screen. This is a useful feature to look for in any password protection scheme because it keeps the password private. If the password is never displayed on the screen, it cannot be "stolen" or compromised by an onlooker. Also note that the type of protection offered by a Macintosh application is different from the basic "write-protection" that is part of the Macintosh system software. The latter is invoked by selecting a file on the desktop then using the Get Info option on the File menu. This gives you size and date information about the file, plus a very useful comment in which to make notes about the contents of the file, as well as the option to lock it, as shown in the upper part of Fig. 8-5.

Note that clicking the Locked box for a file does not prevent a user from reading the file, it only prevents any changes being made to the file. If you attempt to open a locked file, you will get a message like the one shown in the lower part of Fig. 8-5.

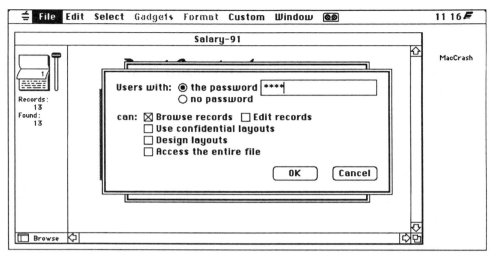

Fig. 8-4. Password protection on the Macintosh.

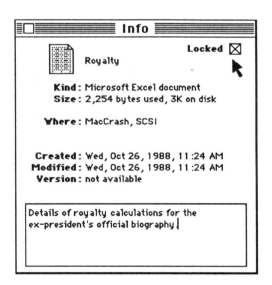

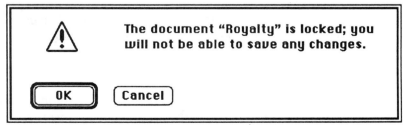

Fig. 8-5. Write-protection in the Macintosh system.

Password Commands

Suppose you are convinced that you need to use password protection on at least some of your data files. The next question is: How do you go about using the commands? Typically password protection is invoked by a simple variation on the program's normal file saving command. In 1-2-3, you type a space and the letter P after the file name when saving the file. This causes 1-2-3 to prompt you for the password. As you can see from Fig. 8-6, an asterisk appears for each letter you type.

```
A:A1:                                                    EDIT
Enter password: ********

A       A        B        C        D       E        F       G       H
1
2    Salary Recommendations                    For:     1991
3
4    First    Last     Hired    Salary   Rating   Raise
5    Alan     Chan     08/14/87  3,301        1     297
6    Bill     Front    08/05/87  1,985        4     114
7    Emma     Wong     05/08/90  2,844        2     228
8    Jane     Dobbs    06/06/88  2,302        7      69
9    Jane     Folsom   08/11/87  3,091        2     247
```

Fig. 8-6. Password requesting 1-2-3.

When the password is complete, you press Enter and 1-2-3 immediately asks you to re-enter the password. This verifies that the password was typed correctly, the assumption being that because you cannot see the word as you type it you might enter a mistyped password the first time. If the second typing of the word does not match the first, the process is cancelled and the save command must be repeated. If both typings of the password are identical, the file is saved and cannot be retrieved from disk without knowledge of the password. Only someone who knows the password can retrieve the file in order to remove the password.

Bear in mind that assigning a password to a file does not protect the file while it is in use. If you open the file by supplying the correct password then leave your computer unattended, the data in the file will be accessible to anyone who has the audacity to use your computer. See Chapter 11 for information about programs that allow you to temporarily "blank" your screen while you are away from your system.

Although you will find most major application programs have tried and tested password systems, you might want to do your own tests on programs that are widely used in your organization in order to reassure yourself on this point. Try attacking the system with the same skills and knowledge that employees have at their disposal. For example, in the case of 1-2-3, you might wonder if the password could somehow be circumvented by using the File Combine command, or, in Release 2.2 or 3, by creating a file link. You should find these back doors firmly closed. However, they are worth investigating because "security" is as much a state of mind as it is a tangible condition. If you are not convinced that a protection scheme is relatively foolproof, it will not help you rest easy.

Questions about Passwords

Obviously each program has its own method of invoking password protection, and this can be learned from the manual. The important questions at this point are:

- What constitutes a *good* password?
- How do you choose and remember passwords?
- How does password protection work?

All of these questions are dealt with in the course of this chapter. The third one is dealt with in the following section.

PRYING INTO FILES

Having entered a password, you might wonder whether such a simple act can ensure the secrecy of the information in the file. Because a vital part of any security system is the sense of security you get from it, a few moments spent examining the effectiveness of password protection is worthwhile. The first step is to look at how information is stored in data files.

Viewing Files

The simplest type of computer file is known as an ASCII or text file, one that is composed of simple strings of characters entered in rows that end in carrier returns. All of the characters used are of the American Standard Code for Information Interchange and can be displayed on a nongraphics display. In the world of PC-DOS, such files are also called DOS files (because they can be created in DOS by using the EDLIN editor or COPY CON technique) or print files (because programs communicate with printers in ASCII and in many programs files can be created by diverting information intended for the printer to disk).

You can use DOS to view the contents of a text file. The TYPE command will list the contents of a file on screen. For example, suppose a colleague has given you a file called SALREC91.PRN. You have a general idea of what the file contains but you want to check the contents of the file. You can use the following command at the DOS prompt:

```
TYPE SALREC91.PRN
```

The results can be seen in Fig. 8-7.

If the file is a long one, it will start to scroll off the top of the screen. The keystroke Ctrl−S will stop and start this scrolling, allowing you to view all of the file.

While a text file contains a simple arrangement of readable characters, the data files created by application software such as database managers or spreadsheets usually have a more complex structure. They are required to contain, in addition to the words and numbers, information about how the data is presented, about relationships between pieces of data, such as fields in a database record, or cells in a spreadsheet model. In Fig. 8-8, you can see an employee database file called SALREC91.DBF. This was created by dBASE and contains salary recommendations. Although the data can be read, the arrangement is clearly more complex than that in a simple text file.

```
C:\>TYPE SALREC91.PRN

Salary Recommendations                    For:      1991

First     Last     Hired      Salary   Rating   Raise
Alan      Chan     08/14/87   3,301       1      297
Bill      Front    08/05/87   1,905       4      114
Emma      Wong     05/08/90   2,844       2      228
Jane      Dobbs    06/06/88   2,302       7       69
Jane      Folsom   08/11/87   3,091       2      247
Joe       Smith    07/25/87   2,750       3      193
Erin      Marissa  08/23/87   2,171       2      174
Nancy     Blass    10/20/89   2,052       3      144
Nina      Smith    08/21/87   1,850       7       56
Peter     Green    08/11/87   3,388       6      136
Sue       Wong     07/27/87   3,390       1      305
Will      Right    11/09/88   1,568       2      125

C:\>
```

Fig. 8-7. Using TYPE to view a text file.

```
C:\>TYPE SALREC91.DBF
[        ° 7              FIRST     C                       LAST
C                HIRED    D             SALARY      N
 Alan     Chan   19870814    3301       1       297.00 Bill    Front   1987080
5    1905       4     114.00 Emma     Wong   19900508    2844        2      2
28.00 Jane     Dobbs   19880606   2302     7        69.00 Jane    Folsom   19
870811    3091       2     247.00 Joe      Smith  19870725    2750         3
    193.00 Erin     Marissa 19870823    2171       2     174.00 Nancy    Blass
 19891020    2052       3     144.00 Nina     Smith  19870821    1850
    7     56.00 Peter    Green  19870811    3388       6     136.00 Sue
Wong  19870727    3390       1     305.00 Will     Right  19881109    1568
      2     125.00
C:\>
```

Fig. 8-8. Using TYPE to view a dBASE data file.

Some data files store information in the form of machine language. While most ASCII codes can be read on screen, machine language is like computer shorthand. You can see this if you use the TYPE command with a 1-2-3 worksheet file, like SALREC91.WK1, which contains salary recommendations, and is shown in Fig. 8-9.

Machine language is used by programmers to issue instructions to the computer and can be read using a special program called an assembler. However, as you can see from Fig. 8-9, its meaning cannot be read directly from the screen with the TYPE command. Machine language is used to store information in less space than a plain ASCII file of the same data would require.

```
C:\>TYPE SALREC91.WK1
   ☻ ↔♦K ☻ ¼|♦ ≡♂o1Bm+┬û $ ïÑëHÑ¬
C:\>
```

Fig. 8-9. Using TYPE to view a 1-2-3 file.

     Most program files are stored in machine code and so using the TYPE command to view a program file like COMMAND.COM produces similarly unintelligible "garbage" on the screen plus several alarming beeps. While the TYPE command does not damage files, it should never be assumed that, because the file appears to contain garbage, it is expendable!

File Formats

The structure of a data file is called the *file format*, and most programs create data files that use a proprietary format, one that is supposedly unique to the program. However, because it is useful for programs to be able to share information, some file formats that began as proprietary are widely used, examples being the DBF format used by dBASE and the WKI format used by 1-2-3. Both of these formats are known by the three-letter extension used with the file name to distinguish the file type (as in SALREC91.DBF or SALREC91.WK1). Several extensions are reserved by program files. These are listed in Table 8-1. Some programs, such as WordPerfect, do not require specific extensions on file names although they do use a proprietary format. In Fig. 8-10, you can see a WordPerfect file viewed with TYPE.

The name of the file is SALREC91.WP5, but the WP5 extension is not required and is merely a convenience to help the user know which program created the file (WordPerfect 5.0). Although rather jumbled, the contents of the file can still be made out as a memo about salary recommendations.

In addition to proprietary formats, several formats have been designed with data sharing in mind. IBM developed the DCA-RFT format for word processing programs (from *Document Content Architecture - Revisable Format Text*). Both Macintosh and IBM PC software can read files in this format.

Another format for sharing is SYLK developed by Microsoft for spreadsheet type data (from Symbolic Link format).

Finding Files

Having seen that the contents of some files are readable with a simple DOS command, and that the format of common data files is widely known, you can begin to

Table 8-1. Program and
Other File Name Extensions.

BAK	Backup copy of a file.
BAS	Program written in BASIC.
BAT	Executable batch file.
COM	Program in compiled form.
DBF	Database in dBASE format.
DOC	Text, required by some word processors.
EXE	Program in executable form.
PAS	Program written in Pascal.
PRN	Print file, in ASCII.
RFT	Revisable Format Text.
SYS	System configuration file.
TXT	Text, required by some word processors.
WK1	Worksheet in 1-2-3 format.
XLS	Excel spreadsheet (not required).

```
?    3,301         1      297
                       Bill    Front   08/05/87    1,905      4         114
Emma     Wong   05/08/90   2,844       2      228
                                           Jane     Dobbs   06/06/88
  2,302      7       69
                       Jane    Folsom  08/11/87   3,091      2         247
                                                                      Joe
     Smith  07/25/87   2,750        3       193
                                       Erin    Marissa 08/23/87    2,1
71     2      174
                   Nancy   Blass   10/20/89    2,052      3       144
                                                                 Nina
  Smith  08/21/87   1,850        7       56
                                   Peter    Green   08/11/87    3,388
     6      136
                   Sue    Wong   07/27/87   3,390      1       305
                                                             Will    Rig
ht  11/09/88   1,568       2      125
                              Please let me know if you have any chang
es to make.

        Fred
C:\>
```

Fig. 8-10. Using TYPE with a WordPerfect file.

understand just how exposed your data is when stored in ordinary files. Indeed, some utility programs make it their job to help you view the contents of files. Hard disk organizers such as QuickDOS II usually have a View command that is a refined version of the DOS TYPE command. In Fig. 8-11, you can see the way QuickDOS presents a dBASE file.

```
Viewing: SALREC91.DBF          Press ESC to exit          (F)ilter: OFF
─────────────────────────────────────────────────────────────────────
♥[♦♦♀  ₧ 7                FIRST      C                        LAST
   C    ▯           HIRED     D    ▯           SALARY    N
              RATING     N                       RAISE     N    ♂▯
        Alan     Chan    19870814      3301       1    297.00 Bill    Front
19870805    1905      4      114.00 Emma     Wong   19900508    2844
2     228.00 Jane     Dobbs   19880606     2302       7     69.00 Jane    Fo
lsom  19870811     3091      2     247.00 Joe     Smith  19870725    2750
   3     193.00 Erin     Marissa 19870823    2171       2    174.00 Nancy
   Blass   19891020    2052      3    144.00 Nina     Smith  19870821    1
850      7     56.00 Peter    Green   19870811    3388       6    136.00 S
ue     Wong   19870727    3390      1    305.00 Will     Right  19881109
   1568      2    125.00→
─────────────────────────────────────────────────────────────────────
Commands: PgUp  PgDn  Home  End  1..9 (9 is fastest)  ↑ ↓  (H)ex  (N)ormal
```

Fig. 8-11. Using QuickDOS to view a dBASE file.

Note the Hex option that allows programmers to read the hexadecimal code used to store the file. Unless you are familiar with hex code, it reveals very little. Many hard disk organizers also have "find file" commands that can locate files based on partial file names or even file contents.

Another PC hard disk organizer that reveals file contents is Magellan from Lotus. This program used a feature called the Viewer to actually show file contents as they would appear in the program that created the file. As you can see from Fig. 8-12, this means that the dBASE file seen earlier in Fig. 8-8 and 8-11 is much easier to read using the Viewer.

When applied to worksheet files, like the one shown earlier in Fig. 8-9, the Viewer is particularly effective, revealing file contents otherwise invisible to the non-programmer. As you can see from Fig. 8-13, the program formats the data as it appears in the program that created the data file.

Magellan can display files in some 40 different formats, including graphics files. However, if the file is password protected, the contents will not be displayed.

Some utility programs, like the text search module in the Norton Utilities, will find files based on their contents. The program is given a series of characters, known as a *text string*, and told to examine the disk to see if any of the files contain this string. Using such a program, an interloper could quickly seek out the right file, as shown in Fig. 8-14.

In order to achieve this result, all that the interloper did was enter the following command:

```
TS *.* salary /S
```

```
Lotus Magellan Viewer          Press RETURN to quit Browsing         LIST
Directory: C:\*.*
   QD2.LOG            FIRST---- LAST---- HIRED--- SALARY--- RATING--- RAISE------
   SALREC91.DBF       Alan     Chan     08/14/87    3301        1      297.00
   SALREC91.PRN       Bill     Front    08/05/87    1905        4      114.00
   SALREC91.WK1       Emma     Wong     05/08/90    2844        2      228.00
   SALREC9P.DBF       Jane     Dobbs    06/06/88    2302        7       69.00
   SALRECL9.WP5       Jane     Folsom   08/11/87    3091        2      247.00
   SALRECP9.WP5       Joe      Smith    07/25/87    2750        3      193.00
   SYM.BAK            Erin     Marissa  08/23/87    2171        2      174.00
   SYM.BAT            Nancy    Blass    10/20/89    2052        3      144.00
   TEST.DAT           Nina     Smith    08/21/87    1850        7       56.00
   TOPSTART.BAT       Peter    Green    08/11/87    3388        6      136.00
   TP.BAK             Sue      Wong     07/27/87    3390        1      305.00
   TP.BAT             Will     Right    11/09/88    1568        2      125.00
   WARN.BAT
   WARN1.MSG
   WARN2.MSG



 File 19 of 33      SALREC91.DBF      5/04/91   6:20p        886 Bytes
```

Fig. 8-12. Using Magellan to view a dBASE file.

```
Lotus Magellan Viewer          Press RETURN to quit Browsing         LIST
Directory: C:\quattro\data\*.*
   SALES.WQ1          A1:                                              READY
   SALES2Q.WK1
   SALES2Q.XLS             A      B       C       D       E
   SALESNOW.WQ1     1
   SALESPER.WQ1     2  Salary Recommendations              For:
   SALESTAT.WQ1     3
   SALREC91.WK1     4  First  Last    Hired    Salary  Rating
   SAMPLE.WQ1       5  Alan   Chan    08/14/87  3,301     1
   SAMPLEF.WQ1      6  Bill   Front   08/05/87  1,905     4
   SCUTS.WQ1        7  Emma   Wong    05/08/90  2,844     2
   SHEET1.WQ1       8  Jane   Dobbs   06/06/88  2,302     7
   SHEET2.WQ1       9  Jane   Folsom  08/11/87  3,091     2
   SLIDTOA.WQ1     10  Joe    Smith   07/25/87  2,750     3
   SMITH@PC.WQ1    11  Erin   Marissa 08/23/87  2,171     3
   SMITHY.WQ1      12  Nancy  Blass   10/20/89  2,052     3
   SSVOL2.WQ1      13  Nina   Smith   08/21/87  1,850     7
   SSVOLREV.WQ1    14  Peter  Green   08/11/87  3,388     6
   SSVOLUME.WQ1    15  Sue    Wong    07/27/87  3,390     1
   STCSTUFF.WQ1    16  Will   Right   11/09/88  1,568     2
   STICKY.WQ1
 File 167 of 207    SALREC91.WK1      5/04/91   6:20p      2,910 Bytes
```

Fig. 8-13. Using Magellan to view a 1-2-3 file.

This tells the text search program (TS) to search all files (*.*) for the text salary, while the /S option tells the program to search through all subdirectories on the disk.

The Macintosh has a number of file location/examining programs. Many of these are installed as desk accessories so that they are available at any time. The Locate program shown at work in Fig. 8-15 can find files based on all or part of the file name or a section of the file contents.

```
Searching C:\salrec19.wp5

Found at line 9, file offset 1,831


Dear Frank:

Here are the [Salary] Recommendations for 1991, based on the agreed ranking
system:

First    Last    Hired    Salary   Rating   Raise
Alan     Chan    08/14/87  3,301        1     297
Bill     Front   08/05/87  1,905        4     114

Search for more (Y/N) ?
```

Fig. 8-14. The Norton Utilities locating a file.

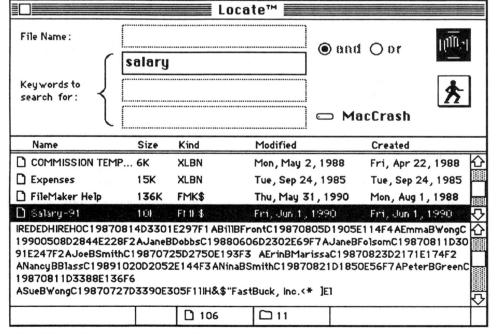

Fig. 8-15. Using Locate on the MAC.

Disguising Files

To combat this ability to locate and examine files, you can use the password protection built into the application you are using. For example, Fig. 8-14 shows how the contents of a memo written with WordPerfect can easily be revealed. However, if a password is assigned to the file, the results are quite different. The file viewed in Fig. 8-14 was password protected and then placed on a disk in drive B. The text search command was issued, but the program could not identify the contents of the file, as you can see from Fig. 8-16.

```
C:\>TS B:\SAL*.* salary
TS-Text Search, Advanced Edition, (C) Copr 1987, 1988, Peter Norton

Searching contents of files

Searching B:\salrec91.wp5

Search Complete

no files found containing the text "salary"

no occurences of the text "salary"

C:\>
```

Fig. 8-16. Failing to find search text on drive B.

Earlier in Fig. 8-9, you saw the way that the simple TYPE command reveals the contents of a WordPerfect file. Using the TYPE command with a similar file after it has been password protected produces very different results. As you can see from Fig. 8-17, the results are unintelligible, the contents of the file are safe from prying eyes.

```
C:\>TYPE SALRECP9.WP5
 WPCⁿ♠  ☺
             0■   ┐▒\@υ@{"\WGXTX.)–_IP½»p◄lg:hlheµ1my`┼`▬☺âê6x¦x°δt⌂iptq♀◄≈ü≈♦C↓r♦V
υS└º♀↓└↑nh¶GδxsVd#,ú–t>ñTY$»╗ t£V&♀t +<├▒╖╨╨╫╥╥╫N39.727AF;0&?;?I^#(>'#'QU+▀╙≥╘R
▒╧╥▒Ç║╟½·αΣÅà°≤σⁿ°ⁿ▄█φµ≡╓☺♀£_7▌▐1
                                   δ¥H▐‡▼=▌=P¿║+1p9=Kè=ⁿ╨╘î╘h6'‡'8r◄V~■––<0yt*.0
;7Jj–└0f‡beRñF2+/
C:\>
```

Fig. 8-17. Viewing a protected WordPerfect file.

Of course, you might need to protect data in files created by programs that lack password protection features. In this case, you can use a utility program like SuperKey that has a file encryption feature. SuperKey is a memory-resident program that provides a variety of desirable features lacking from the normal disk operating system. In addition to file encryption is screen blanking, keyboard locking, and macros that are independent of programs. Because SuperKey is loaded into memory before main application programs and stays resident while you are working, you can call on its services at any time by using a hot-key sequence. Normally this is Alt−/ key. Pressing this combination pops up the menu of commands shown in Fig. 8-18.

Macros	Commands	Functions	Options	Defaults	Encryption	Layout	Setup

Fig. 8-18. The SuperKey menu.

From here you can record *macros*, sequences of keystrokes, that can later be activated with a single key. You can also invoke the Encrypt command and assign a password to any file. For example, the SALREC91.PRN file shown earlier is wide open to snooping, as is the dBASE file. While dBASE contains password protection, you can use SuperKey to encrypt a dBASE file without using dBASE itself. In Fig. 8-19, you can see that SuperKey has been invoked, the Encryption option has been selected, and the name of a dBASE file entered.

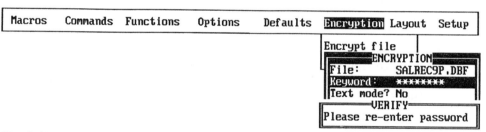

Fig. 8-19. Assigning a password with SuperKey.

The program then asks for a password to be typed in and this is represented on screen by asterisks. SuperKey asks the user to retype the password for verification, after which the encryption takes place. This takes place very quickly and the SuperKey program can then be put away. Anybody trying to see the contents of the file will be foiled, as can be seen from Fig. 8-20.

```
C:\>TYPE SALREC9P.DBF
Ñ·‚#ċ'£ÿHá )óí£("Qö RôNL╚P öQ╨N ₩ ▐z¥'&j(ëJðh'
                                    ê=öΣô 5 ─╱T4ô DJrà╚╠^bfì*
C:\>
```

Fig. 8-20. The file after encryption.

Attempts to read the file using dBASE or any other program that can read files in the DBF format, will result in an error, typically invalid file format. SuperKey does not monitor attempts to access encrypted files and so there is no automatic prompt to enter the password when the file is needed, even if the person attempting to use the file is a legitimate user.

SuperKey has other security applications, some of which are discussed later in the chapter. The encryption that it offers is effective and at two levels. The program comes with Borland's own encryption method, plus the method known as DES, which is described in a moment, and works with all types of files. An option even encrypts text files while at the same time keeping them in ASCII rather machine code. This allows the files to be communicated over some computer-to-computer phone links that can only handle ASCII files. However, the type of password facilities offered by SuperKey have several limitations. These do not concern the strength of the protection itself, which is virtually impregnable, but operation of the program: SuperKey's encryption cannot be automatically invoked to encrypt files whenever they are saved or prompt for passwords whenever they are needed for decryption. In other words, the program does not encrypt "on-the-fly." This requires a more specialized piece of software, such as SoftSafe from Software Directions.

Despite these limitations, SuperKey should not be overlooked as a password protection tool, particularly as it is inexpensive and many users already have a copy. SuperKey can encrypt and decrypt several files at a time, using DOS wildcards, as in SALREC??.DAT, which will include SALREC90.DAT, SALREC91.DAT, and so on. Multiple encryption assigns the same password to each file. Because SuperKey can be commanded from a batch file, it is possible to develop a system that leads the user through decryption of data files at the beginning of a session and then encrypts files afterwards.

THE TECHNICALITIES OF ENCRYPTION

In exploring the question of how password protection works, you have seen how the password-protected file appears to an interloper attempting to view its contents and how some programs handle requests for passwords. What you have not seen is exactly how the scrambling of data within a file is accomplished. You might want some assurance that this is done effectively, otherwise there will be the lingering fear that the hacker/interloper may be able to crack the encryption and decipher the data you have tried to hide. The first piece of reassurance is shown in Fig. 8-21.

This is a diagram of something called *DES encryption*. This is one of the most widely used data encryption techniques and, as you can see from Fig. 8-21, it is not for sufferers of math anxiety. After examining some of the mechanics of simple encryption, the DES method is looked at in more detail.

Practical Cryptography

The aim of cryptography is to develop systems that can encrypt plaintext into ciphertext that is indistinguishable from a purely random collection of data. This

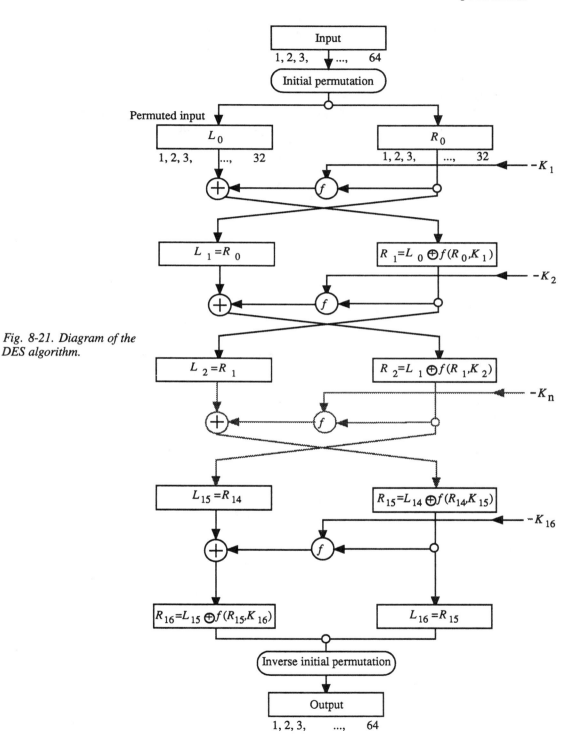

Fig. 8-21. Diagram of the DES algorithm.

implies that all of the possible decrypted versions of the data will be hopelessly ambiguous, with none more likely to be correct than any of the others. One of the simplest ways to create ciphertext is to represent each character or word in the plaintext by a different character or word in the ciphertext, such that there is no immediately apparent relationship between the two versions of the same text. The use of coded messages has ancient and distinguished origins. Writings on the art of cryptography appear as far back as the fourteenth century and there is evidence of the use of codes in classical Egyptian, Greek, and Roman times. Julius Caesar is said to have used a cipher in which the letters of the alphabet are simply shifted three places, as shown here:

Plaintext: A B C D E F G H I J K L M N O P Q R S T U V W X Y Z
Ciphertext: X Y Z A B C D E F G H I J K L M N O P Q R S T U V W

To encrypt a message you find each letter of the message in the plaintext alphabet and use the letter below it in the ciphertext alphabet. Thus the message:

BEWARE THE IDES OF MARCH

becomes

YBTXOB QEB FABP LC JXOZE

The key to this text is 3, which is the number of places the alphabet has been shifted. While easy to use, this cipher is fairly transparent because as soon as the cryptographer identifies one letter correctly, the rest fall easily into place. For example, since "the" is the most common three-letter word, testing QEB against THE reveals that each letter of plaintext has a fixed relationship to the ciphertext, a shift of three to the right.

This type of cipher is known as a *substitution* cipher and although this one is very simple, substitution ciphers can be very powerful. The relationship between simplicity of operation and strength against decryption is central to the selection of ciphers, and can be graphed as shown in Fig. 8-22.

On this chart, the ideal cipher is at position A. Getting to this position is difficult, as you can see if you look at a more complex cipher than Caesar's.

A Cryptographic Scenario

Put yourself in the position of the customs officer attempting to discover when an illegal weapons shipment will be entering the country. After raiding the office of an arms dealer, you are seated at the office computer. You discover a file called ARRIVAL, but when you use the operating system to view the file this is what you see:

YZYG JKZO RZOY XZRR KZRK XUXR JXRZ XUYK

The message is clearly in some form of code. At first glance, the code might strike the uninitiated as hopelessly complex. The person who encoded this text clearly substituted new letters for the original letters of message. However, to the experienced code-

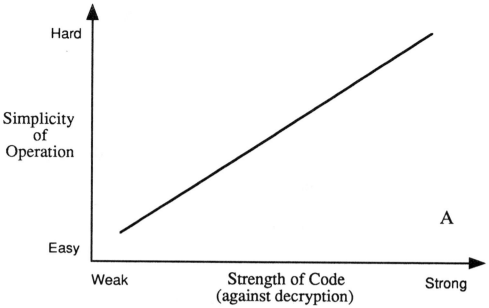

Fig. 8-22. The relationship between simplicity and strength.

breaker or cryptanalyst the task of deciphering this message is quite a simple one. To break the code you first count how many times each letter occurs in the text. This produces a list like this:

R	Z	X	Y	K	J	U	O	G
6	6	5	4	4	2	2	2	1

Next you reach for your table of frequencies, a list showing the relative frequency with which the letters of the alphabet occur in plain, that is, uncoded text, in a specific language. Not everyone has these handy, but they are easy enough to obtain, and two such lists are shown in Table 8-2. You can see the most commonly used letters in English are E, T, R, and so on. Assuming that the original message is in English, you can easily come up with a list that matches code letters to plaintext letters.

R	Z	X	Y	K	J	U	O	G
6	6	5	4	4	2	2	2	1
E	T	R	I	N	O	A	H	S

This gives the following:

YZYG	JKZO	RZOY	XZRR	KZRK	XUXR	JXRZ	XUYK
ITIS	ONTH	ETHI	RTEE	NTEN	RARE	ORET	RAIN

which is fairly easily decipherable as

IT IS ON THE THIRTEEN TEN RARE ORE TRAIN

Table 8-2. Letter Frequency Tables.

English

Letter Frequency by Letter				By Frequency			
A	7.25	N	7.75	E	12.75	U	3.00
B	1.25	O	7.50	T	9.25	M	2.75
C	3.50	P	2.75	R	8.50	P	2.75
D	4.25	Q	0.50	I	7.75	Y	2.25
E	12.75	R	8.50	N	7.75	G	2.00
F	3.00	S	6.00	O	7.50	V	1.50
G	2.00	T	9.25	A	7.25	W	1.50
H	3.50	U	3.00	S	6.00	B	1.25
I	7.75	V	1.50	D	4.25	K	0.50
J	0.25	W	1.50	L	3.75	Q	0.50
K	0.50	X	0.50	C	3.50	X	0.50
L	3.75	Y	2.25	H	3.50	J	0.25
M	2.75	Z	0.25	F	3.00	Z	0.25

Dutch

Letter Frequency by Letter			
A	8.25	N	10.25
B	1.75	O	6.00
C	1.00	P	1.75
D	5.25	Q	0.25
E	19.00	R	6.25
F	1.00	S	4.00
G	3.00	T	7.25
H	2.50	U	2.50
I	6.50	V	2.25
J	1.50	W	2.00
K	2.75	X	0.25
L	4.00	Y	0.25
M	2.75	Z	1.25

Despite the fact that this example was invented to make the decoding process fairly straightforward, it illustrates one of the approaches an experienced cryptographer would take to decipher something that looks at first glance to be very forbidding.

The encryption done in the above example is based on a simple substitution cipher using the password TRICK. The password is written out, followed by the regular alphabet minus the letters in the password. The ciphertext is the alphabet written backwards:

Plaintext: T R I C K A B D E F G H J L M N O P Q S U V W X Y Z
Ciphertext: Z X Y W V U T S R Q P O N M L K J I H G F E D C B A

To encrypt a message, you find the letters of the message in the top line, then read the code letter from the second line. Thus an "A" in the original message becomes a "U" in the coded message or ciphertext. Thus the message

IT IS ON THE THIRTEEN TEN RARE ORE TRAIN

becomes:

YZ YG JK ZOR ZOYXZRRK ZRK XUXR JXR ZXUYK

which can be further mystified as:

YZYG JKZO RZOY XZRR KZRK XUXR JXRZ XUYK

The splitting of the text into equal letter groups is done to further confuse the issue because patterns of word length can be analyzed statistically to reveal underlying text. To decrypt the message when you know the code is easy using the table of equivalents read backwards. Letters in the ciphertext are located in the second line the first line equivalent read off.

To the casual observer not familiar with frequency tables, the above cipher might appear to be quite effective. This points up a basic tradeoff in codes: If you need a basic level of protection, it is easy to get, but also easy to break, at least "for an expert." The qualification "for an expert" is important because you need to keep the role of encryption in perspective. The salient question is, Who can gain from decrypting the data, and what means do they have at their disposal? There is no point investing in powerful encryption hardware or software if those likely to attempt to read your files are not particularly sophisticated.

Implementing Encryption

The procedure used to encrypt data is sometimes referred to as an *algorithm*. In this context, the term is somewhat synonymous with *recipe*. An encryption algorithm is a recipe for scrambling information so that it is rendered incomprehensible. Typically, a parallel decryption algorithm provides instructions for unscrambling.

On a personal computer, encryption can be performed by software, as in the case of 1-2-3 or SuperKey, or it can be implemented through specially designed hardware that speeds up the encryption/decryption process. Encryption can be application specific, as in the mechanisms built into 1-2-3 or WordPerfect. Alternatively encryption can be application independent. This can be done by means of the operating system, or by a program that is closely allied to the operating system. SuperKey is an example of application independent encryption, performed by a memory-resident utility. However, SuperKey is not closely allied with the operating system. A program like Soft-Safe actually intercepts the file save or file open commands sent from an application to the disk operating system and inserts an extra step for encryption or decryption. This is referred to as password protection on-the-fly, and it makes the use of passwords more convenient. Of course, this does increase the time required to save and open files.

The Digital Research operating system for IBM-type personal computers known as DR-DOS, supports password protection but at the DOS level, rather than on-the-fly. This is a step in the right direction because password protection has long been accepted as a standard feature of operating systems for larger computers. It is likely that future versions of personal computer operating systems will incorporate encryption in the file save and open procedures.

When a programmer wants to include an encryption facility in an application, a utility program, or an operating system, several algorithms can be used. Ready-made algorithms exist, or the programmer can develop a proprietary algorithm. Both approaches have advantages and disadvantages. An existing algorithm will have been tried and tested. The level of equipment and amount of time required to break it will probably be documented. As long as the algorithm's level of difficulty is suitable for the application at hand, and the implementation is not too cumbersome, then the customer using the program will probably be satisfied. A proprietary algorithm, one that is not published, runs the risk of being compromised by a weakness that the designer overlooked. On the other hand, if the algorithm is *very* good, distribution of the program can be restricted.

The U.S. government, like several others, reserves the right to restrict the distribution of software that contains powerful encryption algorithms. Because these could conceivably be used by foreign and unfriendly powers to encrypt strategic communications and thereby hinder ongoing successful cryptanalysis. You might see software packages marked, "Not for export, may not be sold outside the U.S." The restriction on distribution of cryptographic methods is one reason for such labelling. Such restriction is in line with the thinking that restricts the sale of certain personal computer hardware to certain countries. The fact that just about any hardware available in the U.S. is freely sold in the Far East, where most of it is made anyway, makes a restriction on hardware practically useless. The fact that cryptanalysis is essentially applied mathematics, a discipline in which many non-American academics excel, makes the restriction on distribution of encryption technology equally dubious.

The bottom line for most personal computer users is that the commercially available encryption products are more than adequate. Only where the highest levels of security are required does the exact choice of algorithm make a difference. One of the most widely used ready-made methods of encryption goes by the name DES.

The Emergence of DES

The two goals for the professional cryptographer are to develop a perfect cipher and to point out the weaknesses in existing ciphers. The professional cryptographer has two main customers are the military and the financial services sector. These are the areas where the highest levels of security are required. Back in the 1960s, IBM saw that the growing role of electronic communications in commerce would create a huge market for reliable encryption methods. Over a period of years, mathematicians and computer scientists at the IBM research lab in Yorktown Heights, New York, developed a cipher called Lucifer that was sold to Lloyds of London for use in a cash-dispensing system. Of course, the NSA, with its ongoing mandate to keep on top of developments in cryptography was in close touch with the project, making regular visits to the lab (the constant flow of personnel between the NSA, IBM, and the mathematics departments of the major American universities tended to ensure that all new developments in the field were closely monitored).

At roughly the same time, the National Bureau of Standards was developing standard security specifications for computers used by the federal government. In 1973, the NBS invited companies to submit candidates for an encryption algorithm to be adopted by the government for the storage and transmission of unclassified information. IBM submitted a variation of its Lucifer cipher and, after extensive testing by the NSA, this was adopted as the nation's *Data Encryption Standard* (DES). The acronym actually refers to a document published as *Federal Information Processing Standards Publication 46*, or FIPS PUB 46 for short. This was published on January 15, 1977. The heart of DES is the Data Encryption Algorithm (DEA) that is described in a publication of the American National Standards Institute, titled *American National Standard for Information Systems-Data Encryption Algorithm-Modes of Operation*, 1983, as referred to as ANSI X3.106-1983.

    Copies of these documents can be ordered from the U.S. government, by way of the National Technical Information Service, U.S. Department of Commerce, 5285 Port Royal Road, Springfield, VA 22161.

The Technicalities of DES

If you are considering purchasing a data encryption product that uses DES, you will want to know how secure it is. The simple answer is: As long as you keep the password a secret, *very*. The only known method of deciphering data encrypted with DES without knowing the key, is the use of brute force. This involves the computerized comparison of plaintext data with encrypted versions of the same data, using every possible code until both versions of the data match. Suppose you use a 56-bit key for the code (more about bits in a moment). The number of possible combinations is about seventy quadrillion. If you could test one trillion possible keys per second it would take 70,000 seconds, or nearly 20 hours to try all combinations. On an average the code would yield about 10 hours after half of all possible combinations had been tested. Given that this amount of time would be required if the attacker had the use of an appropriately programmed, purpose-built super-computer capable of testing one trillion keys per second, you have some idea of the league your attacker would be in. Suffice it to say that for general business purposes, in which the potential benefits to an attacker are less than six figures, the DES provides an adequate level of security.

If you are still not reassured, then you might want to compare the flow chart of the DEA in Fig. 8-21 with the description presented in Table 8-3. Your opponent has to be a party to whom such specifications represent light reading. Technically speaking, the DEA is a combined substitution/transposition cipher, a product cipher that operates on blocks of data 64 bits, or 8 bytes, in length. Remember that a bit is a simple 1 or 0 and with 8 bits you can have 256 different combinations, so 8 bits are often used to represent one character, or byte. Using 56 bits for the key gives room for 7 characters, each of which can be one of 256 possible characters, thus the possible combinations are 256^7 or (2^{56}) or 72,057,594,037,927,940, the number in the region of 70 quadrillion referred to earlier.

Table 8-3. The Data Encryption Standard.

This following description is based on ANSI X3.106-1983, as presented by George Sassoon in *The Radio Hacker's Code Book*:

The input is taken in 64 bit chunks. The key is 56 bits in length. Each 64 bit slice of data is first thoroughly scrambled according to a fixed scheme in an initial permutation (known as IP). It is then split into two 32-bit halves designated left and right. The two halves are then subjected to 16 "rounds" of treatment as follows: at each round, the right half is transferred unchanged to the left half. The right half is also expanded from 32 to 48 bits. This is done by duplicating some bits. The result is then exclusive-ORed with a 48-bit permutation of the 56-bit key.

The output from this operation is then split into eight 6-bit blocks, each of which is subjected to a different Boolean substitution into a 4-bit "S-block." That is, each of the eight "S-blocks" can have an input in the range 0 to 63, and for each input it gives a random-looking output in the range 0 to 15. These substitutions are not in fact random, but chosen by IBM for maximum security. The eight 4-bit outputs from the S-blocks are then recombined via a further permutation (2P) in a 32-bit register. The contents of this will be a thoroughly scrambled function of the original right-hand half of the data input and the 48-bit key permutation. The said contents are then exclusive-ORed with the original lefthand of the input data; and the result of this becomes the new 32-bit right-hand half. The new left-hand half is, as mentioned above, the unchanged original right-hand half.

This process is repeated 16 times. At each stage the 48 bits used for the key area are a different permutation of the full 56 keybits. Finally, the two halves are recombined in the inverse permutation to that carried out at the beginning, and the result is 64 bits of ciphertext. The scrambling is so thorough that changing just one bit in the plaintext input or the key causes the output to become unrecognisably different.

For decryption, the procedure is exactly the same except that the 16 key permutations are used in reverse order. Feed in 64 bits of ciphertext, and out comes the original cleartext.

DES Implementation

A good example of personal computer implementation of DES is the Eracom PC Encryptor, a full length add-on-board for IBM PC, XT, AT, PS/2 Model 30, and compatibles. This sytem provides encryption security for the operating system, program and data files on floppy or fixed disk drives, using the DES algorithm implemented in a VLSI chip (a purpose-built chip that uses Very Large Scale Integration). Options are available for communications and key storage capabilities. Keys used for floppy and hard disk encryption are combined with the individual hardware key mounted on the board before being loaded into the DES Processor. Boards are normally supplied with individual hardware key ROMs, but groups of boards with identical key ROMs can be ordered. The key storage section provides secure storage of up to 240 cryptographic keys (in battery backed CMOS memory) for use at systems and applications software levels.

The board contains the DES Processor, all bus interface logic, a basic system ROM with the kernel drivers required to implement the DES functions and a unique hardware key ROM. It encrypts/decrypts all data either written to or read from floppies or fixed disks that have ROM support. It also contains the system drivers to encrypt/decrypt information as requested by user application programs. All disk transfers are performed using the existing DMA channels. If insufficient DMA channels are available to support the cipher processor, a switch option allows automatic selection of direct I/O to the cipher processor. A factory-fitted option is available that disables standard disk encryption while permitting access to the various cryptographic facilities offered by the PC Encryptor Sub-System at the applications level.

The DES-LOCK from Oceonics is an operating system utility, which uses the DES algorithm to implement all of the approved modes of DES defined by ANSI X3.103. The DES-LOCK software is parameter driven and so can be incorporated in customized batch files on MS-DOS based systems. DES-LOCK employs very secure methods of key management and can be made available on other personal computer systems besides IBM compatibles.

Another DES product is RAC/M, made by Okiok Data Ltd for IBM compatibles. Short for Resource Access Control/Management, the system provides encryption using DES that is transparent to the user. In addition to performing background encryption of data in files on hard disks, hard disk partitions, and tape backups, the product also provides access control, access scheduling, a secure audit trail, key management, password management, secure partitions, secure key storage, and other forms of "tamper proofing." The product supports LANs and micro-to-mainframe communications.

Those who are interested in exploring the DES cryptosystem in depth before investing heavily in it should check out a piece of shareware called Private Line, developed by Surry P. Everett. It is available from Everett Enterprises of Springfield, Virginia. This package consists of a DES encryptor for MS-DOS personal computers and can be used with files in most popular data file formats. The software complies with the NBS requirements for DES systems and the package includes the tests. Private Line can be downloaded from many on-line services such as CompuServe, or complete versions or evaluation copies can be ordered direct from the company. (The term shareware refers to software that you can try for free, but for which you are obliged to pay if you decide to use it.)

A handy Macintosh utility with DES capability is PC Secure, part of Central Point Software's PC Tools for the Mac. This can be run as an application under Multi-Finder or installed as a Desk Accessory, so that is available at any time. When you want to encrypt a file, you run PC Secure and select Encrypt from the PC Secure menu, as shown in Fig. 8-23.

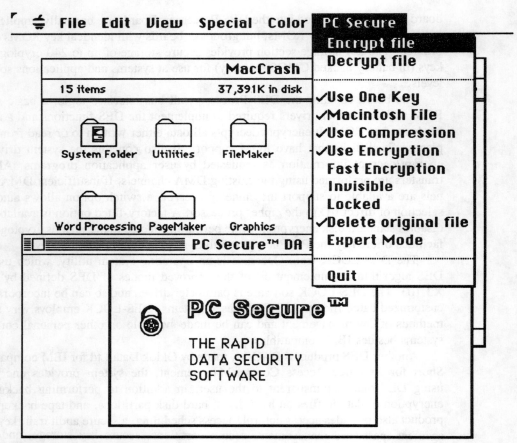

Fig. 8-23. The PC Secure menu.

Note the considerable number of options that can be selected to customize the operation. When you select Encrypt, the currently checked options are used. A standard File dialog box appears from which you can select the file to be encrypted. You are then prompted to enter a password for the selected file, as shown in Fig. 8-24.

As a precaution against short passwords, the program requires a password of at least five characters. The characters are represented on screen by asterisks to prevent snooping. Passwords must be entered twice. Encryption is very quick, handling a 100K Excel document in about 5 seconds on a Mac II, and this includes optional file compression, which saves valuable disk space (the 100K file was reduced to 17K!). Once encrypted, files are displayed on the desktop as padlocked documents, as shown in Fig. 8-25.

The encrypted file can simply be a coded copy of the original file, or it can replace the file. When you want to use an encrypted file, you double click on it. PC Secure is automatically loaded and a password entry prompt appears. The password must be entered twice and asterisks conceal what you type. When a file is decrypted,

r ⇌ **File   Edit   Uiew   Special   Color   PC Secure**

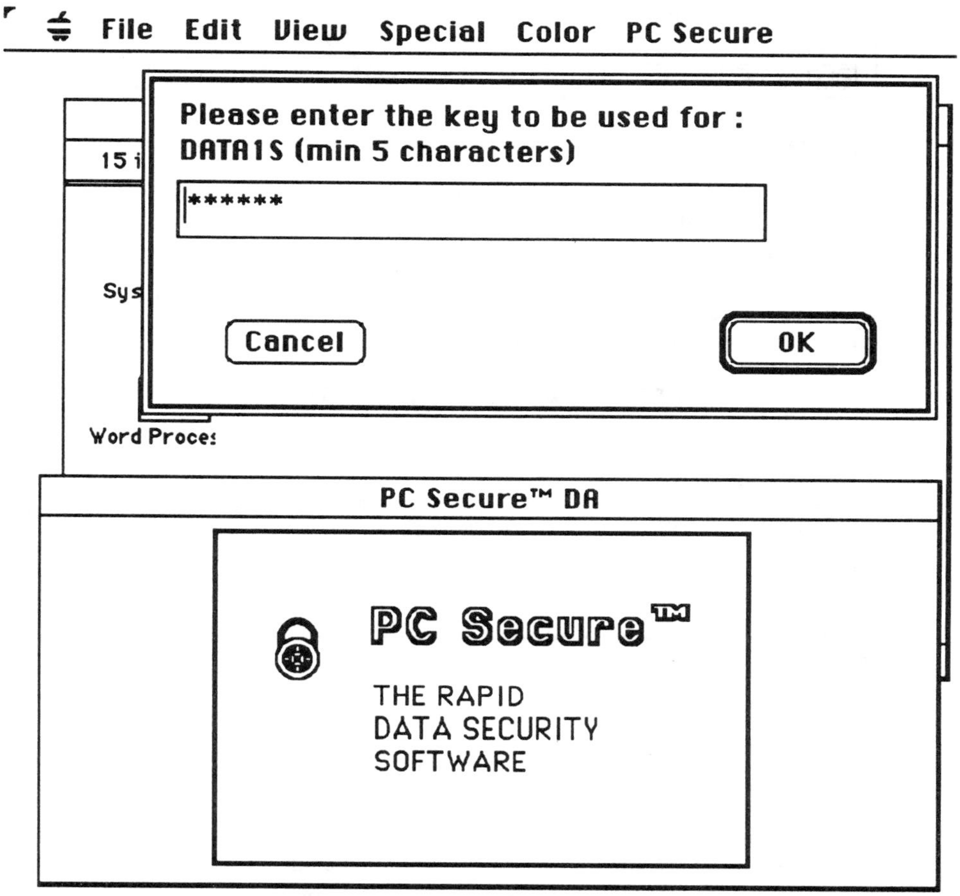

**Please enter the key to be used for :
DATA1S (min 5 characters)**

```
|******
```

(**Cancel**)   (**OK**)

PC Secure™ DA

🔒 **PC Secure™**

THE RAPID
DATA SECURITY
SOFTWARE

Fig. 8-24. Entering a password.

the original file is left on disk and a new file is created with the letters UNSEC added
to the end of the name. This file must then be resecured after changes are made.

PC Secure has a number of desirable features including making files invisible or
read-only. The option to compress documents at the same time they are encrypted
increases the incentive to use the program because it allows users to economize on
disk space. The encryption is fast, even when using DES and compression. Decryption is also quick and can be used while launching an application from double-
clicking on a document.

Although PC Secure does not work on-the-fly, it is nevertheless very useful. It
comes as part of a package of useful utilities, including a file finder called Locate, a
hard disk manager called the Optimizer, and PC Backup, a high-speed alternative to
Apple's hard disk backup utility. Like SuperKey on the IBM, PC Secure on the Mac
offers a choice between DES encryption and faster, proprietary encryption, the latter
being the only option in versions of the program sold for export.

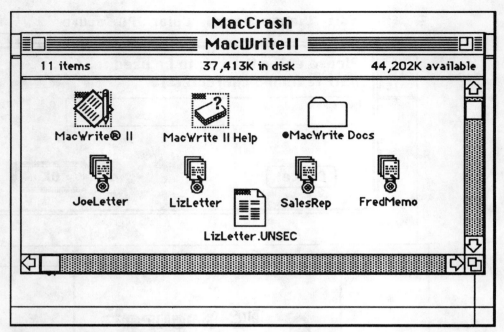

Fig. 8-25. Icons for encrypted documents.

Doubts about DES

If you think the value of your data does extend into the upper six figure region, then you might want to hear about weaknesses in the algorithm behind DES, weaknesses that a determined and well-heeled attacker might try to exploit.

The primary weakness is the length of key provided by the DEA. This is less than half the length of the key used in the original Lucifer cipher developed by IBM. There was considerable controversy over the NBS decision to approve a weakened cipher. Two Stanford University professors, Diffie and Hellman, pointed out that the DEA, as approved by the NBS, would be increasingly vulnerable to attack as computer equipment increased in power and came down in cost. The NBS dismissed any and all criticisms with the kind of righteous indignation typical of such institutions, and the NSA flatly denied any attempts to weaken the cipher. However, the general consensus is that the NSA had done just that, and, as British cryptographer George Sassoon writes, "Although both the U.S. Department of Commerce and IBM deny it vigorously, everyone in the know insists that the NSA enforced a halving of the DES key length to ensure that they themselves could break the ciphers even if nobody else could." Substantiation of this opinion came in 1986 when the NSA announced it would no longer certify the DEA for nonclassified use, less than ten years after the DES was approved!

 In *The Radio Hacker's Code Book* Sassoon points out that this type of behavior on the part of secret agencies is not new. The story of how, during WWII, the British broke the German Enigma machine ciphers is now well-known, but it was kept secret for some thirty years. Sassoon suggests that the probable explanation for this is that, after the war, all the German Enigma machines were collected up and sold to third-world governments, which continued using them, implying that "the British government had access to all their secrets for virtually no further effort."

The original Lucifer cipher used data blocks of 128 bits and a key of 112 bits. If this had been adhered to in the DEA the difference is the number of possible key combinations would have been staggering. While 2^{56}, the current key length, is a number more than 7 with 16 zeros behind it, 2^{112} is more than 5 with 33 zeros behind it. The practical consequence of this weakness in the DEA means that the search for better algorithms is still on, and the DEA is not likely to become established as a standard. New algorithms are constantly being put forward in academic circles and tested by an army of cryptanalysts. Some of those that show the most promise are known as "public key cryptosystems" described in a moment.

There are definitely some positive aspects to DES that recommend it for general business use. The fact that it is a standard means that you can send a DES encrypted file to someone who has DES software and, as long as you also give them the key, they can decrypt the file, even if they do not have the same DES software that you use. The cryptographic weakness of DES can easily be strengthened by double encryption, and you will see some security packages offering this feature. Double encryption more than doubles the difficulty of decryption, making it a task that is well into the realm of super-computers (like the Crays used at the NSA).

Public Key Encryption

Even with a longer key, the DEA would have a major weakness in common with all of the other password systems mentioned so far: The need to keep the password secret. When password-protected data is sent from one place to another, either electronically or by hand, the need to transmit the password to the recipient raises major problems. In cryptography, this is known as the problem of key-distribution. In fact, it is possible to develop cipher systems that enable the key to a particular file to be transmitted openly from the sender to the receiver. Such systems seek to address the classic problem of two people wishing to communicate in confidence, who have never met before, and who are linked only by an insecure communication channel. As Sassoon points out, "We are still no better off with DES than were the Elizabethan diplomats with their nomenclatures when it comes to the problem of key-distribution."

The answer, according to Sassoon and a number of distinguished cryptographers, is a public key system known as *RSA*, after its inventors, Rivest, Shamir, and Adleman. The RSA algorithm combines several mathematical concepts: modulus, exponent, factor, and prime number. For those whose math is a little rusty, the *modulus* of a number is the remainder when divided by a second number. Thus 3 is the modulus of 11 when 11 is divided by 8. Similarly 2 is the modulus of 42 when 42 is divided by 8 or 5. This can be expressed by saying 2 is 42 modulo 8. An exponent is the power you raise another to so 4 exponent 3 is 64 (as in $4 \times 4 \times 4$). The factor of a number is any number which, when multiplied with another number, produces the original number, so that 3,

4, and 6 are factors of 12. Strictly speaking, 1 and 12 are also factors of 12. A prime number is a number which has no factors other than 1 and itself. In other words, a number that can only be divided by itself and 1 (examples being 2, 3, 5, 7, 11).

How RSA Encryption Works

A very interesting phenomenon occurs when you increase a series of numbers exponentially and then find the modulus of each. For example, in Table 8-4, you can see the numbers 1 through 10 raised to powers 1 through 10, expressed modulo 10. Thus 3 times 3 times 3 is 27 and 27 modulo 10 is 7, the number listed in column 3, row 3. In fact, you can see that the results in columns 3 and 7 are the same. This pattern of repetition can be used to advantage. Consider this scenario: Two secret agents, called Black and White, need to exchange information. Black must tell White how many of the enemy's army nine tank divisions are battle-ready. There is no secure channel of communication. Black must communicate a number from 1 to 10 without revealing that number to anyone who intercepts the message. First Black cubes the actual number, that is, raises it to the power of 3. Then Black divides the results by 10 and finds the modulus. Black then tells the resulting number to White. Suppose that the correct number of divisions is 8. The cube of 8 is 512 (8*8*8=512) and 512 modulo 10 is 2 (10 into 512 goes 51 times, with 2 left over). So the message from Black to White is 2. Nobody who overhears this exchange can be sure that this is the actual number or a coded number.

Table 8-4. Modulus Calculations.

	1	2	3	4	5	6	7	8	9	10
1	1	1	1	1	1	1	1	1	1	1
2	2	4	8	6	2	4	8	6	2	4
3	3	9	7	1	3	9	7	1	3	9
4	4	6	4	6	4	6	4	6	4	6
5	5	5	5	5	5	5	5	5	5	5
6	6	6	6	6	6	6	6	6	6	6
7	7	9	3	1	7	9	3	1	7	9
8	8	4	2	6	8	4	2	6	8	4
9	9	1	9	1	9	1	9	1	9	1
10	0	0	0	0	0	0	0	0	0	0

So how does White obtain the correct number? All White has to do is raise the message number to the power of 7 and find the result, modulo 10. Thus 2 to the power of 7 is 128, and 128 modulo 10 is 8. This works for every number from 0 through 9. Although for 4, 5, 6, and 9, the secret number is the same as the original number, this simple technique has several of the elements of the best-of-all-possible coding systems. The person encoding the message does not need to know the key used to decode it, and all the possible decryptions of the ciphertext are indistinguishable from randomly selected messages. In this scenario, the public key consists of the numbers 3 and 10. The secret key is 7.

The RSA algorithm goes much further than this simplistic example, but you begin to get the idea. The following example follows more closely the actual working of the RSA algorithm. White chooses two prime numbers, say 5 and 7. He multiplies these together, producing 35. He then chooses a two digit number at random, say 17. He then sends 17 and 35 to Black as the public key. Black has a message to send. The message is 33. He raises the message to the power of the first key number, 17. He then divides this by the second key number, to find 33 to the power of 17, modulo 35. The result is the ciphertext, in this case 3.

In the meantime, White has created the secret key. He begins by subtracting 1 from each of the two prime numbers and finding the lowest common multiple of the two numbers (5−1=4 and 7−1=6, and the lowest common multiple of 4 and 6 is 12). The secret key is the random number selected as the first key number, modulo the lowest common multiple of the two primes, in this case 5, since 17 modulo 12 is 5. When White receives the encoded message (3), he raises it the power of the secret key and finds the result modulo 35, the product of the two primes (thus 3 to the power of 5 modulo 35 is 33).

Testing the RSA Algorithm

You can see that even with small numbers, some of the mathematics involved is getting serious. The result of raising 33 to the power of 17 is a 28-digit number. Nevertheless, you might think that the code is fairly easy to break. If you know the public key, you just need to find the two prime numbers that are factors of 35. However, the inventors of the RSA algorithm intended it to be used with very large prime numbers, over fifty digits in length. Some commercial implementations of the RSA algorithm use primes over 200 digits in length. With the right hardware and software, prime numbers of this size are relatively easy to find, but when you multiply two of them together, the product is very difficult to factor (try factoring 8633 in your head and compare the effort required with the straightforward factoring of 35; this gives you an idea of the way in which the problem of factoring increases in difficulty when moving from single digit primes to two digit primes, in this case 89 and 97).

The difficulty of factoring hundred-digit numbers provides the strength of the RSA algorithm, but you might think that such a problem, though daunting on paper, would yield easily to the power of the computer. In fact, this is not the case. Even the mathematics of the simple RSA algorithm example stretch the limits of personal computer software. At first glance, a spreadsheet program like 1-2-3 or Excel would seem to be a good place to test the math of the RSA algorithm, but these programs cannot cope accurately with the large numbers created and the results are not reliable. To test the above calculations on your personal computer, it is good old BASIC that fits the bill. The following code works with most recent versions of BASIC as long as they have

MOD and INT functions:

```
10 INPUT "Enter first prime ";P1
20 INPUT "Enter first prime ";P1
30 INPUT "Enter second prime ";P2
40 P = P1*P2:DP1 = P1 - 1:DP2 = P2 - 1:L = DP1*DP2
50 IF INT(L/DP1) = L/DP1 AND INT (L/DP2) = L/DP2 THEN L = L/2 GOTO
60 L = L/2
65 REM Use routine to calculate LCM
70 REM L is Lowest Common Multiple
80 INPUT "Random number ";R
90 PRINT "Publish"R "as Key1 and "P "as Key2"
```

This listing creates the public keys that are given to the person who will be sending the encrypted message. The program can then wait until the message is received, at which point the following code deciphers it:

```
100 INPUT "Ciphertext is ";T
110 S = R MOD L:Y = 1
120 IF S = 0 THEN GOTO 160
130 IF S MOD 2 = 1 THEN S = S - 1:Y = Y*T MOD P
140 T = T*T MOD P:S = S/2
150 GOTO 120
160 PRINT "Plaintext is" Y
170 END
```

The sender of the message uses the following program to encrypt the message using the keys generated above:

```
10 INPUT "Enter Key 1";K1
20 INPUT "Enter Key 2";K2
30 INPUT "Enter message";M
40 Y = 1
50 IF K1 = 0 THEN GOTO 90
60 IF K1 MOD 2 = 1 THEN K1 = K1 - 1:Y = Y*M MOD K2
70 M = M*M MOD K2:K1 = K1/2
80 GOTO 50
90 PRINT "Ciphertext is"Y
100 END
```

Bear in mind that this code is intended for experimental purposes only and is not presented as a reliable or complete implementation of the RSA algorithm. If you try this code, you will find it works as long as you use small prime numbers and a small value for the random number. Also, the number you enter as the message must be an integer greater than zero and less than the product of the two primes.

You might be wondering why the messages in the examples of RSA are numbers rather than the letters used in earlier examples of ciphers. This is simply done to leave out the added step of converting text to numbers. Using a system of codes, such as ASCII, any string of text and digits can be converted into a string of numbers.

Choosing Public Key Systems

The point of the RSA cryptosystem is to provide a means of encrypting information that is not compromised by the distribution of passwords. With secret key systems, such as DES, password or key distribution is a considerable problem. You encrypt valuable with a password because you suspect someone is trying to steal it or tamper with it. This implies that you surmise a motivated and skilled adversary, one who will use every opportunity to discover the password when it is passed from one person to another. This is not the stuff of Bond movies, but a serious practical matter that affects many areas of organized activity, from business to public institutions.

Suppose you have to send an encrypted file containing sensitive accounting data to head office. How are you going to let the recipient know the password needed to access the file? You could make a phone call, if you are sure it will not be overheard and you can be sure that you have the right person at the other end. You could hire a courier, send a sealed envelope, or encrypt the password, but all of these channels present problems. You cannot guarantee that the courier is honest or that the envelope will arrive intact, and the password for the encrypted password will itself have to be transmitted. You can have the recipient of the file provide you with the password before you encrypt it, but this is no guarantee that the password will not be intercepted. There are ways of making matters more difficult for the attacker, and some possible tactics are discussed later in the chapter, but the ideal solution would be to use a key that was useless to the attacker. This is what the RSA cryptosystem offers, encryption that does not depend upon the key remaining a secret, and which allows the receiver of the key to verify its source.

Other systems besides RSA offer secure key distribution. A method called SEEK is patented, trademarked, and marketed by Cylink of Sunnyvale, California. This uses an alternative algorithm for public key distribution. Cylink manufactures a range of DES encryptors that use SEEK for key distribution.

You might wonder how safe the SEEK system is, relative to RSA. Cylink has made available several articles on the subject. However, you should bear in mind some important factors when evaluating such literature. Evidence suggests that ever since the late 1970s when the DES algorithm was endorsed by the U.S. government and the RSA algorithm was published (by colleagues of Diffie and Hellman, vocal critics of the "weakened DES"), various government agencies have been at pains to encourage DES and disparage RSA. There have been well-documented attempts by the NSA and its employees to block conferences on cryptography where RSA might be discussed, and squash National Science Foundation funding for mathematical research that could refine RSA. Conducted under the guise of national security, this campaign has at times sought to include cryptographic research under the provisions of the State Department's International Traffic in Arms Regulations, equating publication of such research with the export of military equipment.

Furthermore, alternatives to RSA, such as SEEK, have been put forward in an apparent attempt to steer potential users away RSA. A prominent figure in the development of SEEK at Cylink was Dr. Lee P. Neuwirth, a former director of a place called the Communications Research Division of the Institute for Defense Analysis. Referring to the time of Dr. Neuwirth's tenure at the IDA-CRD in *The Puzzle Palace*, the controversial book about the NSA, James Bamford states that the IDA-CRD had "the most intimate ties with the NSA." This would seem to suggest that organizations and individuals who are looking for the ultimate in secure encryption might be well-advised to investigate carefully the origins of any systems that are considering adopting.

Even in today's climate of relaxed international tensions there is no reason to think that government agencies are any the less sensitive about technology that offers a high level of security. For example, few Americans who dream of patenting an invention are aware that patent applications are screened for military potential, first by the Patent Office and then by the Pentagon. The U.S. government reserves the right to classify any application as top secret, thus preventing further development, sale, or marketing of the invention. More than one commercial encryption system has come dangerously close to disappearing completely into this bureaucratic black hole.

Given this discussion, it is perhaps not surprising that one of the leading suppliers of RSA technology for computers is a Belgian company. Based in Brussels, Cryptech has an extensive range of RSA products, including purpose-built RSA chips, developers toolkits, and mainframe communications products. Their PC-RSA Security board is a high-performance processor card that gives full RSA capabilities to IBM compatibles. Designed as a toolbox for security projects, the card can be equipped with firmware to provide fast key generation, file encryption, and key distribution.

The Problems of Encryption

Whether you need to use a public key encryption system will depend in the first instance on whether you have to distribute encrypted data. For single users who do not share information, a public key system is largely redundant. Beyond this is the broader question of your assessment of the value of your data and the level of threat. After looking into the workings of some of the most powerful and widely used ciphers, it is time to assess the general value of encryption for data protection. If you rule out torturing the person who knows the password, the only two ways to defeat encryption are to crack the code or to guess the password.

Code-cracking is the focus of attention for theoretical cryptanalysis, which attempts to confirm or deny claims of complete security. It is also the concern of applied cryptanalysis, used by intelligence-gathering agencies attempting to make sense of large numbers of messages the exact origins of which are unknown. The raw data of such messages are simply collections of characters or codes out of which the original meaning must be reconstructed. As you saw earlier, the actual password can be secondary to code-breaking techniques.

In practical terms the second approach, guessing the password, requires knowledge of and access to the program that performed the encryption. This is probably more relevant to personal computer security where there is a likelihood that the source of the data file is known. For example, if you are attempting to get your competitor's pricing data out of a password-protected 1-2-3 worksheet, an illicit copy of which you have obtained, nothing can stop you from loading 1-2-3 and making repeated attempts to retrieve the file using a succession of possible passwords. Indeed, it would not be difficult to imagine a small program written to do just that. A list of typical passwords could be fed to the program and tried one after another until the file was successfully opened. However, only a very directed and determined interloper who would go to such length and the question of "reasonable precautions" again arises. You will need to match the type of security you decide to use against the potential loss from its failure and the resource level of potential attackers.

In most situations, the password protection offered by programs like 1-2-3, SuperKey, or SoftSafe, is effective against those attempting to discern the contents of a file. However, before instituting a program of security that relies upon such systems you might want to review their weak points. Essentially, three ways to attack the password protection schemes used on personal computers exist:

- Guess the password.
- Find out the password.
- Defeat the encryption technique.

The defenses against these attacks are:

- Choosing "hard" passwords.
- Properly managing passwords.
- Using proven encryption techniques.

You can see that these defenses relate to the three questions posed earlier:

- What constitutes a *good* password?
- How do you choose and remember passwords?
- How does password protection work?

So far this chapter has focused on the third question. It is now time to look at the first two questions.

PASSWORD SELECTION AND MANAGEMENT

Having seen how password protection works you know that one of the main weaknesses is "soft" passwords, ones that are easy to guess. The strength of the most complex encryption technology is rendered useless if the password can be obtained.

Soft Passwords

There is no point locking up the password if it is "Opensesame" or "pass" or the last four digits of your home phone number. While such commonly used passwords might defeat an inexperienced user who has inadvertently stumbled on a protected file, there is little chance they will present a problem for the experienced and determined interloper. Indeed, if you know the right people, you can buy extensive lists of commonly used passwords, compiled by experienced hackers. Take the case of the famous Internet worm created by Robert Morris Jr., son of an NSA official (the worm is described in detail in Chapter 10). This program gained unauthorized access to thousands of powerful computers connected on a worldwide network. As the program attempted to spread from system to system, it would encounter password requests designed to keep out unauthorized users. To overcome this access control, the worm program contained a password module. This consisted of some 400 commonly used passwords which were tried systematically, one after another. In an alarming number of instances, the correct password was indeed among those in the list!

Password Positioning

There is clearly a relationship between the ease with which a password can be remembered and ease with which it can be guessed. This relationship presents a dilemma for banks that provide automatic teller machines (ATMs) using personal identification numbers (PINs). The dilemma can be stated like this: If the bank allows the customer to choose the number, the customer will choose a number that is easy to remember, but that could make it easier for someone who has stolen the card to guess the number; if the bank randomly assigns the number to the customer, that makes it harder for the customer to remember, but probably makes it harder for the unauthorized user to guess. Of course, all sorts of qualifications can be placed on this statement. Given a meaningless number to remember some customers write it down and keep it handy, a boon to the thief who gets both the card and the scribbled number. On the other hand, allowing customers to choose their own numbers does not guarantee that they will remember them, or that they will pick a number that an unauthorized user can guess. The relationship between ease of remembering and ease of guessing directly affects how you choose passwords.

Choosing Hard Passwords

The ideal password is easy to remember and hard to guess. In order to work towards such a password, it is first necessary to look at what makes a password difficult to guess. Consider the following criteria:

1. There should be no logical connection between password and the user.
2. There should be no logical connection between passwword and the contents of the file.
3. There should be no discernible relationship between password and the date of the file.
4. The password should contain a mixture of characters, both uppercase and lowercase, plus numbers, punctuation, and special symbols.
5. The password should not be a "word."

	A	B	C	D	E	F	G	H
1	KJDW491	DWDN45	HMKI945	VVXA940	DSFK865	WPEH504	VRHK658	DMJT72
2	UNJB847	PXAD202	RKWX968	GKPY950	PXPA418	EOVF156	PNTQ919	MXAE347
3	SCYB652	LONH301	OIVA509	OMPC753	QMIY24	CGVW777	QPNT75	ILUV415
4	YRHC272	LNQB829	QVPA191	VXRW396	JANK373	DQDH48	BUTQ311	EBFY822
5	UFBT830	QJBQ567	ARFI982	TTRD825	WNHW382	UDYA802	FDEB922	DERO456
6	QFRV580	DFJB382	JTHK458	EVHI521	FLRP900	IMFO408	NQCB323	WFEO563
7	XPMC381	VGUE138	NTEN592	AFYV701	OQQS49	HEPI972	BXWG25	VIKV898
8	XUCT688	IGJU463	OWNR474	VOQJ889	DTPT437	THVA137	ANHO247	NLWE479
9	JXOI452	QSJU86	SKAU634	UVAO923	VKWW15	MFRT871	VNUA518	PLYQ987
10	NDNV343	GISS916	DGLY963	YGSP712	FUEF777	MTIN610	JAKH461	BURM150
11	KQVR812	YTXT790	QTJY480	YACQ501	AVBL833	IXLK390	DLWO301	HHRG270
12	SJCW609	QIBY41	XTIH615	BOBM189	RWNU312	EKVY261	TEHC13	WRMN548
13	KUJK274	GTRO893	LGEB203	NOYW598	WATW254	CSRC662	GFRN427	JJGS594
14	PIWS814	OJFS104	TGTF947	GTJO778	WBIB976	NJUY795	MAUW771	ELUG69
15	DJYN168	FETR741	UNTT323	KCGY966	QTDM122	DANN347	EEHL525	UDQU746
16	DLYL804	DIUW848	DCUB362	HYKH530	NUGL812	LXVY874	OJXS368	TDMG644
17	OUAL84	XXIC384	OAFS631	HNTQ339	UKSK419	YTXY731	WKCF826	SAIM306
18	EDDT936	NCBT450	WNBG219	THRT417	WBKW447	DUDY181	SEGL506	WMRU758
19	HEAB440	XJGK990	HBFA13	FBWG11	DBIH357	VDGW74	EHDE274	FTDF680
20	QLVM337	EUJM999	KFDT328	OSEH135	PWMI765	BFLB356	ODUK738	TYLV333
21	NMMB56	RBFW211	SGJT561	MEPH181	ELSV389	ITJM684	WUND869	OTMA723
22	FOEI853	SGDG712	GIKF820	YFWM683	AGPB527	COHP837	INAC458	HGVV263
23	PKAK400	YVVB771	WRKF489	DAYR706	JCJD271	DHXY36	DYQA400	UWSG438
24	HJWK215	YJUX74	WKCP725	BQPN861	NHTX817	QIMF906	IOMM127	NFCI874
25	NWTA216	EGCY292	NSJA485	LGBS263	FDEA810	BWGB634	TDHE314	IBYM244

Fig. 8-26. Spreadsheet of passwords.

Adhering to the first three criteria will decrease the threat from an attacker who knows the general subject matter of the file, or when it was created and/or by whom, and so use that information to guess the password. The last two criteria ensure that the interloper cannot simply try a series of ordinary words.

Consider the list presented in Table 8-5. This shows some of the passwords found by hackers to be in common use. While all of these words and their like should be

Table 8-5. Commonly Used Passwords.

ABC	DISPLAY	LOVE	PHONE
ABRACADABRA	ELEPHANT	MANAGER	REMOTE
AID	ENTER	NET	SECRET
APPLE	EXTERNAL	NETWORK	SEX
BANANA	FRED	OPEN	SYSOP
CALL	GARFIELD	OPENSESAME	SYSTEM
CENTRAL	HELLO	OPERATOR	TERMINAL
CHECK	HELP	OPS	TEST
COOKIE	IBM	PASS	TESTER
COKE	IDIOT	PASSWORD	TOP
DEMO	KEY	PC	XYZ
DEMONSTRATION	KITKAT	PENGUIN	

avoided, even these words would make reasonably effective keys if they were combined with suitably random numbers. For example, a password like PASS&6873 is very infinitely more obscure than PASS or even Pass. Used without letters, random numbers of at least four digits in length make a reasonably secure password (there are 1,000,000 possible combinations given four digits from 0 to 9). However, just as there are soft words, there are soft numbers, like 1234, 1111, 2222, 0101, and so on. Digits that are readily deducible, such as birthdays, parts of phone numbers, social security and employee identification number, should also be avoided unless disguised or used in conjunction with random text.

The ability of an encryption system to use punctuation and "special characters" is a valuable asset. For example, there are 256 characters in ASCII and only 62 of these are letters (uppercase and lowercase) and numbers. That leaves 194 other characters. Not all encryption systems recognize ASCII codes as valid characters, but many do, including programs like 1-2-3 and WordPerfect. This gives you the ability to use passwords like ☺ or the happy face that is ASCII code 1. Which ASCII codes a password system recognizes should be described in the program's specifications or manual and is worth experimentation. For example, in WordPerfect you would enter the sign for pi, which is ASCII code 227, by holding down Alt while typing 227 on the numeric keypad. The same technique works with Quattro and 1-2-3, although 1-2-3 does not recognize all of the ASCII characters when they are generated in this way. On the Macintosh, plenty of unusual characters can be created by using Option and Shift Option together with regular keys. The PC Secure program described earlier in the chapter allows the use of hexadecimal numbers as well as regular numbers.

Password systems that accept spaces allow you to use phrases as keys. A phrase like Time after time is easy to remember and not difficult to type. However, it is quite difficult to guess as there are 15 characters, the length limit in some password schemes. However, just as words that are easy to associate with the file's creator or its contents should be avoided, so should popular phrases and inside jokes. Again, adding numbers and other characters can strengthen the password, as in Chinatown, 1975.

Selection Systems

Those users who have to enter a lot of passwords might want to set up a system of password selection. One simple but effective method for a single user is to use words from a particular page of a book. This allows the word to be identified in the name of the file without revealing it to others who do not know the system. For example, many people keep a dictionary or thesaurus at their desk. To use this system you select a page at random and use the first word on the page. Suppose you turn to page 67 and the first word is cataclysm. For the first file you have to encrypt you could use 67cataclysm01 as the password. The file name could contain 671 as a code to help remember the word, as in SALES671.WK1. The code is of no use without the word itself. The second file could use the second word on the page, say catacomb, as in 67catacomb02, with the file using 672 as the code. Proceeding in this fashion, you have an ample supply of passwords that can be readily recalled.

Another source of random words and numbers is found in electronic spreadsheets. There is a RAND function in most of these programs that produces a random number between 0 and 1. This function can be used alone, or in combination with a formula to produce a larger number, as in @RAND*1000 in 1-2-3 or = RAND( )*1000 in Excel. To create a whole number, you can use the ROUND function, as in @ROUND(@RAND*1000,0) in 1-2-3 or = ROUND(RAND( )*1000,0) in Excel. Each time you recalculate the formula, you will get a different random number. This can be used to create a list or table of numbers from which to choose passwords. If you prefer to work in letters, you can convert the random number into characters. For example, the ASCII codes for the capital letters A − Z are 65 − 90. To produce a random number from 65 to 90 use this formula

65 + (@RAND*(90 − 65)) or 65 + (@RAND*25)

To convert this to a letter use the CHAR function, as in:

@CHAR(65 + (@RAND*25))

This will produce a letter from A to Z. For a three-letter password use the concatenation symbol, &, to connect three copies of the formula, as in:

@CHAR(65 + (@RAND*25))&@CHAR(65 + (@RAND*25))&@CHAR (65 + (@RAND*25))

Bear in mind that some programs will constantly recalculate formulas created with the RAND function and so you might want to "fix" the formulas by converting them to values (1-2-3 users can employ the Range Values command, while Excel users can use Paste Special Values). In Fig. 8-26, you can see a grid of passwords printed from an Excel worksheet that combines numbers and characters.

One way of using such a spreadsheet is to select passwords according to an index. For example, you could keep a copy of this sheet locked away, select passwords from it when needed. You could use the password as is, or combine it with another word used consistently, such as your name. For example XTIH615Fred, uses the password in column C, row 12. You can record the password in the file name, as in SALES12C.XLS. When you came to retrieve the file you would simply glance at the sheet, see that row 12, column C is XTIH615, and enter XTIH615Fred as the password.

A sheet of passwords like that shown in Fig. 8-26 is not something you would want to stick on the wall next to your computer. However, there are several techniques you can use to store your passwords in plain sight. Consider the word puzzle shown in Fig. 8-27.

By combining a random collection of letters like this with simple mnemonics you can easily keep track of numerous passwords like the ones diagrammed on the right. Suppose you use the spreadsheet program Quattro Pro. To password protect Quattro Pro worksheets you use letters starting in row 4, column 4, that extend in a diagonal like the cell coordinates of a spreadsheet. The password is MBMTGCFY, being 8 characters in length, like Quattro Pro file names. This is fairly easy for you to remem-

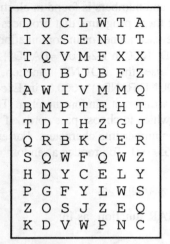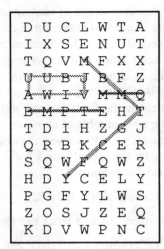

Fig. 8-27. A word puzzle for passwords.

ber, using the mental picture of Quattro=4 and spreadsheet=diagonal, but to anyone else, the table of letters is meaningless, with no combination more valid than any other.

Next you want a password for use with WordPerfect files. You use version 5.0 of WordPerfect. You go to column 5 row 5, and take 8 letters from there, reading to the end of the row and then at the beginning of the next row, like word wrap in word processing. This gives a password of MMQBMPTE, again, easy for you to find the otherwise random table. A user of version 4.2 of WordPerfect might use a 4 × 2 grid of letters, resulting in UUBJAWIV. A similar system can be operated with a favorite quote or a piece of poetry, neither of which will look out of place on your cubicle wall.

Hopefully, these suggestions will prompt you to come up with your own system of password selection. If you have to come up with a lot of passwords, for example, where a whole department is using passwords, then it might be necessary to adopt a centralized system where passwords are given to users, rather than chosen by the users themselves. Indeed, if employees are required to use passwords on files that management will need to access, then a management-controlled password selection system becomes essential. You can set up such a system in numerous ways. For example, there can be a daily password. The manager lets each user know the password for files created on that day. The user then combines the password with his or her initials, thus creating a unique password. Given a list of the daily passwords, the date the file was created, and who it was created by, the manager can determine the password.

The file management limitations of DOS mean that files can only bear the name of the creator if it is made a part of the file name, whereas Macintosh users can use Get Info to annotate files. Also, DOS changes the date on a file whenever it is saved, making the DOS date unreliable as an indicator of when the file was created.

This system has other limits. It leaves files open to any employees who keep track of the daily password. A variation is for each employee to have a unique password which is then combined with the daily password. If employees are given their personal password in secrecy and if such passwords are changed frequently by the manager, then the system becomes considerably stronger. The weak link will be employees not guarding their own words effectively. However, whenever a personal password appears to be compromised, the manager can change it. By keeping track of daily and personal passwords, the manager has access to all files.

Comprehensive Password Management

These comments apply equally to application specific protection, such as that provided by 1-2-3 or WordPerfect, and comprehensive password systems such as that offered by SoftSafe. If you are considering adopting a comprehensive password system, perhaps one which controls system access as well as file access, you must consider several important factors to consider.

Audit Trail. One of the advantages that comprehensive systems can offer over application specific schemes is an audit trail. In simplest terms, this means a record of password usage. This allows you to see who has been using a particular file or system, as well as what access attempts have been made with invalid passwords. The fact that all access is recorded is in itself a great deterrent to wrong-doing as far as insiders are concerned. A computer file or printed report that lists attempted access is an excellent warning system that lets you know that data is under attack. Of course, valid users sometimes enter their password incorrectly, but a good audit trail will record the actual entry, the date and time and system involved. This allows you to distinguish between genuine mistakes and attempted incursions.

Hierarchical Access. There is clearly a danger in demanding that users protect their files with passwords if said passwords are lost or forgotten, or if said employees leave or turn nasty. The need to get at data despite the password is a real one for managers and administrators. For this reason some password systems are hierarchical, that is, they allow for passwords to be applied at several levels. For example, the PC Secure utility for the Macintosh requires a master password be entered when the program is installed. This is a valuable back door for the system owner or administrator. When personal computer resources are networked, a hierarchical password system becomes essential if the system administrator is to control the level at which different users access the network's resources.

Password Log. Managers and administrators might want to be able to check the passwords that are currently being used. Some security systems maintain this information in a password log. Particularly useful in a network situation, such a log allows screening out of inappropriate passwords, such as user names. For example, an organization can easily develop a list of all employee names and initials. This list can be checked against a password log to see if anyone is using his or her name. This has a two-fold effect. In addition to weeding out ineffectual passwords, it discourages the habit of using soft passwords because users know they will be detected.

General Features. The other desirable features in a password protection system are that they are:

- Use a wide variety of characters, including uppercase and lowercase characters, punctuation, spaces, or ASCII or HEX codes.
- Require a minimum key length to prevent short passwords.
- Disguise the key length when password is entered or retrieved.
- Disguise the actual password as it is entered.
- Limit the number of failed attempts at password entry, locking the system or sounding an alarm to prevent attack by a list of potential passwords.
- Vary the number of failed attempts that are allowed.

Ongoing Password System Management

Having gone to the trouble and expense of instituting a password system, you will want to make sure that it is not simply put in place and left to run itself. Password systems quickly lose their effectiveness if they are not enforced, maintained, and monitored. Consider the following points when checking up on password-based security systems:

- Make sure employees are properly instructed in proper password selection and password rules such as minimum length.
- Develop a list of prohibited passwords to cross-check against those in use. Update the list regularly, and perform the cross-check at random intervals.
- Check that procedures are in place to promptly remove passwords assigned to persons who leave the organization. Check that procedures have been complied with, removing all redundant passwords.
- Check procedures to revoke the password of an employee who has been transferred from one department to another.
- If your password system does not have a minimum length requirement, verify the length of passwords being used.
- Some password systems can be activated by macros or scripts, which means that the user's password is kept in a file that might not be protected. Check whether users are employing such systems and verify that they are secure.
- Maintain a log of previously used passwords, listed by employee name.
- Check that you have a readily available up-to-date list of authorized users.
- If users are having difficulty remembering passwords, check the security of procedures for assigning new passwords and coach employees of safe methods of recording passwords.
- Monitor the number of illegal attempts to access files and note any increases.
- Compare passwords used by employees within a single department. Make sure everyone is not using the same password.

An ongoing effort is required to maintain the effectiveness of a password system. Reminding users of the rules and their responsibilities should not be left until a major intrusion reveals a problem. While maintenance operations are somewhat repetitive and boring, they are essential to maximize security.

COMMERCIAL ACCESS CONTROLS FOR DOS SYSTEMS

To give you some idea of the range of solutions now available in the "access control" category, this section presents brief descriptions of several products.

Segregated Files

One approach to providing file access control without completely destroying the open access motif of the personal computer is to create a secure area within the personal computer. This can be used for sensitive material while the rest of the system is freely accessible. The SecretDisk II from Lattice, Inc., creates new "logical" disk drives where all data and programs are always encrypted. Password-protected access can be turned on and off at any time without rebooting. Users can select either the DES algorithm or Lattice's FAST encryption method, which offers virtually the same degree of security but is 40–50 percent faster. Secret disks can be built inside of other secret disks for multiple levels of security, and the encryption algorithms can vary at each level. Files can easily be copied in and out of protected areas. All application programs recognize these drives, and programs can also run from inside the encrypted areas. A companion product, SecretDisk II Administrator, protects data from being lost due to user mistakes or from lost or forgotten passwords.

Another product that uses segregation is SoftSafe, from Software Directions of New Jersey. This product has already been mentioned as a software approach to file access control, offering on-the-fly encryption through the use of secure directories. To begin with, SoftSafe provides hard disk password protection. The controller or owner of this password can then set up seven authorized users of that PC, each with their own password. The owner can also delete users or change any password, and users can change their own password at any time. When working with sensitive data you can hit a hot key sequence to cover the entire screen with the SoftSafe password display. Then, only your password unlocks the machine, protecting your data from unauthorized access. In addition, SoftSafe automatically encrypts data in designated subdirectories, so only the user who generated the file or the computer owner can access the files.

As an added benefit, SoftSafe provides powerful virus protection for your PC. SoftSafe maintains a protected copy of the critical system files and compares these to the working files each time you boot up. If SoftSafe detects tampering, it gives you the option of replacing the infected files with a clean copy, or ignoring the change if it was intentional, such as with a DOS version upgrade.

Lockit II is a software product from Security Microsystems of Staten Island that allows users to create private subdirectories on any hard drive or floppy. This part of a series of products that offer various levels of access control. The Lockit 1 system was described in Chapter 7. The private subdirectories created by Lockit II do not appear on a directory or tree listing and are invisible to most of the common shell programs such as PC Tools, Norton Utilities, 1-Dir, and DOS shell programs. Entering a private subdirectory is done via the Lockit II CCD command, which functions like the DOS CD command except it prompts the user for a password. If an incorrect password is given, CCD places the user back in the root directory. Files stored within a private subdirectory are not accessible unless the private subdirectory is the current working directory. Other Lockit II utilities provided allow users to create, remove, and change the passwords for private subdirectories. Lockit II is completely compatible with DOS and does not require reformatting the hard disk to set up the private subdirectories. Lockit II uses less than 3K of RAM and installs by typing START.

To provide a second level of protection with Lockit II, an optional software encryption program is available to encrypt any file that can contain sensitive information. Because Lockit II depends on a device driver to protect the private subdirectories, it is more secure when combined with Lockit 1.

Lockit III provides a system of menus to limit a user's privileges on a PC. Each user is required to enter a log-on name and password to get on to the computer. Once logged on, each user can be provided an individual set of menus or can be given an access level of 1 to 99 within a general set of menus. Each menu-item can be assigned an access level so that users can only execute those applications that have an access level less than or equal to their own access level. An audit trail log is automatically kept to record the users actions and times on the system. Skeletal menus are provided as well as an easy-to-use menu builder program that allows a system administrator to set up menus of up to 8 levels deep. Menus can contain up to 45 items, and any application that can be executed from the DOS prompt can be run as a menu item. Even DOS internal commands can run as menu items.

Lockit III provides an excellent way to prevent hard disks from being reformatted, programs and data from being stolen, and unauthorized use of the computer. A data encryption program is provided and can be selected to work manually or automatically. Password aging, screen saver, custom logs, and automatic inactivity log-off are just some of the additional features. Lockit III provides a secure shell around DOS and can prevent access to DOS from within most applications.

General Solutions

The security software package Fortress for IBM PCs from Deloitte Haskins & Sells protects files, programs, and DOS functions from unauthorized use and encrypts data. Fortress provides supervisor control and security logging controlled by a menu system, as well as the basic facilities of password protection and encryption.

Crypt Library contains four easy-to-use data encryption subroutines that allow data to be encrypted from your program. Data strings are encrypted using several different methods that can be used separately or in combination. A password is used as the key to the encryption. The data is returned by using the same password during decryption. Without the proper password, access to the data is prevented. The routines perform both the encryption and the decryption functions. Use it once to encrypt your files. Use it again with the same password to decrypt your file. Double encryption can be performed by using the same routine with a different password or by using different routines. The only exception is provided with CRYPTH and CRYPTV. This guarantees that zero data values result in a Zero Encryption. This is to avoid problems with compilers that interpret the zero as the end of the string.

Drivelokr from Glenco Engineering is a software-based access control security system for IBM PCs. Access control can be installed onto floppies or hard disks. Password protection can be provided via the keyboard or one of Glenco's electronic Key Tags. Drivelokr provides restricted access to subdirectories for up to 16 users. These restricted subdirectories cannot be accessed until the user logs on to the system. Any subdirectory off the root directory can be marked as restricted for read-only or read/write access. A disk protected with Drivelokr has three types of users. The first two are authorized and are referred to as the SUPER USER and the USER. The third type is a general unauthorized user. Setting up the restrictions is optimized for simplicity and according to Glenco, "The system administrator need not be a technical wizard."

One piece of software that can make a big difference for a reasonable price is WPHD.COM, available free from on-line services such as CompuServe. Named as an acronym for Write Protect Hard Disk, this program protects hard disks from writing and formatting. This is particularly useful when you let someone else use your PC or when you are trying out new software. Run it once and it protects, run it again and it unprotects. Each time WPHD is run, it toggles the protection off or on. If the DOS FORMAT command is run when WPHD is on, the program will appear to format your hard disk, but it is actually verifying each sector, which does not harm the disk. (Data is not actually lost during a format until DOS writes a new directory and FAT, which WPHD prevents.)

The software File-Guard from Savtec Computer Technology consists of two floppy disks. One is a File-Guard program disk for locking and unlocking files, and the other is a manager's Master Key disk to be held in safe keeping for unlocking all locked files without a password. Once File-Guard is loaded, all instructions are available by pressing the F1 function key. The F3 key brings up a directory display from which you can choose files to be protected. After choosing to lock a file, you need enter your password, which can be up to 11 characters. The same procedure is used to unlock files.

Full-Scale Security

Trispan is a PC and LAN security system from Micronyx UK Limited that implements high-end security for stand-alone and networked PCs by providing:

- System access control, authenticating users before log-on.
- Resource access control, controlling users access to all workstation devices.

- Discretionary Access Control (DAC), limiting *who* can access data, *where* they can access, and *what* they can do with it (read, write, and so on).

Full auditing control logs all machine/user activities and violation attempts. In addition, Trispan provides Common Sign-On with certain LAN and mainframe security systems, an Application Program Interface and Central Site Administration that allows the security administrators to manage the security of a large geographically-dispersed PC population from a single central workstation.

Triumph! is a software version of Trispan, and one of the first software systems to incorporate use of an electronic key for user authentication. Also available from the same company is SIS, the System Integration Support package, which is an application program interface allowing security system developers to add trusted functionality to security systems implemented with Micronyx Trispan and Triumph. SIS comprises C subroutines and documentation allowing application programs to interact directly with the security "kernals" of Trispan and Triumph! to retrieve or set security rules from within an application. SIS thus allows the development of "trusted applications" and seamless interfaces with Micronyx protected workstations.

Complementing the other Micronyx products is Browser, a software product that displays and processes the audit accounting information produced by Trispan and Triumph! All significant PC activities and violations including information about user log-ons, file opens and creates, directory changes, idle time, program executions, and I/O port violations are recorded. By processing the data stored in this audit trail, true accountability of workstation utilization can be achieved. Reports can be produced that provide both security feedback as well as detailed information to help your organization manage and control this asset most cost effectively.

When a simpler approach is needed, Menugen from Microft Technology, Ltd., is a utility used to create password-controlled menus. Anyone with even elementary experience of operating system commands can use Menugen to set up menus to access all regularly used functions and programs on the micro. Users will then always be able to make a menu selection rather than be faced with a system prompt and no help. There is an option to prompt the user for a password before displaying the first menu. Only those program options authorized for that password will then be displayed. A log can then be kept of all selections taken.

Clam Data Protector is an extension of Menugen designed to protect information and programs stored on a microcomputer from unauthorized access. Authorized users are able to run activities and access information very easily by selecting options from user-defined menus or by typing in a command at the DOS prompt. Clam can also keep a record of all use of the micro. Each user has a password that identifies the user to the system and determines which menu options the user will see, and which file he or she can access. Clam is completely fail-safe. Data is protected even in the case of hardware breakdown or power failure.

Stoplock III from PC Security is a software-based access control and encryption device that prevents access to your PC, its files and application programs, directories, disk drives and physical devices by unauthorized users. Supporting up to 32 user-IDs plus that of the system administrator, it offers sophisticated management functions for a systems security administrator (SSA). The SSA can define system defaults and user profiles, file protection parameters, device access, and encryption. The system is monitored by a comprehensive audit trail. Stoplock III can be combined with the Stoplock Security Enhancement Adapter, a printed circuit board that prevents boot-up before sign-on with a valid user-ID and password. This combination is referred to as Stoplock III+.

Stoplock IV is a hardware-based access control and encryption device that prevents access to a PC, its files and application programs, directories, disk drives and physical devices by unauthorized users at the discretion of the systems security administrator (SSA). The system is monitored by a comprehensive audit trail. Security is enhanced by the AutoEncrypt feature that encrypts the entire hard disk. Should the Stoplock IV board be removed illegally, AutoEncrypt ensures the data cannot be read.

Stopper, also from PC Security, prevents the unauthorized removal of the internal components and add-in boards of your PC by securing the cover of the PC to the chassis and preventing power-up of the PC by covering the on/off switch. It is of a heavy-gauge, all-steel construction, including a special high-security key-locking mechanism of the type used by the IBM PC AT. Stopper also provides control of the monitor power port, eliminating unauthorized power-up of the system through the CRT port. The system is powered on and off with the turn of a key.

FOOTNOTE: THE SECRECY/PRIVACY DEBATE

As you might have gathered from this chapter, encrypting data is one of the few aspects of personal computing that comes close to being controversial. While the controversy occasionally ruffles feathers in the halls of academia or the underground corridors of power, rarely does it reach the general media, perhaps becuase the public would rather not think about the issues involved. Attempts by the government to prevent research into disease and pollution rate much higher than arguments over the security implications of applied mathematics.

However, when Rivest, Shamir and Adleman, developers of the RSA algorithm, had their National Science Foundation research grants withdrawn after their original paper was published, they were told to apply to the National Security Agency for further funding, there were clearly some serious implications for the rights of privacy.

Unfortunately, the argument is not simply one of freedom of thought versus government censorship and appropriation of intellectual capital. The power that secrecy bestows upon an individual or organization raises important ethical and political questions. Society as a whole must concern itself with the difficult issues of how much secrecy it is prepared to afford its members and how much oversight is appropriate for those involved in breaking down secrecy.

In recent years, the NSA has made overtures to the private sector to counteract the impression that it is stifling developments in cryptography that could benefit commercial organizations. Consider this statement, made in the IEEE Network Magazine:

> Prime users of a secure network of communications include the banking community who has a need for ensuring that funds, electronically transferred, are sent correctly: a message authentication problem. Similarly, the stocks and securities community, which operates on a computer network, has a requirement that the buy and sell of stocks are authentically sent to and from the correct person. In attempting to assist the private sector to overcome these problems, the National Security Agency, in the National Security Decision Directive 145 (NSDD-145), has adapted its Commercial COMSEC Endorsement Program (CCEP) to permit private sector access to CCEP equipment for ensuring the privacy of communications. (D.B. Newman, J.K. Omura, R.L. Pickholtz, IEEE Network Magazine, April 1987)

For those not familiar with COMSEC it stands for communications security, while IEEE is the Institute of Electrical and Electronic Engineers. At first glance it does appear that genuine assistance is being offered. However, you do not have to be paranoid to notice that one of the three authors of the article in which this statement appears is listed as Chairman of Cylink, which markets an NSA-approved public key alternative to RSA. If the two industrial sectors mentioned, banking and stocks/securities, were to adopt NSA-backed cryptosystems, this would seem to imply that such systems were well understood by, if not transparent to, the NSA. While this might alarm some citizens, others will point out that these areas of commerce have in recent years been the subject of extensive government investigations into insider trading, racketeering, and the laundering of drug money. The ability to penetrate the cryptosystems used in such immoral and illegal activities can thus be presented as a weapon for justice, rather than a blow against the right to privacy.

The dilemma can be presented like this: Suppose you are sending a file by modem from your New York office to an associate in London. You want to control who has access to the contents of the file and so you encrypt it. Should this make it impossible for anyone but you and your associate to read? These days it is generally accepted that any transatlantic telephone traffic is likely to be monitored by at least one intelligence agency. What if the file contains details of illegal arms shipments? Should you be allowed to keep this information completely secret? If the government holds the key to all codes and ciphers in what ways might it abuse this power?

In fact, the state of affairs posed by the last question is assumed to exist by many persons, including me. From the unclassified evidence available today it is reasonable to conclude that, with a few exceptions, the U.S. government does hold the key to all codes and ciphers. In the United States, the NSA has a mandate to monitor the worldwide flow of information, from phone calls to satellite signals. In order to carry out this task, the NSA has a budget many times greater than that of the CIA. A significant and growing proportion of this information is encrypted. Consequently, the NSA has invested millions of dollars in decryption facilities, including its own factory in Virginia for making specialized silicon chips that can speed up computerized code-breaking.

The DES encryption, popularized by the government itself, can now be unravelled in a matter of minutes by specialized super-computers. The one group of ciphers that can still pose problems for code-breakers are the asymmetric algorithms, of which the RSA cryptosystem is most widely known. The evidence suggests government agencies are nervous about this cipher because it is so hard to break. Whether the government has the right to look through the screen of secrecy that encryption allows you to erect around the files on your personal computer is a question that any democratic society should openly and freely debate.

SUMMARY

In some ways this chapter reflects one of the fundamental paradoxes of personal computer security: You can spend a lot of time and effort worrying about something only to find that there is nothing to worry about, if you act sensibly. For the majority of personal computer users, the password protection built into commercial application software provides ample file access control. Standard methods of encryption provide a good gain-to-pain ratio and will withstand all but the most sophisticated attackers, provided that soft passwords are avoided. For data files produced by applications that have no encryption facility, plenty of commercial third-party solutions, from general purpose utilities to specialized security systems, provide file encryption that is virtually transparent to authorized users. Combined with good site access control and a reliable method of system access control, file encryption forms the third, and probably the most reliable level, of static data protection.

Several subjects have been raised in this chapter that will be taken up elsewhere in the book. Chapter 12 looks into the particular problems of nonstatic data, that is, data being transmitted or communicated between sites and/or computers. That chapter also examines the complex matter of access control and passwords management on local area networks. The fact that any password system can be rendered ineffective by sloppy users raises the question of the human factor, discussed in depth in Chapter 13. Protection for systems exposed to prying eyes and inept users during normal operation is discussed in Chapter 11, which examines screen blankers, file deletion, and file recovery. Chapter 10 looks at the particular threat to files posed by virus programs while Chapter 9 looks at the best defense against file loss—proper backup.

*...and every prudent man will sooner
trust to two securities than to one.*
Earl of Chesterfield (1694-1773)

9
File Backup

IF THERE IS one single fact about data security that you should have grasped by now it is that your best protection against data loss is backup, the storing of current copies of all valuable files in a safe place. This chapter reviews some of the many alternatives for file backup such as floppy disks, tape drives, worm drives, and removable hard disks. The relative merits of the various technologies are presented, and specific product reviews are avoided because these too quickly become out-of-date. Indeed, the growing realization of the importance of this area of personal computer usage is reflected in a constant stream of new products claiming to offer faster, more convenient, as well as more cost-effective solutions to the backup dilemma.

THE BACKUP DILEMMA

Backing up computer data is rather like flossing teeth: everyone knows it should be done frequently and thoroughly, most people do it seldom, and seldom do it properly. From the administrative perspective, the dilemma is this: If we invest in hard/software to make backing up less tedious and time consuming, will people use it? Some managers are inclined to take a dictatorial approach and decree that "everyone will back up their data every day, or else." But the problem with this strategy, apart from its tendency to alienate the underlings, is that it is hard to enforce and noncompliance is typically discovered only when something goes wrong, at which point no amount of retribution can compensate for the absence of proper backup.

Why We Don't Do Our Daily Backup

The origins of the problem of inadequate backup can be seen in the way personal computing has developed. While security and backup systems have always been part and parcel of the hardware and software of mainframe computers, many of which were developed for the two most security conscious market sectors (the military and financial institutions), many of the early personal computers were developed with a zeal for "equal access to technology." This meant that backup facilities were initially limited to devices designed to copy files for others to use, rather than archive them for posterity. However, this was not a major problem until the appearance of hard disks for personal computers. When floppy disks were the only way to store data, users were forced to enjoy the advantages of a removable storage medium that could be locked away at night; for those who could afford "dual disk drives" archival copies were relatively easy to make.

With the arrival of hard disks offering fast and capacious storage, the amount of data handled by personal computers increased proportionately, as did the need for faster and easier backup procedures. However, hardware specifically designed to facilitate data backup was slow to appear and involved considerable extra cost. Early efforts to market hard disks paired with backup systems, and thus establish the concept of "don't buy one without the other," did not fair well. The storage capacity of floppy disks did not grow as fast as that of hard disks and floppies remained geared to the size of program files rather than data files. Furthermore, backup facilities within early versions of personal computer operating system software were primitive, in some cases limited to file-by-file copying. This made backup up tedious and slow, which did little to establish the practice as an integral part of running your own computer system.

Today plenty of inexpensive programs simplify backing up hard disks onto floppy disks, and floppy disk capacity has increased considerably. Reasonably priced backup hardware is available and is increasingly perceived as a desirable option. However, the fact that such devices are not universally accepted as a necessity is a continuing reflection of the early neglect of this area, as well as other trends in the history of personal computing. It is important to remember that even today the majority of personal computer users have had little or no formal training. What training they have had has tended to concentrate on breaking down the barriers of computerphobia and mastering complex command systems. Relatively few users have experienced training programs in which they were taught to perform daily backup as an indispensable part of everyday computing.

Unfortunately, this neglect has been reinforced by the general tone of personal computer retailing. Regardless of the intentions of the instigators of the microcomputer revolution, its effect has been to set up a promise of quick fixes and cheap solutions. Early efforts to turn personal computers into household appliances fostered an attitude inimicable to the more serious and tedious aspects of computing. The first wave of inexpensive home computers created the sense that hardware and software should cost less and less. This perception has put tremendous pressure on the profit margins of major vendors who have sought to support current products while developing new ones.

Very few personal computer makers have been prepared to buck the trend and advertise along these lines: "Our systems cost more, are less convenient to use, but are more secure and offer quicker recovery from disaster." As a consequence, the means to secure personal computers from attack and create backups have been, until very recently, perceived as "extras" and, as such, unnecessary. While there are signs that some vendors may now be looking to the added value of security features to give their products a competitive edge, the general tendency has been for organizations to keep adding to their installed base of personal computers without stopping to think about the full cost of supporting and protecting this growth in raw computing power.

What Can Be Done

The problem of getting users to adopt a proper backup regime can be tackled rather like good dental hygiene: Make it easy to do and make people want to do it. Making people want to do something is mainly a question of education. People need to be told why backups are important, and this means more than simply saying, "Because it is company policy." A positive approach is to present scenarios in which backup saves the day. Users should be made aware of the variety of ways in which data can be lost or damaged (without instilling a complete mistrust of the technology). You need not dwell at length on the sinking feeling that comes from seeing the message "error reading hard disk" and remembering that you haven't got a recent backup. The moral of such doomsday scenarios is immediately apparent. The stress should be on the relaxed and comfortable feeling that comes from knowing that you have current backups. An education campaign of this type can make use of the usual channels of organizational communication of meetings, memos, posters, and seminars. The campaign might be started with a special employee meeting, given some depth with a series of seminars, and then reinforced with posters and occasional memos.

Making backup easy to do involves some decisions about hardware and software. What backup media will be used—floppy disks, tape, optical disks, special cartridges? Is specialized backup hardware going to be used? If not, what specialized backup software will be used to assist in backing up to floppy disk drives? If the decision is to rely on the backup commands that are part of the disk operating system, will macros or batch files be created to simplify the procedures?

Beyond these questions are matters of policy, such as how often backup should be done, what files should be backed up, and where the backup media will be stored. Organizations might well want to establish clear guidelines on these matters so that users are clear about what their responsibilities are. Such rules and regulations can be incorporated into an education campaign. To summarize, the answer to poor levels of backup is to:

1. Make backup a policy, not an option.
2. Make backup desirable.
3. Make backup easy.

4. Make backup mandatory.
5. Make sure users comply with backup plicy.

BACKUP STRATEGIES

Before looking in detail at the various hardware and software products that are used to perform backup operations, it is important to look at overall backup strategies. Clearly there is no universal path to quick and easy backup. If there was, we would all be taking it and cheerfully doing our daily backup. The user with unlimited resources has some excellent options, the most attractive probably being rewritable optical disks. But the whole culture of personal computers is shaped by economics and the inescapable fact that most individuals and organizations do not have unlimited resources.

What to Back Up

To make effective use of resources devoted to backup, both the time and the money, you need to develop a backup strategy. It is important to consider what files need to be backed up, and how often the backup should be performed. Begin by considering the type of backup you need.

Image. Some of the first tape backup units for personal computers could only perform a complete and total backup of every file on your hard disk, referred to as an *image* backup. This might strike you as ideal, until you discover that this is a "warts and all" image, created by reading the surface of the hard disk track-by-track, including hidden files, system files, even unused areas and cross-linked files. This poses problems when you have to restore data. If the disk you have backed up dies and you buy a newer, better disk as a replacement an image backup might not fit properly on the new disk. Some systems only allow an image backup to be restored in its entirety, meaning that you get the bad along with the good. However, other systems allow file-by-file restoration of data from an image backup.

In some situations an image backup might be useful, particularly if you take a few precautions and accept a few limitations. The main benefit of an image backup is not completeness, but speed. By treating the contents of the hard disk as continuous stream of data bits, a lot of time that would otherwise be spent searching the disk for parts of specific files is saved. The amount of cross-linking and fragmentation of files on the hard disk can be minimized by making use of a disk optimizer such as Steve Gibson's Spin Rite or the ones found in the utility packages from Paul Mace and Peter Norton. Plan to use the image backup only on the same type of system and hard disk that you are backing up. This will avoid restoration problems due to differences in hard disk design.

File-by-File. The alternative to an image backup is a *file-by-file* backup. This involves the user selecting which files and directories are to be backed up and then the software reading and writing each one in turn. Typically, this takes longer than an image backup, but allows quick restoration of a single file or group of files. A file-by-file backup can also be faster than an image backup when only a small percentage of the hard disk has been used. A file-by-file backup can be complete, including all of the files on the hard disk, but this is different from an image backup. In a file-by-file backup, the files are read individually rather than as a pattern on the disk. You can see this difference diagrammed in Fig. 9-1.

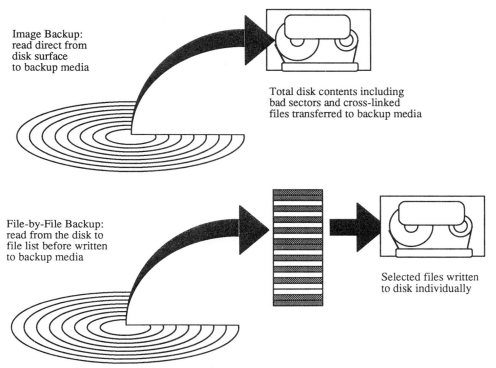

Image Backup:
read direct from
disk surface
to backup media

Total disk contents including
bad sectors and cross-linked
files transferred to backup media

File-by-File Backup:
read from the disk to
file list before written
to backup media

Selected files written
to disk individually

Fig. 9-1. Diagram of file-by-file backup vs. image backup.

When you are choosing the files to include in a file-by-file backup, you might decide you do not need to back up all of your files. For example, you might choose not to back up program files, for example, because you already have the original application-program and operating system disks. However, you should watch out for some subtle points here. A fully-functioning hard disk personal computer represents the result of an evolutionary process. Software has been installed and customized, utility programs have been added, batch files and macros created, system files tweaked for best performance. Recreating a hard disk system after a major crash involves a lot more than just copying back the data and program files. Installation of software can be a lengthy process sometimes involving numerous parameters, the right combination of which was previously determined by considerable trial and error. If you have no backup of configuration or user-preference files, getting the system back to normal can be quite a challenge. A good compromise is to make a complete backup at longer intervals, while backing up data files more frequently.

Now consider what you want to include when performing a data file backup. For example, font files for printers can appear to be data files, but they seldom change and take up a lot of disk space. You might want to omit them from a data-file backup. The same applies to spelling dictionaries and thesauri, which do not change. However, user-defined spelling supplements that are regularly updated might need to be included. The method you use to include or exclude files from a backup operation will depend on the backup software you are using. For example, on the Macintosh, files are marked document or application by the operating system and so backup software on the Mac may have a simple check box for "include applications." Backup software on the PC might have include and exclude parameters based on file extensions. Program files can be excluded by specifying the extensions EXE and COM, plus BAT, SYS, and others if you want to stick purely to data files. If you are consistent in your file naming, you might include all data files by specifying extensions such as DBF, WK1, DOC, and so on.

Incremental. Another type of backup that you need to consider is *incremental*. This refers to backing up only those files that have changed since the last backup. The idea is that successive backups of all data files on a hard disk are likely to include files that were already backed up. This slows down the backup process. Interim backups can be performed that only apply to files that have been added or modified since the last backup. Operating systems can do this by checking the status of files stored along with names and other directory information.

When to Back Up

Having consider what needs to be backed up, it is time to look at when the backup should be made. Obviously this depends on how often the information on a system changes. At the one extreme, a personal computer might operate purely as an information bank, perhaps it is used to look up pricing information. Such a system need only be backed up when the information is updated and the system could go months between changes. On the other hand, a personal computer that records customer orders coming in as fast as they can be typed might have to be backed up several times during a single day.

Most users operate systems that are somewhere between these two extremes. How often you back up typical data files, such as word-processed documents and spreadsheets, depends on how often they change, and this might not be a constant factor. For example, spreadsheets in the accounting department might change quite often while the budget is being prepared, but remain unchanged the rest of the year. So, the backup regime you implement will depend on how you use your computer. The three factors that need to be weighed against each other are:

- The amount of time and effort represented by changes to files.
- The amount of time and effort represented by backing up the files.
- The value of the contents of the files.

The interplay between these factors is not as simple as it might first appear. Take the case of a word processing file, 200K in length, that is accidentally wiped from the hard disk. If the file was created by a legal secretary transcribing dictation the file might represent a few hours work. If the file was created by a budding novelist who is also a two-finger typist, it might represent days, even weeks, of work, each word carefully chosen before being committed to disk. If the legal secretary does not back up the file and it is lost, the negative effects could be minimal. If the dictation tape has not been erased the file can be re-created quite quickly. If the aspiring novelist suffers the same fate, well, we could be talking major tragedy. However, what if the legal secretary's file contains a deposition obtained at great expense and due to be presented in court the very morning the file disappeared from the disk? In this case, it is possible that the failure to make a backup will have very real and costly consequences. On the other hand, if the novelist is unemployed and has no contract to complete the novel, then the financial consequences of the loss of the unarchived file are far less significant.

When you consider that it can take no more than one minute to make a backup copy of a 200K file you might conclude that the bottom line is simple: Back it up! But what if these two users were in fact adhering to an every-other-day backup schedule? The novelist, who created the 200K file over a number of days, might have most of the file backed up, while the legal secretary, who cranked out the 200K in a matter of hours, has no backup because the file disappeared between backups. Your immediate reaction to this might be, put both users on a daily backup routine. However, if the legal secretary creates or edits many megabytes of data a day, making daily backups onto floppy disks will be a considerable chore, one that is all too easily put off. If the data is important enough for daily backup, then it is worth investing in specialized backup hardware to minimize the time and trouble of a daily backup.

Hopefully what these scenarios make clear is that the need to perform backup varies between users and that only after careful consideration of work patterns can a suitable regime be established. When establishing a backup regime, you can combine the three levels of backup described earlier, based on three different intervals:

Interval 3   Total backup
Interval 2   Data file backup
Interval 1   Incremental data file backup

For example, if the interval is days, then every 3 days you do a total backup. Every 2 days you do a data file backup. Every day you do an incremental data file backup. This regime might not be appropriate for all systems. For some users, it would be safe to substitute weeks for days. Indeed, because each user is likely to have a different work pattern a regime might need to be set up on an individual basis. The main point is that every backup does not have to be complete/lengthy, and a schedule of complete and partial backups will require less time, and so stand more chance of being adhered to.

The Rotating Three-Way Split

Having looked at the factors that determine what needs to be backed up and when, you will want to consider the physical handling of the backup media. Where will it be stored? How many copies will there be? What is a good off-site storage location? One possible media management program is based on the generally accepted wisdom of putting your eggs in several different baskets: The rotating three-way split. This involves two sets of backup media, which means that the files are always in three places at once: backup copy 1, backup copy 2, and the original. You begin this regime by making backup copy 1 and storing it in a safe place, off-site, known as location A, as shown in Fig. 9-2.

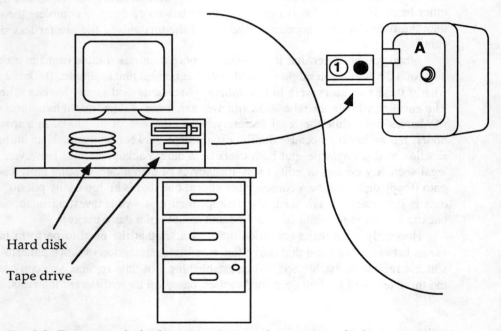

Hard disk

Tape drive

Fig. 9-2. First step in the backup regime is to put the most recent backup copy off-site.

The off-site location can be a bank, the manager's home, a different office of the same company. Very important data might warrant a fire-proof safe.

After a suitable interval, determined by the factors discussed in the previous section, you make backup copy 2. This is placed in location A. You now move backup 1 to a safe place, on-site, known as location B. This might be a locking filing cabinet or desk drawer. This can be seen in Fig. 9-3.

After another interval, you remove backup copy 1 from location B and reuse the media to make backup 3. This is then placed in location A. At the same time backup 2 is moved to location B, and so on, as shown in Fig. 9-4.

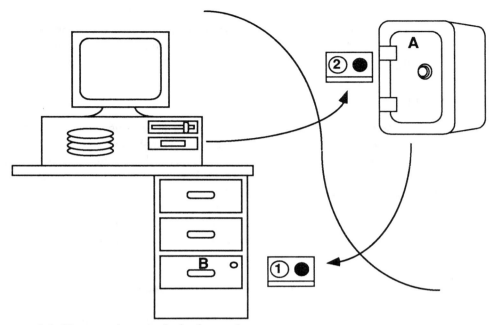

Fig. 9-3. The second step in the backup regime.

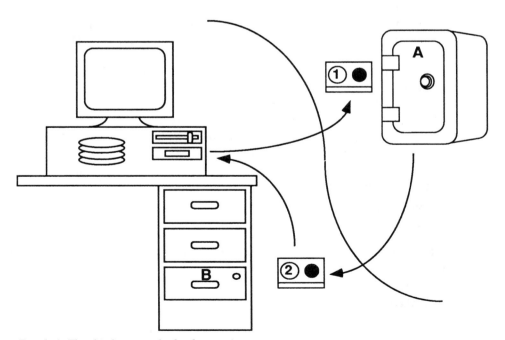

Fig. 9-4. The third step in the backup regime.

The off-site backup is always the most up-to-date. The copy held on-site is only one interval behind. If something happens to the files on the computer the off-site copy can be used. In the unlikely event that something has happened to that as well, you can use the on-site copy as a fall-back position.

Other Routines

For data intensive operations, such as order processing, where large amounts of data are added or altered every day, you can use a day-by-day system. On Friday afternoon, the operator goes to a special filing cabinet and takes out backup media marked Friday. This is used to make a complete backup of the hard disk. The media is locked away over the weekend. On Monday afternoon, the operator goes to the media cabinet and gets out media marked Monday. This is used to make an incremental backup, overwriting the previous data on the media. The same thing happens on Tuesday through Thursday. Incremental backups are made each day on media marked for that day of the week. When Friday rolls around again, the Friday media is used for a new complete backup.

This system has several advantages. The time required for an incremental backup is generally far less than that for a full backup, making the daily routine less burdensome. Nevertheless, if restoration is required, a full set of data can be put together using a week's worth of tapes. Furthermore, up to a week's worth of historical data is available if the operator discovers an error. Suppose that on Thursday the operator discovers an important record has been deleted from a database by mistake. If the deletion occurred less than a week ago, the record will still be on one of the backups. Suppose the operator remembers the error occurred on Tuesday. The Friday or Monday media will contain a copy of the file made before the record was erroneously deleted. The copy can be restored, and the record copied to the current version of the database. If the operator uses the same backup media every day, this type of recovery is not possible.

A variation of this routine requires eight sets of media. Set 1 is used on the first Friday. Sets 2, 3, 4, and 5 are used for incremental backup on Monday through Thursday. On the second Friday you use new media, set 6, keeping the first Friday's backup intact. The next week you reuse 2, 3, 4, and 5 on Monday through Thursday, then on Friday you use new media:

    Third Friday   set 7
    Fourth Friday   set 8

After the fourth Friday you reuse the first Friday's media, set 1. This system assures at least a three-week buffer for reclaiming files.

Backup Timing

You might want to give some thought to the time of day that backups are performed. It seems natural to do the backup at the end of the day, then lock the media away or take it off-site. Because some backup systems such as tape units, allow back-ups to be triggered automatically, some people leave systems on overnight and have the backup performed under software control. This minimizes inconvenience to users and leaving systems running is not considered detrimental to their health or reliability (although monitors should be turned down or off). However, even if the hardware per-forms reliably, there is a problem in that the backup is being performed during a period of high risk. Theft of computers, tampering with files, or disasters such as fires can progress with less chance of detection during the night. An unsupervised over-night backup operation is no protection against these threats. Indeed, if the backup media sits in the computer until a human operator arrives in the morning, it can make a nice present to someone looking to steal data. Of course, you would have the pre-vious night's backup to fall back on, but a day's worth of work will have been lost.

Doing backup first thing in the morning might seem like the answer, but again, an overnight attack threatens a whole day's worth of work. One solution available to com-panies with evening staff is to have them perform the backup before leaving, but there is no easy answer to some of these dilemmas. You will need to weigh the annoyance factor of a "backup before you packup" policy against the potential risks from unat-tended overnight backup. Another alternative for automated backup is to do it at lunch time.

 I know one company that hires a computer science student from the local college to come in at the end of the day and perform backup operations on the company's dozen or so personal computers.

BACKING UP TO FLOPPIES

When users come to back up their data, which will hopefully be sooner rather than later, one of the first questions to be answered is "what media?" All personal computers have at least one backup device: The floppy disk drive. This has meant that the default backup media has tended to be floppy disks. As you can see from the dia-gram in Fig. 9-5, floppy disk drives have increased in capacity over the years.

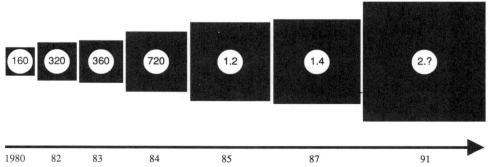

Fig. 9-5. Floppy disk capacity.

Despite this improvement, floppies still represent the low end of the efficiency scale when it comes to making archival copies of information. These days you have several alternatives to floppies, and the alternatives are examined in a moment. However, because no one of these alternatives has yet been accepted as standard equipment on personal computers, the pros and cons of the humble floppy are examined first.

 Two points are noteworthy here. First, the term "floppies" seems to be preferable to, and is definitely shorter than, floppy diskettes, or just diskettes (the rather effete sounding word "diskette" apparently comes from the fact the current disk sizes, 5.25 inch and smaller, were preceded by large 8-inch diameter disks). Second, the statement "all personal computers have a floppy disk drive" can be contended on two counts. The first contention could be that diskless personal computers are available; however, it is generally accepted that such machines are in fact workstations and that a personal computer must, by definition, have local storage (as opposed to remote storage on a network). Also, some radical personal computer designs, such as the Atari Portfolio, use alternatives to floppy disks for their local storage. Nevertheless, the statement is true enough to be valid in our consideration of the relative merits of backup systems.

The Pros and Cons of Floppies

Floppy disks are a cheap backup medium, costing from $1 to $2 per megabyte, depending on the type of disk and how much you want to pay for your disks. Well-tried and tested, floppy disks are generally reliable, widely available, and familiar to all users. All personal computers come with at least one floppy disk drive. Furthermore, floppies themselves are easily duplicated. Given these positive factors, you might wonder why floppy disk drives are not applauded as the idea backup device.

Capacity. Relative to the size of the hard disks they are called on to back up, floppy disks have very limited storage capacity. For example, backing up a 40 megabyte PC hard disk requires the following:

126 older 5.25 inch disks with 360K capacity.
37 newer 5.25 inch disks with 1.2 megabyte capacity.
63 older 3.5 inch disks with 720K capacity.
32 newer 3.5 inch disks with 1.4 megabyte capacity.

While floppies are relatively inexpensive, the cost mounts up when you are talking dozens of disks, and the higher capacity disks are usually priced higher than the lower capacity disks.

The limited capacity of floppies is particularly bothersome when archiving a large file, such as a database. If the file does not fit on one disk, then it must be spread across several, which requires the use of a backup program rather than a simple copy command. This prevents you from using the floppy as a form of on-line storage for large files. In the early days of personal computers, it was possible to argue that the slow speed of floppy disks was offset by their convenience as on-line storage, offering direct access to files. Since then, data files have grown ever larger and it will take considerable advances in floppy disk storage before this argument can be resurrected.

Speed. Floppy disks are relatively slow in operation. A typical hard disk spins at some 3000 revolutions per minute (rpm). A floppy disk might spin at 300 rpm. That gives you some idea of the speed differential between floppies and hard disks. Storing data onto a floppy disk takes time, over a minute per megabyte. Multiplied by the number of megabytes that need to be backed up, this speed factor translates into a boredom factor. Over half an hour is required to back up 30 megabytes, and this is not just computer time, but operator time as well.

Copying data to a floppy disk is not all that takes time; the disk must be formatted first. This places the electronic markers on the disk that the operating system uses to locate files. It takes nearly one and a half minutes to format a 1.2 megabyte floppy disk in a PC. Formatting one of the 800K disks used in a Macintosh takes nearly a minute. While formatting is a one-time procedure and need not be repeated when reusing a set of backup disks, it can still involve time and trouble. Early backup programs required that disks be formatted before beginning the backup procedure, but many newer backup programs offer to format any unformatted disks you want to use. While this is convenient, it adds time to the backup process. One shortcut is to buy pre-formatted disks, now available from many computer supply houses. Another option is to do bulk formatting in-house, using a dedicated personal computer with multiple floppy disk drives, or a floppy disk duplicator that has a formatting mode.

Inconvenience. When you combine the speed and capacity factors with the time taken to insert and remove floppies during a large backup operation, you get a recipe for tedium. Few users look forward to half an hour's worth of disk shuffling at the end of the day, while few managers see it as productive use of time. A full backup every day is not always a necessity, if incremental backups can be performed. But some users find they have many megabytes of files that are updated every day. You cannot perform an incremental backup on a 10 megabyte database file that had several records added during the day, the backup has to be all or nothing, and putting all of it on floppies will probably take a good 15 minutes by the time the paperwork is complete (backup disks need to be labelled).

The sheer quantity of disks required for backing up with floppies poses several problems. A single backup spread across many disks is hard to manage, physically and logistically. If you lose just one disk, Murphy's law dictates that it will be the one that contains the one file that you really need. The disks need careful handling and proper storage. A stack of 30 floppies is an unwieldy package. The older, soft-jacketed disks tend to slip and slide when you stack them, the newer, hard-jacketed disks take up a lot of space (42 of them form a stack 6 inches high). This compares unfavorably with a cassette tape the size of a deck of playing cards holding upwards of 40 megabytes, as shown in Fig. 9-6.

Floppies in Their Place

Having pointed out the weaknesses of floppies as a backup medium, it is as well to highlight some positive factors that might otherwise be overlooked. While floppy

Fig. 9-6. Comparative size of storage media.

disks can be said to be a fairly delicate media, the hard-jacketed 3.5-inch disk are quite a bit tougher than their predecessors, and considerably more convenient since they do not require a separate jacket. In practical terms, alternative backup media, such as tapes and removable hard disks, are just as prone to damage from dust, liquids, and magnetic fields, as floppy disks.

The tedium factor of backing up to floppies can be mitigated. Floppy disks can be very effective for small-scale data backup, or for short term incremental backup. For example, daily backup of word processing files onto floppies is relatively quick and easy. Few typists can produce more than a megabyte a day and so copying from hard disk to floppies at the end of the day is a simple one- or two-disk operation. Some users prefer to store word processing documents directly to a floppy. This is particularly effective if you are using a program that loads the current document into RAM because storing the document on hard disk offers very little speed advantage.

Users who store directly to floppies should make backup copies of their floppies on a regular basis. These can be done very easily on machines with twin floppy drives. Users of DOS can make mirror image copies of floppy disks with DISKCOPY. However, if you are using a floppy disk as primary storage, you should be careful not to use the same disk for extended periods. Adding and deleting files on the same floppy disk for weeks on end can result in a breakdown of the file allocation system, leading to data loss. The DISKCOPY command does nothing to improve this condition, in fact, it simply duplicates it on the copy. From time to time, you should transfer all files from the used disk to a fresh disk using the regular COPY command that copies files one at a time. This will allow DOS to place each file one after another on the disk, in its entirety.

For those who prefer to create documents on the hard disk, a simple addition to the batch file that loads the word processing program can activate a copy operation that archives all changed files onto a floppy disk. For example, a batch file that loads WordPerfect might look like this:

```
ECHO OFF
CLS
C:\WP\DOCUMENTS
C:\WP\WP
CLS
REM Do you want to backup files to a disk in drive A.
REM If not, press CTRL-C then Y and Enter, otherwise
REM Insert blank formatted disk in A and then
PAUSE
XCOPY *.* /A A:
CD\
TYPE MENU.MSG
```

When the user exits from WordPerfect, the files that have been changed since the last time they were backed up are copied to the floppy disk in A. For more on the XCOPY command, look later in this chapter.

A final plus for floppies is the ease with which they can be duplicated. A pair of disk drives and some patience is all it takes to crank out multiple copies of backup disks. Several good utility programs copy floppy disks much faster than the regular DOS commands. Some of these programs can write the format and data files at the same time, thus speeding up the duplication process. This means that a second set of backup disks can be created much faster than the first. There are even dedicated disk duplication machines that can copy disks without using computer time. (A disk duplication machine that can also create blank formatted disks is an excellent investment for a micro-support group or data processing manager becuase users can be issued with pre-formatted disks, avoiding one of the big headaches of personal computer usage—improper or inappropriate disk formatting. See Chapter 11 for more on the format problem.)

DATA, FILES, AND BACKUP TAPE

The use of magnetic tape to store data predates floppy disks. Large capacity tape drives are still used in many mainframe computers and the big tape systems are part of the classic science fiction image of computers, where shiny, wardrobe-size units house fast spinning disk reels.

Pros and Cons of Tape

The primary advantages of tape drives are high capacity and mechanical simplicity. Whereas floppy disks require a moving read/write head that needs to be accurately positioned, the head on a tape drive is stationary, and the tapes simply runs past it. The tape drive's read/write process only needs to deal with one dimension, distance along the tape, as opposed to the two dimensions involved when locating data on the surface of a disk. However, this simplicity is also the shortcoming of the tape drive: Access to a specific location tends to be much slower.

The relatively low cost and operational simplicity of magnetic tape recommended it as a storage medium to the designers of the very first personal computers. They used ordinary cassette tape recorders to store and distribute programs. Indeed, the first IBM PC had a port for a cassette on the back, and some home computers still use this medium. In fact, tape works quite well when all you want to do is load programs into RAM. The shortcomings become apparent when you start storing and retrieving data. Searching the tape from end to end to find a certain piece of data can take a long time. The tape drives used for backup on personal computers address the speed of retrieval problem in two ways, faster tape movement, and some form of tape indexing. To cope with the stress and strain of high speed operation the tape cartridges used for backup are made to a higher standard than regular music cassettes, typically using a metal frame. Also, stronger and wider tape can be used. Music cassettes use a 4 millimeter tape (barely more than $1/8$ of an inch wide). Something of a standard for backup tape cartridges has developed around $1/4$ inch tape. Some systems use the $1/2$ inch tape used in VCRs and the 8 millimeter tape found in some video cameras. Drives that read and write the 9-track tape used on mainframes can be attached to personal computers and employed for backup as well as exchanging data with larger computers.

Indexing to facilitate data location on tapes is achieved by several different systems. Some tape systems use a type of formatting akin to that used on disk drives, laying down a series of marker signals on the tape to allow the mechanism to measure relative positions. This has to be done before the tape can be used for backup. Unfortunately, this type of block indexing or formatting takes time, in some cases as long as two hours for a tape capable of storing 40 megabytes. Tape drives using the DC2000 cartridges use block formatting. You can see a DC2000 cartridge for a QIC tape drive next to a regular tape cassette in Fig. 9-6.

One method of recording data onto tape that avoids the need for pre-formatting is *streaming*, in which the data is fed onto the tape in one continuous stream (leading to the term streaming tape drive, not to be confused with noisy or overheated tape drives, known as screaming and steaming respectively). Streaming tape drives offer fast data transfer to make the initial backup but are somewhat slower when it comes to locating data later.

The type of backup created by a streaming tape drive is usually an image backup, a complete track-by-track record of what is on the drive. Tape drives based on the DC600 cartridge use this method and offer from 150 to 300 megabytes of storage per tape. One disadvantage of not formatting the tape is that it must be erased before it can be reused. The tape mechanism can usually perform this procedure fairly quickly, but it can be annoying when you are in a hurry to make a backup.

A solution to the data location problem used by some streaming tape drives is a method known as *block location* in which the streaming tape drive places signals on the tape at regular intervals as the data is streamed onto it. This allows a file-by-file restoration from an image backup. Another tape recording technique, found on drives that use the 8mm video tape cartridges is helical recording. The data is recorded in diagonal strips across the tape, as opposed to the normal vertical strips. This gives a greater capacity per inch of tape and allows 8mm cartridges to hold up to 2.2 gigabytes of data (that is over 1000 megabytes).

The proliferation of different tape systems can lead to some confusion. A recent review of tape drives for PCs costing under $1000 showed 15 models that used 5 different tape formats. One of the problems with specialized tape recording systems is assuring a constant supply of the tapes. Nobody wants to be stuck with a backup system that uses obsolete media. This fact acts as a natural brake on users adopting any new form of backup that is introduced.

Tape Performances

The speed at which tape drives can back up hard disks varies according to the hardware design and the type of backup performed. Typically the creation of a mirror image backup takes less time than a file-by-file backup. Not surprisingly, you will find that the faster the drive, the higher the price. You will see performance figures quoted showing times from 1 minute per 10 megabytes to 2 minutes per 1 megabyte. When comparing manufacturers' claims, you need to be sure you are comparing like figures. The review articles in computer magazines should be a good source of independent figures that reflect what you can reasonably expect from a particular unit. However, even then you need to make sure that systems are compared on equal terms. For example, one recent review of a streaming cartridge system listed time to back up 10 megabytes as 2.2 minutes, while another article rated the same drive at 11 minutes for 10 megabytes. This is because the second test was based on going from the DOS prompt through the menus, back to the DOS prompt, and included a verification pass. Verifying the integrity of the data backed up onto tape is an important process, one that you will want to use if you are looking for complete security, but it is not always included in a manufacturer's or even a reviewer's performance figures.

Tape Installation

Adding a tape drive to a personal computer system is fairly easy. With many PCs you can mount the tape unit internally, using a half height bay. Otherwise units are external, with their own casing. Many drives, internal or external, are controlled by their own adapter card although some systems can be connected to the existing floppy disk drive controller although this tends to be a slower arrangement than the dedicated card. Macintosh units are typically connected externally via the SCSI adapter. As well as connecting the hardware, you will need to install the software that comes with the unit. This is usually menu-driven that provides all of the options in a straightforward format. Bear in mind that software can make or break a piece of hardware, and you should review the "features to look for" section later in the chapter when looking at backup software.

Other Tape Options

The large tape units that you see on mainframe computers use reels of tape rather than cassettes or cartridges. The data is recorded on nine tracks. This means the tape make nine passes across the head before it is filled up. This gives a good ratio of data to tape, some 3 megabytes per inch. Such tape drives can be attached to most personal computers. This is normally done when you want to transfer data from a mainframe system to a micro. However, the units make good backup devices as long as you have plenty of room. A table top unit the size of an old reel-to-reel tape recorder is attached to the personal computer by a special adapter card. These units are not cheap, but offer considerable capacity and inexpensive media.

You might wonder why a tape backup unit for your personal computer costs over $400 when you can buy a very good VCR for less. One of the main reasons that many hi-tech goods experience a steady decline in retail price is the benefits of high-volume production. Compared to VCRs, computer tape drives are a low-volume specialty item. So, when retail prices for VCRs dropped below $400, some people realized that, given the right programming, they would make good tape backup units for personal computers. Several systems are available, either as a complete unit, or as an interface and software to which you add your own VCR. If you have been thinking of upgrading your VCR and are not sure what to do with the old one, this could be a possibility. VCRs as backup devices do not need all of the fancy facilities such as stereo and picture-in-a-picture that are now available on new VCRs. Because a regular VHS tape can store up to 200 megabytes, and tapes can be bought for less than $10, what sounds at first to be an improbable notion can make a lot of sense.

At the other end of the scale from using your old VCR unit for tape backup, newer compact tape drives offering over 2000 megabytes of storage have been developed to use the small video tape cartridges, known as the 8mm format. These units can cost over $4000 but offer speed and reliability as well as enormous capacity. At the other end of the scale from the old cassette recorders for personal computers are units using DAT technology (short for Digital Audio Tape). This involves a much more sophisticated and accurate method of tape recording which, in audio applications, can exceed the fidelity of CDs. DAT backup units use a high quality 4mm tape and tend to be slightly slower than 8mm tapes. They offer over 1 gigabyte of storage (1000 megabytes plus).

HIGH-CAPACITY REMOVABLE MEDIA

Over the last ten years there have been numerous attempts to popularize storage systems that combine the primary advantage of floppies (removable) with the main advantages of hard disks (high speed/high capacity). None of these attempts have succeeded in establishing a universal standard for data storage, and some have become obsolete. However, several systems of high capacity removable media (HCR) have become well-established and are well worth considering.

On-Line Possibilities

The main advantage of high-capacity removable media is almost instant access to backup files. This is referred to as on-line backup, and it offers a level of convenience that some users will consider worth the usually higher cost of HCR systems. Files can be read directly from the backup media without the need to restore them, and writing data to the media is often much quicker than using a tape system.

Bernoulli Boxes. A good example of HCR is the Bernoulli system from Iomega. This uses a special floppy disk precision mounted in a rigid cartridge and rotated at high speed by a special drive unit. A drive head sweeps across the surface of the disk like a hard drive unit, rather than the fixed track head system used in a floppy drive. When the system was first introduced, the cartridges were close to the size of LPs and offered only 10 megabytes of storage, while the drive units were the same size as the original IBM PC. Now you can get 44 megabyte cartridges that are like 1/4 inch thick versions of regular 5.25 floppy disks, shown previously in Fig. 2-5.

The drives that use these cartridges can be fitted internally in a half height PC drive bay, or connected externally to either PCs or Macs, in single or double configuration. The drives offer read/write times that are comparable to medium speed hard disk drives and can be used as a primary storage device instead of a hard disk. They can be made "bootable" to act as a resident hard disk, or you can boot with a regular floppy or hard disk. With a dual drive unit, you can use one cartridge as the primary drive and the second as a backup device. Because both drives operate at the speed of a hard disk, the time taken to back up one to the other is minimal (4 minutes for 40 megabytes). A single unit can be added to a hard disk system to provide backup facilities. While these units are somewhat more expensive than tape drive units of similar capacity, the advantages in terms of speed and ease of access to archived files are considerable. Like tapes and floppies, Bernoulli cartridges need to be formatted, but the procedure is relatively simple and only takes a few minutes. Because the drives operate on a high-speed flow of air, they do need to be cleaned regularly and are not the best choice for very dusty conditions.

Hard Disk Packages. Despite considerable ingenuity and cunning engineering, the high-capacity alternatives to the hard disk have not achieved the universal popularity of conventional hard disks. This might be because hard disks are obviously solid in construction, reliable, and fast in operation. Furthermore, hard disks are established, proven technology, a fact of considerable importance to buyers reluctant to go out on a limb with unconventional solutions. One approach to removable storage has been to capitalize on the widespread acceptance of hard disks and develop removable hard disk systems. These are literally hard disk drives that can be taken out of the computer. The steadily falling price and size of hard disk drive units has made it feasible to suggest users have several on hand. The cost factor alone would not have made this feasible, but advances in hard disk technology have meant that the normally fragile disk is now quite sturdy, as well as small. A few years ago most hard disks in personal computers were 5.25 inches in diameter. Now most new hard disks are 3.5 inches, and many laptops are using drives of less than 3 inches in diameter.

One company that was quick to see applications for smaller hard disks was Plus Development that introduced the first *hard card*, a hard disk and controller card in one unit that slotted into the motherboard of a PC just like a video adapter or other expansion card. This offered a fast and easy way for owners of older floppy disk-based PCs to gain the benefits of hard disks. Using their expertise in this field, Plus Development created a removable hard disk cartridge system. A half height bay is installed in the PC and the drive unit, smoothly encased in plastic, is plugged into it. The disk cartridges offer 30 megabytes of storage and access times comparable to built-in hard drives. On the down side, the hard disk cartridges tend to cost as much as a built-in drive.

The personal computer manufacturer Tandon offers a slightly different approach. Using self-contained disk "pacs" that are larger than the Plus Development units, the Tandon system requires a special docking bay that can be added to non-Tandon PCs as an external device (needless to say, you can buy Tandon PCs with the docking bay built in). Tandon makes impressive claims for the strength of their 30 megabyte units, able to withstand falling to the floor and a ride home in the briefcase. They also price the disk pacs aggressively, around $200 per 30 megabyte unit.

A slightly different approach to removable hard disks is taken by Stratum Technology in their Datafile. Offering 40, 100, and even 200 megabytes of hard disk capacity, these units are self-contained external hard drives, much smaller than the earlier external drives that appeared for the IBM PC. The advantage of these units is that they plug into the computer through the parallel port, making them very easy to install, attach, and detach. What you get is a hard drive that can be plugged in, used like a regular drive, then unplugged and locked away, or even carried to another machine. You could use such as a primary device, or like a portable tape deck, going from PC to PC backing up data files. To accentuate the security benefits of the drive, the unit has a lock on the front, and only the key holder can power up the drive.

Finally, several systems, among them the Qume Hyperflex and the Verbatim 20-Plus, offer high-density storage on nothing more than oversize floppy disks, sometimes referred to as super-floppies. Using what looks like a 5.25 inch version of a 3.5 inch floppy, hard-cased and with a metal shutter, these drives offer 10 or 20 megabytes of on-line storage at around $20 per special disk. The disks are supplied by Verbatim, a major manufacturer of regular floppies, and so are likely to be available for some time to come. Only slightly slower than most hard disks, these drives offer relatively fast backup at a low cost per megabyte, and might even have a role as a primary storage device, with the advantage of being easily locked away.

Pros and Cons of HCR

While high-capacity removable (HCR) systems offer great speed and convenience, they do have a down side compared with other backup media. The initial hardware investment tends to be more expensive than tape units, and the media itself can also be expensive. A 40 megabyte Bernoulli cartridge is about $80, as compared to $20 for a tape of the same capacity. A removable hard disk can run $300 or more. For this reason, Tandon has tended to dwell on the security benefits of locking away the hard disk pac at the end of the day, rather than its use as a backup device. As backup devices, systems like the Verbatim super-floppy are a good compromise, using relatively cheap media, offering fast on-line backup, and having a high security rating thanks to the ease with which the disks can be locked up.

Redundancy and Backup

One technique used to defend against hard disk failures in large computer systems is called *shadowing* or *mirroring*. This involves reading and writing everything to two disks instead of one. These are two physically separate disks, not two partitions on the same physical disk. The hardware and software necessary to perform disk mirroring on personal computers is just starting to appear, and it offers an interesting line of defense against hard disk breakdown (if one breaks, the other keeps running). There are also potential performance benefits. For more on disk shadowing, see the discussion of the Opus Datasafe, a PC design incorporating this feature, in Chapter 7.

The primary security advantage of disk shadowing is that if one hard disk breaks down, you have a current backup immediately available. The system can be designed so that a disk crash will result in little more than an error message, with disk read/write activity unaffected. Of course, disk shadowing does not protect against user error: Mistakes such as accidental file erasing are faithfully duplicated. Nor is shadowing a replacement for normal backup procedures. However, for critical operations where you cannot afford a disk to go down for even a few minutes, disk shadowing might be the answer. To add disk shadowing to an existing system, you can purchase a special disk drive controller, such as the SmartCache controller from Distributed Processing Technology.

OPTICAL STORAGE

As any music enthusiast knows, the development of optical disks that can store sound has revolutionized the record industry. The convenience and fidelity of the compact disc (CD) threatens to make vinyl recordings, and even cassette tapes, relics of a former age, much like watches with springs. Sound is not the only thing that optical disks can store. Any information, including images and data, can be etched onto the surface of an optical disk, and laser discs are considered by many film buffs to be the preferred medium for archiving movies.

Optical disk systems work by digitizing information and then recording the digital data as patterns on a circular platter. The pattern on the platters can be reproduced very cheaply by modern molding techniques, and the encoded surface can be protected by a clear layer of plastic. When the disk is placed in a drive, it spins at high speed and is scanned by a beam of laser light bounced off the surface. The data is read as reflections from the patterned surface. Their durability and accuracy means that optical disks have great potential as a storage medium for personal computers, but they are not being accepted as quickly as CD players for music.

The Optical Options

The NeXT computer developed by Steve Jobs gives some indication of the medium's possibilities by including an optical drive as standard. However, at this point no clearly dominant format for optical storage exists to enable reading and writing of disks across a wide range of computer models. This is bound to hold back the use of optical drives as primary media for widespread data and software distribution. Nevertheless, optical disks have already established themselves as a viable option as backup devices. Among the positive features of optical storage for data are:

- High density of data (upwards of 400 megabytes per disk).
- Excellent durability of medium.
- Better access facilities than linear media.

On the down side are:

- The drive units and cartridges are expensive.
- The difficulty of altering disks.
- The slow access times relative to the latest hard disks.

In effect, optical drives are a form of high-capacity removable media. They come in three flavors:

- Write once, read many times. Used to permanently archive data, it is a good backup device.
- Rewritable. Otherwise known as erasable, they can be used more like regular hard disks and are good backup devices.
- CD-ROM. Permanently stored data used for reference purposes, CD-ROM is essentially an information distribution media, and not really a backup device.

WORM Drives

The simplest form of optical backup is the WORM, an acronym for Write Once Read Many. As the term suggests, this device writes data to a disk once and then allows you to read it back as often as you want. This is ideal for situations in which large quantities of data need to be archived, and the archives need to be preserved for long periods of time. It is not ideal for daily backup where only the latest version of a constantly updated file needs to be preserved.

The material of the disk is different from that used in musical CDs because it has to be altered by the drive head. The disk is usually sealed in a cartridge with a shutter somewhat like Bernoulli disks. Indeed, the actual disk cartridge is about the same size as a Bernoulli cartridge pictured earlier in Fig. 9-8. Like tapes and magnetic disks, the optical disk used in a WORM drive must be formatted. However, this takes a matter of seconds rather than minutes or hours. Data is transferred to the disk very quickly as well, in the order of megabytes per minute rather then minutes per megabyte.

When attached to a personal computer, a WORM drive can be made to appear like a normal disk drive. A special software "driver" relates the device to the personal computer's operating system. A typical application would be the period-end transfer of company accounting information from hard disk to optical disk. This allows the data from the last period to be removed from the hard disk ready for the new period, but keeps the previous data readily available on the WORM drive. This overcomes an inherent disadvantage of backing up to floppies or tape, since data archived in that way is hard to bring "on-line." Archived files on tape or floppy might have to be restored to a hard disk in order to be used, whereas a WORM cartridge is present for reference just like another hard disk, albeit one that is write-protected. The longevity of WORM cartridges and the fact that they are, by their very design, write-protected, makes them a very secure media for archives.

Another possibility with WORM disks and other optical media is the use of a juke box system. This is a multiple disk holder that shuffles disks in and out of the drive. Made possible by the inherent strength of the optical media, such systems offer many gigabytes of on-line data.

You might wonder what is stopping everyone from going out and buying such ideal backup devices. The answer is cost. The cartridges are expensive and can set you back over $200 apiece, while the drive units are in the $3000 plus range.

Rewritable Optical Disks

The disadvantage of WORM drives, that they can only write to the disk once, is overcome in devices known as rewritable optical disks. These use a variety of different techniques to allow the optical disk to be rewritten while retaining the advantages of large storage capacity and fast data access. For example, Ricoh makes a rewritable optical disk system that combines magnetic and optical technologies. A double-sided cartridge is used to provide 600 megabytes of storage that can act just like a regular disk drive. The average access time is 400 milliseconds, which compares favorably with regular hard disks. The system uses the SCSI interface and can be attached to an IBM PC by installing a SCSI adapter card. Units can be connected directly to a Macintosh because the Mac has a SCSI interface built in.

Rewritable drives and disks are currently even more expensive than WORM drives. However, the general tendency of high-tech goods to drop in price might soon bring them within reach of a wider range of users.

CD-ROM

You may wonder where the term CD-ROM fits into the optical disk picture. Short for compact disc read-only memory, CD-ROM refers to a system of storing data on optical disks in a one-time mastering process, somewhat akin to that used to create old-fashioned LPs. CD-ROM discs are designed to be created by a distributor of information and then mass produced. These discs can be read in CD drives similar to those used in CD music players. In fact, some CD-ROM drives for personal computers can play music as well as store data. The important point is that CD-ROM does not allow the user to write to the disk at all. While this rules out CD-ROM as a backup device in the normal sense of the word, it is still a valuable technology for those working with large quantities of data. For example, an investment advisory service that is using a hard disk to store a large and expanding database of company data downloaded from an on-line service might be better served by a CD-ROM system. Some information services are now providing historical data on CDs. These can be updated on a regular basis. The updating process is simple—you throw away the previous CD when the new one arrives! This is feasible because ordinary CDs cost very little to manufacture in bulk, as opposed to the writable optical media used in WORM drives.

Desktop publishing is another area where the CD-ROM is gaining ground as a distribution media. You can buy large clip art libraries stored this way. Several companies also offer fonts on CD. Agfa distributes over 700 fonts this way, with several hundred on each disc.

COST FACTORS

So far, details of the relative costs of the backup alternatives have not been addressed in any detail. However, they are a significant factor in determining the final backup strategy for organizations and individuals. For example, when comparing WORM drives with tape drives and other systems, few people can ignore the cost of the disk cartridges. These can cost several hundred dollars each. At first this might seem prohibitive but, as you can see from Fig. 9-7, comparison with other forms of storage reveals a different picture.

		Backup Media: Costs & Performance				
Media	Type	MBytes	$/Unit	$/MByte	$/System	Speed Factor
5.25 DD	Floppy	0.35	$0.3	0.86	N A	15.0
5.25 HD	Floppy	1.20	$0.5	0.42	N A	12.0
3.5 DD	Floppy	0.70	$0.6	0.86	N A	13.0
3.5 HD	Floppy	1.40	$1.6	1.14	N A	11.0
QIC 40	Tape	40.00	$19.0	0.48	$400	5.5
QIC 60	Tape	60.00	$24.0	0.40	$600	5.5
DC600	Tape	250.00	$35.0	0.14	$1,200	2.8
DAT	Tape	2500.00	$35.0	0.01	$6,000	4.0
8mm	Tape	2500.00	$40.0	0.02	$5,000	5.0
Iomega	Disk	40.00	$80.0	2.00	$800	4.0
Disk pack	Disk	30.00	$275.0	9.17	$400	3.5
WORM	Disk	650.00	$100.0	0.15	$3,000	4.0
Rewritable	Disk	650.00	$300.0	0.46	$5,000	3.5

Fig. 9-7. Vital statistics on backup media.

This is actually a spreadsheet developed in Microsoft Excel and you might want to create a similar table yourself, updating the figures provided here with ones that are up-to-the-minute. The numbers in this table are only approximate and there are a number of assumptions that must be noted. The $/Unit column is cost per unit of media, that is per disk or tape. The $.System column is cost for the drive unit. No cost is listed for floppy disk drives because at least one of these comes with every personal computer. A graph of comparative costs of media can be seen in Fig. 9-8.

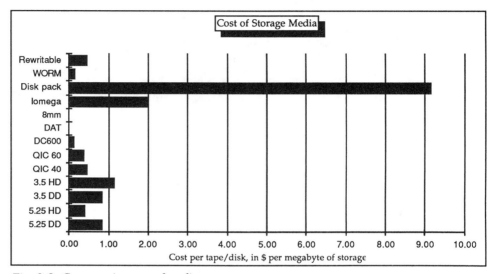

Fig. 9-8. Comparative cost of media.

The QIC 40 and QIC 60 systems use the DC2000 tapes in different lengths. No effort was made to include all of the many standards around for tapes. The disk pack category is a generic one for removable hard disks. The speed factor is number of minutes taken to back up 10 megabytes of data. Bear in mind that some of the media offer on-line storage, whereas others do not. A graph of comparative performance figures can be seen in Fig. 9-9.

EVALUATING BACKUP SOFTWARE

Of course, the hardware you use to back up your data is only as good as the software that drives it. Typically a backup device comes with its own software. Even the floppy disk drives in your personal computer have backup software, the backup and restore commands provided by the operating system. These commands, for the Mac and the PC, are described in a moment.

When shopping for a backup device, you need to avoid being blinded by performance statistics and make sure you look at the software that will operate the system.

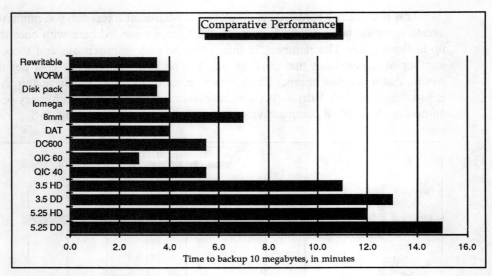

Fig. 9-9. Comparative performance figures.

Features to look for include:

- Menu-driven. If novice users are expected to operate the software it needs an intuitive menu-driven interface that makes selection of source files and target media as easy as possible.

- File selection. You need to be able to include or exclude certain types of files, as well as specific individual files. Directories and folders should be displayed in a way that makes it easy to choose them. The ability to store backup specifications for repeated use is valuable. There should be a clear choice between file-by-file and image backup.

- Overwrite protection. The software should make it clear when it plans to overwrite existing backup information on the media and offer a chance to prevent this.

- Report generation. The software should provide a printed report of a backup session for reference. This can be stored with the media. (Some companies require filing of such reports by users to prove that backup has been performed.)

- Command lines and scripts. To make backup as easy as possible for users, you should be able to set up a single key operation using either a batch file, macro, or script facility. Make sure the software offers you this type of control.

- Timing commands. If the hardware is capable of operating unattended, make sure the software accepts timing instructions so that it can carry out the backup without you.

- Restoration procedure. While the main emphasis is on efficient backup, you cannot ignore the possibility that the backup needs to be restored. Check that the software handles this effectively, offering control over the overwriting existing files on the hard disk.

These are the main features to look for in the software supplied with your backup device. You might also want to check if it is possible to use a different piece of software than the one supplied with the device. A recent review of tape systems for Macintosh computers found that some only worked with the proprietary software while others worked with general purpose backup programs. In some cases, the latter provided considerable performance improvements.

BACKUP COMMANDS IN DOS

It is reasonable to expect any mature operating system to include backup facilities. When IBM introduced the PC-XT, a hard disk version of the original PC, a new version of DOS was provided, 2.00. This included basic backup and restore commands. Over the several upgrades to DOS since then, these facilities have been improved with additional options.

Basic BACKUP

The complementary programs BACKUP.COM and RESTORE.COM should be installed on your hard disk, typically in the DOS directory. Unlike the simple COPY command, BACKUP can spread large files and large groups of files across more than one floppy disk, creating a numbered stack of archive disks. BACKUP lets you choose which files to back up on the basis of path name, file name, whether they have been changed since the last backup, or whether they have been changed since a particular date. The version of BACKUP provided in DOS 3.3 has 11 parameters, listed here:

```
BACKUP<DRIVE> <PATH> <FILENAME> <DRIVE> /A/S/M/F
   /D:<DATE> /T:<TIME> /L:<LOGFILE>
```

<DRIVE> is the drive letter of the *source* drive, the one that is being backed up, typically C:. Some versions of DOS allow you to omit a drive letter but this is not good practice.

<PATH> is the name of directory in which reside the files you want to back up. If you do not specify <PATH>, DOS assumes you mean files in the current directory.

<FILENAME> is the name of the file or files to be backed up. You can use wildcard characters to back up a set of files (? for any character, * for any number of characters). If no <FILENAME> argument is provided, DOS backs up all files in the directory specified by the <PATH> parameter.

<DRIVE> is the letter of the drive that contains the floppy disk that is to receive the backup files, the *target* drive. You must give a <DRIVE> argument, and it must be followed by a colon, as in A:.

/A adds the backup files to the backup diskette, rather than erasing all files on the backup diskette. If you are reusing old disks then this option is not needed because overwriting any existing files on the backup disk is the default action of BACKUP. However, you need to be sure that the disks you are using for your backup contain expendable data. Also note that if your backup occupies more than one disk, all disks but the last one will be filled with files and so using /A will not make any sense.

/S tells BACKUP to include files from all subdirectories of the directory specified in < PATH >. Thus C: \ *.*/S means all files on drive C.

/M tells BACKUP to back up only the files that have been modified since the last backup.

/F formats any floppy disks you use for the backup that are not already formatted. Note that BACKUP uses FORMAT.COM to format the target disk, so FORMAT .COM must be in either the current directory or a directory that is in the command path.

/D: < DATE > backs up all files that have changed since the day you specify as < DATE >. Enter < DATE > just as you would for the DOS DATE command, as in 12-25-91, for Christmas Day, 1991.

/T: < TIME > backs up all files that have changed since the time you specify as < TIME > on the day specified as < DATE >. Enter < TIME > just as you would for the TIME command, as in 13:00 for one o'clock in the afternoon.

/L: < LOGFILE > creates a log file on the disk in the source drive. The log file will show you the date and time of the backup procedure and the path and file name for each file that is backed up, together with the number of the floppy that contains the file, as assigned by DOS. If a log file exists on the source drive, new backup information is added at the end of it, creating a history of backups for the source drive. If you include /L but omit the colon and < LOGFILE >, DOS names the log file BACK-UP.LOG and stores it in the root directory of the source drive.

The various backup options can be combined, so you can back up files in just about any way you like. However, while the BACKUP command exists in versions of DOS numbered 2.0 and later, not all the versions include all the parameters given here, nor are all the versions and releases of DOS compatible with one another. For a list of the options available with a specific version of DOS, check the documentation that came with it. Because of the variations between versions, you should use the same version of DOS to back up and restore files.

The /L is particularly useful when performing large backups that involved numerous disks. The logfile records which disk the files have been placed on. You might want to copy this file from the hard disk to the last of the backup floppies. When you need to restore a particular file you can examine the log, which is a simple ASCII file, using TYPE or a utility such as QuickDOS, and read the number of the backup disk recorded next to the file's name.

Backing Up by Directory

The simplest way to back up files is by directory. You back up all files in a directory by specifying just the path of the directory and the letter of the floppy drive that contains the backup disk. Before you try the following examples, have a formatted blank floppy ready. For example, to back up all files in \WP\DOCUMENTS on drive C, you would type the following:

BACKUP C:\WP\DOCUMENTS A:

When you enter this DOS beeps and displays a message, Insert backup diskette 01 in drive A:. This is followed by this warning: Warning! Files in the target drive A:\ root directory will be erased Strike any key when ready. Unless you have used the /A option, DOS erases any files in the backup floppy disk before it makes the backup copies. This warning gives you a chance to make certain the correct floppy disk is in the drive. When you have put a formatted blank floppy in drive A, you press any key. DOS displays the names of the file as they are copied plus this message:

Backing up files to drive A:
Diskette Number: 01

If you look at the directory listing of the first backup floppy disk, it might surprise you. If you are using 3.2 or an earlier version, you will see the names of the files backed up onto the disk, plus a file like this:

BACKUPID @@@   128   6-05-91   5:30p

This is a small file that DOS stores on a backup floppy disk to identify it. You might also be surprised to see the files you backed up are larger than the originals on the fixed disk. If you are using 3.2 or an earlier version, DOS adds 128 bytes at the beginning of each backup file. This addition contains the path and file name of the file that was backed up and is used by the RESTORE command when it restores files to the fixed disk. The RESTORE command deletes the path and file name information, so the restored version of the file is identical to the one you originally backed up. Users of DOS 3.3 will see a directory listing something like this:

```
Volume in drive A is BACKUP 001
Directory of A:\

BACKUP     001        1015591      6-05-91   6:36p
CONTROL    001           1263      6-05-91   6:36p
           2 File(s)              196608 bytes free
```

If you're using version 3.3, DOS stores all the backed up files in the file called BACKUP.001 and all the path names in the file called CONTROL.001. (On a second backup disk, the extensions would be 002; on a third disk, they would be 003, and so on.) Note that the size of BACKUP.001 corresponds to the total number of bytes in the files it contains; CONTROL.001 contains all the extra information DOS needs to restore those files. This difference from early versions of the BACKUP command is why RESTORE in version 3.3 works only with files backed up with the version 3.3 BACKUP command; the version 3.3 RESTORE command does not restore files backed up with earlier DOS versions.

If BACKUP fills the first floppy disk before backing up all the files specified,

DOS prompts you to put in another floppy. The warning is repeated, referring this time to the second floppy disk as 02. If another floppy disk is needed, then DOS prompts again, increasing the floppy disk number each time. Either before you insert the floppy disks or as you remove them, you should label them with the correct disk number as well as details of the backup. For example:

```
Backup June 5, 1991
All WordPerfect documents
Disk 1
```

The backup disks should then be stored in a safe place.

To back up all of the files in a directory plus all files in all subdirectories of that directory, you use the /S option. For example, suppose you have this directory structure on drive C that looks like this:

```
WP—DOCUMENTS ┬─ MEMOS
             ├─ REPORTS
             └─ LETTERS
```

You want to back up all the files in WP\DOCUMENTS and its subdirectories: WP\DOCUMENTS\MEMOS, WP\DOCUMENTS\REPORTS, and WP\DOCUMENTS\LETTERS. To do this you specify WP\DOCUMENTS as the path and include the /S parameter as follows (making sure you use a backslash in WP\DOCUMENTS, but a forward slash in /S):

```
BACKUP C:\WP\DOCUMENTS A: /S
```

Backing Up Selected Files

You might just want to back up a specific file, such as an important database. You do this by including a file name with the BACKUP command. A database management directory, for example, might contain both databases, which change frequently, and file definitions, which seldom change. You need to back up the actual databases much more frequently than you do the file definitions. The following command backs up only the database files, that is, files whose extension is DB:

```
BACKUP C:\DATABASE\*.DB A:
```

When this command is executed you will see the selected files listed on screen as they are backed up. Only files that have the extension DB will be included in the list.

A printed list of the files on a backup floppy disk is a valuable asset when you come to restore files. You can store this along with the floppy disk itself. There are two ways of doing this. You can capture the backup process on the printer by first turning it on and pressing the Ctrl–Print Screen key before beginning the backup. DOS will display the file names on screen as it backs them up, and it will print them too. When the process is complete press Ctrl–Print Screen again to stop DOS printing.

An alternative approach is to use the /L option to create a log file and then print the log, as in

```
COPY BACKUP.LOG > PRN
```

With some applications you might want to be even more selective about the files you back up. A word-processing directory can easily grow to hundreds of documents and backing them all up would take a lot of time and disks. The BACKUP command has several options that permit backing up only files that have changed since a directory was backed up, or only files that have changed since a particular date.

The /M or modify option of the Backup command backs up only files that have changed since the directory was last backed up. For example, to back up all files in the DOCUMENTS directory that have changed since the last backup you would use:

```
BACKUP C: \ WP \ DOCUMENTS \ *.* A: /M
```

The /D: < DATE > option backs up only those files that have changed since a particular date. Use the /D: < DATE > option to back up the files that have changed since June 5, 1991, by typing:

```
BACKUP C: \ WP \ DOCUMENTS \ *.* A: /D:12-31-89
```

To be really precise about the selection of files, you can use the /T: < TIME > option to specify a time in addition to using the /D: < DATE > option to specify the date.

Adding Files to a Backup Floppy Disk

Normally, the BACKUP command starts by erasing any files on the backup floppy disk. There might be times, however, when you want to back up files from several different directories on one floppy disk or add a file to an existing backup floppy disk. The /A option adds a file to a backup floppy disk. When you use this option, DOS does not warn you that it is going to erase any files from the backup floppy disk. If you are using version 3.3, DOS prompts:

```
Insert last backup diskette in drive A:
Strike any key when ready
```

Note that the prompt specifies the *last* backup disk. This is because only the last disk in of a set of backup disks will have any room on it. Of course, you will only have one backup disk if you are just backing up a few files from several different directories. The /A option allows you to put all the files on the same floppy disk. However, this technique should be used carefully. In versions of DOS prior to 3.3, DOS changes the extension of added files to @01 if they have the same name and extension as files already on the floppy disk, regardless of what the previous extension was before.

The Performance Factor

The BACKUP command offers numerous advantages over the COPY command, not least of which is speed. BACKUP can fill a pre-formatted 360K floppy disk in 30 seconds whereas COPY takes over a minute. The BACKUP command does not require pre-formatted disks since the /F option tells it to format disk as you go. However, formatting is a lengthy process, taking 50 seconds or so per disk (formatting a 1.2 meg floppy takes about the same time as a 360K floppy as the high-density drive spins at higher speed). Pre-formatting of floppies obviously saves a lot of time during the actual backing up process, and many suppliers now offer pre-formatted disks (you can make your own in bulk by using a disk duplicating machine, now available for less than $1000).

Another way to speed up backing up to floppies is keep the number of files per directory to a reasonable limit, say 2−300. If your PC has two floppy disk drives, a further possibility for greater speed is alternating between the two drives. This option is not available with BACKUP, but is offered by third-party backup software. There is a savings of several seconds per disk since no time is wasted taking out one disk and inserting another.

THE RESTORATION

The one command that everyone hopes they will not have to use is RESTORE. This is because you only have to use RESTORE when a file or files that you need is no longer available on the hard disk. This is likely to be because of operator error, malicious attack, or mechanical failure. Fortunately, it is relatively easy to restore a file to a working hard disk from a backup floppy disk.

The RESTORE Command

Assuming that your hard disk is operational and contains the RESTORE command, you merely log onto the hard disk, insert the backup floppy and type RESTORE, followed by the drive letter for the floppy disk and the name of the file to be restored. In the case of a mechanical breakdown of the hard disk, the disk must first be repaired and properly formatted before RESTORE can be used. Files can be restored to a different hard disk than the one they were backed up from, as long as a matching version of DOS is used. The Restore command has 11 parameters:

```
RESTORE < DRIVE > < PATH > < FILENAME > /S/P/M/N/B: < DATE >
/A: < DATE >/E: < TIME >/L: < TIME >
```

< DRIVE > is the letter of the source drive, the one that contains the backup floppy disk. You must include < DRIVE >, followed by a colon, as in A:

< PATH > is the name of the directory *to* which the file is to be restored, as in C: \ WP for the WP directory on drive C. If you omit < PATH >, the file is restored to the current directory of the hard disk.

< FILENAME > is the name of the file to be restored. If you do not give a < FILENAME > parameter, all files backed up from the directory indicated by < PATH > are restored. You can use wildcard characters to restore a group of files

(*.DOC restores all files with the extension DOC). You have to specify either <PATH> or <FILENAME> for RESTORE to work.

/S restores files from all subdirectories of the directory specified in <PATH>, creating those directories if they do not already exist on the target hard disk.

/P tells DOS to prompt for confirmation before restoring files in cases where the hard disk contains files of the same name as those being restored. Normally, when RESTORE sees that a file being restored has the same name as one that is already in place on the hard disk, it will automatically overwrite the existing file. The /P option tells RESTORE to check the existing file and, if it has changed since the last time it was backed up, the user is prompted to confirm overwriting the file.

/M restores only the files that were modified or deleted since they were backed up.

/N restores files that have been deleted from the original source disk since they were backed up.

/B:<DATE> restores only those files that were changed on or *before* <DATE>. The <DATE> is entered as it is for the DATE command.

/A:<DATE> restores only those files that were changed on or *after* <DATE>.

/E:<TIME> restores only those files that were changed at or *earlier* than <TIME> on the day specified by <DATE>.

/L:<TIME> restores only those files that were changed at or *later* than <TIME> on <DATE>.

Note that because the RESTORE command uses the path and file name information added to files by the BACKUP command, you can only restore files that were backed up by BACKUP. The RESTORE command in DOS 3.3 can restore only files backed up with the version 3.3 BACKUP command. Furthermore, although the RESTORE command exists in DOS 2.0 and later, not all versions include all of the above parameters. Check the documentation that came with your version of DOS for a list of the options available. Finally, do not use either the BACKUP or RESTORE commands if you used an ASSIGN, JOIN, or SUBSTITUTE command to alter the way DOS interprets drive letters. Because these commands can mask the type of drive being referred to, RESTORE and BACKUP can end up damaging or deleting either the files you specify in the commands or other files on the disk.

Restoring One File

Despite all the talk of attacks and interlopers, the most common reason for using RESTORE is probably inadvertent erasing or changing of a particular file. You restore a single file by specifying the target drive, path name, and file name with the RESTORE command. You must include the path name if you are restoring a file to a directory other than the current directory; the path name must be the same as the path from which the file was originally backed up. For example, to restore the file MAJOR.DOC to drive C into the directory \WP\DOCUMENTS\, you could enter:

RESTORE A: C:\WP\DOCUMENTS\MAJOR.DOC

This would work regardless of what directory was current. If you made C: \ WP \ DOCUMENTS the current directory, you could use:

    RESTORE A: MAJOR.DOC

Note that the drive and path can be omitted because the file is being restored to the current directory. When you enter the RESTORE command, DOS prompts you for the backup floppy disk:

    Insert backup floppy disk 01 in drive A:
    Strike any key when ready

When you have placed backup floppy 01 in the drive, you press any key and DOS displays the following message

    *** Restoring files from drive A: ***
    Diskette:01

If the file you have specified is on disk 01, then you will name the restored file as it is placed onto the hard disk, otherwise you will be prompted to Insert backup floppy disk 02 and so on, until you reach the disk on which the file is located. When the RESTORE command is completed, you might want to issue the DIR command to verify that the file was restored correctly.

   If the file you want is somewhere in the middle of a fifty-disk set of backup floppies, this procedure might seem somewhat discouraging, but you do not have to insert the disks sequentially. If you have a good idea that the file you want is on disk 8, then you can insert disk 8 when prompted for disk 01. DOS will warn you that the disk is out of sequence, but will allow you to proceed. (Using the log file created with the /L option, you can easily look up which disk the desired file is on to save the guesswork.)

Restoring Groups of Files

   You can use wildcard characters with RESTORE to bring back a group of files. To restore all the files who extension is DOC that you backed up from the current directory you would type the following:

    RESTORE A: *.DOC

When DOS prompts you for the backup floppy disk, press any key. DOS displays the names of the files it restores. Again, you can use DIR to verify that the files were restored.

   If you enter the RESTORE command with a path name but no file name, DOS restores all files belonging in that directory. For example, to restore all the files you backed up from the current directory type:

    RESTORE A:

While the /S option of the BACKUP command backs up the files in a directory and all its subdirectories, the /S option of the RESTORE command restores the files in a directory and all its subdirectories. To restore the files in \ WP and all its subdirectories, you would type:

RESTORE A: \ WP \ *.*/S

Normally a file you restore replaces a file with the same name on the fixed disk. You might not want this to happen, particularly if you have changed the file on the fixed disk since the backup was made. To protect against unwanted changes use the /P (prompt) option of the RESTORE command, which tells DOS to prompt for confirmation if the file on the fixed disk has changed since the backup was made. Suppose you are restoring the group of files *.DOC and have used the /P option. The file MAJOR.DOC has been altered since the last backup. The message DOS presents will be:

Warning! File MAJOR.DOC
was changed after it was backed up
Replace the file (Y/N)?

The /P parameter is essential if you are currently using DOS 3.20 or earlier and want to restore files that were backed up with a previous version of DOS. If DOS asks whether you want to restore files named MSDOS.SYS, IO.SYS, IBMBIO.COM, or IBMDOS.COM, reply N for No. Otherwise, you would replace parts of your current DOS with portions of an earlier version. This really confuses matters and can even prevent DOS from booting from your hard disk.

 DOS has quite a repertoire of frightening messages, one of the horrifying being Warning no files were found to restore, which can easily appear when using RESTORE. The cause is usually an incorrect file specification. Before thinking the worst (that the files were not backed up), check the RESTORE command parameters to make sure that the files you have asked for are correctly specified.

The Archive Attribute

You might wonder how BACKUP decides which files have been backed up and which have not. The answer is in the system of file attributes that DOS uses. As you may remember from Chapter 2, any DOS file can have up to four attributes assigned to it: Hidden, read only, system, and archive. The last of these, the archive attribute, indicates whether the file has been copied or not. The archive attribute is set to On or Yes whenever a file is created or modified. This tells DOS that the file needs archiving. When you back up a file with BACKUP the attribute is changed to Off, or No, meaning that it has been archived. So, because the archive attribute is turned off when a file is backed up and turned on when a file is changed DOS can tell you which files have changed since they were last backed up. BACKUP is not the only program to use this feature. It is used by third-party backup programs and by XCOPY, described in the next section.

If you want to see the archive status of a particular file or set of files you can use the DOS command ATTRIB, as in

    ATTRIB *.DOC

This command will tell you the attribute status of all DOC files in the current directory. The files are listed by name, preceded by letters for any attributes:

    A   archive
    H   hidden
    R   read only
    S   system file

Another way of viewing file attributes is to use the Norton Utilities. The FA program
displays attributes in a more readable list. You can use ATTRIB or FA, or even a hard
disk manager like QuickDOS, to alter the archive status of a file. You might want to do
this for several reasons. Suppose you have backed up all of the files on your hard disk.
A few days later, a coworker gives you a disk containing an important document,
MAJOR.DOC. You create copy this to your hard disk. A few more days later you
decide to perform an incremental backup. This should include all data files that have
been altered and all new data files. However, you check the archive status of MAJOR
.DOC and note that its archive status is not on, possibly because the coworker had
backed it up before making a copy for you. Unless you turn on the archive status, it
will not be included in the incremental backup. To set the archive status of the file
MAJOR.DOC so that it is included in your incremental backup, you would use the
following command:

    ATTRIB MAJOR.DOC +A

THE COPY COMMANDS

The BACKUP command allows you to spread a file or group of files across several floppies. In doing so, it alters the files so that they are no longer directly accessible. Data files backed up with BACKUP need to be restored before they can be
accessed by applications. This means that backup made this way is not "on-line." In
some circumstances, this can be inconvenient. Consider an author who has written
several books about computers. After each book, she backs up the various data files
and chapters onto floppies and deletes the original files from her hard disk to make
way for the next book. The new book requires a description of DOS directories very
similar to the one she wrote in the last book. If the file containing that description was
created with BACKUP, the author first needs to exit from her word processor, issue
the appropriate RESTORE command to get the file onto the hard disk, then return to
the word processor to read the file. If, on the other hand, the backup file containing
the needed data was created with a simple COPY, then the file can be accessed from
within the word processing program, a considerable saving in time and effort. This
illustrates the benefit of creating on-line backup, something you can do with the

COPY, REPLACE, and XCOPY commands that are part of DOS, as well as some third-party hard disk management programs.

The Regular COPY

The most basic form of backup is to copy files from hard disk to floppy with the DOS command COPY. The COPY command allows you to select all files (*.*), or groups of files (*.DOC for all files with the extension DOC), or single files by exact name as in

```
COPY C: \ WP \ DOCUMENTS \ MAJOR.DOC A:
```

which copies the file MAJOR.DOC from the \ WP \ DOCUMENTS directory on drive C to drive A. The drive and directory of the source file(s) to be copied can be stated in full, as above, or the source drive and directory can be assumed, as in

```
COPY *.* A:
```

which copies all files from the current directory to drive A. The target drive can be assumed if it is the current drive, so that

```
COPY C: \ WP \ DOCUMENTS \ *.*
```

will copy all files from the \ WP \ DOCUMENTS directory on drive C to drive A if A is the currently logged drive.

The COPY command can only operate on one source or target directory at a time and cannot provide any further criteria for file selection besides DOS wildcards. There is no way to check for date or archive status. The COPY command does not read or alter the archive status of a file. Furthermore, COPY operates in an "all or nothing" fashion, with no warning when writing over existing files on the target disk with identically named files on the source disk. Further limitations of COPY are that it cannot cope with source files larger than the target disk, or a group of files that needs to be spread across more than one disk. About the only redeeming feature of COPY as a tool for creating on-line backup is the fact that it is an internal command, one that is part of COMMAND.COM and so always available.

The REPLACE Command

To remedy some of the shortcomings of COPY, versions of DOS after 3.1 acquired the REPLACE command. This allows you to perform prompted updating of existing files on a floppy disk and to selectively restore files to the hard disk, including subdirectories. For example, the following command copies to drive A any files in the current drive/directory that have the extension DOC and copies of which already exist on the disk in drive A:

```
REPLACE *.DOC A:
```

The REPLACE command has several parameters:

REPLACE <SOURCE> <TARGET> /A /S /R /P /W

/A stands for add and tells REPLACE to copy only the files on <SOURCE> that do not exist on <TARGET>. This allows you to add files to the <TARGET> disk without replacing files that already exist, useful when updating data files. If you omit the /A parameter, all files on <SOURCE> are copied to <TARGET> just as if you had used the regular COPY command. The /A cannot be used with the /S parameter.

/S applies REPLACE to all subdirectories contained in <TARGET>. Thus, if you specify the root directory of a disk as <TARGET>, the REPLACE command is applied to every subdirectory on the disk (the "s" stands for search as well as subdirectory).

/R causes read-only files on <TARGET> to be replaced, otherwise, such files are not affected by REPLACE.

/P prompts for user confirmation before each file is replaced.

/W waits for a floppy disk to be inserted before starting the REPLACE operation.

Suppose that you have a high-capacity floppy disk on which you store backup copies of regularly updated spreadsheet files. After a spreadsheet session, you want to replace the old copies on the backup floppy with the revised versions from the hard disk. The following command would do that:

REPLACE A:\ C:\123\DATA\ *.WK1

All spreadsheets in C:\123\DATA that had the same name as files already on the floppy disk would be copied to the floppy. You could also tack on the /P parameter, allowing you to avoid updating files to the floppy that do not merit backing up.

Suppose that you have a high-capacity floppy disk on which you store backup copies of general spreadsheet files. After a spreadsheet session, you want to add to the backup floppy all new spreadsheets from the hard disk. The following command would do that:

REPLACE A:\ C:\123\data\ *.WK1 /A

All spreadsheets in C:\123\DATA that were not already on A would be copied. You could also tack on the /P parameter, allowing you to avoid adding files to the floppy that do not merit backing up. Note that the basis for the term "new" is that a file of the same name does not already exist on the target floppy.

Another scenario in which REPLACE is convenient is when you have to return files from a floppy disk to the hard disk. The following command will replace all *.DOC files in the WP directory and all of its subdirectories with files of matching names on the floppy in drive A, pausing for confirmation of each file:

REPLACE C:\WP\ *.DOC A:\ /S /P

The XCOPY Command

Unlike COPY and REPLACE, the XCOPY command, added in version 3.2 of DOS, can be used selectively to copy only files whose archive attribute is on, or to copy only files that have been changed since a date you specify. The XCOPY command has 10 parameters:

```
XCOPY <SOURCE> <TARGET> /A /M /D:<DATE> /E /P /S /V /W
```

<SOURCE> is the name of the file to be copied. You can use wildcard characters to copy a set of files with similar file names or extensions.

<TARGET> specifies where the files specified as <SOURCE> are to be copied. You can include any combination of drive letter, path name, and file name.

/A copies only those files whose archive attribute is on, but leaves the archive attribute unchanged.

/M copies only those files whose archive attribute is on, but turns off the archive attribute. This tells DOS (or any other program) that the file has not been changed since it was last backed up and therefore does not need to be backed up again.

/D:<DATE> copies only files created or changed on or after <DATE>. The date of creation or last change is the date shown in the directory entry for any file. You enter the date just as you do for the DATE command.

/E creates subdirectories in <TARGET> even if they are empty in <SOURCE>.

/P prompts for confirmation before each file specified in <SOURCE> is copied.

/S applies the XCOPY command to all subdirectories contained in <TARGET>. If you specify <SOURCE> as the root directory of a disk, the XCOPY command is applied to every subdirectory on the disk.

/V verifies that the copy of the file on <TARGET> was stored correctly. This can slow the operation of the XCOPY command somewhat, but is good insurance when copying critical data.

/W prompts you to press a key before the XCOPY command begins. This gives you a chance to put in the correct floppy disk before starting to copy files.

Bear in mind that XCOPY.EXE, like REPLACE.EXE, is an external DOS command. This means it must be in either the current directory or a directory that is in the current PATH setting for you to be able to issue the command. As you can see from the above parameters, the XCOPY command offers considerable scope for creating on-line backup files. Like the regular COPY command, XCOPY terminates when the source files exceed the capacity of the target floppy. However, by using the /M option you can overcome this problem.

Suppose you want to back up all DOC files from the current directory to a series of floppies. First issue the following ATTRIB command to make sure that all files have their archive attribute turned on:

```
ATTRIB *.DOC +A
```

you issue the command:

COPY *.DOC A: /M

This copies as many DOC files as will fit on the disk in drive A and then the command terminates. You take out the disk, insert a fresh one, press F3 to repeat the previous command line (COPY *.DOC A: /M) and then press Enter. The command continues copying files, omitting those that were previously copied since their archive attribute has been turned off, indicating that they no longer need archiving. The /A parameter also tells XCOPY to copy only those files whose archive attribute is on but, unlike /M, it does not turn the archive attribute off. With its wide range of options, XCOPY is a valuable tool for hard disk management, particularly within batch file systems.

Third-Party Disk Organizers

Several programs offer a menu-driven approach to DOS file management commands, and these can be very useful to both novice and experienced DOS users. Typical of such programs is QuickDOS. This program displays the current directory of files as a sorted table from which one or more files can be selected using a scrolling highlight bar. A system of tagging is used to mark the files you want a particular command to work with. For example, for selective copying of files from hard disk to floppy, you can browse the list, pressing the space bar to tag individual files. Alternatively, you can apply tags to a group of files using DOS wildcards. In Fig. 9-10, you can see that files with the extension WP5 are tagged.

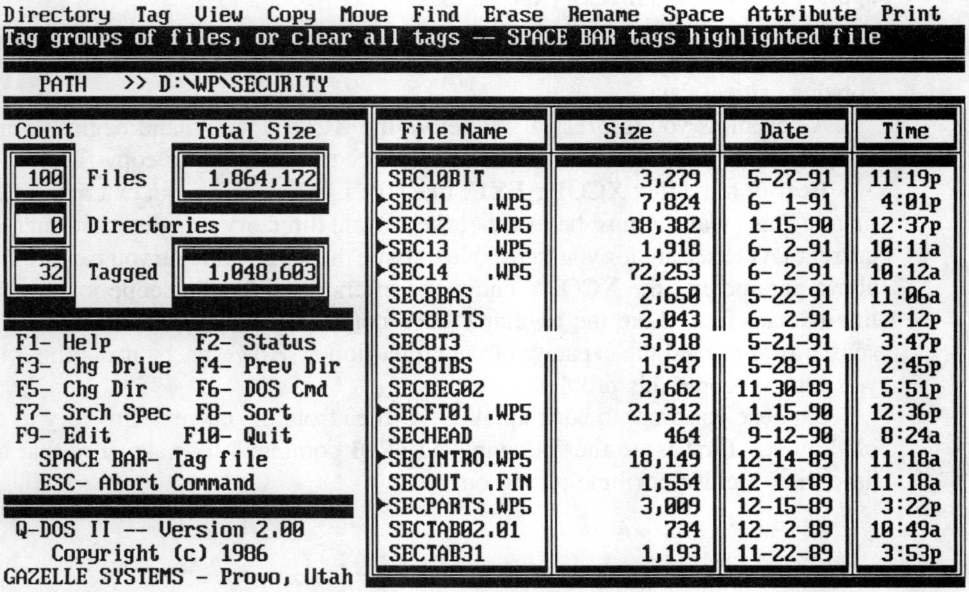

```
Directory  Tag  View  Copy  Move  Find  Erase  Rename  Space  Attribute  Print
Tag groups of files, or clear all tags -- SPACE BAR tags highlighted file

   PATH   >> D:\WP\SECURITY

 Count        Total Size      File Name      Size      Date      Time

 100  Files    1,864,172      SEC10BIT      3,279    5-27-91    11:19p
                             ▶SEC11   .WP5   7,824    6- 1-91     4:01p
   0  Directories            ▶SEC12   .WP5  38,382    1-15-90    12:37p
                             ▶SEC13   .WP5   1,918    6- 2-91    10:11a
  32  Tagged   1,048,603     ▶SEC14   .WP5  72,253    6- 2-91    10:12a
                              SEC8BAS       2,650    5-22-91    11:06a
                              SEC8BITS      2,043    6- 2-91     2:12p
 F1- Help       F2- Status    SEC8T3        3,918    5-21-91     3:47p
 F3- Chg Drive  F4- Prev Dir  SEC8TBS       1,547    5-28-91     2:45p
 F5- Chg Dir    F6- DOS Cmd   SECBEG02      2,662   11-30-89     5:51p
 F7- Srch Spec  F8- Sort     ▶SECFT01 .WP5  21,312    1-15-90    12:36p
 F9- Edit       F10- Quit     SECHEAD         464    9-12-90     8:24a
   SPACE BAR- Tag file       ▶SECINTRO.WP5  18,149   12-14-89    11:18a
   ESC- Abort Command         SECOUT  .FIN   1,554   12-14-89    11:18a
                             ▶SECPARTS.WP5   3,009   12-15-89     3:22p
 Q-DOS II -- Version 2.00     SECTAB02.01     734   12- 2-89    10:49a
   Copyright (c) 1986         SECTAB31      1,193   11-22-89     3:53p
 GAZELLE SYSTEMS - Provo, Utah
```

Fig. 9-10. Selective tagging of files in QuickDOS.

If you want to copy these files to a floppy disk, you select the Copy command from the menu. The command asks if you want to copy the currently highlighted file or the tagged files, then prompts for the target drive. The copy operation is "intelligent" in that it notifies you when a file of the same name exists on the target disk. If the target disk fills up before all of the files have been copied, you are prompted to insert a fresh disk or halt the operation. Even if you have to halt the operation because you have no formatted floppy available, QuickDOS keeps tags on the uncopied files while you prepare a fresh disk, as shown in Fig. 9-11.

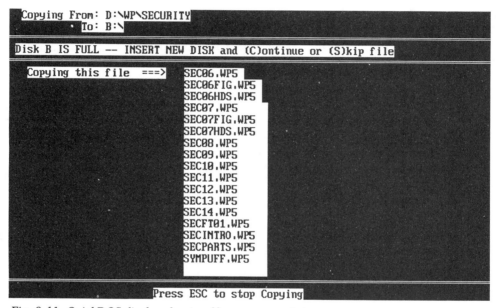

Fig. 9-11. *QuickDOS display showing files not yet copied.*

As you copy and move files, QuickDOS keeps track of space free, aggregate size of files in the current directory, and files tagged.

The program makes it hard to erase or overwrite files accidentally. You can use it to alter file attributes. Third-party utility programs like QuickDOS and its partner Backit are a valuable investment for individual users as well as micro-managers.

 Whenever I visit a client whose PCs need work, I always take my copy of Quick-DOS along. There is no better tool for discovering what files are where and for bringing order to disorganized hard disks. Invariably a client who sees the program in action will ask, "What is that?" and "Where can I get a copy?" The answers are it is the best $89.95 you ever spent, and most mail order software houses.

THIRD-PARTY DOS BACKUP

As sales of hard disk drives for PCs began to take off, a small industry arose to meet the demand for improved backup facilities. Some companies sought to provide hardware alternatives to the floppy disk drive, while others took the "soft" approach and tried to provide backup software for use with floppies that worked better than BACKUP that came with DOS 2.00. Improving BACKUP was not hard. Merely adding a set of menus for parameter selection made the process far less intimidating. However, some developers also saw that improvements could be made in speed of operation.

Menu-Driven Backup

The Backit program from Gazelle Systems, who also make the QuickDOS utility, is a good example of menu-driven backup software. Working from the main screen shown in Fig. 9-12, the user can set parameters and make file/directory selections using straightforward menu options.

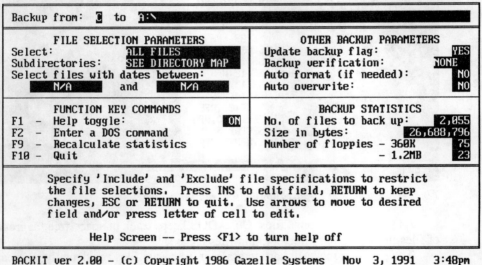

```
Backup  Restore  From-drive  To-drive  Directories  Modified  Specify  Other
Specify 'Include' and 'Exclude' file specifications to restrict selections

 Backup from: C  to  A:\

       FILE SELECTION PARAMETERS              OTHER BACKUP PARAMETERS
 Select:                 ALL FILES        Update backup flag:            YES
 Subdirectories:    SEE DIRECTORY MAP     Backup verification:          NONE
 Select files with dates between:         Auto format (if needed):        NO
        N/A        and        N/A         Auto overwrite:                 NO

      FUNCTION KEY COMMANDS                    BACKUP STATISTICS
 F1  -  Help toggle:            ON        No. of files to back up:     2,055
 F2  -  Enter a DOS command               Size in bytes:          26,688,796
 F9  -  Recalculate statistics            Number of floppies - 360K       75
 F10 -  Quit                                                - 1.2MB       23

      Specify 'Include' and 'Exclude' file specifications to restrict
      the file selections.  Press INS to edit field, RETURN to keep
      changes, ESC or RETURN to quit.  Use arrows to move to desired
      field and/or press letter of cell to edit.

              Help Screen -- Press <F1> to turn help off

 BACKIT ver 2.00 - (c) Copyright 1986 Gazelle Systems   Nov  3, 1991   3:48pm
```

Fig. 9-12. The main menu screen for Backit.

Note the section on statistics that shows the number of disks required, based on the files and directories selected, and the drive units available (Backit supports working with two floppy drives at once to speed up the process). To select directories to be backed up you use a map of the hard disk, as shown in Fig. 9-13.

Files can be excluded from the backup based on user-defined parameters, entered in a simple menu. As you can see from Fig. 9-14, the program and system files can be left out by specifying the extensions COM, EXE, and SYS.

Backit offers several levels of verification, from None, to a special method that is part of Backit, rather than DOS. A sound is made after each disk is filled, prompting

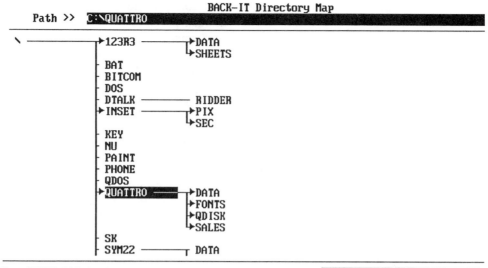

Fig. 9-13. Tagging directories.

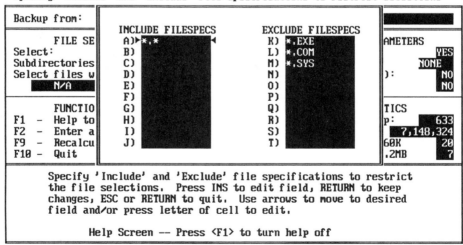

Fig. 9-14. Excluding files.

the user for the next disk. After the backup is completed a report can be stored on disk and printed out for your records.

If you are looking for speed increases in backing up to floppies, Backit does not offer much of a gain over BACKUP, but it does provide a menu-driven interface and much wider range of features. The Fastback program from Symantec offers a fast method of floppy backup because it can format disks and write data to them at the same time. The program requires a more complicated installation that Backit as it takes over the control of the floppy drive from DOS. However, it can format a 360K floppy and fill it with data in less than a minute, compared to a normal format only time of 1 minute and 15 seconds.

MACINTOSH BACKUP

The Macintosh System software, through version 6.0, includes a hard disk backup program that can at best be described as rudimentary. For this reason, most Mac hard disk users will want to get some form of third-party software. Some non-Apple hard disks come with backup software, as do some utility packages such as PC Tools from Central Point Software.

Basic Mac Backup

The program HDBackup that is included on the Macintosh System Utilities Disk 1 provides basic Mac backup onto floppy disks. When you load the program, you get a screen like the one shown in Fig. 9-15.

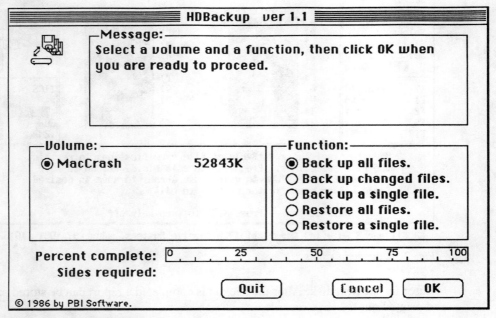

Fig. 9-15. The HDBackup program.

As you can see, you can back up all files, files that have changed since the last backup, or a single file. You can also choose the volume to be backed up if you have more than one. The total size of the storage space used on the volume is listed (in this case 52939K, or nearly 53 megabytes). When you have chosen what you want backed up, the program tells you the total number of disks required (70 in this case) and prompts you to insert a floppy disk. As you can see from Fig. 9-16, you are warned that previous data on the floppy disk will be lost.

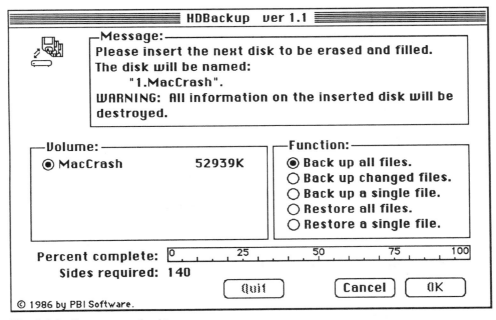

Fig. 9-16. About to start backing up.

Note that the number of disks required is stated as "sides" in case you are still using single-sided disks. Divide this number (140) by two to get the actual number of double-sided disks needed. After each disk is filled the program ejects it and prompts for a new one. A horizontal meter gives a rough idea of progress towards completion. Each disk takes about a minute to fill with data, so this backup will take over an hour.

Third-Party Mac Backup

To get greater control over what is backed up and how the backup is performed, Mac users can turn to a number of alternative backup programs. The PC Tools collection of utilities from Central Point Software includes PC Backup, a respectable and easy to use alternative to HDBackup. The program offers a number of options, as shown in Fig. 9-17.

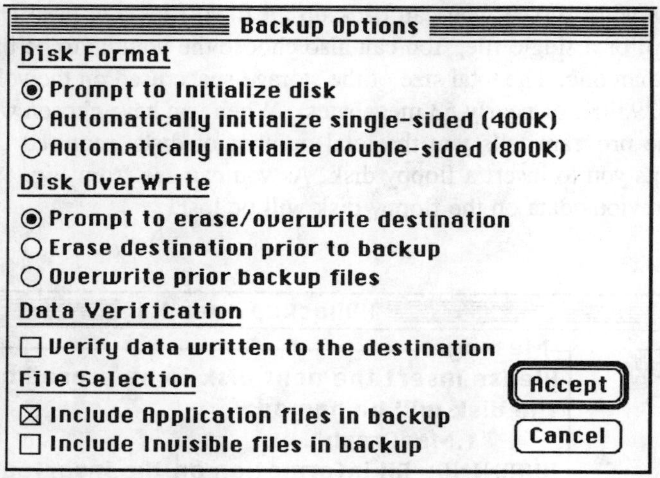

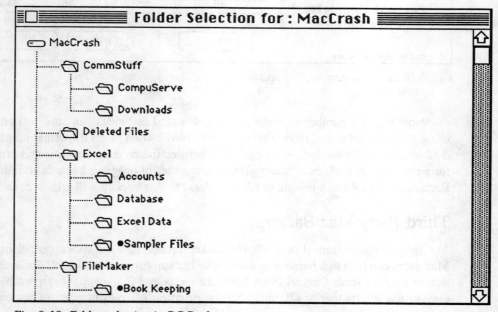

Fig. 9-17. Backup options in PC Backup.

In addition to controlling the formatting and overwriting of disks used for the backup, you can activate a data verification procedure. This slows down the backup but increases its reliability. You can also choose whether or not to include application files, and hidden files such as the desktop. Using a different menu, you can select the folders that you want backed up, using a simple tree diagram of the filing system, as shown in Fig. 9-18.

Fig. 9-18. Folder selection in PC Backup.

You click on folders to select/deselect them. This allows you to include only those folders that contain important data files. The implication is that by organizing your files accordingly, you can substantially reduce the time and quantity of disks needed to back up essential data.

When you have made your selections as to style and content of backup, you are presented with a working screen that meters progress. A set of statistics tells you the number of folders, files, and bytes to be backed up, and the number of disks required, as shown in Fig. 9-19.

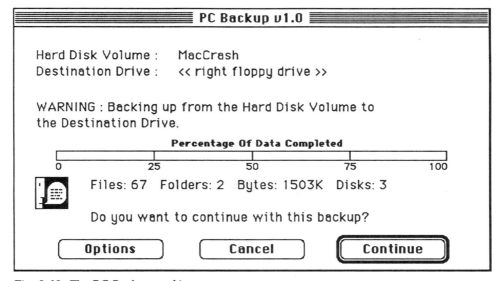

Fig. 9-19. The PC Backup working screen.

After each disk is filled, the program makes an alarm sound and ejects the disk. This is helpful if you are working on something else while the backup is taking place. In fact, you can use PC Backup to perform a backup "in the background." This means that you can continue working on your Mac, editing a document, for example, while the backup is being made. However, the activity of writing to the disk does slow down the Mac considerably and so the response time of programs will be affected, as will the speed of the backing up. Nevertheless, background backup is a useful compromise in some situations.

In foreground mode, PC Backup can fill an 800K disk in 55 seconds, compared with 1 minute 15 seconds for HDBackup. This is still not speedy, but together with the ability to exclude some folders from the backup, the program it makes for a big improvement on HDBackup. When you come to restore files backed up with PC Backup, you have three different ways of handling existing files. As you can see from Fig. 9-20, you can ask the program to prompt before allowing the overwriting of existing files, deny overwriting completely, or enable automatic overwriting.

```
╔══════════════════════════════════════════════╗
║ ▧▧▧▧▧▧▧▧▧▧▧▧ Restore Options ▧▧▧▧▧▧▧▧▧▧▧▧ ║
║ File OverWrite                                 ║
║ ⦿ Prompt to skip/overwrite file                ║
║ ○ Skip file and continue with restore          ║
║ ○ Overwrite file automatically        ┌────────┐ ║
║ Data Verification                     │ Accept │ ║
║                                       └────────┘ ║
║ □ Verify data written to the destination ┌────────┐║
║                                          │ Cancel │║
║                                          └────────┘║
╚══════════════════════════════════════════════╝
```

Fig. 9-20. File restoration options.

Mac Backup Hardware

These days Macintosh users have as wide a range of backup hardware options as PC users, including a variety of tape units, removable high-capacity disks, optical disks, and high-density floppies. Magazines catering to the Mac community regularly run evaluations of these alternatives, and you can check there for current process and performance data. Typically, a tape drive for a Mac will perform at the same speed as one for the PC. However, there has been a tendency for companies to price Mac devices higher than their PC counterparts. This happened when hard disk units were introduced and the trend continued with tape units.

One answer to the problem of expensive Mac hardware is to use a PC as a file server for a Macintosh local area network. A high-speed 80386-based PC, equipped with a large capacity hard disk and a tape backup unit, can be had for much less than a similarly equipped Mac. Furthermore, to operate as a file server, the PC only needs an inexpensive monochrome monitor. Using software and network connectors such as those in the TOPS system from Sun Microsystems, you can hook several Macs to the PC and use its storage and backup facilities. Several configurations are possible. You can use Macs without hard disks and keep all data and program files on the PC hard drive, backing it up regularly with the tape drive. Alternatively you can use Macs that have their own hard drives and back each one up to its own area of the PC hard drive.

 I use an 80386 fitted with a Bernoulli drive. Backing up a Mac II hard drive across the TOPS network to the Bernoulli cartridge takes only 3 minutes per 10 megabytes, and I am using AppleTalk as opposed to EtherNet for the network. Fitting TOPS to a PC is very easy and only requires software installation plus the fitting of a FlashTalk card, or other AppleTalk adapter.

SOFTWARE SAFETY NETS

Backing up on a regular basis is a must for serious personal computer users, a lifesaver when hardware gives out or files are destroyed. However, it is still a damage limitation exercise, a precaution against the time when "things go wrong." There is always a period between backups during which valuable work might be performed, work which can be lost due to error, attack, mechanical breakdown, or power failure.

For example, suppose that you have just designed a brilliant 1-2-3 macro. Before you get a chance to save the file, the lights flicker and your machine reboots. Gone is the macro, and lost is the time it took to design it. If you exercise a positive attitude and immediately start reconstructing your work, you will probably find that reconstruction takes less time than creation. Nevertheless, it is an inconvenience you would like to avoid. Fortunately, you can obtain some measure of protection against the interim effects of such problems as power outages, even if you do not have the budget needed to supply everyone with a UPS.

The Saving Dilemma

Well-trained personal computer users know that they should save work regularly, religiously, and whenever leaving their computers unattended. Unfortunately, as with backup, "knowing you should" does not always mean "doing as you should." Any honest personal computer user of reasonable vintage will own up to at least one major sin of omission when it comes to saving work. To make up for this simple human failing, an increasing number of programs are making provisions for automatic file saving.

WordPerfect. During periods of intense word processing it is very easy to spend several hours totally absorbed in the act of writing and editing. Realizing that exhortations to "save regularly" were ineffective for many users, WordPerfect built an automatic save feature into its bestselling word processor. Activated by the Setup Backup command, the Timed Document Backup feature can be set to store work at regular intervals, measured in minutes. Once set, the program automatically records the current document on disk every so many minutes. So as not to interfere with your file naming system, WordPerfect uses a special file for this operation: WP{WP}.BK1. If you are editing two documents at once, the second one is backed up into WP{WP}.BK2. If things go wrong during an editing session, you can rename these files and then open them as regular documents when you reload WordPerfect. The timed saved feature causes very little inconvenience, particularly if you are using a hard disk. You might occasionally notice a "Please wait" message in the lower left of the screen while the saving to disk takes place. However, even when editing large documents of fifty pages or more, the time taken to save to disk rarely prevents you from typing for more than a few seconds. Using a timed backup setting of 5 minutes on older PCs, 3 minutes on newer, faster models should ensure that you never have to worry about whether you issued the Save command.

Quattro Pro. When Borland International decided to design a spreadsheet program to challenge 1-2-3, they saw that an advantage that could be offered is the ability to recover quickly from errors human and mechanical. Recovery was instituted on several fronts. First of all an Undo feature was added, this allows users to change their minds after issuing a command. Second, a feature called Transcript was incorporated. Transcript keeps a constant record of all keystrokes performed by the user. This keystroke log can then be played back just like a macro, allowing complete reconstruction of an unsaved worksheet after a power failure or other disaster.

1-2-3, New Releases. The designers of 1-2-3, Lotus Development Corporation, were keen to maintain the product's lead in the field of spreadsheet software and so designed error-recovery features into releases 2.3 and 3.1. These include an Undo key.

FileMaker. One of the most keystroke intensive applications on a personal computer is database management, involving as it does, the entry and updating of many records. Regular saving of database files is a must. However, the leading database for the Macintosh, FileMaker, does not have a Save command on its File menu. Instead, it automatically saves all changes whenever they are made. Because this is done incrementally, using a buffer system, the program is not slowed down by constant disk-writing; nevertheless, the user is assured that all work is always saved.

Third-Party Disaster Recovery

For users of programs that do not have built-in error-recovery, a number of third-party products available can restore a personal computer to predisaster form. These include Bookmark from Insight Development, Inc.

In the long run, we might see widespread adoption of the solution offered by Emerson electronics, with their combination hardware/software, Flash Card. This is a unit that delivers battery power directly to the motherboard of a PC in the event of a power supply failure (either at the mains or at the PC's power unit). The user receives a timely warning to save data files and exit applications. If the power outage continues the system is shut down, but a complete image of the current state of the PC's files and memory is maintained by the unit and so, when the power returns, the software can restore the unit to predisaster status.

SUMMARY

The evidence suggests that we are not born with good backup and file saving habits. Such habits are difficult to impose upon others. In the end, we must all take responsibility for making sure our data is backed up, and set a good example for those who might be influenced by our behavior. Within organizations, it is up to management to take the lead in establishing a livable regime of data backup. The value of files, the frequency with which they are altered, and the means available to back them up must all be evaluated. To repeat the key points made earlier, managers and administrators who are serious about personal computer security must:

1. Make backup a policy, not an option.
2. Make backup desirable.
3. Make backup easy.
4. Make backup mandatory.
5. Make sure users comply with backup policy.

Finally, you may want to place the following crude but effective summary, penned by an anonymous office worker, on the notice board:

Oh woe betide those who fail,
Some may even land in jail,
At the very least they'll shake and quake,
When their boss finds out what was at stake.
Tell this to all smug users you know -
Backup! backup! before you're told to go.

The invisible worm/That flies in the night/
In the howling storm.../Does thy life destroy.
William Blake, *The Rose*

10
The Virus Threat

THIS CHAPTER DESCRIBES how to protect against what is probably the most widely publicized threat to personal computer security: malevolent programs. Such programs, which interfere with the normal operation of a computer system, go by several names, including worms, logic bombs, trojan horses, and viruses. Each of these names reflects a different approach to malevolent programming but the name *virus* has captured the public imagination, with its strong analogy to unseen, quick-spreading, life-threatening biological forces. In fact, *virus* is now widely used as a general term for all types of malignant programming, including those that do not fit a strict definition of the term.

GOOD NEWS AND BAD NEWS

Of all threats to personal computer security, viruses have by far the highest public profile. On the other hand, many users have never experienced a virus attack. Before going into detail about what constitutes a virus, I want to put the matter of virus attacks into perspective. Unfortunately, a true perspective is very difficult to attain due to an almost complete lack of reliable statistics from which to gauge the true scale of the problem.

Have You Been Infected Lately?

Plenty of opinion polls support the view that personal computer users are very concerned about virus attacks. However, opinions about viruses are different from facts. When it comes to assessing just how many people have actually experienced a

337

virus, rather than how many are worried that they might, the statistics are less conclusive. The number of individuals and organizations prepared to give an honest answer to the question, "Have you been infected lately?" is limited.

In the October 1989 issue of the British publication, *Mac Magazine*, a senior manager at the stockbroking firm SG Warburg claimed that every company using Macs in the U.K. had experienced a problem with viruses, saying "Viruses are far more prevalent than manufacturers would like to make out." This view might have been colored by the fact that SG Warburg experienced several outbreaks of the Mac virus nVir on networked systems used for graphical analysis of stock market trends.

The June 1989 issue of the U.S. magazine *Mac User* could not verify an infection level in Macintoshes greater than ten percent, but was keen to present that as a low estimate, saying "by virtually all estimates more than ten percent of all Macs have been infected." Grounds for seeing ten percent as a high estimate come from David Ferbrache, a Ph.D. student in Viral Replication strategies at Heriot-Watt University. When asked by *Mac Magazine*, he estimated that only ten percent of business users have had "any contact" with viruses. However, he did suggest that in the academic community, where there are fewer access controls and more sharing of software, the figure probably rises to forty percent.

A reader survey by *Mac Magazine* showed less than a quarter of those responding had experienced viruses. Even fewer respondents said they thought the virus threat was exaggerated, while over half said they took preventative action against viruses. This might be seen as an indication that more people have actually experienced viruses firsthand than admit to having experienced them. The picture that emerges from a review of the statistics is of a phenomenon that is being widely reported and taken fairly seriously, but without clear evidence of the true scale of the threat that it poses.

The good news seems to be that number of cases in which viruses become active on personal computers is smaller than you might have been led to expect by the more pessimistic or alarmist figures. This conclusion was stated in the *PC Buyer's Guide* in the April/May 1990 issue: "The fact is viruses are rare." While it is possible, even perhaps quite likely, that the extent of infection varies according to country, type of hardware, and user classification, the fact is nobody has yet arrived at a reliable figure for how likely you are to encounter a virus. Such a figure, like a reliable estimate of the amount of money businesses lose due to breaches in computer security, is perhaps impossible to obtain. As *Mac Magazine* observed, "Estimates of the incidence of viral attacks vary widely because most companies are loathe to admit that their security is lax for fear that clients will lose confidence in them." Perhaps the one statement that can be made with some certainty is that viruses are not as rampant as some reports have suggested.

When I began work on this book, I installed a virus protection program on the machine used for the research files. Over an eighteen-month period, literally hundreds of floppy disks and dozens of programs from a wide variety of sources passed through the system. Not one virus showed up, until I deliberately purchased a disk that was rumored to be infected, even then, the infection did not do any damage.

Expert Opinion

The fact that you will not encounter viruses on every disk you buy, or in every program that you download, should be of some comfort as you read the rest of this chapter. Unfortunately, you will not find any absolute answers to the virus problem. These days fewer and fewer people are prepared to say that if you do A, B, and C, then you will be virus free. Security experts have been burned too often to give such undertakings. Consider the following advice: "A good rule to use is that all software that is run on any machine of importance, should come from a reputable source. 'Reputable source' does not exclude diskettes on the front of reputable magazines..."

This advice was given by Dr. Alan Solomon, operator of a very valuable data recovery service, supplier of inexpensive anti-virus software, and publisher of Virus Fax International. He wrote this in his advice column in the February 1990 issue of *CONNECTIVITY*, the newsletter of the British IBM PC User Group. Less than six months later, the not unrespectable British magazine *PC Today* unwittingly distributed 40,000 free disks that were later reported to be infected with a virus known as Ogre, the unpleasant effects of which are described later in this chapter.

The problem for experts is that even such apparently sound advice as that given by Dr. Solomon is liable to be undermined by some new manifestation of twisted thinking and malignant programming. The basic rule he suggests is a good one. The sad fact is that even "reputable" sources can fall victim to virus attacks. All reputable magazines that were in the habit of including free disks for readers had to review their vetting and duplicating procedures after the infamous incident.

Another expert, Don Parker of the research institute SRI, interviewed at the end of 1989, also underestimated the extent to which malignant programming has established itself as a permanent part of the computer scene. According to the *Times* of London, he suggested that "This year's [1989] bout of computer virus scares is expected to be the last." Mr. Parker's reasoning, after many years spent studying the phenomenon of hackers, was, "Hackers fast lose interest after a great deal of news attention." This statement might be true of hackers that meet a narrow intellectual definition of the term, but clearly plenty of individuals skilled in programming are still prepared to sabotage the work of others. Furthermore, even if it turned out that 1989 was the last year in which a virus was written, that would not in itself prevent the spread of pre-existing viruses. Plenty of viruses can easily re-emerge after long periods of inactivity.

The Layered Approach

So far this chapter has offered some good news and some bad news: Virus attacks might be rarer than reports suggest, but even experts in the field can misjudge from where the next threat is going to come. The good news for readers who have heeded the advice given in the preceding chapters is that the layered approach to security that this text has been developing gives you a head start in defending against viruses. To briefly reiterate the elements of this approach, they are:

Access Control
- Site—Controlling who can get near the system.
- System—Controlling who can use the system.
- File—Controlling who can use specific files.

System Support
- Power—Keeping supply of power clean and constant.
- Backup—Keeping copies of files current.

This chapter adds a third layer of System Support, referred to as *Vigilance*—keeping tabs on what enters, or is likely to enter, the system. By exercising vigilance, users and administrators alike can prevent, or at least, minimize, the effects of malevolent programming.

To be vigilant, users need to know what they are defending against. The defenses need constant updating to remain effective. Vigilance also involves an ongoing program of security checking, review, and education. Beyond this, it can affect hardware and software purchasing decisions.

In the case of the virus threat, vigilance first means knowing what viruses are, the methods of attack they use, and what constitutes a healthy regime of computer operation and maintenance. Secondly, it involves the use of software that prevents or warns of virus attacks. Thirdly, hardware buying choices might be affected, with systems that are more inherently virus-free being preferred. The measures that go together to make up an effective response to the virus threat will be discussed in this chapter, after a look at what exactly viruses are and where they come from.

WHAT VIRUSES ARE

The first step to securing your personal computer against the effects of malevolent programming is to understand the different types of programs that make up the virus threat and how they operate. To extend the medical analogy suggested by the term virus, personal computer users need an accurate picture of the risk of infection. No good is served by portraying viruses as lurking on every disk. This encourages everyone to see all operating glitches as virus symptoms: Viruses get blamed for user errors, program bugs, and hardware failures. On the other hand, to be effective in protecting a system, you need to know which paths of infection viruses can take, how to recognize an infection, and how to react to that infection.

Defining the Term Virus

Unfortunately, when you start to peruse the literature on this subject, one of the first things you notice is the lack of complete consensus about the basic terminology. For example, one book might dismiss worm as an early term for virus, while another makes an important distinction between worms and viruses. Given this lack of consensus, the definitions advanced here, while reasonably consistent with the majority of definitions, cannot yet be regarded as definitive or official.

The term *virus* has been appropriated as a generic term for all manner of malignant programming. However, the most basic definition of a virus is "a program that has the ability to replicate itself." A slightly more elaborate definition was put forward by Fred Cohen, who in 1983, carried out some of the first experiments with virus code. His definition was "a program that can infect other programs by modifying them to include a slightly altered copy of itself."

Despite the medical overtones, this type of definition makes a virus sound like quite a benign, if somewhat exotic, piece of programming. Indeed, Cohen's book *Computer Viruses: Theory and Experiments* suggested that viruses could have a positive role, a suggestion that has provided later practitioners of the art of virus-making with a tentative raison d'etre.

From an academic perspective, there is some argument as to whether viruses are inherently benign or malignant. Definitions of viruses are often shaded by their context. For example, Steve Gold, writing as a hacker in *Hugo Cornwall's New Hacker's Handbook*, describes a virus as a program that has the ability to "copy itself to and from disks, into systems, and over networks." Nothing particularly malignant from that definition, you might say. Indeed, the whole book presents the activity of *hacking*, defeating computer security measures, as a legitimate, legal, and worthwhile undertaking. Hugo Cornwall passed on to Gold the task of preparing the 1989 edition of this very popular book because it conflicted with his new role as a computer security consultant (under his real name, Peter Summer). Since then, Gold has appeared in computer magazines as an ex-hacker/security expert. In this context he defines a virus as "a program that infects a computer system, usually by introducing a program to the computer's hard disk and/or memory that inhibits the computer's function either wholly or partially." Disruptive tendencies are seen here as an inherent part of what constitutes a virus (for more on hacking in general, see Chapter 13).

While there has been considerable discussion about the potential for *good* viruses, perhaps as part of message delivery systems on networks, the general consensus is that the term *virus* should be restricted to software that is inherently disruptive. A virus carries out its task of replication by altering files, usually program files, attaching itself to them and spreading from one to another, much like a virus attacks and spreads among cells. The files modified by the virus act as carriers for the virus, leading to the definition "a self-replicating file modification."

The very act of modifying files means that the presence of a virus causes disruption to normal operation, in addition to which the virus program can be written to carry out a specific task, like playing a tune at a certain time every day. While this may not seem like a particularly disruptive task, it is almost impossible to write a virus that can carry out such a task without interfering with the normal operation of the host system, if for no other reason than that the programmer cannot possibly predict conditions on all of the host computers to which the virus will spread.

A lot of viruses attack operating system files, meaning that they have the potential to disrupt a wide range of users. Other viruses attack a particular application. Consider the virus that attacks dBASE data files, those stored with the DBF extension. The virus reverses the order of bytes in the file as it is written to disk. The virus reverses them back to normal when the file is retrieved, making the change transparent to the casual user. However, if the file is sent to an uninfected user, or if the virus is inadvertently removed from the host system, the data is left in a scrambled state.

The Worm Turns

In the last chapter the acronym WORM was introduced, standing for Write-Once Read-Many, a type of optical disk drive used for archiving data, and as such, a defense against breaches of security. In the context of malignant programs, *worm* is used figuratively. According to some experts, a worm is a program that spreads parts of itself across many different computers that are connected into a network, the parts remain in touch with, or related to, each other, thus giving rise to the term worm, a segmented insect. Naturally, this has a disruptive effect on the host computers, at the least eating up empty space in memory and storage, and wasting valuable processing time.

The distinction between worms and viruses is sometimes hotly debated. The lack of consensus was clearly evident during discussions of the Internet/Morris incident, described in detail later in this chapter. For example, one science correspondent observed that "Internet, the massive American computer network, came under attack from a worm: a type of computer virus which enters a network, and then replicates itself a number of times on the connected computers." However, a computer magazine stated that "Because it performed no other function, and didn't disguise itself as another type of program, most knowledgeable people have been calling the Internet program a 'worm' rather than a 'virus,' although there is some dissent about this." Yet another report described a worm as "a type of computer virus which enters a network, and then replicates itself a number of times on the connected computers."

There is no doubt that the Internet worm did replicate and did cause a lot of problems. It created a large number of mutant programs that consumed so much memory space and processor time that eventually ground several thousand computers to a halt. More destructive worms might erase files. Even without malicious intent, communications on the network are likely to be disrupted by any worm as it attempts to grow from one area to another. Most people agree that a worm is typified by independent growth rather than modification of existing programs. The difference between a worm and a virus might be characterized by saying a virus reproduces, while a worm grows. You could even distinguish between a worm *infestation* and a virus *infection*, although this may be taking the distinction and the analogy too far.

Worm programs have been more harshly described as "program code that destroys data held in memory or storage." The implication being that worms cannot operate without negatively affecting the computers that "host" them. Like viruses, worms can be left dormant within legitimate code to be triggered later by such events as a particular date or a certain number of uses of the host program. Malevolent code that is triggered like this can also be described as a *logic bomb*.

Logic Bombs

One of the oldest forms of malevolent programming seems to be the creation of dormant code that is later activated or triggered by specific circumstances. Typical triggers are events such as a particular date or a certain number of system starts. Stories abound of disgruntled programmers planting logic bombs to get back at employers deemed to have been unfair. Several logic bombs have been planted in order to extort money ("pay up or the computer gets it"). This requires paying or finding the malevolent code and removing it. The latter option can be extremely costly when the system is a large mainframe computer.

Take the case of Donald Burleson, a 40-year-old programmer at the Fort Worth based insurance company, USPA. In September 1987, he was fired for allegedly being quarrelsome and difficult to work with. Two days later, approximately 168,000 vital records erased themselves from the company computers. A logic bomb had gone off, wreaking havoc with the files that were the lifeblood of USPA!

People who still think of Texas as the land of cattle ranching and roughneck oil workers might be surprised to learn that the state's computer crime division is one of the most sophisticated in the country (due in part to the early lead taken by Texas in computerizing its financial transactions, notably oil and gas tax reporting). Burleson was caught after investigators went back through several years worth of system files. They found that two years before he was fired Burleson had planted a logic bomb, a destructive virus which lay dormant until he triggered it on the day of his dismissal. He became the first person in America to be convicted of "harmful access to a computer."

Trojan Horses

A piece of destructive software that achieves distribution and invasion by masquerading as something else, like the horse made by the Greeks in the Trojan Wars, is referred to as a *trojan horse*, or *trojan* for short. Once the legitimate program is loaded, the trojan code can go to work erasing data. This was the case with the "AIDS disk," distributed in 1989, that purported to be an informational program about AIDS but soon started messing with files on any computer that loaded the program. This particular trojan also attempted to extort money from users, offering to recover, for a fee, data that it had erased/hidden.

While virus programs gain entrance to a computer system by hiding within a normal program, typically part of the operating system, and then spreading to similar programs within the new host, trojan software depends upon being attractive or interesting to prospective users. Such was the case with a trojan that troubled Mac users in 1988. The so-called Sexy Ladies HyperCard stack dished up the promised pictures, but also erased data on the computer that loaded it. Many of the people who loaded the AIDS disk did so out of natural curiosity about the contents. They were rewarded by data loss and threatening messages.

A Programming Stew

In practice, a piece of subversive programming might contain more than one of the elements discussed. For example, a piece of trojan software, such as a free computer game, might be the carrier of a virus, which operates like a logic bomb. The user loads the game program onto a hard disk, and this causes the virus to infect files on the hard disk. From there, it spreads to each floppy disk used in the computer. The logic bomb waits until the thirteenth time the operator turns on the system. At that point, it activates a worm that grows until all sectors of the hard disk are filled.

As you can see from this simple scenario, the aim of a trojan is to slip past a computer's defenses. The main aim of a virus is to spread itself as fast as possible. For example, the virus might attach itself to an operating system file. Every time the user copies data to a new floppy disk, the virus is transferred to the new disk that, when inserted in a different computer, attaches itself to system files in that computer. It does not take much imagination to see how quickly and how far an outbreak of a particular virus can spread.

A recurrent nightmare for software companies is that a virus will infect program disks sold to customers. This nightmare became a reality for Aldus Corporation when a Macintosh virus got into a training disk included in a commercial product. Prompt detection, an accurate list of customers, and widespread coverage in the computer press allowed the company to prevent the problem getting completely out of hand. However, the questions of liability and responsibility get quite complex. For example, if a computer dealer supplied a typesetting company with a program disk that was infected, and the typesetter unwittingly passed on the virus to its own clients, perhaps on data disks, who would be liable for the losses incurred by the clients of the typesetter?

In situations like this, mutual assistance to eliminate the virus should be the order of the day, with recriminations reserved for the creator of the virus, not its innocent victims. When an attack of this nature does occur, a precise definition of the miscreant program is far less important than prevention and elimimation. This chapter and the rest of the book has followed the convenient practice of referring to all miscreant programs as viruses. However, in situations where the distinctions are of practical importance, they will be highlighted.

WHERE THEY COME FROM

The different kinds of malevolent programs may find their way onto your computer by several avenues. First consider the main routes for getting any information onto your computer. Ranked in terms of their potential as a route for infection, these are:

- *Disks*—Floppy disks, removable hard disks, ROM chips, and other media.
- *Ports*—Communications ports, network interfaces.
- *Input devices*—The keyboard.

Direct Infection

The use of an input device to infect your personal computer with a virus would require that someone sit down at your keyboard and type in the virus program. This is not impossible; some virus programs are remarkably compact and would not take long to enter. However, although this is a primary path for malevolent programming on mainframe systems, it is probably the least common method by which personal computers get infected.

Protection against direct infection is firstly a matter of preventing unauthorized use of your computer, and secondly, of detecting infection by an authorized user. A password protection/user-logging security system will prevent unauthorized use and show who has used the system. This is a valuable deterrent against infection by an authorized user, what one might call insider-infection.

Phone Infection

More common than direct infection of personal computers is infection from software transmitted over the phone. This does not mean another computer calls up your computer and infects it. What happens is, you download software from another computer, perhaps a bulletin board, and the software turns out to be infected. As the manual for Corbin Vaccine, a virus-detection program puts it: "Some viruses come from free programs placed on electronic bulletin boards—programs that appear to be innocent, useful utilities but really are vehicles for carrying the seeds of destruction."

An example of this is ARC513.EXE, a utility that claimed to offer file compression and archiving features like those found in ARC.EXE, a legitimate and very useful shareware utility. When ARC513.EXE is run it does not compress files, it destroys track 0 of the floppy or hard disk!

There have even been cases of malevolent programs masquerading as anti-virus software. A program pretending to be a new version of the legitimate virus-fighting Flu_Shot was found to render hard disks unreadable.

The programs are actually trojan horses in that they gain entrance to your system because they look attractive but do something other than you are led to expect. Some are not virus carriers, they only perform direct actions like destroying files. Others bring with them a virus that then starts infecting your files. Fortunately, operators of legitimate bulletin boards have been in the forefront of the fight against virus and take effective steps to prevent their services from being a means of infection. A good bulletin board will only allow programs to be posted after they have been checked by the system operator (SYSOP). If you upload a program to the bulletin board, it will not immediately appear for others to download. The SYSOP will copy with file onto a sanitized and isolated system and thoroughly check the file for signs of a virus.

As a user of bulletin boards you should not rely solely on the protection offered by a good SYSOP. After all, SYSOPs are only human and an infectious or malignant file might slip through the screening process. You should always check downloaded software on a safely backed up computer, preferably on an isolated system. If you do find problems, you should let the SYSOP know immediately. Bulletin boards are a valuable forum for the exchange of ideas, tips, and helpful information. The world of personal computing would be a sorry and stunted place without them. Some large companies have taken to banning the use of bulletin boards by employees because of the risk of virus infection. A more enlightened approach would be to institute proper procedures and facilities for the vetting of downloaded software.

The Infected Disk

The manual for Corbin Software's virus detection program Vaccine warns that "Viruses often are acquired from illegal copies of commercial software that someone modified precisely because they felt morally incensed at the act of illegal copying." Very few virus-writers have given reliable accounts of their motives, so the accuracy of this assertion is difficult to verify, but the implication is irrefutable: You should avoid bootleg software. Failure to do so can lead to all manner of problems, not just virus infection. If you buy your software in sealed packages from a reputable source and observe the terms of the software license agreement you stand to gain a lot. Some of the benefits are:

- Software that is *almost certainly* virus free.
- Warranty rights.
- Support rights.
- Proper documentation.
- Freedom from blackmail.
- A righteous feeling.

The consequences of being prosecuted for using an illegal copy of a software package are clearly a threat to peace of mind and personal security, if not to the security of data.

The question of exactly what constitutes bootleg software is discussed in more detail in the next chapter. Most users should be able to recognize illegally copied software. This ranges from disks with hand-written labels offered by a friend or associate to crude copies of original packaging. The latter are rare in Europe and the U.S., but quite common in the Far East. The former have been encountered by most of us at one time or another, accompanied by statements like: "Here's that game program I was telling you about;" "Go on, take it, it's only a copy;" or "Just copy this utility onto your hard disk, you'll love it."

The ethics of this sort of activity are discussed in the next chapter, as are three types of software that may be legitimately shared without payment: public domain, shareware, freeware. The bottom line is that commercially produced software costs money, and trying to save money by using illegal copies is a risky business. If you do use a bootleg disk that turns out to carry a virus, you will find very few people sympathetic to your plight.

For organizations, the risk of using bootleg software is two-fold. In addition to the risk of virus infection from a bootleg disk, illegal use of software by any members of the organization exposes the organization to prosecution, fines, and embarrassing publicity. This applies to both home and business use. The increasing use of computers to work at home in the evenings and on weekends means that the ban on using bootleg software has to be observed at all times. Take the laptop home, load up a bootleg games disk your kid brought home from school, and you could infect a computer that then returns to the workplace, where it proceeds to infect others.

This is not to say that all bootleg software is riddled with viruses, or that friends and associates will knowingly infect each other's computers, but viruses are hard to detect without special software and an infection can be passed quite unwittingly. The best rule of thumb is to insert no disk into your computer unless you know exactly what is on it, where it has come from, and who you can complain to if it turns out to be infected.

VIRUS AWARENESS

Unfortunately, the blurring of distinctions between worms, trojan horses, and viruses that has so confused some personal computer users is typical of press and television coverage of the subject. Apparently, the media finds it easier to avoid explaining a group of complex terms when one simple one will do, even if the simple approach is inaccurate, or even downright misleading.

The Scare Factor

Reporting the discovery of a new piece of trojan software as a virus outbreak overlooks that fact that only those computers which load the trojan program are at risk. This is quite a different risk from a spreading virus infection, which can place all new programs under suspicion, even ones from reputable suppliers. Similarly, news of a worm program spreading through a network of research computers needs to make clear the fact that only computers connected to the network, running the network operating system, are at risk. The Internet/Morris worm was never a threat to personal computers in general. The program only attacked Sun and DEC VAX systems running a particular version of Unix. This fact was not immediately apparent to many people who saw news coverage of the event.

The sensationalized treatment of viruses in the media frequently gives rise to outbreaks of unwarranted anxiety among personal computer users, and considerable misunderstanding among those who are not familiar with the way in which computers work. In many cases the virus threats that are publicized are not as widespread or as serious as the reports make out. First reports of the Internet/Morris incident were wildly exaggerated. Internet had no useful classified information as many reports claimed. Not all of the 150,000 computers on the network were involved as some reports suggested. In fact, only about 1 in 25 were affected. Talk of hundreds of millions of dollars worth of damage eventually boiled down to a total cleanup cost of $95 million, and even this figure has been questioned.

The point is that the waste of time and effort directly attributable to malevolent programs is bad enough without alarming people unnecessarily. After a big virus scare, less computer-literate users waste time and effort worrying about attacks that do not materialize. The only possible benefit of media scare stories is a heightened awareness of the problem in general. This does make it easier for those within an organization who are concerned about security to successfully advocate the adoption of a defensive approach to personal computer management. The effects can be beneficial just as long as organizations distinguish between the bogus "security experts" that scare stories tend to lure out of the woodwork, and those with genuine solutions to offer.

The Front Line of Education

These days all responsible personal computer users, and those responsible for groups of users, need a basic level of knowledge about "the virus threat." This includes an understanding of how malevolent programs enter a system, and how they are likely to manifest themselves. While the main emphasis must be to help users to protect their systems, it is equally important to educate users as to what a rogue program can and cannot do. This helps to head off the problems of users pinning any and all problems on phantom code lurking in their system.

 Some microcomputer support staff have observed that the publicity about viruses has produced a subtle change in the pattern of many distress calls. Whereas users tended to ask "Could it be I pressed the wrong button or something?" They now tend to wonder "Could it be a virus or something?" Unless users have a good grasp of how their personal computers work, they will have difficulty distinguishing between user error, mechanical error, and intrusive programs.

The best and first defense for the individual user faced with the threat of virus attack is a good working knowledge of the problem, which can be obtained from this chapter. The best defense for organizations is well-informed users who understand how such programs are transmitted.

As most personnel managers know, well-informed users do not grow on trees. They are the product of good hiring, training, and communication practices. By instituting a virus awareness program that incorporates the facts set out here, possibly as part of an overall security awareness program, and by laying down a set of operational rules tailored to the organization's use of personal computers, the threat can be greatly minimized.

An effective anti-virus defense is an active defense, constantly on the alert for the latest developments. To keep them abreast of the latest threats, organizations can subscribe to a virus update service, like Virus-FAX, dedicated to keeping micro-managers posted on the newest developments. This particular service consists of regularly faxed bulletins, plus a commitment to broadcast urgent news as and when it happens. A service like this can help to minimize the effects of new viruses and trojan horses like the AIDS disk, described in detail later in this chapter. Such services look set to be a permanent feature of personal computing, as long as there remain highly skilled programmers to whom the development and release of viral code is an acceptable activity.

For individual users, such a service might not be economical. Fortunately, many computer magazines have eschewed the sensationalism of other publications and now provide responsible and up-to-date coverage of virus threats. Regular perusal of such magazines should provide the individual user with sufficient information about the latest threats.

Further Defenses

After a well-informed user community, the next line of defense is to install a specialized piece of software known as a *virus-detector*. Placed in each personal computer, such software can alert the user to the presence of most viruses before they have time to cause damage. The virus can be removed and its spread within the organization can be minimized. A number of these programs are described later in this chapter.

Despite access controls, security awareness campaigns, and virus-detection software, managers attempting to protect large numbers of personal computers from viruses will continue to face problems due to the sheer volume of new software and data that users generate/accumulate. Any manager who has tried to impose complete control over everything that enters every disk drive, will know that this is an unpopular and impractical strategy. A policy like this is likely to make users resentful, and tempt some to break the rules, just because they are there to be broken. However, the alternative need not be completely *laissez-faire* computing.

Suppose management were to provide users with a no-questions-asked virus-vetting service. This would be run on an isolated test-bed computer that contained no data of any value, but was configured with the latest virus-detection software. Users could bring along any disk that they were even thinking of putting into their computers. This disk could be checked for viruses without risk of contaminating other systems. The disk could then be certified virus-free.

By providing a facility of this type management could then expect to enforce a policy of "no-uncertified software" without appearing to be unreasonable. By testing *any* disk, it would be possible to extend the virus-detection to one of the most dangerous areas for virus-infection: recreational and home use.

Basic Rules

Before going into further detail about viruses and how they operate, it is useful to summarize the basic rules to be followed in defending against viruses:

1. Know what you are putting into your computer.
2. Know the warning signs of a malevolent program.
3. Use a virus detector to watch over your system.
4. Use an isolated machine to test software that might be suspect.

THE VIRUS MAKERS

Before looking in more detail at viruses and ways of defending against them, it might be helpful to take a moment to ask why people create these programs in the first place. Theories to explain the existence of virus programs involve equal parts computer science and psychology. The supposition is that such programs are almost as old as legitimate computer programs, although documentation of early virus attacks is sketchy (as with other areas of computer security, victims are reluctant to admit they have been attacked; details of attacks are often more a matter of rumor than of record).

The Early Days

Cases of disruptive programming in the 1960s tended to revolve around disgruntled programmers seeking to sabotage large mainframe computer systems on which they had worked, or threatening to damage data or programs in an effort to extort payment. In some cases, the goal of the attacker was to gain what he or she saw as "rightful" compensation, denied due to disagreement with an employer. This gave rise to a series of attempts to justify miscreant programming. However, early mainframe systems were often closely guarded and access to them was severely restricted, which tended to restrict the scope of such attacks.

In fact, the tight controls on computer access struck some programmers as frustrating, even repressive. They saw the bypassing of controls as a legitimate undertaking as well as a test of their skills. Feelings such as this have persisted and now form part of the "hacker ethic" discussed in Chapter 13. Those who object to limits on free access to information tend to see each new limit as a challenge. In turn, this has led some to see all legitimate programming as something to be probed and questioned, its weaknesses attacked. Thus we have the "I wrote it to show up weaknesses in the operating/security system" defense of virus making. Users who have lost time and data to viruses tend to equate this with a vandal who has just thrown a brick through a window turning round and claiming he was merely performing a stress test on the glass.

Back in the 1970s, mainframe computers were expensive tools which, by their sheer cost, tended to restrict access to the power of computer technology. Furthermore, it was military, financial, and government institutions that got the bulk of the computer power. A desire to put computer power in the hands of the people was a significant factor in the emergence of the first personal computers in the 1970s. Regardless of the intentions of the companies who started making such machines, it soon became clear that personal computers were going to foster a populist attitude to information and bring programming skills to a much wider cross-section of the population.

The spread of programming skills has had many positive effects; however, it must be remembered that the ability to create programs is a form of power, and power must be exercised responsibly. These days, the population of would-be programmers is not vetted for excessive self-confidence, immaturity, paranoia, vindictiveness, or malice.

All of these traits can be found in viruses that have broken out on personal computers in the last ten years.

The young hacker who thinks he has created a benign virus, one designed to simply display a message of peace on a certain day for example, might not have sufficient maturity to appreciate the potential for unexpected side effects, let alone the potential for a less-benign programmer to subvert the virus code for more malicious purposes, like displaying a message of extortion.

The Ambivalent Image

The perception of "hacker as hero" was quite common during the first half of the 1980s as movies like *War Games* popularized the image of the idealistic computer-literate youngster outsmarting adults, in this case showing them the folly of relying on computers in the cold war. This image became tarnished as the intentions of hackers came under suspicion. In 1987, it was still possible to describe the German Chaos Computer Club as "known for discovering security breaches in data processing systems," and say of their penetration of computers belonging to institutions like the German Research and Experimentation Institute for Aviation and Aeronautics, the European Space Authority, and NASA that "The affected institutions can consider themselves lucky that the intruders were only hackers, who had no interest in using the information they had obtained for unlawful purposes."

Since Ralf Burger wrote this in his book *Computer Viruses: A High-Tech Disease*, published in 1987, a number of German hackers have been convicted of espionage. With the publication of the *Cuckoo's Egg*, Cliff Stoll's account of the affair, we know just how much time and effort that such activities can waste.

A less charitable view of the activities of virus writers is taken by Howard Upchurch, the author of a widely circulated document designed to help Macintosh users get rid of Scores, a particularly nasty virus:

> A virus is an organism that attacks and feeds off a host until either the virus or the host dies. A so-called Scores virus has spread throughout the Macintosh community. This virus, however, is a nasty piece of software written by a demented individual. Just like a living organism, it reproduces itself and has spread like an epidemic.

Stopping the spread of this epidemic involved inoculating users with information about how to recognize the virus, how to eradicate it, and how to prevent further infections.

Unfortunately, the dissemination of detailed information about how viruses work can actually contribute to their spread. Efforts to document viruses have themselves become something of a dilemma. One of the first works on the subject, *Computer Viruses: Theory and Experiments*, by Fred Cohen, actually gave examples of virus code. This practice has remained controversial despite claims that it is important for the subject to be dealt with openly and viruses cannot be gotten rid of by making them secret.

An interesting example of this dilemma is found in Burger's book, quoted earlier, which presents numerous examples of virus code that the reader can experiment with. This can be seen as positive, enabling anti-virus programmers to better understand the problem; but the negative view sees would-be virus-writers getting a helping hand from such information. In the light of subsequent events, one particular passage in this book gains considerable poignancy. In discussing press treatment of virus attacks, the author points out that a *Newsweek* article on viruses in February 1988, entitled "Is Your Computer Infected?" appeared on the same page as another article entitled "A Case Of AIDS And Malpractice." The observation is made that, "In part, it seems as though a hysteria is spreading among computer users which nearly equals the uncertainty over the AIDS epidemic." The parallel between AIDS and the spread of virus programs has been made by many people, including those attempting to make the connection between safe sex and safe computing for the purposes of marketing computer security devices. However, the words quoted above gained new significance when, in 1989, thousands of legitimate computer users received a disk marked:

AIDS Information, Introductory Diskette, Version 2.0

Users who followed the installation instructions on the label soon found an encryption scheme had been invoked that altered information on the disk in such a way that the machine's hard disk was locked up and could not be used. Once locked in this way, the machine would only respond to commands by displaying a warning that "The lease for a key software package has expired." It went on to insist that users should pay the leasing fee for the AIDS software to receive a renewal disk to regain the use of their machine. The disk is shown in Fig. 10-1.

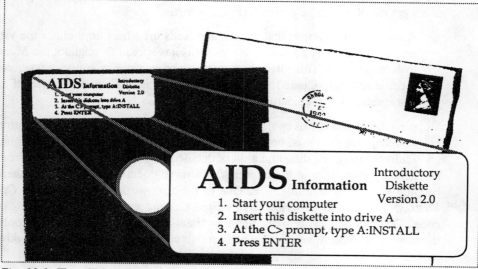

Fig. 10-1. The AIDS disk.

Skill Maturity

As you might expect, creating a piece of software that can accomplish such amazing feats as self-replication is quite a challenge to programmers. Plenty of evidence indicates that early work on viruses was done out of a sense of challenge rather than malice. Unfortunately, while writing self-replicating code is hard, it is almost impossible to write such code so that it reproduces without interfering with the normal operation of the comptuers that it infects.

You might speculate that skilled though they might be, programmers who write and release virus code are not mature enough to acknowledge their limitations. Some viruses have been released by programmers sure that their code will spread without negatively impacting carriers. The nVir virus that spread through Macintoshes in Europe is not designed to do any damage, but it causes printing problems and system crashes that can erase data in memory. The author of the original is reputed to have wanted to inspire others to write more effective anti-virus software. A thriving market in such software now exists but most users wish it was not necessary. The main achievement of the author of nVir is to waste a lot of other people's time and money and give less well-balanced programmers the basic code to create their own viruses. Several strains of nVir are now out there causing yet more trouble.

The goal of the purely neutral virus might be achievable, *if* everyone used their computers in the same way, with the same mix of devices, program versions, utilities, and commands. The real world of personal computing has an almost unlimited number of variations on a standard operating environment. It is perhaps failure to accept that they cannot foresee all of the possibilities for disruption presented by this state of affairs that causes most virus writers to miscalculate the effects of their creations.

Malice Aforethought

Some virus infections are undeniably intended to do damage. The Scores virus that has plagued Mac users was definitely designed to attack applications developed by Electronic Data Systems. The fact that it spread to systems that had nothing to with EDS or its applications is another indication of how hard it is to predict the effects of releasing a virus. Scores causes general printing problems, damage to Excel files, and other disruption, apart from the fact that getting rid of it wastes valuable time and energy.

VIRUS EXAMPLES

This text assumes that you want to protect against, rather than experiment with, viruses. For this reason no how-to instructions for virus-making are provided. However, to defend against viruses, you need to know the sort of actions they can produce. To this end, several cases are cited in this chapter. Because there is considerable defensive value in having a list of known viruses handy, Appendix C provides the basis for such a list, although, given the speed with which a new virus can appear and spread, the list cannot claim to be either complete or up to date. What you should get from the list and this chapter is a good sense of how viruses manifest themselves and how they can be defeated. The following sections describe several viruses, one trojan horse, and a worm.

    For those with a legitimate reason to experiment with viruses, that is, people like bulletin board operators who must protect their systems against virus infections, there is a program called the Universal Viral Simulator made available by the society of bulletin board operators, the National BBS Society of San Jose, California.

A Yankee Doodle Dandy

This virus, which gets its name from the tune it plays, infects IBM compatible personal computers running DOS. The virus will infect any COM or EXE file on any disk, as long as the file is larger than 33 bytes to begin with. Referred to as an indirect action file virus, it causes COM files to grow when infected. The amount of growth is about 2800 bytes. The date and time settings on the file are not altered by the act of infection. The main evidence of the virus is hearing Yankee Doodle, at 5:00 P.M.

The way the virus works is to load itself into memory when you run an infected COM or EXE file. Any COM or EXE file loaded after that is then also infected. Files which have been marked read-only are not protected. The virus sets their file attribute to read/write, infects them, then resets the attribute after infection. The critical error handler in DOS is disabled while the file is being infected. This prevents write-protected disks from producing an Abort, Retry, Ignore message.

The virus has been encountered in both the U.S. and Europe. The overt action of the virus is to play Yankee Doodle, at 16:59:53 by the DOS clock. In some versions this happens every day, that is, every time the clock reads this exact time. Other versions of the virus do not play the tune every time. Because of the similarity to another virus, called Vacsina, and the fact that at least two different versions of Yankee Doodle have been found, with provisions for version numbers and upgrades, it looks as if there will be further versions of this virus. The routine for playing the tune is quite easy to modify, so variants could play a different tune, possibly at a different time of day.

A Real Ogre

While the Yankee Doodle virus spreads by going memory-resident when an infect EXE or COM program is run, another sort of virus operates by infecting the boot sector of disks. The boot sector is the first part of a disk that the operating system reads. Consequently it contains important information about the disk, such as which version of the operating system created the disk, and so on. You can see a boot sector from a normal formatted MS-DOS floppy disk in Fig. 10-2, as revealed by the Norton Utilities.

This book is not the place to go into great detail about the information displayed, but you can see that the version of DOS used to create the disk is MS-DOS 3.3. The important point is that the contents of the boot sector go into memory as soon as a disk

```
 Boot area ══════════════════════════════════════════════ Hex format ═
  Sector 0 in Boot area                                  Offset 0, hex 00
EB34904D 53444F53 332E3300 02010100 02E00060 09F90700 ♦4£MSDOS3.3.◙◙◙,◙α,`○·•,
0F000200 00000000 00000000 00000000 00000000 00000012 *.◘,..............‡
00000000 0100FA33 C08ED0BC 007C1607 BB780036 C5371E56 ....◙.·3└░╨╝,|▬•╗x,6╫7▲V
1653BF2B 7CB90B00 FCAC2680 3D007403 268A05AA 8AC4E2F1 ▬S┐+!╢δ,ⁿ¼&¬=,t♥&è♠·è╙╒±
061F8947 02C7072B 7CFBCD13 7267A010 7C98F726 167C0306 ♠▼ëG◙║┐+¡√╛=!!rgá►!ÿ≈&¬!♥♦
1C7C0306 0E7CA33F 7CA3377C B82000F7 26117C8B 1E0B7C03 ¬!♥♠♫!úúú?!ú7!▸ ◙≈&◄!¥▲δ!♥
C348F7F3 0106377C BB0005A1 3F7CE89F 00B80102 E8B30072 ╟H≈≤◙7!¶₁♠?!δf,¶◙◙◙|.r
198BFBB9 0B00BED6 7DF3A675 0D8D7F20 BEE17DB9 0B00F3A6 ↓┤√╣δ,╢}≤ªu∩ì╜}╣δ,≤ª
7418BE77 7DE86A00 32E4CD16 5E1F8F04 8F4402CD 19BEC07D t↑╜w}δj,2Σ=¯^▼Â♠ÂD◙=↓┘}
EBEBA11C 0533D2F7 360B7CFE C0A23C7C A1377CA3 3D7CBB00 δδí¬♥3╥6δ!■↳6<!í?!ú=!¶,
07A1377C E84900A1 187C2A06 3B7C4038 063C7C73 03A03C7C •í?!δI,í↑!*♠!;@8♦<!s♥á<!
50E84E00 5872C628 063C7C74 0C010637 7CF7260B 7C03D8EB P☼N,Xr╟(♦<!t♀◙♦?!≈δ!♥♦δ
D08A2E15 7C8A16FD 7D8B1E3D 7CEA0000 7000AC0A C07422B4 ╨è,§!è¬}¥▲=!Ω,,p,╝◙└t¶
0EBB0700 CD10EBF2 33D2F736 187CFEC2 88163B7C 33D2F736 ♫╗•,→δ23╥6↑!■╥è¬;!3╥6
1A7C8816 2A7CA339 7CC3B402 8B16397C B106D2E6 0A363B7C →!è■*!ú9!╟╟BY¬9!▲╥╥◙6;!
8BCA86E9 8A16FD7D 8A362A7C CD13C30D 0A4E6F6E 2D537973 Y╨â◙¬ⁿ}è6*!=!!╟♫Non-Sys
74656D20 6469736B 206F7220 6469736B 20657272 6F720D0A tem disk or disk error♪◙
5265706C 61636520 616E6420 73747269 6B652061 6E79206B Replace and strike any k
65792077 68656E20 7265616E 790D0A00 0D0A4469 736B2042 ey when ready♪◙.♪◙Disk B
6F6F7420 6661696C 7572650D 0A00494F 20202020 20205359 oot failure♪◙.IO       SY
534D5344 4F532020 20535953 00000000 00000000 00000000 SMSDOS   SYS...........
00000000 000055AA          Press Enter to continue    ......U┐
1Help   2Hex    3Text   4Dir   5FAT   6Partn  7      8      9Undo   10QuitNU
```

Fig. 10-2. Boot sector as displayed by Norton Utilities.

is read. This means that a virus infecting the boot sector gets into a system very quickly.

A boot sector virus does not need to be on a disk that is bootable, that is, contains a copy of the operating system. If you insert a non-bootable floppy disk in floppy drive A of a hard disk PC, close the drive door and boot up, you will get the message Non-system disk or disk error. Replace and strike any key when ready. This message has been read from the floppy! When you take out the floppy and press any key the system does not reboot, it simply carries on. The contents of RAM are not flushed out. Virus code could have been loaded from the non-bootable disk along with the message you just read. The viral code can go to work almost immediately. The virus can then spread by placing itself on disks formatted by the infected system.

An example of this type of virus is *Ogre*, sometimes called *Computer Ogre* or *Disk Killer*. If your computer gets infected with Ogre, it will pass itself on through floppy disks you create with the computer, plus, it can render hard disk data useless. If you leave an infected computer on for 48 hours, then access the hard disk during the following hour, you will trigger the destructive part of the virus. The screen clears and the following messages appear:

Disk Killer—version 1.00 by Computer Ogre 040/01/89.
Warning, Don't turn off the power or remove the
diskette while Disk Killer is processing,
PROCESSING

The virus then encrypts your hard disk, making it inaccessible! The reason for including this virus as an example is that it was the subject of a major "false alarm," one of the less obvious indirect effects of viruses. In July of 1990, a damaged copy of this virus was found on a free disk distributed by a British computer magazine. Free disks are a feature of computer magazines in Europe, and this particular one contained a copy of the shareware program PowerMenu. Ironically PowerMenu is a useful security tool, providing password-protected menus for access to programs on a PC.

The tell-tale signs of Ogre are:

- The boot sector of infected disks is abnormal.
- When present on a floppy disk, the disk will have 3K of bad sectors.
- When it is active, 8K of memory is lost.

The first two of these three signs were present on the free disk. In Fig. 10-3, you can see how the boot sector of the disk differs from a normal disk, shown earlier in Fig. 10-2.

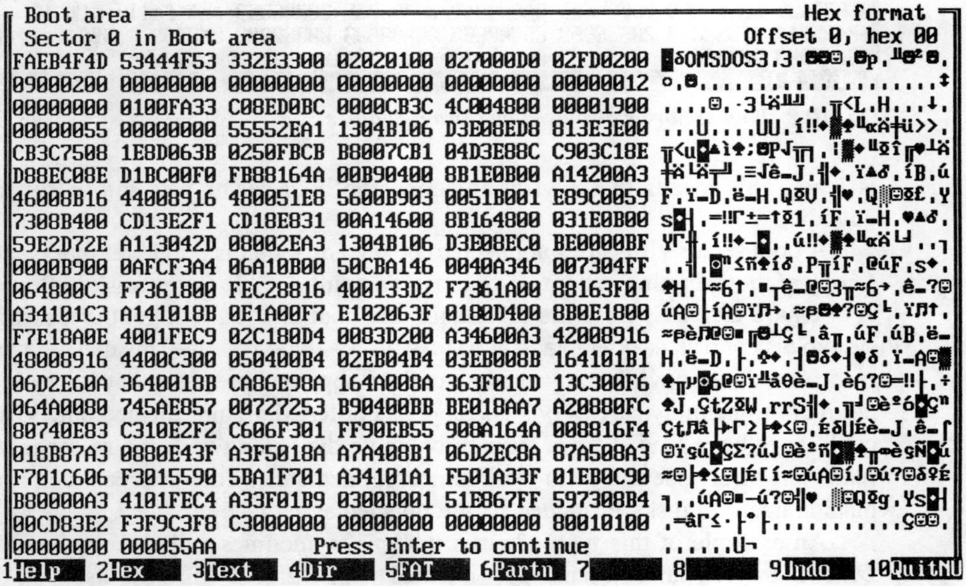

Fig. 10-3. Abnormal boot sector from an infected disk.

Upon detecting these signs of infection, several very vigilant users informed the magazine, which informed the media of the problem as a method of warning potential victims. Having distributed 40,000 magazine/disk packages, most of which were sold to be sold on newsstands, the decision could not have been an easy one. Fortunately for everyone involved, it transpired that the virus code was damaged. However, the magazine made the mistake of telling callers that the virus could only go to work if the infected disk was used to boot up a computer, and that the distribution disk could not be made bootable. In fact, as mentioned earlier, a boot sector virus does not need to be on a bootable disk to infect a system.

Beyond the general confusion and embarrassment, there were other negative implications. The use of free disks as a method of distributing software was placed under considerable scrutiny. Many other magazines had to reassess the procedures used to prepare and duplicate disks. Some considered taking out insurance against infections, thus placing pressure on the cover price. Furthermore, a "useful" piece of viral code was placed into the hands of a wide range of individuals, some of whom might be tempted to try their hand at a variation of Ogre.

The *MacMag* Virus

First press reports of this Macintosh virus appeared in February 1988, although it was launched in December 1987 by Richard Brandow. He was then publisher of *Mac-Mag* magazine in Montreal, Canada. He claims that the virus was intended as a simple message of peace, designed to pop up on Macintosh screens on March 2, the anniversary of the introduction of the Mac SE and II. The virus infects the System file, but does not directly affect applications. After March 2, the virus erased itself. A classic example of a virus designed to be benign but in reality having nasty side effects: It played havoc with System folders, resulting in thousands of hours of lost work. The virus spread to Europe and became the first virus to infect a commercially available personal computer product.

How this came about is a classic case of virus infection. The president of a software company in Chicago loaded a computer game, called Mr. Potato Head, on his personal Macintosh. He was unaware that the disk was infected. He only ran the game program once, but it was enough to infect his Mac. Some time later his company, MacroMind, was developing a training disk for Aldus. The infected Mac was used to work on the training disk, which was then sent to Aldus. A disk-duplicating machine at Aldus copied the infected disk for three days. Half of the infected disks were distributed to customers. The other half were warehoused. Upon discovery of the virus, infected packages were recalled.

The AIDS Disk

Between 8 and 12 December 1989, thousands of personal computer users around the world received in the mail the free disk pictured earlier in Fig. 10-1. The disks were sent by a company called PC Cyborg Corporation, and contained a program written to evaluate a user's risk of contracting the HIV virus according to answers given to a series of questions about the user's life-style. The disks had professionally-printed labels and were mailed in white envelopes to names taken from various mailing lists of known computer users.

Negative Effects. An unknown number of recipients, estimated at between 500 and 1000, proceeded to load the disks according to the instructions on the label. The program required a hard disk and the installation copied the program to the hard disk.

Some observant users noticed that the installation process had created a series of hidden files and directories on the hard disk, but apart from take up space the program did not at first appear to have much impact on the host system. However, after a certain number of reboots (in most cases 90), the program proceeded to encrypt the entire contents of the hard disk, effectively denying users access to their own data, with no obvious way to reclaim it.

The AIDS program did offer a way of getting back your computer. The first operation performed by the program when installed was to print out an invoice for payment. After locking up the hard disk, it displayed this message: The lease for a key software package has expired. It went on to insist that users should pay a lease renewal fee for the AIDS software in order to regain the use of their hard disk. The fee, based on the term of the lease was either $189 or $378 and was to be sent to a post office box in Panama City.

The Reaction. The PC user community reacted very quickly to this problem, developing a program that would remove the trojan and return control of the hard disk to the user. A computer magazine, who had, in good faith, sold a copy of its mailing list to Cyborg Corporation began to receive calls from subscribers about the disk. The magazine started an investigation into the source and operation of the disk and its contents. Arrangements were made to produce a clean-up program which would remove the hidden files and directories set up by the installation routine. Removal of these installation files was a relatively simple process for knowledgeable individuals with the requisite software utilities. However, it was felt that non-technical users would be at risk unless a special clean-up program was freely available. Such a program was written, tested, and distributed free of charge worldwide on various computer networks by lunchtime December 13. In the meantime, postal and other authorities were closing in on the address in Panama City, attempting to find out who was behind this mailing.

The next technical step in combating the disk was to identify the encryption algorithms used during the disk-locking process. The goal was a program able to recover the use of the disk on a machine where the program had been "triggered." After further testing of the AIDS disk, a decryption program was developed that completely reversed the encryption, restoring an affected machine to the state it was in before the AIDS program was installed. Within days of the problem being discovered, a second clean-up program was released which incorporated the functions of the first and was capable of recognizing what state the machine was in and then taking appropriate action.

The Implications. While the reaction by the global computer-using community was impressive and certainly helped to minimize the negative impact of this trojan program, perhaps what is most remarkable about this incident is that more than a handful of users actually installed the program. Along with each disk there was a small sheet of paper that gave details of how to run the program. The sheet carried details of "Limited Warranty" and a "License Agreement." Some people described this document as being in "almost illegibly small print" but it could be read, as this is part of what it said:

> There is a mandatory leasing fee for the use of these programs; they are not provided to you free of charge . . . If you install these programs on a micro-computer . . . you thereby agree to pay PC Cyborg Corporation in full for the cost of leasing these programs.

If this was not enough cause to pause, the text went on to say that in the event of a breach of the license agreement, PC Cyborg Corporation reserved the right to use what were ominously referred to as "program mechanisms" to ensure "termination of your use of the programs." There was also a warning that these program mechanisms would adversely affect other program applications on the computer.

There is some debate as to whether or not this license "agreement" or any of its conditions are legal, particularly because the disk comes under the heading of "unsolicited material."

However, the important point from a security perspective is that there was some form of warning with the program. Only users ignorant as to basic software rights and the potential of trojan programs could have proceeded to install the program before learning more about it.

The Internet/Morris Incident

The most widely reported case of computer tampering took place in November 1988, when Robert Morris, Jr., a 24-year-old post-graduate student at Cornell University, released a worm/virus onto Internet, the massive American-based international computer network. This network consists of Unix-based computers in research facilities such as U.C. Berkeley, Purdue University, and Lawrence Livermore Laboratories. Although some of the institutions connected to this network carry out classified defense work (Livermore is "famous" for its design work on nuclear weapons), none of the computers connected to Internet contain classified data.

The Attack. The method used to introduce the worm has been described as "relatively straightforward." The operative term here is "relative" because you have to be very Unix-literate to understand how it worked. Basically, Morris wrote a program that examined the password file of computers on the network. This file contains the sequences of letters that have to be typed by users in order for the computer to recognize them and gain access. The password file contains the password of all users, but they are encrypted using a highly efficient coding algorithm to prevent intruders from reading them.

The worm program consisted of a version of the algorithm which carried out the encryption. It generated passwords, using a list of commonly used passwords, then encrypted them and compared them against entries in the password file. The program was highly successful in finding passwords. At one site more than eighty percent of the passwords were "guessed" by the worm. This is because, as pointed out in previous chapters, users who pick their own passwords choose one that is easily memorized or that can be derived easily, such as variants of their user name.

Another aspect of the Internet network used by the worm was in the mailing software. Normally, this is used to send messages from one computer to another. The worm took advantage of undocumented features in this program to send information to other computers on the network that resulted in the creation of other worms. If this wasn't frightening enough, the worm was capable of much more sophisticated actions. For example, it contained the ability to plant trojan programs that could be activated later, and local viruses that would have a character of their own and so could not be traced back to the worm.

The Results. In the end, the worm infected more than 6000 computers and closed down major parts of the Internet network for several days while the rogue program was eliminated. You can get an idea of the level at which Morris was working from the fact that it took about 6 hours for a team of 18 UNIX wizards at U.C. Berkeley and Lawrence Livermore Laboratories, to figure out what caused the problem and to develop a fix. Beyond this was a lot of discussion about how to close up the programming loopholes that Morris exploited. In fact, when he was later put on trial under the 1986 Computer Fraud and Abuse Act, Morris claimed that the worm was written to expose these weaknesses in Unix and Internet. Some experts in Unix led credence to this defense, pointing out that many users had complained about the very things that Morris brought into the limelight.

The Consequences. For Robert Morris, Jr., the main consequence was over a year of uncertainty as he was investigated, indicted, tried by a jury, and finally convicted, under the 1986 Computer Fraud and Abuse Act, in January 1990. The verdict set several legal precedents and was seen as a vindication of the Act, which some experts thought would be inadequate against "hacking" offenses. In the long term, Morris, a brilliant programmer and son of a leading computer expert at the NSA, might not find his career prospects seriously affected by what happened.

The immediate consequence for the public was all manner of media hype and not a little confusion. A number of television news broadcasts even went so far as to show footage or quotes from the movie *War Games* to illustrate their stories about the Internet worm. In fact, there is no worm or virus in the movie, which has no relevance whatsoever to the Internet case (one opportunistic station quickly scheduled a showing of the movie itself, using the headlines to promote the movie).

For Internet and the people who control the standards for the Unix operating system, the consequences were, after the cleanup, considerable tightening of security. It could be argued that things are safer now than before the attack, and got safer quicker than if the attack had not come. Personal computer users had really no consequences. The worm was not written to be passed to personal computers on disk. Most of it was written specifically for Sun and Digital Equipment Corporation VAX systems running BSD Unix. Unless you were running this type of system and connected to Internet during November 1988, you have nothing to fear from a practical perspective.

We all need to consider wider implications. The Internet network is essentially operated by the U.S. government. In recent years there has been a massive increase in funding by U.S. government agencies looking into security provisions in computer networks. The Internet/Morris incident is a reminder that much still needs to be done. As one writer observed: "It provides stark evidence that, compared with nuclear strikes and action by deep-penetration units, the infection of a defense computer network by a worm is both effective and highly cost efficient."

General Symptoms

The above are just a few of the unpleasant surprises sprung by the writers of malevolent programs. Appendix C has short reports on a number of other viruses. However, there are several good reasons to resist the temptation to compile a definitive list of viruses. For a start, such lists, like a doctor's apothecary tend to give the impression that the problem is worse than it is. Many viruses have more than one name and some have their own names although they are merely variations on other viruses. There is a natural tendency to overestimate the impact of a new virus infection, which gives many viruses a scare value that is disproportionate to the threat they pose.

It would be helpful if a list of virus symptoms could be drawn up. Unfortunately, few symptoms are unambiguous. There are many possible explanations for files disappearing or messages saying Error reading drive C. Such events do not necessarily herald a virus infection. Some virus symptoms are unmistakable, such as a message announcing the presence of the virus. Other symptoms are less obvious and can be difficult to detect without operating system utilities or a program designed to spot virus activity. Such programs are well worth buying. If you prefer not to rely on such software, what you must do is watch for anomalies, such as:

- Less memory than usual.
- Loss of disk space.
- A change in the size of operating system files.
- A change in the appearance of the file directory.
- Missing files that you know you did not erase.
- Difficulties reading files or disks.

When such anomalies arise, you will need to explore them, possibly using tools such as Norton Utilities or PC Tools. Refer to the later section on remedies for how to proceed if a virus appears to be the culprit.

DEFENSIVE MEASURES

Purveyors of petroleum for automobile consumption are fond of pointing out that "Your engine will only perform as well as the gasoline you put in it." A similar statement can be made about personal computers: They only perform as well as the software and data that you put in them. If you have complete control over what goes into your personal computer and only put in "clean" software, then you will be free from viruses. However, few users have complete control of their machines. Furthermore, it is getting increasingly risky to take someone else's word for the fact that a piece of software is clean.

No Free Software

Without software, computer hardware is of little use. Software is what turns an overpriced door-stop into a desktop publishing system, a budget analyzer, or a corporate databank. When you are putting together a personal computer system, it is not unreasonable to budget as much for software as for hardware. However, many users are reluctant to spend their money in these proportions for several reasons, summarized here and discussed at greater length in the next chapter:

- *Low perceived value*—Hardware looks and feels like it is worth more than software.

- *Lack of real value*—Many purchasers of full price software have been disappointed by the level of support they have received.

- *Nobody pays the price*—Seeing friends or competitors saving money by violating license agreements with apparent impunity is a big encouragement to follow suit.

What many personal computer users tend to overlook is that there is a lot to a software package besides a manual and some disks. A good package will include telephone support and a favorable upgrade policy. Other benefits to look for include an on-line users forum for exchanging tips, and access to qualified training. From a security perspective, the bottom line is this: When it comes to acquiring software there are several other ways to save money than using stolen/borrowed goods, all of these pose less potential threat to your security and that of your data. A simple scenario can illustrate this.

Suppose you manage 20 personal computers. You want them all to run WimpWriter, which lists for $495. Street price is $350. Buying one copy for each will cost $7000. You buy bootleg versions for $30 each. You save $6400, that is $7000 − (20 * $30). Suppose you get a virus infection from the bootleg disks. Half of your systems are affected before it is stopped. The data on 10 hard disks must be recovered, and you have to call several clients and make the embarrassing announcement that the data disk you sent them was infected. Is this worth $6400? The question is even easier to answer when you discover that if you had approached the makers of WimpWriter, you would have been able to negotiate a site license for around $3000, including several days of on-site training, free upgrades to the next version, and special hotline support.

Obtaining Safe Software

Security comes at a price and whatever route you take to obtain safe software it is likely to have a higher initial cost than unsafe software. The following are some of the proven methods of obtaining software together with comments on their relative security from virus infection.

Do-It-Yourself. The one way to be absolutely sure of the contents of a computer program is to write it yourself. In the early days of personal computing, many users did just that. They used a simple language, like BASIC, to write their own programs. However, this is an impractical source for many users, the most obvious reason being that writing programs involves skills and knowledge that many users do not have the time to acquire.

Creating your own programs is not simply a question of developing enough skills to write a program that works. Any program that is to be entrusted with valuable data must be well-written, to prevent accidental data loss. The program should also include the appropriate security mechanisms to protect against nonaccidental data loss. Beyond developing the program yourself, you must take steps to keep the contents of the program secret, particularly details of the security measures you have built into it.

The fact is that even professional programmers rarely work "from the ground up" when writing commercial software. For a start, most commercial programs are *application* software, that is, they work with an existing operating system and allow the operating system to handle most of the basic input/output functions. Beyond that, many programmers make use of routines, algorithms, and libraries that were developed by someone else. This saves a lot of time and effort. For example, suppose you need your program to treat part of the computer display as a window, separate from the rest of the screen. Using the pre-written windowing routine that came the programming language allows you to accomplish this task without having to re-invent the wheel. Building parts of the program from standard blocks of pretested code is undoubtedly efficient. However, it does mean that the programmer has to assume the code to be virus free. Indeed, the programmer who uses someone else's programming language has to assume that the language itself is safe.

Hire a Programmer. Instead of writing your own programs, you can pay someone to write one for you, either as an employee or as a contract worker. Immediately the task is assigned to someone other than yourself an element of trust enters the picture. This can be approached from a personal angle and a professional one. A solid contract with the programmer is essential, as is a good working relationship. If the programmer is an employee, you should own the full rights to the software developed on your time. Full-time programmers are an expensive proposition for small organizations. A short-term contract programmer might be a better proposition. However, there might be an extra charge if you want the rights to the source code developed by the programmer. A good compromise arrangement is to have a copy of the source code deposited with a third party, such as a lawyer, as insurance against such eventualities as the bankruptcy or death of the programmer. This also provides a measure of protection against malevolent programming.

Software Houses. Rather than hire a programmer directly, you can contract with a group of programmers, known as a *software house*, for a piece of software. Your protection here is the reputation of the software house, its quality control procedures, and a solid contract specifying redress against any malevolent elements in the resulting program. Even so, it still makes sense to bargain for a copy of the source code or to have it deposited with a third party.

Off-the-Shelf. For many users, both corporate and individual, off-the-shelf software would appear to be the most cost-effective source of software, and one that is reasonably safe. For general-purpose programs such as word processing, this impression is probably correct, but when it comes to more complex tasks such as accounting, there are definite tradeoffs in using canned software. Beyond a point, ready-made programs do not allow you to make the necessary changes to adapt the program to your own precise needs. While some database management programs, such as dBASE, are virtually a programming language in their own right, allowing the development of sophisticated and highly specialized programs, this again raises the questions of who is to do the programming, and how reliable they are.

Other off-the-shelf programs such as spreadsheets have macro features that make possible customized operations, but these require a lot of work to be reliable. Spreadsheets designed by nontechnical staff might lack security features built into professionally written applications. As with any build-it-yourself program, customized spreadsheets raise these questions:

- Who will document it?
- Who will support those who use it?
- Who will maintain it after the designer moves on?

It is important to answer these three questions about any piece of software you are considering using.

Further Software Precautions

You should also consider some additional factors when acquiring software. Even if, like most personal computer users, you are opting for off-the-shelf software, you can take certain steps to make the acquisition less dangerous.

Have Faith. Buying off-the-shelf software means putting your faith in the integrity, longevity, and vigilance of the manufacturer. These factors make a strong argument in favor of products from established companies with a good track record.

Use Caution. Not purchasing the very latest in software has advantages. Usually, software publishers are under intense pressure to meet pre-announced ship dates for new products or new versions of old products. This pressure can lead companies to ship a product that is not quite ready. Recipients of this "first run" act as guinea pigs, just like the first people to buy a new car model. The manufacturer can take care of this with bug fixes, patches, additional drivers, and other such techniques. The early buyers have to deal with these retroactively, while those who buy a month or so after initial release usually find they have been incorporated into the product, which is now "stable."

Source Code. You are very unlikely to get a copy of the source code of a commercial software package. Normally, you have to take it on faith that nothing evil is lurking in the code. In this area there is safety in numbers: If several hundred thousand users have already tried a piece of software, it is probably safe to use.

Signed, Sealed, Delivered. Whenever you acquire new software, you should make sure that all the disks are in a sealed envelope/bag/sleeve. The disks should also arrive write-protected. This means that the write-protect notch on a 5.25-inch disk should be covered, while the write-protect hole on a 3.5-inch disk should be open. You might find that some master disks are not write protected. This is usually because of a copy protection scheme that requires a "write enabled" disk, or an installation procedure that requires writing to the original disk. Both of these should be avoided if at all possible. Obviously, disks that are shipped in a write enabled state are more susceptible to virus infection.

Registration. Whenever you purchase legitimate copies of software, you should register them with the manufacturer. This is an area that is often overlooked by organizations, much to their loss. Registering software establishes the connection between user and manufacturer. All responsible manufacturers encourage product registration, and some even offer modest incentives to encourage users to register. The manufacturer can then provide news of product upgrades, enhancements, and add-ons. More important still, problems with the product, such as a virus infection, can be communicated directly to users as soon as they are discovered.

Centralized Distribution. Users who manage other users might want to consider centralizing the distribution of software. If all software that goes onto the organization's computers is centrally screened for viruses, there is far less likelihood of infection. If instituted, such a system should apply to both original installations and upgrades. A further safety measure is to make copies of original programs as soon as the media arrive, then place the copies in the keeping of a third party. You might even have the third party witness the copying. Apart from providing useful backup, this procedure ensures that, if the program is ever suspected of starting a virus infection, you have proof of the source of the infection.

Beware Free Gifts. One of the most insidious threats to personal computer security is the "free" disk that contains a malevolent program. It is tempting to recommend that users swear off such disks altogether, but this would be narrow-minded and in a sense would be an admission that the writers of destructive programs have won. There are legitimate reasons to dispense free disks. The main motive to do so is marketing, either through product demos or shareware.

The *product demo* is usually either a slide show affair of sample screens with explanatory text, or a version of the real program that is somehow limited or crippled, perhaps lacking a file save feature. *Shareware* is fully operational software that you are free to go on using, if you pay the license fee, a sort of "try-before-you-buy" approach to software sales. Both demos and shareware are important as a communication channel because of the high cost of full-scale advertising campaigns for new products, and the difficulty of conveying in print what a program can do. Useful and innovative programming might need to be seen to be believed. Often the work is done by small outfits that lack the funding to advertise extensively. Distributing free demo or shareware versions of programs means users get a hands-on feel for the product. In

Europe, you will find free disks included with computer magazines. In the United States, you can pick them up at computer shows. Free disks are sometimes offered with hardware or software packages, and magazines might have coupons for them.

The sad fact is that any such disk could be carrying a malevolent program. As a general rule, a disk you ask for is safer than one that is unsolicited. A disk containing a demo version of a commercial product is probably safer than a disk containing share-ware culled from bulletin boards. However, these statements are all relative: Any disk that you do not pay for, any disk that is not distributed in a sealed package with a proper warranty statement, should be checked for malevolent programming.

Downloading. If you find on-line bulletin boards to be a useful source of soft-ware, you should exercise caution over which bulletin boards you use, and how you handle freshly downloaded programs. Download only from reputable sources, and check them regularly for news of any problems with software that has been made available. If possible, test software using the procedures described in the next section, and make sure you have a virus detector installed.

The Safety Test

Suppose you have just received a disk which is supposed to contain *the* most use-ful operating system utility you can imagine. What procedures should you use to check that the disk is genuine and poses no threat to your programs and data? By using one or more of the following techniques, you should be able to weed out most malevolent disks.

Discrimination. Before the disk enters your computer, you should evaluate it using standards the exact opposite of those you would apply to people:

- All disks are not created equal.
- You can tell a lot about a disk from its cover.
- It does matter where it came from.

What you need to do is determine the disk's risk factor, the appropriate level of suspi-cion with which to treat the disk. If it is professionally produced and packaged, comes from a leading name in software publishing, and arrives in response to an enquiry you made, then the risk factor is low. If it arrives unsolicited in an envelope with no return address and only a photocopied sheet of instructions, the risk factor is high.

You should satisfy yourself on the following questions:

- Does the disk have a professionally printed label?
- Is there a company name and address on the label?
- Have you heard of the company?
- If the disk came in the mail, is there a return address?
- If the disk has been handed to you, how reliable is the donor?

Bear in mind that positive answers to these questions are not a guarantee that the disk is free from malevolent programs. However, the more negative answers you get, the more thorough you will need to be in applying further tests.

A similar set of questions can and should be applied to software that has come from an on-line bulletin board.

- Is the bulletin board reputable?
- Does the program come with documentation?
- Is the program author clearly identified, either in the documentation or by the bulletin board?

When you have decided the risk factor associated with the disk/program you can proceed to one of the following tests.

Disk Test. Before installing, copying, or booting from a newly arrived disk, examine it with either operating system utilities or a virus detection program. Some virus detection programs can examine software and disks for tell-tale virus *signatures*, or disk and file attributes that have been discovered in known viruses. If you have such a virus detector, use it to start your test of the new arrival. Otherwise, a variety of common disk operating system utilities can be combined into a pretty effective do-it-yourself test.

A good first step is to get a directory of the files on the disk. Check that the directory listing match the disk label. Check that the total size of the files plus the free space on the disk equals total disk space. For example, in Fig. 10-4, you can see a directory listing for a 360K disk that does not seem to add up. Running CHKDSK reveals the hidden files that are responsible.

```
C:\>dir b:

 Volume in drive B has no label
 Directory of  B:\

COMMAND  COM     25307   3-17-87  12:00p
CHKDSK   COM      9850   3-18-87  12:00p
        2 File(s)    273408 bytes free

C:\>chkdsk b:

   362496 bytes total disk space
    53248 bytes in 2 hidden files
    35840 bytes in 2 user files
   273408 bytes available on disk

   655360 bytes total memory
   331056 bytes free

C:\>
```

Fig. 10-4. Checking out a disk.

You will want to know what the hidden files are. This can be done with a disk examiner, like Norton Utilities or PC Tools. The disk contents should be examined with such a program anyway. As well as hidden files, look for bad sectors on the disk, sometimes used to hide virus code. In Fig. 10-5, you can see how bad sectors show up in Norton.

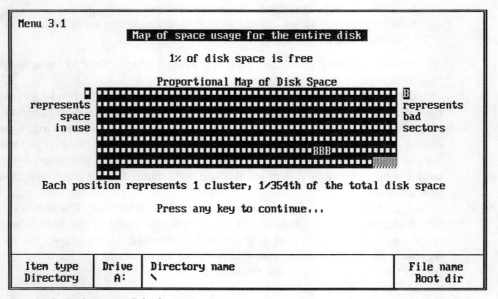

Fig. 10-5. Disk map with bad sectors.

You might also want to examine the boot sector of the disk to see if it looks normal (use a known clean disk to make the comparison). After this, you can view the program files themselves, using a file viewing utility to look at the contents of the file for clues as to function and source. In Fig. 10-6, you can see a program called PMAP being examined in QuickDOS.

While most of a program file is unintelligible to the nonprogrammer, a section of the file might contain messages to be displayed on screen. These are often stored in plain ASCII and so can be read. They offer important pointers as to the program's true purpose and origins. Try the end of the file, a popular place to store this sort of information.

A program file freshly downloaded from a bulletin board should also be checked. Many users download files to a floppy disk rather than to a hard disk. This helps to isolate the file and in most cases does not delay the downloading process since communications software can usually receive data and write to disk at the same time. A lot of downloaded software is archived, compressed into a smaller space to speed up the telephone transfer. Program files and documentation might be compressed into a single file. You must uncompress the file into its component parts to examine it. Check that the parts are as claimed on the bulletin board listing. Review the documentation for credibility, and use a file viewing utility to look at the contents of the file for clues as to function and source.

```
Viewing: PMAP.EXE          Press ESC to exit          (F)ilter: OFF
```

```
Ä⊗⊗]♦_U ^≡]ⁿW▲_▼Ï~
î⩘ÂE♦Ï~Ðèⓧⓔ]ⓔⒺM♦ëU♦ëuⓀÂE
r♦3÷δⓄⓄÇ┬┘⊙ Ï⊗ëuⓆâ-
▼_^Ïσ]├UÏ∞UWÏ~♦Ï♦Ï]ⒺÏM♦ÏU♦ÏuⓀÏ)
=↕WÏ~♦èⓧⓔ]ⒺⒺM♦ëU♦ëuⓀÂE
r♦3÷δⓄⓄ5┬┘⊙ Ï⊗ëuⓆ_^Ïσ]├ UÏ∞UWÏ~♦Ï♦Ï]ⒺÏM♦ÏU♦ÏuⓀ u
Ï~ⓀÄ⊗⊗]♦_=↕W▲îⒺÂⒺ"Ï~Ⓚî⩘ÂE♦Ï~♦èⓧⓔ]ⒺⒺM♦ëU♦ëuⓀÂE
r♦3÷δⓄⓆ╫μ┘⊙ Ï⊗ëuⓆ_^Ïσ]├ UÏ∞Ï^♦î_♦î•î⓪ⒺↀWⓌ♦Ïσ]├ UÏ∞WÏ~♦▲•Ï▪3Ⴑ┤  ⅀«Ⴄ≈┘èF♦ÏⱮⅉ2«0ⓐ♦tⓐ3
 Ï‖_Ïσ]├UÏ∞Wⓐ•Ï~♦3Ⴑ┤  ⅀«Ⴄ≈┘0èF♦² ⅀«GⓐⒸ♦t♦3ႱδⓐÏ‖┃ⁿ_Ïσ]├ UÏ∞Ï^♦Ï┃ë•
Ⴑt◄,Ⴄ‹•s♦♦aê•Cè•
Ⴑu┃╢Ⴄ]├UÏ∞Ï╫î╫⩘Ⴑ Ï~♦Ï▪ÏN┃ⓝⓢèF♦è⍺≈‖⊙ tⓐ┤I┬0⦁⅀‼‖⎯Ï⋅ô]├ ÏN
 ÏF♦ÏU♦Ï~ⓀW▲•ⁿô
Ⴑt‼â⋅
uⱮⓓⱤⱮy
‖⎯≈ⱤâⱮ ≈┌Ï≈A3Ɱδ Ⴑtⓐ≈±ô≈±Aⓢⱪ♦ⓑ<9uⓑ♦ⁱ¬Ï┬δ├uⱤê♦0¼â♦èD ìDⓄ;‖┌²X_^Ïσ]├ UÏ∞ÏU♦┤A=↕ⓔⴀσ
UÏ∞ÏF♦Ï^
δ♦Ï^ⱭuδÏF♦≈πÏσ]┬Ⓚ ≈πÏⱪUÏF♦≈f
♦ⱪUÏF♦≈πⱭ┬Ïσ]┬Ⓚ                    MS Run-Time Library - Copyright (c) 1988, Microsoft
 Corp◄            ⊙ ⊙   pmap %d.%d%d Copyright (C) 1986-1988 by The Cove
Software Group/C.J.Dunford
```

```
Commands:  PgUp  PgDn  Home  End  1..9 (9 is fastest)  ↑ ↓  (H)ex  (N)ormal
```

Fig. 10-6. Viewing a program.

Testing, Testing

If no anomalies have appeared yet and the disk/program risk factor is fairly low, you might want to proceed to install and run the program. If you have just one personal computer at your disposal, and if it has a hard disk, you should first make sure your hard disk is backed up. Then make a backup copy of the new disk/program. At this point, you can proceed to install and run the program. However, you might want to take several further steps to test the new software before accepting that it is "clean." Check the following section on infection indicators for more about testing a new program.

In offices with several computers, a lot can be said for designating one as a guinea pig, a test machine where software can be run without fear of serious harm. This machine should be run in isolation from all others, that is, it should not be connected to a network. Several configurations work well.

Floppy Disk Systems. At last there is a use for the aging dual floppy micro that nobody wants! For all their limitations, floppy disk machines have real security pluses. You can designate one such system as your virus test bed. Make sure that no important data or program disks are placed in the system. You can then boot the system using a verified and write-protected copy of the operating system. After this, you can insert a suspect disk with impunity and proceed to run the programs on the disk, looking for the infection indicators described in the next section.

 Depending upon your hardware and your level of technical expertise, you can create a temporarily "floppy only" system out of a hard disk system by disconnecting the power supply to the hard disk. If you are comfortable opening up the system unit, something you should only do when the machine is unplugged, locate the cable from the power supply to the hard drive. With this disconnected there is no possibility of data of the hard drive being damaged. You can then plug in the unit, insert a bootable floppy, and turn it on. This might not work with some hard drive controllers and some PC AT type systems will require a change to the setup program to work in floppy-only mode.

Hard Disk Systems. At last there is a use for the slow 10 megabyte hard disk micro that nobody wants! Instead of junking that old system, set it up to test software. Make sure only expendable copies of data and programs are placed on the hard disk. Install any virus checkers and operating system utilities you might need, then install the suspect software and proceed to test. While this might seem like a waste of a machine it might well be a justified use of resources for larger offices. A hard disk system can do a more thorough check for malevolent programs than a floppy disk system. The infamous trojan, the AIDS disk, required that users install it on a hard disk.

Removable High-Capacity Disk System. If you needed one more reason to invest in a removable high capacity disk system, this is it! When it comes to testing software this arrangement really shows its security potential. A high-capacity cartridge can be used as a virus test bed with little fear of infecting other disks or damaging valuable software or data. If you use bootable cartridges, you should create a special one for testing, loaded with sample data and software, operating system utilities, and virus detectors. Make sure it is clearly marked as a special disk and do not put any floppy disks containing valuable data into the machine while tests are being run. If you boot from a floppy disk, make sure the boot disk is write-protected before testing.

Infection Indicators

When you are ready to install a new piece of software and test it for malevolent effects, you need to know what to look for. As was pointed out earlier in this chapter, it is difficult to list non-ambiguous symptoms of a malevolent program at work in a typical computer system. A file might no longer be readable for many reasons; a virus attack is only one of them. However, under the controlled conditions of a test, a virus is easier to spot.

The first step is to get a clear picture of the state of the computer before the new program is installed. All directories and files need to be logged. This can be done by using a variety of operating system utilities. For example, on a Macintosh the File Print Directory command gives you a useful list of files, as shown in Fig. 10-7.

You can supplement this with a program like MacTree by Andy Peterman, distributed by Software Research Technologies. This gives a visual display of folder/directory structure. You can see the results in Fig. 10-8.

On an MS-DOS system, you can use a program like Norton's Find File to print a complete file listing (including hidden files). In addition to file names, it is important to log file sizes and dates as many viruses alter size and/or dates of files. You can see part of a Find File listing in Fig. 10-9.

System Folder

Name	Size	Kind	Last Modified	
Aldus Prep	26K	PageMaker 3.01 d...	Thu, Mar 17, 1988	4:26 PM
Apple File Exchange	245K	application	Tue, Sep 5, 1989	12:00 PM
AppleShare	45K	Chooser document	Mon, Jul 11, 1988	12:00 PM
Backgrounder	6K	System document	Sat, Apr 30, 1988	12:00 PM
Canvas Prefs	6K	document	Fri, Jul 31, 1987	5:07 AM
Capture	5K	Startup document	Mon, Sep 12, 1988	10:56 AM
Claris Fonts	27K	MacWrite® II doc...	Thu, Jul 20, 1989	10:47 AM
Clipboard File	14K	System document	Mon, Aug 6, 1990	8:53 PM
Color	3K	Control Panel doc...	Tue, Sep 5, 1989	12:00 PM
CPSDeleteTracking	6K	Startup document	Wed, Sep 21, 1988	11:10 AM
DA Handler	8K	document	Tue, Sep 5, 1989	12:00 PM
DCA-RFT/MacWrite	59K	Apple File Exchan...	Fri, Dec 9, 1988	12:00 PM
FileMaker Temp	--	folder	Mon, Aug 6, 1990	8:31 PM
Finder	108K	System document	Thu, Mar 1, 1990	9:24 AM
Finder Startup	2K	System document	Mon, Jul 30, 1990	5:07 PM
Finder(keys)	2K	document	Mon, Jan 22, 1990	1:42 PM
Fonts	1,2...	Font/DA Mover d...	Wed, Jun 20, 1990	6:59 PM
General	15K	Control Panel doc...	Mon, May 8, 1989	12:00 PM
General.apd	12K	document	Sun, Feb 21, 1988	11:14 PM

Fig. 10-7. A Macintosh File Print Directory listing.

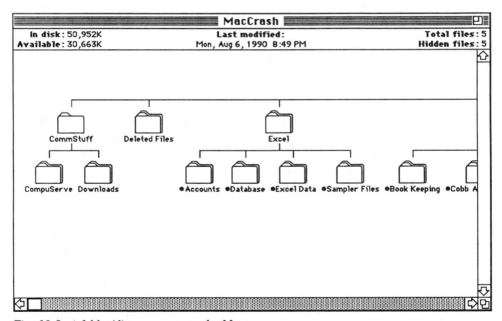

Fig. 10-8. A folder/directory tree on the Mac.

Another area to watch for suspicious changes is memory. Check the amount of free memory before and after installation. The figures should be the same. Installation alone should not leave any code in memory. Use CHKDSK on DOS machines and About the Finder on Macs for this information.

```
C:\>ff *.* /p
FF-File Find, Advanced Edition, (C) Copr 1987, 1988, Peter Norton

C:\
        io.sys              22,398 bytes   12:00 am   Tue Feb  2 88
        msdos.sys           30,128 bytes   12:00 am   Tue Feb  2 88
        123R23              <DIR>           7:01 pm   Tue Oct 22 91
        BAT                 <DIR>          12:40 am   Tue Jan  1 80
        COL                 <DIR>           1:26 pm   Fri Aug 23 91
        DOS                 <DIR>          12:03 am   Tue Jan  1 80
        INSET               <DIR>           1:58 am   Thu May 18 89
        KEY                 <DIR>          12:36 am   Tue Jan  1 80
        NU                  <DIR>          12:22 am   Tue Jan  1 80
        PHONE               <DIR>           9:28 pm   Thu Jan  4 90
        QDOS                <DIR>          12:19 am   Tue Jan  1 80
        QT                  <DIR>           8:38 pm   Fri Nov 22 91
        QUATTRO             <DIR>           1:47 am   Thu May 18 89
        SK                  <DIR>          12:18 am   Sun Mar  3 91
        SYTOS               <DIR>           5:16 pm   Fri Nov 22 91
        TOPS                <DIR>          12:07 am   Tue Jan  1 80
        TP                  <DIR>           3:57 pm   Tue Jul 23 91
        VACCINE             <DIR>           2:32 pm   Sat Dec 16 89
        backup.m_u          82,432 bytes    2:45 pm   Sun Nov  3 91
        23.bak                  40 bytes    8:48 pm   Thu Oct 24 91
Program paused; press any key to continue...
```

Fig. 10-9. A Find File listing.

After installing the suspect program, you should look to see what changes have been made to the system. A decent piece of software will always tell you when directories are being added or files altered. Unannounced changes should be monitored closely, as should any additional bad sectors, hidden files, or screen changes. Macintosh users should pay close attention to the contents of the System folder while DOS users should watch for changes in AUTOEXEC.BAT and CONFIG.SYS.

Once the program has been installed and any system changes noted, you can proceed to run the program. After exploring the program's commands, you should exit and again check disk and memory status for unexplained changes. Watch for virus code that is left memory-resident, reducing available memory. Obviously a new program will take up disk space, but watch for any sudden unexplained loss of free disk space.

At this point, you might want to load and unload the program a number of times. This can trigger virus code that is initially dormant. You might also want to reboot the system a number of times for the same reason. A batch file or macro can be set up to automate a cycle of loading or rebooting. After a few hours of this, you can return to look for any manifestations of infection. Beyond this, you might want to leave the system on but idle for a 24-hour period. Idling for a day will allow any time-of-day triggers to be activated.

While these tests might sound like a lot of trouble, they do not apply equally to all software. The more dubious a program's origins, the more thorough the testing it will require. A virus detector that looks for virus signatures can be used instead of a complete cycle of tests.

Rules to Work By

Being vigilant about the software that enter your system will go a long way towards protecting it from viruses and trojans. If you use access controls to extend that vigilance to the times when you are not around to oversee what is happening to your computer, you can feel reasonably confident that you will avoid the immediate effects of malevolent programming. To sum up the defensive measures discussed here, the following sets of rules can be promulgated, first for the individual user, and then for the manager of users.

Rules for all:
1. Observe site, system, and file access security procedures.
2. Always perform a backup before installing new software.
3. Only use reputable software from reputable sources.
4. Install a virus detector.

Rules for managers of users:
1. Make sure that access control and backup procedures are observed by all users.
2. Forbid the use of unchecked or unapproved software.
3. Check all new software with a virus detector before installing it or issuing it to users.
4. Stay informed of latest developments in malevolent programming through a virus alert service.
5. Keep staff informed of latest trends in viruses so that they know what to look for.
6. Make use of activity/operator logging systems so that you know who is using each system and what it is being used for.
7. Encourage the reporting of all operational anomalies and match these against known virus traits.

DEFENSIVE TECHNIQUES

In addition to carrying out the measures discussed and observing the rules, some other techniques might be helpful. Their appropriateness depends on your level of exposure to virus infection.

Encryption

Files that are encrypted are harder to infect than ordinary files. Several of the anti-virus programs described later in this chapter work by encrypting program files, thus defending them against virus infection. While viruses that spread by means of data files are rare, they are not impossible. You might already have adopted the use of encryption on important data files for other security reasons. Protection from virus damage and infection is another reason to add to the list.

Deception

Most viruses target program files, particularly operating system files. One way of finding out if there is a virus attacking your computer is to make up some dummy files for the virus to attack. For example, under MS-DOS, the extension .COM or .EXE indicates an executable program. Naturally, these dummy files should not be called, but you can check their contents regularly. Viruses in such a system naturally try to attach themselves to the dummy files. In these files, an infection can be recognized more quickly, and counter measures can be initiated before the damages become too high. The dummy files essentially take on a buffer function.

Disguise

Because viruses tend to attack certain files that are identified by their names, you can rename the files so that the virus ignores them. A virus looking to infect EXE files can do no damage to them if there are no EXE files on the disk. To give this impression, you could rename all EXE files to have the extension HPE, for Hidden Program EXE-type.

Unfortunately, you cannot run an EXE file if it does not have the EXE extension. The same is true of COM files. If you rename CHKDSK.COM to CHKDSK.HPC then enter CHKDSK at the DOS prompt, you will get the message, Bad command or file name. To get around this limitation, you can use a batch file to run programs that have been disguised. The batch file uses a parameter to identify the program by the first part of its name. The batch file then alters the file's extension so that it can be run. When user quits the program, the extension is returned to its disguise. Suppose you call the batch file RUN.BAT. You would then run the disguised file CHKDSK.HPC by entering RUN CHKDSK at the DOS prompt. The contents of RUN.BAT might look like this:

```
@ECHO OFF
IF EXIST %1.HPE GOTO HPEFILE
IF EXIST %1.HPC GOTO HPCFILE
ECHO File not found!
GOTO END
:HPEFILE
REN %1.HPE %1.EXE
%1
REN %1.EXE %1.HPE
GOTO END
:HPCFILE
REN %1.HPC %1.COM
%1
REN %1.COM %1.HPC
:END
```

This routine means that the user does not have to enter, or even know, the secret file extension. While renaming all COM and EXE files on a typical hard disk might seem like hard work, there are shortcuts. A number of DOS utilities allow you to execute a command across subdirectories. For example, the public domain utility SWEEP would work like this:

```
SWEEP REN *.EXE *.HPE
```

Executed from the root directory, this command would change all EXE files to HPE files. Using RUN.BAT does add a small slice of time to program loading and exiting, but this is not really a problem on a hard disk system.

While this sytem has the benefit of being simple and free, it has several potential snags. An existing system of batch files used to launch programs might need altering, as might a menu program. Some application programs call other programs while they are running. For example, some applicataions invoke the DOS program PRINT .COM, DOS and the applications would get confused if this was stored as PRINT .HPC. However, if you are reasonably competent in using DOS, you might want to try the rename system.

ANTI-VIRUS HARDWARE

In the fight against viruses, the most obviously useful piece of hardware is an access control system, something that requires a user-specific key, token, or password for log-on. Apart from excluding the casual interloper, this sort of system acts as a strong deterrent to those who might be in a position to infect the system. Only the foolhardy will persevere knowing that an audit trail is in place that will allow the system administrator to identify the perpetrator of any acts of sabotage.

A more subtle defense measure is to use a personal computer with a ROM-based operating system. By burning the operating system code into a read-only memory chip, manufacturers create complete protection against viruses that modify operating system files. In recent years, there has been an increase in the use of ROM for operating systems. In part, this has been made possible by the increasing stability of "standard" operating systems, such as MS-DOS. When Toshiba was designing its first notebook style computer, the T1000, it placed MS-DOS 2.11 in ROM. This version offers all of the features that a modest personal computer needs. User-definable parameters, such as those stored in CONFIG.SYS, are written in a special area of battery-backed RAM. This system allows users to devote floppy disk space to application programs and data, rather than take up space with operating system files. This translates into increased functionality for a machine with only one disk drive. Tandy found that placing DOS and its Desk Organizer software in ROM made its entry-level Radio Shack PCs easier for novices to use.

The disadvantage of ROM-based operating systems is the need to change a chip when you want to upgrade the DOS version, but there are several ways of simplifying this process, including easy-access ROM sockets and new ways of packing ROM. The advent of pocketbook computers has led to credit-card sized memory packages, which can be either RAM or ROM. If the operating system came in this format, upgrades could be handled with ease.

ANTI-VIRUS SOFTWARE

As soon as some programmers started releasing viruses on personal computer systems, other programmers began the task of designing software to detect viruses. For some, this was a simple question of survival: They could not continue using their own systems and developing new software if they were not able to guarantee the integrity of their systems. Some took the "white knight" approach and started releasing copies of their anti-virus software to the public at low or no cost. Some felt that commercial distribution was necessary in order to finance research into the finer points of virus detection and prevention.

Anti-Virus Strategies

Although there are now dozens of different anti-virus packages from which to choose, many of them use similar strategies. Because it is impossible for a virus to infect a file without altering the file, the two basic strategies are to check for changes to files, and prevent changes to files. Checking for file changes usually involves recording information about uninfected or clean files and then repeatedly comparing the files to this reference information. Because every personal computer must use operating system files many viruses are designed to infect one or more of these files. A clean copy of the operating system can be checked against the operating system files every time the system is booted.

Preventing changes to files is not as simple as it sounds. You cannot simply write-protect your operating system files and expect that to keep them safe from virus infection. Some viruses, for example Yankee Doodle, can change the write-protect status of a file, alter the file, then return the write-protect status back to protected. One method of write-protection that does defeat viruses is hardware write-protection. There is no way software can override the write-protect tab on a floppy disk. For this reason, a write-protected boot disk is a good way of preventing changes to essential system files. This system simulates having the operating system in ROM, a handy hardware ploy. Some access control software packages can simulate hardware write-protection for hard disks.

File Comparisons

The logic behind the file comparison strategy is described by Jim Murphy in the documentation to his program, FCBIN.EXE, released to the public domain. Because many of the early IBM PC viruses attacked COMMAND.COM, he decided to try using the MS-DOS program FC.EXE to check a hidden, clean copy of COMMAND .COM against his working copy each time he booted up his sytem. Named as an acronym for file compare, the program FC.EXE is provided with MS-DOS does much the same thing as the COMP program in PC-DOS, that is, compare one file against another, line by line, reporting on the differences.

Murphy found that the problem with using FC.EXE for an automated check that stops only if a particular file is changed, is that "FC.EXE does not create an errorlevel code after it terminates." As you will recall from Chapter 7, errorlevel codes are used by DOS programs to indicate a certain condition. The ERRORLEVEL is a single digit code, from 0 to 9, that can be left in memory by a DOS program or command when it is completed. Batch file utilities use error-level codes to carry out branching, and Murphy wanted to use a line in his AUTOEXEC.BAT such as

```
FC CMDCOM.TRU COMMAND.COM
```

where CMDCOM.TRU is clean copy of COMMAND.COM. Ideally the batch file would then continue:

```
IF ERRORLEVEL 1 GOTO WARNING
IF ERRORLEVEL 0 GOTO QUIT
:WARNING
ECHO Warning – COMMAND.COM does not match CMDCOM.TRU!
GOTO END
:QUIT
ECHO Okay – COMMAND.COM matches CMDCOM.TRU
:END
```

To get around the fact that FC.EXE does not in fact return an errorlevel, Murphy decided to write his own File Compare utility that would create an errorlevel code: "I called my program FCBIN.EXE (File Compare Binary); it is written in Turbo Pascal version 4.0 and it will compare any file, reporting all the general differences, such as Date and Length, and that the bytes did not compare. It also tells you at which byte the first difference occurred."

There are several ways to use FCBIN.EXE in a batch file virus checking system. Murphy suggests creating a subdirectory called ZROOT to hold uncontaminated copies of all the files in the root directory. The file copies in ZROOT can be renamed for additional safety (COMMAND.COM as CMD.BAK, CONFIG.SYS as CFG.BAK, and so on). The FCBIN.EXE program is available on a number of bulletin boards, complete with the source code so that you can verify the program's workings. Look for it under the colorfully descriptive name of CONDOM.ARC.

A more complex approach to virus checking through file comparison is provided by Checkup, a shareware program written by Richard B. Levin, and available through BBSoft, of Philadelphia. Checkup is able to detect viral infections by comparing a file's size, its incremental checksum, and its total checksum to previously stored values based on clean versions of the file. File size is the number of bytes in the file, recorded in the directory. A checksum is a number created by adding together the binary values in a file. All program files consist of a series of binary values and these can be added up for each byte, each block of bytes, or for the whole file. Checkup breaks a file into a series of randomly sized blocks of data. These data blocks can vary from one byte to near the total file size. Checkup's dynamic block size allocation allows files as small as one byte to be accurately checked.

When requested to check a file, Checkup scans and compares every byte of the target file with the recorded baseline values on a block-by-block basis. If the recorded file size, any of the block checksum comparisons, or the checksum totals do not match, Checkup alerts the user that the target file has been altered and possibly infected. Checkup's incremental file checksum technique has advantages over simply adding the bytes in a file and comparing past and present checksum totals. Future viruses might be intelligent enough to calculate a host file's checksum total, pad their own code with dummy characters to maintain total checksum integrity, and then infect. Such viruses, says the author of Checkup, would defeat other checksum calculation programs, but not Checkup since it looks at the file in sections and, according to the program's author, ". . . it is impossible for a virus to maintain an accurate intra-block checksum. This is especially true when the checked block size varies from one byte to near the total file size; the method for calculating the checksum is unknown, and the results are encrypted."

A commercial implementation of the file comparison strategy is Vaccine from Corbin Software (unfortunately, so many people seized on the word "vaccine" as a product name for anti-viral software that you need to know which "vaccine" you want). The first thing you notice when you buy Corbin Vaccine is the serious approach to virus infection. There is a label sealing the disk in its folder that says: "Warning! Do not use if YOU didn't break this seal!"

Corbin Vaccine works by storing a record of what a clean version of DOS looks like, then comparing this record to the working version you boot up with. Corbin recommends that if you do not have a genuine, unaltered "sterile" copy of your operating system, you should purchase an updated version right away, pointing out that "they are not expensive compared to the data you might lose." Corbin Software sells genuine MicroSoft operating systems and in sealed, "sterile" packages, as do many other legitimate software firms. The Vaccine documentation warns you not to trust "an operating system that has been handed to you by a friend, or one that came pre-installed on the hard disk of your computer. Get an original that you can trust."

This theme is echoed throughout the instruction manual which begins the installation instructions with "Open your genuine operating system disk package. Make sure that the write-protect tab is covering the notch on the right side of your 5.25 inch disk, or the slide is moved to the protected position on a 3.5-inch diskette."

By including the command VACCINE in your AUTOEXEC.BAT, you can have the program check your operating system files every time you bootup. The program tells you the status of the check. If the working versions of the operating system files match the master copies the message is no viruses found. If there has been a change, the message is this:

Your system has been infected: please re-boot with your original DOS disk in drive A: and refer to your VACCINE MANUAL for further instructions. DO NOT USE YOUR SYSTEM WITHOUT RE-BOOTING!

An infection can be cured by replacing the old operating system files with fresh, healthy ones from your "sterile" disk. The Vaccine documentation walks you through this process, which consists of uses the SYS command on your sterile DOS disk, then copying COMMAND.COM onto the hard disk.

Corbin's documentation points out that there can be other kinds of viruses in your system, besides those, referred to as type "A" viruses, that reside in modified operating system files. Defined as type "B," these other viruses lurk in application programs and only affect your system when you use these programs. Type B viruses are typically less dangerous than type A viruses because they can be localized to damages that occur only after running a certain program. However, the Vaccine documentation points out that:

> Normally, for a virus to reproduce and spread, it has to attach itself to a certain part of your computer's basic input/output system and thus be invoked whenever you do any disk copy operation or modem communications . . . there is one kind of type B virus that can spawn type A infections: if an application is copied to your hard disk that contains code which can repeatedly write clandestine code every time you use the application, then your system will get an infection every time you use that program.

Because Vaccine checks out your system every time you boot, it informs you of the effect of this type of virus. You can quickly find the virus by disinfecting your system, then running each program that you used in the last session and typing VACCINE after running each program. You can track down the problem to a specific program this way. Although Vaccine does not automatically locate a type B virus, it will tell you as soon as the system has become infected, and you can pin it down by trial and error.

The Vaccine documentation also points out that many programs are called automatically by your AUTOEXEC.BAT file, or are loaded by your CONFIG.SYS file:

> If you get a new infection report every time you boot up, you might remove the device drivers and programs called in the AUTOEXEC.BAT file one at a time (use a program editor or EDLIN to edit the files), until you cure the infection.

The Encryption Approach

A different approach to protecting programs from virus infection is to encrypt them, rendering code and programming techniques indecipherable. This makes hacking or modification of the program much more difficult, though not impossible. An example of this approach is a program called COP, an acronym for Command Obfuscation Processor, by Jack A. Orman, of Southaven, Massachusetts. To encrypt a typical program such as XCOPY.COM, you would enter the following at the DOS prompt:

```
COP C: \ DOS \ XCOPY.COM encryption-key
```

COP will read the program and use the key to write a modified version back to the disk. The modified version is encrypted and makes disassembling of the program very difficult. Programs modified by COP will still run from the DOS prompt and perform just as the original.

Keith P. Graham at the PC-Rockland BBS in New York has written a program called ICE that scrambles and compresses COM files, which makes it very difficult for a virus to alter the original COM program. ICE also compresses the files without affecting functionality. This means the files take up less disk space, and might actually load faster. The format of the ICE command is similar to that of COP and can be included in batch files:

    ICE FILE.COM encryption-key

ICE will compress and scramble the COM file and replace the original. As with COP, it is important to have a backup of the original COM file. ICE is distributed as freeware, meaning that it remains the property of Keith P. Graham, but you are allowed to share it with other users as long as no fee is associated with the copying of distribution of the program other than nominal disk copy or access charges.

The name ICE is an acronym, used by the award winning science fiction writer William Gibson in his brilliant first novel, *Neuromancer*, published in 1984. He describes a military role for virus programs: "Tried to burn this Russian nexus with virus programs . . . We were running a virus called Mole. The Mole series was the first generation of real intrusion programs . . . Icebreakers . . . Ice from *ICE*, intrusion countermeasure electronics." In my opinion, Gibson's novels *Neuromancer, Count Zero*, and *Mona Lisa Overdrive* are required reading for anyone studying the implications of modern technology.

FURTHER ANTI-VIRUS PROGRAMS

This section presents further examples of anti-virus software. Most of the examples are commercial programs and are likely to have been updated since this was written. Thus comments about the limitations of certain packages cannot be taken as gospel. This is a rapidly moving area of software development and new, improved versions are constantly appearing. The bottom line is there are very few excuses left for not having some form of anti-virus software installed on your personal computer.

Mac Products

It has been suggested that an outbreak of the Scores virus in its Washington office is what prompted Apple Computer to provide an anti-virus program free to users. The program, called Virus RX, lists damaged applications; INIT, CDEV and RDEV files; invisible files; altered system files; and altered applications. The program reports different levels of concern, from simple comments to dangerous to fatal. Damaged applications are the first to be listed. These have not been infected by the virus, but they will not work and should probably be removed from your disk.

Next the program lists all INIT, CDEV, an RDEV files (such as the Easy Access, Mouse or AppleShare files) in your System folder. Many of these are common, but you should make sure you know why they are on your disks. Some files are normally invisible; Virus RX checks these and lists them. The documentation provided with Virus RX explains how to determine if you have a virus and how to remove the infection. Virus RX is available free on Delphi, CompuServe, other networks, various computer bulletin boards, and through your local Apple dealer. It is designed primarily for the Scores virus described earlier.

Probably the most comprehensive anti-virus package for the Macintosh is SAM from Symantec. Standing for *Symantec Anti-Virus for the Macintosh*, SAM is a suite of programs that can identify viruses according to known virus signatures and warn against virus-like interference with files. Symantec provides a subscription service that allows SAM to be updated to include information about any new viruses that emerge. As with all software purchases, you should check the version number if you are considering buying a copy of SAM, to make sure that it is the latest. If you then subscribe to the update service, you should be safe from once and future infections.

Another powerful commercial anti-virus package for the Macintosh is Virex, from HJC software of Durham, North Carolina. More straightforward to use than the more comprehensive toolkit provided by SAM, Virex looks for known viruses and anomalies that might be attributable to viruses. The program has an option to repair files and remove viruses although replacement of files with uninfected copies is the preferred option. Capable of being run by an inexperienced Mac user, Virex is available on a site license basis for large organizations.

Virex was written for HJC Software by Robert Woodhead, author of the shareware program Inteferon (proceeds from registration fees are actually donated to charity). This is also a "known virus identifier" that is a very useful utility to have around when you are checking new software. You can see a typical Inteferon report in Fig. 10-10.

The top part of the window lists virus signatures of which this version of Inteferon is aware. Several of these are not named viruses, but system manipulations typical of virus activity. As the Inteferon documentation explains, the "SNEAK" virus signature might actually be caused by legitimate program. In fact, that is what has happened in the example illustrated: The TOPS networking software is erroneously identified as being infected. Fortunately, the TOPS 3.0 documentation mentions this discrepancy, and points out that the commercial version of Inteferon, Virex, overcomes this anomaly (the user community has virus writers to thank for one more level of compatibility problems).

In the Inteferon documentation, Woodhead recommends the Vaccine "cdev" by Donald Brown that warns of attempts by viruses to modify files, as well as the Ferret program, designed to locate and remove the Scores virus. A further shareware product that is useful for detecting Macintosh viruses is the VirusDetective, written by Jeffrey Shulman of Ridgefield, Connecticut, and seen at work in Fig. 10-11.

This is a desk accessory that can check a whole disk or a single directory at once, comparing files therein against virus signatures. This is very handy to use when you

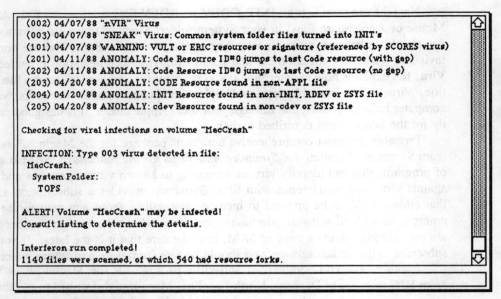

```
(002) 04/07/88 "nVIR" Virus
(003) 04/07/88 "SNEAK" Virus: Common system folder files turned into INIT's
(101) 04/07/88 WARNING: VULT or ERIC resources or signature (referenced by SCORES virus)
(201) 04/11/88 ANOMALY: Code Resource ID#0 jumps to last Code resource (with gap)
(202) 04/11/88 ANOMALY: Code Resource ID#0 jumps to last Code resource (no gap)
(203) 04/20/88 ANOMALY: CODE Resource found in non-APPL file
(204) 04/20/88 ANOMALY: INIT Resource found in non-INIT, RDEV or ZSYS file
(205) 04/20/88 ANOMALY: cdev Resource found in non-cdev or ZSYS file

Checking for viral infections on volume "MacCrash"

INFECTION: Type 003 virus detected in file:
 MacCrash:
  System Folder:
   TOPS

ALERT! Volume "MacCrash" may be infected!
Consult listing to determine the details.

Interferon run completed!
1140 files were scanned, of which 540 had resource forks.
```

Fig. 10-10. An Inteferon report.

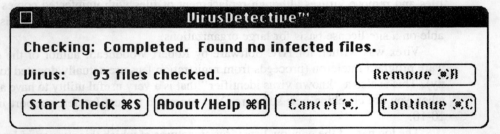

Fig. 10-11. The VirusDetective DA.

received a new disk, particularly as the program accepts user input as to what virus features to check. The screen shown in Fig. 10-12 is used to define resources to be flagged by the VirusDetective.

This feature allows the more technically literate user to add the features of new viruses and keep the VirusDetective up to date. The latest versions of all this and other shareware virus-fighting programs can be found on reputable Mac bulletin boards or obtained through user groups.

Some DOS Anti-Virus Programs

A host of software products are designed to help users of MS-DOS systems defend against virus attacks. Symantec, makers of the SAM product for the Macintosh, also make a comprehensive anti-virus product for DOS. The following are representative of the products available.

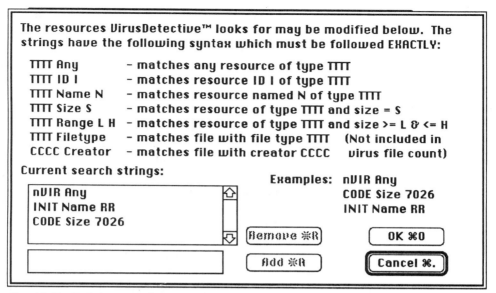

The resources VirusDetective™ looks for may be modified below. The strings have the following syntax which must be followed EXACTLY:

TTTT Any	– matches any resource of type TTTT
TTTT ID I	– matches resource ID I of type TTTT
TTTT Name N	– matches resource named N of type TTTT
TTTT Size S	– matches resource of type TTTT and size = S
TTTT Range L H	– matches resource of type TTTT and size >= L & <= H
TTTT Filetype	– matches file with file type TTTT (Not included in
CCCC Creator	– matches file with creator CCCC virus file count)

Current search strings:

nVIR Any
INIT Name RR
CODE Size 7026

Examples: nVIR Any
CODE Size 7026
INIT Name RR

Remove ⌘R   OK ⌘O

Add ⌘A   Cancel ⌘.

Fig. 10-12. Defining virus features to be searched.

Data Physician. Produced by Digital Dispatch of St. Paul, Minnesota, this is a collection of programs for defending DOS-based personal computers from viruses and logic bombs. Datamd is the main virus protection, detection, and removal program, allowing you to detect whether an unauthorized change has occurred in any file or system area on your disk. The program also allows the removal of certain types of viruses. Two programs, Disklock and Padlock, provide an intelligent disk write-protect function. Attempted writes to disk, such as a virus might use as it attacks a system, are intercepted. These programs also provide protection against logic bombs that do not spread on their own, but can attack in much the same manner as a virus. A program called Novirus works with the data created by Datamd and runs virus detection in background mode while you perform other tasks on your system. Novirus can be helpful if you have many files to watch over, or if you want continuous security monitoring. Antigen allows virus protection to be installed directly on any executable program. Each time a protected program is run, it checks itself for tampering and is capable of removing certain types of viruses on its own. This is useful when the protected program needs to be widely distributed and you want it to continue to be protected. Finally, a device driver called Viralert can be run in the background to intercept changes to executable and operating system files (files with EXE, COM, and SYS extensions). VirAlert also watches for changes to the boot record, and any disk formatting attempts.

C-4 Antiviral Shield. Another comprehensive product for IBM PCs and compatibles is C-4 Antiviral Shield, from InterPath of Santa Clara, California. This is a TSR program that monitors all system activity, including program loads, BIOS calls, interrupt requests, and accesses to system and application files. The program runs a constant check on activity characteristic of viral replication such as attempts to write to executable programs or DOS system files, access to a disk's boot sector, and attempted modification of COMMAND.COM. The C-4 program also checks for activities that indicate a virus is active and attempting to destroy or corrupt the system, including access to the system's file allocation table, low-level formats, and other low-level disk access requests.

If a virus does enter your system, C-4 will identify the virus and prevent it from infecting any existing programs on your disks. It will freeze the virus and display a warning window, identifying the name of the offending program and the name of the file or disk area where it was attempting to replicate itself. Likewise, if your system was infected prior to installing C-4 and an existing virus attempts to activate, it will be frozen before it can cause harm, and you will be notified.

Disk Watcher. Written by Raymond M. Glath of RG Software Systems, Willow Grove, Pennsylvania, Disk Watcher is a combination viral protection and disaster prevention package. The first program automatically checks all active disk drives and the computer's RAM for the presence of certain hidden virus characteristics when the computer is started. This program can also be run on demand at any time to check the disk in a specific drive. Disk Watcher itself is a TSR program that, when installed, monitors ongoing disk activity while you are working in other applications, using a series of proprietary algorithms that detect the behavior characteristics of many different virus programs. Disk Watcher has the ability to differentiate between legitimate input-output (I/O) activity and the I/O activity of a virus program. When an action occurs indicative of a virus attempting to reproduce itself, alter another program, set itself up to be automatically run the next time the system is started, or attempting to perform a massively damaging act, Disk Watcher will pop up. You will then have several options, one of which is to immediately stop the computer before any damage can be done.

Whenever the "Stop the computer" option is selected, both the application program screen image and Disk Watcher's screen image will be automatically sent to the system printer before the machine is stopped. This helps in performing an effective analysis of the problem. Disk Watcher also protects against certain other mishaps such as formatting of the hard disk, the system date and time not being set, and unintentionally pressing Print Screen.

Dr. Panda Utilities. The Dr. Panda Utilities from Panda Systems of Wilmington, Delaware, detect virus, worm, and trojan horse programs. Dr. Panda is a three-part software approach. The virus detection utility, called Physical, compares essential system files and user-selected files against a unique installation record. The system status is reported on-screen each time Physical is run. If a file has been changed, the file name is displayed onscreen. Any change in a system file, *.SYS, *.COM, *.EXE, *.OVL, or other program file might indicate a virus. Physical also reports the name and location of all hidden files on a disk at each operation.

A program called Labtest displays the hidden ASCII strings of a selected file after reporting warning messages for calls bypassing DOS. Through a function key interface, users can scroll through the file onscreen, perform basic editing functions, and direct output to a file or printer. Help screens are available to assist in identifying and analyzing potentially destructive code.

The Monitor program automatically intercepts disk operation calls that request a format of any drive or writes to the file allocation table of the first designated hard drive, typically C. The user can also select additional disk operations for checking (Read, Write, Verify) at installation. Control of a program passes to the keyboard at each interrupt with a Proceed/Bypass option. Monitor is particularly effective against trojan horse programs that destroy data immediately as part of their operation.

FoundationWare Vaccine. The Vaccine program from FoundationWare of Cleveland, Ohio, is a virus protection program particularly suited to networked computers. When installed on a hard disk, Vaccine continually tests files for the presence of any viruses without interrupting the computer's normal operation. If Vaccine detects a virus, it will prevent the virus from damaging the system and at the same time alert the user to the danger. Vaccine also protects against logic bombs. If a logic bomb tries to override the operating system with an illegal "write to disk" command, Vaccine halts the process and flashes a warning.

Vaccine can be used to isolate the hard disk from the rest of the system, thus providing a safe environment for testing dubious software. Vaccine is designed to allow a system manager to control what software can exist and be utilized on a system, thus preventing the use of unapproved software. For additional usage control, Vaccine has a tracking feature that enables an administrator to know what software has been run and when.

Vaccine from World Wide Data. Vaccine from World Wide Data Corporation of New York is a software viral protection package consisting of the Vaccine program, and two other utilities, Antidote and Checkup. Antidote scans your disk for all viruses known to World Wide Data. It then notifies you if any of them appear to have attacked any of your programs. Checkup keeps a record of the state of your system and informs you if any of your executable files (.EXE and .COM) have been changed since the last time Checkup was run.

Vaccine is a memory-resident program. Once you run it, you can continue to use your system as you normally do. Vaccine automatically and transparently checks every exceptional situation. If any program you run tries to alter your system in a suspicious way, Vaccine warns you about what the program is trying to do and gives you the chance to stop the destructive operation.

When Vaccine is loaded, no memory-resident program is permitted to remain in memory unless its name has been declared legal to Vaccine. No program is permitted to perform an absolute write to any device or to modify another executable program unless the user specifically and intentionally grants it permission. Memory addresses are checked as well to prevent any virus from corrupting the programs and data loaded in a system. Trusted and approved programs that might otherwise trigger Vaccine are listed in an exceptions file. Typically this includes the names of all programs that change memory tables or install themselves as resident.

Flu_Shot. One of the first programmers to release a shareware program to counter viruses was Ross Greenberg of Software Concepts Design in New York. He released the program as Flu_Shot, along with some choice comments, "There exists a low-level form of dirt who gets joy out of destroying your work." Perhaps because of the efficacy of the program, or the candor of his accompanying remarks, Flu_Shot fell victim to a particularly insidious form of sabotage. Whereas the legitimate Flu_Shot was distributed as FLUSHOT1.ARC in the first version and FLUSHOT2.ARC in the second, someone put out a file called FLUSHOT4.ARC which was in fact a trojan that trashed hard disks.

Greenberg opted to call the new and improved version of his original program Flu_Shot + to distinguish it from the imposter. The program offers customized write-protection, checksum file comparison, and TSR warnings. A file called FLUSHOT .DAT is stored in the root directory on drive C. This data file allows you to write- or read-protect entire classes of programs. This means you can write-protect all COM, EXE, and SYS files. You can even read-protect BAT files so an interloper cannot determine what name you used for Flu_Shot + when you invoked it.

Additionally, you can automatically check programs when you first invoke Flu_Shot + to determine if they've changed since you last looked at them. This part of the program uses the check-summing technique and allows you to tell if a protected program has been changed (some viruses can alter write-protected files). Check-summing can be invoked each time you load the program for execution. Flu_Shot + can also warn when an unauthorized program is loaded into memory as a terminate-and-stay-resident program. Some viruses use the same techniques as utilities like Borland's SideKick and SuperKey to act on your system or monitor it for "triggers" or "hot keys" while you are working with application software. You can register legitimate TSR programs in the FLUSHOT.DAT file and then Flu_Shot + will advise you if any other programs are loaded.

Ficheck 4.0. A slightly different approach to virus fighting is taken in the program Ficheck written by Chuck Gilmore of Gilmore Systems in Beverly Hills, California. One of the problems with well-established blocking programs like Flu_Shot is that intelligent viruses may actually look for them and attempt to circumvent the monitoring functions they perform. To avoid detection Ficheck is not actually installed on the hard disk. It simply resides on a floppy disk; when run, it records a complete and detailed picture of the entire fixed disk, logging it to a file. Ficheck records the date, time, size, attribute, and CRC (cyclic redundancy check) of every file on the hard disk. Whenever you decide to run it again Ficheck looks for differences in all these areas and alerts the user to any changes. Changes potentially mean a virus is at work because viruses have to alter files in some way in order to spread themselves.

Ficheck allows the user to organize his or her own checking program and does not slow down the computer during normal operation. The program would run well with a floppy boot disk system, recording the log file on the boot disk for a checkup on startup.

Mace Vaccine. Paul Mace Software of Ashland, Oregon, has proved a life-saver for many PC users. The package known as Mace Utilities is one of the leaders in hard disk format recovery and file deletion reversal. Mace has its own Vaccine program, a memory-resident utility designed to warn when unusual attempts are made to access vital disk areas and system files. This includes not only a computer user or virus, but also by any application that has no business modifying vital areas of a disk.

One nice feature of Mace Vaccine is the ability to increase or decrease levels of protection. The default protection, Level 1, write-protects the specified drive against access to vital areas and system files. Permission is required before any vital area or file can be modified. Level 2 provides all Level 1 protection of vital areas and files plus it write-protects the entire drive against all attempts at direct access. Programs that are denied direct access include viruses, the FORMAT command, CHKDSK/F, DEBUG, and disk reorganizers such as Mace UnFrag, Disk Optimizer, Norton SpeedDisk, and disk sector editors such as Norton and PC Tools.

SoftSafe. The SoftSafe program, described as a password-protection and file-access-control utility in Chapter 8, is also marketed as providing virus protection. SoftSafe's manufacturer, Software Directions of Randolph, New Jersey, has included a file comparison feature. SoftSafe maintains a protected copy of the main system files and compares these to the working files each time the system is booted up. If SoftSafe detects tampering, it gives the option of replacing the infected files with a clean copy, or ignoring the change if it was intentional, such as with a DOS version upgrade.

In addition to this, SoftSafe offers password protection of hard disks, allowing one "owner" to create up to seven authorized "users" for each PC. The owner can also delete users or change any password, and users can change their own password at any time. Also, SoftSafe's lock-out feature provides a hot key sequence to cover the entire screen with the SoftSafe password display. This prevents over-the-shoulder snooping, and, because only the correct password unlocks the machine, it protects data from unauthorized access during short periods away from the computer.

IF YOU ARE INFECTED

So far the emphasis in this chapter has been on identifying, deflecting, and defeating viruses without much discussion of what to do if you are unfortunate enough to have your computer(s) infected by one. In fact, this is a very difficult area to address in a general text. For a start, the large number of different viruses, each with different effects and methods of spreading, makes generalization difficult. However, the following points should provide a place to start. I hope you will excuse shorthand terminology used in the title for this section.

Detection and Disinfection

The first question to answer is, "How do you know you are infected?" It is important to sort out actual virus infections from other problems that have similar symptoms. Of course, you might be infected with a virus that needs no detection software to announce its presence. If your computer is playing Yankee Doodle Dandy at five o'clock everyday and nobody in your office is claiming credit for this musical interlude, you know you have a case of the Yankee Doodle virus. However, many symptoms are ambiguous, such as a file erased or a program malfunction. One of the most reliable indications that you have a virus infection is a message from a virus-detection program. As a rule, these come with instructions for removing infections caused by the specific or group of viruses that the program can detect. For example, the Corbin Vaccine described earlier tells you to refer to the manual when an infection is detected. The manual then walks you through the disinfection process.

Some virus-detectors that search for known viruses also provide automated cleanup facilities. This is possible in the case of well-known viruses such as Scores and nVir on the Mac since their actions are well-documented. Virus detectors that alert you to changes in key files can tell you which files are affected, but you will usually have to repair the damage yourself. Typically this involves:

- Restarting the system using a write-protected, certifiably-clean copy of the operating system.
- Making sure that you have backup copies of the infected files.
- Removing infected files from the system, either by erasing, or by copying onto clearly marked floppies.
- Replacing affected program and operating system files with clean copies.
- Determining if any previous backup files are infected.
- Possibly reclaiming important data from infected files.

Seeking Help

In a number of situations, an attack from malevolent program warrants a call for outside help. If a personal computer user is faced with anomalous phenomena ("really weird things happening with the computer") that cannot readily be explained by an informal committee of the organization's most computer literate members, then it is time to look beyond the organization. The two reasons for this are:

- Expert advice will lead to a faster and safer resolution of the problem.
- This might be a new strain of virus and the wider user community needs to be alerted.

You have several options when looking for outside help. If the problems appear closely linked to a specific piece of software ("this only started happening after we installed WimpWriter"), then the software manufacturer may be of assistance. However, you cannot reasonably expect support staff at a software company to help you deal with a virus on your system unless they know it came from their package.

Perhaps the next step is to contact a user group. Both individual users and organizations can belong to user groups. These are typically organized within cities according to brand of machine or operating system, as in Berkeley Macintosh Users Group (BMUG). Apart from being a valuable source of information about the latest products, these groups, by pooling knowledge, experience, and expertise, can often provide a lot of help in tackling a virus outbreak. User groups can sometimes be found in the phone book or through dealers and manufacturers. Local computer magazines often carry listings.

Beyond this, professional security experts can assist you in identifying viruses and recovering data. A certain amount of care needs to be exercised in selecting an outside consultant to help you with a virus problem. At the very least, you should ask for references and credentials, some verifiable evidence that the consultant has experience in this area. You should get a clear statement of likely charges and look for some sort of performance-related payment arrangement. This consultant is likely to want to charge for time worked regardless of outcome. You will not want to pay unless you get results. For more on selecting a reliable consultant, see Chapter 13.

SUMMARY

No reliable statistics on the amount or value of data lost because of malevolent programming exist. The actual number of cases is probably less than you might suppose from media reports of virus outbreaks. However, one reason that the effects of such programs has not been greater is the speed with which detailed news of their operation has been spread throughout the user community. Another reason is the rapid creation of free or inexpensive anti-virus software. This reflects a real commitment on the part of personal computer users to protect the freedoms they currently enjoy, the freedom to use communication links and the freedom to share files, with reasonable assurances that security will not be threatened by so doing.

In this chapter, you have seen that some of the security products mentioned in previous chapters have reappeared. The defense against viruses is really an extension of the layered approach to overall security that this book advocates. Once you control the following

- Who gets near the computer,
- Who uses the computer,
- Which programs and files can be accessed,
- How often backup is performed.

You are already well on the way to protecting against viruses. You will probably want to add a good working knowledge of how viruses operate, and make sure you:

- Know from where your software comes.
- Test any uncertified software on an isolated system.
- Regularly use virus detecting software.
- Make regular backups.

A further precaution that might be worthwhile is to make sure all use of the computer is logged in such a way as to identify the users, thus discouraging abuse by authorized users. If your computer is connected to others via the phone and/or a network, then you will want to ensure that these links are secured against viruses. For more on networks see Chapter 12, where you will also learn more on securing phone links. For more about hackers and other human factors in malevolent programming, see Chapter 13.

Anything a scientist can invent,
another scientist can uninvent.
Peter Duffy

11
Software Piracy and Pitfalls

THIS CHAPTER LOOKS AT a number of issues relating to software and security: Programs that protect your personal computer from prying eyes while you are away from your desk; formatting of disks; recovery of erased files; and software piracy, the illegal copying of programs. Some of these subjects might not at first appear directly related to personal computer security, however, in the course of this chapter their relevance should be made clear.

SOFTWARE PIRACY

If you make an illegal copy of a piece of software, there is a possibility that you will be prosecuted for doing so. No stretch of the imagination is required to see that such a prosecution, with its adverse effects on career, bank balance, and peace of mind, would be a threat to your personal security. If you supervise someone who uses your organization's time and equipment to make an illegal copy of a piece of software, there is a possibility that you will be liable for this illegal action. A number of legal questions surround the extent of this liability, such as how much you knew of, condoned, or encouraged this illegal copying, but it is a potential threat to your security and that of your organization. It should go without saying that organizations that condone or encourage illegal copying of software are simply creating a rod for their own backs. Beyond any moral arguments about the ownership of intellectual property and the charges made for its use, the fact that unauthorized copying of software is illegal means that to do it, or condone it, creates a threat to security. For this reason all users of personal computer software should be clear as to what constitutes illegal copying, otherwise known as software piracy.

What Constitutes Piracy

An illegal copy of a piece of software is a copy made in violation of the terms under which the software is licensed. Within broad limits defined by law and precedent, those terms are dictated by the owner of the software and can vary considerably. The owner is not the person who goes into a store and pays money for the software, but the person who created/wrote/published the software, the legal entity, be it an organization or an individual, that owns the copyright on the software.

The person who "buys" a software package actually purchases a license to use the software. The owner of the software is free, within certain legal parameters, to dictate the terms of that license, including the precise conditions under which copies can be made. As an example of this consider the license agreement for 1-2-3 Release 3, reproduced in Fig. 11-1.

LOTUS LICENSE AGREEMENT

BY OPENING THE SEALED DISK PACKAGE YOU AGREE TO BE BOUND BY THE TERMS OF THIS AGREEMENT WHICH INCLUDE THE SOFTWARE LICENSE AND THE LIMITED WARRANTY (collectively the "Agreement"). THIS AGREEMENT APPLIES TO YOU AND ANY SUBSEQUENT LICENSEE OF THIS SOFTWARE PROGRAM ("software").

IF YOU DO NOT ACCEPT OR AGREE TO THE TERMS OF THIS AGREEMENT, DO NOT OPEN THE DISK PACKAGE. PROMPTLY RETURN THE UNOPENED DISK PACKAGES AND ALL OTHER MATERIAL IN THIS PACKAGE WITH PROOF OF PAYMENT TO YOUR AUTHORIZED DEALER WHERE YOU OBTAINED THE PRODUCT FOR A FULL REFUND.

Lotus Development Corporation (Lotus) retains ownership of the enclosed program. This program is licensed to you for use under the following conditions:

PERMITTED USES/YOU MAY:
 • Use the software on any compatible computer, provided you use the software on only one computer at a time.
 • Use the software on a network, file server or virtual disk provided that access is limited to one user at a time and that you have the original copy of the documentation and the program disks.
 • Dedicate this license for use with 1-2-3 Release 3 Server Edition as described in the 1-2-3 Release 3 Server Edition License Agreement.
 • Permanently transfer the software to another user if you transfer the documentation and all disks and the other user agrees to the terms and conditions of this Agreement.

PROHIBITED USES YOU MAY NOT:
 • Make copies of the documentation or program disks, except as described in the documentation.
 • Loan, rent, sub-license, or otherwise transfer the software or the documentation, except as provided above.
 • Alter, modify or adapt the software or documentation, including, but not limited to, translating, decompiling, disassembling, or creating derivative works.

This license and your right to use the software automatically terminate if you fail to comply with any provision of this license agreement. Upon termination you will destroy all documentation and disks.

Lotus retains all rights not expressly granted. Nothing in this Agreement constitutes a waiver of Lotus' rights under the U.S. Copyright laws or any other federal or state law.

Fig. 11-1. License agreement for 1-2-3 Release 3.

In many ways, buying a piece of software is like buying a book. The main difference is that we traditionally make a closer identification between the material substance of a book and its contents and we use different terminology. The person who buys a book is not free to make copies of it. The author and/or publisher own the *copyright*. The purchaser of the book acquires a limited license to the contents thereof. The detailed terms of this license are contained in an established set of laws, but these days many books contain a short summary of the terms as shown in Fig. 11-2.

Copyright © 1980, by A. N. Author. All rights reserved.
Except as permitted under the Copyright Act of 1976, no part of this publication may be reproduced or distributed in any form or by any means stored in a database or retrieval system.
Except for use in a review, the reproduction or utilization of this work in any form or by any electronic, mechanical, or other means, now known or hereafter invented, including xerography, photocopying, and recording, and in any information storage and retrieval system is forbidden without the written permission of the publisher.
This book is sold subject to the condition that it shall not, by way of trade, be lent, resold, hired out, or otherwise disposed off without the publisher's consent, in any other form of binding or cover other than that in which it is published.

Fig. 11-2. Copyright agreement in a book.

License Agreements

Software license agreements are really a formalized statement of rights similar to those that automatically pertain when you purchase a book. Software publishers feel the need to formalize the relationship in terms of a license agreement for a number of reasons, perhaps the most obvious being the ease with which a copy can be made. A small utility program can be copied from one disk to another in a matter of seconds. In some cases, copying does not even require a disk. Software that is installed on a network can be loaded by several different users at the same time, creating illegal copies that exist only in computer memory.

Another reason for a formal licensing agreement is the fact that some software authors are more creative in the disposition of the rights than others. Indeed, an author may give up all rights of ownership in a particular program, making it *public domain*. A public domain program can be freely copied without charge. Another category of software is *shareware*. In this case, the owner of the copyright retains the right, but allows limited copying and sharing of the program in order to effect a type of try-before-you-buy distribution. If someone gives you a copy of a piece of shareware and you decide to use it on a regular basis, then you send a license fee to the publisher.

This method of distribution has been favored by small publishers who cannot afford the enormous expense of a commercial product launch. In part, shareware is a reaction against the tendency towards oligopoly in personal computer software, whereby a few big name products dominate a particular market, their prices kept high in part to fund the advertising budgets needed to maintain market share. Operating by what amounts to an honor system, several companies have done quite well with shareware. Typically, there are other incentives for registering shareware besides honesty, such as complete documentation, free upgrade to the next version, and so on. In most cases, the fee for registering a piece of shareware is quite reasonable, which helps to keep people honest.

Between shareware and public domain software lie several forms of copyright that can be lumped together as *freeware*. With freeware, the author retains copyright, but gives permission for widespread copying. This may be accompanied by a request for donations to a favorite charity, or other voluntary conditions of use. Many Macintosh users are familiar with this type of licensing as it has been favored by many community-minded programmers writing for the Mac. A lot of early anti-virus software was distributed in this manner.

The main point to bear in mind about all forms of software licensing is that when you buy a software package you do not really gain anything in physical terms. What you get is a license to use a piece of thinking that is contained in a set of disks and manuals. Suppose you have just purchased 1-2-3 Release 3. You sit down at your computer and open up the package to get at the disks. So far you may have been unaware of the distinction between owner and licensee. However, a big sticky label on the plastic bag containing the disks reminds you:

Warning: Do not break this seal until you have read the license agreement.

At this point, the license agreement becomes required reading. Having read words similar to those in Fig. 11-1, and having decided you can live with this agreement, you open the package and install the software. When you load the software, you get a further reminder of who owns the copyright, as shown in Fig. 11-3.

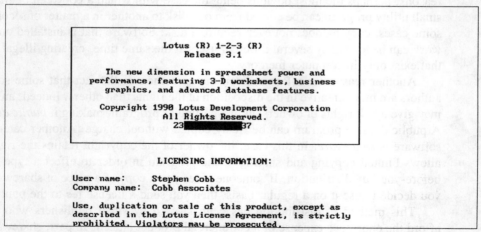

Fig. 11-3. On-screen copyright notice.

One reason for this type of opening screen copyright message, used by many software companies, is that failure to declare copyright can lead to loss of copyright. Usually such screens appear momentarily then give way to the main program. Other packages will require users to press a key to get past the copyright notice, thus making it impossible to argue, "I never saw it."

In the early days of personal computer software, license agreements were often difficult and burdensome reading. Borland International was one of the first companies to come up with a simplified, no-nonsense license statement, an example of which is given in Fig. 11-4.

BORLAND BUSINESS PRODUCTS
NO-NONSENSE LICENSE STATEMENT

This software is protected by both United States copyright law and international copyright treaty provisions. Therefore, you must treat this software just like a book, except that you may copy it onto a computer to be used and you may make archival copies of the software for the sole purpose of backing-up our software and protecting your investment from loss.

By saying, "just like a book," Borland means, for example, that this software may be used by any number of people, and may be freely moved from one computer location to another, so long as there is no possibility of it being used at one location while it's being used at another or on a computer network by more than one user at one location. Just like a book can't be read by two different people in two different places at the same time, neither can the software be used by two different people in two different places at the same time. (Unless, of course, Borland's copyright has been violated or the use is on a computer network by up to the number of users authorized by additional Borland licenses as explained below.)

Fig. 11-4. A simplified software licensing agreement.

As you can see, this agreement addresses a special area of software licensing: Programs that are used to make other programs. In this sense a piece of software is not unlike a book. One of Borland's first successes as a software publisher was Turbo Pascal, a simple but powerful programming language that enabled users to write their own programs. Borland soon supplemented the programming language with program examples and collections of same program code, known as *routines*. These sample programs and routines gave programmers the foundations and building blocks for creating new software. At some point, Borland needed to draw the copyright line between what the programmer created and the original tools and materials provided by Borland. The company's fairly liberal attitude on this question proved attractive, and Borland's languages have a loyal following among programmers.

Finer Points

Most license agreements specify that you may only use the software on one machine at once. In some cases this is further restricted to "install on one machine at once." This is where the differences between a book and piece of software begin to emerge. You can use a book just about anywhere and carry it with you. Software cannot be used without a computer, and, until recently, few computers could travel with you. This led to the dilemma of the person who uses a piece of software to do their work in the office, and needs to carry on working at home, during the evening or on the weekend.

Before the arrival of the laptop, people overcame the inconvenience of carting a desktop computer from office to home and back, by purchasing a second computer for the home. If the software being used is a single disk, it can be carried from one machine to another. This does not seem to be a problem: The software is only being used on one computer at once. However, if the user makes a copy of the software to leave at home the situation becomes less clear. There is a possibility that both copies could be used at the same time, which would be a violation of most commercial license agreements.

While the growing complexity of software has made single disk application software a rarity, the advent of hard disks made the installation of multiple copies of large programs that much easier. When a user installs a program onto two hard disk computers at different locations, the original intention might be that only one will be used at a time, but the fact is that both can be used simultaneously, and often are. In many cases, piracy is not a deliberate rip-off, but rather something that insinuates itself into general business practice.

The Extent of the Problem

Before going into any more detail about software piracy, it is important to get an idea of how many users violate software license agreements. The answer is probably about half! In 1990 a survey of 2000 members of the great British public by MORI found that of those who regularly use a personal computer either at home or at work, 43 percent admit to having used software illegally. This is not a case of cheap games software skewing the figures. MORI also surveyed 300 senior British managers and found that 55 percent of those using personal computers at work copy software in violation of license agreements. One in three companies admitted to having no control over software duplication.

According to calculations by MORI on the basis of their findings, the revenue lost to illegal copying cost the software industry in Britain £300 million in 1989. That is half a billion dollars! There is no reason to suppose that the situation in the U.S. is any better. In fact, Britain has tough copyright protection legislation which has outlawed products like Copy II PC which facilitate the duplication of copy-protected software.

Casual Copies and Counterfeiting

The boom in sales of laptop personal computers in the late 1980s might have meant a reduction in illegal copying, eliminating the need to keep copies on two machines, instead it has probably contributed to the problem. The typical scenario goes like this: Executive uses PC at work; executive wants mobile computing capability; buys PC-compatible laptop plus desktop-laptop link; copies software from desktop to laptop; uses laptop on the road while someone back at the office, where there are never enough PCs to go around, uses the exec's desktop computer and now illegal software copy.

As soon as disks began to emerge as the standard medium for software distribution, efforts were made to prevent unauthorized copying, to enforce the honesty of a user who installs the same copy of a piece of software on two machines with the intention of only using it on one machine at a time. The key disk and dongle methods of copy protection, discussed later in the chapter, are the prime examples of this. They allow the copying of software onto more than one machine, but only one key is provided per software license purchased. On the face of it, this is not a great inconvenience for the legitimate user who simply has to carry the key from one machine to the other. However, such protection techniques have an implicit message of mistrust, and they work far less conveniently in practice than on paper. Take the user with a second copy of the software on the home computer. If the user leaves the key disk at the office he or she is faced with being unable to use the software at home, even though it is not being used at the same time at the office.

If a software license forbids the installation of the software on more than one machine at once, then this might be seen as an excessive restriction, preventing the itinerant user from enjoying access to a product for which good money has been paid. Definition of the term "install" becomes critical as well, because it could be argued that copying a key disk protected program onto a hard disk is not installing it on that machine, since the program will not run "as is." Some license agreements forbid, and some copy-protection systems prevent, making copies of the original software disks. Some users feel that this is unfair. They want to be able to make several copies to be stored separately as backup, thus helping to guarantee uninterrupted access to the program. The legality of restrictions on archival or backup copies is a matter of debate. In England, the 1988 Copyright Act specifically outlaws the sale and use of devices whose purpose is the circumventing of copyright protection schemes. It does not matter whether you think you have a right to another copy for backup purposes, using a program like Copy II PC is illegal.

The type of piracy that occurs when a company buys one copy of 1-2-3 and installs it on three computers can be distinguished from the type of operation in which copies of 1-2-3 are sold commercially, often in packages that are made up to look like the original 1-2-3. This is counterfeiting, a practice that occurs in many areas of commerce where a copyrighted design or brand name carries a premium. If you know where to look, you can buy counterfeit jeans, perfumes, luggage, and more. The extent to which software is counterfeited is hard to gauge, but there have been some major seizures in recent years, involving tens of thousands of illegal copies.

While some people make a distinction between bootleg software (privately-made, hand-labelled, pirated copies) and counterfeit software (commercially distributed look-alike copies), both are clearly illegal under the present system of intellectual property rights. Some people think those rights need to be changed, but neither form of piracy is the right way to achieve this. In fact, the private pirating of software is tougher to stop than large-scale counterfeiting, particularly when users cling to such justifications as "it's only one copy."

Apart from the ethical and legal transgressions involved in piracy, there are other negatives. The preceding chapter pointed out that pirated software is a serious source of virus infection, and viruses pose a significant security threat to data, programs, and normal operations. The use of illegal software also opens up the door to the extortionist and blackmailer threatening to turn a company in for license agreement violations. Software companies are always interested in hearing about organizations who condone illegal copying of their software, and there are industry watchdogs that react very quickly to such claims (these include the Federation Against Software Theft, the Business Software Alliance, and the Software Publishers' Association).

WHY PEOPLE CHEAT

Why people are not prepared to pay full price for software, why they are prepared to cheat to get a "good deal" is that the cost of a fully functional personal computer system can easily consist of equal parts of hardware and software.

Low Perceived Value

Most people would agree that software just doesn't appear as valuable as hardware. The value of software is intangible, buried in the lines of finely crafted code that most users never see. Take an accounting program that outwardly consists of a ring bound manual and half a dozen floppy disks. The material cost of making up each copy is a few dollars, yet the selling price per unit might be as much as the personal computer it is designed to run on. This is because writing the program might take thousands of programmer-hours.

Some software publishers have tried to use packaging to alter the perceived value of their products, producing bigger and fancier boxes, more substantial manuals, and so on. However, the gap in perceived value is difficult to remove. This is because of the steady decline in absolute hardware prices, which contrasts with the steady rise in absolute prices for software. This can be seen in the graph in Fig. 11-5.

This graph shows that the street price of a basic business microcomputer has steadily declined, while the cost of business software has not. Of course, hardware and software have improved over the years. Today's entry-level machine is yesterday's top of the line. Today's spreadsheet does things unthinkable in earlier versions. Measuring relative power of hardware and software is difficult and tends to be subjective. Even if you alter the graph to take into account the power factor, there is still a gap. There has been a steady rise in raw computing power per dollar without a corresponding rise in applied power, as shown in Fig. 11-6.

The lack of perceived value in software presents an obstacle for software publishers trying to get what they see as a fair price for their products, one which covers past product development, research into new products, support of existing products, and the huge bill for marketing. Most of this marketing is aimed at beating out competing products and little effort goes into educating the consumer as to the large and very real costs of product development. As a consequence, many people resent paying full price for software and some will take every opportunity to avoid paying it. A positive PR campaign by software companies and their trade organizations could do a lot

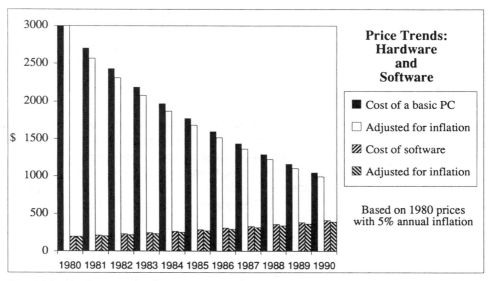

Fig. 11-5. Hardware and software price trends.

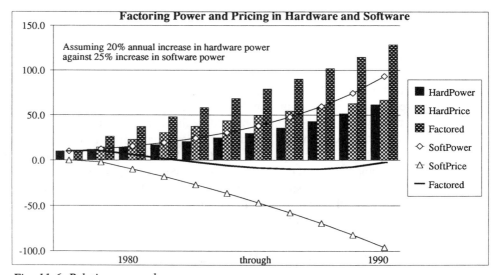

Fig. 11-6. Relative power changes.

to reverse this perception. It might be a more effective antidote to piracy than the "bootlegger as criminal" campaigns that have been mounted in the past.

Lack of Real Value

Unfortunately, in the fast-paced and fiercely competitive world of personal computer software there have been a lot of broken promises. At various times different software companies have failed to deliver the levels of support to which customers of high priced packages felt they were entitled. This has left some users feeling "why pay more for a legitimate copy when you do not get more." The antidote to this perception is a greater effort by software companies to keep faith with customers.

Everyone Else Does

When one company sees another enjoying the productivity benefits of computerization without paying the price, there is a big temptation to follow suit. If $50,000 worth of computer equipment is required to stay competitive, and your competitor paid only $25,000, you will not be able to enjoy the same profit margins if you pay full price. This type of argument is familiar at a personal level when it comes to breaking all sorts of inconvenient rules: "Everybody else does." The fact that so doing is foolish should be adequate dissuasion.

The Liberation Ethic

The first microcomputers were not developed by giant corporations looking for a new consumer market to monopolize. They were developed by some very unique individuals who were not unfamiliar with the radical political and social movements of the late 1960s and early 1970s. Some saw microcomputers as bringing computing power, once the prerogative of giant corporations and the military, to the masses. A lot of programs were created and distributed by individuals with no thought of personal gain. As commercial interests threatened to become the dominant influence on the direction of hardware and software design, a backlash developed in which commercial software was seen as a "rip-off" and making a copy for personal use was "liberating" the technology that had been appropriated by the software publisher.

Today some programmers still do not believe that software should be a commercial commodity. They write programs that are then given away. It remains to be seen whether this approach will ever pose a threat to commercial publishers. However, the idea of "liberating" commercial software by making illegal copies is a dangerous one. It belongs with "all property is theft" in the trash can of simplistic responses to the inequalities and injustices of life.

A HISTORY OF COPY-PROTECTION

Over the last dozen or so years, numerous techniques have been developed to prevent illegal copying of software. Most of the major software companies have used one or more of these techniques at one time or another, although the trend over the last five years has been to drop copy-protection from products. The last major company to do this was Lotus, whose 1-2-3 package was probably the most widely sold copy-protected program. Most of the techniques used to prevent illegal copying and spread of software fall into two categories of disk-based and hardware-based. The disk-based techniques involve tinkering with the distribution disk to make it difficult to copy.

Hardware-based techniques usually involve use of a key device, without which the software cannot be used.

Key Disks

Floppy disks are the main form in which personal computer software is distributed. Floppy disks are also very easy to copy. The two main techniques that operating systems use to copy disks are file-by-file and image. In a *file-by-file* copy, each file from the source disk is copied onto a formatted target disk. The *image* copy simply transfers a track-by-track image of the source disk onto the target disk. In this case, the target disk does not need to be preformatted; the image that is transferred includes the format.

It is possible to design a disk so that part of the contents are hidden and not transferred from source to target in either a file-by-file or image copy. It is also possible to write instructions on a disk that are activated by the copying process. Thus a disk might be set up so that attempting to copy it will scramble a small but vital part of the program code, rendering the program unusable. A less drastic alternative would be to hide a vital part of the copy-protected program on the original disk so that it could not be copied to another floppy or to a hard disk. This requires that the original disk be placed in the computer while the program is loading, in order for the program to read the "key" section. This is known as the key disk approach, and it has been the most widely used form of copy-protection.

The best known application of this technique was Lotus 1-2-3, which was copy protected until 1989. When loading protected versions of 1-2-3, the program would read the serial number and display it on screen. The serial number was embedded on a special "master" disk supplied with the package. The program was designed not to load without reading this serial number. The number could not be copied to another disk by normal DOS commands. Two master disks were provided when you bought the package, giving you a backup in case one was damaged. With a floppy-disk-only computer the scheme was not too restrictive as far as program loading was concerned, but users who somehow damaged both master disks found that waiting for Lotus to send a replacement was highly inconvenient and not without cost.

Tokens

As hard disks became more popular users found that even when they copied the bulk of the 1-2-3 program to the hard disk, the master disk had to be in a floppy drive for 1-2-3 to read the serial number. This was highly inconvenient because it slowed down the loading process and led to problems when users left the disk in the floppy drive, preventing normal system start-up for the next user. Lotus attempted to overcome this problem with a technique that copied the serial number from the master floppy onto the hard disk. The problems with this were less obvious, but in some ways even more insidious. The special disk-writing used to embed the serial number on the hard disk caused problems for backup and restore operations, and these problems were often hard to diagnose. Users often found out too late that the serial number could be wiped out by formatting of the hard disk or a hard disk crash. This meant writing to Lotus for a replacement because the copy-protection scheme actually transferred the serial number like a token from the master floppy to the hard disk.

A similar token system was adopted for a while by Ashton-Tate who were keen to prevent bootlegging of dBASE III Plus. The token system used by dBASE was annoying in the extreme because it took a long time to write the token from the floppy to the hard disk and to remove it back to the floppy when the program was being transferred from one machine to another. When a token was removed from a system, it had to go back onto the correct copy of the program disk, otherwise the token was lost.

     I well recall setting up a network of six machines running dBASE and having to perform nearly two dozen token transfers in the process of arranging the hardware to the client's needs. However, the token system was better than one short-lived Ashton-Tate copy protection experiment that involved a disk deformity, an extra hole in the disk. Some users claimed that their floppy drive read/write heads were actually damaged by this technique, which was quickly dropped.

A slightly different token scheme was used by IBM with its Drawing Assistant program and other software in the same series. The program disks had a set number of copy tokens and the token count was reduced by one each time the disk was copied. This permitted a fair number of copies, more than two, but usually less than six.

Dongles

One of the most effective copy protection systems is a hardware/software combination involving a device called a *dongle*. A dongle is a small circuit board containing a microchip which can generate/store a serial number. The dongle is plugged into one of the computer's ports. Under the control of software, the computer is instructed to check periodically for the presence of the dongle: If it is not there, the software stops. The hardware is usually encased in epoxy resin to prevent tampering. An example is pictured in Fig. 11-7.

The first dongles to be produced in any quantity were designed for the Commodore PET personal computer in the early 1980s. Like many early personal computers, the PET had a number of spare ports, allowing the dongle to be used without interfering with other input/output. Readers kicking themselves for not having invented the dongle can take some consolation in the fact that its fortunes have been at best "mixed."

After the IBM PC was introduced and started to become a standard, dongles went into decline. This was due mainly to the lack of suitable ports in which to insert them. The first IBM PCs did not have a serial port as standard, and the color model did not even come with a printer port! The monochrome model had a parallel printer port, but parallel ports are not easy to program, and to be used on this port a dongle has to be "transparent" to let the printer work normally. These days any self-respecting personal computer comes with several ports built-in and the technical problems of trans-

Fig. 11-7. A typical dongle.

parency have been overcome. By some accounts, the popularity of dongles amongst software authors is on the increase.

The great advantage of dongles in copy protection is that programs can be tied to a single dongle by giving them code numbers, to which the customer is not privy, that have to match before the program can work. This means that, however many copies are made, they work only on one machine. The only drawback of dongles versus key disks is cost. The cheapest version might, in bulk, run about $2 a unit, but this is a substantial addition to a computer game selling for $20. On the other hand, it is a small proportion of a $200 to $400 word-processing program.

More sophisticated dongles have been developed which include cipher keys, such as a random number that has to be subtracted from the program to make it work. This enables the manufacturer to "license" how many computers could use the software, and even identify a particular user. Now a variety of dongles on the market plug into the serial or parallel port or keyboard socket or internal bus slot. The majority of dongles are serial or parallel types, although the internal bus variety is gaining popularity because of its speed and physical security.

Wherever a dongle is inserted it has to produce a "key" or "sequence" that cannot be generated elsewhere. The three general types of dongle are the key-of-the-door, the RAM type, and the pseudo-random number generator (PRNG). A key-of-the-door dongle typically delivers 8, 16, or 32 bits of data. The program it is protecting checks to see if this "key" is correct and continues accordingly. This type of dongle gives the least security: It is possible to "debug" a program protected with a dongle of this type and bypass the part of the software that accesses it. There has to be a point in the software where it says something like, "Has the dongle compared correctly? If Yes, carry on; if No, then abort." The hacker simply changes the Yes/No branches to make the program work without the dongle.

A RAM dongle usually holds 64 or 128 bits of user-definable password-protected data. This dongle is rather like the key-of-the-door type except it is easier for the program author to alter what the program expects to come from the dongle, such as a date or a counter. To make either dates or counters effective, the program must write to the dongle. To do that, it must write the password first. Because these passwords are relatively short, it will not take a determined hacker long to guess it and rewrite a counter back in. Furthermore, unless the software company originally buying these RAM type dongles has a unique or "special" dongle made, a hacker can buy a similar one with the same "write" passwords and therefore duplicate the software. If you are a software developer looking to use a dongle to protect your software, be absolutely sure that nobody can buy dongles with the same internal sequence that you are receiving.

The Pseudo-Random Number Generator (PRNG) dongle contains hardware that will produce a very large nonrepeating sequence of random numbers (in excess of 1 million bits without repetition). They do, of course, repeat their own sequence on request.

When using a dongle to protect software, the methods fall into two main headings, key-of-the-door and encryption. With the key-of-the-door method, any of the discussed dongle types can be used. The programmer places a copy of the dongle's output somewhere in his code. When the protected software is run, it examines the dongle and checks that the bytes produced are the same as those placed within the program when it was originated. This dongle data can be anything from one to four bytes for the key-of-the-door type dongle, up to a practical limit of about 500 if a PRNG dongle is used.

The encryption method is by far the most effective way to protect software from illegal use, although it is not as easy to implement as the key-of-the-door method. One method of encryption to protect software is to take say, one kilobyte of code or data, the same amount of pseudo-random data from a PRNG dongle, then exclusive-or the two together. This produces one kilobyte of pseudo-rubbish where the program code or data used to be. The program eventually sold to the end user will have areas of code that can reverse this process each time the program is run, or each time a certain part of the program is activated. The program will now work only with a suitable dongle. For further security, the program could destroy or re-encrypt this data after use. The anti-debugging advantage here is that without the dongle in place, it is not possible to decrypt the "pseudo-rubbish."

Despite the advances in dongle technology, which mean that they are now completely compatible with other hardware and do not interfere with normal operation of the computer, there remain several objections. Users still seem suspicious of something they have to plug into their machine. It is a nuisance, particularly if the computer has to be relocated to make room for the dongle sticking out of the back. However, perhaps the most obvious problem is that of the user who wants to work with two programs, both of which require dongles. Only the adoption of an industry-wide standard for dongle design would allow such an arrangement without conflicts, and who knows how they would all be plugged together. For this reason alone it is likely that dongles will remain a specialty item. It is unlikely that large corporate purchasers of software will accept hardware-based copy protection.

Other Methods

Several other methods of copy protection have been used, with varying degrees of success. Some games software requires that the user answer a question, the answer to which is in the documentation, making the pirating of the disk alone ineffective.

Other game manufacturers experimented with codes on their packaging. When the program was loaded, the user was required to type in the colors in the correct sequence to begin the game. In theory, it was impossible to run the program without the original packaging to refer to. In practice, of course, it could easily be written down and passed on by hand.

One system now used extensively is software registration, whereby the serial number and the user's name is written into the software when it is installed. This information appears whenever the software is loaded. The idea is that you will not want to be caught running software that says it is licensed to Joe Blow, Fred's Tool Emporium when your name is Bill and you work for Bill's Real Estate. This is only effective against casual piracy and people with scruples. In most cases, you can copy the original program disks before they are installed and so each copy can be installed by the illegal owner.

Retreat from Protectionism

A constant stream of customer complaints about the inconvenience of copy-protection finally began to wear down those companies who had adopted it. Also, there was evidence to suggest that sales were being lost to nonprotected work-alike programs. A further nail in the coffin came from the decision by some major customers, such as the U.S. government, to insist on protection-free software.

The government, particularly the military, argued thus: We have a right to make archive copies of programs that we buy. Copy-protection is a dangerous infringement of that right. In critical applications at critical times, it is not reasonable to send off to the manufacturer for a replacement disk. After all, the silos and bunkers could be overrun in the time it takes to get a new master disk for the spreadsheet program used to calculate defensive strategy.

 While few people took seriously the image of a bullet-dodging courier scrambling over the barbed wire, key disk in hand, the basic point was sound: As personal computers take on more and more critical tasks, there is no room for copy-protection schemes that might impede maintenance or disaster recovery operations.

The leading software manufacturers began to have second thoughts about copy protection. At the Softcom 85 exhibition in Atlanta, Georgia, Seymour Rubenstein of Micropro announced they were dropping protection from their new WordStar 2000 package. Users of the earlier, unprotected, WordStar were not upgrading to WordStar

2000 as fast as Micropro had hoped, and the copy-protection was seen as a major factor. Micropro felt it had lost a lot of sales of WordStar due to piracy, but some people argued that lack of copy protection had helped WordStar become an early standard for word processing.

At the same conference, industry analyst Will Zachman warned, "Any company laying plans on the basis of copy protection is heading for disaster." In 1986 Software Publishing Corporation, makers of PFS File, a popular copy-protected filing program, removed copy protection from their programs, and Microsoft dropped it from their MS-DOS software. In 1988, Lotus started dropping protection from its products as new versions were released, and by 1990 all products were protection-free.

A number of companies announced their about-face on this issue with the face-saving line: Copy-protection is no longer needed now that the public properly understands the legal framework of software licensing. What few people in the industry were willing to admit was that copy-protection was not really working. Human ingenuity being what it is, for every copy-protection system, an unprotect product soon appeared.

Justifiable Illegality

When, in 1973, the U.S. made fifty-five miles per hour the maximum speed limit on all roads, regardless of traffic levels and traveling conditions, many people felt unfairly inconvenienced, particularly those living in the wide open spaces of the west. Some people ignored the speed limit. When the highway patrol started to use radar devices to check speed limits and levy fines, some people felt justified in using a piece of equipment that gave early warning of radar devices. Increasingly sophisticated, difficult to detect radar devices inspired increasingly sensitive early warning devices. The personal computer software industry experienced a parallel form of technological escalation in the copy protection stakes.

The arguments used to justify breaking the speed limit also provided a parallel for those wishing to circumvent copy-protection. Copy-protection schemes were said to be inconvenient, an unfair imposition upon honest users, a source of system errors and malfunctions, and a failure at their intended task.

Inconvenient. Few people would deny that copy protection is inconvenient. Publishers of software tended to underestimate the inconvenience and claim it was a necessary evil that ensured maximum revenue collection, and hence better funding for new and improved products. Users were constantly finding new forms that this inconvenience could take. For many users of copy-protected products, it was this feeling that they were acting as guinea pigs that was most objectionable. The main problem facing designers of copy protection systems is the same as that facing virus-writers: Predicting how the scheme will interact with the practically infinite combinations of hardware and software that exist outside the software lab.

Perhaps the most common mistake in the checkered history of copy protection has been to assume that a piece of software is purchased and installed, just once, by one person, on one machine. In reality, the use of software is much less straightforward.

Programs often need to be re-installed and de-installed as hardware is upgraded, as systems are reconfigured, as patterns of work change. This fact of office life made copy protection schemes much more of a problem in practice than on paper.

 I was recently visiting the offices of a company that used a dongle-protected financial charting program. There were technical problems with the machine on which the program was normally used. This necessitated temporarily transferring the program, and dongle, to another system. The only available computer was installed in such a mass of cables that reaching a port into which the dongle could be plugged involved moving furniture and relocating the computer so that there was room for the dongle.

It would appear that few people have taken the time to study what really happens in offices that make extensive use of personal computers. Unfortunately, what studies are done tend to be carried out by computer companies, with their own offices as the subject. This produces a distorted picture of what is likely to happen.

Unfair. Users who have no intention of illegally sharing software and organizations with strict internal controls on software copying, find it particularly galling to have to put up with the inconveniences of copy protection. They also object to software companies passing on the cost of protection schemes designed to protect against a minority of irresponsible users.

Errors. Many users find personal computers daunting enough without the added complications of a copy protection scheme that requires a key disk, token, or dongle. The difficulties of complying with the requirements of these devices only increased the likelihood of errors, and added one more layer to the already complex process of setting up and running a personal computer. In addition to problems resulting from the intimidation factor, and the complication factor, some copy protection schemes simply imposed hardware and software problems. They would not work properly with certain hardware and software combinations, requiring users to forego preferred configurations in order to use the copy-protected software.

Failure. The final charge leveled against copy protection schemes is that they do not work. Users with sufficient knowledge and experience can circumvent most protection mechanisms. This gives rise to the feelings of unfairness among less knowledgeable users, and to a roaring trade in protection-defeating software written by those who know how. Users wanting the benefits of unprotected access therefore have to pay to defeat something they did not want in the first place.

Such were the main arguments used to justify violations of software licensing agreements and circumvention of copy-protection schemes. Once it was clear that people were prepared to do this, products appeared that made the task a lot easier.

The Copyist's Weaponry

The main weapon to be used by those wishing to circumvent copy-protection was called a bit map copier. This tells the computer to scan a floppy disk track by track, without activating any instructions, until it has worked out the entire layout. This makes it possible to avoid any protective "booby traps" and reproduce the original in pristine condition without triggering the security systems. Under trade names such as Locksmith, Copywrite, and Copy II PC, the bit map copiers promised to allow anyone to duplicate programs at will.

In fact, bit map copiers did not provide a complete solution. Early versions of programs like Copy II PC allowed you to create a copy of the 1-2-3 key disk, they did not remove the need for hard drive users to insert key disk when loading 1-2-3. As hard disks proliferated, programs that allowed you to dispense with the key disk became popular. There was still the problem of escalation. Old versions of Copy II PC could not unprotect new versions of 1-2-3, and so on. As copy protection systems developed more intricate ways of writing to disk, Central Point Software, makers of Copy II PC brought out a circuit board that was placed between the floppy disk drive controller and the drive in order to more precisely control reading and writing of disks. To many users and publishers of software, it began to appear as though copy-protection was a technological race with no winners, except for the makers of protect/ unprotect products.

The Big Debate

The open sale and advertising of protection-defeating devices caused outrage among software publishers convinced they were losing revenue to pirated copies. The makers of the products defended them on several grounds. Firstly, they were intended and clearly marked "For archival purposes only, within the limits of existing licensing law." Secondly, they were in fact a boost to sales of copy-protected software, because people who saw a pirated version of a product and liked it tended to go out and buy a legitimate copy. The seller of one protection defeating product, Interface-3, quoted in the book *The Electronic Pirates*, by John Chesterman and Andy Lipman, put it like this:

> Piracy is a load of rubbish. It doesn't affect sales in any way. We've been selling products of this kind [protection defeating] for two years and, if anything, it's increased sales [of regular software]. Interface-3 doesn't encourage piracy. After all, when people hear a record, they go out and buy it. Hearing encourages people to buy.

Of course, you might counter that people who hear a record they like, often tape it without the artist getting anything. Nevertheless, claims of revenue losses due to piracy have always been matched by skepticism in some circles. For example, Chesterman and Lipman quote Jim Stockford, a contributor to the *Whole Earth Software Catalogue*. Stockford said, "These software people are not missing much . . . I do not believe any company is really being ripped off by the use of pirated computer programs." The crucial phase here is "really being ripped off." Because it is a proven fact that illegal copies are made and used, how is it possible to argue that software companies are not being ripped off? Several points can be made in defense of this argument. Whenever a software company cites figures for the amount of revenue lost through pirating, the figures are usually based on the assumption that each pirated copy being used represents one unit of lost revenue, yet there is reason to question this assumption. There is no proof that users of pirated programs would actually go out and buy the same programs if all illegal copies were confiscated. In many cases, they could choose a less expensive competitor with similar features. Furthermore, there is a case for saying that some sales have been spawned by pirate copies. A user who is introduced to a program through a pirate copy, and finds the program very helpful, might then decide to buy a legitimate copy to get the latest upgrade, complete documentation, or telephone support.

Only extensive research can reveal the true extent of the impact of piracy on software revenues. Certainly software companies are free to press their case and encourage compliance with license agreements. More imaginative licensing arrangements, such as site licenses, could go a long way toward eliminating what appears to be a major area of revenue loss: Organizations that buy one legitimate copy of a program then issue illegal copies to employees. Piracy is likely to continue; the level at which it does will be determined by a number of factors:

- The cost of legitimate copies.
- Perceived value of the software.
- Ease of copying.
- Practical value of the software.
- Effectiveness of copyright-awareness campaigns.

The Future of Copy Protection

All of the major business applications for personal computers are now free of copy protection. Named-user software registration seems to be well on the way to a standard practice. Meanwhile, dongle makers are becoming more sophisticated. It is now possible to have such features as user definable battery-backed RAM, password settable read-only DOWN counters (that reduce by one each time the program is used), internal password generation without the need for encryption software external to the dongle, internal bounce-back encryption of bytes, and user-definable serial numbers. However, the bottom line is that a dongle has to be attached somewhere, and until there is a standard dongle port that accommodates multiple dongles, this technology will remain limited to a few specialized packages.

ONLOOKERS AND INTERLOPERS

In Chapter 8, file access controls were examined. Password protection of files on personal computers was shown to be increasingly easy to implement. However, even the strongest password protection must be removed when the file is being edited. This opens up a window of opportunity for the IHI or *in-house interloper*. A fact of office life is that opportunities exist to access forbidden information when someone is working on that information. This access can be as casual as reading the screen over the legitimate user's shoulder, or as intentional as using an unattended machine on which a forbidden file has been left in memory by a legitimate, although careless, user. While it is not pleasant to suspect coworkers and colleagues of such behavior, it might be realistic to do so at times, and take appropriate precautions.

Over the Shoulder

If you work in an open office you might find it convenient to be able to blank your computer's screen at will. Programs called screen-blankers do this. Some of these are public domain and can be found on bulletin boards. Others, such as Pyro for the Macintosh, are sold commercially. Occasionally display adapters come with their own blanking facility. Some monitors, notably older monochrome models, can actually deteriorate if the same image stays on the screen for an extended period of time. This fact led to the development of timed screen blankers that dim the display if the computer is unused for a set period of time. A number of commercial and public domain programs offer both timed and user-activated screen blanking.

Pad-Lock. A rather handy desk accessory for Macintosh users is Pad-Lock, which began life as a shareware program from Mike Whittingham of Wilton, Connecticut. This provides password-protected screen blanking, plus a warning when someone has tried to use your Mac while you were away. In Fig. 11-8, you can see the initial Pad-Lock screen where a password is being entered. The user has selected Pad-Lock from the DA menu and typed a password. Note the miniature padlock icons representing characters of the password.

Fig. 11-8. Entering Pad-Lock.

You will also note that in Fig. 11-8 the "leave a message" box has been checked. This tells Pad-Lock that you want to enter your own message for anyone who tries to use the computer while you are away. The message entry screen can be seen in Fig. 11-9.

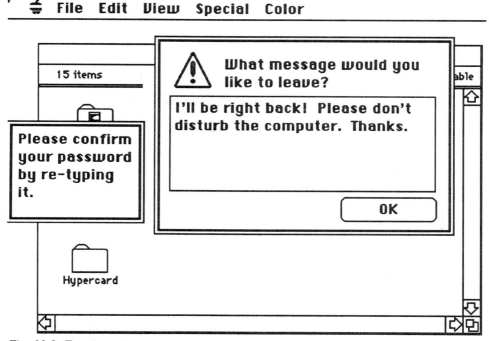

File   Edit   View   Special   Color

15 items

Please confirm
your password
by re-typing
it.

⚠ **What message would you like to leave?**

I'll be right back! Please don't disturb the computer. Thanks.

OK

Hypercard

Fig. 11-9. Entering a message.

The default message is quite a mild one. There is plenty of scope for giving sterner messages. When the message has been confirmed the screen goes blank except for a padlock icon that bounces around (the underlying desktop is unaffected and can be restored by the rightful user). The bouncing padlock lets everyone who sees it know that the computer is still on and prevents accidental unplugging ("I thought it was turned off"). Suppose someone tries to use the computer? A message box like the one in Fig. 11-10 appears on the blank screen.

Anyone can try to enter a password, but only the correct one removes the screen blanking. Furthermore, the message makes it clear that the owner does not want the passing user to go any further. When an incorrect password is entered, Pad-Lock reacts by issuing a warning that is likely to scare off all but the most determined interloper. You can see the warning in Fig. 11-11. Clicking OK at this point blanks the screen and returns the bouncing Pad-Lock.

Finally, the legitimate user returns. Pressing any key brings up the password entry screen seen in Fig. 11-10. After entering the correct password, the screen is cleared

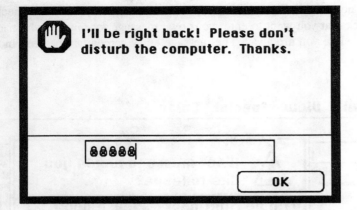

Fig. 11-10. The message box.

Fig. 11-11. The breach of security warning.

and work can continue. However, if someone has tried to use the computer, Pad-Lock gives the message shown in Fig. 11-12 before allowing the user to resume work.

This system is very effective. While entering a password every time you leave your computer might seem like a pain, the protection you get is considerable. Pad-Lock works well on machines like network file servers that need to be on all the time but allow little actual access to the system. In Fig. 11-13 you can see the bouncing Pad-Lock icon and a sterner message of warning to an interloper.

Fig. 11-12. The Welcome Back message.

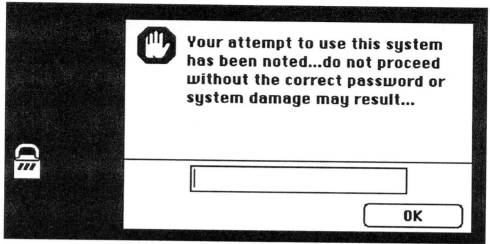

Fig. 11-13. *Tough warning.*

SuperKey. One way for DOS-based machines to temporarily control hardware access and screen display is a macro program such as Borland's SuperKey, mentioned earlier in the book as an encryption utility. This program has been around for quite some time and is one of the most reliable terminate-and-stay resident programs for PCs. You can use the program's macro and screen-blanking features to devise a system of keystrokes that offer protection from casual interlopers. For example, if you have loaded SuperKey, you would follow these steps to create a pair of macros that shuts off the screen and then turn it on again using the keystrokes Ctrl−0 and Ctrl−1:

1. Begin defining the macro by pressing Alt−= (Alt plus the equal sign). Now press Ctrl−0.
2. Press Alt−1 to bring up the SuperKey menu and type F for Functions, followed by S for Screen off.
3. Press Alt− (Alt plus the minus or hyphen key) to end the macro.
4. Now begin the second macro by pressing Alt−= followed by Ctrl−1.
5. Press Alt−1 to bring up the SuperKey menu, and type F for Functions followed by O for Screen On.
6. Press Alt− (Alt plus the minus or hyphen key) to end the macro.

Be sure to use the Macro Save command to store these macros on disk if you want to keep them. Use a file name such as SCREEN.MAC. You can now turn the screen on and off with Ctrl−0 and Ctrl−1 (if these keys are needed by other programs, you can select a different pair).

To make this operation password protected you can use the following in place of the previous step 2:

2. Press Alt−/ to bring up the SuperKey menu and type F for Functions followed by K for Keyword. Now press Alt−/ again and type F for Functions followed by S for Screen off.

Now when you press Ctrl−0, SuperKey will prompt for a keyword. After you have typed a password and verified it, the screen will blank. To return the screen, you must type the password again and then press Ctrl−1. It is unlikely that a casual interloper will be able to bypass this system to see what is actually on your screen. To protect against someone rebooting the computer to gain access, you can use one of the many boot protection systems described in Chapter 2, or invoke the SuperKey keyboard lock with a line in your AUTOEXEC.BAT, such as

```
KEY /FKpassword
```

where *password* is your password. This command will lock the keyboard until the correct sequence of letters is entered.

Key Files

In earlier chapters, you saw that a number of security measures for DOS-based personal computers are implemented in the AUTOEXEC.BAT and CONFIG.SYS files. If circumstances warrant, you might want additional precautions to protect these files from prying eyes. If the wrong person were to view or alter these files, they could defeat or short-circuit your file and system access controls.

The first step to protecting these files is to make them read-only, using the ATTRIB command, as in

```
ATTRIB +R CONFIG.SYS
ATTRIB +R AUTOEXEC.BAT
```

This prevents changes being made to the file. Obviously, you will have to reverse the read-only status to make your own changes to the file, but this is not a great chore. For added protection, you can also use a utility like Norton or QuickDOS to change these files to hidden status, thus preventing the casual observer from finding the file to alter or delete it, or even examine its contents. It is even possible to alter COMMAND .COM so that it looks for something other than CONFIG.SYS and AUTOEXEC.BAT when starting, but this is a risky procedure and probably not worth the risk that it will prevent other programs from functioning correctly.

FORMATTING, ERASING, AND RECOVERING

All operating systems must provide commands for erasing unwanted files. Many personal computer users know that the commands used to prepare new disks for data storage, known as *formatting* or *initializing*, also erase files. Careless or willful misuse of such commands poses a significant threat to the security of valuable data. On the other hand, it is often possible to recover data that has apparently been erased. This is one of those double-edged facts of computing life that make it so interesting. Failure to understand this aspect of disk storage can have serious consequences for security. If you are not careful, you could write off deleted files prematurely, or falsely assume that sensitive data have been deleted, when in fact they are recoverable. (On more than one occasion an organization has sold a used computer thinking that all its data had been cleared from the hard disk, only to find that an enterprising purchaser has reconstructed sensitive files.)

More about Disk Storage

For an operating system to store information on a disk requires that the storage space be structured. This structure is called a *format*, a magnetic grid by means of which the disk drive can assign an address to any part of the disk. As you can see from Fig. 11-14, the space on the disk is divided into concentric circular tracks, which are further divided into sectors (Fig. 11-14 shows the format of a floppy disk, but a hard disk is formatted in essentially the same way).

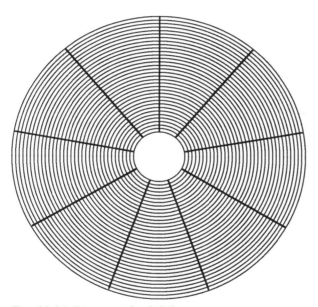

Disk Format

40 circular tracks
9 pie-shaped sectors
9 x 40 = 360 boxes
known as sectors
each storing 512 bytes
= 184320 bytes or
180 kilobytes per side
180 x 2 = 360K per disk

Fig. 11-14. Diagram of a disk format.

Different operating systems and different sizes of disk use different numbers of tracks and sectors, which is one reason why all floppy disks are not sold preformatted. Most computers format both sides of the disk since the read/write head in the floppy disk drive can scan both sides of the disk at once. On a 360K floppy disk, the arrangement on each side is 40 tracks divided into 9 pie-shaped wedges or sectors. This produces, per side, 360 cells, also known as *sectors*, each of which can store 512 bytes, or half a kilobyte. This means each side stores 180K (360 × .5). The whole disk can thus store 360K (180K × 2).

Most files are larger than the 512 bytes contained in one sector. For this reason the operating system sets a minimum allocation unit for disk storage. This is rather like the minimum unit of time used by the phone company when charging for phone calls, as in "for every 3 minutes or part thereof." Operating systems allocate disk space in groups of sectors, known as *clusters*. For example, on a 360K floppy disk DOS uses clusters made up of two sectors. Even a 50 byte file would take up two sectors, making 1024 bytes the smallest storage area on the disk. Thus a file that is 2345 bytes in size uses up three clusters because $2345 \div 1024 = 3$ (when rounded up to the nearest whole number).

Formatting

The FORMAT command is used by DOS to prepare new disks to store data while on Macintoshes formatting is called *initializing*. The format is a set of signals written on the disk by the operating system and organized into a structured storage space. Without a format, a disk cannot store files. Both hard disks and floppy disks require formatting. However, there is a subtle difference between formatting a hard disk and formatting a floppy. Formatting actually takes place at two levels. Low-level or physical formatting involves the actual laying down of the electronic marks on the disk to indicate the physical locations of the tracks and sectors, while high-level or logical formatting involves organizing the function that each sector will perform.

When you format a floppy disk, both low- and high-level formatting is carried out at once. Most hard disk formatting performed by end-users is only high-level formatting. To perform a low-level hard disk format involves either specialized disk management software or direct access to programs stored in ROM on the hard disk controller card. This is why the effects of a user accidentally formatting a hard disk can be reversed, and why something besides the FORMAT command is needed to ensure that all trace of data is wiped out when you really need to erase it.

The high-level or logical aspect of the format actually assigns tasks to specific areas of the disk. One sector is designated the first sector on the disk. This sector is known as the *boot sector* and stores basic information about the disk. As you saw in Fig. 10-11 in the previous chapter, the boot sector on a DOS disk carries the DOS version number, information about the size and capacity of the disk, and, if the operating system files are not on the disk, the "Non-system disk" message. Formatting also sets aside two sets of sectors, one for the file allocation table or FAT and another for the directory. The rest of the disk is then divided into data clusters. The FAT records the allocation of files to data clusters, while the directory records the names of files stored on the disk, plus file dates and sizes. You can see a floppy disk directory displayed in Fig. 11-15, using the Norton Utilities.

In the column headed "Cluster," you can see the number of the first cluster occupied by each file. If you use a utility program to view the FAT, you will see empty clusters represented by zeros while occupied clusters are numbered. Most files contain a special code that marks the end of the file, known as an end-of-file marker (EOF). In Fig. 11-16, you can see the FAT for the disk shown in Fig. 11-15, with one EOF marker for each file.

```
┌ Root dir ═══════════════════════════════════════════ Directory format ┐
│ Sector 15 in root directory                              Offset 0, hex 00 │
│                                                              Attributes    │
│Filename Ext      Size       Date       Time     Cluster   Arc R/O Sys Hid Dir Vol│
│                 ════════   ════════   ════════  ════════                   │
│BACKIT   EXE      62464    12/02/89    5:40 pm       2      Arc             │
│BKCOLOR  COM       7087     2/23/87    6:06 pm     124      Arc             │
│BKREPORT EXE      15360     2/23/87    6:06 pm     138      Arc             │
│BKSTART  EXE      16896     2/23/87    6:06 pm     168      Arc             │
│REPORT   BAK        192     8/09/91    3:06 pm     201      Arc             │
│                 unused directory entry                                     │
│                 unused directory entry                                     │
│                 unused directory entry                                     │
│                 unused directory entry                                     │
│                 unused directory entry                                     │
│                 unused directory entry                                     │
│                 unused directory entry                                     │
│                 unused directory entry                                     │
│                 unused directory entry                                     │
│                 unused directory entry                                     │
│                 unused directory entry                                     │
│                                                                            │
│                         Press Enter to continue                           │
│1Help   2Hex    3Text   4Dir    5FAT    6Partn  7      8      9Undo   10QuitNU│
```

Fig. 11-15. A disk directory displayed.

```
┌ FAT area ═══════════════════════════════════════════════ FAT format ┐
│ Sector 1 in 1st copy of FAT                           Cluster 2, hex 0002 │
│                                                                            │
│   3      4     5     6     7     8     9    10    11    12    13    14     │
│  15     16    17    18    19    20    21    22    23    24    25    26     │
│  27     28    29    30    31    32    33    34    35    36    37    38     │
│  39     40    41    42    43    44    45    46    47    48    49    50     │
│  51     52    53    54    55    56    57    58    59    60    61    62     │
│  63     64    65    66    67    68    69    70    71    72    73    74     │
│  75     76    77    78    79    80    81    82    83    84    85    86     │
│  87     88    89    90    91    92    93    94    95    96    97    98     │
│  99    100   101   102   103   104   105   106   107   108   109   110     │
│ 111    112   113   114   115   116   117   118   119   120   121   122     │
│ 123 <EOF>    125   126   127   128   129   130   131   132   133   134     │
│ 135    136   137 <EOF>   139   140   141   142   143   144   145   146     │
│ 147    148   149   150   151   152   153   154   155   156   157   158     │
│ 159    160   161   162   163   164   165   166   167 <EOF>   169   170     │
│ 171    172   173   174   175   176   177   178   179   180   181   182     │
│ 183    184   185   186   187   188   189   190   191   192   193   194     │
│ 195    196   197   198   199   200 <EOF> <EOF>     0     0     0     0     │
│   0      0     0     0     0     0     0     0     0     0     0     0     │
│   0      0     0     0     0     0     0     0     0     0     0     0     │
│                                                                            │
│                         Press Enter to continue                           │
│1Help   2Hex    3Text   4Dir    5FAT    6Partn  7      8      9Undo   10QuitNU│
```

Fig. 11-16. Viewing the FAT.

Between the FAT and the directory, DOS has enough information to handle storage of data on a variety of different-sized disks. When a hard disk is formatted, all entries in the FAT and directory are wiped clean, literally "zeroed out" because the entries are replaced by zeros. This leaves the files intact, but with no apparent way of knowing what their names are or where they are stored. While it is possible to recover data at this point, it is a considerable inconvenience to say the least. In the interests of security, you should try to prevent accidental/belligerent formatting of disks as well as take steps to make recovery from such actions as painless as possible.

Protection against Formatting

In any office, it makes sense to control the formatting of disks. On DOS computers, the first step is to make sure you are using a recent version of DOS. These offer greater safeguards against accidental formatting of hard disks. In versions 3.3 and later, the FORMAT command will not work without a drive letter, preventing any ambiguity over which drive will be formatted.

The classic accident that occurred with DOS 2.0 when attempting to format a floppy in drive A, was to enter FORMAT, with no drive specifier, while DOS was at the C> prompt. Without any warning, not even "insert disk in drive," the FORMAT command proceeded to wipe out drive C.

When you are using DOS 3.3 and enter FORMAT C: you get the following fairly unambiguous message:

WARNING, ALL DATA ON NON-REMOVABLE DISK
DRIVE C: WILL BE LOST!
Proceed with Format (Y/N)?

For added protection on DOS systems, the FORMAT.COM file can be removed. Removing FORMAT.COM from all but a few machines is a good idea, allowing only reliable users to perform formatting. Also, supplying employees with preformatted disks, now available in most standard sizes from computer supply stores, makes a lot of sense.

A further step is renaming FORMAT.COM to something like WIPEOUT.COM. This helps to emphasize the dual role of the program, forcing a command line entry like:

WIPEOUT A:

You can also write a batch file called FORMAT.BAT to perform a format using the renamed FORMAT.COM file.

```
@ECHO OFF
CLS
IF %1NOTHING = = NOTHING GOTO MESSAGE
BEEP
```

```
ECHO Do you really want to format the disk in drive %1 ?
ECHO Press CTRL-C to abort or
PAUSE
WIPEOUT %1
GOTO END
:MESSAGE
BEEP
ECHO You must say which drive, as in "FORMAT A:"
:END
```

To format a disk in drive A using this batch file, the user enters:

```
FORMAT A:
```

The batch file then beeps to catch the user's attention and asks the user to confirm the command, echoing back the drive letter entered by the user, as in

```
Do you really want to format the disk in drive A: ?
Press CTRL-C to abort, or
Strike a key when ready . . .
```

If the command is confirmed, then the actual FORMAT.COM program, disguised by renaming as WIPEOUT.COM, issues its own warning, Insert new diskette for drive A.

If the user has not entered a drive letter, the FORMAT.BAT routine takes the user to MESSAGE, a section of code that beeps a warning and reminds the user of the correct usage. An alternative batch file might prevent formatting of drive C by looking for C: as the parameter. The code might look like this:

```
@ECHO OFF
CLS
IF %1 = = C: GOTO MESSAGE
BEEP
ECHO Do you really want to format the disk in drive %1 ?
ECHO Press CTRL-C to abort or
PAUSE
WIPEOUT %1
GOTO END
:MESSAGE
BEEP
ECHO Illegal request, cannot format drive C:
:END
```

Beyond these batch file tactics, some programs warn of or prevent formatting of a hard disk. Several of these, including the shareware WPHD.COM, were described in previous chapters. Some anti-virus packages detect and thwart attempts to format the hard disk as this is a favorite ploy of malevolent programs.

Recovery from Formatting

What can you do if you find a hard disk has been accidentally/malevolently formatted? The first step is to stop anyone attempting to use the hard disk. Although the operating system has lost track of where and how the data on the disk is stored, the underlying data structure is still there, and some programs can recreate your files from this information. On DOS machines, both Paul Mace and Peter Norton Utilities can do this. The reason they can do this is that DOS stores subdirectories as files in their own right. The information in these subdirectory files provides vital clues as to what files were on the disk and where. By using fairly sophisticated algorithms, Norton and Mace can piece the files back together.

The success of this type of recovery operation depends to a certain extent on how "clean" the hard disk is, that is, how "unfragmented" the files are. Files get *fragmented* when they are stored in noncontiguous clusters. The first few files on a disk are stored in contiguous clusters, but then when files are erased, they leave holes in the pattern of clusters. As fresh files are added, they fill in the holes. If the added files do not fit exactly into the space left by erased files, then parts of the files are stored in separate areas of the disk. The more fragmented files get, the harder it is to recover them.

Fragmentation of files can be minimized by regular use of a disk optimizer. However, this is not the only maintenance action that you can take to maximize the chances of a successful format recovery. Both Mace and Norton offer programs that record comprehensive FAT and directory information in special disk files. If the disk is formatted, the format recovery software can identify this special file on the disk and use the details to perform a much more reliable recovery. By regularly updating these special files, you are essentially taking out insurance against an unintentional format.

On a Macintosh, you can use a program like PC Tools Deluxe to help you recover from a format. Like DOS, the Macintosh operating system uses hidden files to locate, open, and close files and applications. Normally this information is placed on a reserved area of the disk. If this area is damaged, corrupted, or wiped out by formatting, the entire disk can become unreadable, despite the files themselves being intact. PC Tools includes an INIT called CPS Delete Tracking (for Central Point Software) that maintains an up to date reflection of the hidden information on a separate part of the disk. The program copies everything required by the system into an invisible storage file. This can be used by the Mirror utility to rebuild the disk after a format or crash.

In the next section, you will read how to deal with the opposite problem—making sure that all of the data on a disk is erased. Suppose you are selling off older hard disk personal computers to make way for newer models. In the interests of confidentiality and propriety, you decide to erase all of the files off the hard disks. You use the operating system's file delete commands. Someone points out that it might be quicker to reformat the hard disks. In either case, you have not consigned the files to oblivion. If the buyer is reasonably computer-literate, he or she will be able to reconstruct much of what was on your computers, a fact that could prove anything from embarrassing to downright damaging.

 In June 1990, the once-mighty-but-by-then bankrupt merchant bank and trading house Drexel Burnham Lambert held an auction to liquidate assets. Over a hundred hard disk computers were sold. Several gigabytes of hard disk storage changed hands. In the right hands, some of the information that had been stored on those disks could prove far more valuable than the hardware itself. To the best of my knowledge, no measures were taken to ensure that the data on the auctioned hard disks were rendered unrecoverable.

ACCESS AFTER THE FACT

The files in which you store data on disks are surprisingly hardy. This fact is not always immediate apparent, particularly if you have experienced messages like "Bad command or file name" or "Error reading file." However, with the notable exception of complete mechanical failure, disk files, both floppy and hard, are more difficult to destroy than you might think. In a number of circumstances, data that you thought had been destroyed can actually be resurrected. For those of us that have accidentally erased the wrong file or formatted the wrong disk, this is good news, but for those who want to get rid of data in order to prevent others from getting hold of it, the longevity of files is an annoying, if not downright awkward, fact of life.

An Old Trick

When you issue the operating system's DELETE or ERASE command to remove a file from disk storage, you do not actually get rid of the data in the file. With the proper tools, the data can still be read from the disk. At least one computer literate screenwriter has employed this personal computer equivalent of the classic detective ploy of a seemingly blank notepad revealing the impression left by the person writing on the previous sheet. Obviously, the fact that "erased" files can be read has serious security implications. To understand how erased files can be recovered, and how permanent erasure can be effected, it is first necessary to understand how an operating system keeps track of information on a disk.

 Note that reversing an operating system's file erase command is different from the use of the trash can on a WIMP interface such as the Macintosh (in this context WIMP stands for windows, icons, mouse, and pull-down menus). Macintosh users erase files by dragging the file's icon to the trash can, which then swells, as shown in Fig. 11-17. The trash can is periodically emptied by the operating system or by the user, but at any point before it is emptied, the trash can be opened by the user and the file returned to the desktop. This type of "file erase undo" feature is built into the operating system and is distinct from low-level undeleting.

The previous section pointed out that most files take up more than one sector on a disk. Indeed, disks are organized in groups of two or more clusters. Large files are

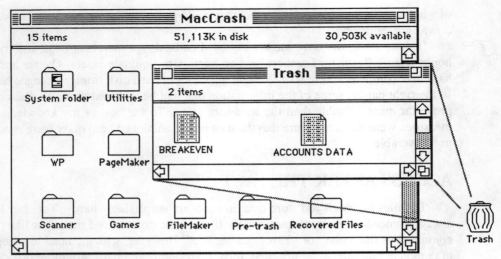

Fig. 11-17. Trash icon.

spread across many clusters. The file allocation table, or FAT, is the list maintained by the operating system showing which sectors are used by what files. When you delete a file, you want to free up space on the disk. However, the operating system does not clean out the sectors that were once occupied by a deleted file. This would make deletion a lengthy process. Instead, the FAT is altered.

When you erase a file with DOS, the first letter of the file listing in the FAT is removed, effectively removing the file from the directory listing and making it inaccessible to normal applications. You can see the effect in Fig. 11-18, where one of the files listed in Fig. 11-16 has been erased.

Immediately after a file is deleted, the data still occupies the clusters it did before the delete command was issued. In fact, the data will remain where it is until DOS overwrites the vacated space to add further files to the disk.

Applications such as Norton Utilities and Mace Utilities are able to read the FAT and give you a chance to replace the first letter of a file that was erased. These programs can then use the information in the FAT to find data that belongs to the file, scanning the clusters of the disk until as much as possible of the file has been recovered. If you delete a file accidentally and then use one of these unerase programs right away, you should be able to get all of the data back. In Fig. 11-19, you can see Norton Utilities listing erased files within a hard disk directory.

You can see that the first letter of each file name is a question mark. To unerase a file, the user selects from the file list then enters a suitable first letter. After this, the program proceeds to reconstitute the file. In many cases, this is virtually automatic and the entire file is unerased. When parts of the file have been overwritten, a partial unerase is possible and the program allows for user input in the rebuilding process. Norton offers a Quick Unerase program that can often recreate a whole group of deleted files with little or no user input.

```
┌ Root dir ══════════════════════════════════════ Directory format ┐
│ Sector 15 in root directory                        Offset 0, hex 00 │
│                                                         Attributes   │
│Filename Ext     Size      Date      Time    Cluster  Arc R/O Sys Hid Dir Vol│
│                ·                                                     │
│BACKIT   EXE    62464   12/02/89   5:40 pm      2     Arc            │
│BKCOLOR  COM     7087    2/23/87   6:06 pm    124     Arc            │
│BKREPORT EXE    15360    2/23/87   6:06 pm    138     Arc            │
│BKSTART  EXE    16896    2/23/87   6:06 pm    168     Arc            │
│σEPORT   BAK      192    8/09/91   3:06 pm    201     Arc            │
│             unused directory entry                                  │
│             unused directory entry                                  │
│              unused directory entry                                 │
│              unused directory entry                                 │
│              unused directory entry                                 │
│             unused directory entry                                  │
│              unused directory entry                                 │
│               unused directory entry                                │
│                unused directory entry                               │
│                unused directory entry                               │
│                unused directory entry                               │
│═══════════·══════════════════════════════════════════════════════│
│          Filenames beginning with 'σ' indicate erased entries       │
│                   Press Enter to continue                           │
│1Help   2Hex   3Text   4Dir   5FAT   6Partn  7      8      9Undo  10QuitNU│
```

Fig. 11-18. Showing a file erased.

```
┌───────────────────────────────────────────────────────────────────┐
│ Menu 2.2 part 1                                                     │
│                  Select erased file or sub-directory                │
│                                                                     │
│              Create file            ?ecnu02.pix                     │
│              ?ec08-10.pix           ?ecnu03.pix                     │
│              ?ec08-15.pix           ?ecnu04.pix                     │
│              ?ec08-17.pix           ?ecqd2.pix                      │
│              ?ec12t1.pix            ?ecsym.pix                      │
│              ?ec12t2.pix                                            │
│              ?ec12t3.pix                                            │
│              ?ec12t4.pix                                            │
│              ?ec12t5.pix                                            │
│              ?ec12t6.pix                                            │
│              ?ec12t7.pix                                            │
│              ?ec8-01.pix                                            │
│              ?ec8-02.pix                                            │
│              ?ecnu01.pix                                            │
│                                                                     │
│                  18 entries to choose from                          │
│                  Speed search: ▓▓▓▓▓▓▓▓▓▓▓                          │
├─────────────┬───────┬──────────────────────────┬──────────────────┤
│ Item type   │ Drive │ Directory name           │     File name     │
│ Erased file │  C:   │ \INSET\PIX               │    Create file    │
└─────────────┴───────┴──────────────────────────┴──────────────────┘
```

Fig. 11-19. Norton Utilities listing erased files.

You can perform unerasing of files on the Macintosh at two levels. Files that are dragged to the trash can are still on disk and selectable as long as the can icon appears stuffed. You only have to double click on the trash can to see the files and move them back onto the desktop. However, many applications empty the trash can when they load. As soon as the trash can is emptied, you need to get some extra help if you want to unerase a file.

One utility that helps undelete Mac files is the MacTools part of the PC Tools Deluxe for the Macintosh. You select Undelete Files from the Disk menu, as shown in Fig. 11-20.

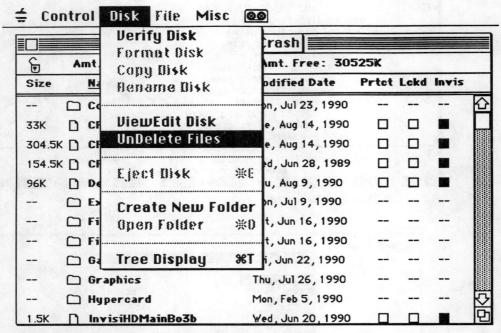

Fig. 11-20. Undeleting files on the Macintosh.

The three methods to choose from are delete tracking, tag recovery, and resource forks. The most reliable is *delete tracking*, which makes use of a hard disk logging file, similar to that employed by Mace and Norton format recovery utilities on the PC. This file is used to recover from disk crashes and accidental formatting, as well as assist in unerasing. In Fig. 11-21, you can see a list of erased files displayed by the delete tracking method.

After selecting the files to be recovered, all the user has to do is click Continue. The program places the recovered files in a special folder, creating the folder if one does not already exist. You can see the results in Fig. 11-22.

The other methods of unerasing offered by PC Tools are slower and less reliable. The resource fork method reads the disk block-by-block checking each block to see if it contains a *resource fork* (this is the half of the two-part Mac file structure which stores file type, location, and so on, the other half being the *data fork*). When a resource fork is found for a program that has been deleted, the program attempts to

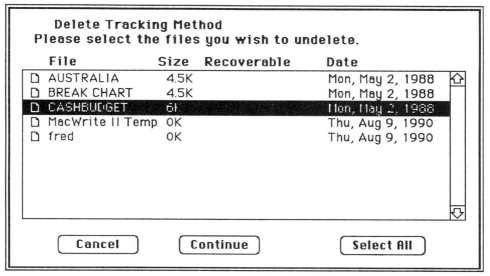

Fig. 11-21. Erased files on a Mac.

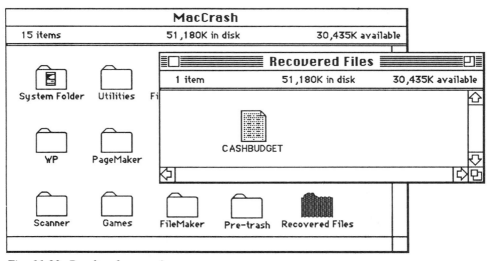

Fig. 11-22. Results of un-erasing.

rebuild the file using a "best guess" method. This works well if the file is stored in contiguous sectors, less well if the file is fragmented. The resource fork method is valuable for use on damaged disks without a delete tracking file.

The other method of recovery on the Mac, using tag bytes, works by exploiting a feature of the Mac disk operation that uses a 12 byte section of disk space as a "tag" for each 512 byte sector. The tag stores information about what is stored in the sector, and it is possible to use this information to rebuild damaged or erased files.

The Complete Delete

When you are managing sensitive data files you may want to make sure that deleted files really are removed from the disk or put them beyond the reach of file recovery programs. A good measure of how important this can be for maintaining security is the fact that there exists a U.S. Department of Defense specification for file erasing (known as DoD 5220.22-M). You can ensure complete file erasure in several ways. A number of operating system utilities provide "complete delete" capability. One important point to bear in mind is that ordinary reformatting of a disk will *not* completely erase files, because there are format recovery programs designed to reverse this process.

Wipe Out. Two programs provided in the Norton Utilities provide a "complete delete." One is called Wipedisk, the other Wipefile. Both can eliminate all trace of a file from a disk. This is accomplished by overwriting the space previously occupied by an erased file. The character used to do this is normally binary 0, but the user can select a different character. Both programs meet DoD requirements, which specify that an alternating pattern of 0s and 1s be written over the file data, three times, followed by a write of a random value. The last write is then verified.

The Wipefile program is used together with a specific file name to remove a file's entry from the FAT and the directory, *and* remove all trace of its data from this disk, overwriting it with meaningless values. DOS wildcards can be used to wipe groups of files, and there is a pause option to provide for file-by-file confirmation of the command. On the other hand, Wipedisk can be used to blank out an entire disk, accomplishing what formatting fails to do by writing meaningless data across the entire disk. The Wipedisk program has an option that can be used to clean up after the normal DELETE command, wiping only that portion of a disk that is occupied by erased files.

Macintosh users will find a disk-wiping routine in the disk Optimizer section of PC Tools for the Mac. Reflecting the tasteful possibilities of the Mac's graphic interface, the program animates a pencil erase while it works. You can see the program screen in Fig. 11-23. Note the two options for Erase.

The documentation for PC Tools reflects the dilemma of file erasing. After describing the first erase option there is this note: "Erasing is permanent. No erase files can ever be undeleted." The manual goes on to describe the Erase 3 times options, which does a more thorough job of erasing: "Although it is slower than the previous selection, it would be *nearly* impossible for anyone to reconstruct a deleted file after you have erased it three times." There is no emphasis on *nearly* in the manual.

SUMMARY

The IHI or in-house interloper is probably the toughest opponent in the battle to defend the integrity and confidentiality of your data. Techniques are available to prevent file access, either from disk or from the screen. There are ways of ensuring that

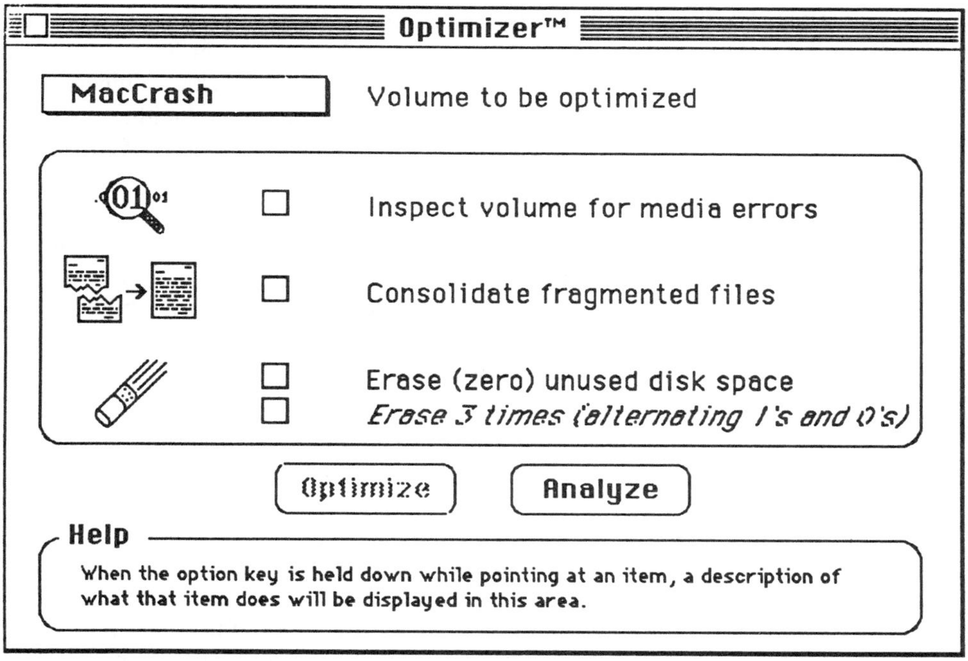

Fig. 11-23. Performing a complete erase on the Mac.

data is completely removed from storage. The persistent and computer-literate insider is not easily defeated. For more on the human aspects of security, see Chapter 13.

For individuals and organizations interested in complete security, counterfeit and bootleg programs pose few dilemmas. You simply do not use them or countenance their use. If you find copy protection schemes annoying, you have, as a software consumer, the option not to purchase packages that are thus protected.

For those who are hoping that questions of copyright and copy protection will just fade away, the message is: Do not hold your breath! You can rely on technology to keep raising issues of intellectual property rights that grow thornier almost by the day. Some individuals and software companies have turned to the courts to try and create or maintain revenue, by copyrighting or even patenting key elements of software design, elements that are as central to standard programming practice as the steering wheel is to car making. Few judges or patent office officials have a real grasp of the issues unique to computer technology. To grasp the implications of this, you only have to think about what might have happened if Henry Ford had been given a patent on a "circular device for directional control of a land vehicle."

The point is that intellectual property rights are a fairly recent phenomenon in human history. Officials are having a hard time coping with modern developments, like computer programs, and their validity in traditional areas such as words and music is increasingly probed by such technology as digital sound reproduction and sampling. From a historical perspective, copyright concepts appear full of contradictions and shortcomings. Mozart enjoyed no effective copy protection on the tunes he wrote, while Lennon and McCartney did; whatever your tastes in music, it is hard to argue that copyright either fosters or proscribes true genius (neither does it preclude adulteration: Advertising campaigns have cheapened the sounds of Mozart and Lennon and McCartney alike).

Some people in the computer industry, myself included, are calling for a fresh approach to intellectual property, one that encourages and rewards creativity and removes the incentive to stake out and defend ideas as though they were unique tangible assets, incapable of being improved upon. After all, there might have been a "first" steering wheel on a land vehicle, but the idea, borrowed from boats, was so obvious that it is likely a lot of people thought of it independently at about the same time.

Scrolling lists within a window on a computer screen might well be considered an equally obvious idea, but if someone is given a patent on it, using common sense when creating programs could quickly become an expensive proposition (Apple Computer's HyperCard program faced a legal challenge from the owner of a U.S. patent that pertained to the scrolling of data within windows, while computer maker Tandy claims a patent on the "clamshell" design of laptop computers in which the screen folds over the keyboard for transportation). While proof of independent parallel development can be a valid defense against copyright infringement, it is no defense against patent infringement.

An organization is now devoted to the cause of intellectual freedom in programming. This organization, the League for Programming Freedom, is based in Cambridge, Massachusetts. Continued use of legal restraints on creative programming could lead to a resurgence of the "pirating as liberating" attitude, and a renewal of the original hacker ethic. For more on hackers and other human aspects of computer security, see Chapter 13.

12

Network and Communication Security

THIS CHAPTER EXAMINES the security aspects of intercomputer communications. This subject includes local area network security, where personal computers are communicating with each other over a system of cables. It also includes the security of micro-to-mainframe links, where personal computers are exchanging data with larger systems, and the security of modem connections where a personal computer is communicating over telephone lines. Establishing a connection between two or more computers has two basic implications for security:

- You have more to lose.
- You have more ways to lose it.

THE COMBATANTS

The suggestion that connecting computers increases the potential for loss might seem overly pessimistic but it is not. The positive side of intercomputer communications is that there is much to be gained from the electronic sharing of information and conveying of data. However, these gains bring with them increased risks in keeping with the natural principle of more to gain means more to lose. The connection between two computers opens up a new front for the attacker who can use it either to get at the data being transferred or to penetrate one or more of the connected systems, as shown in Fig. 12-1.

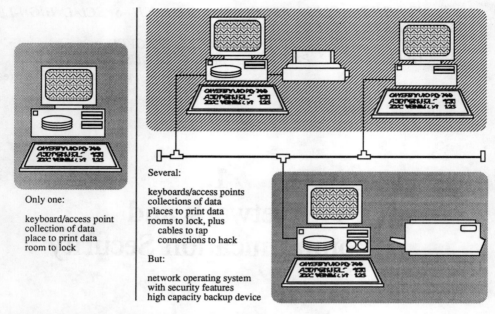

Only one:

keyboard/access point
collection of data
place to print data
room to lock

Several:

keyboards/access points
collections of data
places to print data
rooms to lock, plus
    cables to tap
    connections to hack

But:

network operating system
with security features
high capacity backup device

Fig. 12-1. Attack and risk of connected vs. stand-alone systems.

The Attackers

The increase in potential gains from a single successful penetration of security makes the connected computer a far more promising target for the attacker. The promise is further accentuated by the assumption that intercomputer connections reflect the value of data being handled by the systems: It is usually assumed that organizations only go to the trouble of networking computers if the information they are handling is of value to the organization.

While some individual users employ intercomputer communications, it is an area of security that is more typically associated with organizations. This is one reason that the cast of characters in this chapter is slightly different. Connecting computers requires a coordinated effort by several parties within one or more organizations. The enhanced target that such connections create might attract a more sophisticated attacker. You still have to worry about IHIs (in-house interlopers), as well as DISEMs (disgruntled employees, for whom intercomputer connections might represent a target for acts of belligerence). What you may also need to consider are hackers, who live and breath intercomputer communications.

 Few definitions in the lexicon of computer-speak are as hotly contested as that of *hacker*. As in other areas of language, arguments over the correct definition of the term reflect a deeper debate, in this case over proper role of information technology in society. Chapter 13 reviews the arguments over what constitutes hacking, while Fig. 12-2 summarizes the type of activity it encompasses.

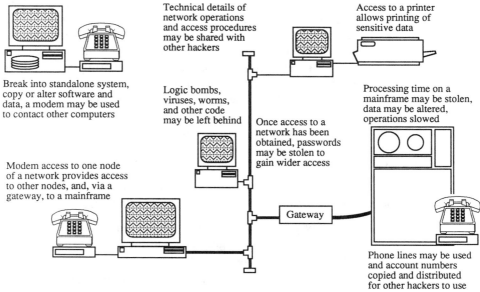

Fig. 12-2. The manifestations of hacking.

Technical details of network operations and access procedures may be shared with other hackers

Access to a printer allows printing of sensitive data

Break into standalone system, copy or alter software and data, a modem may be used to contact other computers

Logic bombs, viruses, worms, and other code may be left behind

Once access to a network has been obtained, passwords may be stolen to gain wider access

Processing time on a mainframe may be stolen, data may be altered, operations slowed

Modem access to one node of a network provides access to other nodes, and, via a gateway, to a mainframe

Gateway

Phone lines may be used and account numbers copied and distributed for other hackers to use

The Defenders

While substantial benefits can be gained from connecting computers so that they can share information electronically, computers working together, like citizens living together, must conform to certain rules of behavior and observe collectively agreed protocols. New levels of responsibility are demanded of users seeking the benefits of networking. Invariably, the need arises for some responsibilities to be centralized, for some decisions to be delegated. Hence, this chapter introduces a new character, known as the network administrator, the system operator, or the system administrator.

Whatever the name, the job is pretty much the same: Organize, coordinate, protect, and police the connections between computers. This character might also be the micro manager, the person responsible for managing an organization's personal computer resources. Large organizations might have numerous networks, each with its own administrator responsible to a central manager of information technology. Whatever the scale of the network, or structure used to manage it, the important point is that setting up and running a networking involves serious security issues, and these are more likely to be handled effectively if responsibility for them is assigned to a single person.

THE FIELD OF COMBAT

In this chapter, the term network will be used to refer generally to any group of connected computer systems, regardless of size. The term *local area network* (LAN)

is used for two or more personal computers in the same area connected in order to share resources, either hardware or software. The definition of *same area* is what distinguishes a local area network from a *wide area network* (WAN). Typically, same area means same office, same department, or same building. In other words, any area in which computers can be directly connected without resorting to long distance telephone lines, satellite links, or microwave transmissions. However, as communications technology grows more sophisticated, the distinction between WANs and LANs is getting increasingly blurred. For example, users on a LAN might connect to remote computers through a network modem, and so on.

Security Implications

The act of establishing connections between computers, either locally or over considerable distances, has several important security implications:

- Normal security problems associated with an unconnected computer system are multiplied by a factor, roughly equal to the number of computer systems connected together. This can be referred to as the *multiple factor*.

- Opening up channels of communications between computer systems, providing access into a computer through one port or another, creates a new security area which can be called the *channel factor*.

- Taken together the multiple factor and the channel factor create a unique set of security problems, known as *network security* or possibly *manifold security*.

An Expanding Theatre of Operations

Networks of connections between large computer systems have been around for many years, and an established body of knowledge referred to as network security deals with the question of how to provide the integrity of information on these large-scale networks. Unfortunately, not all of this knowledge is directly applicable to personal computers because of major differences in design and application. By now, it should be clear that most personal computer operating systems are lacking in security features. Personal computer hardware has little in the way of built-in access control. Personal computers are rarely located in secure or controlled environments. Consequently, the term "manifold security" might better suit the situation confronting those responsible for looking after personal computers that are required to communicate. After all, with so little in the way of security measures built into the raw material of a personal computer system, opening up new channels of access is, at face value, a very risky proposition.

One factor that is certain is that this area of security is not one that you will be able to ignore for long. Estimates vary, but you can probably count on a 40 percent annual growth rate for personal computer networking. In the summer of 1990 Microsoft U.K. set up a new network division to "cash in on an expected 40 percent annual growth rate in the U.K. networked PC marketplace." More and more organizations are looking to connect their personal computers to each other and/or to larger computers.

The Multiple Factor

The security of computers that are connected must start with individual computer security. You cannot combine a number of insecure computers into a network and create a secure system from the top down. While any decent network operating system does contain extensive security measures, examples of which are given later in this chapter, these are defeated or weakened if the individual systems are not secure. This means that intercomputer security begins with everything in the book so far. According to the layered approach that this book advocates, each computer connected to another must be:

- Protected by site, system, and file access control.
- Supported by suitable power and data backup facilities.
- Watched over by a vigilant operator/administrator.

The multiple factor implies that protecting two computers is at least twice as difficult at protecting one. You might liken this to the difference between babysitting one child and babysitting two. There are pluses and minuses to this arrangement. The two children might entertain each other, and so require less input from the babysitter, but they might also argue and create a level of disturbance that a single child could not achieve. Besides, however well behaved the children are, the babysitter has to feed two mouths and wipe two noses.

Connected computers have positive security aspects. If all of the important files used by five users are stored on one machine, then a fast, automated file backup system is more cost effective, and likely to be carried out more frequently and reliably than if it was left to each of the five users with less sophisticated backup facilities. A backup power supply is also more likely to be used on a machine that is serving several users. From a software perspective, the network operating system can add security features not found in ordinary operating system.

The negative aspects of networking include the fact that a security attack on one networked computer has the potential to open up many computers' worth of data. This makes the networked computer a much more attractive target, and consequently puts it at greater risk than a stand-alone computer. The damage and disruption that a virus can cause is far greater when a networked computer is attacked. The potential fall-out from the errors, omissions, and malicious actions of individual users is magnified when they are network users. A higher degree of user supervision is thus required. However, this is not always forthcoming: Users accustomed to the freedom and independence of stand-alone computing may find it irksome to submit to the rules for network users.

The Channel Factor

In previous chapters, you have seen how the layered approach to security is built up. So far, the concern has been the protection of personal computers as separate entities, vulnerable to abuses by users putting information in, or taking it out, via disk, screen, and keyboard. The layered approach to stand-alone security can be summarized like this:

Access Control
  Site   Controlling who can get near the system.
  System   Controlling who can use the system.
  File   Controlling who can use specific files.

System Support
  Power   Keeping supply of power clean and constant.
  Backup   Keeping copies of files current.
  Vigilance   Keeping tabs on what enters the system.

This arrangement needs to be expanded whenever a computer system is connected to another system. Intercomputer connections involve opening channels of communication between machines. The third level is thus *channel protection*, which can be divided into three areas:

Channel Protection
  Channel control
  Channel verification
  Channel support

Individual users who are not in the practice of connecting their personal computers with other computers might find it difficult to relate to the problems of channel protection. However, to paraphrase a tired jingle: "Sooner or later, you'll be connected!"

The cost of LAN hardware is slowly falling while the simplicity and functionality of LAN software is rising. More and more organizations see LANs as a major part of their overall information technology strategy. Micro-to-mainframe links are expanding as micros become better able to work effectively with large amounts of downloaded data. The use of on-line databases, bulletin boards, and electronic mail facilities is steadily rising. Channel protection will become increasingly important in all three areas: LANs, micro-to-mainframe connections, and on-line services.

Channel Control. To look on the dark side, a connection between two computers is one more way for an attacker to steal, delete, and corrupt information, or otherwise undermine normal operations. To prevent a channel of communication from becoming an avenue of attack, you need to control who can:

- Open a channel.
- Use a channel.
- Close a channel.

Clearly the first step is to ensure that proper site and system access controls are in place. The next step is to decide who needs to use a particular channel and then restrict access to authorized users. In network terms, this might be a matter of using password-controlled logging-on procedures.

Password protection can be used for mainframe connections as well. Most commercial on-line services require an account number and password for access, and these should be closely guarded. However, it is possible for damaging telephone connections to other computers to be made via a modem without a password. For this reason, system access control should be particularly tight on personal computers equipped with modems.

Channel Verification. To be on the safe side, you should think of a channel of communication as a path through enemy territory. Whatever passes along that runs the risk of being ambushed. Secure communications involves ongoing verification of:

- The identity of users.
- The integrity of data.
- The integrity of the channel.

Users of a communication channel should be required to identify themselves, whether the connection is a network hookup, a modem, or a mainframe link. When you are on the receiving end of intercomputer communications, that is, acting as the host for users calling in, you need to be able to verify the claimed identity.

One of the most important requirements for secure communications between computers is verification of identity. On a local area network, this might mean that each user has an ID number and a password, both of which must be entered before login can be completed. Of course, entry of a valid ID number/password combination does not guarantee the identity of the person using them, but a simple deterrent to impostors is the physical presence of the network administrator who can actually see who is working at each station. The network software will tell the administrator who claims to be using the system, and a tour of the LAN can provide visual verification of these claims. In large installations, where the administrator might not be expected to put a name to every face, assistance might be provided in the form of photo-ID tags. Alternatively, the network administrator might have a file of employees' photos matched to ID numbers.

When data is being transferred via a communications channel, it is subject to possible distortion, tampering, or theft. Verifying the integrity of the channel means making sure that this does not happen. Most communications software includes some form of error checking. At a rudimentary level, this can check that the amount of data received matches the amount transmitted. More sophisticated methods confirm details of the transmission.

Verifying the integrity of the channel also means making sure nobody is listening in, or preventing the theft of anything useful if someone is. This is best accomplished by encryption. You will need to assess the likelihood of anyone attempting to intercept or overhear your communications. If the risk is high enough, then you can encrypt important communications, using a variety of devices. Some software systems encrypt all network and telephone line traffic. Hardware encryption/decryption devices can be placed at each end of a communications link. Some of these are combined with data verification systems.

Channel Support. Intercomputer communications can only be established when a large number of different parameters are properly coordinated. Once established, communications need to be maintained. This requires a high degree of reliability in communications hardware and software. The need for reliability and protection centers on those components that serve more than one user, and is in proportion to the number of users served. For example, in a local area network where one personal computer is acting as a file server for others, disruption or failure of the server can have far greater consequences than the breakdown of a personal computer working on its own. Once established, channels of communication must be supported, or else those tasks that depend upon them will be jeopardized.

Taken for Granted

Although a lot of work is involved in establishing intercomputer connections and they might require significant changes to the pattern of work in the organization, you will find that the organization is quick to take new channels of communication for granted. On the whole, this is a positive tendency, contributing to efficient use of the technology. However, awareness of the security implications of the new connections must be maintained.

The fact that a group of personal computers arranged in a LAN can perform far more sophisticated tasks than a group of unconnected machines has meant that LANs are now performing *mission critical* work, data processing assignments that are essential to the organization's continued existence. The level of security awareness must match the value of the work being carried out by the network. Indeed, LAN performance is increasingly measured by standards once reserved for mainframe and minicomputers. There is talk of *uptime requirements*, the amount of time the system is required to function continuously without interruption. The idea of *fault tolerance* enters the picture, meaning the ability of the system to keep functioning despite component failure or other faults.

NETWORK BACKGROUND AND TERMINOLOGY

Used generically, *network* refers to any group of connected computer systems. The term *LAN* is used to describe two or more personal computers in the same area connected in order to share resources. The resources that are shared can be hardware or software. Shared hardware typically includes mass storage devices such as hard disks and output devices, such as printers and plotters. Shared software consists of data files and/or programs.

Topologies

Several possible arrangements of machines in a LAN are referred to as *topologies*. One is essentially a circle, usually referred to as a *ring* topology. Another arrangement is a *star* topology configuration. This is diagrammed in Fig. 12-3, along with the *trunk* or *bus* topology.

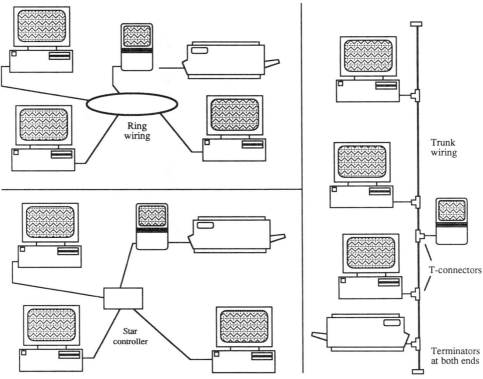

Fig. 12-3. Ring, star, and trunk topologies.

The physical size of a local area can be extended significantly through the use of bridges and gateways. A *bridge* is a combination of hardware and software that enables you to connect one LAN to another and communicate across the connection as though it was a complete entity. The LANs being connected can be of the same kind, or they can be two different types of LAN. You can see a bridge diagrammed on the left of Fig. 12-4.

A *gateway* provides a network with a high-speed communication to a large computer. By means of the gateway, which is usually a combination of hardware and software, users on the network can access data and software on the large computer, just as though they were directly linked to it as a terminal. You can see a gateway in the arrangement shown on the right of Fig. 12-4.

Local area networks with bridges and gateways are at the upper end of the scale. In its simplest form, a LAN is just a piece of cable and a set of commands, a combination of hardware and software. The cable wires the computers together. The commands control the communications between the computers. Commands that control communications are often referred to as *protocols*. Thus software commands that are supposed to work across a network must conform to the appropriate network protocols. After looking at some of the history behind personal computer networking, the distinctions between network hardware and software will be examined.

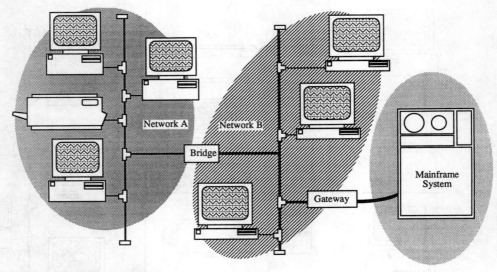

Fig. 12-4. A bridge and a gateway.

Network History

To understand the merits of LANs relative to other approaches to computing, you need to look at the history of the small computer. If you define a computer as a data processing device that has facilities for data input, storage, and output, as shown in Fig. 12-5, then the first "personal" computers were those developed in the mid-1970s by such companies as MITS, which marketed the Altair, and later Apple, which put out the Apple 1 in 1976.

These computers were personal in that the four essential elements (input, storage, processing, and output) were self-contained in one unit, capable of being grouped together on one person's desktop. This was quite a break from previous systems that were centrally located and provided storage and processing to a number of different users. You can see this distinction diagrammed in Fig. 12-5.

The large central computers were referred to as *mainframes* because they consisted of numerous components assembled in a large framework, one that might occupy a whole room specially designed to accommodate it. The mainframe computer, with its centralized storage and multiple users who shared its processing power, was a natural evolution from the early days of computing. The first computers only came into being through the combined efforts of teams of scientists and engineers. In order to make these machines economically feasible, their power was shared. Computing time was parceled out around the clock. Because not everyone who needed computer power could afford the great expense of building one, connections were made from the central computer to remote terminals to allow access.

While the advent of computer power was welcomed by many companies and gov-

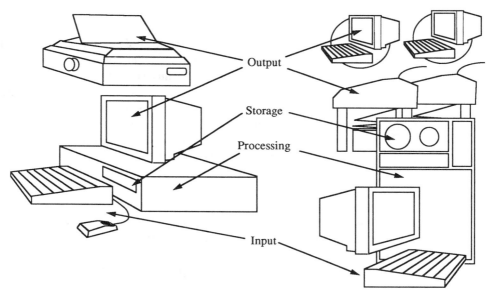

Fig. 12-5. Elements of a computer system.

ernment institutions, the original centralized, multiple user systems had several disadvantages. They imposed a need for coordination between the different users. Sometimes this meant scheduling of work for certain times of the day. Often it meant uniform procedures were centrally imposed. Making changes to improve programs required consensus, followed by lengthy programming efforts to achieve changes that were often outdated before they could be implemented. Individuals eager to apply computer power to their specific tasks found this restrictive.

The Personal Computer Arrives

When the personal computer appeared, it promised to free computer users from central authority and restrictions. Individuals could set their own work timetable and no longer had to wait for a free terminal. Users who were willing to learn how to run the personal computer could organize their data in a way that made sense to them, and make immediate changes to system design and procedures rather than submit changes to lengthy approval and implementation processes. However, the early models of personal computer were limited in their storage capacity and this seriously hampered their ability to cope with tasks such as database management. In the early 1980s, the advent of hard disks that worked with small computers offered increased storage and opened up new applications. However, at that time, these disks were perceived as expensive. For example, in 1983, you had to pay about one-and-a-half times as much for a hard disk drive as you did for the computer itself. At this price point, the idea of sharing a disk between computers made sense.

The Network Idea

In addition to the savings that it offered, the idea of sharing a hard disk appealed to some systems managers because this is the way earlier computers had worked, sharing large storage devices between many users. Thus early attempts to connect personal computers into a network had both economic and philosophical justification. Although there was clearly going to be a cost involved in connecting computers, it was thought that this would be offset by the sharing of hard drive costs. One of the first personal computer networks was Omninet from Corvus, introduced in 1981, and designed primarily to provide multiple user access to a central hard disk drive. Along with the central hard drive, you could have central tape backup facilities, thus providing protection against data loss for all users.

The cost of networking could be further offset by the savings from additional printers. In the early 1980s, a good letter-quality printer could cost more than a computer system. Because nobody prints all the time, people sought ways to make greater use of printers shared between workers. Several personal computers with floppy disks networked together, and sharing a common printer and a hard disk were seen as an economic alternative to everybody having their own hard disk and printer.

There were other reasons for wanting to network users together. Almost as soon as individuals found uses for the personal computer, they had need to share the data between several people. Consider a simple database of clients. The person who designed the database might want someone else to type in the existing client list. Typically this meant giving up the computer so that the typist could enter the information. The alternative was to have the data entry done on another computer and transferred back to the original by means of copying to and from floppy disks. Thus was born the infamous "sneaker net" that saw people swapping disks from machine to machine. When the clients have been entered into the database, several people might want to sort the list and print out their own copies: More sneaker net as copies of the database proliferated to different computers. The benefits of wiring everybody together quickly became apparent.

A further reason for wiring personal computers together was the need to transfer data between dissimilar machines. Early personal computers for business came from several different companies, each with their own system of managing files. The way data is arranged on a disk is called the *disk format*, and the way data is arranged in a file on the disk is called the *file format*. Even today, competing companies use different disk and file formats. Early users of personal computers saw the potential of a network of computers to overcome the problem of data stored onto disk by one company's computer not being readable by another company's system. There were also hopes that networks would facilitate access to data stored on large computers. If users of small computers could share a single link to a large computer, it would increase the cost effectiveness of such a link.

More Reasons to Connect

The circumstances that gave rise to the desire to network personal computers have changed somewhat since the early 1980s. The price of letter-quality printers and hard disks has declined significantly. This means that it is more feasible for everyone to have a hard disk, and some form of printer. However, the economics of sharing devices have not gone away. Some printers, such as laser printers that support Post-Script, remain relatively expensive and there is a strong economic argument for sharing these and other new peripheral devices, such as typesetters, CD-ROM drives, and scanners. Although the relative cost of some equipment has changed, today's networks are still based on the idea of sharing. They allow users of connected computers to share the elements of storage space, data, and peripherals.

In many ways the need to share is greater now than it was when personal computers first entered the office. The extreme diversity of systems in the early years of personal computers has given way to increasing standardization. However, today's offices have to contend with the two standards derived from the IBM PC and the Apple Macintosh. The existence of multiple standards means that there is an ongoing need for techniques and tools that facilitate the exchange of data between the two worlds. Several aspects of data sharing have recently increased in importance. One of these is electronic mail, a means of distributing messages and documents to different users on a network. With more and more workers getting computers on their desks, electronic mail becomes increasingly practical as a means of communication and sharing specific data with specific individuals.

Another way in which the sharing of data is becoming more important arises from the snowball effect of computerization: The more people who have computers, the more data there is on computers that needs to be shared. More and more users want to connect to mainframes, the large centralized systems that many companies and government institutions still use to accumulate data. There is also a need to connect networks with other networks. The implication is that incidence of network-related security problems will increase in the years ahead.

Network Organization

When the first networks were designed, the traditional paradigm of the central computer was still very influential. Early systems envisioned one particularly powerful personal computer supporting a number of less powerful machines. The powerful computer would have the expensive hard disk and would be the centralized storage for the network, dubbed the *file server*, as seen in Fig. 12-6.

In early networks, this file server could not be used for anything but serving and was called a *dedicated network server* or *dedicated file server*. Omninet and Novell's first NetWare followed this pattern. Later networks such as Apple's AppleShare,

IBM's PC Network, and Sun Microsystem's TOPS, can also be configured with file servers, but they can also be arranged in ways that dilute the relative important of the file server.

A personal computer that is attached to a network to use the storage and computing power of a server is called a *client*. As you can see from Fig. 12-6, a typical client computer might consist of a keyboard, monitor, and system unit with single floppy disk drive and network interface. A client computer is often referred to as a *workstation*. A workstation might have limited storage of its own but will usually have at least a floppy disk from which it can read files. The workstation's floppy disk is also used when the system is turned on. A disk with the programs connecting the client to the network, the *sign-on* procedure, is placed in the drive. This is sometimes referred to as a *boot disk* (as in pulling the system up by its own bootstraps, not kicking it). For some networks, you can buy client computers without disk drives. These are referred to as *diskless workstations*, and they have their sign-on procedures stored in ROM or nonvolatile RAM. A diskless client computer or workstation thus has no data storage facilities of its own.

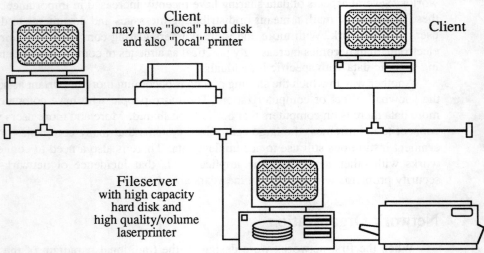

Fig. 12-6. A file server and client.

You might wonder what distinguishes a client computer or workstation from a computer *terminal*. The usual distinction involves the processing power of the client. Although a diskless client does not have storage facilities, it does have computing power, which a terminal does not. When performing a task, the client can use both programs and data that are stored on a file server, but the processing of data is done on the client, by the client's CPU, the *central processing unit*. You can see this distinction in Fig. 12-7.

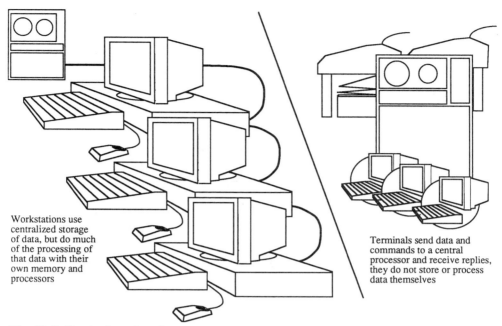

Workstations use
centralized storage
of data, but do much
of the processing of
that data with their
own memory and
processors

Terminals send data and
commands to a central
processor and receive replies,
they do not store or process
data themselves

Fig. 12-7. Terminals and workstations.

Communication between users and computers usually follow one of three models. The early model is the dumb terminal connected to a powerful central computer. The client/server network model has intelligent terminals, machines that have their own computer power, borrowing storage and other resources from the server, a computer that is usually more powerful that the clients it serves. The third model is peer-to-peer communications, in which each computer has client and server capability. This is sometimes referred to as a *distributed network architecture*. These three arrangements are diagrammed in Fig 12-8.

Two more terms that are useful in describing network operations are *local* and *remote*. From the perspective of a workstation on the network, resources such as hard drives and printers that are attached to the file server or other workstations are described as *remote*. Resources that form part of the workstation are *local* in terms of that workstation. This is diagrammed in Fig. 12-9.

CURRENT NETWORK OFFERINGS

Writing about the current state of affairs in LAN technology is a bit like trying to sketch a wave. Every week, new products announced alter the overall picture. Some standards have emerged in the last few years and, although these will doubtless continue to evolve and change, the basic descriptions given here should hold true for some time.

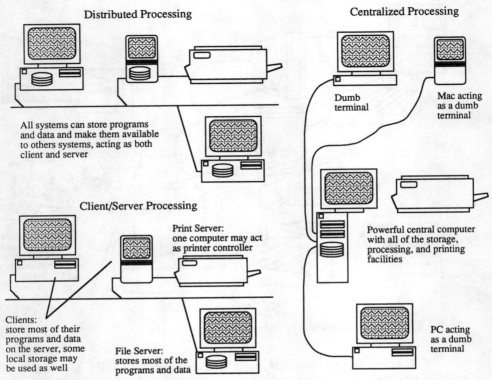

Distributed Processing

All systems can store programs
and data and make them available
to others systems, acting as both
client and server

Centralized Processing

Dumb
terminal

Mac acting
as a dumb
terminal

Powerful central computer
with all of the storage,
processing, and printing
facilities

PC acting
as a dumb
terminal

Client/Server Processing

Print Server:
one computer may act
as printer controller

Clients:
store most of their
programs and data
on the server, some
local storage may
be used as well

File Server:
stores most of the
programs and data

Fig. 12-8. The central, client/server, and distributed architectures.

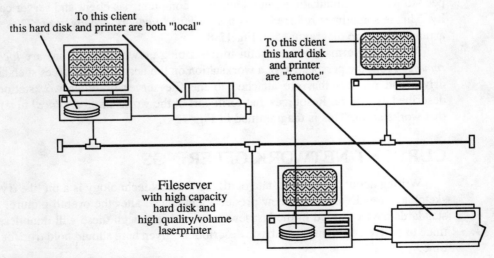

To this client
this hard disk and printer are both "local"

To this client
this hard disk
and printer
are "remote"

Fileserver
with high capacity
hard disk and
high quality/volume
laserprinter

Fig. 12-9. Local and remote resources.

Network Protocols

The commands that control communications between networked personal computers is referred to as *protocols*. Various companies have developed protocols. These tend to have names that sound like specific products when in fact they refer to a general technology rather than a single piece of hardware or software. Some of the major players in networking are reviewed here. The following are systems used to enable communication between computers, they are not software programs that manage such communication.

ARCnet. Datapoint's ARCnet was originally developed in the 1970s as a network for minicomputers, computers that are between mainframes and personal computers in terms of power and number of users supported. Many vendor companies have licensed the ARCnet technology, and many brand names of ARCnet are now available for personal computers.

Ethernet. One of the most popular network systems is Ethernet which originated in a joint project of Digital Equipment Corporation (DEC), Intel Corporation, and Xerox Corporation. Most major computer companies offer Ethernet-based networks (although IBM has long been a hold-out in this field). Ethernet was not originally developed as a personal computer network, but in 1983 the 3COM company introduced its EtherSeries network for personal computers. In simplest form, Ethernet is a standard method of connecting computers. Network software such as Novell and TOPS will run on networks that follow the Ethernet standard. To connect PCs or Macintoshes to Ethernet cabling requires an Ethernet adapter or interface card and Ethernet driver software. In the case of TOPS running on Ethernet, the driver is referred to as EtherTalk because it is an adaptation of the AppleTalk protocols to the Ethernet cabling system. Unix-based computers often come with a built-in Ethernet interface but require EtherTalk drivers to run on a TOPS network.

IBM Networks. The IBM technology referred to as *Systems Network Architecture* (SNA) is not a network for personal computers, but rather a system for connecting to larger computers, as well as an overall strategy for distributing data. In 1983, IBM announced a wiring system for networks called the *token-ring* standard. However, the IBM PC network that was released in 1984 used technology from a company called Sytek and did not follow token ring standards. IBM did agree with Microsoft to incorporate network support in version 3.1 of the IBM PC operating system (called PC-DOS if you buy the IBM brand, MS-DOS if you buy the generic offering from Microsoft). All subsequent versions of DOS have maintained this network support. IBM's first actual token ring network products were released in 1985, and networks based on this standard are now quite widespread. Both the IBM PC network and the token ring support a set of protocols called *NETBIOS* and so you will see some network products advertised as NETBIOS compatible.

Apple's Network. The Macintosh computer from Apple comes with a hardware interface to LocalTalk, a low-cost cabling system. Apple uses LocalTalk to connect LaserWriters to Macintoshes and the software that drives communications over *LocalTalk* cabling is built into the Macintosh system software. The LocalTalk driver is referred to as *AppleTalk*, more formally, the *AppleTalk Network System* (ANS). AppleTalk's seven-layer architecture is similar to the Open Systems Interconnect (OSI) model established by the International Standards Organization (ISO). AppleTalk supports peer-to-peer communications between networked devices. However, the network software that Apple sells, called *AppleShare*, adopts the dedicated network file server model in which on Macintosh is used to run the network, a network that can include PCs as well as Macintoshes. To put these terms in perspective: AppleShare is a network product that uses LocalTalk cabling and AppleTalk protocols.

By building network support into the Macintosh, Apple gave a big boost to the whole idea of networking in the office, preparing for the day when all manner of computer resources would be tied together for greater productivity. Indeed, although the LocalTalk connection is built into Macintoshes, the AppleTalk protocol can run on other media. Technically defined, LocalTalk is shielded twisted pair wiring. AppleTalk will also run on unshielded twisted pair, such as Farallon Computing's PhoneNet, on Fiber-Optic LAN from DuPont Connector Systems, and on EtherNet coaxial cabling.

Network Operating Software

Once you have cabled your computers together, you need a software program to manage the communication between machines. This is referred to as *network operating software*, typical examples being NetWare from Novell and TOPS from Sun Microsystems. The latter will be reviewed here as an example of this type of software. TOPS began life as The Web, a low-cost network for the early CP/M personal computers, put together by Nat Goldhaber who saw a need to connect the new machines. Goldhaber rejected the classic central computer paradigm and decided that a network of personal computers would work best if it was decentralized. The guiding principle of TOPS is that it transcends boundaries between operating systems, providing what is referred to as interoperability. Computers that are themselves controlled by different operating systems can deal with each other as though they had the same operating system. This allows TOPS to present itself in familiar terms to users of different systems, improving the learning curve for new users and reducing the need for technical autocrats who control the network.

When TOPS is loaded in a computer, it catches all the commands that are addressed to the operating system, either DOS on the PC or OS on the Macintosh. TOPS examines the command and passes it on, to local equipment, or to remote systems, as shown in Fig. 12-10.

Suppose you are using a PC running TOPS, and you issue a command to open a file that is on a remote Macintosh. TOPS takes the DOS command to open a file and translates it to a Macintosh operating system command that means the same thing. As a user, you see nothing of this activity except the result. To accomplish its goals of power and ease of use, TOPS employs the decentralized concept of distributed servers. TOPS allows each user to be both server and client, as is described in the next section. This provides flexibility and direct end-user control, promoting sharing of

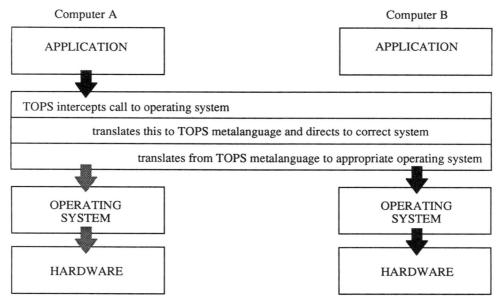

Fig. 12-10. How TOPS works.

responsibility for the network, rather than concentrating it in the hands of an administrator.

TOPS runs on Macintoshes by using the LocalTalk ports cabled together with unshielded twisted pair telephone wire, with simple telephone jacks for connections. Instead of driving the LocalTalk ports with AppleTalk, TOPS uses its own LocalTalk driver, called *FlashTalk*, together with TOPS network software.

TOPS developed the special LocalTalk driver called FlashTalk to operate at 770 Kbps (that is 770,000 bits per second), twice that of Apple's LocalTalk. This higher speed was first implemented on the FlashCard, an interface card for the IBM PC that allows PCs to run TOPS network software and print to LocalTalk printers such as the Apple LaserWriter. Later came the TOPS FlashBox, a connector for the Macintosh that enabled FlashTalk's higher speeds for Macintoshes on a TOPS network. TOPS also has drivers for Ethernet networks so that TOPS users can take advantage of the higher speed of the Ethernet system and still have the ease of use of the TOPS network software.

To recap, local area networks consist of hardware connecting two or more personal computer systems, plus network operating software to control communication between the systems. Users of a local area network can share storage and output facilities. They can also exchange data between systems on the network, even if the systems are otherwise incompatible. After looking at the security implications of network hardware, several examples of security arrangements within network operating software are examined.

THE NETWORK HARDWARE SECURITY ANGLE

Installing a LAN involves combining a number of computers with additional hardware and software. Some network hardware opens new fronts for security attacks, while other hardware can actually provide increased security. At the most basic level, hardware purchased to create a network adds a further area of potential loss from theft. However, the right combination of network hardware can make data on a network harder to steal or corrupt than if it were stored on a stand-alone system. The main hardware components of a LAN can be grouped as follows:

- *Cables* carry signals between the computer's network interface and the rest of the LAN.

- *Interfaces* and *connectors* interface between the network cabling and the main circuitry of the computer or connect cables to interfaces and cables to cables.

- *Expanders* or *peripherals* supply shared facilities like printing, facsimile transmission, and connections between networks or to remote computers (personal or mainframe).

- *Security components* provide backup, redundancy, and access control.

Cables

The cables used to form a LAN range from simple telephone wire, to coaxial cable like that used with televisions, or optical fibers. The installation of LAN cables can be a very expensive and disruptive undertaking. Some office buildings are now constructed with cables already installed to avoid the time and expense of retrofitting. The value of the cable itself is usually not so great as to make a tempting target for thieves, but the installed cable does represent a significant asset, which needs proper protection. Cables should be installed professionally, in such a way as to minimize the risk of accidental cutting, abrasion, or other damage. If data is the lifeblood of the organization, then network cables are its arteries. The most common threats to cabling can be summarized as:

- *Interference*. The data traveling along the cable is altered by electrical fields. These might be generated by power cables for heavy machinery, or by radio and microwave equipment. Metal cables are normally shielded to prevent such interference (fiberoptic cables do not suffer from this problem).

- *Cable cutting*. The connection made by the cable is broken, preventing the flow of data along the cable. This can happen when equipment is moved or the structure housing the data is altered.

- *Cable damage*. Normal wear and tear can weaken the shielding that preserves the integrity of transmitted data, or damage the cable itself, leading to unreliable communications.

For most organizations, these problems come under the category of natural dangers, similar to those faced by a lot of other office equipment. However, they could also be seen as a means of attacking a network if the sole aim was to disrupt its operation. Conceivably, network cable could provide a new front for attack by the determined interloper seeking access to your data. This could be done as follows:

- Tapping in or establishing an unauthorized connection on the network (proper system administration and password log-on procedures would make it difficult to establish user privileges on the network, but data flowing through the network would be in danger).
- Listening in without actually establishing a new connection, data can be overheard and thus compromised.

Cable does not have to be physically penetrated for the data it carries to be revealed, thanks to the EMI factor (electromagnetic interference, described under eavesdropping in Chapter 7). Because it does not emit electromagnetic radiation, fiberoptic cable is impervious to eavesdropping. But fiber and copper cables alike can be tapped. Even bending fiber optic cable sharply will allow light to escape, as will slight cracks in the insulation. While it is more difficult to tap fiber than coax, it is still possible. The moral, as *LAN Magazine* put it, is "People who don't need to access the cabling shouldn't be allowed to."

Interfaces and Connectors

Despite the growing acceptance of LANs as a way of increasing the productivity of personal computers, the majority of personal computer models still do not come complete with a network interface. This means that for most machines a network interface is an added extra, usually in the form of a circuit board installed in the system unit. The Apple Macintosh does have a LocalTalk network interface built in, but if you want to use a different type of network, such as EtherNet, an EtherNet interface has to be added. If a computer does not have room for an internal network interface card, then it is usually possible to add one as an external device, cabled to the computer. This is the case with some portable computers and with some Macintoshes that require EtherNet interfaces.

From a security perspective, network interfaces do not pose much of a problem. While internal network interfaces do add to the value of personal computers, only the most sophisticated thief would single out such machines. External interfaces can be seen as one more piece of equipment that can go missing, but securing them to desks is easy enough to do. In fact, network interfaces can be given a positive security role. By providing a locking network connection, a workstation's use of the network can be controlled independently of the network software or workstation access control. For example, the computer accessory supplier, Inmac, sells a unit that locks coax connectors and secures them to PCs, as shown in Fig. 12-11.

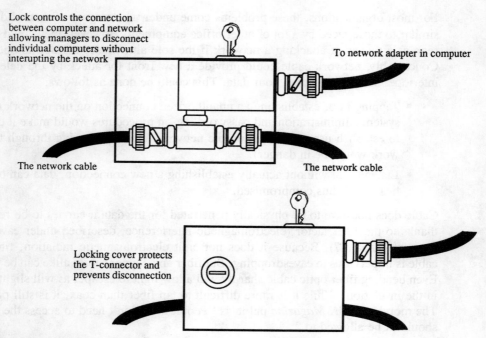

Lock controls the connection between computer and network allowing managers to disconnect individual computers without interupting the network

To network adapter in computer

The network cable

The network cable

Locking cover protects the T-connector and prevents disconnection

Fig. 12-11. A locking network connector.

Expanders and Peripherals

One of the reasons for networking computers is to spread the cost of acquiring expensive peripherals that are shared between many users. These peripherals include laser printers, typesetters, optical drives, facsimile transmitters, modems, and gateways to other networks or mainframe systems. Some of these components present potential security problems. For example, several users on a network might share a single laser printer. This often leads to a situation in which one or more users are having their documents printed at a printer they cannot see. It should go without saying that printed documents are a very vulnerable form of data. There is no point using password protection on the payroll database if payroll reports are likely to be sitting in a print tray where those who should not read them can.

Access to network devices designed for communication beyond the network might need to be controlled, such as gateways, mainframe connections, network modems, and network fax machines. Remember the need for channel control, and make sure that only authorized users can make the connections that network devices provide.

Security Components

For the interloper seeking access to data on a network, the most promising line of attack is a network workstation. This must be protected very carefully. There must be systems in place which prevent unauthorized users from logging on to the network, copying information off it, or even printing data from it.

Of course, a network will not be efficient if it is turned into an inaccessible fortress. The network administrator might want to classify networks users in order to impose the appropriate level of security. This is a suggested three-level system:

- *Administrative level.* Those who design, maintain, and run the network. This might be the administrator alone, or more likely a small group of support and managerial staff.
- *Trusted users.* Those who are competent, stick to the rules, and whose work benefits from greater freedom of access to the network.
- *Vulnerable users.* Those who are lacking in competence, are excessively curious or belligerent, or are for any reason not to be trusted.

These levels can be reflected in the number of barriers to system access that are erected, and the type of access rights granted once log-on is accomplished, as well as the level of supervision and frequency of compliance checks made.

Network Access Control. Here you can use any number of the defensive weapons mentioned earlier in the book, depending upon the value of the data you are protecting and the sophistication of likely attackers:

- Restrict access to workstation areas through keys, ID cards, smart-cards, biometrics.
- Restrict workstation powerup through keys, ID cards, smart-cards, biometrics.
- Password-protect network sign-on.
- Password-protect all sensitive data areas and restrict programs on a "need to use" basis.
- Log all workstation activity, identified by user ID.
- Password-protect or lock out all copy-to-floppy operations on workstations.
- Monitor all copy-from-floppy operations on workstations.

The Diskless Workstation. Clearly there is a need to prevent the copying of programs and data off the network onto floppy disks and to eliminate the possibility of viruses and other malevolent programs being copied from floppies onto the network. On the other hand, the person responsible for running the network needs wide-ranging access to all drives. One answer is to provide vulnerable users with diskless workstations.

Many makers of PCs now have diskless offerings. These units use essentially the same architecture as the standard IBM PC architecture, but with the important difference of no floppy or hard disk drive. The user stores data on the network server's hard disk. By eliminating the disk drive, diskless PCs make it difficult to introduce viruses onto the network. Diskless PCs also prevent users from stealing corporate information or software.

You might wonder how a PC can work without a disk; after all, how can it load the disk operating system and the network operating system? The most common solution is to place operating system instructions in ROM. With DOS burned into ROM chips, it cannot be corrupted by a virus, pirated, or erased by a user. Network interface cards can be fitted with network ROM, so that when the diskless PC is turned on, everything loads from ROM and the connection to the network is made. Operating system details specific to individual workstations can be stored in battery-backed RAM or writable ROM, allowing each one to be configured with its own password and so on.

Diskless PCs offer other benefits over regular personal computers, like taking up less space on the desk, and operating more quietly (many do not need a cooling fan). However, users accustomed to a full personal computer might resent being "downgraded" to a diskless unit. These units are easier to "sell" to new operators or when a complete change in working patterns is introduced.

 Users judged too vulnerable to be allowed their own floppy drive, certainly do not deserve direct access to a printer. Be sure that vulnerable users print on monitored devices.

Protecting the Server

The most important part of the network is the server. The concentration of data on the server, in terms both of quantity and sensitivity, makes it essential to protect it from all eventualities.

Securing the Server. Servers are not room-sized mainframes. They can be carried away, or at least wheeled away. Even if you have not used physical tethering systems on your workstations, you should consider it for the server and its immediate peripherals. The room housing the server should be off limits to anyone but the LAN administrator. People who do not need to use the server should not be allowed near it. Printers and other peripherals should also be kept away from prying eyes (why password-protect the payroll if the mail clerk can watch the paychecks being printed?).

Backing Up the Server. It goes without saying that regular and frequent backups will be made of data on the server. See Chapter 9 for more on backup devices and regimes. Given the importance of the server and the amount of data it handles, you might be able to justify some of the more exotic backup options. Particularly attractive are rewritable optical on-line backup systems. These are fast and offer large capacity (500 megabytes and more per disk). Multiple drives can be arranged in "jukebox" systems that provide several gigabytes of storage with automated disk loading mechanisms.

A number of tape backup units are designed specifically for LAN operation.

Remember that file server backups are a particularly valuable resource and they should be kept in locked storage. A set of backups should be moved off-site regularly to a secure location. Beware of slower tape backup systems that have to be left running overnight, which often means undersupervised. Also, be careful to whom you delegate backup duty. Some backup systems require that the backup station be logged in with supervisor or administrator privileges. Giving an untrusted employee this type of access could be dangerous.

NETWORKING AND FAULT TOLERANCE

Networks, like individual personal computers, must function when you need them to, and keep functioning. *Fault tolerance* is the ability of your network to continue functioning in the event of a major problem or catastrophic breakdown, with no damage to data and with no perceptible change in operation. Most commonly, fault tolerance entails a redundant piece of hardware that automatically takes over in case the primary component fails. However, fault tolerance can mean as little as storing duplicate file allocation tables and directory entries on separate areas of the same disk, or simple read-after-write verification which ensures that data is never written to a bad sector on the disk.

Relatively Tolerant

Not every network will require the same degree of fault tolerance. Fault tolerance usually involves additional costs and so you will want to weigh these against your uptime requirements. The basic question to answer is: What happens if the network breaks down? If you stand to lose serious money or goodwill from such an event, then you need to consider investing in some form of fault tolerance. For example, although the author's data is of great importance to him, he can survive if his network goes down for an hour or two. A catalog sales operation using a LAN for order taking, inventory control, and cash receipts would be badly hit by any corruption of its data, and could not tolerate extended network downtime. Not only would the company lose transactions made since the last backup, but also it would lose potential customers while the computers were down. Similar scenarios can be imagined for banking, trading, and reservation systems.

Fault tolerance has several levels. At the ultimate level, every hardware component is duplicated, even triplicated, to ensure nonstop network performance. The most common form of fault tolerance is at the low end, where the only replicated component is the one responsible for nine-tenths of network failures—the file server hard disk. This is the part of the network most prone to failure because it is the only part with moving parts. Moving parts can wear out, break down, or otherwise malfunction. Apart from catastrophic failure, sectors of the disk surface often go bad under normal usage, and data written to these sectors will be corrupt. Fault tolerance, therefore, entails not only redundancy but error detection.

Duplexing and Mirroring

The first fault tolerant systems were implemented with a second disk drive that was a mirror image of the first. Any data that was written to the first drive was also immediately written to the second. If the primary drive failed for any reason, the secondary disk would take over, allowing the first drive to be replaced without disrupting file server operations. Referred to as *disk mirroring* or *disk duplexing*, this is still the most widely used method of fault tolerance. Some companies make provisions for disk mirroring in their network operating systems. These include Performance Technology of San Antonio, Texas; Novell of Provo, Utah; and Univation of Milpitas, California. Other companies add on hardware, software, or a combination of both to mirror data to a secondary disk.

Even within the area of disk mirroring are different levels of redundancy and fault tolerance. While most duplicate the data from one disk to another, some duplicate only critical data to the secondary disk. Keep in mind that mirroring need not mean only two disks; it is not uncommon for a disk to be mirrored by two or more backup disks. Although the use of the terms mirroring and duplexing is debatable, the generally accepted difference is that the latter uses two controllers. If you feel that the potential failure of the controller card poses a threat to the network, two disks can be duplicated using two controllers. Although controller failure is less likely than hard disk failure, there are those who cannot afford the risk. Of course, the level of redundancy implemented should be determined by the importance of the system.

A positive spin-off from duplexing is that it improves network performance. With two separate controllers, the system has split-seek capability. Not only can users read files simultaneously, but the server can determine which disk can service a read request more quickly. A server with duplexed drives can also read from one disk, write to another, then, once the read is finished, mirror the data that had been written to the secondary disk. The Opus Datasafe computer, described in Chapter 4, provides intelligent disk duplexing with considerable performance gains through a single smart controller.

While not everyone agrees that duplexing entails more than one controller, most agree that no matter how you define the degrees, duplexing involves a greater degree of redundancy than mirroring. In basic intent, however, the terms are synonymous. Both involve backing up data in real time to a secondary disk that can take over automatically if the primary disk fails.

Product Samples

A software approach to fault tolerance for NetWare LANs is used by LAN Services of New York in their LANshadow. This automatically backs up the file server to a secondary server, including all files, NetWare bindery information, and directory trustee rights. LANshadow uses something called a "recursive directory traversal routine" to search through the directories on the primary, or source, server. In the copy phase, it copies only those files that are missing or not up to date on the secondary, or target server. Similarly, in the delete phase, it deletes all files on the target server that are no longer on the source server. LANshadow always maintains a lot of its activities as it copies and deletes files to and from the backup server. The log includes the date and time at the start of the cycle, the phase, path and names of all files copied or deleted. LANshadow allows the network manager to manipulate the number of copy cycles, as well as the delay time between cycles.

A less intense form of fault tolerance involves backing up data rather than making hardware redundant. NetBack from Cheyenne Software of Roslyn, New York, allows administrators of NetWare LANs to reconstruct the file server and its bindery database. Bindery information such as printer definitions and login scripts are stored as individual objects in what Cheyenne calls a VaultFile, the storage utility included with NetBack. The VaultFile can be fed into NetWare while reconstructing the server, eliminating the need for rekeying all those trustee rights. Not only can NetBack be used to restore a server, it can also be used to create a duplicate server, complete with trustee rights.

While LANshadow and NetBack offer software-oriented solutions to fault tolerance, the disk mirroring system from Distributed Processing Technology of Maitland, Florida, is accomplished completely through hardware. SmartCache Mirroring is based on the company's SmartCache disk controller, which works with virtually any LAN operating system. The controller automatically writes a copy of all data to a second drive. The controller supports enhanced small device interface (ESDI) drives as well as ST506 and run length limited (RLL) drives. According to DPT, mirroring in hardware reduces both the software overhead that additional mirroring software requires, as well as the necessity of developing software for each operating system environment.

Software overhead is a significant fact in disk mirroring systems. Depending on the method used to determine whether or not a server is working, the overhead can be as high as 70 percent. Writing data to one or more disks is not enough; the system must also be able to determine when one of the disks has failed. FaultNot Technologies of East Kingston, New Hampshire, manufactures completely redundant file server systems based on both 80286 and 80386 technology, with two servers mirrored to a "hot" standby. It also provides Error Detection, Isolation, and Recovery software. Known as EDIR, this package detects any hard server fault and reconfigures the system to full operational status in less than a minute, while maintaining mirror images of both servers on the standby. This level of redundancy is not inexpensive, and prices of such systems are into five figures.

There are two approaches to redundant file servers. In the *consensus-based protocol*, an odd number of hosts are each given the same algorithm to execute. If all agree, then it is assumed there is no problem. If there is a conflict, the majority rules. The other approach is called the *deterministic processor method*. A "watchdog processor" monitors redundant hosts. Both hosts perform the same tasks, have dual-ported memory, disk drives, and an I/O subsystem, but only one actually drives the I/O subsystem. Using the consensus-based protocol can cost 60 to 70 percent of the available computing power, whereas the deterministic processor approach only expends between 12 to 15 percent.

Paradoxically, as fault tolerant systems become more sophisticated, it becomes harder to determine when a component has failed, especially in a system where every component is duplicated. The best solution is to triplicate components, and the one that two out of three agree is faulty is the one that has failed (this level of sophistication is rare in personal computer LANs).

Atlantic Microsystems of Salem, New Hampshire, offers two levels of fault tolerance for PC LANs, Me2 Disk Protection and Me2 System Protection. Me2 Disk Protection is a software product that transparently mirrors all data written to one hard drive to a secondary drive. These two drives together are called a "shadowpak" and appear as a single disk drive to the operating system. If one drive has an error, Me2 Disk Protection automatically switches to the other and notifies the user of the failure. The user can then either continue working on the surviving drive, or halt operation until the first drive is repaired, so as to be assured data redundancy. Me2 Disk Protection comes in both single-user and network versions.

Me2 System Protection combines both hardware and software for a fault tolerant solution. It consists of two System Interface adapters, a connecting cable and software. Two 286s or 386s are connected by placing an adapter in each computer. When a computer fails, Me2 System Protection switches control to the other computer and continues processing without interruption or data loss. Typically, Me2 System Protection provides fault tolerance for the network server. The primary server handles all the network activity and also backs up data to the secondary server through the connecting cable. When the primary server fails, the secondary server is brought up within a matter of minutes. Atlantic Microsystems OEMs its Me2 technology to 3Com. Me2 Disk Protection for Network File Servers lists for $1595. Me2 System Protection lists for $8995.

Disk Power Mirror from Performance Technology (PT) is the fault tolerance capability for PowerLAN operating system. The file server is outfitted with a duplicate disk and controller, and all data written to the first disk is also written to the duplicate disk. Although it has duplicate controllers, once mirroring begins, users can only access the primary disk. PowerMirror offers a few other options as well. If the critical data on only one logical volume of the disk needs to be mirrored, PowerMirror will only duplicate the writes to that volume, saving disk space. PowerMirror also supports more than one duplicate disk.

When a write to either the primary disk or any of the duplicate disks fails, that disk is removed from any further access and the write is completed to another disk. PowerMirror also time stamps a disk immediately after a successful write. After a failed disk has been repaired, the system examines all the mirrored disks and copies the one with the most recent time stamp (the one that has been most recently updated) over all the disks. This resynchronization assures data integrity. In case of a power failure, PowerMirror will force a resynchronization, because the disks could have identical time stamps but different data, if the power failed before the data was mirrored.

The Novell Approach

In 1985, Novell announced System Fault Tolerant (SFT) NetWare. Novell offers three levels of fault tolerance with SFT NetWare. Level 1 is available with Advanced

Level NetWare and NetWare ELS 2.0. (NetWare ELS 1.0 has no fault-tolerant capability.) Level 2 is available with SFT NetWare. Level 3 is available in NetWare 386.

Level 1 of NetWare provides a relatively low-level of fault tolerance, focusing on disk fix functions rather than mirroring data. That is, Level 1 systems are more concerned with ensuring that data remains uncorrupted than with keeping the system running continuously. Level 1, available with both Advanced NetWare and NetWare ELS 2.0, includes Hot Fix, read-after-write capability and power protection. Hot Fix prevents data from being written to a bad sector on the disk. After writing data to the disk, the system checks to make sure the data is readable. If this read-after-write verification fails, then the sector is flagged as bad and the data is rewritten to a good sector. While Level 1 does nothing to ensure that the system will continue to run in the event of a disk failure, it does protect data.

Level 2, shipped with SFT NetWare, includes mirroring and duplexing as well as transaction tracking. The Transaction Tracking System (TTS) available with Level 2 allows any application to define a series of operations as a transaction. This is an advantage for database management-intensive systems. The whole transaction, all of the related operations, must be completed to be written to the disk. If services are interrupted for any reason, and the transaction has not been completed, it is entirely abandoned, and the database is returned to where it was last known to be consistent.

Level 3 includes the feature of Levels 1 and 2, plus mirrored servers. With Level 3, all data written to one server can be duplicated to a second server. The servers are completely synchronized and communicate with one another. One is designated as the primary server, and if it fails to respond, then the secondary server assumes it is down and takes over. When the primary server is repaired and comes on-line again, then the servers are resynchronized and the primary server once again takes over. Level 3 is aimed at mission-critical environments and applications. System and data integrity are mandatory in a mission-critical environment. A mission critical application is one that can never go down.

The Power Factor

Ultimately, a truly fault-tolerant network is not only completely redundant but includes power protection and tape backup as well. Power protection is simple enough: Plug any critical workstation into a UPS (*uninterruptible power supply*, for more details, see Chapter 6). Certainly the network file server deserves a UPS, many of which now have the ability to signal the file server, through a cabled connection, that mains power has failed and there is only a limited supply of power in the UPS batteries. Network software like Novell Netware has the ability to respond to this signal and warn the administrator who can then take the necessary steps. This includes making sure that all files on the server are saved before the system is shut down.

If all workstations are on UPS systems an outage would not prevent the network administrator from communicating with users via electronic mail, issuing a "save all work" order. If the outage is likely to be prolonged, the administrator can organize an orderly shutdown. Some systems will shut down the network for you, logging out clients in an orderly fashion and making essential backups while there is still backup power available. These intelligent power supplies allow you to run operations unattended and provide an extra measure of security and convenience.

The Cost of Fault Tolerance

Disk mirroring is invaluable in any business that relies on point-of-sale transactions, inventory tracking, or any situation where you cannot afford to go back and re-enter data. It all depends on the value you place on your employees' work. Any number of things can and will go wrong, from a small sector on your server's hard disk going bad to an entire server going down, the potential fallout from which is frightening. However, a fault-tolerant system is designed solely to save you money. It is possible to buy a system far more redundant and expensive that you need. Most people need only to protect their data; for many, a regular tape backup will suffice. Others need completely redundant systems.

Consider not only the value of your data, but the value of your system to the overall operation. Can you survive a few hours of downtime? Also remember that user error is one of the biggest threats facing a network. Training, awareness, and attention to detail can save more money than expensive fault tolerance products.

Some people will argue that tape backup overlaps with disk mirroring. However, disk mirroring is done continuously, whereas tape backup is done at intervals, say every night or once a week. One cannot be substituted for the other, and a completely fault tolerant network will have both. With disk mirroring alone, you always run the risk of your data falling victim to user error. Remember that not only the writes, but also the deletes are mirrored to the secondary disk. Any data mistakenly erased or corrupted is gone immediately, and if you do not have tape backup, it is gone forever. While tape backup offers a measure of data protection, it does nothing for those systems that need to stay up. A disk crash can cost a catalog company or airline untold lost revenues while the computers are down.

THE NETWORK SOFTWARE SECURITY ANGLE

In a typical personal computer LAN, the network software allows a computer with a hard disk to make space on that disk available to others, usually by giving it a special name. Other users can then access files in that area, store their files there, and load programs from that area. A file server, a computer that makes its hard disk available to others, clearly represents an added security risk. You must control who can initiate such sharing and who is allowed to be a client, that is, a user of the shared area. You must also control the boundaries of the shared area, ensuring that clients cannot gain access to the rest of the file server. On the other hand, clients will want to be sure that they can control use of the connection they make to network. If clients feel that their local resources are exposed to others because of connection to the network, they will be loathe to make that connection. The security implications of LAN operations can best be illustrated with a realistic example.

The TOPS Example

Like most personal computer network software, TOPS can be run either through a set of menus or by direct commands. The latter approach allows automation of such operations as making local disks available or accessing remote disks. In Fig. 12-12, you can see TOPS running in menu mode on a PC.

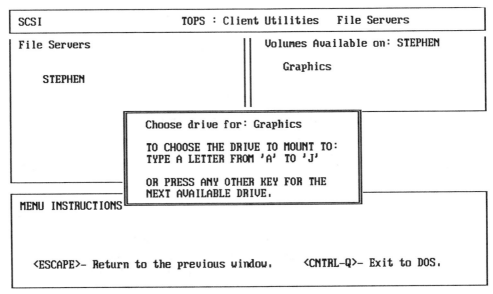

Fig. 12-12. Mounting a drive with TOPS.

Each computer on the network must have a unique name to distinguish it from the others. The network name for the computer in Fig. 12-12 is SCSI, shown in the top left-hand corner of the screen. The box on the left of the screen lists the network station STEPHEN as a file server, meaning that at least part of the storage capacity on the personal computer called STEPHEN has been made available to others, a process known in TOPS-speak as *publishing*. The shared areas available on STEPHEN are listed on the right as *volumes*. In fact, the file server STEPHEN only has published one volume called Graphics.

The user of SCSI wants access to the area called Graphics on STEPHEN; in TOPS-speak, SCSI wants to become a *client* to the file server STEPHEN. In fact, the user in Fig. 12-12 has requested access, a process known as *mounting*. The box in the center of the screen is telling the user to give this remote storage area a drive letter, by which the file server area will be known to the client. If the user types E, then the client computer will gain a new drive E. In Fig. 12-13 you can see that in this case the user typed J, and the result is shown on the TOPS menu.

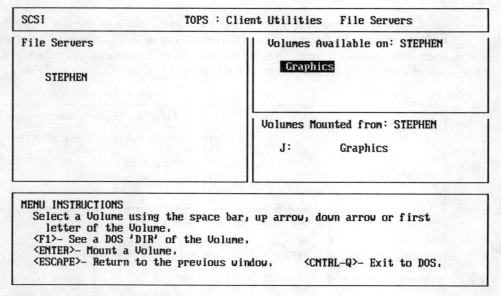

```
SCSI                    TOPS : Client Utilities   File Servers

  File Servers                         Volumes Available on: STEPHEN

      STEPHEN                               Graphics



                                       Volumes Mounted from: STEPHEN

                                          J:        Graphics




  MENU INSTRUCTIONS
    Select a Volume using the space bar, up arrow, down arrow or first
       letter of the Volume.
    <F1>- See a DOS 'DIR' of the Volume.
    <ENTER>- Mount a Volume.
    <ESCAPE>- Return to the previous window.        <CNTRL-Q>- Exit to DOS.
```

Fig. 12-13. The drive successfully mounted.

When the user of SCSI returns to DOS, the command DIR J: will be valid. The files on file server STEPHEN in the published area called Graphics will be listed, and the client user SCSI will have access to them. The actual listing can be seen in Fig. 12-14, where J is shown to contain a file and several subdirectories.

The names look a little odd because this is actually a Macintosh hard disk. Even though SCSI is a PC, the files and subdirectories on the Mac called STEPHEN are readily accessible, and the drive appears to DOS just like any other. If you look at Fig. 12-15, you can see the actual folder called Graphics on the Mac that was published by STEPHEN and mounted as drive J by SCSI (note that STEPHEN is the network user name established by TOPS, whereas MacCrash is the name of the hard disk on the Macintosh file server).

When TOPS has to show a Mac directory on a DOS system, long folder names are truncated and those that begin with the black dot character are shown beginning with the percent sign. The spaces permitted in Mac names are replaced with underlines when TOPS passes the information on to DOS.

TOPS Security

The main point to note at this stage is that TOPS allows a server to share or publish *part* of a hard disk, rather than the whole thing. This feature provides basic secu-

```
C:\>dir J:

Volume in drive J is Graphics
Directory of   J:\

BOW_SAMP    <DIR>      1-10-90    9:11p
FRED         62586     6-01-90    4:42p
GRAY_SAM    <DIR>      1-10-90    9:11p
%ALDUS_F    <DIR>      5-24-90   10:02p
%CANVAS     <DIR>      6-25-90   11:16p
%MACDRAW    <DIR>      6-27-89    9:54p
%MACPAIN    <DIR>      1-14-89   12:59p
%MISC_AP    <DIR>      6-01-90    1:39p
       8 File(s)   30244864 bytes free
```

Fig. 12-14. The DIR listing for J.

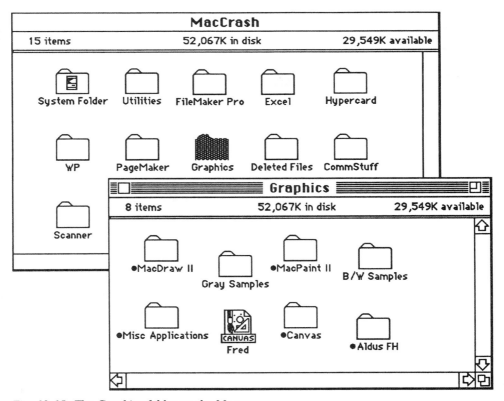

Fig. 12-15. The Graphics folder on the Mac.

rity: If you do not want another user to access certain files on the server, you keep those files in a folder/directory that is not published. In this example, the client who has mounted the Graphics folder cannot get to files in the PageMaker folder, or any other area of the server.

Beyond the ability to maintain strict segregation of files, TOPS offers password control over volume mounting. For example, the user of STEPHEN could have published the volume Graphics with password protection. This would mean that only clients who have the password can mount Graphics. Prospective clients can see a password protected volume listed on the menu, but when they attempt to mount it, TOPS inserts a step between the request for a drive letter shown in Fig. 12-12, and the completing mounting of the volume shown in Fig. 12-13. This step is seen in Fig. 12-16.

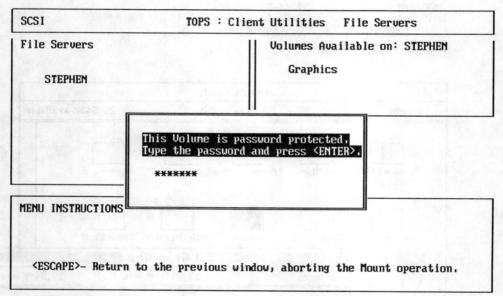

```
 SCSI                    TOPS : Client Utilities    File Servers

 File Servers                          Volumes Available on: STEPHEN

       STEPHEN                                   Graphics




                      ┌─────────────────────────────────────────┐
                      │ This Volume is password protected.       │
                      │ Type the password and press <ENTER>.     │
                      │                                          │
                      │     *******                              │
                      │                                          │
 MENU INSTRUCTIONS    └─────────────────────────────────────────┘


    <ESCAPE>- Return to the previous window, aborting the Mount operation.
```

Fig. 12-16. Password request.

Note that as the client types the password it is obscured by asterisks. If the password is correct, then the volume is mounted and access continues unhindered. An erroneous password terminates the request.

Establishing password protection is easy for the file server to do. In Fig. 12-17, you can see that the system called SCSI is now acting as a file server, publishing the directory C: \ 123R3 \ DATA as a volume called DATA. The password has been entered by the user, and is temporarily visible on screen. Also note the Mode setting. This is currently R, for read-only, meaning that even when the volume has been mounted by a client, files can only be read from it, they cannot be saved onto the volume.

Suppose that a Mac user wants access to files in the 123R3 \ DATA directory of drive C of the system called SCSI. You can see the Macintosh version of the TOPS menu in Fig. 12-18. The Mac that is attempting to become a client in this case is STEPHEN, and the MacCrash hard disk on this system is listed on the left of the menu. The list of file servers on the right shows SCSI as a PC icon, which has been

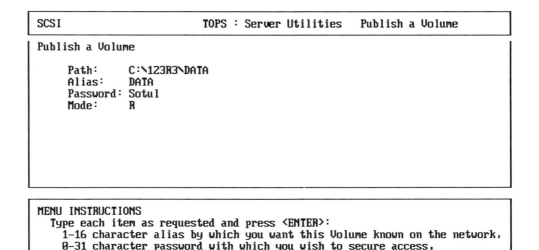

Fig. 12-17. Publishing a volume.

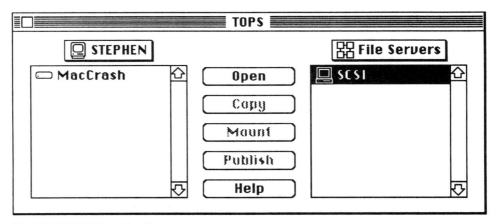

Fig. 12-18. TOPS on the Mac.

selected. Note that the Mount and Publish buttons are gray at this point, indicating that a volume must first be selected before it can either be mounted or published.

If the Open button is clicked, a list of published volumes on SCSI is revealed, as seen on the right of Fig. 12-19, where the volume DATA is listed. The DATA icon has been selected and the Mount button is available. By clicking on the MacCrash hard disk icon, a list of the folders on that disk can be revealed, as seen on the left of the menu in Fig. 12-19.

Note the appearance of the Graphics folder, which has a different icon. This is how TOPS shows a volume that has been published for other users on the network.

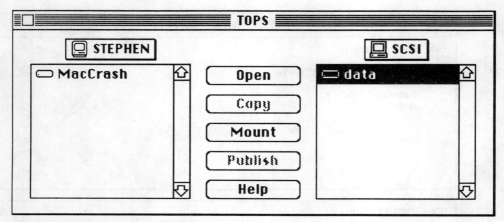

Fig. 12-19. Mounting on the Mac.

When the DATA icon is highlighted and the Mount button is clicked, TOPS attempts to make the \ 123R3 \ DATA directory on drive C of the PC called SCSI available to STEPHEN. However, as you have already seen, that directory was published with password protection, and so a password requested appears, as shown in Fig. 12-20.

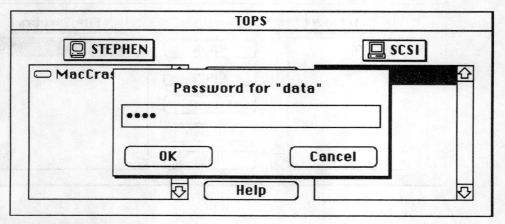

Fig. 12-20. The password request.

The successfully completed operation can be seen in Fig. 12-21, where the PC drive can be seen mounted on a Mac.

SECURITY ON NOVELL NETWORKS

For a more comprehensive look at security factors in the design of a network operating system, turn to Novell's Advanced NetWare. One concept central to Novell

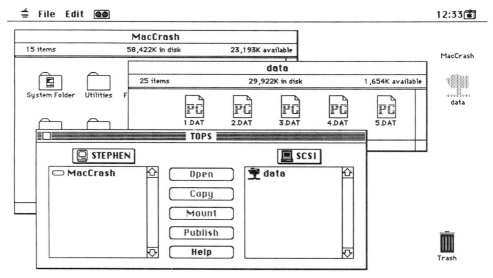

Fig. 12-21. PC drive mounted on a Mac.

and many other networks is the network administrator, the person responsible for overall management of the network. Such a position is deemed essential to coordinate the diversity of users on the system as well as the large number of important decisions that need to be made about how data and programs are organized and who gets access to what.

In terms of NetWare security, each network has a set of access privileges defined as Supervisor. The Supervisor account is controlled and operated by the network administrator. Advanced NetWare provides a powerful set of security mechanisms for security-conscious network administrators. A central security facility directs a range of security alternatives, including:

- Account level security.
- Password level security.
- Directory security.
- File security.
- Internet security.

Each of these mechanisms is accessible either through utilities that accompany Advanced NetWare or through program level commands that can be issued at the command line.

The Bindery and Named Objects

Advanced NetWare's security facility is implemented as a small special-purpose database called the Bindery. Each NetWare file server has a Bindery and uses this to administer the security of its local resources, services, and accounts. The Bindery and other aspects of the NetWare operating system work together to provide a foundation upon which a number of security mechanisms can be built, including account, password, directory, file, and internet security. The main aim of these mechanisms is to give network administrators the capability to design a secure, protected operating environment based on the individual requirements of each user, workgroup, department, and organization in an installation. Thus, varying degrees of freedom and restriction can be mixed to form the ideal security environment.

The Bindery is actually a database of named objects. An object can be a user, resource, user group, or any other logical or physical entity that has been given a name. Associated with each object in the Bindery is a set of properties that contain the information known about the object. These properties include passwords, internet addresses, a mail directory, a list of authorized users, and so on. Two types of properties, items and sets, are attached to Bindery objects, allowing a complete representation of each object's attributes. *Items* are string values used to store miscellaneous information about the object, examples being network addresses, passwords, and accounting information. *Sets* are lists of other object ID numbers, for example, a list of authorized users, a list of the members of some group, or a list of the groups in which an object belongs.

Clients desiring to access network services and resources initiate a connection with the network operating system by sending a login request. The operating system scans the Bindery and reads the client's Bindery information into memory. The client is then asked to supply the appropriate password and its ID is placed, along with all security information, into the server's connection list. The client is then said to be "logged in." In this way, resources with security levels above the level of the requesting client will not be "visible" and hence, cannot be read, written, or destroyed by the client.

Security Masks and Status Flags

Each Bindery object has a security mask associated with it. This is a one-byte field that controls which clients can find the object and which clients are allowed to add properties to the object. The first half of the byte (known as the first nibble) specifies the security level required to read the object. The second nibble specifies the security level required to alter the object. Five different security levels are defined:

0   Access is allowed to all clients even before logging into the server.
1   Access is allowed to all clients who have successfully logged into the server.
2   Access is allowed only if the station requesting access is logged in as the object it is attempting to access.
3   Access is allowed only to those clients with Supervisor status or Supervisor equivalence.
4   No clients are allowed to access this object. Access is allowed only to the server.

Suppose an object has a security mask of 13, that is 1 for the first nibble, 3 for the second. This means the object can be read by any client that has successfully logged into the network, but can be altered only by clients that have Supervisor security clearance. Like objects, each property also has an associated security mask. Access to each property is allowed or denied in the same manner as it is for the security levels.

In addition to a security mask, each object and each property has an associated *status flag*. The status flag is used to determine whether the respective property is an item or set and the expected lifetime of the object or property. An object or property might be dynamic in nature and therefore can be erased during system initialization. Static items or properties must be explicitly removed by the Supervisor. These features are diagrammed in Fig. 12-22.

Named network objects are collected together in the Bindery
Each object has a list of associated properties
Each object and property has a Security Mask and Status Flag

Fig. 12-22. Security masks and status flags.

Groups, Equivalence, and Supervisor Access

One of the most powerful features of the NetWare security implementation is the ability to place objects into sets, called groups. Suppose you have a group of users in an intra-office department. Each user has been assigned a user ID. Users might then be grouped into a set. Users in another group might be placed into another set. Yet another group might be divided into several sets. Each group could then be assigned rights according to the type of network access necessary for their responsibilities.

Each group might also be referenced by name. For instance, a group called DATA ENTRY would be given rights to write and view in specific directories, while rights to delete could be withheld. This mechanism allows network administrators to greatly simplify the security process while retaining absolute control.

In addition to these features, some existing objects might have detailed security assignments. Objects entered into the Bindery needing to have equal rights with an existing object might simply be designated as equivalent to the existing object. This is accomplished with a Bindery property known as SECURITY EQUALS, attached to each client Bindery object. SECURITY EQUALS is a set property and lists other client Bindery objects to which the client has equivalent privileges.

When clients correctly identify themselves to the server, the server gathers all group and equivalence information about them. These access rights are then logically ORed (added together) with the clients' rights mask. The network operation system uses the resulting rights mask while servicing the clients' requests.

Current server implementations include an object named *Supervisor*. The Supervisor is defined by the network administrator and has access to all network resources, except the Queue Management System. Another Bindery object, named *Operator*, controls all administrative privileges for the queuing system.

Login Scripts and Profiles

As was mentioned earlier, clients initiate a connection with the network operating system by sending a login request. After the operating system has read the client's Bindery information into memory, it asks the client to supply the correct password and its ID. Following successful login, the operating system views the client as a consumer with a set of rights. These rights are defined by the client's security mask and status flags. The client, however, has not established a processing environment. For this reason, the login program also executes a configurable batch file called a login script that initializes environmental variables, maps network drives, and can control the client's program execution.

To make network administration easier, a test for group membership has been incorporated into the login script services. This allows the administrator to perform many functions on the basis of workgroup membership and expands the usefulness of groups beyond that of security. Virtual drive mappings can also be configured based on the various groups that a user belongs to.

Advanced NetWare uses the Bindery to implement the login procedure and login script. Part of the login procedure initializes the client's security privileges while the login script initializes the client's environment. The result of these two processes is referred to as a user profile. In essence, this profile becomes the client's window onto the network.

Security Checks

Advanced NetWare provides a collection of security restrictions that allow the system administrator the flexibility to restrict user login and server access. These include account expiration dates, login time restrictions and accounting, all of which require a workstation to satisfy certain conditions to remain logged in. Advanced NetWare performs a security check to make sure all connections satisfy these conditions.

Every half hour, the NetWare operating system checks each workstation connection to make sure that it has the right to continue receiving services from the server. If the NetWare OS determines that the workstation does not have the right to remain attached, then an "automatic logout" process is begun. Initially, a message is broadcast to the workstation asking the user to log out. After four minutes, if the user has not logged out, the NetWare OS broadcasts another message informing the user that the connection will be terminated in one minute. One minute later the connection is cleared.

Expiration Dates and Disabled Accounts

An account can be disabled without actually being deleted from the server Bindery. Users with disabled accounts are denied access to the server until the Supervisor enables the account. If an account is disabled while in use, the connection is terminated during the next half-hour security check. The Supervisor account cannot be disabled.

An account expiration date can be affixed to any account except the Supervisor account. Any attempt to log in after the account expiration date causes the NetWare OS to disable the account. The expiration date is effective at midnight on the specified date; therefore, any active accounts affected by the expiration date are disabled during the next half-hour security check. The Supervisor can enable the account at any time.

Station and Time

Server access periods can be defined for each account, in half-hour increments for each day of the week. Users attempting to log in during unauthorized periods are denied access to the server. Users who are connected to the server when their authorized time period expires are subject to the half-hour security checks. Any time restrictions attached to the Supervisor account will be enforced.

A client's login capabilities may be restricted to specific physical network numbers and individual node addresses. Restrictions can apply to entire networks of workstations or to individual workstations scattered across an internet. Also, a limit can be placed on the number of concurrent connections for individual clients. This applies to concurrent connections with individual servers and does not apply to internet connections. If the client has already logged in from the specified number of stations, any further login attempts will be rejected by the server until one of the existing connections is logged out. If the Supervisor does not set a connection limit on an account, that user can log in from as many stations as desired. Connection limits placed on the Supervisor account will be enforced.

Intruder Detection and Lockout

The intruder detection facility in NetWare allows the Supervisor to set a threshold which determines whether an attempt to break into an account is being made. The threshold is specified as a number of incorrect login attempts during a specified length of time. If the incorrect login limit is reached in the specified time period, an audit note specifying that an intruder was detected is generated. This appears on the file server so that the network administrator can take appropriate action. The audit note includes the time of detection, the account name, and the physical node address of the intruding workstation. The incorrect login count will be reset to zero when a correct login occurs or if a period of time greater than the threshold time period has passed since the last incorrect login attempt.

In addition to generating an audit note, the Supervisor can specify that an account should be locked if an intruder is detected. If the Supervisor specifies that the account should be locked, a time period that the account should remain locked must also be specified. The time period can be from one minute to over a month. The lockout feature can be used to discourage breaking into an account by trying random passwords. For example, the definition of an intruder might be three successive incorrect password attempts, after which the account is locked for fifteen minutes. This means the would-be intruder can only try fifteen passwords in an hour, effectively discouraging the use of lengthy lists of soft passwords. The Supervisor has the ability to clear a lock on any account should a legitimate user need access.

If account lockout has been activated on the server, the Supervisor's account will also be locked if an intruder is detected attempting to break into the Supervisor's account. A lockout on the Supervisor's account can be cleared from the server's console.

Password Level Security

Advanced NetWare's security includes an optional password for each client account on each server. Once the client supplies the appropriate password, the client inherits a predefined view of the network's resources. Therefore, the password protects the client's tailored view of the network. The following security features allow system administrators to configure the way passwords are enforced on an account basis.

Mandatory Passwords. For those accounts which require mandatory security, the system Supervisor can flag the account, mandating a password. This feature can also be used on the Supervisor's account.

Forced Periodic Password Changes. In addition to mandatory passwords, individual accounts can be forced to change passwords at regular intervals. The interval is specified in days. Once the expiration date arrives, the login program will warn the user of the need to change the account password. In addition, a number of "grace logins" can be specified. A grace login is one that is allowed after the specified interval has expired. The account is disabled once the grace logins are used. This requires the user to talk to the Supervisor before further access to the account is allowed. This feature is not supported on the Supervisor account.

Passwords Changeable Only by Supervisor. The Supervisor can specify that an account password cannot be changed by the user. This is useful for accounts such as GUEST where the Supervisor wants to set the account to no password, or a password that is known to all who should use the account. The user will not be able to change the password even though he knows the current account password.

Minimum Acceptable Password Length. The Supervisor can specify a minimum acceptable length for a client's password. All passwords submitted by the client must comply or they will be rejected by the NetWare OS.

Required Unique Passwords. If the Supervisor flags an account requiring a unique password, the NetWare OS will track the previous eight passwords used by the account. When the account specifies a new password, the user is forced to enter a unique password, one that has not been used the last eight times.

Password Encryption. All passwords are encrypted with a nonreversible encryption algorithm before they are stored on the server disk. This prevents people with direct access to the server from finding passwords. In addition, the Supervisor is no longer allowed to view a user's password. This will allow a user to use the same password on several servers, without the Supervisor on one server knowing his password on the other servers.

Directory Level Security

The network operating system provides a mechanism to grant and revoke access rights to specific users at any level within a directory tree. Each directory can have attached to it a list of trustees (clients) and their access rights. These lists are accessed by network clients only through secured network primitives.

Directory trustees correspond to objects within the Bindery. All users requesting service within a specific directory must own an object ID in the server Bindery (be a member), and be assigned access rights within the specific directory. Trustee access rights are stored in a one-byte mask with the following format:

0   Read from files in this directory.
1   Write to files in this directory.
2   Open existing files in this directory.
3   Create files in this directory.
4   Delete files in this directory.
5   Has parental rights in this directory. (Parental rights include the ability to create and delete subdirectories, and the right to make other objects trustees of this directory or its descendants.)
6   May search this directory.
7   May modify the status flags of files/subdirectories in this directory and rename files.

By combining these separate privileges, a system administrator can tailor trustee access rights to suit a wide variety of installation security requirements. Some users, for instance, might only require search, open, and read privileges, while others might require the freedom to create subdirectories and files.

Directory Maximum Rights Masks. In addition to the rights granted to each trustee individually, each directory has associated with it a maximum rights mask that indicates which access actions might occur in the directory. The trustee's access mask is logically ANDed with the directory's maximum rights mask to obtain the set of actions the trustee might actually perform. Consequently, a client with delete privileges will not be able to use them if the maximum rights mask does not allow that privilege in that specific directory.

File Level Security

The file server strictly enforces file access security to ensure that clients are allowed access only to those files they have been granted rights to access. In addition to the constraints imposed on a client by his directory access rights, each file has a file flag mask that controls its access characteristics. The file flag mask bits are defined as follows:

Bit 0:   Set if the file is read-only.
Bit 1:   Set if the file is hidden.
Bit 2:   Set if the file is a system file.
Bit 3:   Set if the file is an execute-only file that can be executed but not copied or read.
Bit 4:   Unused.
Bit 5:   Set if the file has been changed since the last archive.
Bit 6:   Unused.
Bit 7:   Set if the file is shareable by multiple clients.

In fact, when file flags and directory access rights are properly administered, they present a powerful capability to design a secure multi-user environment.

Internet Security

In an internet, the NetWare system architecture guarantees a secure and reliable distribution of services. Security for each subnet is handled by the local server on the network offering the requested services. Therefore, internet resources with security levels higher than those of a requesting client, regardless of the client's location, will be "invisible" to the client and hence cannot be read, written, or destroyed by the client.

For the developer who requires more control, NetWare's open architecture and programming interfaces offer the capability to develop custom login applications. A client using a custom login procedure can be kept completely unaware of services and resources his application is accessing. Internet clients can be separated from entire groups of servers and resources through this capability. In fact, developers can incorporate services and resources from throughout the internet into an application without the user having any knowledge of the process, or the location and identity of the resources. Thus, valuable resources can be physically removed and logically hidden from any or all network clients.

These mechanisms are enhanced by the inherent security of the network server. The server file system is not accessible from the server itself. This means that the only access method, short of stealing the machine or disk drive, is through the network operating system which, in turn, administers system security. By definition, then, Advanced NetWare provides the capability to design a truly secure multiuser environment.

TELEPHONE CONNECTIONS

Local area networks are not the only means of making intercomputer communication. Computers can communicate with each other over great distances by using telephone lines. Communications with distant computers are sometimes referred to as *remote* or *wide area* communications. A large central computer that stores data accessed by others is called a *host*, while the distant computer calling in to the host is referred to as a *remote system*.

Hardware and Software

For computers to talk over the phone requires modems. A *modem* turns computer data into signals that are transmitted over the phone. At the other end of the line, another modem converts the signal back into data. The conversion process is known as *modulation*, and modem is a conjunction of *modulator-dem*odulator. Essentially a modem is a circuit board and can be fitted internally in a personal computer or housed in an external box connected to the computer by a cable.

Most personal computer operating systems only have minimal support for modems and so a special piece of software, a communications program, is required in order to control the modem. For one computer to call another the following is necessary:

1. Both computers must have modems properly attached and communications software loaded.
2. The host computer, the one receiving the call must be placed in "answer mode," that is, the communications software must program the modem to answer the phone and respond to the incoming call.
3. The computer initiating the call must dial the number of the computer receiving the call.
4. When the call is answered a series of exchanges must take place, known as *handshaking*, to establish the connection.
5. There must also be an agreed exchange of messages to let users of the two systems know that they are communicating. This can be as simple as sending a carriage return in each direction, but in practice it should involve some form of caller verification, such as ID number and password.

On the Line

With so many reports going around of hackers wreaking havoc by illicitly accessing computers via modems, it is easy to get nervous about fitting one to your personal computer. For this reason it is important to stress that nobody can access your computer via its modem unless:

- The computer is turned on.
- The modem is connected to a phone line.
- The communications software is programmed to answer the phone.

As you will already know if you have tried to set up a modem with the intention of having it answer the phone, it takes a concerted effort to open up a computer to incoming calls. It is a relatively complex operation, involving the coordination of numerous different parameters. Answering the phone is not something a person is likely to do "by accident." That said, it is important to know what precautions to take in situations where you need your computer to answer the phone.

The most basic precaution is a *caller verification system*. At the very least, this requires the person calling your computer to enter an ID, a name and/or number that your computer can check against a list of authorized user IDs. If the ID given is not on the list, the computer can hang up or offer the caller another chance to enter a correct ID. Only a limited number of chances should be given before the call is terminated. Beyond this, you might require a password as well as an ID.

Most of the methods of attack used by hackers and other intruders, keen to conduct unauthorized explorations of your computer, depend upon outsmarting the caller verification system on the host computer. The following are typically the steps followed when breaking into a computer over the phone:

1. Find a computer to call. This can be done by all manner of means. Numbers can be gleaned from company literature, documents, trash, and employees. Repetitive dialing devices can dial all numbers in an area until a computer answers (the technique used in the movie *War Games*).
2. Make the call and check the response (login procedure, type and length of ID and password). Experienced hackers can tell a lot from the response they get when a computer answers the phone. The request for an ID or password may reveal the number of characters expected, or even the type of characters (words or numbers).
3. Keep trying. The hacker will not hesitate to keep calling until the logon attempt matches the expected parameters and the required logon information is discovered.

From this it is simple enough to propose a series of basic countermeasures:

1. Keep your number secret. Unless you are operating a public dial-up service treat computer phone numbers as highly sensitive information, revealed on a need-to-know basis. If you need extensive electronic communications with a lot of people, use a third-party system, such as MCI Mail or CompuServe Information Services. These provide a well-policed forum for information exchange without exposure to your organization's computer systems.
2. Limit repeated access attempts. Do not allow more than three attempts to log in before breaking the connection and forcing the caller to try again.
3. Reveal as little as possible in log-on procedures. This is one area where you do not want to be user-friendly. For example, do not prompt the caller to "Enter your six digit ID number." A cryptic prompt such as "WAY?>" will suffice. If a caller enters an incorrect ID number the message "Invalid Response" is better than "Sorry, the ID number you entered has too many digits." Authorized callers can be trained to use the system without the benefit of such giveaways.

Who Is There

It should be clear by now that one of the most important requirements for secure communications between computers is verification of identity. Entry of a valid ID number/password combination does not guarantee the identity of the person using them, but in the case of local area networks a simple deterrent to impostors is the physical presence of the network administrator, who can actually see who is working at each station. When dealing with remote communications, direct physical verification of identity claims is not so easy. The following are some of the techniques you can use to get around this problem.

Call-Back. One of the most powerful techniques to prevent unauthorized remote access is to deny it completely. This is possible if the central system calls the remote one, rather than the other way around. A simple system is to schedule calls for set times. Suppose that you have several remote offices that report their daily transactions to a central computer. Instead of placing the more valuable central computer in potentially dangerous answer mode, the central computer can be programmed to call each remote office in turn. The computers in the remote offices only need to be placed into answer mode for a short period of time to receive the pre-arranged calls. If these can be made during business hours, they can be monitored.

Several factors that work against this type of closely monitored arrangement are: the need to make the calls outside normal business hours and the inflexibility of pre-scheduled calls. The latter difficulty can be circumvented by a call-back system. This operates at the convenience of the remote user. When remote users are ready to connect to the central system, their communications software dials the central system, which answers the phone. After interrogating the remote system to determine who is calling, the central system hangs up, then dials the remote system. Several safeguards can be incorporated into this approach, plus it has the potential to permit remote users to call in from anywhere and avoid expensive long distance charges.

When the central computer interrogates the caller prior to the call-back, an ID and password can be required from the remote system. The phone number given by the remote system can be checked against a list of authorized users. Call-back systems make it much harder for intruders to log on. Although there are hacking techniques such as adding false numbers to the list of authorized callers and redirecting the outgoing call from the central system to the remote, they are difficult to implement. A call-back system certainly makes your computer a less attractive target.

One potential disadvantage of a call-back system is that the central computer might get left in answer mode for long periods of time. Time can be the hacker's best weapon. The more often the hacker can make an attempt to break in, the more likely it is that the effort will eventually succeed. Defensive measures include limited retries before the host hangs up, a call-logging feature that lets the caller know each attempt is recorded, and limiting access hours to those times when the system is attended.

The Temporary Password. One of the biggest weaknesses of password protected access is the failure by users to come up with difficult passwords, and to keep changing the passwords. As mentioned in Chapter 8, hackers have lists of typical passwords. If your log-on system permits repeated attempts to log on, then the hacker can run through the list. Once a good password is discovered, you can bet it will be used more than once. Regularly changing passwords is as important as using "hard" ones. One approach is to give potential callers a password that expires within a fairly short period of time. You can even use voice calls ahead of computer calls to give "instant" passwords that are good for one call only.

The Automatic Problem

In an effort to make it as easy as possible for remote users to access a central computer, a lot of communications software can carry out the entire sequence of operations necessary to dial up and log into a computer. This automated login is performed with features known by names like *scripts* or *command files*. Convenient as they might be for the user, these features can pose a security problem in that they record, on disk, the caller's ID and password. This can make it a simple matter for someone exploring the caller's computer to steal this vital data.

You can see a typical log-on sequence in Fig. 12-23, viewed with an ordinary file handling utility. In amongst various codes used by the script, the ID and password are clearly visible. Look for communications software that can encrypt log-on files, or work with files encrypted by third-party packages. Make sure users are aware of the value of these log-on files and protect them accordingly.

```
Viewing: COMSERV.ACT              Press ESC to exit           (F)ilter: OFF

{ Autologon file for CompuServ Network }
   twait(1, "sec")            { wait for 1 second }
   "$03"                      { send Cntl-C character }
   cwait("ID:")               { wait until 'ID:' string received }
   "76530,102$0d"             { send login id followed by carriage return }
   cwait("word:")             { wait for pass'word:' prompt }
   "UR@CIS1234$0d"            { send password followed by carriage return }
   invoke handykey            { invoke another file which defines some keys }




Commands:  PgUp  PgDn  Home  End  1..9 (9 is fastest)  ↑ ↓  (H)ex  (N)ormal
```

Fig. 12-23. An automated login file.

MICRO-TO-MAINFRAME

Another form of intercomputer connection is the micro-to-mainframe link. Many organizations that employ personal computers for data analysis and projections use mainframe computers to deal with the mass quantities of day-to-day data that is the raw material of information. This is particularly true of data that must be processed in real-time, such as sales transactions, invoices, orders, and so on. One way to make sense out of this raw data is to copy some of it to a personal computer where it can be analyzed by database and spreadsheet software. Because mainframe computers usually have security procedures built into the operating system, these links are typically well-protected to begin with, but several areas need attention.

Well-Defined Responsibility

To establish a micro-to-mainframe link often requires coordination between two different parts of an organization or between two separate organizations. When the link is created, there should be a clear understanding about security responsibilities. The mainframe system is likely to have ID/password facilities. You will need to decide who assigns passwords and who polices them to verify user identity.

Both sides of the channel need to beware of blanket access rights. The micro side should only be given access to the mainframe at the minimum level required for the planned exchanges of data. Mainframe access details should be closely guarded on the micro side. If higher level access if given and the micro side fails to protect it, there could be nasty recriminations. Similarly, the mainframe side must be prepared to do its part in policing connections from the micro end.

Identity Verification

As with other aspects of intercomputer communication, it is important to make sure that the people who use the micro-to-mainframe link are indeed who they claim to be. A system of ID numbers and passwords is a minimum requirement. If the micro is a long way from the mainframe, then you need to consider some of the remote verification techniques mentioned in the previous section. If it is possible to verify user ID by visual checks, this should be done frequently to let users of the link know that posing as another user will not work.

Bulletin Boards and On-Line Services

Numerous commercial "on-line information services" provide both generalized and specialized information to modem-equipped computer users. These are run on computers equipped with many incoming lines and protected by sophisticated login procedures. Even more bulletin boards are run by individuals and small organizations, and are often operated from a personal computer with a large hard disk and just a few incoming lines. Both bulletin boards and larger services, such as CompuServe, Genie, and BIX, provide software files that callers can download onto their own machines. In some cases, these are just the sort of valuable but specialized programs that larger software companies cannot be bothered to distribute. Other files are more frivolous, from games to pornographic images.

To what extent you wish to avail yourself of the opportunity to download software depends upon your situation. If you have confidence in the person or organization offering the files, who should thoroughly test them for viruses and other malevolent code, then downloading can be a very useful source of software solutions. Whatever the source, you are advised to check out downloaded files on an isolated system before putting them into use anywhere near valuable data. Bear in mind that downloaded software is rarely free. At the least, you might be paying for the phone call, which can be lengthy if the file is large. You might be paying a time charge or subscription to the service. Once you have downloaded the software you might find that it is shareware, which you must register if you are going to use it and want to get upgrades and complete documentation.

QUICK LINKS

One other form of intercomputer communication deserves attention: The direct connection of two personal computers. It has always been possible to send files from one personal computer to another, but until recently the process was clumsy and slow, meaning that this was a likely way to lose data. In recent years, file exchange has been made very easy by packages such as LapLink.

Originally designed to overcome the compatibility problem posed by the 3.5 inch disks (which just will not work in 5.25 inch drives, no matter how you fold them) used on laptop PCs, these computer linking packages got a big boost when IBM introduced the PS/2 range with 3.5 inch drives as standard. Featuring menu-driven copying of files between machines, using serial or parallel ports, programs like LapLink are very handy and, when copying from hard drive to hard drive, mush faster than copying to floppies. Like most other tools, such programs can also be abused, in this case by someone wishing to copy data quickly, and without using a floppy disk drive.

HOT LINKS

Finally, it is worth mentioning other forms of communication that can be damaging to your personal or organizational security.

The Printed Word

The personal computer has not yet brought about the paperless office, and the printed word is still very potent. When confidential information is printed off your computers, it should be handled only by those who are trustworthy. Beware of networked printers that spew out everybody's reports next to the coffee machine where all and sundry can read them.

Photocopiers

Information duplication is not only accomplished by copying files to floppy disks. If sensitive data has to be put on paper, make sure copies are strictly controlled. Special papers are designed to prevent photocopying, and these should be used where applicable.

Fax Machines

Facsimile transmission is a rapidly growing form of communication, one that is increasingly integrated into computer operations. If you have stand-alone fax machines, make sure you know what is being sent and to where. If you have fax machines in computers, make sure you trust the users. If you have a networked fax facility, make sure it is password-protected and has full call logging and accounting to discourage and discover abuse.

Mobile Phones and Satellite Links

Whenever you put information into the air, be it in radio waves, microwaves, or sound waves, you make it possible for someone else to take it out. Against the unquestionable convenience of the latest forms of voice and data communication must be set the question mark of interception. Apart from a dedicated band of amateurs who spend a lot of time tuning in whatever waves they can, sometimes using very sophisticated equipment, there are professionals who specialize in this area of eavesdropping. Having company data intercepted and decrypted by a radio buff is embarrassing. When professionals are involved, it can be decidely damaging.

SUMMARY

Opening up computers to gain the benefits of sharing information and physical resources also opens up new channels through which data can be lost and intruders can gain access. However, by taking the proper precautions, the benefits of information and resource sharing can be achieved and obtained without incurring unacceptable risks. Indeed, network operating systems for personal computers provide security features that are not found in regular operating systems. When a network is installed, access controls can be instituted. More sophisticated backup facilities can be employed cost-effectively by personal computers running on a network. For the most part personal computer networks are not subject to the same sort of threats as the large Unix and mainframe networks, which have featured in the more sensational virus and hacking stories.

The telephone lines can be employed by personal computer users without too much fear of opening up a door for intruders. The main weapon in securing the connected computer is a clear understanding of how intercomputer communication works. By understanding the technology involved, you will be able to pinpoint the weak links in the chain and take the necessary steps to strengthen them.

Hell is other people.
Jean Paul Sartre

13
Hackers and Other Human Factors

THIS CHAPTER FOCUSES on the human aspects of computer security. These include not only that mysterious creature known as the hacker, but also such everyday phenomena as the disgruntled employee, and the unsympathetic manager. The relatively short length of the chapter should not be taken to indicate that this is the easy part of the problem. Without the human factor, computer security would simply be a question of uninterruptible power supplies, automated backups, and fault-tolerant hardware.

THE PEOPLE PROBLEM

For readers who find the technical side of computing to be baffling, frustrating, even intimidating, the news is not good: Humans are even more complex and difficult to understand than computers. If you are a people person, someone who enjoys interaction with others, you might find that you have a better handle on the human aspects of computer security than less gregarious/more technically-oriented colleagues, but you are warned that taking charge of the human side of the computer security problem is not a burden to be shouldered lightly. After all, humans create the need for security, and aside from the effects of rare and random acts of nature such as tornadoes or earthquakes, humans pose the biggest threat to security.

This chapter does not attempt anything so grand as an explanation of human behavior, it merely attempts to put in perspective the human issues surrounding the need to protect and preserve valuable data and functions entrusted to personal computers.

The People Perspective

The recommendations made in this chapter are probably more subjective than any others in the book, and so it is reasonable to expect an up-front declaration of my biases. I am firmly on the side of people over technology, that is to say, computers should be treated as tools to serve humans, and not vice versa. From this, you can infer that:

- Security within an organization cannot be divorced from other aspects of the organization, such as the goals and activities of the organization, its personnel policies, and its overall management.
- Sound personnel policies are the most cost-effective security measure an organization can institute.
- Without sound personnel policies, attempts to achieve security through purely technical means will not achieve maximum possible efficiency.

The People Involved

Contrary to media myths and popular misconceptions the main human threat to computer security is not hackers, but ordinary people who work with computers. As should be clear from previous chapters, a person with only average computer literacy can seriously impair security in plenty of ways, from erasing and corrupting data to stealing files.

The Disgruntled. Few personal computers are equipped with enough safeguards and security devices to prevent an angry user from wreaking havoc with valuable files. Personal computers are tools, and just as the harmless hammer is a practical impossibility, so is the personal computer that is safe from the authorized user. The best defense against employees abusing legitimate access is to make sure you know what frame of mind users are in. Any manager worthy of the title should be sensitive to signs of dissatisfaction or unrest in an employee. The time to act is when these signs first appear. Negative attitudes should be brought to the employee's attention and an attempt made to resolve the underlying problem.

Managers responsible for large groups of employees often delegate authority and receive feedback through a system of supervisors. The responsibility of management is to make sure that the feedback is timely and honest, ensuring that particularly acute cases of disaffection are quickly recognized. Obviously, some underlying problems are not easily resolved. Difficulties in the national and local economy are usually beyond management control. However, if management can foster a spirit of solidarity across all levels of the organization, then it is possible to prevent discontent from turning inward on the organization. Security is best served when dissatisfaction and resentment are deflected away from the organization.

The Curious. Some people are naturally curious. Others are downright nosey. To such persons, the amount and type of information that is stored on some personal computers make them irresistible targets of attention. Managers and supervisors should be alert to users straying from their normal area of work. If an activity logging system is in use, this can be checked for attempts to access unauthorized areas. Employees should be left in no doubt as to which areas are accessible and which are "no-go." There should be some consensus on this, meaning that management should avoid imposing restrictions for their own sake.

It follows that organizations using an "open" style of management will have fewer secrets, and hence less need to erect security barriers. If management is seen to be keeping employees well-informed and encourages employee participation in the decision-making process, then curiosity is less likely to turn into prying.

The Incompetent. The statement, "I didn't erase it on purpose," does not make it any easier to recover lost data. The truth is that carelessness and lack of proper training are two of the biggest threats to the security of your data. In general, the responsibility for carelessness rests with the individual employee, the responsibility for proper training rests with management. The two levels at which carelessness and lack of training affect security on personal computers are normal computer operations and security operations. If normal computer operations are not performed correctly, then data might be erased and corrupted causing considerable loss of time and effort. The second level is security operations. Most security measures are ineffective if they are not properly utilized. Negligence in backing up or locking up can prove expensive.

Management must ensure that employees know how to use applications properly. Management must ensure that employees are properly aware of their security role and the importance of fulfilling it. Employees have a duty to perform to the best of their ability and to comply with the security rules.

As has been stressed on several other occasions in this book, the mushroom approach to management seems particularly ill-suited to organizations utilizing expensive and powerful technology. For those not familiar with the mushroom theory of management, it states, "Keep them in the dark most of the time and just open the door every once in a while to **** on them" (meaning: renew the compost). It is hard to argue with the statement that technology is most efficient and productive in the hands of those who understand it best. This implies that there is little to gain from restraining the natural tendency of personal computer users to better understand their hardware and software the more they use it.

The Management Challenge

Several experts have observed that the rapid spread of personal computer technology presents a challenge to traditional styles of management. Wariness, regimentation, coercion, and restriction need to give way to trust, interaction, consensus, and freedom to grow. Making the most of information technology requires that you put faith in the people who work for you. If they do not merit that faith, you hire replacements that do. You have to have confidence in your ability to hire the right people, and not simply rely on paper qualifications. You must have the necessary self-confidence to allow employees to perform to the best of their ability. You must command the respect required to ensure that the limits and controls you impose are observed.

THE PEOPLE SOLUTION

Without doubt, the single most effective computer security measure an organization can take is engendering a loyal, well-informed, competent, and contented work force. This makes security not only a personnel management issue, but also a matter of overall organizational philosophy. To make gains in productivity through the use of personal computers, an organization pays a price in terms of vulnerability. This is a simple fact of life, just like the vulnerability that comes from relying on any power tool. To minimize this vulnerability, you take suitable precautions and engage in a program of user education to ensure that the tool is used correctly.

Well-Paid

You cannot buy loyalty and dedication, but workers who exhibit these qualities should be rewarded. You cannot expect to hire skilled workers for unskilled wages, but you might consider hiring undertrained workers and training them. Well-paid does not necessarily equate with highest-paid. A pay scale that is equitable and fair can go a long way towards increasing loyalty and minimizing disaffection without having to be top dollar.

Well-Educated

Whether you hire unskilled workers and train them or pay the going rate to attract skilled workers, you have to realize that training is an ongoing process. If you do not help your employees to improve their skill and knowledge levels, they will go to an employer who will. You might invest in training for people who jump ship anyway, but this is usually an indication that something else about your organization is below par. It goes without saying that if you train people to new levels of ability, you must pay them commensurate with that ability.

Beyond the question of specific skills, it would appear that the full implications of personal computer technology are best grasped by people with a well-rounded education. Indeed, much of the personal computer industry was created *ab initio* by people from all walks of life with little in common but their ability to understand and capitalize upon the possibilities that the emerging technology presented. In most cases this ability can be seen to originate from either a well-rounded education, or a wider than average breadth of experience. Individuals of this type tend to be somewhat intimidating to the old school of management, but offer the best potential for organizations able to channel and reward their energies and abilities. It is short-sighted to see well-qualified and capable people as a security risk, versus the safe option of the slow-witted underachiever. The safest information technology workers are those that are properly managed, motivated, and rewarded.

Well-Aware

Management has a responsibility to make sure that all staff are fully aware of the need for computer security and the measures that must be taken to maintain it. If you have any doubts about the level of security awareness in your organization, consider launching a security awareness campaign. This can be as important to the well-being of the organization as quality control, customer service, and other aspects of business that are regularly highlighted by management. You can start with a security-awareness week, complete with seminars, slogans, and surveys. Follow that up with posters, newsletters, and refresher courses. Every effort should be made to place security in a positive light. It is not a matter of management mistrusting employees, indeed, it is often managers who leave the biggest holes in security barriers. It is a case of all levels of the organization, from janitor to C.E.O., working together to protect the organization for the good of its members.

HACKERS

Turning now to that particular group of humans known as hackers, the first observation to make is that they are invisible. For a group of people variously accused of wreaking havoc on government computer networks, stealing millions from financial institutions, and creating world-shaping breakthroughs in computer technology, they are curiously low profile. Unlike some other social stereotypes, hackers have no consistent public image. Furthermore, public appearances are not part of their lifestyle. In fact, it is exceedingly difficult to even define who they are, beyond some bland generalization such as people who explore and experiment with the workings of technological systems.

Images of Hacking

Several images of hacking have been influential in shaping public perception. By reviewing them, it is possible to get an idea of the breadth of the field of activity that this one term encompasses.

War Games. In this 1984 movie a basically good, "kid-next-door" teenager discovers, through his hacking mischief, simple but fatal flaws in the U.S. government's top secret, super-secure, defense computer computer. The impression is given that hacking, though mischievous, can save us from those who put too much faith in computers or use them to make moral decisions.

The Morris-Internet Incident. This was the first virus infection to receive headline attention. The media's lack of accuracy and tendency to exaggerate gave the impression that the personal computer in your office was at risk, when in fact the virus inhabited an on-line network. The virus maker was not glorified, but condemnation was mixed with admiration for his impressive programming skills.

The Cuckoo's Egg. Clifford Stohl's book, *The Cuckoo's Egg*, details the detection and pursuit of hackers who were attacking U.S. government computers. While the book clearly indicates the serious problems hacking can create, it does little to dispel the mystique surrounding those who inhabit the complex computer network that permeate universities, laboratories, and research organizations.

The Hackers Handbook. Written by a man using the name of Hugo Cornwall, this book was first published in Britain and actually told readers how to go about exploring on-line services, including those to which access was not authorized. Later updated by Steve Gold (not his real name), who had been arrested for hacking into the British videotext service called Prestel, the book did a lot to put hacking in perspective, with the authors claiming it is essentially harmless and talking of a code of ethics to which real hackers should adhere.

The Lack of Definition

The terms *hacker* and *hacking* have joined the special group of words and phrases that are battlefields for political and moral argument. (Other examples include *patriot* and *liberal*.) Such arguments are characterized by a high level of emotion, and repeated protestations as to the true meaning of the words in contention. As different factions lay claim to such words and the right to define them as they see fit, their usefulness in ordinary discourse seems to be diminished. This is certainly the case with hacking. To some people the essence of hacking is an innocent technological curiosity that is essentially beneficial to human progress. From this perspective, hacking was the driving force behind the development of personal computers and many other aspects of information technology. To others, hacking is a willful and dangerous disregard for the rights of others, including electronic breaking and entering, the trashing of valuable data, and the fraudulent use of stolen account numbers.

Clearly, the gulf between these two extremes is a wide one, full of muddled and convoluted definitions that attempt to encompass elements of both extremes. The term hacker becomes a slur or an honor depending upon your point of view. The hacker can be convincingly portrayed as either hero or villain, and both images are correct until there is a single agreed definition of hacking. In the absence of such a definition, it is necessary to qualify the terms of the debate so that discussions can continue. The following is an attempt to categorize the various activities that are currently called hacking by one or more factions in the debate. You are left to decide which of them is true hacking, the domain of the real hacker.

Passive Hacking

Passive hacking is the exploration of systems with an eye to understanding how they work and what information they contain. There is no desire to alter the way the system works or use for gain the information discovered. This is relatively harmless hacking, although there can be negative effects. The intruder might leave open "doors" into the system that more active hackers then exploit. The simple act of examining files could result in accidental damage. Processing time could be consumed and network channels blocked.

Active Hacking

Active hacking is exploration plus attempts to alter the way the targeted system works, tinker with it, and use the information discovered, possibly to further explore.

A typical example is breaking into the password file to collect passwords that can then be used for further attacks. In the *Hacker's Handbook*, Steve Gold describes hackers making changes to a password system to lock out employees of the British phone company, in a successful attempt to disrupt a public demonstration of a new videotext service. Some people enjoy this sort of activity and fall back on the "we were showing them how weak their security was" defense. More sinister is the use of access and account numbers to enable a hacker to use services, including the telephone, without charge. This simply fuels additional hacking.

Hired Hacking

The account of hacking by Clifford Stohl in *The Cuckoo's Egg* shows that, as with all activity on the fringe of legality, there is the potential for it to be turned "to the dark side." Hacking for pay poses a serious threat to society as well as to commerce because just about every institution, from the military to schools and hospitals, now relies on computers. Although the cold war might be over, the world is not yet at peace. The mobilization of military forces against Saddam Hussein revealed just how reliant on computers and communications the world's armies have become. Virus attacks as an offensive weapon, as described by science fiction author William Gibson, are not beyond the realm of possibility.

HACKING AND THE LAW

You might think that it would be automatically against the law to commit the electronic acts of voyeurism, breaking and entering, and theft that constitute a significant part of hacking. In fact, until recently, the legal status of hacking has been far from clear. This was largely because of the difficulty of finding traditional definitions of crime that could be applied to the high-tech deeds committed by hackers.

In recent years, many Western countries have passed new legislation to cover the many aspects of hacking. In the U.S., many states decided not to wait for federal action and passed state legislation outlawing some aspects of hacking, usually making it possible to arrest someone for damaging records, releasing malignant code, or trespassing in unauthorized areas. There have now been convictions for committing most of the acts that constitute hacking, and most countries seem keen to make it clear that hacking is not an acceptable pastime.

On the other hand, some voices have been raised in defense of hacking, most notably Apple Computer cofounder Steve Wozniak and former Lotus executive Jim Manzi. Some circles fear that legislation and legal rulings made by those who do not fully understand the world of computing could create an excessively restrictive environment, one in which creativity would be stifled.

ANTI-HACKING PROTECTION

While the debate over who hackers are and what constitutes hacking is considerable, nobody is denying that for some people breaching computer security is a form of recreation. The immediate concern of this book is the implications of this fact for the security of your computer(s).

Concrete Protection

If you have read any of the preceding chapters of this book, you will know that there are plenty of hardware and software products available to help you secure your computers and data against attack. You can also implement plenty of inexpensive practical measures to improve security. These cover attacks from inside your organization and from outside forces. Taken together these can be summarized as:

1. Setting up access controls for sites, systems, and files. This makes sure that only authorized users can get to valuable files.
2. Make sure the controls are used. Let users know that there are penalties for failure to comply.
3. As well as keeping people out, access controls should record who comes in, who uses systems, and who makes use of files.
4. Make sure that all valuable data is backed up and all critical systems can be brought back quickly in case of a successful attack.

What you have here is concrete protection, tangible steps that create and maintain security. Beyond this are aspects of security that are intangible. Referred to as theoretical protection, this involves the right attitude, an appropriate level of awareness, as well as something called pre-emptive thinking.

Theoretical Protection

The idea behind theoretical protection is that you must understand the nature of the threats that you face in order to maintain effective security against them. Theoretical protection is not provided by machines, but by the people running those machines. The first and second rules of theoretical protection can be stated thus:

- Complete security is attainable only when all threats have disappeared.
- All threats will never disappear.

Two of the biggest mistakes to make in security are overestimating the strength of the security systems you have in place, or underestimating the ingenuity of the attacker, which often amount to the same thing. Theoretical protection aims to prevent these mistakes and is characterized by attitude, awareness, and a suitable amount of forward thinking.

Attitude and Awareness. To make the most of concrete security measures, you need to understand the problems. You need to know the most likely sources of attack, the most likely targets, and the appropriate levels of response. The correct attitude with which to approach security issues is somewhere between the extremes of complacency and paranoia. Only an attitude that is appropriate to the situation can avoid being ineffectual on the one hand, and counterproductive restrictions on the other.

Installing an expensive perimeter security system and insisting that all computers be locked away at night is pointless if your most likely attacker is an insider selling copies of data files to your competitor. Subjecting loyal employees to intimidating biometric access controls is pointless if the most likely method of attack is external eavesdropping on your mainframe uplink.

A useful exercise in attitude and awareness is to imagine your car has broken down in a rough part of town. If you act in a scared and paranoid manner, you are inviting trouble. On the other hand, swagger too confidently and you might provoke a challenge. You leave ostentatious accoutrements locked in the car rather than carried like flags proclaiming your status. You avoid eye contact as you walk to the nearest phone, but you walk confidently so as not to reveal fear. You are alert to your surroundings, calculating potential threats, and preparing suitable responses—negotiation, fight, or flight. You are working on contingency plans in case none of these options succeed, how to minimize the losses and the injuries. All of this is theoretical security, and it must be used in conjunction with concrete security (in the scenario—the police whistle, can of mace, and so on) to inform and guide its application.

Pre-emptive Thinking. Much of the theory of security applies across many different fields of human activity, from banking to national defense. In all areas, those responsible for security must constantly think through all of the possible threats, particularly those that have not yet materialized but which new developments in science and technology have made feasible. For example, consider the cellular car phone. Immediately recognized as a productivity tool by businessmen who spend a lot of time on the road, these devices have sold like hotcakes. They sold particularly well in Silicon Valley, a hotbed of entrepreneurial activity, crisscrossed with a highway system that regularly grinds to a halt. Not long after car phones started to become popular, radio enthusiasts found you could tune in conversations using specialized radio equipment. This fact quickly went from merely interesting to downright alarming as businesses realized that their mobile phone calls could be tapped. The point is that in some cases, company security was breached because people failed to anticipate the threat of eavesdropping. Pre-emptive thinking would have put cellular phone users on guard before some of them said things they later came to regret.

When it comes to computer security, the implications of new technology are particularly difficult to grasp, resulting in particular need for pre-emptive thinking, the anticipation of new threats. Apart from the fact that it often takes a long time for all of the implications of new developments in computers to be understood, the profession is thick with people of exceptional ingenuity and intelligence, not to mention irreverence and audacity.

SUMMARY

Engendering loyal, well-informed, competent, and contented workers is the best computer security measure you can take. Remember, it is people who lose, steal, or compromise valuable information. If you know your staff, work closely with them, understand them, and educate them, you will be in a much better position to prevent breaches of security and to recover from them when they occur, as inevitably they will.

   The less need an organization has to keep secrets, the less need it has for security. The organization that is excessively defensive is likely to spark resentment and provoke attack. On the other hand, a benevolent view of people needs to be tempered with realism. The organization that fails to anticipate the next form of mischief or dishonesty is likely to suffer as a result.

   There will always be people who get a kick out of electronic trespassing, exploration, and eavesdropping.

*I fear none of the existing machines; what I fear is
the extraordinary rapidity with which they are becoming
something very different to what they are at present.
Should not that movement be jealously watched, and
checked while we can still check it?*

Samuel Butler, *The Book of Machines*, 1872

14
Conclusions and
Future Developments

ONE OF THE MAIN AIMS of this book has been to provide practical assistance to
those seeking to protect personal computer resources and the information they are
used to manage. Another was to give some theoretical basis for making decisions
about security. Although only in its second decade, the world of personal computing is
already so complex and multifarious that specific advice to meet every possible set of
circumstances is beyond the scope of a single text. This means that it is important to
have some basic guidelines and principles from which to work, rules of thumb that
can be applied as new situations arise. Throughout the book lists of rules, tips, and
suggestions have been presented. This chapter pulls these lists together, and gives
them a spin, an orientation, towards the future.

GRAND SUMMARY

The following lists recap, in abbreviated format, the main points of the book:

Personal computer security is:

- Letting personal computers get on with what they do best.
- Freedom to enjoy the benefits of personal computers without negative consequences.
- Freedom to use personal computers without fear of disruption or outside interference.

As computer technology advances, the distinctions between different types of computers continue to get blurred. A personal computer is a small computer designed around a central processing unit that is contained in a single integrated circuit or micro-chip, the microcomputer contains all of the basic features of a larger system, but together in a single unit serving a single user. The unit might actually be several small boxes cabled together, but the whole thing will fit on or under a desk, providing one person with the ability to enter, process, store, and retrieve data, without reference to or assistance from any other facilities.

The users of personal computers are:

- Private users. These people use personal computers for their personal enjoyment or benefit. Work that they perform with the personal computer is for themselves and not for an organization. These users own the personal computers they use. They must take care of their own security, which faces a limited number of threats.

- Group users. These people use personal computers as part of their work for an organization. In most cases these users work on personal computers owned by the organization. These users have a responsibility to support the security policies of the organization. They face a wide range of threats.

- Supporting users. These people support, assist, or manage, group users. They have some level of responsibility for the personal computer resources of an organization. These users must implement security programs and policies that cover every possible area of threat.

Not enough users:

- Know exactly what is stored on their computer.
- Perform regular backups.
- Use password protection.
- Use all the locks that exist between their data and the outside world.

Value in a personal computer system consists of:

- The hardware itself.
- The software used by the hardware to process information.
- The information that is processed.
- The system's ability to continue doing the processing.

Value of information in a personal computer consists of:

- The value to you.
- The value to others.
- The negative value.
- The value of immediate access.

Planning for personal computer security involves:

- Risk evaluation: What are the risks, and what is the value of what is at risk.
- Security policy: What practices should be followed, what devices used, and what is the allocation of responsibility.
- Contingency plan: What should be done to recover from a major security incident.

Risk evaluation should answer these questions:

What are you trying to protect?
What is its value to you or your organization?
What are you trying to protect against?
What is the likelihood of an attack?

The major areas of threat are:

Fire, destroying equipment and files.
Common theft, taking equipment and files.
Vandalism, damaging equipment and files.
Equipment failure, damaging files.
Screw-ups, damaging files.
Virus damage, damaging files.
Earthquake, destroying equipment and files.
Unauthorized access, leaking sensitive data.
Data theft, spreading data without fee.
Fraud, diverting funds by computer.

For security planning, you need to know this about your hardware:

Serial number.
Date of purchase.
Vendor.
Warranty period.
Maintenance contract.
Current location of equipment.
Current location of manual.

For security planning, you need to know this about your software:

Serial number.
Original version number.
Date of purchase.
Vendor.
Software registration.
Current location of manual.

Current version number.
Date of last update.

You need to know this about each station:

- Is there a keyboard lock? This should be used.
- Who has the key(s)? These should be controlled.
- How skilled is the user? Low level of skill means a potential source of data loss, high skill level could weaken effectiveness of simple defense.
- Does the software being used have undo capability? This should be turned on.
- Does the system have format capability? Remove if practical, or install protection.
- Does the system have unerase and unformat capability? If not, install.
- Is a disk optimizing program installed/used? If not, install.
- Is personal software used? If so, is it guaranteed/approved?
- How complex is the operating environment? The more complex, the greater the potential problems.
- What type of backup device is installed? The first line of defense—only diskless personal computers lack a backup device.
- Is there an automated backup procedure? If not, install one.
- Is the backup media stored securely? If not, why do backup?
- Is the backup performed regularly? Use backup file dates or operating activity logs to check this.
- Is the computer connected to another system, either by modem of local wiring? If so, protect access with suitable controls.

Categories of data to be protected:

- Decision-critical: Data that is used as the basis of decision-making, for example, budget projections, or current inventory.
- Operational: Data that is an integral part of operations, for example, daily transaction accounts, time sheets.
- Archival: Data that is retained for record-keeping purposes, for example, purchase orders, invoices, and correspondence.
- Convenience: Data that is retained because it might be useful at some point in the future, for example, expired contracts kept because the language might be used in new contracts.

Always ask:

What can go wrong?
How often can it happen?
What will be the consequences?
How certain are the answers to the first three questions?

Perform risk analysis by describing:

1. What could go wrong?
2. What the impact would be?
3. What should be done to minimize 2 and prevent 1?
4. How should you react when 1 happens anyway?

To support users within an organization:

- Post security rules.
- Circulate regular security warnings.
- Formulate security incentives.
- Institute security checks.
- Open a security hotline.

The "Top 20" lines of defense are:

1. Users who are responsible, trustworthy, knowledgeable, and who have incentives to uphold security policies.
2. Clearly-defined security policies based on regularly updated risk analyses, backed by a contingency plan, administered by well-defined organizational structure.
3. Regularly made and safely-stored backup copies of all important files.
4. Controlled access to the site where computing takes place.
5. Controlled log-on to computing systems and monitoring of usage.
6. Controlled access to files within systems and monitoring of activity.
7. A clean and uninterrupted supply of power to essential systems.
8. A comprehensive database of hardware and software resources together with registration of ownership.
9. Insurance against natural disasters, fire, fraud, and theft, covering direct and indirect losses.
10. Well-maintained equipment, backed by maintenance contracts, with provision for "loaners" in case of equipment failure.
11. A well-policed scheme for authorizing all software used and all copies made.
12. Controlled access to all channels of communication between computers, whether by phone lines or network cabling.
13. Centralized responsibility for network security to ensure effective use of security services within network operating software.
14. Shielding against electronic eavesdropping and line-tapping where appropriate.
15. Controls on output devices, ensuring that screen displays and printed reports are only seen by those who need to, plus all sensitive printed materials, floppy disks, manuals, reports, and other "loose" information.
16. Controls on hardware to prevent unauthorized removal, disconnection, or tampering.

17. Regular security awareness meetings to maintain an appropriate level of interest, concern, and compliance.
18. Incentives to enforce security compliance.
19. Disincentives to penalize security lapses.
20. A sense of proportion, ensuring that security procedures do not become excessively restrictive and thus counter-productive.

THE LAYERED APPROACH

Throughout the book, successive security measures have been portrayed as a series of layers, each complementing the other to build up a comprehensive pattern of protection. The complete picture can be seen diagrammed in Fig. 14-1, and summarized as follows:

Access control
  Site   Controlling who can get near the system.
  System   Controlling who can use the system.
  File   Controlling who can use specific files.

System support
  Power   Keeping supply of power clean and constant.
  Backup   Keeping copies of files current.
  Vigilance   Keeping tabs on what enters the system.

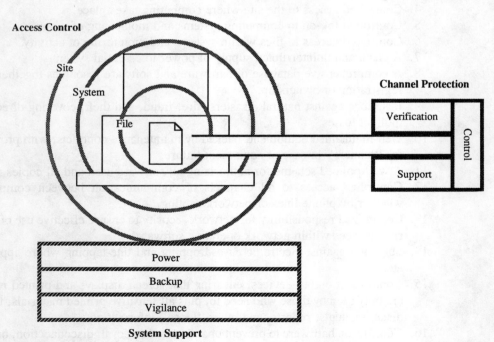

Fig. 14-1. The layered approach to security.

Channel protection
> *Channel control*   Who can open a channel, use a channel, close a channel.
> *Channel verification*   The identity of the users, integrity of the data, integrity of the channel.
> *Channel support*   Keeping the channel in good working order.

THE NEXT FRONT

Guessing what the future holds for personal computers is not easy, and on the whole this book has avoided making definitive statements about what will happen next. There is little point in statements such as "by 1999 we will all be using retinal scan access control units." For a start, there is no way to know what the personal computer of 1999 will look like. For example, if we are all using notebook-size computers by then, security will be a different story (controlling access to something that can be locked away in a desk drawer is quite different from keeping a desktop unit on the desk). However, some general trends can be discerned and these will be examined, after a suitable disclaimer.

The Problem with Prediction

The history of the personal computer industry is littered with false predictions. These range from product release dates to announcements of "The Year of *Trend X*." While some speculation about the future is useful, you would think that company executives would have learned by now not to go overboard with claims about what will happen next. Two factors in particular seem to doom such claims: The recurrence of good ideas, and persistence of the power gap.

The Recurrence of Good Ideas. People tend to write off any idea which is hailed as a step forward, but then falters in the marketplace. This leads analysts to overlook the potential of such ideas to reappear in new and more commercially viable guises. A good example of the recurrence of good ideas is ROM-based software. Prior to 1985, several personal computers appeared with the capacity to accept ROM-based software, as opposed to software loaded from disk. These included the Acorn BBC Microcomputer and Hewlett-Packard 110 laptop (into which you could plug 1-2-3 on a chip). Both machines failed to capture significant market share in the U.S., and sales were discontinued within a few years. Now it seems that some form of ROM, possibly the credit card chips used in sub-laptop machines, might emerge as a preferred means of software distribution, being hard-to-copy, tamper-proof, and more reliable than floppy disks.

The Gee-Whiz Gap. New technology can be described, and applications for it can be imagined, long before working prototypes are made. Working prototypes can be publicized long before commercial production begins. The first commercially produced product sells for more than the clones that follow. Taken together, these facts of technological life in the world of personal computers mean that there is often a long gap between the initial enthusiasm for new hardware and software developments, and the widespread use of products embodying those developments. This poses a problem for those who prognosticate about future trends in the industry because such persons are often privy to the latest developments, often as they emerge from the smoke of speculation, and certainly well before they hit the shelves of your local dealer. It is all too easy for an experienced user to enthuse over a new piece of hardware or software without realizing that it solves a problem that the rank-and-file user does not yet realize exists. The point is that future trends cannot be reliably predicted purely on the basis of the latest gizmos to emerge from the labs. You have to look at what users will be trying to accomplish by the time the new technology hits the streets. For example, a promising new device for shielding against electronic eavesdropping will not seem so promising if there is a big rush to low voltage laptops with color LCD displays and fiberoptic cabling.

The Trends

While the specifics of future developments are hard to pin down, and the art of prediction notably flawed, some general trends are unmistakable:

- Personal computer security will continue to be a major concern of business and institutional users.
- Intercomputer connections will increase, placing relatively greater emphasis on network security in the broadest sense of that term.
- Personal computers, particularly in network configurations, will handle more of the work previously done by larger mainframes, work that is mission critical.
- Personal computer technology will become increasingly sophisticated, with computers continuing to get smaller and more powerful.
- Technology in general will become increasingly sophisticated, opening up new chinks in whatever security systems are put in place.

A bleak picture can be painted; security threats are on the increase just as personal computers reach the point where they are being assigned critical tasks. Each new item of defensive technology seems doomed to defeat at the hands of increasingly sophisticated attackers wielding yet more technology.

The optimistic perspective is that the personal computer is maturing as a technology, finally receiving attention in those areas, such as security and reliability, which were not important when the personal computer was not taken seriously. The awareness of security is growing rapidly. A few basic security measures can result in a tremendous increase in security. Only further down the road towards maximum security will each new measure have only a minimal impact. You can see this diagrammed in Fig. 14-2.

Products to Look For

Having cautioned against predictions, some specific future developments can be anticipated.

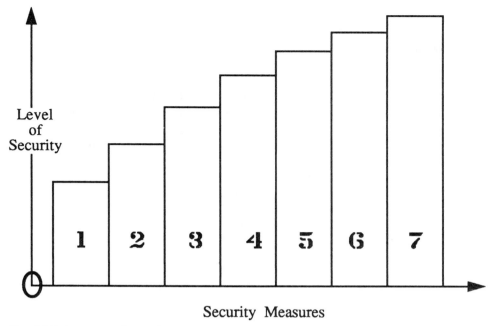

Fig. 14-2. Incremental security.

Secure Systems. Look for more personal computers to be fitted with security features as standard, including custom BIOS and operating system extensions to provide user identification, file access control, and so on. Also look for more security features to be included in future releases of the major operating systems. Look for more and more users to switch from desktop systems to laptops, which are easier to lock away and use screens that cannot be read by electronic eavesdropping equipment.

Fault Tolerant Systems. Look for more sophisticated personal computer hardware, particularly in the area of file servers, with built-in fault tolerant features, such as disk duplexing, integral uninterruptible power supplies, and automated backup.

High-Capacity/Speed Removable Media. Look for more and more megabytes in smaller and smaller packaging, such as the 20 megabyte floppy and the 2-inch hard disk. Adopting high capacity/speed removable media is probably the single biggest hardware step you can take towards greater security. Backups are easier, quicker, and more secure. Data can be locked away. High capacity/speed removable media will solve many of the problems that come from leaving valuable data trapped on top of your desk in a suitcase-sized box with holes in it.

Biometrics. For those situations that warrant biometric access control of user access control, smaller, cheaper, and more accurate devices will be coming onto the market. (To go out on a limb: The development of hand-writing recognition systems for pen-operated "notebook" style computers might well result in cheap electronic "sign-on" systems.)

Fax. Few methods of communication have grown as fast as fax, largely because of its convenience factor. Increasingly users are integrating fax devices into personal computers. Be aware that the ability to send data straight from a hard disk file to a piece of paper on the other side of the world in a matter of minutes, creates considerable security problems. Fax is a valuable tool, to the bad guys as well as the good.

Encryption and Communications. All manner of systems are being developed to permit communications from anywhere to anywhere of anything, from voice to fax to files. Users of such systems will need to be particularly vigilant against eavesdropping, interference, and interception. You can assume that anything you or your communications provider can beam from one place to another can be picked up by either the well-equipped professional or the ingenious amateur. Use of encryption for all sensitive information would seem to be inevitable. However, with desktop computers now capable of almost as many calculations per second as the most powerful super-computer of five years ago, all systems of encryption now have to be seen as at least a little bit suspect.

CONCLUSION

The goal of personal computer security is to protect and foster the increased creativity and productivity made possible by a technology that has so far flourished with a minimum of controls, but which finds itself increasingly threatened by the very openness that led to its early success. To achieve this goal, you must step from an age of trusting innocence into a new era of realism and responsibility, without lurching into paranoia and repression.

Technology itself is neutral, it lacks any moral content. The users of technology determine whether it is applied to positive or negative ends. The most cost-effective long-term approach to personal computer security is the promotion of mature and responsible attitudes among users. Lasting security will not be achieved by technology, nor by constraints on those who use it. True security can only be achieved through the willing compliance of users with universally accepted principles of behavior. Such compliance will increase as society as a whole becomes increasingly computer literate, and users understand the personal value of the technology they use.

Appendix A
Company Listing

THIS APPENDIX PROVIDES a list of companies offering relevant security products. Every effort has been made to include here all companies whose products are mentioned in the text, plus others who have related offerings. This listing is roughly alphabetical by company name. A number of non-U.S. companies are listed; to call these companies, you must use the appropriate international dialing codes.

Given the speed with which the computer industry changes, the accuracy of addresses and phone numbers cannot be guaranteed. Detailed product descriptions have also been avoided because specifications are subject to such rapid change. Nevertheless, this should be a good starting point. In future editions of this book, the list will be updated.

Absolute Security Inc.
63 Great Road
Maynard, MA 01754
(508) 897-1991
Management, audit, and security controls for PC LANs.

AEG (UK) Ltd.
217 Bath Road
Slough, Berks, SL1 4AW
United Kingdom
0753 872101
Fire protection and uninterruptible power supplies.

AES Corporation
285 Newbury Street
Peabody, MA 01960
(508) 535-7310
Access controls, protective doors, corporate security. Specialized security equipment and services.

AOE International, Inc.
2137 Flintstone Drive
Tucker, GA 30084
(404) 934-2244
Strategic and tactical level encryption systems for voice and facsimile.

American Power Conversion Corp.
350 Columbia Street
Peace Dale, RI 02883
(401) 789-5735
  Backup power supply systems.

Astronautics Corporation of America
P.O. Box 523
Milwaukee, WI 53201
(414) 447-8200
  Makers of COP (Communication Oriented Processor), an intelligent communication control system which adapts and directs data flow between selected resources, regardless of their characteristics.

Atalla Corporation
2304 Zanker Road
San Jose, CA 95131
(408) 435-8850
  Leading vendor of customer identification, card management, network interchange, electronic data interchange (EDI), and computer security solutions.

AutoSIG Systems
P.O. Box 165050
Irving, TX 75016
(214) 258-8033
  Signature recognition systems.

A & G Security Electronics Plc.
Wrigley Street
Oldham, Lancs OL4 1HW
United Kingdom
061633 3033
  Electronic intruder and fire detection, personal attack/emergency systems and communicators.

Belling Lee Intec Ltd.
540 Great Cambridge Road
Enfield, Middlesex EN1 3QW
United Kingdom
01367 0080
  Technology for protecting electronic equipment and systems against interference, including Tempest.

BBSoft (Richard B. Levin)
9405 Bustleton Avenue
Philadelphia, PA 19115
(215) 333-6922

Computer Sciences Company Ltd.
Finance and Security Division
Heathcoat House
20 Saville Row
London W1X 1AE
United Kingdom
01439 6252
   Consultants in security strategy, security reviews, risk analysis, PC security, and network security.

Computer Security Consultants Inc.
454 Main Street
Ridgefield, CT 06877
(203) 431-8720
   Computer-based tools designed for security staff: Contingency Plan, Directives and Procedures, Audit and Review Diary.

Computer Security Consultants "Coseco" International B.V.
Westblaak 91
3012 KG Rotterdam
The Netherlands
010 4331977
   Interactive, PC-based automated risk assessment software.

Computer Security Ltd.
Oliver House
18 Marine Parade
Brighton, East Sussex
United Kingdom
0273 672191
   Products for securing electronic information within data processing systems and networks.

Concord-Eracom Nederland BV
Hoekenrode 8
1102 BR Amsterdam
The Netherlands
020 913 781
   Development and implementation of custom security systems, delivery of hard and software security components.

Computer Accessories Corporation
6610 Nancy Ridge Drive
San Diego, CA 92121
(619) 457-5500
   Backup power supply systems.

Campbell Engineering Company
2540 Bates Avenue
Concord, CA 94520
(415) 689-7212
 Site access control including card readers, PINs, and biometrics.

ComNetco Inc.
2475 Lamington Road
Bedminster, NJ 07921
(201) 781-7940
 Enclosures both floor standing and wall mounting electronic equipment, RFI shielded.

Computer Power, Inc.
124 West Main Street
High Bridge, NJ 08829
(201) 638-8000
 Backup power supply systems.

Coopers and Lybrand Associates, Ltd.
Plumtree Court
London EC4A 4HT
United Kingdom
01822 4552
 Specialist security consultants.

Core International
7171 North Federal Highway
Boca Raton, FL 33487
(407) 997-6055
 Makers of tape backup units for all types of personal computers.

Cotag International
Mercers Row
Cambridge CB5 8EX
United Kingdom
0223 321535
 Hands-free access building control systems.

Cryptech
Lloyd George Avenue 7
B-1050 Brussels
Belgium
32 2 645 2931
 Wide range of encryption and security devices for computers of all sizes, covering RSA and DES technology.

Cuesta Systems Corporation
3440 Roberto Court
San Luis Obispo, CA 93401
(850) 541-4160
   Manufacturer of uninterruptible power supply systems for network and stand-alone personal computers.

DRS Power Products, Inc.
2065 Range Road
Clearwater, FL 34625
(813) 443-0345
   Backup power supply systems.

Data Encryption Systems Ltd.
Edbrook House
Cannington, Bridgewater, Somerset TA5 2QE
United Kingdom
0278 653 456
   Dongles used for portable data security and for corporate users to stop internal software copying/stealing.

DMR Group Inc.
1200 McGill College Avenue
Montreal, QB H3B 4G7
Canada
(514) 877-3301
   Consultancy and support in security, including risk assessment, security reviews, security policy, encryption, access controls, and contingency planning.

Data Innovation Ltd.
39 Mark Road
Hemel Hempstead, Herts HP2 7DN
United Kingdom
0442 50312
   Cryptographic products, packet switching encryption, comprehensive authentication, and key management systems.

Data Processing Security Inc.
200 East Loop 820
Fort Worth, TX 76112
(817) 457-9400
   Security management surveys, physical security, data security appraisals, and disaster recovery plan development.

Datastripe Ltd.
461 London Road
Camberley, Surrey GU15 3JA
United Kingdom
0276 684 066
     Card readers/encoders designed for inclusion in terminals, access control devices, tills and so on.

Datong Electronics Ltd.
Clayton Wood Close
West Park, Leeds LS16 6QE
United Kingdom
0532 744 822
     Personal and executive anti-bugging devices.

Digital Dispatch, Inc.
55 Lakeland Shores
St. Paul, MN 55043
(612) 436-1000
     Data Physician is a set of programs designed to help protect PC-DOS or MS-DOS computer systems from software viruses and logic bombs.

Director Technologies, Inc.
906 University Place
Evanston, IL 60201
(312) 491-2334
     Disk Defender, a powerful anti-virus system.

Deloitte Haskins & Sells
128 Queen Victoria Street
London EC4P 4JX
United Kingdom
     Security software for microcomputers and security consulting.

Disk Technologies
P.O. Box 1750
Winter Park, FL 32789
(407) 645-0001
     Makers of removable hard disks for laptop PCs.

Diebold Incorporated
P.O. Box 8230
Canton, OH 44711
(216) 489-4000
     A wide range of security products including alarm monitoring, access control, and video surveillance.

Digital Dispatch, Inc.
55 Lakeland Shores Road
Lakeland, IN 55043
(800) 221-8091
    Anti-virus programs.

Digital Pathways Inc.
201 Ravendale Drive
Mountain View, CA 94043
(415) 964-0707
    Large data and computer network access security systems.

Dorado Systems Corporation
1842 Sabre Street
Hayward, CA 94545
(415) 783-2000
    Encrypted magnetic stripe cards and readers used with access control systems.

Dowty Information Systems Limited
Newbury Business Park
London Road
Newbury, Berks RG13 2PZ
United Kingdom
0635 33009
    Secure modems multiplexers and network management products.

Emerson Computer Power
3300 South Standard Street
Santa Ana, CA 92702
(714) 545-5581
    Backup power supply systems.

EDP Security Inc.
7 Beaver Brook Road
Littleton, MA 01460
(508) 486-8080
    Automated contingency planning.

Eccleston Technology
351 Lichfield Road
Aston, Birmingham
United Kingdom
021327 7626
    Emergency, standard, and uninterruptible power supplies.

Edicon, A Kodak Company
95 Allens Creek Road
Rochester, NY 14618
(716) 271-2950
    Photo image management systems for computerized security databases.

Ecco Industries
130 Centre Street
Danvers, MA 01923
(508) 777-7750
    Voice recognition systems.

EyeDentity
P.O. Box 3U327
Portland, OR 97208
(503) 645-0567
    Retinal scan identity systems.

Encore Computer Corporation
6901 West Sunrise Boulevard
Ft. Lauderdale, FL
(305) 587-2900
    Computer systems with a secure implementation of the Unix operating system.

Ensign Communications Ltd.
6/7 The Omega Centre
Sandford Lane
Wareham, Dorset BH20 4DY
United Kingdom
09295 6553
    Secure communications access controllers and data call logging equipment.

Ernst & Whinney
2000 National City Center
Cleveland, OH 44114
(216) 861-5000
    A full range of information security services to clients throughout the world.

Europa Sysems Ltd.
Mill Works
Tonbridge Wells, Kent TN9 1PE
United Kingdom
0732 353 217
    Physical security devices, including locks that prevent unauthorized access to the on/off switch, power locks, and floppy disk locks.

Exide Electronics Corp.
3301 Spring Forest Road
Raleigh, NC 27604
(919) 872-3020
   Backup power supply systems.

First Inertial Systems
61 Lower Road
Harrow, Middlesex HA2 ODE
United Kingdom
01864 7534
   Access control systems.

Fischer International Systems Corporation
4073 Merchantile Avenue
Naples, FL 33942
(813) 643-1500
   Comprehensive personal computer data security software.

Fingermatrix
30 Virginia Road
North White Plains, NY 10603
(914) 428-5441
   Fingerprint identity systems.

FoundationWare
13110 Shaker Square
Cleveland, OH 44120
(216) 752-8181
   System management software to protect the integrity of data, prevent user errors, and automatically recover in the event of a hard disk crash. Also Vaccine, a commercial anti-virus product.

GPT Data Systems
Secure Systems Business
Elstree Way
Borehamwood, Hertfordshire WD6 1RX
United Kingdom
01953 2030
   Secure communications processors providing special security features for such applications as network interfaces, file servers, and terminal access control.

Gelosia Limited
17-19 St. Georges Street
Norwich, Norfolk NR3 1AB
United Kingdom
0603 617506
   HMX cipher system, a proprietary algorithm of enormous strength and flexibility.

Glenco Engineering Inc.
721 West Algonquin Road
Arlington Heights, IL 60005
(312) 364-7638
   Copy protection products and tools.

Gretag Data Systems
Althardstrasse 70
CH-8105 Regensdorf
Switzerland
   Encryption and authentication, in data network for commercial customers and institutions.

General Power Systems
1045 South East Street
P.O. Box 65008
Anaheim, CA 92805
(800) 854-3469
   Backup power supply systems.

Art Hill
936 South Kensington Avenue
La Grange, IL 60525
   Vaccine 1.3, shareware anti-virus software.

Hotsite CompuSource
110 MacKenan Drive
Cary, NC 27511
(919) 460-1234
   Fully equipped recovery centers, relocatable shell facilities, PC-based disaster recovery planning services, and data communications network backup.

Information Integrity
P.O. Box 1219
Sausalito, CA 94966
(415) 332-7763
   Consulting and research in information systems security.

Inmac (UK) Ltd.
Westerly Point
Bracknell, Berks RG12 1EW
United Kingdom
0344 424 333
   Catalog of computer supplies includes a range security equipment for PCs. Also in the United States.

IOMEGA1821
West 4000 Street
South Roy, UT 84067
(801) 778-3000

Makers of high-capacity removable disk systems, known as Bernoulli boxes.

ITT PowerSystems Corp.
1371 State Street, Suite 598
Galion, OH 44833
(419) 468-5200

Backup power supply systems.

International Electronic Technology Corporation
1931 Mott Avenue
Far Rockaway, NY 11691
(718) 327-1119

Supplier of security systems to protect microprocessor controlled equipment from unauthorized use and theft.

InterPath
4423 Cheeney Street
Santa Clara, CA 95054
(408) 988-3832

C-4 Antiviral Shield, anti-virus software for PCs. Tracer Virus Detector, commercial anti-virus software.

Jane's Information Group
Defense Data Division
Sentinel House
163 Brighton Road
Coulsdon, Surrey CR3 2NX
United Kingdom
017631030

Data on many areas of security, market intelligence reports, on-line services, journals, or confidential market reports.

Jaguar Communications Limited
Upper Marlborough Road
St. Albans, Herts AL1 3UU
United Kingdom
0727 41311

Data encryptors for point-to-point dial up links.

Jerry Fitzgerald & Associates
506 Barkentine Lane
Redwood City, CA 94065
(415) 591-5676

Information security consulting, development and sales of security-related software.

Jones Futurex Inc.
10933 Trade Centre Drive
Rancho Cordova, CA 95670
(916) 635-3972
DES and Mac products employing ANSI Standards X9.9 and X9.17 where appropriate.

Kaldo Electronics Co., Inc.
6584 Ruch Road
Bethlehem, PA 18017
(215) 837-0700
Backup power supply systems.

Kinetic Software Corporation
240 Distillery Commons
Louisville, KY 40206
(502) 583-1679
PC security software products.

Lattice, Inc.
2500 South Highland Avenue
Lombard, IL 60148
(312) 916-1600
Data encryption software packages.

LeeMah DataComm Security Corp.
3948 Trust Drive
Hayward, CA 94545
(415) 786-0790
Makes and designs communications security hardware to protect against unauthorized access on dial-up lines.

Lindgren RF Enclosures, Inc.
400 High Grove Boulevard
Glendale Heights, IL 60139
(312) 307-7200
Designing, manufacturing, installation, and testing of RF shielded enclosures for government, commercial, and medical use.

London Internal Security Systems Ltd.
67-69 Trinity Road
London SW17 7SD
United Kingdom
01767 778819

Designers, manufacturers, and suppliers of security, communication, and surveillance systems.

Paul Mace Software
499 Williamson Way
Ashland, OR 97520
(503) 488-0224

Mace Vaccine, a commercial anti-virus program, plus Mace Utilities, comprehensive operating system tools, including file and format recovery.

MIS Training Institute
498 Concord Street
Framingham, MA 01701
(508) 879-7999

Training, consultation, and publication in the fields of internal auditing, EDP auditing, and Information Security.

MLH Software Systems
1007 Chelten Parkway
Cherry Hill, NJ 08034
(609) 795-5257

NoVirus, shareware anti-virus software.

MPPi Ltd.
2200 LeHigh Avenue
Glenview, IL 60025
(312) 998-8401

Personal computer access control, encryption, and physical theft prevention.

MPL Power Systems Ltd.
Bilton Way
Hayes, Middlesex UB3 3NF
United Kingdom
01848 9871

Manufacture and installation of specialized power supply and protection systems for computers, aviation, and other critical loads.

Management Advisory Services & Publications
P.O. Box 81151
Wellesley Hills, MA 02181
(617) 235-2895

Consulting, management training (seminars), and professional publications on computer security, EDP auditing, and internal controls.

Micro Security Devices (PC Guardian)
118 Alto Street
San Rafael, CA 94901
(415) 459-0190

A complete range of data and theft protection products, including hardware devices, software security, and firmware boards.

Micro Expert Ltd.
95 Ditchling Road
Brighton, Sussex BN1 4SB
United Kingdom
0273 571989
　　Access control and audit trail software for personal computers.

Microft Technology Ltd.
The Old Powerhouse
Kew Gardens, Surrey TW9 3PS
United Kingdom
01948 8255
　　Personal computer security software.

Micronyx UK Limited
33 Linford Forum Drive
Linford Wood, Milton Keynes MK14 6LY
United Kingdom
　　Manufactures and markets a family of products to secure both networked and stand-alone personal computers.

Mordon Management Systems, Inc.
4480 Whittelodge Crescent
Mississauga, ON L5R 1S9
Canada
(416) 568-1428
　　Consulting in access control software and disaster recovery.

Motorola Ltd.
Colvilles Road
Kelvin Estate, East Kilbride G75 OTG
Scotland
03552 39101
　　Designer and manufacturer of secure microcomputers for Smart Card and Conditional Access systems.

Mynda Marketing and Manufacturing Co. Ltd.
Unit 6, Vauxhall Trading Est.
Duddeston Mill Road
Saltley, Birmingham B7 4RA
United Kingdom
0213591747
　　Manufacturers and designers of the Mynda secure storage systems.

NCR Corporation
1700 South Patterson Boulevard
Dayton, OH 45479
(513) 445-5000
Development and production of security hardware/software products for use in financial and retail environment.

National BBS Society
6226 Channel Drive
San Jose, CA 95123
(408) 727-4559
Universal Viral Simulator, available commercially to BBS (bulletin board services) operators to test their security systems.

National Computing Centre Ltd. (Security Division)
Oxford Road
Manchester M1 7ED
United Kingdom
061228 6333
Consultancy in all aspects of IT security, public and in-house courses and seminars, and publications.

Nordnet SDC AB
Bangardsgatan 6
S-582 31 Linkoping
Sweden
131149 80
Distribute and develop security systems for user identification and security in data transmission.

North American Morpho Systems, Inc.
1145 Broadway Plaza
Tacoma, WA 98402
(206) 383-3617
Biometric identification/verification systems and components in a highly parallel, distributed architecture for high-speed performance, high accuracy, and reliable operation.

Northern Computers
4915 South Howell Avenue
Milwaukee, WI 53207
(414) 769-5980
Manufacturer of small, medium, and large access control systems.

Oceonics SPL Ltd, Sypro Division
Gloucester Trading Estate
Hucclecote, Gloucester GL3 4AE
United Kingdom
0542 371044
Security studies and policy definitions through the implementation of secure systems to the lifetime support of such systems.

Okiok Data Ltd.
3945 St. Martin Boulevard West
Laval, Montreal, QB H7T 1B7
Canada
(514) 681-1681
Manufacturer of access control and data security products for microcomputers.

Jack A. Orman
Box 858
Southaven, MS 38671
Shareware program to encode a .COM program to make the data or programming techniques indecipherable.

PC Security Inc.
420 Lexington Avenue, Suite 1714
New York, NY 10170
(212) 949-1825
PC security products.

PC Power & Cooling, Inc.
31510 Mountain Way
Bosnall, CA 92003
(619) 723-9513
Makers of the InnerSource 2110, an internal UPS for PC systems.

Paxdata Ltd.
Communications House
Primrose Hill
Kings Langley, Hertfordshire WD4 8HX
United Kingdom
09277 61966
Secure modems and communications products.

Peat Marwick McLintock
1 Puddle Dock
Blackfriars, London EC4V 3PD
United Kingdom
01236 8000

A wide range of computer audit, control, and specialist computer security services.

PIDEAC
800 Livermore Street
Yellow Springs, OH 45387
(513) 767-7425
Personal identity verification systems.

Peter Norton Computing Inc.
100 Wilshire Boulevard 9th Floor
Santa Monica, CA
(213) 319-2000
A wide range of tools for supplementing personal computer operating systems, including file and format recovery.

RAM Computer Services Plc.
Synergy House
Eldon Place
Bradford, West Yorks
United Kingdom
0274 736 455
PC security software with transparent, automatic in-line encryption/decryption, subdirectory control, user access control, audit trail, and security log of system usage.

RSA Data Security Inc.
10 Twin Dolphin Drive
Redwood City, CA 94065
(415) 595-8782
Providing privacy and authentication solutions to OEM's and end-users on a wide variety of computing platforms. The RSA public-key cryptosystem is the technology basis for encryption and digital signatures in most of the company's products.

Racal Guardata
309 Fleet Road
Fleet, Hants GU13 8BU
United Kingdom
0252 622144
Comprehensive range of data security systems.

Racal Recorders Ltd.
Hardley Industrial Estate
Hythe, Southampton S04 6ZH
United Kingdom
0703 843 265
Make Elfin, a secure voice and data logger providing a log of both spoken and computer transmitted information.

Rainbow Technologies Inc.
18011-A Mitchell South
Irvine, CA 92714
(714) 261-0228
External hardware key approach to software protection (dongles).

Recognition Systems
1589 Provincetown Drive
San Jose, CA 95129
(408) 257-2477
Hand geometric recognition systems.

Robot (UK) Ltd.
Building 33
East Midlands Airport, Derby DE7 2SA
United Kingdom
0332 812 446
Slow scan video surveillance and other digital CCTV surveillance equipment.

Rodan Engineering Company Limited
5 Millbrook Business Park
Jarvis Brook
Crowborough, East Sussex TN6 3JZ
United Kingdom
0892 655188
Heavy-duty shredders for the destruction of files, disks, cassettes, and other types of products where the use of an obsolete product or article is to be prevented or made impossible for various reasons.

Rothstein Associates Inc.
13 Spring Pond Drive
Ossining, NY 10562
(914) 941-6867
Disaster recovery and business continuity planning.

Software Directions, Inc.
1572 Sussex Turnpike
Randolph, NJ 07869
(800) 346-7638
SoftSafe is a comprehensive security system for PCs.

Systems Designers
1 Pembroke Broadway
Camberley, Surrey GU15 3XH
United Kingdom
0276 622 44
PC-based information security and virus detection software and hardware.

Sola Electric
1717 Busse Road
Elk Grove Village, IL 60001
(312) 439-2800
    Backup power supply systems.

Scicon Networks
Wavendon Tower
Wavendon, Milton Keynes MK17 8LX
United Kingdom
0908 585 858
    Software access control systems.

ThumbScan
335 Eisenhower Lane South
Lombard, IL 60148
(312) 932-8844
    Fingerprint recognition systems.

Vault Corporation
2192 Anchor Court, Unit C
Newbury Park, CA 91320
(805) 499-5978
    Manufactures the Prolock disk for copy protection systems.

Virus Fax International
S&S Enterprises
Weylands Court, Water Meadow
Germin Street
Chesham, Bucks HP5 1LP
United Kingdom
0494 791900
    A newsletter that keeps you up-to-date on virus threats, faxed for speed (their fax is 0494 791602).

Viteq Corp.
10000 Aerospace Road
Lanham, MD 20706
(301) 731-0400
    Backup power supply systems.

Unison Technologies, Inc.
23456 Madero
Mission Viejo, CA 92691
(714) 855-8700
    Backup power supply systems.

World Wide Data Corp.
17 Battery Place
New York, NY 10004
(212) 422-4100
   Vaccine, a commercial anti-virus product.

——————Appendix B——————
Going On-Line for Security

ON-LINE BULLETIN BOARDS and databases provide a particularly powerful medium for the rapid spread of news and the world-wide exchange of information. When you equip your personal computer with a modem, you can connect with other users to share knowledge, views, and ideas. The on-line medium can be used to warn users of new viruses and other threats, and also to ask other users for help in solving virus-related problems. Specialized security programs can be distributed electronically, and updated very quickly.

One of the largest on-line systems for personal computer users is CompuServe (the full name is CompuServe Information Service, often abbreviated to CIS). You can now connect to CIS from most countries. Contact CIS for more detailed information on rates, subscriptions, and services:

CompuServe Information Service, Inc.
P.O. Box 20212
Columbus, OH 43220

The following list shows security-related files available on CompuServe, with file name, system, date, and size. The date refers to when the file was placed on the service, a process referred to as *uploading*. The act of receiving the file on your personal computer is referred to as *downloading*. Most communications programs allow you to use an error-checking system referred to as a *protocol*, such as XMODEM, to copy the file across the phone lines without disrupting the contents. Many of the files are compressed. IBM files that have the extension ARC can be unarchived with a program called ARCE. Mac users will find SIT files are unpacked with a program called Stuffit.

While IBM and Mac files are listed here, CIS has files for users of other systems such as Amiga, Atari, and so on. Some of the programs offered are freeware, others are shareware, meaning that if you use the program you must send payment to the author.

Name: NOBRK.ARC
System: IBM
Date: 05-Apr-88
Size: 5760
Description: A device driver to intercept Ctrl−C and Ctrl−Break. Install in CONFIG.SYS to secure system during boot. Enable and disable from the command line by writing to the driver with the included utility. Intended for systems with more than one user, or for systems with confidential material. Can be used at any time to prevent a

user from breaking into DOS. Install in 304 bytes in the BREAK OFF mode. Uploaded by author: Benjamin Diss.

Name: IFCRC.ARC
System: IBM
Date: 18-Mar-88
Size: 10234
Description: Control execution of DOS commands on CRC. IFCRC.EXE allows you to control execution of a DOS command in a batch file based on the CRC value of that file. The program can also be used to display the CRC value of any DOS file. It can be used to check a daily transfer from a remote site or even used to check for computer viruses. (Anyone with the intelligence to alter your COMMAND.COM without changing its CRC value probably would not waste his time writing a virus.)

Name: GS.EXE
System: IBM
Date: 05-Apr-90
Size: 76229
Description: GuardSet/Sentry customizable security. Create your own unique encrypt/decrypt program(s), especially for an automated log-on/off type of PC security system. Data integrity is assured, even in the event of a power loss during processing. Choose from many security levels, from very simple to virtually impregnable. Shareware $20. Programs, manual, and examples on self-extracting file. Phone support available from author. Another $20 gets you one-of-a-kind setup for even greater security.

Name: MSECRE.ARC
System: IBM
Date: 27-Nov-88
Size: 17024
Description: Memory-resident notepad for passwords and short name. The text is saved to 5.25 inch disks (only) and cannot be listed or deleted (by even DEL *.* or FORMAT) by regular means. Might not work on some 5.25-inch drives. Ideal for storing highly confidential information (passwords, etc.). Shareware. Uploaded by author Masaaki Sawada.

Name: PASS20.ZIP
System: IBM
Date: 10-Jun-90
Size: 33024
Description: PASSBOOT version 2.0 is a simple yet very useful computer password utility. Easy to setup and use. Use PASSBOOT to require a password when computer is booted or use from a batch file to add security to individual programs. User-selectable password with data encryption. Includes executable program and documentation. Shareware, fully functional, uploaded by author.

Name: PASSWO.ARC
System: IBM
Date: 21-Dec-88
Size: 1408
Description: PASSWORD is a small, easy to use computer security package. It prompts the user for a password before continuing. The default password can be changed and stored on the hard drive. A product of NECTAR software written in assembler, it is complete with documentation.

Name: DCSCAN.ARC
System: IBM
Date: 17-Oct-89
Size: 22746
Description: DataCrime anti-virus program, scans the specified disk and checks all COM & EXE files for the Datacrime (Columbus Day, Friday the 13th) virus. It is *very* fast because it only checks for three known strains (1168, 1280, and Datacrime 2). Note! Columbus Day has come and gone, but these viruses do not explode till you run the infected programs—you still should check for them. This is a *free* utility provided by Sector Technology.

Name: WCOM30.ZIP
System: IBM
Date: 29-Jan-90
Size: 16896
Description: This is version 3.0 of the WatchCom program. In theory, some viruses could attach themselves to one of the hidden system files (IO.SYS, IBMBIO.COM, MSDOS.SYS, and IBMDOS.COM) or the COMMAND.COM file. Then when the time is right, they corrupt your disk. WatchCom keeps track of your system files and will notify you if a change is noted. Put it in your AUTOEXEC.BAT routine, and have your files checked every time you boot up your computer. User supported.

Name: COLUMB.ARC
System: IBM
Date: 15-Sep-89
Size: 14080
Description: A set of programs that provides protection against the so-called Columbus Day Virus. Generally useful for programs that wipe out the partition table on the hard disk. The program stores the partition info on a floppy and can later restore that saved data onto the hard disk. Includes C source code, is public domain, and has no copy restrictions.

Name: INTCHA.ARC
System: IBM
Date: 03-Feb-88
Size: 9088

Description: This program allows you to detect if any program changes the interrupt vectors, or the interrupt routines, in your IBM (or compatible) system. All vectors or entries changed are listed. You can save a configuration to disk for comparison to a later configuration. Author: Dave Bushong, author of "Trojans."

Name: V-CHK.ARC
System: IBM
Date: 03-Jul-88
Size: 49280
Description: V_CHECK Series 1.0 was written to perform several tests on important and system files to provide a minimum of security in protecting software from the sting of some viruses. V_CHECK consists of six programs (no TSR) and has Turbo C source code available. Uploaded by author.

Name: EXERU.EXE
System: IBM
Date: 26-Nov-89
Size: 23691
Description: This can check if file size or date/time was changed. Check if BIOS and DOS changed. Request passwords. Check if other required software, such as TSR utilities, were already run.

Name: NOVIRU.EXE
System: IBM
Date: 05-Oct-89
Size: 39178
Description: Two similar anti-virus programs. The simpler one is in source and compiled format. The compiled versions are for DOS and OS/2. Complete instructions are included for protecting your executable files from nasty viruses. These programs are copyrighted by Sansaska Systems and are placed into the public domain *only in the current versions*. The second program is in compiled format only. Happy Columbus day.

Name: AIDSOU.ZIP
System: IBM
Date: 18-Dec-89
Size: 37248
Description: Program by Jim Bates, Bates Associates, U.K., to get rid of PC Cyborg trojan horse. *Caution*: Run SCAN version 1.8v52 (file SCAN52.ZIP) to determine if your system has this trojan horse, before using AIDSOUT.ZIP.

Name: AVS220.ZIP
System: IBM
Date: 23-Aug-90
Size: 74446
Description: AVSearch V 2.2 is a virus search program. Program searches for 135

virus strains in memory, partition table, boot record, and files. Has many options and a short description. AVSCrc, also included, is a CRC program. This package remains copyrighted, but you do not have to pay for use. Uploaded by coauthor.

Name: CKANS2.ARC
System: IBM
Date: 15-Nov-88
Size: 31104
Description: Anti-virus program that checks for harmful ANSI codes. Version 2 of CHKANSI; it checks text or any other file for harmful ANSI codes that might be embedded. ANSI codes embedded in a text file are capable of redefining your keyboard keys when the file is typed (i.e.: ERASE *.EXE). Use this program to scan those files before typing them! This is a family application (will run equally well with DOS or OS/2). This version runs on all CPU's. Uploaded by author.

Name: FICHK5.ARC
System: IBM
Date: 01-Jan-89
Size: 114060
Description: Non-TSR virus detection/file tracking system. Version 5 of "Fixed Disk File Integrity Check" system. Preventive medicine program for your entire disk system(s). Logs/checks entire file system for file size, date, time, attrib, CRC, and our unique MCRC because CRC alone is not adequate. Also logs/checks the master boot record/partition table and interrupt vectors. Reports on discrepancies found on these checks plus added/deleted/renamed files/directories. Uploaded by author.

Name: PROVEC.ARC
System: IBM
Date: 29-Jul-88
Size: 12288
Description: This program will prove that it can make an altered copy of a file and maintain its original CRC. It also explains how to get a system that is capable of detecting these changes based on our unique Modified CRC (MCRC) check.

Name: VACI15.ARC
System: IBM
Date: 29-Mar-89
Size: 21504
Description: Vaccine is a program to help protect you from the so-called virus programs. There are programs circulating that play tricks with your system and wipe out your hard disks. They "infect" your operating system and spread to other disks. Vaccine gives you some protection. Version 1.5 adds ability to bypass check. Not memory resident. Author Art Hill.

Name: VTAC47.ZIP
System: IBM

Date: 27-Aug-90
Size: 23552
Description: Tenacious little TSR that stops file infection and disk corruption from virus and trojan-horse programs. Easy to use; it is specially designed for those who hate anti-virus programs. Uses only 5K memory (shareware).

Name: CHKUP.EXE
System: IBM
Date: 29-Apr-90
Size: 134072
Description: Rich Levin's CHECKUP Version 3.9, the leading user-supported virus detection system. Thousands of users world-wide. Fast, accurate, and easy to use, CHECKUP detects all viruses—past, present, and future—without requiring software updates. Documentation includes an overview of anti-virus programs and protection techniques. Shareware registration fees are $24.95 for home users and $49.95 for office users. Rename to CHKUP39.EXE. Uploaded by author Rich Levin.

Name: ICHECK.ARC
System: IBM
Date: 09-Jul-90
Size: 9603
Description: ICHECK Version 1.00. This program saves and verifies the size and checksum of a list of files with the purpose of detecting the spread of viruses. Requires DOS 3.0 or higher. Shareware.

Name: FSP16.ARC
System: IBM
Date: 14-May-89
Size: 63284
Description: FLU_SHOT+, Version 1.6. An anti-virus program and winner of PC Magazine's coveted Editor's Choice for anti-viral products (issue 8/89). This version has some minor bug fixes, some enhancements, and better documentation. Includes boot-sector CRC, and more informative screens. Table driven, it allows you to protect files or classes of files from virus and Trojan activity. Shareware, $14.

Name: VALIDA.COM
System: IBM
Date: 16-Feb-88
Size: 8576
Description: VALIDATE can be used to alert you to unauthorized changes to critical files. For example, it can be used to validate COMMAND.COM to check for a system virus. It uses a proprietary checksum that can be keyed to make your checksum unique. This version (1.2) has a much-improved check algorithm. It is virtually impossible to change any part of a file without detection. To get the documentation, just run validate with no command line parameters.

Name: TECH.ARC
System: IBM
Date: 17-Sep-88
Size: 39552
Description: This is an anti-virus program that goes into your AUTOEXEC.BAT and checks every time you boot your system. (A complete system check takes about 3 seconds on a 4.77 MHz PC, so it won't slow you down.) This program is a must for SYSOPs and users alike. Unpack with ARC-E.

Name: CHECKG.ARC
System: IBM
Date: 07-Oct-89
Size: 14923
Description: A program to check *.COM files for the presence of either of two hexadecimal strings that could be embedded there by the Datacrime virus. Based on information from National Institute of Standards and Technology as reported in Government Computer News. Executable only provided, with *.doc file.

Name: PPUTIL.ZIP
System: IBM
Date: 25-Feb-90
Size: 23808
Description: Ping-Pong Virus Utilities (PPUTIL) is a set of two programs that will identify and remove the infamous ping-pong virus from an infected DOS hard or floppy disk. Shareware.

Name: MIC.ZIP
System: IBM
Date: 28-Jul-90
Size: 24832
Description: Module Integrity Check, M.I.C. attempts to detect the presence of a virus by flagging changes to program files. It scans all directories on your disk for COM, EXE, BIN, SYS, and OVR files and records file size, date, time, and a PARTIAL CRC checksum into a disk file. For each run, the file is compared to the previous run, and differences are flagged. Easy to run and fast; it scans my 200 program files in about 45 seconds. Shareware, fee requested but not mandatory.

Name: VCHECK.ARC
System: IBM
Date: 17-Jun-89
Size: 9984
Description: This program is a small virus check that a friend keyed in from *Computing Now*. I found it useful when trying new software obtained from several BBSs. Download with a protocol. Unpack with ARC.E.

Name: DEFEND.ARC
System: IBM
Date: 15-Oct-89
Size: 49271
Description: Computer Defender will fight and protect your computer from computer viruses. It is fully menu driven, and any user can operate it. Shareware. Uploaded by author Michael Dorio.

Name: MORE.ARC
System: IBM
Date: 01-Jan-89
Size: 8150
Description: This program effectively replaces DOS's TYPE and MORE commands. It is specifically designed to combat ANSI bombs, hidden commands which can tell your ANSI device driver to reconfigure your keyboard for malicious purposes. Copyrighted, but free for nonprofit use. Version 1.00 uploaded by author. Download with a protocol, unpack with ARC-E.

Name: VIRUS2.ARC
System: IBM
Date: 14-Jan-89
Size: 7936
Description: Version 2.0 of Virus Stopper. Memory-resident program monitors computer activities, prevents computer from performing seven known virus or Trojan Horse operations (like FORMAT C: or DEL *.COM) without user permission. New version has new checking, fewer false alarms. Package also contains separate program to write (and DELETE) protect individual files. Also prevents accidental deletions. Unarc with PKXARC. $10 registration.

Name: FIND17.ARC
System: IBM
Date: 17-Jun-89
Size: 23727
Description: Finds and eliminates the "1701" virus that attaches itself to any .COM program to add 1701 bytes to the length of the file, then lets the program keep on functioning normally until the bomb goes off.

Name: DAYCHE.ARC
System: IBM
Date: 07-May-88
Size: 2206
Description: DAYCHEK.ARC contains DAYCHECK.BAT DATECHECK.COM and the necessary documentation to set up for automatically running CHECKUP.EXE version 1.4 (stored here as CHKUP.ARC) once each day at first boot and to run CHKDSK /F once each week so that we forgetful ones will check for virus invasion. This version does not require EBL and runs in a regular DOS environment. It can be

used to modify your AUTOEXEC.BAT file (recommended). Download with a protocol, unpack with ARC.E.

Name: BOOTRE.ZIP
System: IBM
Date: 11-May-90
Size: 17693
Description: Save and restore the boot sector from any drive, A: to F:. Also shows the boot sector. Documentation gives some technical info. Good to backup boot sectors in case a virus infects them. Uploaded by author Ron Freimuth. Free program.

Name: NOVIRU.ARC
System: IBM
Date: 12-Mar-88
Size: 27648
Description: NoVirus 1.01 is a small program to put in your AUTOEXEC.BAT that monitors your system files, alerting you if they have changed. It is small, quick, and has a slick interface.

Name: CHECKU.ARC
System: IBM
Date: 26-Mar-89
Size: 13120
Description: Checkup is an anti-virus utility that checks if your files have changed and keeps a complete log of all changes and deletions. Very fast, very accurate and very easy to use. Great!

Name: DVIRUS.ARC
System: IBM
Date: 04-Nov-88
Size: 3868
Description: Text file from Usenet with directions for dealing with the virus described in the newspapers on November 4. Does not affect any microcomputers. Only affects VAXes and SUNs and currently only those on Internet. (An excellent example of how fast news, and help, can spread via on-line service.)

Name: BS200.EXE
System: IBM
Date: 15-Sep-89
Size: 39250
Description: BSearch v2.00 with CRC checking is a virus checking program. It keeps an index of files with size, CRC-16 and CRC-32, and lets you verify that files have remained the same. Also included is some info on the new Columbus Day or Datacrime virus that formats track 0 of your hard disk on October 12. The Datacrime virus has been verified . . . it does exist! User supported. Self-extracting archive. Download with a protocol.

Name: VGUARD.ARC
System: IBM
Date: 15-Aug-89
Size: 3119
Description: A small device driver to protect an IBM PC (or compatible) computer system against the Friday the 13th virus (a.k.a. Israeli or Jerusalem virus). Intercepts DOS interrupt 21h, and aborts any program that calls functions used by the virus. Device driver so installed before the virus has a chance to infect it, even if a program called by AUTOEXEC.BAT is infected. Includes source. Uploaded by author.

Name: EXPEL.ZIP
System: IBM
Date: 22-Feb-90
Size: 73216
Description: This is Version 1.1 of the Virus Control Device. Includes a selective write-protect function, 9 different levels of CRC checks, and a Sample and a Track function: the Sample function permits you to extract a sample of the viral code in case of infection. This sample is then used by the Track function to test all other files of the system. This approach is efficient to clean a system even if the CRC archive is built after the beginning of the infection.

Name: VACCIN.ARC
System: IBM
Date: 14-Jul-89
Size: 8794
Description: A program to defeat Jerusalem, Hebrew, or Friday 13th virus. This program (with documentation) searches all files .COM and .EXE and kills virus. Download with a protocol, unpack with ARC-E.

Name: CLEANP.ZIP
System: IBM
Date: 11-Aug-90
Size: 52419
Description: Cleanup 4.3V66 kills and removes computer viruses, and in most instances it repairs infected files, reconstructs damaged programs, and returns the system to normal operation. Cleanup works for all viruses identified by the current version of McAfee Associates' SCAN. It searches the entire system looking for the virus that you wish to remove. This version adds 27 additional virus types. Shareware, $35.

Name: NETSCN.ZIP
System: IBM
Date: 11-Aug-90
Size: 37262
Description: NETSCAN v66 is the network version of VIRUSCAN. It scans network virtual drives and identifies any pre-existing PC virus infection in the file servers.

When used with Viruscan on the individual workstations, can identify 133 major virus strains.

Name: SENTRY.ZIP
System: IBM
Date: 11-Aug-90
Size: 15630
Description: SENTRY 2.09 works on DOS v4.0 and newer, plus divisions larger than 32 megabytes as well. Sentry uses a unique approach to finding virus. Prior TSR approaches have numerous weaknesses, primarily because TSRs cannot prevent viruses from directly interfacing with the system I/O controllers. Thus, over half of existing viruses cannot be stopped or detected by such products. Shareware $25.

Name: VC100.ZIP
System: IBM
Date: 11-Aug-90
Size: 57796
Description: Central version 2.0 is a shell program that simplifies the use of Virus-Scan and CleanUp, both virus programs from McAfee Associates. It provides a menu-oriented environment that does away with the need to memorize command line parameters. It is ideally suited for locations such as college computer labs. Mouse can be used. Has a built-in screen saver. Shareware, $25. Requires CGA/EGA or VGA display systems.

Name: VCOPY.ZIP
System: IBM
Date: 11-Aug-90
Size: 32502
Description: VCOPY 0.4V66 is a replacement program for the DOS copy command that checks for viruses as it copies. It prevents infected programs from entering your system, and it identifies infected diskettes during the copy process. VCOPY implements all functions of the DOS 3.3 COPY command, and uses the identical switches. It is about 10 percent slower, then, than the normal DOS COPY command. Free program.

Name: VSHLD.ZIP
System: IBM
Date: 14-Sep-90
Size: 41476
Description: VSHIELD 2.0V66 now prevents infection from 31 new viruses discovered since version 64. VSHIELD is a small TSR program that prevents viruses from getting into your system. 2.0V66 can identify and prevent infection from 133 major virus strains and 213 substrains. Shareware. $25.

Name: VSUM08.ZIP
System: IBM
Date: 11-Aug-90
Size: 83286
Description: VIRUSSUM contains information for the identification, detection and removal of MS-DOS viruses. It allows the user to understand what a virus generally does, how it activates, what it is doing to their system, and most importantly, how to get rid of it. Free program.

Name: DGLOCK.ZIP
System: IBM
Date: 10-Jul-90
Size: 51728
Description: Protect your computer from unauthorized users! David Gerrold's notorious LOCK utility installs in your AUTOEXEC.BAT file, or can be called manually. Allows permanent and one-time passwords. Temporarily disables Ctrl−Alt−Delete reboot. Keeps a log of attempts to break in. Runs on any size screen. Release 2.10 fixes Ctrl−Break bug, replaces earlier version. Shareware.

Name: PK193B.EXE
System: IBM
Date: 02-Jul-90
Size: 36863
Description: The famous POWERKIT do-everything utility. It offers keyboard enhancement (large keystroke buffer with window, fast, slow, or no keystroke repeat; stop on a dime; adjust wait time), printer output to screen, escape from hung programs, screen blanker, password protect your machine, auto-repeat macros, access pop-up utilities inside programs that commandeer INT 9, shell out to DOS, fast warm boot (mainly for T1k's), more. Adjust options at the touch of a hot key. Shareware.

Name: AVS220.ZIP
System: IBM
Date: 23-Aug-90
Size: 74446
Description: AVSearch version 2.2 is a virus search program. Program searches for 135 virus strains in memory, partition table, book record, and files. Has many options and a short description. AVSCrc, also included, is a CRC program. This package remains copyrighted, but you do not have to pay for use. Uploaded by coauthor.

Name: DN.EXE
System: IBM Windows
Date: 11-Aug-90
Size: 76800
Description: METZ Desktop Navigator version 2.44 is a comprehensive file and disk manager for Microsoft Windows. Create, Rename, Copy, Move, and Delete directories. Run, Print, Copy, Move, Rename, and Delete multiple files. Screen saver, lock

system, file finder, clock, and more. This version is compatible with Windows 2.x and Windows 3.0. See included DESKNAV.DOC for details. DN.EXE is a self-extracting archive file.

Name: LOCK-ZIP
System: IBM Windows
Date: 19-Sep-90
Size: 47104
Description: METZ Lock version 1.3 is a security application for Microsoft Windows. Lock is password-driven and will prevent unauthorized use of your system. Lock has several configuration options, as well as a customizable screen blanking feature. This version is compatible with Windows 2.x and Windows 3.0. See included LOCK.DOC for details.

Name: LO.SIT
System: Mac
Date: 17-Apr-89
Size: 66944
Description: LockOUT 2.0 password protection is from BEYOND, Inc., in Tucson, Arizona. It comes as an INIT, DA, and FKey. The INIT stops people from using your Mac at startup time by asking for a password. The DA and FKey can be used from inside applications or in the Finder.

Name: SECURE.SIT
System: Mac
Date: 29-Jun-89
Size: 130304
Description: SecureINIT virus protection application, Version 1.7.2. Can check all applications, save any HD configuration, and restore it on startup, also it will give your Mac the absolute maximum protection available against almost everything: viruses, unwanted modifications, polluted drivers, system crashes, etc.

Name: LOCKFL.SIT
System: Mac
Date: 08-Sep-90
Size: 31616
Description: Folder Locker/Unlocker allows you to password-protect folders on your disk. Once protected, the contents of a folder cannot be examined, deleted, replaced, etc., unless the folder has been unlocked using the password. This is a limited functionality version of the full product. It still permits protecting one folder and the overall security is reduced over that of the full product

Name: GUARD
System: Mac
Date: 03-May-89
Size: 40448

Description: Guard Dog version 2.3, with password, software security system for any Macintosh. Version 2.3 includes the long-awaited password. Registered owners received this free in the mail. Please register with Nemesis Systems if you use it.

Name: FILEZE.SIT
System: Mac
Date: 05-Dec-87
Size: 31232
Description: File Zero is a handy utility to completely erase files from a disk so not even a disk editor can retrieve any information. Use it for company, private, or trade secrets, data, proposals, etc. This product is shareware. SIT format.

Name: ZORBA.SIT
System: Mac
Date: 06-Jun-90
Size: 20608
Description: Zorba is a quick-and-dirty security program. Its function is to hinder unauthorized users from using a Mac, by demanding a password upon startup. If a correct password is not entered after three attempts, the program will attempt to shutdown the Mac. Features include hidden typing, master and regular passwords, optional screen saver, user log for access attempts, reminders to change password, desktop hiding, and more. Free. Written by Jon Wind.

Name: ENIGMA.PIT
System: Mac
Date: 21-Aug-87
Size: 21632
Description: ENIGMA is a general file encryption utility. ENIGMA can encrypt/decrypt all kinds of files: text, applications, fonts, spreadsheets, etc. The Packit III file contains a brief text documentation file. This upload is for a friend. It is shareware.

Name: LOCKEM.PIT
System: Mac
Date: 21-Aug-87
Size: 20736
Description: LOCK'EM UP is book disk, password protection utility. It will log all failed attempts to boot the disk. The Packit III file contains a short documentation file. This upload is for a friend. It is shareware.

Name: PASSWO.BIN
System: Mac
Date: 17-May-90
Size: 7680
Description: PasswordMaker makes it easy to generate a secure password for on-line systems, mail servers, etc. It generates truly random passwords in several formats making it easier to have a password that will be safe.

Name: SECURE.PIT
System: Mac
Date: 27-Jul-88
Size: 14848
Description: Secure is a simple utility to help you safeguard access to your computer system. It displays a model dialog which prompts for a password, and will not relinquish control until the correct one is entered. Unlike some similar programs, Secure works equally well under MultiFinder. This Packit III file contains the program plus a short documentation file. By Gary R. Voth.

OTHER ON-LINE SERVICES

While CompuServe is very popular, and probably the largest company of its type, it is not the only on-line system of interest to personal computer users. The following are some of the other services available (also note that many manufacturers are now providing on-line bulletin board systems as part of their support services).

BIX
Operated by *Byte* Magazine
One Phoenix Mill Lane
Peterborough, NH 03458
(603) 924-7681
Heavily oriented to computer users, particularly programmers and developers. An excellent way to keep in touch with the latest technical development in personal computing.

GEnie
Operated by General Electric
(800) 638-9636
An acronym for General Electric Network for Information Services, GEnie is used by numerous vendors, including Microsoft, to provide on-line support. Special-interest groups are organized into roundtables. There are also general services such as airline bookings and reference databases.

Delphi
Operated by General Videotex Corporation
3 Blackstone Street
Cambridge, MA 02139
(617) 491-3393
An inexpensive PC-oriented service with news, shopping and general features as well as useful files you can download.

Appendix C
A Catalog of Viruses

In THE CHAPTER ON VIRUSES, several examples of this particular form of programming were described so that you could get an idea of what you are up against. This appendix provides, in summary form, information about further examples of the species. If you need a complete and current listing of viruses, you should consider subscribing to one of the virus reporting services listed at the end of this appendix.

VIRUSES ON MS-DOS SYSTEMS

Name: Alabama
Target: Any EXE file on any writeable DOS device.
Type: Indirect action, file virus.
Symptoms: EXE files grow by 1560 bytes.
Impact: When the hour changes, a display is triggered that says "SOFTWARE COPIES ARE PROHIBITED BY INTERNATIONAL LAW" then "BOX 1055 Tuscambia ALABAMA USA." After this, the computer hangs.

Name: Blackjack, 1701/1704
Target: Any COM file on any writeable DOS device.
Type: Indirect action, file virus.
Symptoms: COM files grow by 1701 bytes (in other versions by 1704 bytes).
Impact: When triggered, the characters on the screen gradually crumble into a heap. As each character falls the speaker clicks. The crumble is enabled by any system date between October and December 1988, or else by the virus going memory-resident when the year is 1980 and the date is subsequently set to 1989 or later.
Notes: There are many versions of this virus, for example Fallboot, a boot sector virus. Some variants trigger the crumble at different times and some have even greater impact, such as a low-level disk format. However, there are also harmless "joke" programs that produce a screen crumble.

Name: Brain (Pakistani, Lahore)
Target: The boot sector of any 360K diskette.
Type: Boot sector virus.
Symptoms: You see Brain as a volume label on floppy disk. Infected disks have 3K of bad sectors.
Impact: No significant effects.
Notes: Also Ashar, an early version of Pakistani Brain.

Name: Dark Avenger
Target: All but the smallest COM or EXE files on any writeable DOS device.
Type: Indirect action, file virus.
Symptoms: COM files grow by 1800 bytes. EXE by a similar amount.
Impact: It writes a sector that starts "Eddie lives . . . somewhere in time," to a random sector on the hard disk at random intervals. There is no major negative impact from this virus.
Notes: Variations include Eddie 2 (COM files grow by 651 bytes).

Name: Datacrime (1168)
Target: Any COM file on any writeable DOS device, but does not infect COM-MAND.COM.
Type: Direct action, file virus.
Symptoms: COM files grow by 1168 (or 1280) bytes.
Impact: On October 13 each year and every day thereafter until December 31, the virus puts up the message "DATACRIME VIRUS RELEASED 1 MARCH 1989" and then does a low-level format of the hard disk of cylinder zero, all heads up to head eight.
Notes: Variations of this virus include Datacrime II (similar to Datacrime, but affects both COM and EXE files including COMMAND.COM).

Name: Dbase
Target: Any COM file on any writeable DOS device.
Type: Indirect action, file virus.
Symptoms: COM files grow by 1664 bytes, and 1884 bytes are subtracted from the top of conventional memory. The virus creates a hidden file in the root directory called C:\BUGS.DAT.
Impact: The virus garbles all files with a DBF extension by interchanging pairs of bytes. It keeps a list of these files in the hidden BUGS.DAT file. Three months after this file is created a damage routine is triggered, but there is a bug in the code and it does not work.

Name: Denzuk (Venezuelan, Search)
Target: Floppy disks.
Type: Boot sector virus.
Symptoms: If you have a color monitor, whenever you do a warm boot on an infected machine, you see the red DENZUK logo. You will also find the volume label changed on floppy disks.
Impact: If Denzuk finds the Brain virus on a disk, it removes Brain and replaces Brain with itself. Denzuk assumes that all disks are 360K so it uses track 40 to store code and replaces the original boot sector with a 360K boot sector. This will have no ill effect on a 360K disk, but it will cause problems on all other capacity disks.

Name: Fu Manchu (2086)
Infect: Any COM or EXE file on any writeable DOS device.
Type: Indirect action, file virus.

Symptoms: COM files grow by 2086 bytes, EXE by a similar amount. When you do a warm boot, it clears the screen and types out the message "The world will hear from me again!"

Impact: If you type Fu Manchu while the virus is resident, it types back "Fu manchu virus 3/10/88 - latest in the new fun line!" If you type Thatcher, Reagan, Waldheim, or Botha, it adds "is a *xxxx*," where *xxxx* is one of four crude words. If you type one of the two most common four-letter swear words it backspaces over them. The virus will also reboot the computer at random times.

Name: Italian (Ping Pong, Bouncing Ball)
Target: The boot sector of any floppy or hard disk on 8086 or 8088 computers.
Type: Boot sector virus.
Symptoms: Once every half hour, if you are accessing the disk, a bouncing dot is triggered. Infected floppy disks have one cluster (1K or 512 bytes) of bad sectors. Hard disks lose one cluster (usually 2K).
Impact: No significant effects. Does not affect 80286 or 80386 machines.
Notes: Variations include Big Halian (generates a diamond shape instead of a dot and can infect 80286 and 80386 machines).

Name: Jerusalem (1813, Israeli, PLO, Friday 13th)
Target: Any COM or EXE file on any writeable DOS device.
Type: Indirect action, file virus.
Symptoms: COM files grow by 1813 bytes, EXE files grow by about 1808 bytes. COM files grow once, EXE files grow indefinitely until they become too large to load into memory. COMMAND.COM is not infected.
Impact: On every Friday 13th, any program you run is deleted. On all dates, 30 minutes after the virus is installed, the computer slows down and at the same time a small black rectangle opens up on the screen.
Notes: Apparently first sighted by a student at Hebrew University and first mentioned publicly in one of Israel's daily newspapers on January 8, 1988. What called attention to the virus was an error in the virus code itself, which caused it to mistake previously infected programs as uninfected. Some programs were infected as many as four hundred times, and the growth in size of the program was noticeable. This one was discovered before its D-Day, but it had infected university and military computers before it was detected.

Name: Lehigh
Target: COMMAND.COM, any disk, any computer.
Type: COMMAND.COM virus.
Symptoms: COMMAND.COM does not grow, but the date/time is changed.
Impact: After the virus has copied itself four times, it trashes the disk by writing code from the BIOS to sectors 1-32 of a disk. After this has been done, the virus displays a string from the BIOS. This is one of the very first viruses, seldom seen outside the U.S.

Name: Ogre (Computer Ogre, Disk Killer)

Target: The boot sector of any writeable floppy or hard disk.

Type: Boot sector virus.

Symptoms: 8K of memory is lost. The boot sector is abnormal. A floppy disk has 3K of bad sectors.

Impact: If you leave your computer on for 48 hours and access the hard disk during the following hour, the virus triggers. It clears the screen and puts up "Disk Killer - version 1.00 by Computer Ogre 040/01/89" then "Warning," "Don't turn off the power or remove the diskette while Disk Killer is processing," followed by "PROCESS-ING." The virus then encrypts the hard disk, making it inaccessible.

Name: Oropax

Target: Any COM file on any writeable DOS device.

Type: Indirect action, file virus.

Symptoms: COM files grow between 2756 and 2806 bytes.

Impact: One in four times that Oropax goes memory-resident, it plays one of three tunes every few minutes. The tunes are "Stars and Stripes Forever," "Symphony Number 40" by Mozart, and "The Blue Danube" by Strauss.

Name: Saturday 14th (Durban)

Target: Any COM or EXE file on any writeable DOS device.

Type: Indirect action, file virus.

Symptoms: COM and EXE files grow between 669 and 684 bytes.

Impact: Every Saturday 14th, it writes 100 sectors of rubbish to the first sectors of drives D, C, B, and A, in that order.

Name: Stoned (New Zealand, Marijuana)

Target: The partition sector of hard disks, the boot sector of floppies in drive A.

Type: Partition sector virus.

Symptoms: Every eighth time you boot up the infected system, you see the message, "Your PC is now stoned."

Impact: No intentional damage, but a bug in the virus causes it to overwrite the directory entries for files 33−48 on high-density 5.25-inch disks, and causes similar problems on 3.5-inch disks. On some hard disks, it overwrites part of the FAT.

Name: Syslock (Macho, 3551)

Target: Any COM or EXE file on any writeable DOS device.

Type: Direct action, file virus.

Symptoms: COM and EXE files grow between 3551 and 3566 bytes.

Impact: If "Syslock=@" is in the environment, the virus does nothing. Otherwise it works its way down the disk, converting each occurrence of "Microsoft" to "Macrosoft" (or Machosoft in the Macho variant).

Name: Tenbytes (1554)

Target: Any COM or EXE file on any writeable DOS device.

Type: Indirect action, file virus.

Symptoms: COM files grow by between 1554 and 1569 bytes, and EXE files by 1514 and 1529 bytes.

Impact: Every year during September to December, whenever DOS writes to a file, the first 10 bytes to be written are omitted, and 10 bytes of garbage are added at the end of the write.

Name: Vienna (648, 1-in-8, Austrian, Dos62)
Target: Any COM file on any writeable DOS device.
Type: Direct action, file virus.
Symptoms: COM files grow by 648 bytes.
Impact: One infection in eight deliberately trashes the file instead. Eventually COMMAND.COM is infected and whenever the computer is started up, it keeps rebooting. (In some cases, the machines just hangs.)
Notes: Variations include Lisbon where one infection in four makes the file unusable; then when COMMAND.COM is infected, the computer hangs on boot up; the virus puts "@AIDS" at the start of the file.

Name: Yankee Doodle
Target: All but the smallest COM or EXE files on any writeable DOS device.
Type: Indirect action, file virus.
Symptoms: COM files grow by between 2771 and 2900 bytes. EXE files also grow.
Impact: At 5:00 PM the virus plays "Yankee Doodle Dandy."
Notes: There are many variants of this virus, including Vacsina, an early version, which has no major negative impact.

Name: Zerobug (Zero Eater)
Target: Any COM files on any writeable DOS device.
Type: Indirect action, file virus.
Symptoms: COM files grow by 1536 bytes, but if this virus is in memory you do not see the increase in file size because the virus conceals this.
Impact: A face moves way down the screen eating all the zeros.
Variants: Agiplan, first described in a West German newspaper.

Name: 405
Target: Any COM file on any writeable DOS device.
Type: Direct action, file virus.
Symptoms: Files smaller than 405 bytes grow to that size. Programs larger than 405 bytes do not change but no longer function.
Impact: Infected programs no longer run.

Name: 4096 (Century, 4K)
Target: Any executable file on any writeable DOS device.
Type: Indirect action, file virus.
Symptoms: Executable files grow by 4096 bytes, but if the virus is in memory, you do not see the increase in size because the virus conceals this.
Effect: The virus installs a routine on the partition sector of hard disks (which makes it inaccessible) and the boot sector of any floppy disk in drive A. When you boot from such a disk, (from September 22 to December 31st) you get a display that says

"FRODO LIVES." However, there is apparently an error in the virus and when it is called, the machine often hangs.

Name: June 16th (Pretoria)
Target: Any COM file on any writeable DOS device.
Type: Direct action, file virus.
Symptoms: COM files grow by 879 bytes (or grow to 1758 bytes if they would end up less than that size).
Impact: On every June 16, it scans through the root directory of the drive it has been looking at and converts any file name it finds to the name "ZAPPED."

Name: 765 (Periume)
Target: Any COM file on any writeable DOS device.
Type: Indirect action, file virus.
Symptoms: COM files grow by 765 bytes.
Impact: After an infected file has been run 80 times or more, a message is put on the screen before the program is run. If you type 4711 in response to this, the programs continues to run, if you type anything else, the virus puts up a second message and terminates the program with an errorlevel return code of 1.

VIRUSES ON MACINTOSH AND OTHER SYSTEMS

Name: MacIn Virus
Description: Written by a West German and posted to CompuServe in a HyperCard stack, the virus is disguised as a resource that inserts itself in a system trap handler (the place where the computer catches errors so they won't cause system crashes). The virus destroys hard disks and the applications that run on them.

Name: Scores Virus
Description: First mentioned in *MacWeek*, April 1988, but in existence since at least February 1988, and possibly as early as September 1987, this virus infiltrated several government agencies, Apple sales offices, and the Mac of an unidentified senator, as well as *Macworld* and *Macintosh Today*. First dissected by John Norstad and Bob Hablutzel, Scores has several time-delay features. It is designed to attack two custom applications called ERIC and VULT, but it will infect anything. Several days after infecting a Mac system, the virus attempts to locate and modify any files with the creator code of ERIC or VULT. The code of the virus is written to make the targeted program dysfunctional.

The virus lies dormant for two days after infection. After two, four, and seven days, various parts wake up and begin their mischief. Two days after the initial infection, the virus begins to spread to other applications. After four days, the second part of the virus wakes up. It begins to watch for the VULT and ERIC applications. Whenever VULT or ERIC is run, the system bombs after 25 minutes of use. After seven days, the third part of the virus kicks in. Whenever VULT is run, the virus waits 15 minutes, then causes any attempt to write a disk file to bomb. If there are no disk writes for another 10 minutes, the application will bomb anyway.

Deleting the infected resources is not enough to remove the virus, because the virus recognizes the attempt and modifies its resource identification and memory location when probed by resource utilities. ResEdit "thinks" that the virus resources have been deleted, but they have been renamed and will return when the Mac is restarted. Apparently, the virus does not attempt to spread itself over networks. The Scores virus causes printing problems, system crashes, application crashes on launch, and damage to Excel files.

Name: J-nVIR
Description: Seems to have broken out in Zurich. This is an exact copy of an nVIR type B virus, the only obvious difference being the renaming of the viral resource to Jude. All current anti-virus detection programs recognize this as being an nVIR clone and will prevent infection.

Name: WDEF
Description: Has been detected at a number of sites including the Universities of Georgia and Texas. This virus appears only to infect the invisible desktop files used by the Finder. The virus spreads from file to file, but does not infect applications, data files, or system files. In fact, the only tell-tale signs leading to its detection were caused by a bug that resulted in the slowing down of window updates and unusually frequent crashes on certain Macs.

WDEF seems not to attempt any damage. It appears to do little more than spread from disk to disk. However, other bugs in the software might result in problems later. Jeff Shulman, author of Virus Detective 3.1, recommends adding the following search string to his program in order to detect the virus:

CREATOR = ERIK & Resource WDEF & Any

Disks or individual desktop files can then be searched from Virus Detective's main window. WDEF can be eliminated from a disk by simply rebuilding the desktop.

Name: MacMag Virus
Description: First mentioned in print in a UPI report February 12, 1988. The virus was launched in December 1987 by Richard Brandow, publisher of *MacMag* magazine in Montreal, Canada. It was supposed to be a simple message of peace, designed to pop up on Macintosh screens on March 2, the anniversary of the introduction of the Apple Macintosh SE and Macintosh II. The virus infects the System file, but does not directly affect applications. After March 2, the virus erased itself. Although this virus was designed to be benign, it had some nasty side effects: It played havoc with System folders. The virus spread to Europe and the West Coast; it is the first virus to infect a commercial computer product. It was inadvertently passed to Aldus and appeared on some copies of their software.

Name: Amiga Virus
Description: A boot sector virus that, after a certain number of disks have been infected will print a message: "Something wonderful has happened. Your Amiga is alive!!!," then "Some of your disks are infected by a VIRUS Another masterpiece of

the Mega-Mighty SCA." On an Amiga floppy, the boot block consists of the first two sectors on the disk. Because the virus overwrites this, the information on the disk is lost.

Name: Atari ST Virus
Description: A warning of this virus was posted on Usenet on March 26, 1988, by Martin Minow. Once installed, the virus will copy itself onto every disk used, except any that are write-protected. It tests an uninfected disk to see if it contains the virus, replicates, then keeps count of how many times the disk is used after that. When a certain limit is reached, the virus writes random data across the root directory (the central directory) and file allocation tables (which contain the bitmap record of unused sectors) for the disk, making it unusable. The virus then removes itself from the damaged disk. The virus does not affect hard disks.

TROJAN HORSES

Trojan horses are malevolent lines of code slipped into otherwise innocent programs. While viruses replicate, trojan horses do not. Some are written from scratch, while others are adulterated copies of legitimate programs. Some begin destruction within minutes of infection, others perform as legitimate software for weeks or months, then touch off a logic bomb. They can scramble data, erase files, or damage the file allocation table.

Name: Xmas Tree
Description: First sighted December 9, 1987. Written as a prank by a West German student, it started out in a European academic computer network (Bitnet) then jumped through electronic gateways to five continents and to the internal E-mail system of IBM. In the IBM internal E-mail system, a holiday message promised to draw a Christmas tree on the screen if someone would type the word Christmas on the computer. When they did, it drew a tree but it also sent a copy of itself to all of the other network mail addresses kept in the user's electronic address book. Along with a very primitive tree (made of capital Xs), a message was displayed: "A very happy Christmas and my best wishes for the next year. Let this run and enjoy yourself. Browsing this file is no fun at all. Just type Christmas."

Once opened, the program rarely accepted commands to stop. Operators who turned off their terminals to try to stop the Christmas message lost electronic mail or unfinished reports not saved in the computer. The Trojan infected so many machines that it brought IBM's global electronic mail network to a halt, disrupting the system for 72 hours. Plant officials were forced to turn off internal links between computer terminals and mainframe systems to purge the message. A virus was written to follow and destroy the Christmas trojan horse and then self-destruct in mid-January. The trojan horse was generally stamped out by Monday, December 14, 1987.

Name: Turkey Trojan
Description: A program that was being passed around via ARPAnet and some other

computer networks, called Turkey and was supposed to draw a picture of a turkey, but it did not. Instead, it erased all of the unprotected files in the directory.

Name: Run.me
Description: Posing as a graphics program that plays "The Star-Spangled Banner" and displays the American flag. It actually attacks the hard disk and erases the data on it. Reported in the *New York Times*, May 19, 1987.

WORMS

Essentially, worms are memory crunchers that rewrite themselves successively through the computer's memory. The programs on individual computers are the segments, which remain in communication with each other. Almost any program can be modified to incorporate the worm mechanism.

Name: Xerox PARC Worm
Description: In 1980, John Shoch at the Xerox Palo Alto Research Center devised a worm that wriggled through large computer systems looking for machines that were not being used and harnessing them to help solve a large problem. It could take over an entire system.

Name: VM Worm BITNET
Description: VM users on Bitnet encountered a worm disguised as a utility program. When logging on in November in 1988, they found a new EXEC called DIR. This purported to list VM/CMS files in a convenient MS-DOS format. When run, DIR produced the promised listing, but all was far from well. Hidden within the code was a worm, whose major purpose was to replicate itself throughout the network.

After it had been run from an unsuspecting user's terminal; the EXEC was programmed to send itself to all net addresses found in the current NAMES and NETLOG files. Reminiscent of the CHRISTMAS EXEC that cluttered the network three years earlier, and that reappears from time to time, it quickly set about its task. Many sites, no doubt, received the file before one watchful recipient took the trouble of listing the REXX code.

It became clear that its purpose was not only to cause disruption as there was found to be a time-bomb hidden away in the code, too. Remember, this was late November 1989. The EXEC's time bomb was due to detonate if run during 1990.

Every execution of the DIR command checked the system date. If this reported later than 1989, the program was set to start erasing files in users' accounts.

Luckily, the network used to distribute this potentially damaging code also brought about its apprehension. Within hours, urgent warning messages had been issued. Concerned system administrators were able to offer guidance to their users, and as a follow-up, a second EXEC had been written to check systems and disable the DIR EXEC. These combined actions ensured that disruption and damage were kept to a minimum.

Name: Shockwave Rider Worm
Description: A fictional worm created by writer John Brunner in his novel *The Shock-wave Rider*. This has been mentioned as a major influence on Robert Morris, Jr., designer of the Internet worm. In Brunner's novel, worms were used by rebels to undermine a dictatorial government wielding power through a computer network. The worms could not be killed as they were designed to be self-perpetuating so long as the network existed. Even if one segment was inactivated, a counterpart of the missing portion remained in store at some other station. The worm then automatically subdivided and sent a duplicate head to collect the spare groups and restore them.

RECOMMENDED READING

The following books have been referred to in the text and are recommended for further reading on computer security and the issues raised.

Electronic Pirates: The DIY Crime of the Century, 1989. An excellent overview of the problems of copy protection, pirating, and the copyright problems raised by technology.

Computer Viruses: A High-Tech Disease, Ralf Burger. Abacus, 1988. An interesting work that includes examples of virus code, raising interesting questions.

The Shockwave Rider, John Brunner. Ballantine, 1975. A novel in which computer systems and worms feature strongly.

Neuromancer, Count Zero, Mona Lisa Overdrive, William Gibson. Ace Science Fiction. A trilogy that is the best in cyber-punk fiction. Required reading for those concerned about the future of computers and the planet.

The Radio Hackers Handbook. Duckworth, 1987. Contains interesting and practical details of encryption systems, including some routines in BASIC and assembler.

Hugo Cornwall's New Hacker's Handbook, by Steve Gold. Century, 1989. An excellent way to find out what hacking is all about.

Cryptography: An Introduction to Computer Security. 1989. For those interested in the mathematics behind encryption (not for those who suffer from math anxiety).

VirusFax International, a newsletter about the latest virus threats (see the listing in Appendix A).

The Puzzle Palace, James Bamford. Penguin, 1982. A ground-breaking work that revealed so much about the workings of the National Security Agency that it was nearly banned. Excellent history of code-breaking, plus insights into government eavesdropping on private and commercial communications.

Electromagnetic Man, Simon Best and Dr. Cyril Smith. Dent, 1989. Required reading for all concerned about the health effects of working with computers and other electronic equipment that emit non-ionizing electromagnetic radiation (Winner of Book of the Year Award, *Journal of Alternative Medicine*).

Electropollution, Roger Coghill. Thorsons, 1990. Further required reading for those concerned about the health effects of working with computers and other electronic equipment.

Index

Other Bestsellers of Related Interest

DISASTER RECOVERY HANDBOOK
—Chantico Publishing Company, Inc.

Could your company survive if a tornado struck today? You'll find everything you need for coping with your worst-case scenario in this book. Among the other issues covered are plan formulation and maintenance; data, communications, and microcomputer recovery procedures; emergency procedures. Action-oriented checklists and worksheets are included to help you start planning right away—before it's too late. 276 pages, 88 illustrations. Book No. 3663, $39.95 hardcover only

ENHANCED MS-DOS® BATCH FILE PROGRAMMING—Dan Gookin

This new guide leads you through the development of versatile batch files that incorporate the features of the lates DOS versions, commercial batch file extenders, and utilities written in high-level languages such as Pascal and C. The companion diskettes packaged with the book include all the significant batch file programs described—plus all the utilities and their source codes. 360 pages, 71 illustrations, two 5¹/₄" diskettes. Book No. 3641, $24.95 paperback, $34.95 hardcover

MICRO TO MAINFRAME DATA INTERCHANGE
—2nd Edition—Michael Simon Bodner
Reviewers said this about the first edition:
". . . provides a wealth of information . . . is well worth the time it takes to study it carefully."
        —Library and Information Science Annual

This newly revised second edition of a classic in its field confronts the issues involved in the efficient transfer of information. Bodner focuses on the techniques used in data file exchange on local area networks and micro-to-mainframe links. He provides updated information on error control, file structures, data security, and more. 304 pages, 124 illustrations. Book No. 3399, $34.95 hardcover only

DATA DICTIONARIES FOR DATABASE ADMINISTRATORS—Robin J. Vinden

This straightforward guide shows you, in clear, easy-to-follow language, how to use data dictionaries to manage your database. The emphasis is on establishing procedures for setting up a data dictionary and maintaining basic rules of data control. Graphs and line drawings illustrate key points. You'll discover new and practical ways to manage and ensure the integrity of stored data. 192 pages, 15 illustrations. Book No. 3515, $17.95 paperback, $29.95 hardcover

HARD DISK MANAGEMENT WITH DOS®
2nd Edition—Dan Gookin
". . . a comprehensive guide to hard-disk management under MS-DOS."
        ALA Booklist

This valuable resource of utilities, applications, and management tips takes you from day-to-day basics to your system's most advanced capabilities. Designed to streamline your use of hard disk computers, this comprehensive sourcebook covers . . . file organization, batch file programming, menu generating, backing up procedures, solutions to hard disk/data security, and performance enhancements. 384 pages, 66 illustrations. Book No. 3490, $19.95 paperback, $29.95 hardcover

BUILD YOUR OWN 80486 PC AND SAVE A BUNDLE—Aubrey Pilgrim

With inexpensive third-party components and clear, step-by-step photos and assembly instructions—and without soldering, wiring, or electronic test instruments—you can assemble a 486. This book discusses boards, monitors, hard drives, cables, printers, modems, faxes, UPSs, memory floppy disks, and more. It includes parts lists, mail order addresses, safety precautions, troubleshooting tips, and a glossary of terms. 240 pages, 62 illustrations. Book No. 3628, $16.95 paperback, $26.95 hardcover

THE ILLUSTRATED HANDBOOK OF DESKTOP PUBLISHING AND TYPESETTING—2nd Edition
—Michael L. Kleper
"This . . . tome is simply incredible. . . . Fabulous book."   **—John C. Dvorak,** *PC Magazine*

Use this guide to create dazzling printed pieces once possible only with traditional ink-and-press methods. The first edition emerged as the standard reference for desktop publishing in the Macintosh and IBM® PC environments. Now Kleper has expanded his coverage to include optical character recognition, telepublishing and facsimile machines, electronic imaging, and pre-press production methods. 952 pages, 1,350 illustrations. Book No. 3350, $34.95 paperback only

MICROCOMPUTER LANs—2nd Edition
—Michael Hordeski

Pull together a multi-user system from your stand-alone micros. With this book, you gain an understanding of how networking actually happens. This comprehensive source helps you make the right decisions and cut through the confusion surrounding LAN technology and performance. You'll evaluate your alternatives intelligently, set up networks that allow for growth, restructure or upgrade LAN configurations, and effectively manage network systems. 384 pages, 135 illustrations. Book No. 3424, $39.95 hardcover only

WRITING BETTER TECHNICAL ARTICLES
—Harley Bjelland

Published technical articles is a sure bet to enhance your professional career. With this unique new style-book, you can develop the writing and editing skills needed to get published! This guide leads you through all the steps between the idea and the sale. The author targets the shorter technical article, but his techniques are equally well suited to all types of technical writing, including books, manuals, proposals, and letters. 208 pages, 40 illustrations. Book No. 3439, $12.95 paperback, $19.95 hardcover

NETWORKING WITH BANYAN® VINES®
—Edwin G. Laubach

Master the sophisticated Banyan VINES software with this practical approach to networking. Laubach offers essential guidelines for setting up and using an effective VINES operation. Anyone from the first-time network builder to the experienced VINES user will find tips and practical examples throughout the text, including: network topologies, StreetTalk protocols, creating groups and services, wiring centers, maintenance and disaster recovery, and more. 336 pages, 88 illustrations. Book No. 3405, $21.95 paperback only

THE WORDPERFECT® BOOK—3rd Edition
—Leo J. Scanlon

Follow these step-by-step procedures to simplify a wide range of everyday writing jobs using WordPerfect. Examples drawn from actual applications help you learn a variety of useful tips, tricks, and shortcuts. Take maximum advantage of WordPerfect's power and put all the valuable new features of 5.1 to work for you. You'll construct and format tables, access pull-down menus, use a mouse to select commands and operate on text, display and print mathematical equations, and import information from a spreadsheet. 368 pages, 98 illustrations. Book No. 3616, $17.95 paperback, $27.95 hardcover

THE FAX HANDBOOK—Gerald V. Quinn

This comprehensive guide explores what a fax machine can do for your business's bottom line, and explains all of the elements of owning and operating a fax machine. You will understand how fax machines work, and why they have become as crucial to today's workstation as the photocopier. This book also gives you set up and operation guidelines for your fax. You'll find tips on power supplies, connecting to the telephone, and the best locations for the machine within the workstation. 160 pages, 42 illustrations. Book No. 3341, $8.95 paperback, $16.95 hardcover

OLD TIME RADIOS! Restoration and Repair
—Joseph J. Carr

Restore classic vacuum-tube and transistor radios easily and inexpensively! This book gives you the transistor theory and practice you can use on radios produced in the '50s and early '60s. You'll find the history, theory, and practical operation behind these old-time home radio sets, and the detailed instructions and schematics you need to repair or rebuild them. 256 pages, 247 illustrations. Book No. 3342, $16.95 paperback, $25.95 hardcover

LEARN DOS—GUARANTEED!
—Richard P. Cadway

Use DOS as the tool it was intended to be! This book tells you how to make MS/PC-DOS work for you, without making you digest an encyclopedia of specialized information and technical jargon. Cadway concentrates exclusively on the most important DOS commands and most basic hardware installations—he explains what the major parts of DOS do, how the file system works, and just enough DOS to install and use your applications effectively. 192 pages, 28 illustrations. Book No. 3331, $14.95 paperback only

THE ILLUSTRATED DICTIONARY OF MICROCOMPUTERS—3rd Edition
—Michael F. Hordeski
Praise for the 2nd Edition:
". . . one of the most comprehensive topic-related books that we've come across."   —*Computing*

Rapid technological changes since the second edition of this highly rated microcomputer dictionary mean an additional 1,500 entries. Its comprehensive coverage of the latest terminology includes explanations of desktop publishing, networking, communications, graphics, and much, much more! 448 pages, 445 illustrations. Book No. 3368, $19.95 paperback, $29.95 hardcover